Thomas Jefferson Clayton

Rambles and Reflections

Europe from Biscay to the Black Sea

Thomas Jefferson Clayton

Rambles and Reflections
Europe from Biscay to the Black Sea

ISBN/EAN: 9783744760201

Printed in Europe, USA, Canada, Australia, Japan

Cover: Foto ©Andreas Hilbeck / pixelio.de

More available books at **www.hansebooks.com**

RAMBLES

AND

REFLECTIONS.

EUROPE

FROM BISCAY TO THE BLACK SEA AND FROM ÆTNA
TO THE NORTH CAPE WITH GLIMPSES AT
ASIA, AFRICA, AMERICA AND THE
ISLANDS OF THE SEA.

THOMAS I. CLAYTON.

CHESTER, PA., 1892.

PREFACE.

The following letters are published in book form more as a souvenir for my friends than for general distribution. I have received many flattering letters requesting copies of the newspapers in which they were originally published, but which I have been unable to furnish. This book is intended to supply that demand.

The first series of letters was published in 1869, before the Franco-Prussian War. In that year I saw Paris as it will, perhaps, never be seen again. It was the most glorious period of the Empire of Napoleon III.

The second series was published in 1873, after France's humiliation and during the World's Fair, at Vienna, a display that has never been equaled by any exposition that it has been my good fortune to see.

In 1888, I made an extended tour of Europe, from Sicily to the North Cape and from Paris to Constantinople. The letters of this series give faithful pictures, as far as I was able to paint them, of my experience and observations during six months of the most active and, to me, the most interesting period of my life.

In 1889 I visited Spain and Northern Africa and have endeavored to give my impressions of the places I visited during the three months I spent in those interesting countries.

The last series of foreign letters was written in 1892, and is confined to France, Italy and Africa.

I trust the letters from Florida, Havana, Jamaica and Bermuda, written during the winters of 1890 and 1891 will prove interesting to those who have, as well as to those who have not visited those places.

The letters describing my hunts in Arkansas and Virginia will recall some pleasant recollections to the old friends who were my partners upon those pleasant occasions and will be enjoyed by all who are fond of the sports of the field and are friends of the dog and gun.

I have supplemented my book with a Biographical sketch

of the Clayton family in America, which will, of course, be only interesting to my immediate relatives and nearest friends.

As these letters were the hasty compositions of leisure hours and transitory observations, I cannot expect them to be free from just criticism, especially as I am conscious of many grave errors and defects in diction as well as in style. For the want of time and patience, I have concluded to republish them without much revision, trusting to the indulgence of the generous reader, who, I am quite sure, will agree with me that it is much easier to criticise the writings of others than to employ our own pens with perfection.

The book contains faithful records of my first impressions of the manners, customs and characteristics of the Old World as I have seen it, and if it will give information, pleasure or pastime to my friends, to whom it is respectfully dedicated, my only object in its publication will be attained.

T. J. C.

v

TABLE OF CONTENTS.

XXXV.

XXXVI.

XXXVII.

XXXVIII.

PART II.

VII.

VIII.

IX.

X.

XI.

XII.

XIII.

XIV.

XV.

XX.

XXI.

BIOGRAPHICAL SKETCH

OF THE CLAYTON FAMILY, WITH SOME PERSONAL RECOLLECTIONS
OF BETHEL AND BRANDYWINE HUNDRED.

PART I.

PATERNAL LINE.

MATERNAL LINE.

PART II.

PART III.

New York to Queenstown—Parting Scenes—Life on the Ocean Wave—Gambling and Drinking—Cockney English—First Sight of Ireland—Queenstown and Cork Harbor—European Hotels.

Cork, Ireland, June 1869.

I left New York on the 12th inst., and arrived at Queenstown on the 21st. Our voyage was pleasant, and the winds and weather propitious. It may be interesting to describe life on the sea. To the reflecting mind a trip across the Atlantic is full of profitable lessons. I took my stand on the promenade deck where I could observe both cabin and steerage passengers as they came on board. Old men wept as they bade farewell to their sons, and the heaving bosoms of tender maidens indicated the heart struggles within as they parted from their lovers, perhaps to meet no more. A poor lad, apparently in the last stages of consumption, seemed loth to quit the fond embrace of his weeping mother who, as a forlorn hope of restoration, had consented to his departure. I do not think she will see him again. From these sad parting scenes I concluded we were to have a melancholy trip, but we had not been at sea twenty-four hours before I was led to modify my views. For four days I saw but few sober men. The only amusement was drinking and gambling. They bet on everything, from the toss of a penny or turn of a card to the run of the ship ; one gentleman bet £80 (about $400 American gold) on the toss of a penny. The other party to the wager pocketed the money as coolly as a beggar would a penny. The second day out was Sunday, and although we had five clergymen on board no one proposed religious service, not even *myself ;* I confess I forgot the day. I saw one of the clergymen coolly looking on at a game of euchre, with a sovereign on each corner. That night he fell out of his berth and dislocated his shoulder ; the poor fellow was under the doctor's hands for the rest of the voyage. I asked one of his companions how it happened. He said, " Oh, he *smoked* too much."

The cabin passengers were a mixture of all nations, and were composed of Americans, Irishmen, Englishmen, and Frenchmen, with a few Italians, Spaniards, Germans, and Scotchmen. One fellow was quite a character. He delighted in the name of Captain. He had been all over America, and was ready to swear that it contained nothing worth seeing, not even a rose. His seat was opposite mine at table. We had

oranges after dinner ; he called the steward and demanded a
knife and fork ; said he : " *Hi* never could *heat han horange*
without a *fowk*, *hit* seems so dem'd *vulgaw*." Turning to his
companion, a Captain in the English army, he said : " How
joli it will be to get *'ome* to *hold Hengland ; hafter hall hit his
the honly* place *hon hearth* for men and *'orses.*" I suggested
that it also produced some very fine *asses ;* after which suggestion I did not presume to raise my eyes for full ten seconds,
expecting all the time the concussion of a champagne bottle
with my head. Upon presuming to look up I was met with a
withering scowl from all the English passengers at our table.
The captain of the ship remarked that the American gentleman was inclined to be *jokeful.*

Off the coast of Newfoundland we encountered a dense
fog. With the greatest effort I could not see twenty yards
from the ship ; withal it was exceedingly cold ; we saw no ice,
but felt it in the air. The officers on duty were very vigilant.
A watch of four sailors kept a sharp lookout ahead A bright
light was placed at the masthead, and the steam whistle was
blown every half minute during the entire night. The greatest danger at sea is from fire and fogs. Had a ship or iceberg
crossed our path you would, perhaps, never have heard from
us. From this time until we first saw land, officers and passengers were *tolerably* sober. The day before we saw land was
Sunday ; we had the regular Church of England service for
the sea. I was promenading on deck, and observed the officers
anxiously looking northeast, where I observed what I supposed
was the dim outline of a cloud. It proved to be the bleak
and rocky coast of Ireland.

The ship accommodations and fare were all that could be
desired. Clean berths, good attendants and obliging stewards.
From 5 to 7 o'clock A. M. we had coffee ; at 9, breakfast ; at
12, lunch ; dinner at 4 P. M., and supper from 7 to 9 P. M.
Custom requires passengers on quitting the ship to leave a
sovereign with the stewards and attendants, usually distributed
as follows : 10*s.* to the head table steward, 6*s.* to the bed steward, and the balance to the cabin boy and bootblack.

Our steamer did not enter the harbor at Queenstown, but
signalled by means of rockets, and was met in the channel by a
steamboat which took off the passengers and mails for Queenstown. The town is situate upon an abrupt bank and previously
to 1849 was called *Cove.* It was then visited by the Queen,
and has since been dignified by its new name. It is beautiful
and picturesque, built in tiers or terraces upon a hill nearly as
abrupt as Fairmount, facing the wire bridge at Philadelphia.
The hill rises so high behind the town that a person standing
on any of the eminences can look down the chimneys of the

houses on the lower tier. Great labor has been expended on the streets; they are as smooth and clean as a floor, and as hard as the *hearts of the Irish landlords.* From Queenstown southeast the prospect is charming. Cork harbor and passage lie in front and around it to the right. It is the finest harbor in the world, and. could afford shelter to the entire English fleet. Spike Island lies directly in front. It is a convict depot, with room for two thousand prisoners. Rocky Island, also in view, contains a powder magazine hewn into the solid rock, in six chambers. It contains 10,000 barrels of gunpowder. Hawbowline is an island opposite Spike. It has a fresh-water tank holding 5000 tons of water. It was in this harbor that Drake took shelter when pursued by the Spaniards. He was so effectually hidden in Cross Haven Creek that they believed his escape to be the work of magic. His hiding place is known to this day as "Drake's Pool." The finest hotel in the place is the Queen's; it fully equals the Girard House, Philadelphia. It is, of course, conducted on the European plan, containing drawing-room, coffee-room, and *salle a manger* for gentlemen and ladies, and a commercial room for merchants, tradesmen, etc. The scale of prices varies, the drawing-room guests being charged about one-third more than those of the commercial room.

Meals will be served for the drawing-room guests either in their chambers, *salle a manger*, or drawing-room, as desired, and at any hour. Everything is itemized in the bill. Upon the whole, my impressions of Ireland are good.

II.

QUEENSTOWN TO KILLARNEY—OLD CASTLES—CORK—SHANDON—ROYAL NAMES—IRISH FARMERS--FROGS AND SNAKES —BLARNEY CASTLE—BEGGARS—LAKES OF KILLARNEY— MUSICAL ECHOES—ST. JOHN'S DAY AT KILLARNEY.

LAKES OF KILLARNEY, June, 1869.

From Queenstown to this place, by way of Cork, is about seventy-five miles. It is eleven miles from Queenstown to Cork by rail, and fourteen by river. Tourists should by all means choose the latter; the scenery is really superb. The shore rises in groves and hills crowned with splendid edifices, public and private. Two castles are passed. The one at Monkstown, erected by Anastatia Goold,. in 1636, is now a ruin. The other, known as Blackrock, stands upon a promontory, and at a distance looks like a formidable old castle. It is of comparatively modern construction. It was from this place that William Penn, who had been converted at Cork to Quakerism, embarked for America.

Cork is quite a considerable town. It contains about eighty thousand inhabitants; its population *decreases* about six thousand in ten years. This is true of all the cities and towns of Ireland. The river Lee, upon which it is built, forks at the city; the town is built on the swamp between the forks, and on the high hills on the north and south of both branches. It takes its name from its location, *Corcagh*, the original Irish name, meaning a swamp. It is one of the oldest towns in Ireland, and was the site of a Pagan temple, which was destroyed in the seventh century. The streets of the older parts of the city are very narrow, ranging from four to thirty feet; Grand Parade and St. Patrick's Streets, however, are from eighty to one hundred and fifty feet wide, being wider in some places than others. The Imperial Hotel is fully equal to any second-class hotel in America. It fronts upon Pembroke Street, barely twenty-five feet wide. The streets in the old part of the city run in every conceivable way, making all kinds of angles, circles, triangles, elliptics, and now and then, for one square, a straight line. The quays are built of solid oblong granite blocks, and are walled up on both sides of the river's branches, at least six feet above high water. The town is united by six bridges of solid masonry. The public buildings are really a credit to the city. The court house and the county jail are noble edifices, far superior to any of the class in Pennsylvania. It also contains stores on Grand Parade and St. Patrick's Streets, equal to those of Market Street, Philadelphia. It boasts of eight scientific institutions, but as an offset I counted thirty-three pawnbrokers. I noticed a peculiarity in the numbering of the houses, which I am told prevails all over Ireland. The numbers begin on one side at the commencement of the street and run consecutively to the end, then turn and come down the other side—thus No. 10 St. Patrick's Street is opposite No. 130 on the other side of the street. The city contains some splendid churches. The most celebrated has been neglected since Cromwell took the town and melted all the church bells into cannon. The steeple or Shandon, to which I refer, is of solid masonry, and one hundred and twenty feet high, standing upon a hill on the north side of the north branch of the Lee. It has yet a good chime of bells.

> "Those Shandon bells,
> Whose sound so wild, would,
> In the days of childhood,
> Fling round my cradle
> Their magic spells."

I heard them, and can bear witness to their sweetness. The town delights in royal names ; you see them on everything, such as the Imperial Hotel, the Royal Victoria, the Queens, the Prince of Wales, the Princess Royal, Prince Arthur, the King's Arms, etc., etc. The country around Cork is naturally fertile, but badly cultivated. The land is mostly owned in England, and is cultivated by tenants who, as a rule, hold at sufferance from year to year. The farms contain from one to ten acres, with no barns or houses ; if a tenant was to build himself a house his rent would be at once raised. I noticed as an emblem of Justice, the Goddess on the court house held in her hand an old-fashioned pair of *steelyards*, banished from America long ago because of their *uncertainty*. I suppose it to be a true emblem of English justice for poor Ireland.

There are plenty of frogs around Cork. I saw a fine large one on the bank of the lake. I said to my coachman : " I thought you told me that St. Patrick banished from Ireland all the frogs, toads and snakes." "Oh," said he, "That's not a frog, that's only a *waterjack*." The castle and lake of Blarney are about five miles from Cork. The castle is now a ruin ; it was built by Cormac McCarthy, in 1446. The massive donjon tower that remains is 120 feet high, and must have been indeed a strong, and I would say, from its ruins, an impregnable place, before the introduction of gunpowder. I kissed the Blarney stone, a somewhat perilous task, as it is about six feet down from the parapet, and while performing the devotion your head is down and your heels up ; by holding firmly to the two iron bars, with the assistance of your guide, who holds you by the *feet*, the *feat* can be accomplished. The groves and lake of Blarney are lovely and romantic ; they have been the theme of many Irish songs. The *Reliques* of Father Prout alludes to them and the "stone."

"There is a stone there
   That whoever kisses,
Oh ! he never misses
   To grow eloquent.

"'Tis he may clamber
   To a lady's chamber,
Or become a member
   Of Parliament "

A short distance from the castle is a cave said to lead to the bottom of the lake, 360 yards off. As we approached it we heard the *fiddler* of Blarney *sawing* away on " *Yankee Doodle*." There were five tourists in our party ; of course we gave him sixpence each, after which you should have heard the *blarney*, for it was beyond description. Rabbits are quite thick, and birds fly around the streets of Cork as tame as chickens. The crows are also numerous, and as tame as pigeons ; this is because of the severity of the game laws ; no one in Ireland is allowed to carry a gun without royal permission, and a license in his pocket.

The most striking peculiarity of Ireland is its *beggars* ; they importune you at every step. Cork is full of them ; I saw ten at once make a raid upon a gentleman and lady while walking on the Mardyke, a very beautiful promenade, about a mile long, with stately elms on both sides and arches every few yards, from the apex of which are suspended lamps which give it a most enchanting appearance at night. From Cork to Killarney we passed several ruined castles. The railroads are far superior to ours in construction ; so with the common roads, they are all in splendid order ; no wooden bridges, they are all of stone, even the platforms along the road are built of dressed stone.

The railway hotel is decidedly the best in Killarney. It is built of square dressed stone ; the walls are three feet thick ; it contains everything necessary for a first-class hotel, and has one hundred large, airy, and elegantly-furnished guest chambers, coffee-room, commercial-room, large drawing-rooms, *salle a manger*, and breakfast-room. It is well kept, and the prices are reasonable.

On the 25th inst., I visited the "Lakes of Killarney," a most charming place. No tongue can tell or pen describe, the ever-changing scenery. It must be seen to be comprehended. Its lakes, glens, cascades, and mountains present to the eye a panorama of unequalled loveliness. The journey through the lakes and over the mountain passes, by carriage, foot, and boat, is at least 31 miles. I only gave it one day, and went the whole journey. At one point our guide played an air on his bugle ; the whole range of mountains took up the echo ; he was hid from our view, and had we been ignorant of its origin, we would have thought the mountains full of musicians. While passing the Gap of Dunloe we overtook about forty gentlemen enjoying a picnic. They recognized me, and insisted on me joining them ; I was fatigued, and gladly partook of their refreshments. The remaining gentlemen of our party supposed I had found a company of American friends. They could not be convinced that we had never met before, until informed by the landlord that they were members of Trales Lodge, F. A. M., No. 379, spending St. John's day at the Lakes. God bless the craft around the globe ! I sat with them that night at *table lodge* at their hotel and was royally entertained.

I leave Killarney with regret. I feel that I shall not look

upon its like again. But one thing marred my enjoyment—its *beggars* ; it *beggars* description to do them justice. They followed us four miles over the mountain, and could not be scolded, coaxed, or kicked away. At the town of Killarney —a very mean place—I met a bare-headed, bare-footed mendicant friar, with gown and cowl, and shaved head, an old rope for a girdle, and rosary hanging by his side ; just such a picture as you have often seen in old paintings.

III.

KILLARNEY TO DUBLIN—IRISH RAILWAYS—THE PEASANTRY —AN IRISH AMERICAN—PRE-HISTORIC ROUND TOWERS— BOGS—DECREASING POPULATION—AMERICAN FARMING IMPLEMENTS—DUBLIN, ITS BRIDGES, GARDENS AND PUBLIC BUILDINGS.

DUBLIN, June, 1869.

From Killarney to Dublin is 185 miles, we pass through parts of Counties Kerry, Cork, Limerick, Tipperary, Queens, Kildare and Dublin. The route is through the heart of Ireland. While the railways are superior, the cars are inferior, to those of America. One of our palace cars would be a wonder here. In the railway car no conductor accompanies the train ; the passengers are locked in, and at certain stations an agent presents himself, requesting a sight of your ticket. Sickness or other emergency must be endured until a station is reached. Tipperary and Queen's counties look bad to an American. The fields are deserted, and the rich meadow lands abandoned to sheep grazing. The ditches and mud fences are broken, and the once beautiful hedges are ragged and trodden down. I noticed the ox-eyed daisy and thistle in great abundance in the fields, hedges and roadside. The land looks as if it had once been well cultivated, but it is certainly not now. In vain the traveller looks for a farm-house or barn, instead of which he sees but mud hovels and huts, in which a Pennsylvania farmer would *blush* to his cattle. These are the dwellings of the Irish peasantry. As the train approached the line of Queen's County, I observed a farm-house and barn, such as are seen all over America. I asked an old man at the station who owned it. He said it had been built about ten years ago by an " *Irish American.*" " Does he live there yet ?" said I. "Oh, no, he sold out and went back to America, four years ago."

Several interesting ruins are passed ; one of the most perfect old round towers in Ireland stands at Clondankin. It is eighty-four feet high. The telegraph poles throughout Ireland are not ten feet high ; they look like dwarfs, compared with ours. I have not seen an orchard in this part of Ireland. In Limerick I saw some middling well-timbered woodlands ; we pass hundreds of acres of bog-lands. A bog is not a swamp ; the turf is sometimes cut ten feet down, without the interference of water. It burns quite cheerfully, and leaves a white ash. The general face of the country is not unlike that along the line of the railroad from Marcus Hook to Philadelphia, substituting ditches, mud walls, and ragged hedges for fences, and dividing the fields into patches of from one to three acres. Queen's County looks to me worse than Tipperary ; both have enormously decreased in population during the last twenty years ; the latter from 153,930 in 1641, to 90,650 in 1851 ; County Kildare looks better ; its lands lie well, are mostly rich and rolling, and seem pretty well cultivated. It looks somewhat like New Castle County, Delaware, without its farm-houses and barns, but with better roads and bridges. The water-power of Ireland is enormous ; nature could not have better distributed its rivers and creeks. As I approached Dublin I saw all the modern American implements of farming, such as mowing machines, threshing machines, horse-rakes, hay-spreaders, cultivators, etc., etc.

Dublin is a very interesting and handsome city. It contains more elegant public buildings, monument, and works of art, within a comparatively small compass, than any I have yet seen. It has about 250,000 inhabitants, but is decreasing. It is beautifully situated on both banks of the river Liffey, which is about as wide as the Schuylkill at Market Street. The river is walled with dressed stone on both banks at least 15 feet higher than high water mark. It is spanned by eight substantial stone and iron bridges. The shipping comes up to Carlisle Street bridge. The King's bridge is the furthest up the river, say about two miles from Carlisle bridge. Wellington, Essex, Richmond, Wintworth, Queen's and Barrack bridges intervene at nearly equal distances. A short distance below Carlisle bridge the river expands into a noble bay. The principal objects of interest in the city are : Nelson's Monument, 121 feet high ; the Post Office, Custom House, Rutland . Square, the Rotundo, Newgate Prison, the scene of Fitzgerald's execution in 1798 ; the King's Inns, the Four Courts, the Royal Barracks, Phœnix Park, containing 1750 acres, in which stands Wellington's Monument ; the Old Castle, Col lege Green, with the statue of William III ; Trinity College, with its statues of Moore, Burke and Goldsmith ; Marion Square, St. Stephen's Square, Exhibition Palace and Winter

Garden, Porto Bello Garden, St. Patrick Cathedral, (said to stand over the well where the Old Saint baptized his converts) and Christ Church. The beggars are not quite as many as at Cork and Killarney, but too thick for comfort. Articles of merchandise are about as high as in Philadelphia, and the people about as happy. I leave it this afternoon for Belfast and the Giant's Causeway.

IV.

DUBLIN TO GIANT'S CAUSEWAY—HIGH RENTS—DROGHEDA—
CROMWELL'S CRUELTY—BOYNE WATER—ORANGEMEN OF
ULSTER—CROSSES OF MONASTERBOICE—TOMB OF KING
MUREDACH—MELLIFONT ABBEY—TEN COUNTIES AT ONE
COUP D'OEIL—LONG DAYS—BELFAST—FAMILIAR NAMES—
PHILADELPHIA LEDGER OBITUARY POETRY—JAUNTING
CARS --KEEP TO THE LEFT—GIRLS FARMING—GIANT'S
CAUSEWAY—PORTCOON CAVE—WHO BUILT THE CAUSE-
WAY?—DUNLUCE CASTLE—SEA BATHING.

GIANT'S CAUSEWAY, July, 1869.

From Dublin to this place, *via* Belfast, is 187 miles. The country traversed is most interesting, and contains some renowned places. The fields are large, well cultivated and green with pasture, flax, barley, oats and potatoes. The farmers pay a perpetual rent, ranging from one to seven pounds per acre. Several manufacturing towns, somewhat resembling Upland, are passed. I spent a day at Drogheda, a very old town, about 37 miles north of Dublin, situated upon the famous river Boyne ; it was once a walled city. A fine specimen of the wall, known as St. Lawrence's Gate, still remains. On the south side of the river are the remains of St. Mary's Abbey, founded in the reign of Edward I. Magdalen Steeple is a very fine ruin on the north side of the river, and is all that remains of the famous church of the Dominican Friars, where the Irish chiefs submitted to Richard II. Cromwell sacked the town, and indiscriminately slaughtered its inhabitants, from the effects of which it has never recovered. The bitter memories of the siege are still fresh with the people, and the name of the Protector is one of execration ; they tell of little babes found, the day after the slaughter, sucking at the dry breasts of their murdered mothers. There are a few good buildings in the town, but the suburbs are miserable mud hovels, one story high, thatched with straw, without floors or chimneys, and swarming with wretched creatures in the most abject poverty. I saw pretty little, bright-eyed girls, nearly naked, in the streets, and smart little boys begging for a living. The railroad bridge over the Boyne is superior to any I have seen in America. It is of solid masonry, and consists of fifteen arches of 61-feet span, and a centre arch of 250 feet. Large shipping can sail under it.

About two miles up, on the north bank of the river, an obelisk 150 feet high, marks the spot where William of Orange commenced the attack upon his father-in-law, King James II. The spot where James stood and surveyed the battle, as well as that occupied by William, is pointed out by the guide. Some of the entrenchments can still be seen. This is the anniversary of the battle : it was fought July 1, 1690, and has been annually celebrated ever since by the Orange men of Ulster. Red and orange-colored flags are now flying from the steeples of Episcopal churches between here and Belfast, commemorative of the event and mobs of men and boys may be seen flaunting orange-colored flags, and singing insulting sectional songs by day, and by night congregating around immense bonfires, and hooting, yelling and screaming around the Catholic churches, for the apparent purpose of inciting to riot and bloodshed. The Catholic population of this place is twelve to one of the Protestant, and they are commendable for their good behavior, as they seem determined to avoid a conflict, by looking in silent contempt upon the disgraceful proceedings of their Protestant neighbors.

For twelve shillings a car and driver, who also acts as guide, can be hired to conduct the tourist to Monasterboice, Slane and Mellifont, making a journey of about twenty-five miles circular from Drogheda. At Monasterboice, in a solitary field, stands an old round tower and two chapels in ruins, with three elaborately sculptured stone crosses, one of which is twenty-seven feet high, and has stood perhaps a thousand years in its present position over the grave of some Irish king. The tomb of King Muredach, who died A. D. 534, is near the round-tower. The name is quite legible in Irish characters upon the slab over his grave. The round-tower is 110 feet high, and, like all of its kind, is of pre-historic antiquity. It was doubtless an object of traditional reverence when the chapels were built, perhaps by St. Patrick, as King Muredach's death was only about 100 years after that of the old saint.

Mellifont Abbey, about three miles west of Monasterboice, was built A. D. 1142, by O'Carrol, Prince of Orgiel. It contained at one time 140 monks. Slane, three miles further, contains a fine old ruined abbey, which commands one of the finest views in Ireland. It is said that ten counties may be seen from its towers. The view is truly fine.

The time by rail from Drogheda to Belfast is about five hours. The days here in July are very long; daylight commences at 2.30 A. M., and ends a little before 10 o'clock P. M. Belfast is a pretty and clean city, but too much like the towns of America to require special notice. Signs of industry are exhibited everywhere, and consequently beggars are few. I was struck with the familiar names on the business signs, and on the grave-stones in the burial-grounds, such as Gamble, Ward, Wilson, Johnson, Brown, Shaw, Taylor, McCay, and other Delaware county names. Perhaps some of the old settlers of the county came from this place. Judging from the obituary poetry on the tomb-stones, the Philadelphia *Ledger* must have found its way here as early as 1831. I copied some of its poetry from an old headstone—

> "With suffering sore, a long time bore,
> Physicians was all in vain.
> But death him seized
> And God was pleased.
> A happy release from pain."

There are no omnibuses or street railways in Ireland; short journeys are made in *jaunting cars*. As a rule the sidewalks in all the cities are paved with cobble-stones instead of brick. I have also observed that the guage of the wheels of the vehicles is of a different width, thereby obviating the formation of ruts, and keeping the streets and roads level. If the traveller were to observe the American rule and keep to the *right* he would be going *wrong*.

There are no brick in Ireland like those of Philadelphia; here they are of a yellow mud color, giving even to new buildings an old appearance. On my journey from Belfast to Portrush at Ballymena, I saw an apple orchard, the first I have observed in Ireland.

It is quite common here to see full grown girls spreading hay with their *hands* instead of *forks*. Grass and garden vegetables grow in abundance to within a few feet of the sea-shore, which is very abrupt and rugged, giving indubitable evidence by its charred and cracked rocks of plutonic formation. From here to the Causeway the coast looks as if its rocks had been belched up from the infernal regions in a state of fusion, and suddenly cooled by contact with the sea. The seaweed grows in great abundance upon the rocks, and is gathered and burnt by the peasants, who sell the ashes to the chemists for the manufacture of potash.

The coast from Portrush to the Giant's Causeway is calculated to inspire sentiments of pleasure as well as wonder. In entering Portcoon and Dunkerry caves, nothing is wanted but the smell of sulphur to transform them into the portals of

Pandemonium. I fired my pistol in Portcoon cave, and the
effect was like the discharge of a battery of artillery.   Tradition says this cave was the home of a hermit giant, who was
fed by seals from the sea.   The Causeway proper cannot be
described, it must be seen to be enjoyed.   It also has its
tradition.   The peasants tell you, with great earnestness, that
it was built by Fin M'Coul, the champion of Ireland, to afford
a passageway to Scotland, that a famous Caledonian giant
might cross over without wetting his feet, as he had threatened
that he would come over and whip Fin, were it not for the
wetting of his feet.   After the Causeway was finished he
crossed over and got wofully thrashed, but with becoming
Hibernian generosity, Fin allowed his former rival to remain
in Ireland, and gave him his daughter to wife.   As he did not
desire to return, the Causeway was neglected and broken up
by the angry sea, what is now seen being all that remains of
the famous work.

Dunluce Castle four miles west of the Causeway, is the
most picturesque ruin in Ireland.   It rests on a precipitous
mass of rock, 150 feet high, boldly facing the ocean.   Portrush
is the Cape May of Dublin and the North.   The ladies bathe
by themselves in linen suits, but the gentlemen go in *nude*.
The fair ones do not seem at all shocked, but promenade the
shore in perfect *nonchalance* while the gentlemen are bathing.
At Bangor, which is the watering place for Belfast, the entire
shore was lined with gentlemen, bathing in *all the simplicity of
nature*, and the ladies on the boat did not even turn their
heads, or "look with downcast eyes."   So much for the customs of the country.   I have now finished my tour in Ireland.
It is a fair land, its people are kind and hospitable; an American feels that he is not friendless in Ireland.   To-morrow I
embark for England.

V.

FROM IRELAND TO ENGLAND—LIVERPOOL—HOW TO EXPLORE
AN OLD CITY—U. S. BONDS—THE SUDDEN CHANGE FROM
PAPER MONEY TO GOLD—BIRKENHEAD—CHESTER—THE
ROWS AND ROMAN WALLS—PHŒNIX TOWER—AN OLD
MONK'S DESCRIPTION OF CHESTER—CATHEDRAL EPITAPH
UPON THE TOMB OF A DEAD SON—HORSES.

LIVERPOOL, July, 1869.

Liverpool is about half as large as Philadelphia, and lies
nearly due east from Dublin.   The sun rises here about twenty-

five minutes ahead of Ireland, although Paddy is loath to admit the possibility of the sun rising anywhere earlier than in Ireland.

By taking ship at 8 P. M. at Dublin, Liverpool is reached at 6 A. M. next day, and by one not subject to *mal de mer*, a pleasant sleep may be enjoyed upon the bosom of old ocean. Liverpool possesses nothing worthy of especial notice, except perhaps its splendid docks and quays, mud colored brick and sombre appearance. I am becoming accustomed to winding streets and begin to rather like them. A little exercise of brain, tongue, and eyes, will conduct the intelligent traveller through the most irregularly constructed city of Europe. They have all been built without any previous plan, but afterwards enlarged and beautified, as a native forest would be pruned to convert it into a public park. London was originally a fort, and Liverpool a fishing town. The roads converged to these points, and new ones were made as the towns grew in importance, and as they generally followed the lines of the farms and hillsides or the bank of some stream they would, of course, be crooked and irregular. As the town grew, the roads became the principal streets, and, for convenience of access from one to another, the cross streets were made. This was the outline : the streets, lanes, and alleys for private dwellings being subsequently filled in. They all have a central point or grand trunk street, which can easily be found by observing the convergence of the old principal streets into it. By impressing on the mind the courses of the grand trunk and its principal branches, together with their names, and the names and localities of the most notorious places, squares, monuments, gardens, parks, and public buildings, and by observing the sun by day and the polar star at night, the traveller may bid defiance to guides and cabmen, and without fear walk over every city in Europe.

With the exceptions just noticed, Liverpool looks very much like an American city. United States 5-20 bonds and greenbacks are plenty here, and can be converted into gold without difficulty for their full value, though the better way is to procure a draft, or letter of credit before starting abroad. All American travellers tell the same story as to the sudden change from paper to metallic currency. As soon as the traveller is assured that he can get gold for his draft, he doesn't want it ; he draws a few sovereigns in coin and the balance in Bank of England notes, and soon hates the sight of silver, and spends the copper to get rid of it. It will be the same in America in a week after resumption. The bank notes here are different from ours, being about twice as large as a greenback, and printed without any engraving, on fine and strong white paper.

Birkenhead occupies the same position to Liverpool that
Camden does to Philadelphia. It is about the size of Chester,
Delaware County. The name of Chester inspired me with a
desire to see the town from which our Chester derived its name.
It lies nearly south, and is about an hour distant from Birkenhead by rail. It is admitted to be one of the most remarkable
old towns in England, if not in Europe. Before Christ it was
a considerable town and has preserved its ancient form to a
wonderful extent to the present day. It has its old gates of
entrance and exit, and its old Roman walls standing entire.
They are about three miles long, and afford a delightful promenade, and splendid views around the town. The public
square outside of the walls is full of Roman antiquities, constantly being exhumed. In 1821, a fine and well-preserved
Roman altar was dug up bearing the following inscription :—

NYMPHIS ET FONTIBUS
Leg. XX. V. V.——

which in English would read, "To the Nymphs and Fountains, the 20th Legion, the invincible and victorious" (dedicate
this altar). As I walked around the wall I observed a mould-
ering old turret, known as Phœnix Tower. The inscription
over its ruined portal tells the rest. Here it is :—

"King Charles
Stood on this Tower
September 24th, 1645, and saw
His army defeated
On Rowton Moor."

The streets are most singularly constructed. The sidewalk or foot-path, apparently runs through the middle of the
houses ; below are shops on the level with the street, above
are chambers, and on each side stores. Ramulph Higden, a
monk of Chester Abbey, whose chronicles were published A.
D. 1495, gives the following description of the town: "The
City of Legions, that is Chester, in time of Britons was head
and chief city of all Venedocia, that is North Wales. There
lay a winter the legions of Julius Cæsar sent for to win Ireland.
And after Claudius Cæsar sent legions out of the city to win
the islands that he called Orcades. This city hath plenty of
live land, of corn, of flesh, and specially of salmon. This city
receiveth great merchandise and sendeth out also. North-
umbers destroyed this city sometime, but Elfleda, Lady of
Mercia, builded it again, and made it much more. In this city
had been ways under earth with vaults and stone work, wonderfully wrought, three chambered works, great stones engraved
with old names therein. This is that city that Ethelfrede,
King of Northumberland, destroyed, and slew there fast by

nigh two thousand monks. This is the city that King Edgar came to sometime with seven kings that were subject to him."

The old Cathedral of St. Werbug, built upon the site of a Pagan temple to Apollo, which it is said itself supplanted a still older fane of the Druids, stands so near the city wall that the uncouth rhymes on the tombstones may be read without descending. This ground was a place of sepulture before the Christian era. Among the quaint old verses and epitaphs I read one which touched a tender cord. Here it is :—

"Thou art gone, sweet boy, to death's dark shade,
    To never—never fading bliss ;
We could have wished thou'dst longer staid
    To share with us thy smiling kiss.
But God was pleased to call thee hence
    And save thee from this life of care ;
He called thee while in innocence
    His mercies better gifts to share.
Remember how I danced and sung,
    And clasped thee in my fond embrace,
Delighted with thy prattling tongue,
    Thy sparkling eye—and lovely face.
Thou should'st have closed thy father's eyes,
    And laid him in his native clay ;
But gone before me to the skies,
    I pray thoul't meet me on the way."

The face of the country between Liverpool and Chester wears very much the same appearance as some parts of Delaware. It is undulating rather than hilly, and is better cultivated than the land in Ireland. The farm-houses are not equal to those of Pennsylvania, and the barns few and poor. The horses, however, are the finest for heavy work I have ever seen. I saw draught horses in Liverpool almost as large and strong as elephants. I think the English iron plough is superior to any American one. I wonder it has not been adopted by our Pennsylvania farmers, as it would suit the soil, is very strong and steady, and yet of easy draught, and can be managed with one hand in the stiffest sod.

VI.

LONDON, July 1869.

From Liverpool to London by rail is about 200 miles, the route is through the bowels of the land, for which reason the journey should be made by day ; but the anxiety to reach the metropolis often induces many travellers to journey by night, a practice to be condemned. One of the objects of travelling should be to see the general face of the country, and to ob-serve, by comparison, its distinctive geographic features, as well as its style of cultivation and improvement. The speed attained upon this line is very great, averaging fifty miles an hour. The locomotive enters the centre of the city of London, but not on any of the streets ; the entrance was effected at enormous expense, by tunnelling and bridging. The passing train can be sometimes heard, but never seen. My impressions of the high state of English agriculture have not been realized; I have seen nothing superior to the well cultivated farms of our own State. Britain depends more on her traffic than her soil for her prosperity. Her merchants are truly princes, and her traffickers the honorable of the earth. If Paris is France, so London is England. To say it is a great city would be a tame expression ; it is an immense, and in many respects, a wonderful place. Its enormous docks, royal palaces, renowned antiquities, old abbeys, cathedrals, monuments, parks, and places of amusement, together with its mongrel population of 3,500,000 souls, of all classes and characters, from beggars, burglars and professional thieves, up to its peers, princes and royal heads, dwelling in habitations as distinctive as its classes, from the Royal Palace, resplendent with dazzling brilliancy and gorgeous light, down to the pestiferous haunts and noxious dens, where the light of the sun is never seen, all contribute to our wonder, or, if nothing more, furnish food for our serious reflection. London contains many objects of interest which no visitor should fail to see, among which are the British Museum, the National Gallery, the Zoological Gardens, the Crystal Palace, the Parliament Houses, Westminster Abbey, the Tower and St. Paul's Cathedral. The Museum contains specimens of antiquity, art, sciences and curiosity, so systematically arranged as to at once commend themselves to the intelligent mind. Fossils can there be seen ranging from the earliest developments of animal life, and regularly progressing through millions of ages up to the last and highest type, that of a human skeleton imbedded in a hard rock of solid limestone. Every known metal and mineral, salt or rock, is there represented. So in botany, zoology and geology. In the department of antiquities may be found the footprints of every step in human progress. Those from Nineveh, Babylon and Egypt, are the most interesting and confirmatory of the Holy Scriptures. The library contains either the original or a fac-simile of every known book or manuscript. I saw there a deed on papyrus in a plain, bold hand. It was exhumed with a mummy, and purported to convey a lot of ground in Memphis. It was at least four thousand years old, but in form it was identical with the deeds of the present day. The translation, with very little alteration, would pass for the work of a Chester conveyancer for a lot of ground in the South Ward, for I observed it had been sold *subject to a mortgage*. The student of universal knowledge could learn more in a month, in the British Museum, of practical education, than could be acquired in years of theoretical research. In the National Gallery at Trafalgar Square, are some of the rarest and best paintings in the world. Paul Veronese's Family of Darius, is considered among the best; it cost £14,000. A fine opportunity is afforded of comparing the works of modern masters with those of the ancient school. I observed a work of Raphael, and an unfinished piece by Michael Angelo, as bright and fresh as when they received the last touch of the brush, while some works of comparatively recent date, although equally beautiful in outline, were manifestly deficient in color, being dim and faded. As I journeyed toward the Tower, I paused a moment at London Bridge, and stood where Macaulay says the future traveller from New Zealand will stand upon its broken arch and sketch the ruins of St. Paul's.

Near the bridge stands the Monument, from the top of which an excellent view of London is had. It is 202 feet high, and stands just that distance from the spot in Pudding Lane, where the great fire of 1666 began. It was erected by Sir Christopher Wren. It bore an inscription which was erased in 1829, and which conveys a good idea of the bigotry of the age. It read as follows : "This pillar was set up to perpetuate the memory of the most dreadful burning of this ancient city, began and carried on by the treachery and malice of the Popish faction, in the beginning of September, A. D. 1666, in order to the carrying on of their horrid plot for extirpating the Protestant religion and old English Liberty, and introducing Popery and Slavery.''

All we know of our fathers is taught by the monuments they have left behind them. Man is naturally vain and inclined to imagine the age in which he lives the most perfect the world has ever known, but, after looking upon the ruins of time and glancing at the remains of ancient greatness, we are bewildered and amazed in the mere attempt to comprehend the glory of the olden time.

The art of war was perfect 4000 years ago ; all we know of music and the fine arts are but poor imitations of ancient models. Our best efforts at architecture are but copies of Grecian Temples.

London was a city before the birth of Christianity. In its growth it has absorbed all the surrounding villages and towns within a radius of twenty miles. The fire of 1666 destroyed 13,200 houses—400 streets were laid waste. The rebuilding of the city shows a peculiar trait of English character. They never change anything once deliberately adopted. The Pudding Lane, where the fire began is '' Pudding Lane''. still. The great architect, Sir Christopher Wren, urged the authorities to lay out the city on a new and greatly improved plan suggested by his experience, but with the disposition to do as their fathers had done, and that they might not infringe on private rights, they resolved to rebuild the city just as it was before the fire, with all its old bends, crooks, twists, hills, hollows and irregularities. Recent excavations however have demonstrated that the present city, in the older portions, is at least sixteen feet higher than it was in the days of Roman occupation. Old Roman roads, baths and foundations are constantly being exhumed below the bottom of the cellars of the present city.

London covers an area of about eighty square miles of solid buildings. Its three distinctive landmarks are Westminster Abbey, St. Paul's Cathedral and the Tower. The tombs and monuments of the old abbey are the marble records of English history. ''They harmonize its confusion and shed light upon its darkest pages.'' The present structure escaped the great fire. It was commenced by Edward the Conqueror upon the site of a ruined monastery. Its ground plan is that of a Latin cross. Its length including the chapel of Henry VII. is 530 feet ; its breadth at the transept is 203 feet. The towers are 225 feet high. William the Conqueror was crowned here with great pomp in A. D. 1065. The chapel of Henry VII. was added during the reign of that prince. To see the abbey under the most favorable conditions it should be entered by

the western door. When the eye surveys, and the mind for
the first time comprehends its vast proportions, the sensation
is one of wonder and surprise. The nave, the side aisles, the
mass of marble columns and monuments, the organ and the
grand eastern arch, beautified by the soft and tinted shades of
the decorated windows, present a scene of indescribable beauty.

Every inch of space on the side walls and niches has been
utilized by a profusion of memorials of the dead, some in
good, others in very bad taste. Above the line of the tombs
are dreary and solemn looking little chambers, once the dwelling places of the monks. The nine adjoining chapels have
been constructed so as to give them the appearance of being a
part of the same edifice.

The chapels contain the tombs, effigies and ashes of England's mightiest dead. Sebert, who died A. D. 616, was the
first and George II. the last king here interred. It has been
a royal burial place for over twelve hundred years. Among
the many royal tombs I particularly noticed that of Eleanor,
the beautiful Queen of Edward I. While in Palestine the
Saracens employed an assassin to murder Edward with a
poisoned dagger. In his struggle he received a wound in the
arm. Eleanor sucked the poison from the wound and saved
his life. She was the mother of the first Prince of Wales.
She died at Harby in 1291. Edward followed her body to
Westminster and to commemorate her worth and his grief he
set up a cross at every place where the funeral procession had
stopped, the last place being at the village of Charring, which
has ever since been known as Charring Cross. It is now in
the heart of London.

The traveler will also notice the tombs of Mary Queen of
Scots, the little princes murdered by Richard III., the effigy
of Henry VII. and the royal vault of George II. One of the
most interesting tombs contains the remains of Lady Margaret
Douglass, daughter of Queen Margaret of Scotland. It represents a beautiful lady reposing upon a finely chiseled altar.
The inscription says : '' This lady's great-grandfather was
Henry VII. ; her cousin Edward VI. ; her brother James V.
of Scotland ; her son Henry I. of Scotland ; her grandson
James V. ; having to her great-grandmother and grandmother
two queens, both named Elizabeth ; to her mother Margaret
Queen of Scots ; her aunt the French Queen ; her cousins Mary
and Elizabeth, Queens of England ; her neice and daughter-
in-law Mary Queen of Scots.'' This would seem to an
American to be royalty enough concentrated in one body to
satisfy even a woman. She was said to have been very beautiful. Her first husband, Sir Thomas Howard, died in prison ;
his only crime was his marriage without the assent of Henry

VIII. She afterwards married the Earl of Lenox, by whom she had Lord Darnly, the second husband of Mary Queen of Scots and father of James I. of England. Near her tomb is that of her most unfortunate daughter-in-law, Mary Queen of Scots ; she was remarkable for her rare beauty and doubtful virtue. Her first husband was the Dauphin of France ; her third was Bothwell, a rough soldier. After seventeen long years of imprisonment she was beheaded by order of her cousin, Queen Elizabeth. And so we might continue for days, reading the inscriptions and commenting upon and reviewing the lives of those here interred.

A favorite resort is the Poets' Corner. Near the tombs of Addison and Lord Macaulay we observe a marble slab set in the wall. Its inscription contains but four words—" O Rare Ben Johnson." The effect of a stroll among these tombs is to engender a desire to know something of the lives of the ones in whose honor they have been erected. We naturally look up their biography and by an association of ideas we never forget what we thus learn. I would, perhaps, never have known of the early struggles of the grand old poet if I had not been struck with the quaintness of his epitaph. Ben Johnson's father recognized his son's talent and took great pride in his education, but when he died Ben lost his best friend. His mother married a bricklayer who thought it a waste of time to study Latin in the school where Ben's father had placed him, so he took him from school and set him to laying bricks. At the building of Lincoln's Inn his subsequent benefactor found him with Horace in one hand and a trowel in the other. Near his memorial may be seen a small portion of the tomb of Lady Ann of Cleve. She was married to Henry VIII and was received by him with great pomp on Black Heath, January 3, 1539. In the following July he divorced her. His only ground for divorce was that " she was too Dutch for him." Touched at this insult she, with great dignity, retired to private life under the new name of " Lady Ann of Cleve." She lived to see her rival beheaded for infidelity to the King. Near by repose the ashes of the still more unfortunate Queen Annie. Richard III. after murdering her husband, and marrying her, conceived a passion for Elizabeth, sister to the little princes he had murdered in the Tower. To make room for his marriage with Elizabeth he poisoned Annie, but he did not live to capture Elizabeth, having been slain by the Earl of Richmond, afterwards Henry VII. Richard was a cunning, brave and blood-thirsty brute.

> "Not shaped for sportive tricks
> Nor made to court an amorous looking glass ;
> Cheated of feature by dissembling nature,
> Deformed, unfinished, sent before his time

> Into this breathing world, scarce half made up,
> And that so lamely and unfashionable
> That dogs barked at him as he halted by them."

In the days of pious frauds, the monks of Westminster Abbey invented and circulated the legend that St. Peter, in person, assisted by holy angels and amid a glorious display of heavenly light, dedicated the abbey the night before the day appointed by King Sebert for that ceremony.

Westminster Abbey is undoubtedly the first landmark of London. In my next letter I will try to say something about St. Paul's.

———

VII.

St. Paul's—Sir Christopher Wren's Monument—Tombs in the Crypt—Wellington's Funeral Car—Benjamin West—View from the Ball—Great Bell—Travel on London Bridge—The Tower—Arms and Armor—Colt's Revolver Four Hundred Years Old—Axe and Block—Koh-i-Noor for Sixpence—Traitor's Gate—Anne Boleyn—Philadelphia in Canada—Alabama Claims—English Jealousy of America.

LONDON, July, 1869.

Passing down Whitehall Street, the Strand, Fleet and Ludgate Streets, about two miles nearly due east from Westminster Abbey, we arrive at the next landmark, the magnificent Cathedral of St. Paul, one of the largest churches in the world and with capacity to hold twenty thousand persons. It is the most prominent object in London. The lofty dome can be seen for many miles. The cathedral stands in the centre of an enclosed churchyard at the head of Ludgate Hill.

A church existed here four hundred years before the Norman conquest. The present edifice was erected upon the site of the one that was destroyed by the great fire. Its architect was Sir Christopher Wren. It was thirty-five years being built and he lived to see it finished. Over the north door, in letters of gold, may be seen the following inscription :—

" SIR CHRISTOPHER WREN—Si monumentum quæris, circumspice ! "

A free translation of this inscription is a request to the beholder, if he is endeavoring to find Wren's monument, to look around him. In other words, the whole cathedral is his monument.

This church is also built upon a ground plan of a Latin cross five hundred and fourteen feet long by two hundred and sixty-six feet wide. From the pavement to the dome is three hundred and sixty-five feet, a foot for each day in the year. It covers two acres and sixteen perches of ground and cost $3,700,-000 in gold at a time when the purchasing value of a sovereign was twice as great as it now is. It occupies the site of a Druid Temple, remains of which were found when digging for the foundations of the church. The first christian church of St. Paul was commenced by King Ethelbert, A. D, 610. King Athalstan was buried in it and his son Edmond Ironsides was crowned in it. Canut had his palace hard by ; his courtyard extended to the river. It was there he rebuked his courtiers by commanding the tide to rise no higher. During the civil wars the church was converted into a stable. The soldiers amused themselves by playing ten pins on the long level aisles.

The interior of the present edifice is decorated by fifty elaborate marble monuments in commemoration of England's great men. Upon entering the building the first impression is that the interior is unfinished. The building is so immense that the fifty marble monuments are not a sufficient relief to the apparently naked walls.

In the crypt are the tombs of Wellington, Nelson, Wren and others. On entering the chamber containing the Sarcoph-agus of the Duke of Wellington, the effect is somewhat start-ling. There stands the colossal funeral car which carried his remains to their present resting place. The six great wheels are of solid brass, cast from the cannon he captured in Spain. Three enormous horses, all harnessed and equipped, draped in black velvet, seemed only to await the driver's word to start. It stands under the dome, a dim light giving to the whole chamber a solemn and sombre appearance. In emerging from the vault I saw the name of Benjamin West, cut upon a slab of marble. His remains repose beneath it. He was born in Delaware County at Swarthmore, and was deemed worthy of a burial place with the hero of Waterloo. For a small fee, trav-elers may climb from the crypt to the ball that surmounts the dome. The view from the balcony on a clear day (hard to find in London) comprends the whole city, the tortuous Thames and surrounding country. The great bell weighs four and a half tons and is ten feet in diameter. The hours are struck, but it is only tolled when one of the Royal family dies. Its solemn tone in the quiet evening sweeps over the metropolis and is often heard far into the suburbs.

As we journey east from the Cathedral we may pause awhile at London Bridge. It is the first bridge coming up the river. Most of the ships anchor, or go into the docks below.

The travel over it is enormous. From early daylight till far into night the bridge is crowded. Two great lines of vehicles and foot travellers may be seen, one coming, the other going from London to Southwark. A penny toll for each person and six pence for each wagon, would yield a revenue of one thousand dollars a day.

About a mile further down the river stands the Tower of London, one of its most ancient landmarks. Within its walls some of the gayest and many of the saddest scenes of English history have transpired. It was founded by Julius Cæsar and was the nucleus of the old city. It contains specimens of all known arms, from the war club to the Needle gun. It was from a revolver 400 years old that Col. Colt got the idea of his pistol. The old Warder told me that he saw Colt closely examining the pistol. He then got an order from the Constable of the Tower and went with it into an adjoining room where he took it apart and made careful drawings of its several parts. About two years afterwards Colt produced and patented his pistol. The quantity of arms and their fantastical arrangements, forming centre pieces, flowers, imitations of the sun, cornices, railing fountains, etc., has a confusing and somewhat bewildering effect upon the mind. Besides its museum of ancient arms and armor, it contains 300,000 stand of the most approved weapons always ready for use.

The horse armory contains the life-sized models of the mounted Kings of England from Edward I. to James II. They are clad in the actual armor they bore in life. The lances, coats of mail, saddles, shields and other accoutrements of the old warriors, clearly convey to the mind the contrast between the battle of Hastings and the bloody field of Waterloo.

Among other curiosities in the Tower, I saw the block, and felt the edge of the axe, used to decapitate prisoners of state. Anne Boleyn, Lady Jane Gray, her husband Lord Dudley and many other unfortunate players in the bloody game of "Crowns," have laid their naked necks upon this terrible block. It is of oak, but the blood of its victims has stained it to the color of mahogany. The marks of the axe upon it are very distinct and suggestive of the many tragic scenes in which the old piece of wood has played a prominent part.

For an extra six pence, they show the visitors the crown jewels including the famous koh-i-noor diamond—(I afterwards learned the supposed diamond was an imitation.)

The walls of the Tower enclose about thirteen acres of ground. The moat has a circumference of about half a mile. There are twelve towers around the walls ; the center building is called the White Tower. Every lover of ancient history must be interested in this hoary relic of a by-gone age. William, the Norman, dwelt in it as a place of safe retreat where he could seek shelter and at the same time awe his rebellious subjects.

A simple list of the renowned prisoners, who, during the past thousand years have pined away within these walls, would fill a good sized book.

The entry from the river is through the " Traitor's Gate." It is a gloomy, low arched passage with a heavy iron port-cullis and drawbridge. The great, the beautiful, even the Royal have passed beneath this ominous portal to exchange dreams of glory for the fatal block. Illustrious captives have sighed out a lifetime in the dungeons of the tower. In one of these chambers the Duke of Clarence had his dreadful dream the night before he was drowned in a but of port wine by order of his villainous brother, the Duke of Gloster. I read it, as so graphically repeated in Shakespeare's play of Richard III. At the foot of the staircase of the White Tower, years after the murder, the bones of the little princes of Edward IV. were found and were buried, as before stated, in Westminster Abbey.

In 1487, the beautiful Elizabeth of York, sister of the murdered princes, married Henry VII. in the tower. Henry had avenged the murder of her father and brothers by slaying Richard in the battle of Bosworth Field. As to the victor belong the spoils, Henry married Elizabeth. If Richard had been successful, he would have married her. All England rejoiced at her restoration, if not upon, at least by the side of her father's throne. Sixteen years afterwards she was buried from the tower. The procession passed to Westminster Abbey where her remains still repose. She was the grandmother of Lady Margaret Douglass, the inscription upon whose tomb I have already given.

On the 29th of May, 1533, the fair Lady Anne Boleyn was received at the Tower by Henry VIII. with great pomp and amid a melody of trumpets and a mighty peal of guns. " Beauty and sprightliness sat upon her lips, and in readiness of wit she was unsurpassed." Three years after, while dining with her gay friends, she was arrested by order of the King and again entered the tower, the place of her former triumphs. She inhabited the same royal apartments, but never saw the King again. She was tried for unfaithfulness to Henry, was convicted and on the 19th of May, less than three years from her coronation, she laid her neck upon the block already mentioned and her head was struck off at a single stroke of the axe whose edge I have just felt and find it sharp and keen, ready for a thousand more. Her mutilated body was thrust into an old chest and no one to this day 'knows where it was buried. Catherine of Arragon was avenged !

The last King crowned in the tower was Charles II. Since then its glory has departed. Before leaving England I must do her the justice to say that in many things we might improve by her experience. She encourages bravery in her soldiers, she fosters the arts, patronizes the learned and rewards those who serve her. The government of her metropolis is dignified and economical. She holds private rights more sacred than we do and seems to have more reverence for time-honored customs. But, while the majority of her people are well informed, many are lamentably ignorant of everything outside of England. I met a Member of Parliament at Graves End who thought Philadelphia was in Canada and that California was a city on the Pacific Railroad. When I informed him that Philadelphia was one-fourth as large as London and only about 100 miles West of New York, he gave me an incredulous look and remarked that he did not know it was so far out West. He wound up by asking if there were any buffalo around Philadelphia. I told him there were BULLS and *bears* in Third Street, but if he wanted to hunt buffalo he would have to go to Lake Erie, where he would find them so plentiful that they had named the city of Buffalo after them.

We must not, however, charge a nation with the faults or follies of an individual. They do not deny their sympathy with the South during our rebellion, and candidly admit that it was because they thought we were growing great too fast. All their professions, however, of love for the "Great Republic," as they now call our country, are false and hollow; they are evidently a little jealous of our growing strength. They are very uneasy about the Alabama controversy, and exhibit great anxiety for its settlement ; yet not a man can be found in favor of the payment of the damages. At the theatre a few evenings since, I heard a popular actor sing a song evidently made for the occasion, as it touched all topics of local excitement, such as the Irish church bill, Life Peerage, &c. The chorus to each verse, as nearly as I can remember it, ran thus:

> " But all is yet uncertain.
> I have no cause to doubt it.
> It may be yes. It may be no.
> That's all I know about it."

The whole song was coolly received until the last verse was reached, which ran as follows:

> " Now in the Alabama case
> The Yankees want their bill.
> But will they get it? Not for Joe!
> I do not think they will.

It won't be yes. It will be no,
I have no cause to doubt it.
It shan't be yes. It shall be no.
That's what I know about it."

This verse was received with prolonged shouts of applause, encored two or three times.

As a people the English are undoubtedly brave and intelligent. They are slow to enter a quarrel. They count the cost and are reluctant to embark in doubtful wars, but he reads English character amiss who attributes this reluctance to cowardice. They often bluster to their equals and bully their inferiors, but history is too replete with their great and obstinate struggles to leave a doubt as to their courage. Let us also remember, when we cast calumny on the British name, we foul the nest in which our own eagle was hatched. While yielding nothing that is our due, let us accord to England all that is her right, that the peaceful relations now existing may never by any fault of ours be disrupted. "With all her faults we love her still."

VIII.

LONDON TO CARLISLE—HOW TO SEE LONDON—ENGLISH AND AMERICAN PRONUNCIATION—CRYSTAL PALACE—DOCTORS AND LAWYERS—CARLISLE—WIND MILLS—MARYS PRISON—A GIANT'S GRAVE—KING ARTHUR'S ROUND TABLE—LONG MEG AND HER DAUGHTERS.

CARLISLE, ENGLAND, July, 1869.

From the smoke and fog of London, on my way to Scotland, I tarried here for a day. I have experienced no difficulty in finding any desired place in London. To thoroughly know the city it is necessary to walk over it, avoiding hackney coaches as much as possible. The locality of a place, like a geometrical problem, is never forgotton when discovered by unassisted effort. By the assistance of a map, any desired number of walks may be arranged, and although the streets are almost innumerable, and never more than a few squares long, by sketching the principal ones and noting the prominent squares and public buildings, it is not difficult to comprehend the whole city. The names of the streets are never changed; those familiar to the readers of ancient literature may still be found just where they were in the days of Shakespeare The citizens have adopted a very simple rule by which any spot referred to is mentally located. They associate it with

the most prominent object in the vicinity, thus : Ask for
Drury Lane Theatre, the answer will be "Covent Garden," a
famous fruit and vegetable market. I had occasion on my
first arrival to ask for the post-office ; the answer was: "St.
Martin le Grand, St. Paul's," meaning it was upon the street
known as St. Martin le Grand, which street was near St.
Paul's Cathedral: It is advisable, of course, to so arrange the
daily walks as not to duplicate any previous route—invariably
pronounced here "root." I observe some difference between
English and American pronunciation. In proper nouns they
almost invariably here pronounce the letter "a" as it is sounded in the word "father." The words "either" and "neither,"
they pronounce as if written "*ither* and "*nither*,"' giving the
"i" its first long sound as in "ice." Their orthography also
in some respects differs from ours. They spell cider, *cyder*,
jail *gaol*, labor, *labour*. They call baggage, *luggage*, pantaloons they call *trousers*, The word *farmer* here has a meaning entirely different from the same word in America. It
means a *renter*. I noticed in some of the advertisements relating to the Crystal Palace, the word was spelled *Chrystal*.

The Crystal Palace has lost but little of its original interest, and although some ten or twelve miles from the city, it
is visited by from three to ten thousand persons daily. The
great and commendable effort of its managers seems to be, to
make it as highly educational as possible. The building is
enormous, yet graceful. It is nearly one-third of a mile in
length, and over three hundred feet in width, and so high that
forest trees could grow under its roof. It contains *fac-similes*
of almost all the architecture and sculpture of successive ages,
including one of the exhumed palaces of Pompeii. I saw
here a cast of one of the great crosses at Monasterboice. It
was so perfect that, until informed to the contrary, I was sure
it was the original which I had seen less than a month ago,
standing near Drogheda, in Ireland. The grounds contain
over two hundred acres, and are laid out in delightful gardens, groves, lakes and cascades, relieved by life-sized representations of all the extinct antediluvian animals and reptiles,
from the mastodon down to a lizard thirty-five feet long.
Some of them appear to be browsing upon the reeds and rushes
in which they stand, others just crawling from the water ;
some are sleeping upon the rocks, and yet others half hid in
the mud. It would be a very hard day's work to give even a
cursory look at all that is here exhibited. In emerging from
a small wood, skirting a twenty-acre lake, I came upon one
of the best artificial geological studies in the world. It covers
several acres, and displays nearly all the rocks forming the
earth's crust, from the old red sandstone up to the latest

tertiary beds, including veins of coal and fossil remains. A
little further up the hill is a *jac-simile* of a Derbyshire lead
mine. I also noticed in the South Kensington Museum the
same highly educational arrangement of industrial production,
showing at a glance all the different processes of the manufacture of various articles, from a farthing's worth of iron ore
through all its processes until it is worth $1000 in watch
springs. I particularly noticed at the latter place an exhibition of the chemical analysis of every known article of food
and drink, from tea up to whisky, and from an oyster up to
roast beef. The elementary matter was so arranged as to
show, by comparison, the quantities of each kind. The
water, gelatin, fibrin, albumen, fat, and earthy matter contained in each kind of fish, flesh and fowl, were clearly shown,
as also the water, alcohol, sugar, citric, malic, and tartaric
acids, and fusel oils in the various wines and liquors used as
beverages.

The division of labor is carried to excess in London, and
has been applied to the professions of law and medicine to a
ridiculous extent. The physicians make certain diseases
specialties ; the result is that each disease has its doctor, and
if the patient does not know his disease he cannot choose a
physician, and may therefore die before he knows what ails
him. Divisions in the legal profession are still worse. It has
its attorneys, barristers, solicitors, proctors, counsellors of the
inner and outer bar, special pleaders and sergeants. The
poor client often requires the services of the whole batch,
in which event Heaven help his purse. In America the entire
duty is performed by one lawyer.

Carlisle, where I now rest, is about three hundred miles
north of London, and one hundred miles from Edinburgh,
which lies due north from here. The country is very beautiful, but no more so than some American rural scenery. There
are no barns, no forests, and no fields of Indian corn, so
charming to an American eye. Although the water power of
the country is good, I observed old fashioned wind-mills, such
as Don Quixote made war upon, on many of the hills ; and I
saw on my journey, several men threshing wheat in the open
field with old-fashioned flails. Carlisle is about the size of
Wilmington, Delaware. It is a very old town, having been
at one time a Roman station. The castle, now in ruins, was
built by William Rufus. Robert Bruce besieged it, but un-
successfully. After the union of the Scotch and English
crowns, the city sank into decay, but now appears to be flourishing again. The lofty and massive tower of the castle still
remains. It contains a very deep well, and excites more than
ordinary interest, as the place where Mary, Queen of Scots,

was imprisoned on her flight to England. Seventeen miles
south of here, we passed through the old town of Penrith ; it
is about the size of Chester, Delaware County. It was laid
waste by an army of 30,000 Scots, in the reign of Edward III.
Its castle, which is now in ruins close to the line of the road,
was dismantled by the adherents of Cromwell. A subterranean passage leads from the castle to Dockray Hall, which is
three hundred yards distant. The grave of a Caledonian
giant, who must have been a rival of Goliath of Gath, is
pointed out in the churchyard. The head and foot-stones,
covered with unintelligible Runic characters, stand fifteen
feet apart. Two miles distant is what tradition declares to be
his cave. It shows evident marks of having been inhabited,
having traces of a window, doorway, and grate. It is very
difficult of access. A short distance from the town is another
curious relic of the olden time, consisting of the remains of a
Druidical place of judicature, called "King Arthur's Round
Table." About six miles from the town are the remains of a
Druid temple, consisting of a circle of upright stones, ten feet
high, with a large altar stone in the centre. The circle is 350
feet in circumference. It is undoubtedly one of the oldest
relics of antiquity in England. It is called, here, "Long
Meg and her daughters."

I find some very ignorant people about here, who barely
know that there is such a place as America, but whether it is
an island or continent, or situated in Asia or Africa, they
cannot tell. Methinks Dickens might have found subjects
enough for his sarcasm without leaving his own country.

IX.

CARLISLE TO EDINBURGH—THE CASTLE—COLTON HILL—
ARTHUR'S SEAT—HOLYROOD—MARY'S CHAMBER—RIC-
CIO'S BLOOD HAWTHORNDEN—ROSLIN CASTLE.

EDINBURGH, July, 1869.

This is modern Athens, and the handsomest city I have
yet seen. It is built of dressed stone upon the sides and summits of precipitous hills, almost approaching the dignity of
mountains. Some of the houses are ten stories high, fronting
on the lower street, and only three stories on the upper one.
They rise one above the other in tiers, and when lit up at night
by gas present a very brilliant appearance. There are two
great dales running east and west through the entire city, laid

out in delightful gardens, ornamented by fountains, monuments and statuary. The ranges of hills are united by waterless bridges, from the battlements of which we can look down into the tallest chimneys. Castle Hill is 383 feet high ; on its summit stands the ancient castle of Edinburgh, pronounced here *Edinburro.* It presents an appearance strikingly unique. It was the nucleus around which the city arose. From its ramparts the view is magnificent. The whole city and surrounding country seem to lay at the beholder's feet. Much historical interest attaches to the old fortress. Various and daring have been the exploits of its captors and defenders, the last of which was Sir William Kirkaldy. For his heroic defence on behalf of his queen, the unfortunate Mary, he and his brother were hanged at the Cross. The regalia of Scotland, consisting of Bruce's crown, made in the fourteenth century, with the sword of state and sceptre, are exhibited in one of the chambers of the castle, strongly guarded by sentries and iron bars. Another chamber with its furniture is also open to the public. It is the one in which Mary Queen of Scots gave birth to James II. of England, after she had fled from Holyrood Palace.

Colton Hill, about a half mile east from the castle, is also too steep for building purposes. Its summit is decorated by several monuments, and an astronomical observatory, the top of which is 350 feet high, and affords also a most superb prospect. But the most commanding altitude is the peak, known as Arthur's Seat. It rises from the gardens of Holyrood Palace, which lie at the foot of Cannongate Street. At the highest point it is 822 feet above the level of the sea. Its ascent is not difficult from the east ; facing the west it is nearly perpendicular. In ascending the hill the spot is seen where Jennie Deans is said to have met the ruffian Robertson, in Scott's novel of the *Heart of Midlothian.*

From Arthur's Seat the whole country for twenty miles around is under the eye, including the Frith of Forth, seaport town of Leith, the island where one of the scenes of Macbeth is laid, several villages, mountains and lakes, rendered immortal by Sir Walter Scott. On a clear day may also be seen the Lammermoor hills, the scene of one of Scott's most fascinating novels, while at the foot of the hill repose the palace and ruined chapel at Holyrood, and the city of Edinburgh. On the shoulder of the hill, near the palace, are the ruins of St. Anthony's chapel, mentioned in one of Scott's songs :—

" Now Arthur's seat shall be my bed,
    The sheets sall ne'er be fyled by me ;
Saint Anton's well shall be my drink,
    Since my true love's forsaken me."

The Palace of Holyrood, when not occupied by the Queen, is open to the public under certain restrictions, easily overcome by any who desires to see it. It is the most interesting spot in Scotland. The abbey is in ruins, but the castle is kept in repair. The apartments of Mary Queen of Scots are kept as nearly as possible as she left them, after the murder of her Secretary Riccio. There stands her bed, and work basket, with some unfinished fancy work The table at which she was taking her tea stands just where it did when Lord Darnley entered and fondly put his arm around her waist, while his gang proceeded to murder the poor Italian. The stains are still upon the floor where they left him all night weltering in his blood. In Lord Darnley's chamber, his portrait, together with that of the Queen, painted when she was Dauphiness of France, hang upon the wall. If she was as beautiful, and he as simple as their portraits represent them, it was indeed an ill-starred match. That she had a fool for a husband will hardly be questioned, but whether she was justifiable in murdering him, is a more doubtful subject. The general opinion among the most impartial here is, that she in her youth was an artless, amiable and confiding woman, but becoming soured by disappointment in her husband, and enraged at the disgrace he had put upon her, she became revengeful, artful and corrupt. Had she been as ugly as Mary, Queen of England, surnamed the Bloody, her admirers would have been fewer. Her portrait cannot well be looked upon without attraction by her inimitable beauty, and as the mind naturally associates a lovely face with a good heart, we jump to the conclusion that the excellencies of her soul were only equalled by the elegance of her person. Cleopatra was beautiful, so was Delilah, but let the shade of Mark Antony and the ghost of Samson answer as to their goodness or virtue. The disposition seems to be to carry the doctrine " *de mortuis nil nisi bonum*," too far when we canonize the defunct Queen for her religious faith and praise her for her perfidy to her husband. That she was an accessory, if not a principal in his assassination, will hardly be doubted. Had she openly plunged a dagger in his heart, it would have been comparatively pardonable, but she enticed him by her charms, and with words of tenderness and love induced him to lodge in Edinburgh, where she could *care* for his comfort and provide for his wants. A terrible explosion of gunpowder, her unaccountable absence from the house, the shattered remains of the building, and his dead and mangled body among the ruins of the house she had provided for him, all point to her as his murderer. Her subsequent conduct confirms the suspicion. How can her admirers excuse her willing but romantically arranged capture by her accomplice in crime, her pretence that he had forcibly abducted her, and when the offer of her relief came, her declining to be freed from his captivity ? When Shakspeare said :—

"The evil that *men* do live after them,
The goo t is oft interred with their bones,"

he of course had no reference to *women*, for the good they do lives after them, the bad is often interred with their bones, especially if they are pretty. So let it be with Mary.

Among the many charming places around Edinburgh, Hawthornden and Roslin chapel are prominent. The former can be reached by rail in about an hour. The sequestered glen bursts upon the traveler just when he least expects it. By a simple path over an apparently uninteresting country, he suddenly comes upon the fairy stream of Esk, with its deep dell, great caverns, copsewood and cascades. The path winds along the water's edge, with the crags and cliffs of the high banks on either side. The castle, now in ruins, stands upon the cliff of a rock at least one hundred feet above the water. Cut in the solid rock under the castle is a deep well from which a passage leads to several large caves and curiously shaped rooms, all cut out of the solid rock. When they were made or by whom no one can tell, but their purpose is easily divined. They were intended for dwelling places in times when habitation above ground could not be enjoyed. About two miles down the stream, by a most delightfully romantic path, sometimes winding along the water's edge, at others coursing over the cliffs overhanging the stream, and deeply shaded by copsewood, Roslin Castle stands, and about two hundred yards further up the hill is the chapel. The former is a ruin, the latter is pretty well preserved. Many are the traditions told by the guides and keepers of the two old buildings. Among others they say that on the night previous to the death of any of the Lords of Roslin, the chapel appears all in flames. Sir Walter Scott's ballad of Rosabelle refers to it :—

" O, listen, listen, ladies gay !
    No haughty feat of arms I tell ;
Soft is tue note, and sad the lay,
    That mourns the lovely Rosabelle.
O'er Roslin all that dreary night,
    A wondrous blaze was seen to gleam ;
'Twas broader than the watch-fire's light,
    And redder than the bright moonbeam.
It glared on Roslin's castled rock,
    It ruddied all the copsewood glen ;
'Twas seen from Dryden's groves of oak,
    And seen from caverned Hawthornden."

X.

EDINBURGH TO ROTTERDAM—DYKES AND CANALS—WIND-
MILLS AND BLACK COWS—HOLLAND BEND—CURIOUS CUS-
TOMS—LIFE IN THE STREETS—SMOKERS AND EATERS—BAD
DRINKING WATER—LIVING EXPENSES—THE MENU.

ANTWERP, August, 1869.

To go from Edinburgh to Rotterdam, by steamer, requires
about two days and a half. From the hills of Scotland to the
plains of Holland, the contrast is striking, but not disagreeable. As the old sailor became tired of the Italian sky and
longed for the fogs of London, so the traveler wearies even of
mountaïns, dales and glens, and rejoices at the level sea and
the unbroken plain. To see Scotland you gaze upward, but
you look down upon Holland. The land lies several feet below
the level of the sea. The great canals, some of which are
larger than many of the rivers of England, are in some places
fifteen feet above the surface of the fields. The whole country
seems to have gradually subsided, as it would have been impossible to have walled out the sea and built the immense
dykes and canals without some elevated spot at which to commence. As well might Archimedes have moved the earth
without a resting place or fulcrum for his lever. The manner
of raising the water from the ditches up to the canals is as grotesque as it is efficient; they check the encroachment of the
waves by the action of the winds. I counted twenty-seven
windmills in a row, working like giant slaves day and night,
having no other employment than pumping up the superfluous
surface water. The canals answer the double purpose of drainage and internal commerce. Small steamboats run upon them
without difficulty and carry cattle and produce from the farms
to the centre of the cities of Amsterdam and Rotterdam, which
are nearly as full of canals as Venice. It is no uncommon
sight to see children fishing from the windows of their parents'
houses facing on the canals. The fields present an appearance
of the most exuberant verdure for pasture unequalled in the
world. The banks of the dykes and canals are perfectly clean
and free from reeds, rushes, or other useless weeds. On my
way from Rotterdam to the Hague, I saw at one *coup d'œil*
several thousand cattle grazing over miles of meadow, in the
finest pasture I have seen since I left America. A red cow is
not to be seen in Holland; they are spotted black and white.
If the Hollanders owned the marshes between Marcus Hook
and Philadelphia, they would soon convert them into a bovine

paradise. Their industry is unremitting ; men, women, children, and even puppies work. An idle dog is not found in the land ; they make them do all the churning, and haul almost cart-loads of butter, eggs and vegetables about the streets for sale. The consequence of all this industry is a well-fed and comfortably clad people. The English language is only spoken at the hotels, but most of the citizens speak French. In Antwerp the French predominates, the streets being named first in French, then in Dutch. The singularly irregular architecture of the city of Rotterdam is at once noticed by a stranger. The finest buildings are neither *plumb*, *level* nor *square*. They lean every conceivable way, and are both lopsided and twisted. It is not uncommon to see a three-story house three feet out of plumb, with the adjoining one perhaps leaning the other way. In the narrow streets the tops of the houses from the opposite sides seem endeavoring to embrace, but unable to obtain the coveted kiss, lest they should fall at each other's feet. Upon inquiring the cause of all this crookedness, I was informed that it was originally because of the swampy nature of the ground, the buildings having settled during erection, but that it afterwards became fashionable to build them so, that they might be like their neighbors. It is not the only bad fashion which has been followed here, for I observe the ladies have the *Grecian*, as badly as the houses have the *Holland bend*. The same thing is observable at the Hague as well in the houses as the ladies. They have some curious old customs here. For instance, the sign of an apothecary is not, as with us, large bottles of red and blue water in the windows, but consists of a full-sized human head, carved in wood and painted as nearly like life as possible, with the mouth wide open, and in some cases containing an enormous pill, which he seems to be trying to swallow. It is placed on a bracket over the door, and is as unanimously adopted by all druggists as the *Pompey* is in America by tobacconists. The drollest thing I have seen here was a bulletin affixed upon the door of one of the fashionable houses, and which the passing citizens seemed to read with great satisfaction. It read as follows : " *Der kraamvrouw en het kind zijn naar ornstandigheden* "— (the mother and her babe are doing as well as could be expected) I was informed that the custom of the country requires the advent of every baby to be thus announced. In some places in Holland the event is published by hanging upon the knob of the front door a little board covered with red fringed silk. If the little stranger be a girl, a small piece of white paper is pasted on it. In case of twins they hang out two. The maidens from sixteen upwards wear white bobbinet caps, and on holidays and evenings, in company with their beaux, resort to the gardens and spend their leisure hours in drinking beer, making love, and listening to the music, which is always of the very best kind. The young men are well-made, hale and rosy-cheeked fellows, and the maidens are really pretty, but not to be compared with the young ladies of Delaware and Delaware County. I do not think *they* have their superiors in the world, at least I have not found them yet. The wives and daughters of the farmers here work in the fields the same as the men. I actually saw them mowing and working potato ground with milch cows harnessed to harrows, and with bridles and bits in the cows' mouths like horses. On the other hand, the wife is in every respect her husband's equal, and participates in all his pleasures. She is consulted on every subject, and has equal access to the family treasury ; indeed she is almost invariably the treasurer.

On Saturday nights and Sunday afternoons the town presents a very lively appearance. The whole population seem to be in the narrow streets, and as they have no sidewalks for foot passengers the consequence is they are full to overflowing from house to house. The absence of sidewalks is observable all over Holland ; where one is found it is the exception, not the rule, and is always considered as the exclusive property of the owner of the house in front of which it is. Whole squares are often obstructed in front of restaurants and cafes with tables and chairs, where men and women, especially on Sundays, are eating, drinking and smoking. In some streets I noticed iron bars placed across the foot-paths at intervals of about twenty feet, as a gentle intimation that it was *no thoroughfare.* Thus men, women, maids, donkeys, dogs and carts are all compelled to move in one compact mass along the streets together, and they seem to have a mutual respect for each other.

The people of Holland are good eaters, though they make but one full meal a day. The rule at the hotels, at the *table d'hote,* is for the guests to go through the entire course, the last of which is cigars, but, like the wines, they are charged extra in the bill. It is not considered a breach of etiquette for gentlemen to smoke in the presence of ladies ; the luxury is indulged in everywhere, except at church, even in the drawing-rooms and parlors of the elite. The principal reason why so much beer and wine are drunk in Europe, is the miserable and unwholesome water found there. I have not tasted a glass of good cold water since I left Philadelphia ; it is all strongly impregnated with lime and very hard. Those who do not drink wine have to resort to soda water, which is almost as expensive as wine. It cost at the hotels nine pence per

glass, which is equivalent to eighteen cents, American silver.
The general idea in America that everything is cheaper in
Europe is simply erroneous. To live here as one would live
in America the cost is about the same. The fact is, the people
here do not indulge in the luxuries of American life. But few
can afford to keep horses and carriages ; fewer still can own
their own houses. Some articles are undoubtedly much
cheaper, while others are more expensive.

A hotel breakfast generally consists of a cup of coffee or
tea, with bread and butter and boiled eggs, or cold roast, or
corned beef. For supper nothing is taken but a cup of tea and
bread and butter. The majority do not sup at all. The *table
d'hote* is the principal meal, and is generally taken from 4.30
to 6.00 P. M. The second class live chiefly on bread, milk
and vegetables, seldom indulging in tea or coffee, and rarely
in beef. For flesh they resort to bacon, and eat freely of the
cheaper varieties of fish. Salmon often sells for two shillings
per pound. The great number of courses named in the bills
of fare at the hotels is often more dependent upon the skill of
the cook than the variety of viands, some of the fancy dishes
being but skillful inventions for saving the previous day's
fragments.

XI.

ROTTERDAM TO BADEN-BADEN—BRUSSELS AND WATERLOO
  —THE RHINE—HEIDLEBURG—GAMBLER'S PARADISE—
  OLD CASTLE OF BADEN—RIDE THROUGH THE BLACK
  FOREST—GREAT FORTIFICATIONS—STAR SPANGLED BAN-
  NER—CONJUGAL NIGHT SCENE—NO FENCES—VINEYARDS
  —WOMEN IN HARNESS.

BADEN-BADEN, August, 1869.

This is the gamester's paradise and the blissful resort of
the gay world. It is a beauty spot on Nature's face. The
town, like a charming but abandoned woman, reclines upon
the banks of the river Oos, a limpid mountainous stream ; she
is arrayed in wealth's most voluptuous attire, and decked with
jewels of countless value, the price of her shame, and the
revenue of her perverted trade. She is surrounded by mountains from whose summits the enchanted eye looks down upon
the broad valley of the Rhine, and from whose base forever
gush exhaustless springs of water, pure as nectar. Baden-
Baden must be seen to be fully understood. It is decidedly a
gay place. It lies at the entrance of the Black Forest, interesting as the seat of so many legends and superstitious tales.

At the top of one of the highest mountains stand the ruins of the old castle, one of the most extensive in Germany, and the dwelling place, in A. D. 1190, of Herman III., after his return from the Holy wars. The carriage drives through the Black Forest and over the mountain are most enchanting, and the aroma from the mountain firs most exhilarating. Instead of indulging in play, I invested a sovereign a day in a carriage, guide and pair of splendid black horses, and made excursions in every direction through the forest and over the mountains, and was repaid by a ravenous appetite and an exuberant flow of spirits without the aid of wine. The animated scenes within and in front of the *Conversations-haus*—which is simply a magnificently fitted up gaming palace, with drawing-rooms, reading and dining-rooms, concert hall and promenade—do not begin until about 7.00 P. M., and continue in unabated vigor until midnight, during which time fortunes are hazarded and lost. Ladies from eighteen to eighty spend their whole evenings at the tables, and gamble away an incredible sum of money. During the play, while animated by the excitement of the game, some of them showed traces of rare beauty ; but I noticed them next morning in the gardens, where they resorted for recuperation, and upon the cheeks of every one I saw sad traces of the serpent's tooth, and from their careworn and haggard looks, I fear the poison of his sting was rankling in their hearts. Many of them have once been beautiful and all talented ; but alas for human nature ! the one has been betrayed and the other perverted. An idea can be formed of the extent to which play is here indulged in, from the fact that the keeper of the establishment pays a rent of about $50,000 per annum, and defrays all the expenses of the concern, which amount to as much more.

In my journey from Antwerp, I spent three days at Brussels and the field of Waterloo, and two full days on the Rhine from Cologne to Mayence. I also stopped a short time at Heidelberg, which is a very beautiful place, but, in my judgment, not comparable with Baden-Baden. Brussels is called, by those who have seen both cities, Little Paris. Both it and Antwerp are completely encompassed with most gigantic fortifications. An American can form but a poor idea of these immense military works, as nothing of the kind was ever seen in the United States.

The old bulwarks have been converted into boulevards, and make most magnificent streets around the towns. Before proceeding to the field of Waterloo I visited the spot where the Duchess of Richmond gave her grand ball to the Duke of Wellington on the eve of the battle. '' The eyes that then looked love to eyes that spoke again, have long since been

closed forever, but the sound of revelry at night is still heard
in Belgium's capi'al.'' I have often *heard* of the inspiring
effect of a familiar air upon the ear of a wanderer in a foreign
land ; but I *felt* it here. There were seven passengers in the
coach, of which I was the only American. The bugler played
several airs without attracting any particular attention ; after
a moment's rest he readjusted his horn and suddenly struck up
in splendid style the " Star Spangled Banner." I confess the
effect was so electrical that despite every effort at stoicism,
my eyes filled with tears and my thoughts were immediately
transferred from the conflicting scenes of strife and blood so
intimately associated with Waterloo, to the now peaceful fields
and sunny plains of my own dear native land. A drive of
about three hours through a luxuriant and well-cultivated
country brought us to the Battle Monument, an immense
mound of earth surmounted by an enormous Belgian lion. It
requires about four hours to survey the field, and by the assistance of a good guide and a history of the battle at hand, more
can be learned of the tremendous conflict and decisive victory
of June 18, 1815, than by months of study. It does not require much imagination, while looking at the bullet marks
upon the walls and the broken and shattered inclosure of the
garden, known as the Poste d'Hougomont—which stands to-day
very much as the battle left it—to reproduce upon the surrounding hills the contending armies, surging like an angry
sea to and fro amid the smoke and confusion of the battle, the
beating of drums, roaring of artillery, charges of the cavalry,
groans of the wounded and moans of the dying. Many persons visit Waterloo, but few see it. Like those who visit and
merely glance at the superb masterpiece of Rubens in the
Cathedral at Antwerp, without taking time to study it, they
go away disappointed.

There is but one step from the sublime to the ridiculous,
and I must be pardoned for making the sudden descent. On
returning to Brussels, fatigued by the long drive and four
hours' walk I retired early to bed. I was suddenly aroused
by a tremendous row between an English tourist and his wife
in the adjoining room, and as the transom over the communi-
cating door was open, the noise was more distinctly heard.
He had evidently left her in the hotel, and gone out to *see the
town.* She had left the candle burning for him, but it had
exhausted itself before his return. In endeavoring to sneak
into bed without awakening his wife, he ran against the table,
upset the wash-stand and broke the pitcher and basin to atoms,
and at the same time fell himself sprawling on the floor, yelling as he fell, " Where in 'ell's the candle ?'' " Where have
you been all night ?'' screamed the wife. " Hall night ! hit's

honly 'alf past ten ; I've just come from the theatre. You're always lecturing me, and if you don't stop it we'll 'ave han halmighty row. So I caution you not to do it." Just then the treacherous town-clock struck three. "There," said the indignant wife. "I knew you were deceiving me ; you've been at some bad house and left me here all alone among strangers. You'll break my heart, so you will. Oh, boo-woo-woo." A soothing scene followed, entirely too affecting for vulgar ears, so I gave a very loud cough, which seemed to have a marvellous effect in quieting the impending storm. Methought I heard a smothered kiss and an affectionate utterance, something like that made by a cow when her calf wanders too far away, and all was quiet as a grave ; he had doubtless convinced her of his innocence, for next morning they were as loving as turtle doves.

On my journey from Brussels to Cologne I noticed what I had also particularly observed around Brussels, the entire absence of fences or inclosures. Even the roads were unfenced and not a horse, cow, or sheep could be seen anywhere, except in the fields at work. The land is good and undulating, but cultivated on a very small scale, the cattle being kept in stalls and the grass being mowed for them every day. The entire country is divided into small patches, composed of oblong and irregular squares, varying from a few feet to a few acres, giving to the face of the country a checkered appearance, not unlike an immense patch-work bed quilt ; here a patch of deep green potatoes, there one of light green oats, adjoining one of bright yellow mustard, red clover, purple-topped turnips, wheat, barley and cabbages.

One of the most interesting journeys in Europe is from Cologne up the Rhine as far as Mayence. Of course it would be utterly impossible to give anything like an adequate description of the scenery in the narrow limits of a letter. Those who have traveled up the Hudson can form some idea of it, but nothing can supply the historical interest connected with every mile of the Rhine ; its mountains, castles, villages and vineyards passing like a panorama before the eye are entirely beyond description, and are superlatively beautiful.

A vineyard, however, while remarkable for the great labor bestowed on the terraces on which they are planted, often extending up the side of a mountain so steep that it would be otherwise impossible of ascent, has no particular beauty about it, and is not half as attractive as a well-cultivated field of corn. The vines are planted about three feet apart, tied to rough stakes, and never permitted to grow over four feet high. They are in some places planted from the mountain top down to the river edge, the flow of which is very rapid, and in this respect not unlike the Susquehanna at Harrisburg. It is no uncommon sight to see women in harness performing the duties of mules and horses along the tow-paths up the Rhine, while big lazy-looking men are sitting on the deck, or steering the boat and smoking their pipes.

———

XII.

BADEN TO GENEVA—BALE—LES ILLUSION PERDU—GRAND SCENERY—MONT BLANC—PURE AND FOUL WATER CANNOT FLOW IN ONE STREAM—FIRST SIGHT OF A GLACIER —FIFTY MILES BY DILIGENCE—MOUNTAIN ROADS IN SAVOY—VALLEY OF CHAMOUNI—OPTICAL DELUSION— ADVENTURE OF A YANKEE ON A GLACIER—DANGEROUS PASSES—RIVER ARVE—STARS AND STRIPES IN SWITZERLAND.

GENEVA, August, 1869.

I have escaped from the allurements of Baden-Baden, and have taken refuge in this old Calvinistic town, chiefly inhabited by clock-makers, jewellers and millionaries, and more remarkable for the natural beauty of its situation than its monuments of art. I broke my journey at Bale, and was fully compensated for the time there expended. Its quiet demeanor is in fine contrast with its gay neighbor of Baden. It contains two of the finest churches I have seen on the continent. The one remarkable for its well-preserved antiquity, the other for its modern architectural beauty. The old Cathedral of Bale was founded by Henri II., and is about 900 years old. It has suffered from war, fire and earthquakes, but still presents its original appearance, in this respect unlike many of the old monuments of Europe, which instead of being restored have been reconstructed and spoiled by the confusion of architecture. The new church of St. Elizabeth is a magnificent modern structure of the purest gothic order, and is composed entirely, within and without, of dressed and ornamented stone. If not destroyed by violence, it will begin to be admired a thousand years from now. Bale is the republic of Switzerland where the air is supposed to be too pure for kings to breathe, but I am inclined to think that their absence depends more upon the height of the mountains than the purity of the air. I rubbed my eyes and picked my ears, expecting of course, to see those beautiful maidens—pictures of which I had seen in my youth, with their little straw hats, crooks, ribbons and white petticoats, and to hear the shepherd's pipe or the echo

of his merry song as he guarded his sheep and led them from
the waterfall of the mountains to the pastures of the valley.
All was vain! The mountains, meadows and cascades were
visible, but instead of the maidens, cottages, shepherds and
flocks, I saw nothing but ugly old hags with immense goitres
like pelicans, performing the triple duty of shepherd, child's
nurse and knitting stockings. In some places instead of sheep,
they were guarding herds of black hogs. And thus the
romance and poetry of youth is ever blurred, blighted and
disappointed by the stern realities of life. As I advanced
toward Geneva, and even along the far-famed valley of Chamouni, it got worse instead of better. All along the route I
saw women and girls performing the labor of horses and mules
as well as the work of men. They not only reap the grain
and mow the grass, but they carry on their backs the hay and
grain from the fields to the barns. I saw them staggering
under loads I would not have put upon a horse.

The scenery, however, is superlatively grand. The Alps
are in constant view, and the mountains and valleys are studded with cities, villages and cottages. The line of the road
passes from Lausanne to Geneva, along the entire northwestern
shore of the lake, which is about fifty miles in length, and affords
a most perfect view of the Alpine hills and Mont Blanc,
which, although fifty-one miles distant by diligence, does not
seem more than ten miles off. The waters of the Lake of
Geneva are crystal clear, and at a short distance look as blue
as indigo. Stones and shells can be seen on the bottom in
thirty feet of water. The city of Geneva is situated at the
extreme southwest end of the lake, where it empties into the
Rhone. The rapidity of the current is startling, it darts under
the bridges like an arrow and propels the machinery of great
factories by under-tow water-wheels. No races or water
courses are necessary, the force of the current entirely super-
seding the weight of water required. About half a mile below
the town the river Arve joins the Rhone. The confluence is
very remarkable, they run together for a mile or two in the
same channel without mixing, the line of each river being as
distinctly marked as if one were oil and the other water.
After thus flowing side by side for some time, they gradually
mingle, and then the pure waters of the Rhone assume the
character of the muddy waters of the Arve, and from the
most limpid it becomes one of the most murky of rivers.
While contemplating the purity of the one thus soiled and
corrupted by the filthiness of the other, it seemed like a lesson
of nature, teaching the inevitable fate of virtue when attempting to run in the same course with vice, she is sure to become
soiled and eventually corrupted, for although the Rhone is

much the greater river, after its confluence with the Arve it loses its character for purity and assumes that of the defiled one it has received into its bosom.

On a clear day Mont Blanc can be distinctly seen from Geneva, and the sight of it has certainly a very exhilarating effect on one seeing it for the first time. The desire to ascend it and stand upon its glaciers is irresistible, and must be gratified even at the expense of a hundred francs and two days' journey in a diligence, or, in other words, in an old-fashioned stage coach drawn by six horses, three abreast. The journey is very charming ; I need not describe it to the fathers of Delaware County ; they remember the ante-railroad days ; what the stage coach was then there, is precisely what the diligence is now here, from Geneva to Chamouni, which is at the foot of Mont Blanc. Our diligence contained sixteen passengers ; the road is up hill nearly the entire fifty-one miles, but by changing horses three times, Chamouni is reached in twelve hours. The journey back is performed in eight hours, because of the descending grade. At some places the greatest skill is required to keep the coach from striking the rocks on either side of the road, at other places it is so tortuous that it is with difficulty the precipices along the mountain sides are avoided. The Emperor Napoleon is, however, having a new road built which is to be opened next week, and which will greatly facilitate travel from Geneva to Chamouni.

I will not attempt to describe the valley of Chamouni ; abler pens have failed to do it justice. At some favorite spots its scenery is enchantingly beautiful, leaving upon the mind of the beholder a vague presentiment of unreality from which it is difficult to realize that he is gazing upon snow and ice, and at the same time inhaling the aroma of flowers and blossoms, luxuriantly flourishing in richly cultivated gardens and meadows, overhung by barren peaks and rugged crags. As we crossed a rustic bridge over the Arve, about seventeen miles by road from Chamouni, the coach suddenly stopped ; at the same time the driver cried at the top of his voice : *" Voila le Mont Blanc au gauche."* All eyes were instantly turned to the left, and there, comparatively not five hundred yards distant, loomed up the great white mountain, as bright as unsoiled snow, and glistening in the beams of the fast declining sun like burnished silver. A picture approaching the reality of this scene would be rejected as an exaggeration. We could not realize the fact that the mountain was twelve miles distant in a direct line, but the consumption of three hours of hard driving before we reached our destination, convinced us of the truth. A young American gentleman from Chicago, with the usual and often reprehensible conceit of his countrymen, on the day after our arrival, ascended one of the spurs of the mountain without a guide, and as a consequence spent the entire night upon the mountain, having lost his path and nearly his life, in wandering over the glaciers, rocks and tortuous paths. The whole village was as a matter of course alarmed for his safety, and our fears were not relieved until the next morning about nine o'clock, when he came to the hotel more dead than alive, having had neither shelter nor food for twenty-four hours. The known paths are sufficiently dangerous and difficult, without seeking " new ones which we know not of." The path from Montanvert to what is known as Le Jardin is in some places quite difficult, passing for some considerable distance over what are called the *ponts* along the side of a nearly perpendicular rock. The rock is passed by means of steps about two inches wide by six or seven in length, cut in the side of the rock ; a slight loss of the centre of gravity, which is maintained by hugging closely to the side of the rock, would be certain destruction, as the glacier is 300 feet below. The slight danger, however, adds amazingly to the enjoyment of the adventure ; like every other taste of joy, it must have its corresponding perils to give zest to the pleasurable emotions thereby awakened.

The best view of the range of Mont Blanc is had from Mount Flegere, on the opposite side of the river. The path is good and smooth, and by three hours' hard walking the summit may be reached, when the entire range lies under the eye, and the lovely valley of Chamouni, with its villages and meadows, may be seen for miles. Of the innumerable needles and peaks, pointed out and named by the guide, two only fastened themselves on my mind. No person having once seen can ever forget *Aiguille Dru* and *Aiguille Verte*, presenting the appearance of a gigantic Gothic cathedral, with two enormous towers frowning down upon the *mer de glace*. It requires a day to visit this glacier in order to form a perfect idea of its magnitude. By simply ascending Montanvert, which can be done in two hours, crossing the glaciers and returning by *Mauvais Pas* requiring two hours more, an adequate judgment cannot be formed of this immense sea of ice. By extending the journey over the *ponts* to the *junction de Tacul*, and from thence to Le Jardin, which will require seven hours more on the ice, the mind is enabled to partially comprehend its magnitude. I have no doubt but that it is over a mile thick in some places. It has been melting for thousands of years, and will continue to melt thousands of years to come, before it disappears, which it must eventually do. It extends down to the valley, and forms the source of the river Arve, which gushes full formed from under an immense arch, formed by the melting of the ice. It is said that four thousand Americans have visited it this year. I observed the United States flag floating from the roof of every hotel in Chamouni, with that of England and France ; no others are seen. Are these three the only nations of the earth ? American travelers have a good reputation, and I hope they will maintain it, though a sacred regard for truth compels me to say that I have met some fools from my own country ; they are, however, the exception to the rule, and are composed chiefly of a class distinguished for a lavish display of diamonds and jewelry, and scarcity of brains. I leave here to-morrow for Paris where you will, per- haps, hear from me for the last time, as from there I shall embark for home.

XIII.

GENEVA TO PARIS—-HUNDREDTH ANNIVERSARY OF THE BIRTH OF NAPOLEON I.--PARIS IN A BLAZE OF GLORY— L. N.—A PEASANT'S ADVICE—WAITING FOR SUNRISE— THE BASTILE--LETTRE DE CACHET--COLUMN OF JULY--TEN THOUSAND RAMPART GUNS DISCHARGED BY ONE ELECTRIC SPARK—FIRST SIGHT OF PARIS—WHY IS PARIS SUCH A PLEASANT PLACE ?—-GATE OF HELL—-AMUSEMENTS— CHURCHES—SCHOOLS—SALOONS—-THEATRES--GALLERIES OF ART—-MUSEUMS—SOIREES—-BALLS—SHOPS—RESTAU- RANTS—BOULEVARDS—THE DEVIL IN PARIS—HISTORY— CHARACTER OF THE PEOPLE—MONKEYS WHEN PLEASED— TIGERS WHEN IN A RAGE—PLACE DE LA CONCORDE—THE NATIONAL RAZOR—REIGN OF TERROR—NEW PARIS—THE TUILLERIES—COUP D'ETAT OF 1851—WALLS OF PARIS— PERE LA CHAISE—FRENCH FEMALE MODESTY--KING LOUIS PHILLIPE—TALKING POLITICS PROHIBITED--A TRAVEL- ER'S LIFE NOT AN EASY ONE.

PARIS, August, 1869.

While in the village of Chamouni I saw workmen engaged in the apparently vain task of planting great forest pines in the shadeless streets of that picturesque town. As the trees had no roots my curiosity prompted me to inquire of one of the laborers the object of such a strange work. With a look of mingled contempt and amazement he replied in French : " Is it possible that Monsieur does not know that the fifteenth of this month is the one hundreth anniversary of the birth of the Great Emperor ?" I informed him that I was an American, which I hoped would excuse my ignorance. The rootless trees were to decorate the naked squares, and were to be orna-mented with flags and Chinese lanterns very much as a child would decorate its Christmas tree. "If I were Monsieur" said the workman, "and had the money Monsieur has, I would be in Paris on the fifteenth to see the grand fete. Paris will be seen as it never has appeared before. Ten thousand can-non will be discharged by one instantaneous electric spark just at sunrise. The first ray upon the Golden statue of Lib-erty on the Column of July is to be the signal for the grand event."

I had been wandering among the mountains of Switzer-land, and enjoying nature in all its rugged grandeur. I never wearied in climbing its craggy peaks, in walking over its fertile meadows or sailing upon its placid lakes. Even its cold and cheerless glaciers had an enchantment that seemed to chain my soul a willing captive to their icy charms. I had resolved to cross over into Italy and visit Rome, only three days distant, and leave Paris as an epicure would his dessert, until the last of the feast, but the disinterested advice of this peasant of Savoy induced me to break up my previous arrange-ments and go at once to Paris. By traveling at night as well as by day, I reached Paris on the morning of the fifteenth. The day was bright and the scene charming. Every town along the route was decorated with tri-colored flags, triumphal arches were erected in the principal streets and wreaths of immortelles were upon the monuments. The groves and gar-dens at night were gaily illuminated, while the happy citizens amused themselves with music, dancing, rural plays and promenades. On every monument, church, public building and market place, the eye met the monogram of the Emperor, "L. N." in letters of gold. No word but of praise was heard, as well of the Great Emperor as for his nephew the present ruler of France. Can the glory of Napoleon III. ever fade or the star of his prosperity set? God only knows. Time must answer.

Our train halted without the city walls in the Bois de Vincennes. Every eye was turned toward the Column of July, in the Place de la Bastile, to catch the first ray of sun-light upon the Genius of Liberty on its top. While waiting for sunrise I endeavored in fancy to rebuild the Bastile and re-people it with the many prisoners of State whose lives have been smothered within its cruel walls. The royal dames and proud chevaliers who had died in rags and filth or had been starved in its deep mouldy cells or iron cages, and whose neg-lected skeletons were found when the accursed den was forever destroyed, will never be known. The word of the king, or his *Lettre de Cachet* often fraudulently obtained, opened the merciless gates and closed them upon the proudest, bravest and best citizens of France.   When once within the Bastile no power save that of the King could liberate the prisoner. They had no *Habeas Corpus* to bring him face to face with his accuser.   After a few anxious inquiries by relations and friends he was as completely forgotten as if in his grave. I afterwards saw in one of the museums of Paris an original *Lettre de Cachet.*   It had been issued by Louis XIV.   It read as follows : " *C'est par mon ordre et pour le bien d'Etat que le porteur a ce present a fait ce qu'il a fait."*   The English of which is :   "It is by my order and for the good of the State that the bearer of this letter has done what he has done." The Bastile was destroyed by the people July 14, 1789.   The fourteenth of July has been a fete day ever since.   The keys were presented to General Washington.   The Column of July was erected to commemorate its destruction.   The column is 155 feet high, and is entirely of metal.   It is a beautiful Corinthian column which supports a golden globe upon the top of which, with outstretched arms, facing the west, poised on one foot, stands the statue of the Genius of Liberty, as if about to depart westward.   In his right hand he holds a burning torch, in his left hand a broken chain to indicate that the flame of freedom like natural fire must be confided to a strong hand. When the sun arose on the fifteenth of August, 1869, there were over 4,000,000 persons in Paris.   In breathless suspense we awaited the given signal.   Suddenly the simultaneous and con-centrated roar of 10,000 great rampart guns belched forth the glad tidings that the one hundredth anniversary of the birth of the Great Emperor had arrived.

.I cannot express the feeling I experienced on entering for the first time a city of which I have heard so much.   It is surrounded by forests, groves and gardens, and ornamented within by statuary, fountains and boulevards.   When I stood in the garden of the Tuilleries and looked up the beautiful Avenue Des Champs-Elysees as far as the Arc de Triomphe I felt indeed that I was in the Elysian Fields and was enjoying an exquisite view of celestial scenery, but the Bacchanalian revels of fallen Angels and the stern demands of hunger soon admonished me that I was yet mortal and still in this sin cursed world.

There is an enchanting charm about Paris hard to explain because the result of so many causes.   It is laid out with great taste, the air is pure and climate congenial.   It is embellished and adorned by all that art can bestow or wealth command.   One does not become fatigued in Paris as in other places, its pleasures do not satiate desire, nor its pains make the body weary.

The compactness of the city adds much to its charms. Its native population is about 2,000,000 and it usually contains 1,000,000 strangers. While it has four times as many inhabitants as Philadelphia, it is only about one-third as large in territorial limits. When we remember that the 1,000,000 strangers are mostly there for pleasure and to spend rather than to make money, we can form some idea of its gaiety. This immense population is confined within a circuit of about twenty-one miles, yet the city contains over one thousand miles of streets. Fancy, if you can, a grand avenue like Broadway, one thousand miles long, with no square without some object of interest. Whichever way we turn some noble edifice, beautiful column, triumphal arch, colossal monument, bridge, museum, church, palace, fountain, garden or park attracts the attention. Another contribution to its charms is its fresh, clean and bright appearance. If fatigued we can take a chair in some delightful flower garden or in front of a good cafe. The flower beds have no fences nor forbidding notices to warn the citizen that he must "keep off the grass."

The city is built of a soft, chalk-like stone of a mellow yellowish color. It forms the sub-stratum upon which the city stands. It is from this that " Plaster of Paris " is made. In the old part of the city the quarries have been converted into catacombs which undermine about one-tenth of the surface of the city. They contain the bones of over 3,000,000 dead, fantastically arranged and built in on the face of the walls, presenting in the gas light a ghastly picture. Openings have been made to admit the air and channels to carry off the water. Pillars support the vaults. Ninety steps have been cut to carry the visitors to the gloomy caverns. The place of entrance is called Barriere d'Enfer, or " Gate of Hell."

The atmosphere of Paris is usually so pure that the whole city can be seen from any of its elevations. The smoke ascends in a straight column to the clouds, while in London it hangs like a pall and is so dense that one can see but a few squares even from the dome of St. Paul's. Paris is well governed. The police, like trained soldiers, are always ready for instant service. They never converse with citizens except upon subjects of duty If your cabman should become intoxicated, or be arrested for any breach of municipal regulations, the Sergeant-de-ville takes him in charge and, that you may suffer no inconvenience, he puts one of his reserve force in the driver's seat, who politely carries you to your destination.

Much of the pleasure of Parisian life depends upon its system of public amusement. The various desires of the human heart seem to have been provided for and a free amusement selected for every phase of gratification. Are you of a

religious disposition ?   Such churches and sacred institutions
are nowhere to be found.   They are always open and contain
the most interesting relics of christianity. · If the visitor is of
an intelligent turn of mind, such schools, salons, galleries of
art and museums are nowhere to be seen.   Here you may look
upon the remains of ancient as well as the gems of modern
art.   There are paintings in the Louvre worth a fortune to be
seen, studied and enjoyed as freely as the air is breathed.   The
soldier has his museum of artillery and war with maps, plans
and models systematically arranged, illustrating the world's
great battlefields and presenting a mass of most useful information in a most attractive form.

Singular as it may seem, the first theatres of Paris only
represented sacred subjects and were patronized by pious
citizens, priests and church members.   They soon degenerate
to their present style.   When Napoleon became Emperor he
suppressed all the low and vulgar ones.   Only nine of the best
were licensed, but after the restoration, the drama was so encouraged that Paris now has forty theatres, some good and
respectable, others very common and vulgar.   The government pays annually to the French opera 1,000,000 francs. The
Theatre Francais receives annually 240,000 francs as an encour-
agement for classic comedy.   It is estimated that six thousand
persons daily frequent the theatres of Paris.   The theatres are
required to pay a license tax of ten per cent. of their profits,
which is distributed to the poor.   This source of revenue alone
in 1867, amounted to $5,000,000.   The government also
awards two annual prizes for the four best plays represented
during the year, one of five thousand francs and the other of
three thousand francs.

The great social charm of Paris is its soirees or private
entertainments given by the opulent citizens.   The resident
families in fashionable life give weekly receptions from the
opening to the close of winter.   No invitation is required.   In
the course of a month a stranger may see all the prominent men
and women in political, literary or fashionable life at these
soirees.   It is not improper to attend several on the same night.
Long stays are not expected.   The only form required is a
decent suit, gloved hands and the announcement of the name,
and after a salutation to the host movement within and éxit
are free.   If one wishes to attend a soiree of the nobility the
auspices of his diplomatic representative will be required.

The public balls also afford a fine opportunity to see
high life of French as well as foreign society.   Everybody
goes to the balls.   Scandal is absolutely unknown.   Good
public manners and a polite demeanor are all that is required
to secure respect and an entrance into the best society.

Paris has many other attractions. It is the paradise of milliners, mantua makers and shop-keepers. The ladies all love Paris. The fair one may spend her time and her husband's money without limit. The women are free from the cares of housekeeping. Many citizens have but a sleeping place and live in the streets and take their meals at the restaurants. The making of a cup of coffee is about all the cooking done in the dwellings. The man servant is the *fac-totum* of the establishment while the *femme de chambre* keeps the sleeping apartments in order All the washing is done at the laundries. The Emperor would not feel degraded by being found at his meals in a good restaurant. There are about 3000 of them now in the city fitted up with great taste and patronized by the best society. The history of these restaurants is amusing. In 1765 a French cook fitted up a house for the sale of refreshments. He chose for his sign a Latin parody upon a well-known passage of Scripture : " Venite ad me omnes qui stomacho laboratis, et ego restaurabo vos." The experiment was a success, and the word " Restaurabo " in the parody was the origin of the word *restaurant* now so general all over the world.

The boulevards in summer are filled with well-dressed crowds, either promenading or seated in groups among the green trees and thousand lights in front of some fashionable restaurant with neatly dressed waiters in white caps and aprons, ready to serve you with any desired refreshments, on little tables provided for that purpose. If it is desired, meals will be served at any named place. All you have to do is to bargain for the number of dishes and all the cares of the table are over. The variety of dishes runs from fried snails to horse-flesh steaks. It is no uncommon thing to find four hundred dishes named on one bill of fare.

While Paris is such a paradise of pleasure, a sacred regard for truth compels me to confess that all the baser passions find fuller freedom here than in any other city. The devil in Paris is the same individual but of politer mien than his namesake in other cities. Here he is a gentleman of culture and prides himself upon his good manners. He shows you the way to hell with a patronizing smile ; he points out its smooth and attractive path enlivened by the sweetest music and planted with the choicest flowers. For such as seek forbidden pleasures, the city presents her Jardin Mabile, Tivoli, students' balls, exhibitions of living statuary, and innumerable other palaces of impure enjoyment, garnished with most alluring attractions for the unwary traveler or confiding youth. The government has established rules for houses of prostitution and grants them an annual license. The emperor has given to the citizens of his Capital a *carte blanche* for every enjoyment, subject to but one condition, that of good public order. Impoliteness, rudeness, rowdyism or boisterousness, even in the most abandoned resorts, will not be permitted. The most fastidious ear will seldom be offended either by day or night in the streets. You must seek the impure Goddess, but her shrine is easily found. There is a certain abandon in Parisian life which, however reprehensible, is certainly very seducing.

Before the Roman conquest, Paris was a Druid fort upon the isle of St. Louis. It was surrounded with great marshes and heavy forests full of hungry wolves. The Louvre takes its name from a bloody struggle between the citizens and a pack of half starved wolves. Louvre in French has the same meaning as wolf in English. The Gospel was first preached here by St. Denis, A. D. 250; he suffered martyrdom on a hill on the north part of the city, ever since called *Montmartre* —or the Martyr's Hill. Some, however, maintain that the name is a corruption of *Mons Martis* or Mars Hill. Five or six old-fashioned windmills still stand on the hill from the summit of which all Paris can be seen. It is 300 feet above the Seine. It was in the old church on Montmartre that Ignatius Loyola, on the fifteenth of August, 1534, founded the Order of Jesuits, a society whose influence has been felt by every government of the world.

In the year 1466, a law was enacted guaranteeing protection to all the malefactors of the world provided they became resident citizens of Paris. It was soon filled with murderers, robbers and political offenders from surrounding nations which is supposed to in some degree, account for the marked nervousness and excitability of the Parisian French, who are said to be like monkeys when pleased but tigers when in a rage. All history proves the Parisian French, in their times of peace and tranquility to be merciful and kind hearted, but when their passions are aroused they are blood-thirsty and desperate almost to insanity. Their tragedies are the saddest and their comedies are the most frivolous. Paris presents to-day many monuments of her tragic history. The Obelisque du Luxor in the Place de la Concorde surrounded by beautiful fountains and statuary, stands on the spot once occupied by the Guillotine. The rabble made merry over its bloody work and sportively called it the National Razor. So many of the best citizens had their heads shaved off by this blood-thirsty *barber* that it became necessary to dig a canal from the Guillotine to the Seine to carry off the blood, just as a butcher would dig a trench from his slaughter house to the nearest stream.

In those days some overburdened peasants presumed most respectfully to ask the aristocratic Assembly to reduce their taxes that they might with the money saved buy bread for their children. One of the proud deputies in his speech upon the subject said : " If the peasants cannot afford to buy bread let them eat hay—the taxes must be paid." Shortly afterwards the wheel of fortune turned. The tax payers were elevated to political power and their first act was to decapitate the orator and march through the streets of Paris with his head on a pole and a wisp of hay in his mouth, much to the amuse· ment of the merry citizens who thought it a *capital* joke. Were it not for the eternal vigilance of the ruling powers, scenes as extravagant, as tragic and as bloody would be wit· nessed in the streets of Paris to-day. There is a political party here called Communists, who hold secret meetings and advocate a return to the convention, the Guillotine and the reign of terror as the only remedy for imperialism and royalty.

Napoleon III. takes every precaution that human foresight can suggest to guard his imperial throne. He has removed all the cobble stones from the streets to prevent the building of barricades. In 1830, four thousand barricades were sud· denly made from the cobble stones torn up from the streets. The Emperor does not intend that this shall happen again. Grand avenues, under the pretext of improving Paris have been opened in straight but radiating lines from strategic centres, so as to put the entire city under the guns of a few well posted batteries. No power of France, save treachery from within, can dethrone Napoleon III. He floated into power on a wave of popular inconsistency. While liberty slept during the night of December 1, 1851, as confident of security as we now are of the perpetuity of our Republic, he entered her Temple and when she suddenly awoke on the morning of December 2, she found the Republic of the night before metamorphosed into an empire with its former President as its emperor. Na- poleon has dwelt in the Tuilleries in comparative safety, during the past eighteen years. A political thunder storm may result in his ejectment as summarily as the departure of his royal predecessor. Human tenure of earthly power is very uncer- tain. God reigns, and earthly rulers, despite their greatest precautions, are set up and removed from place and power as easily as a piece from the chessboard by the master of the game.

The *coup d'etat* of December 1, 1851, marked an era in the improvement of Paris never witnessed by any other city. Gigantic fortifications and new walls have been built. The approaches to the city are guarded by seventeen casemated forts situated at convenient distances, connected by a series of strategical roads. The walls and forts are armed with 2813 cannon, including 575 heavy rampart guns. Paris can never be taken by assault, it may succumb to famine. I am half inclined to believe that these immense walls and fortified positions are as much intended to awe the unruly citizens within the city as to defend 'hem from possible enemies from without.

I suppose the time will come, if Paris continues to improve in the future as she has in the past, when the walls of Napoleon III. will be removed, and their place be converted into a new line of boulevards just as the old walls were torn down three or four times for that purpose. The city has always been of an oval shape encircled with walls. As the population spread and the city outside the walls increased to accommodate its rapid growth, new systems of bulwarks were erected further out and the old ones were torn down and converted into streets. Boulevard, in French. means a bulwark. All the great boulevards were formerly the bulwarks of the city. They now contain its finest and most imposing buildings, theatres, churches, restaurants and hotels.

There are four cemeteries within the walls, the most fashionable of which is Pere La Chaise, near the eastern wall. It occupies a commanding eminence, from the heights of which the whole city can be distinctly seen. Pere La Chaise was the confessor of Louis XIV., and had his country seat upon the beautiful hill now occupied by the cemetery. It was a battlefield between the French and Russians in 1814. A single grave in Pere La Chaise cannot be secured now under seven hundred francs. This great necropolis contains about 98,000 monuments, some in good but many in very poor taste. There are days when 100,000 people visit the cemetery. The most celebrated monument is that of Abelard and Heloise which to this day is often wreathed with flowers by some unknown fair one. It is looked upon by the French maidens as the true shrine of disappointed love.

I may be pardoned for referring to the little monument over the grave of the daughter of *Madamoiselle* Mars. *Miss* Mars was never married, but had a little girl baby which she buried in this cemetery, and erected over it a monument, the inscription upon which informs us that the ashes of the little one beneath it was the *only* daughter of *Miss* Mars. Miss Mars, was a celebrated actress and great favorite with the French people. She was freely received into the best society. You cannot find a French lady or gentleman who can see the slightest impropriety in what would, with us, be considered as a publication of her own shame. The want of sensibility upon this subject may be accounted for from the fact that one-third of all the children born in Paris are illegitimate. The fault is generally supposed to be with the men, who are inclined to looseness and profligacy ; the women as a rule are fair, vivacious, neat and industrious and make good, thrifty wives. The entire care of the family is left with the mother, who at the same time often manages two or three restaurants and super-intends one or two shops. I do not believe that the women of Paris are less virtuous than their sisters of other large cities. I saw hundreds of shop girls at their earnest religious devotions on Sunday at Notre Dame. Bad girls do not pray.

Before leaving Paris I visited the Palace of the Tuilleries and saw its chambers, halls and saloons, so long the dwelling place of royalty. With its magnificent furniture and gorgeous embellishments it is a very interesting monument of the olden time. From 1830 to 1848, this palace had been the quiet residence of Louis Philippe. During all that time France was tranquil and gave no sign to warn the king of approaching danger. As far as outward appearances indicated he was beloved by the fickle French people. He delighted to promenade the streets in citizen's dress, with nothing to distinguish him from his subjects except his peculiarly benevolent face and unassuming demeanor. On the night of February 23, 1848, while the king was enjoying a chat with some friends in the chamber of the palace now called "The King's Cabinet," the people of Paris were throwing up great barricades and preparing for a successful revolution. About 8 o'clock on the morning of the twenty-fourth, the king was for the first time warned of approaching danger. A feeble attempt was made to change the Ministry and concede to the popular demand for a dissolution of the Chamber of Deputies, but it was too late. Soon after the unfortunate king was informed that his soldiers were fraternizing with the insurgents and that all was lost. The king supposing that his submission might appease the infuriated multitude and induce them to accept the Count of Paris as king, gave orders that no resistance should be made. In a few minutes the crowd penetrated the Court of the Palace, the king fled and the monarchy of 1830 was no more. The king with the queen and a few attendants passed up under cover of the southern wall of the Garden of the Tuilleries to the Place de la Concorde ; he paused a moment at the spot where Louis XVI. had been beheaded about fifty-six years before for "opposing the people." He at once retraced his steps to where a small one-horse carriage was standing, which he immediately entered and in a gallop departed towards St. Cloud never to enter Paris again. The Tuilleries then became the residence of the President and afterwards the Emperor Napoleon, where he still dwells in apparent safety. The chambers of the palace formerly occupied by King Louis Philippe have been preserved very much as they were when he so unceremoniously left the palace.

The Emperor spares neither labor nor expense to please and gratify his people. They may enjoy every pleasure with the single exception of that most exquisitely delightful of all American enjoyments, the privilege of talking politics. It is a thing interdicted and must not even be thought of. He builds them elegant opera houses and theatres, as well as splendid churches. It is a mistake to suppose the French to be a nation of infidels. I found their churches about as well filled as those of London. Infidelity was a fungus of the dark days of the revolution, just as a field of wheat may be blighted by the mildew of a foggy night, but it does not follow that every subsequent crop will be equally blasted.

Were it not for my anxiety for home, I would like to spend at least a month in Paris, but I begin to be fatigued by the hardships of my rapid traveling, and will quit Europe in a few days for home. The life of a traveler is one of more than ordinary labor, and if he would improve his hours, and hope to return to his home benefited in body and enlarged in mind, he must not waste his moments, neither must he indulge in the soft luxuries and enchanting allurements which constantly beckon him to forbidden pleasures. Like Ulysses, he must not trust to his own strength, but while sailing by the Siren Isles, he must lash himself to the mast, stop his ears, crowd the sails and bend the oars, until he is entirely out of reach of their bewitching songs. Those who suppose the pleasures of traveling can be enjoyed without its hardships, will be sadly undeceived before they have advanced far. There is, nevertheless, something very invigorating in the constant change of climate and scenery, otherwise the repeated annoyances would be unendurable. The successful traveler must retire late and arise early, walk over cities and plains and climb mountains. To-night he may have a downy pillow for his head, to-morrow night a board, or the musty berth of a badly ventilated ship. With health and strength and *not too much baggage*, the enjoyment, however, far exceeds the annoyance.

XIV.

On Ship Once More—Lonely Female Passengers—Love on the Sea—Mrs. Studtgardt—Cocktail Club—A Ship in Distress—Southern Men on the Ship.

Queenstown, Ireland, July, 1873.

With a fair wind and flowing sail, a smooth sea and staunch ship, we sailed from New York on the nineteenth, at 2 P. M., and arrived at this port to-day at 7 P. M. A novice is very much surprised at the rapidity with which a cargo is received and discharged. The passengers with their baggage are not permitted to come on board before 11 A. M. The ship is advertised to sail at 1 P. M.; there is always some delay and there are generally some passengers who arrive at the last moment. Just as the plank was half withdrawn, a lady with five great Saratoga trunks arrived; one minute longer and she would have been left behind. Her excuse was that she hadn't time to fix her hair. The bustle of the embarkation is very amusing, officers yelling, crew swearing, steam whistling, passengers out of breath and carriages coming in a gallop; no time to dispute with *Jehu*, who is provokingly slow in getting out the baggage, and for his life can't make change for a five dollar bill which a passenger was fool enough to hand him. When the order comes for all but passengers to leave the ship a scene follows, of kissing, crying, embracing and sobbing, which beggars all attempts at description. Of course everybody is interested in the tears of a pretty woman. I am not singular in this respect. I began at once to look for her; she was sitting in the rear of the ship, her beautiful eyes in a flood of tears, her face buried in her handsome young husband's bosom who, for some unknown cause, at least unknown to me, was not to accompany her; but little Charley, a bright-eyed boy of about six years, was to go with her in papa's stead. He evidently felt his responsibility as he strutted about the deck in his new sailor clothes, happy as a lord. For four days Charley's mother did little but sigh and gaze upon a miniature likeness, which at short intervals she drew from her heaving bosom. The intervals grew gradually and beautifully longer until about the fifth day out, when the sunshine from the face of a very handsome young Englishman began to dissipate from her fair countenance the sombre clouds of grief for the absent one. It was truly marvellous to observe with what disinterested anxiety he would inquire about little Charley's health; how gently he would nurse, caress and pet him, and how sweetly Charley's mother would smile upon the polite and *obliging* young gentleman. The miniature of Charley's papa appeared no more. A stranger to the first scenes of the voyage would have sworn they were lovers, and by my soul, I believe they were ! " Faith," said an Irish gentleman from Cincinnati, who had left a young wife of thirty behind, ".I begin to tremble for myself; I'm losing faith in the virtue of *men*, or the honesty of *women*." " O, 'tis nothing but a little amusement," said an elderly Scotch lady. True, thought I. 'tis nothing ; but

> "Is whispering nothing?
> Is leaning cheek to cheek? is meeting noses?
> Kissing with inside lip? stopping the career
> Of laughter with a sigh; (a note infallible
> Of breaking honesty)   *   *   *   *
> Skulking in corners? wishing clocks more swift?
> Hours, minutes? noon, midnight? and all eyes blind
> With the pin and web, but their's, theirs only
> That would, unseen, be wicked? is this nothing?
> Why then the world and all that's in it is nothing,
> *   *   *   *   *   *   *   *
>   *   *   nor nothing have these nothings,
> If this be nothing."

Mrs. Studtgardt was a buxom dame from Chicago of about forty summers. About the third day out she told me her name ; said that she was alone, and was on a visit to Germany to see her relatives. She was very desirous to be introduced to a handsome young German on board, because she said the poor fellow seemed *so* lonely ; she could speak German and she had no doubt that the charms of her conversation would relieve his apparent solitude. To get rid of her I effected an introduction, and it was very pleasant to see how happy I made them both. Of course I thought her a spinster, but to my unutterable grief, I learned just before we landed at Queenstown, that she was married, and had left Jake at home to attend the children while she visited the *Vaterland*. Upon informing my Irish friend of this painful news, he raised his pious eyes to heaven and exclaimed in apparent despair : " O, woman, thy name is frailty," and with a sigh kissed his wife's photograph.

We had about one hundred cabin passengers on board and but little fun. The trip was to me a very tedious one, not even a storm to relieve the monotony, and with the exception of a *moral* story or *chaste* song, spiced now and then with a *modest* joke from the young gentlemen of the Cocktail Club, whose headquarters were the smoking room, there was little to laugh at during the entire voyage.

On our seventh day out we had a genuine sensation. The full rigged British bark Silver Cloud, with all sail set, bore down straight across our bow. In a few minutes we observed her ensign at half mast, with the union down, an emblem of distress. In a moment all was excitement, the engines were stopped and life boats manned and despatched to the distressed ship. A boat was also sent from the bark ; they met about half way between the vessels within hailing distance. "What's the matter" shouted the Captain, through his trumpet. The response came : "Man very sick ; don't know how to treat him ; send your doctor." He was immediately sent, but soon returned and sent a large package of *Cholera* medicine to the bark. They had but six seamen and were of course greatly alarmed. I was standing near the captain when he received the response to his question. I went at once forward, but rumor had beaten me. I heard one passenger tell another that the cholera had killed all the ship's crew, and that the captain and dog were all that were left to man the ship. It reminded me of the reliability of the war news we used to receive in America.

There were three Southern gentlemen passengers on the ship, from South Carolina, Alabama and Louisiana. At first they were very bitter in expressing their opinions about the government, but they soon grew more conservative. The gentleman from Alabama hoped only for a stable government when Grant should be King, at which remark the Englishmen present expressed great delight. Upon ascending to the deck to take our after dinner smoke, my South Carolina friend gave my arm a quiet touch, and whispered in my ear, " Don't mind Alabama, he has suffered like myself ; however we may differ at home, abroad we will be countrymen." That simple remark has made me that man's friend forever. I will go from here to Limerick and from thence to Londonderry, where you may hear from me again.

—————

XV.

Second Visit to Ireland—Street Nomenclature in Cork—Scene in Court—Irish Hospitality—A Yankee After a Fortune—The City of the Violated Treaty —Cathedral of Limerick—Memento Mori—The Lost Bells—The Shannon—Mishap to an English Tourist —The Coleen Bawn—Kilrush—An Irish Fair at Ennis—Pigs and Wit.

GALWAY, IRELAND, August, 1873.

This is my second visit to Ireland and I find it, if possible, more beautiful than ever. I visited again the church of Shandon and paid the bell-ringer a shilling to play the old

air, "Shandon Bells." The bells are eight in number and
have a very sweet tone. Each one is as large as the old State
House bell at Philadelphia. We were under the surveillance
of two policemen who dogged our heels to the very top of the
tower, which is one hundred and twenty feet high. From the
top of the tower the view of Cork is very fine. The whole
town and many miles of the surrounding country lie at your
feet. In Cork, like London, they never change the name of
anything. Its street nomenclature is somewhat remarkable,
such as Cat Lane, Rag Lane, Cock-pit Lane, etc.

The courts were in session and I concluded to pay them a
visit. The Judge's coach, with footman in livery and cock-
aded coachman, surrounded by eight dragoons with drawn
swords, came galloping down the street. Two dragoons went
before, two behind and two on each side of the coach. When
the coach stopped opposite the court house the dragoons
formed in single file on the opposite side of the street with
their horses' heads facing the court house, while two lines of
soldiers were formed, making a passage between the lines
from the coach to the court house door. Then the Sheriff in
his gold lace uniform and hat in hand approached the coach
door from which his Lordship alighted arrayed in a flowing
black robe and gray wig. The tipstaves walked before them
backwards into the court house, while the dragoons blew a
blast upon their trumpets. The same ceremony is always enacted upon the adjournment of the court. The court rooms
are formed something like a funnel or inverted cone. The
jury box is in reality a box about four by ten feet in which
the jury are locked up, and is about six or seven feet above the
level of the floor. The jury locked like twelve very wise *owls*
in consultation over a dead horse. The witness had not a very
strong voice and the Judge was a little deaf, so the counsellors
set a chair on the table at which they were taking notes, and the
witness was made to mount the table and sit on the chair about
three feet from the Judge's nose, with lawyers all around him.

I spent a very pleasant evening with Mr. Welsh to whom
I had been introduced by my Irish friend from Cincinnati. I
enjoyed his hospitality very much. Mrs. Welsh's tea was
only surpassed by her husband's punch. He is a true type of
an Irish merchant, with good sense, good spirits, quick wit
and a kind heart

I met one of my fellow-passengers promenading upon the
quay ; he was a regular Yankee, with blue swallow-tail coat
and brass buttons, short waist and big collar. He wore an
old-fashioned stovepipe hat, the brim of which rested on his
nose ; a cigar was in his mouth and both hands well down in
his pantaloons pockets. He had kept himself very quiet on

the ship, and as I had not spoken to him before, I hailed him with a "good morning, sir." "How d'ye doo?" was the reply. I asked him if he was going to Dublin. As quick as lightning came the reply: "Well, I rather guess that's the calculation." He was in search of a lawyer, and claimed to be heir to a fortune in Ireland of £2,000,000, only $10,000,000. He had $4000 in his pocket to fee lawyers with, and he "Guessed that would fetch his fortune if anything on airth would." I felt sorry his estate was not in Philadelphia and I his lucky lawyer.

From Cork I visited Limerick, the city of the violated treaty. It is a very old looking town, some parts of which are in complete ruins. It was once a royal city, enclosed by a stone wall of prodigious proportions and defended by a magnificent castle. The ashes of Munster's mighty kings repose in the old cathedral, but her strong walls are broken down and her mighty castle is in ruins. The marks of Cromwell's cannon are very distinct upon the castle walls. It was at one of the eastern gates where the women made a gallant fight and beat back the invading English with no other arms than stones in their stockings. In the year 1691, William III. besieged the city and was several times repelled with great slaughter by the Irish people, commanded by Sarsfield, Earl of Lucan, who caused a large cannon to be mounted on the top of the steeple of the cathedral commanded by one of his best gunners and which did great havoc among the enemy. The place occupied by this gun was one hundred and twenty feet high, the steeple being of massive stone masonry. At last a chain-shot from one of the enemy's guns cut the gunner in two and silenced the gun. This shot is exhibited among the relics of the church. This cathedral is a very well-preserved edifice. We find it referred to in history as early as the twelfth century.

Among the tombs and monuments of the church, deeply cut in black marble, is the following singular inscription, in English characters :—

Memento Mory.

Here lieth little Samuel
Barinton that greate under
Taker ———— of famous cittles—
Clock and chime ma'ter
He made his one time goe
Early and latter but now
He is returned to god his cre
Ator
The 19 of november then he
Scest an for his memory
This here is pleast by his
Son Ben, 1693.

From the steeple the view of the town and surrounding country is most charming. The green fields of Erin, with the beautiful Shannon, the most magnificent of Irish rivers, may be distinctly seen for twenty miles around. The population of Limerick is about 46,000, and like that of most Irish cities, does not increase. The chime of eight very large bells is of great antiquity. They were bought from an old church in Italy. It is said an old Italian gentleman, who had never wandered outside of the range of the bells, when he awoke and missed their music upon the morning of their removal, became very melancholy, and after months of disconsolate mourning, he left Italy in search of his lost bells. After years of wandering he sailed up the Shannon, and as he approached the city on a bright Sunday morning in May, he recognized the sound of his long-lost bells and, as was supposed by his attendants, he swooned away overpowered with delight, but when they came to more closely examine, they found he was dead.

The Shannon is the only river in Ireland worthy of the name. It is 240 miles long and runs through ten counties ; at some places it is very narrow, at others it expands into a glassy lake several miles wide. The shores on both sides are in the highest state of cultivation, and the scenery most enchanting ; studded with old ruined castles and ornamented with splendid new ones. I sailed for eighty miles down the river from Limerick to Kilrush. The sun was shining splendidly over the boat, but we could see refreshing showers, for which Ireland is so noted, falling in five different directions. The river at Tarbet is about nine miles wide and was as rough as the Atlantic. An English tourist lost his hat and came near falling overboard ; he was very much frightened. " *What !*" said he " *hafter traveling hall hover the hearth ham hi to be drowned hat last hin the blasted Shannon ?*" " Holy mother," said an Irish patriot, "shure and you might be drowned in a much more ignoble stream."

Our boat passed the dark and stormy waters, where the Coleen Bawn was drowned by the foster brother of her lover. On the shore may be seen the ruined church where she was buried. On landing at Kilrush I learned that there was to be a great fair held at Ennis, the assize town of county Clare. As I had never seen a genuine Irish fair, I determined even at the expense of a twenty mile ride in a jaunting car, to visit it. I did not grudge the ride, as it took me through some of the richest and best cultivated lands I had ever looked upon. I saw at Ennis, sheep which sold for £3.10 each, which is about equal to $17.50 in American gold. I made my dinner on a mutton chop, as large as an ordinary sirloin steak, and withal as tender and sweet as a three months' old lamb.

Ennis is a very queer looking old town. The river Furgus runs through it and supplies it with all its water. At one place you may see a dozen old crones in the water up to their knees, washing foul linen, hard by a hostler or peasant boy watering his sheep and cows, or washing his horses, and close by a kitchen maid drawing a supply of the same water for *cooking* and *drinking*. The town was crowded to overflowing with peasants, pigs, sheep, cows and horses.

A bed in a hotel could not be obtained at any price. I gave an old woman, with a bushy head of red hair, five shillings for a bed, made on an old settee, in a barn-like chamber, over a saddler's shop and was glad to get it. Persons were there from England, Scotland and all parts of Ireland to buy stock. The fair opened at 4 o'clock in the morning, and presented a scene which must be witnessed to be comprehended. It had rained all night ; the fair grounds consisted of the open lots and streets of the town south of the Furgus. This is the old part of Ennis, where the best street is not over fifteen feet in width. Amid the mud, manure and puddles of foul water, the enormous crowd of men and animals surged, bartered, swore and drank whisky, while the pigs kept up a concert of squealing, relieved now and then by bellowing of bulls and bleating of sheep. The peasantry were there, male and female, in their Sunday clothes. The men in corduroy breeches, blue woolen stockings and heavy soled shoes. Their coats were mostly of homemade gray cloth, with very long tails and enormous collars. The girls looked better than the men ; they wore short petticoats, which exhibited to great advantage their well developed limbs.

Everybody seemed excited ; most of the bargains were made in a loud and boisterous manner, I expected every moment to see a row, but in this I was disappointed, the reason was quite obvious ; her Majesty's constabulary were there in force. The most amusement was found in the pig department. Most of the peasants owned but a single pig, which would be held by its proprietor by a rope of grass around its hind leg. Some of the pigs were in donkey carts and seemed quite contented beside the young woman who drove the cart. The air was full of true Irish wit which seemed to bubble out like water from a spring. The following is a fair sample. An English swell with some lady friends were looking at the fair, and to amuse the girls he pretended to a peasant that he wished to buy his pig. Winking at the girls he inquired its price. "Sure," said paddy, "offer me his value and I'll soon tell ye his price, for there's not a man in all Clare I'd rather sell him to than yer honor, for I know you'd treat him well, seeing ye look so much alike." My friend from Cincinnati,

says this wit was borrowed from Glover who gives a scene
very much like it.   The bystanders laughed, the swell
sneaked off, but paddy never as much as grinned ; he only
gave a half wink, and stood scratching his bushy head.

The fair broke up in the afternoon amid the wildest scenes
of confusion, the roads leading out of Ennis were crowded
with the returning peasantry, and not caring to prolong my
stay, I left for Galway which can only be reached from here
by a circuitous route of about 200 miles.

XVI.

GALWAY—-ATHENREY—-BALLY-DAVID CASTLE—-SPANISH
COSTUMES AND CUSTOMS—EMPTY DOCKS AND STORE-
HOUSES—LYNCH CASTLE AND LYNCH LAW—KING OF THE
CLADDAGH—LONDONDERRY—THE CURSE OF CROMWALL
—SIEGE OF DERRY—A SLOW PLACE FOR BUSINESS—
PORT RUSH BATHING SCENES.

LONDONDERRY, August, 1873.

From Ennis on my way to Galway, I stopped at Athenrey,.
which in English means the *King's Ford*.   I never saw such
a stony country.   All the fences are built with stone, and the
fields are full of large piles of them, resembling at a short
distance, cocks of hay.   We passed several old ruined castles,
which are so thick in this part of Ireland that they excite but
little interest in the traveler and none in the inhabitants.   At
Athenrey there is a very well preserved old ruin, known as
Bally-David Castle.   The town is very ancient, the walls,
castle, convent and abbey are all in ruins.   A battle was
fought here in 1315, in which the Irish were defeated.   From
Athenrey the face of the country improves very much, but I
was greatly disappointed with Galway.   I expected to find a
thriving town, instead of which it proved one of the sleepiest
places I have ever visited.   It requires an hour's notice to
procure. the simplest meal.   There is but one barber in the
town, and he don't shave, but makes his living at hair cutting
at three pence a head.   The citizens have all a foreign air,
and one seems surprised to hear them speak English.   They
dress like Spaniards, and it is said have Spanish manners,
which is accounted for from the fact that the town was once a
Spanish settlement and had a great Spanish trade.   The men
wear red vests and short Spanish cloaks lined with red, while
the ladies adorn themselves with Spanish head dresses, and
wear short red petticoats.   When walking in the streets they

wear a kind of Spanish mantle which entirely covers the head,
falls in graceful folds over the shoulders, and is clasped tightly
by the hand under the chin. The poor as well as the rich
dress in this way. The houses are built like those in Zara-
gosa and other Spanish towns. They are of stone, very large,
without any cornice to the roofs, with immense gable ends
facing the streets, many of which are without sidewalks.
The entrance to the dwellings is by a large arched way without doors, but closed at night by an iron gate; the doors to
the houses are from the inside of the arched way.

Galway has been a very rich town; the evidences and
remains of immense wealth are to be found all over it. The
docks are like those of Liverpool, and must have cost an enormous sum to build them. It also contains great storehouses and
splendid quays, but her docks are entirely deserted, her storehouses all empty and in ruins, her quays only occupied by
miserable fishermen, and her fine old mansions, where wealth
and luxury once abounded, are now the habitations of vice
and poverty. Like a poor and decayed old gentleman who has
seen better days, the town appears to be arrayed in the cast-off
garments of happier times, but withal there is a dignity in its
demeanor, even in its desolate and distressed condition, which
awakes pity and demands respect. The old Lynch Castle still
stands, but the abbey is in ruins. The castle is square and
heavy-looking; it is profusely ornamented, and the balustrade
decorated with the heads of mythical animals. It was from
the window of this castle that James Lynch Fitz-Stephen, who
was Mayor in 1493, hung his own son. He had sent his son
to Spain on business; while returning the son conspired with
the crew, murdered the captain, and seized the ship and cargo.
One of the party discovered the horrid business to the Mayor.
He tried his son, and as he was found guilty, he condemned
him to death. It was thought that as the condemned was an
only son the Mayor would not execute the sentence. All his
relatives interceded for the pardon of the youth. The father
fixed a day to announce his determination, and early on the
morning of the time appointed the son was found hanging by
the neck out of one of the windows of his father's house.
Some suppose that this was the origin of our word "lynch-law."

The lower part of the town is called the *Claddagh*. It is
a miserable conglomeration of one-story hovels, inhabited by
about 5000 sturdy fishermen. They have their own laws and
customs, and are looked upon by the townspeople as an inferior
race. They have a head chief, whose boat bears a white flag,
who is called the " King of Claddagh "; he decides all matters of litigation among the tribe. Among their customs is
the marriage gift of a boat by the bride's father upon her

wedding day, and the marriage ring is an heir-loom passing from the mother to her daughter from generation to generation. They seldom marry with the townspeople, whom they in turn consider interlopers and inferior to the *Claddagh*.

I left Galway at 11 A. M., and arrived in Londonderry about 11 P. M. of the same day. The country from Galway to Derry is very beautiful, rich, rolling and in some parts almost mountainous. The fields which are very small and irregular in shape, present a most pleasing prospect to the eye. The shades of green are as various as the fields; from the deepest hue to the lightest shade.

I find Londonderry, or Derry as it is here called, a very remarkable town, containing many objects of deep interest to the traveler.

On my way to Derry I heard a peculiar Irish *curse*, which I had never before heard. There was in our compartment a young swell who, from the time he entered the car, did nothing but smoke cigars and tell obscene stories to the great disgust of a very pious-looking fellow passenger. Upon stopping at one of the stations a priest was about entering our compartment, when our pious friend with a look of deep concern, ejaculated as he jumped from the car: "May the curse of Cromwell be on you, ye blackguard." Then addressing the priest, he exclaimed: "Holy father, don't enter the car or ye'll be stifled with smoke and horrified by the corrupt conversation."

My first day in Derry was Sunday, and like a good christian, I went to church in the cathedral, by which I killed two birds with one stone: Said my prayers and got to see the interior of the old church; for it being a Protestant church, is somewhat difficult of access on week-day. The Catholic churches are always open. They afford convenient resting places for the weary traveler; and while he often only enters to gaze upon the beautiful paintings and noble architecture, he seldom leaves without a feeling of reverence and religious awe. The Cathedral of Derry was built in 1633. It is a fine old building and remarkably well preserved. I copied the following from an old black marble slab in the vestibule :—

"Ano. Do. 1633, Car. Regis 9.

If stones coulde speake
Then Londons prayse
Shoulde sound who
Built this church and
Cittie from the grounde."

The walls of the city are in perfect order; they are from fifteen to fifty feet wide and form a very pleasant promenade around the city; of course they would afford no defence against modern artillery. The city is located on the west side of the river Foyle, about forty miles from the sea. Derry in the Irish tongue means "thick wood." The city was built by the citizens of London during the reign of James I. and is remarkable for the sieges it has withstood. The appearance of the town from the opposite side of the river is very picturesque. Its population is about 20,000. The monument erected to the memory of Rev. George Walker, in 1828, is one of the most interesting objects in the city. It is a very handsome Doric column surmounted by his statue.

The people of Derry never weary in recounting the incidents of the last siege. They tell of a letter which was dropped at Dumbartin, county Down, where the Earl of Mount Alexander resided, informing him that all the Protestants of Derry, men, women and children, were to be massacred on the 9th of December, 1688; of the wild alarm with which the whole town was seized; how in the confusion which followed, some apprentice boys muttered something about shutting the gates; how the authorities of the city vacillated between hope and fear, until some Irish troops appeared on the opposite side of the river and sent their officers over to take possession of the town in the name of King James, when some nine of the apprentice boys ran to the main guard and seized the keys just as he, by order of the Mayor, was about delivering them to the enemy and when Lord Antrim's soldiers were within 60 yards of the city gate. They also tell with great particularity how, during the siege which followed and which lasted 105 days, the people suffered from starvation, when a mouse sold for six pence, a rat for two shillings and a morsel of horse pudding for five shillings. They point out the place where the besiegers had thrown a boom across the river to prevent provisions from coming to their relief by water. How the boom was broken by a provision ship, which from the violence of the shock rebounded and went ashore on the enemy's side of the river, and how just as the enemy in great joy were about boarding her she fired a broadside into them, the shock of which extricated her from her perilous position, when she floated again into deep waters and relieved the city after 2300 of the citizens had died of hunger; all of which must be taken *cum grano salis.*

I have no doubt the people of Derry were very brave, but they were somewhat slow in preparing for their defence, and from all I could see, the present inhabitants in this respect are worthy sons of their tardy sires, for I went to a bookstore to buy a map of the city at 9.30 A. M. on Monday morning, and was coolly informed by a boy in attendance, that they did not open the store for the sale of goods until 10 A. M. I had a letter of introduction to an attorney of the city, and walked from the bookstore to his office; it too was shut, and on inquiry I was informed that the lawyers did not open their offices until 10 A. M.   So I left Derry in disgust and went to Port Rush to treat my eyes with a glance at the beauties of Erin in their bathing costumes, *a la chemise*, which when wet exhibited in great perfection the natural outlines of their angelic forms. The men go in *a' la naturel*.

I will sail to-morrow for Liverpool and expect a splendid view of the entire northern coast of Ireland.   From Liverpool I will go by rail to Hull and from thence by sea to Hamburg.

XVII.

DERRY TO HAMBURG—DUNLUCE CASTLE—A RUGGED COAST —MANCHESTER FROM THE CARS—LEEDS—HULL — ENGLISH VIEWS OF SLAVERY IN 1834 AND 1864—A CLEVER FELLOW IN ENGLAND—THUNDER STORM IN HAMBURG— LONELINESS IN A CROWD—A FUNERAL—ON TO BERLIN.

HAMBURG, August, 1873.

I sailed from Derry for Liverpool on the morning of the 5th inst.   The weather was delightful and the sky remarkably clear for this climate.   The river Foyle is ten hundred and sixty-eight feet wide and forty-three feet deep opposite Derry. The bold shore and cheerful rural scenery, with the mountain ranges in the back ground, present a charming picture in looking upon which the eye never wearies.   Our ship hugged the entire north coast of Ireland so very closely, that the sheep could be seen with the naked eye grazing in the green fields, and all the little villages and hamlets from which the blue smoke at eventide so gracefully curled, were plainly visible, adding essentially to the beauty of the picture.   The old castle of Dunluce, perched like a hoary sentinel upon its ocean-beaten rock, could be seen in its minutest details.   It stands upon the summit of a perpendicular rock, 1000 feet above the sea.   The entire surface of the rock is occupied by the castle walls, which are in appearance but a continuation of the perpendicular sides of the rock.   The castle must have been absolutely inaccessible, except by the drawbridge across the yawning chasm.   This castle was the scene of a most villainous act of treachery in 1642.   General Munroe visited it as the guest of the Earl of Antrim and was honored with a splendid entertainment.   Munroe took advantage of his host's hospitality, seized his person and his castle, and conveyed the Earl a prisoner to the castle of Carrickfergus.

We passed between the coast and Rathlin island, upon which many fine ships have been wrecked. This coast is very dangerous in rough weather. A ship-wrecked crew would not have the slightest chance of escape by the shore, as it is for many miles a rugged and precipitous rock, rising almost perpendicularly several hundred feet above the surface of the sea, the terrible roar of which can be heard for many miles as it dashes against the rocky coast and seems, even in calm weather, to lash itself into an uncontrollable fury. We passed so near the causeway, that the peculiar formation of the basaltic rocks, with their five and six-sided columns could almost be counted. So clear was the atmosphere that the coast of Scotland could be seen across the channel without the aid of a glass. We lost sight of Ireland about sun-set, passed the Isle of Man during the night, and sighted the Welsh mountains about 7 A. M. the next morning, arriving at Liverpool about 9 A. M. Not caring to tarry in Liverpool, as I had seen it twice before, I took the 11 A. M. train for Hull, which is nearly due east upon the other side of the island. I passed through the city of Manchester and formed a very contemptible opinion of the town. It is hardly fair, however, to judge a city by its appearance from a railway car. It was black with the smoke of ten thousand enormous chimneys, which seemed to rival each other in belching forth the blackest kind of smoke; withal the houses are built of sombre gray and very coarse brick and are covered with red tile, or heavy slate, very rough and ugly. The homeliness of the town was, however, greatly relieved by the busy hum of machinery and the active industry of its inhabitants.

I stopped two hours at Leeds and found it a very important and thriving town. The business part of the city is almost as smoky as Manchester, and is built of the same ugly gray brick, but the residences of the better classes are very handsome and are built of square dressed stone, which is found in great abundance in this vicinity. It is very easily dressed, as it comes from the quarries in great flat flakes and naturally breaks square. The only really handsome women I saw in England were here. The younger ones had a very fresh and rosy look, but the more elderly had a rather heavy and coarse appearance. After all our American ladies are the handsomest women in the world at forty. It is the age at which a woman should be in her prime, yet here at that age they all look like men dressed in feminine attire.

I arrived at Hull about 7 P. M. and was very agreeably disappointed with the place. I found it the third city in the

kingdom, having a commercial importance only equalled by
London and Liverpool. It stands upon the most noble of English rivers; its streets are clean and well paved, and its docks
are truly wonderful works.   It is situated at the point where
the river Hull falls into the Humber, twenty-two miles from
sea.   The country around the town is very flat, hence its extent cannot be judged of from a distant view.   The old part
of the town is very primitive in appearance, with the same
narrow streets and fantastic style of architecture found in all
old English towns.   The new part of the city is really beautiful, the better class of buildings being constructed of the same
kind of mellow colored stone of which Paris is built.   The
history of the town dates back about 700 years; its present
population is about 125,000.   It was the birthplace of William
Wilberforce, the great English abolitionist.   It contains a
splendid monument, with the statue of Wilberforce upon its
top.   The base of the monument contains this inscription:

"Negro slavery abolished, 1st Aug., 1834."

The wicked thought would intrude itself upon my mind
that if the Southern Confederacy had been, as the English
people freely confess they hoped it would be, a success, Hull
might have had another monument equally as conspicuous,
with the statue of Alexander H. Stevens or Mr. Jeff. Davis
upon its top, and the inscription upon its base : " *Negro slavery
re-established, 1st Aug., 1865.*"   I suppose it is uncharitable
to think of such things, especially as the English people *now*
seem wonderfully kind and appear to have a true and devoted
attachment to their American cousins.   They say we managed
the Alabama claims with great cleverness.   *Clever* is a great
word here ; they never say one is skillful, adroit, intelligent
or smart, but that he's very *clever.*   They apply the word
altogether to the intellectual, rather than to the social qualities
as with us.   From Hull regular lines of steamers sail to all
parts of the earth ; I never saw so many ships in any one place
as are here collected.

I embarked from its port in the good ship Fairy for Hamburg, on Wednesday night and reached that city this morning
at daybreak, being two days and a half making the voyage.
I retired to my berth about 11 o'clock P. M , and was soon
dreaming of home, listening to the prattle of sweet little voices
and enjoying the smile of a still sweeter face, when suddenly
a lurid flash and deafening peal of thunder aroused me from
my slumber, scattered all my happy dreams and awoke me to
realize that I was thousands of miles away, a stranger in a
strange land.   I heard a great noise upon the deck, and a confusion of tongues worse, if possible, than the jargon of Babel.
My first thought was that the boiler had burst and we were in

—no matter where. I looked out the port hole of my state room and discovered it was daylight and that our ship was safely moored in some strange harbor, with old warehouses and wharves around us, in a thunder storm. I felt relieved when I saw the rain, for I knew it never rained in the place where I at first thought we were. "Don't be alarmed, sir," said the steward, "we're safe at Hamburg."

The sun rises about six hours sooner here than it does in Philadelphia. The storm was soon over, and when I saw the sun rise I felt that his was the only familiar face I could look upon. One who has never realized the loneliness of suddenly finding himself transplanted from a country where every word is clearly comprehended and every shade of thought perfectly expressed, to a land where every word is but gibberish and every look a vacant meaningless stare ; where one neither comprehends the language nor is understood when he speaks, can not conceive or form any clear idea of the feeling of despair which for a moment overcomes the heart. To suddenly awake and find you had lost both hearing and speech would give some idea of the situation of your humble servant in Hamburg.

Everything here is different from England or America ; the civilization, manners, dress and money, even the dogs bark in Dutch. I offered a porter a shilling to carry my luggage to a neighboring hotel ; he shook his head and said "*nine-nine.*" What, thought I, *nine* shillings for carrying a carpet bag a few short squares ? I'll carry it myself first. The steward laughed and explained that *nine* was *no;* he asked him in Dutch how much he would carry the luggage for ; the rascal wanted *fifteen schellings.* I was about toddling off with my own luggage, when the steward explained that a schelling in Dutch was less than a *penny* in English money, whereupon my wrath subsided and the porter soon conducted me safely to my hotel.

It is truly wonderful with what facility one accommodates himself to circumstances. After a few hours spent in wandering about the town I began to feel quite at home. True, it required a little *cheek*, but every traveler must have a good supply of that commodity or he had better stay at home. I could call for my *bier* and *cigaren*, and enjoy myself in "mine inn" as comfortably as any other Dutchman. Even the names on the signs seemed familiar ; such for instance as *Carl Schurz, Tobacke und Cigaren Fabrick; Johann Freiderick Hartranft, Haarschneiden und Coffeuric—etc., etc.* (1) I met

---

(1) Time has destroyed the point in the intended play upon the names of Carl Schurz and J. F. Hartranft. When the letter was written one was a leader in the Senate, the o her Governor of Pennsylvania. Their namesakes in Hamburg were tobacconists and barbers.—"There is nothing in the name."
T. J. C. (1892).

a funeral coming down the street; the hearse was drawn by a
pair of black horses, each horse led by a man, and both men
and horses dressed in long black robes; the hearse was followed by eight *hired* mourners, also arrayed in long black
robes; these were followed by three carriages, conveying the
priests and family of the deceased.

The hotel at which I am stopping is one of the best in the
city, very large, and beautifully situated upon the lake in the
centre of the town.   In England and Ireland they gave us no
napkins at meals; here they are as large as table-cloths.
When spread out on the lap both ends hang on the floor and
cover even the feet.

The omnibuses and street railway cars are two stories high
and look very odd.   The third class cars on the railroads are
also in some instances two stories high.   It is no uncommon
sight to see women with wooden yokes fitted to the back of the
neck and resting upon the shoulders, with enormous baskets
hanging at each end of the yoke, filled with vegetables, which
they peddle about the streets, or with buckets filled with water
for household purposes, and which they carry from one end of
the town to the other.

The city of Hamburg is really a very interesting town.
It was founded by Charlemagne, A. D. 803, and has houses
now standing in the ancient part of the city one thousand years
old.   They resemble those of Rotterdam, and lean every way,
and are twisted in various shapes.   The streets of the old part
are narrow and crooked; there are no sidewalks; the houses,
some of which are six stories high, project at each story from
one to two feet over the lower stories into the street.   The
city is situated on the river Elbe, about sixty miles from its
mouth.   It has a population of about 225,000.   Upwards of
five thousand sea-going vessels annually enter and quit its
harbor.   It was visited in 1842 with a fearful conflagration
which destroyed about a fourth part of the city, which has
been entirely rebuilt with very handsome modern buildings.
The new part of the town is not surpassed by any city in
Europe.   The gardens, groves and boulevards, lakes and
promenades of Hamburg, are constructed and kept up on a
gigantic scale.   A beautiful lake, of over a mile in circumference, is situated in the centre of the city.   I leave here to-
morrow for Berlin.

XVIII.

HAMBURG TO DRESDEN—MORE ABOUT HAMBURG—CONTRAST
  BETWEEN NEW AND OLD CITIES—PROTESTANT AND CATH-
  OLIC CHURCHES—SUNDAY IN EUROPE—BERLIN—THE KING
  AND HIS CABMEN—UNTER DEN LINDEN—MONUMENT OF
  VICTORY—DRESDEN ART GALLERY—MADONNA DI SISTO
  —IMMODEST PAINTINGS—THE GREEN VAULT—AN ADVEN-
  TURE IN THE ZOO.

DRESDEN, August, 1873.

After taking another stroll through Hamburg, I was compelled to modify my views of the town. The old fortifications
have been destroyed and their places converted into beautiful
parks and gardens. The entire suburbs somewhat resemble
Fairmount Park at Philadelphia, on a small scale, with the
city in the centre of the park.

There are certain general features common to all European
towns, They all have an old and a new quarter ; they are all
comparatively finished, having no scattered suburbs with brick
yards and town lots for sale. On emerging from the thickly-
populated and closely-built streets, you at once enter the cultivated fields or beautiful gardens. They are all built in the
form of an irregular circle, with wide avenues, like bent
hoops, enclosing the town. These avenues follow to a certain
extent, the course of the old city walls, and many of the best
streets now occupy the place of the removed bulwarks. The
old part of every town has crooked, narrow, and very irregular
cross streets, without sidewalks, which cut at various angles
the circular streets. They all have their museums of antiquity and art, and their old cathedrals, and after you have
seen one you have seen all, especially after having visited
Westminster Abbey, the old Cathedral at Cologne, and Notre
Dame at Paris, the Louvre and British Museum. I have
become really weary in wandering through museums and visiting churches, except, of course, for rest and devotion.

The traveler abroad must remark the singular contrast
between the Protestant and Catholic churches. The former are
always shut except during service, and if you wish to see them,.
the sexton must be found and feed for the favor ; when entered,
they are cold, damp and unhealthy resting places. On the
other hand, the Catholic cathedrals are always open, well ventilated, clean and highly ornamented, affording to the weary
sojourner a refreshing rest, and seldom failing to inspire him
with feelings of gratitude and devotion.

The general face of the country, farms, villages and modes of country life have also certain general features of resemblance.   There are no fences ; the earth is cultivated in patches ; the cattle are either watched by herdsmen or tethered. The peasant women all work in the fields, make hay, mow, spread manure and plow, often with a bull in rustic harness, while the implements of farming are of the rudest, primitive kind.   The peasant women generally go bareheaded as well as barefooted, but when they do wear shoes they are either all of wood or have wooden soles, while their hats, when they have any, resemble a tin wash basin upside down, the rim assisting to balance the burdens they bear upon their heads.

The farm lands of the continent, as a rule, are not as fertile as those of England, Ireland or America, nor are they as well cultivated.   The entire country from Hamburg to Berlin is a flat, sandy plain, with no timber, except such as may be seen among the sands of New Jersey.   The villages and country towns are composed of squalid one-story buildings, covered with thatched straw or coarse red tile.   Barns are unknown in Germany, and but few of the modern improvements in farming have been introduced.   The government of the German Empire seems to have devoted all its energies to the art of war ; the cities are crowded with soldiers, well dressed, armed and equipped.

Sunday is never observed as with us in America.   The same labor goes on in the field and the stores and markets are all open in the cities.   I inquired of the waiter at my hotel in Hamburg if the trains ran on Sunday.   He gave me a look of perfect amazement as he replied, "Certainly sir ; why not ? It is only a holiday for the rich ; not for poor men or horses."

The military spirit is so rampant in Prussia that even the inferior officers on the railway give their superiors the military salute as they pass.   Upon my arrival at Berlin, although hundreds of cabmen were in waiting, none of them moved from their seats, or made the slightest effort to obtain a passenger.   I endeavored by signs to induce one to take me to the Hotel de Metropole, but he flatly refused without an order from the officer in charge of the station.   I could not find a person who could speak either English or French.   I saw an omnibus a short distance off marked *Hotel de Saxe*, so without knowing where it would take me, I jumped in and soon found myself in a very good commercial hotel where one of the waiters spoke a little English.   I learned from him that King William became disgusted with his noisy cabmen, and ordained by la v that they should not take a passenger, move from their seats or open their mouths, until called by one of his officers at the station, who should furnish to every decent applicant a ticket with the number of the cab upon it.

Berlin, the capital of Germany, is situated on a flat, sandy plain, about the centre of the empire ; its population is 830,000, of which 25,000 is its garrison of soldiers. The river *Spree* runs through the town ; it is no larger than Chester creek at Chester. The waiter at the hotel made a very bad pun upon the name of the river. "Why," said he, "is Berlin such a jolly town?" I gave it up. "Because 'tis always on the same old *Spree.*" The old part of the city is just like all other old European towns. Its markets are just what might have been seen twenty-five years ago at Market Street, Philadelphia, from the wharf up to Third Street, on market days ; they are held here in the open squares, each person bringing his own booth or shed. They present a very active scene of old-fashioned animation.

The new part of Berlin is undoubtedly very handsome, and at a first glance quite imposing and grand in appearance, but when you come to a closer inspection, you discover all the apparently majestic stone buildings ornamented with finely chiseled statuary, are but plastered brick, painted in imitation of the stone of which Paris is built. The chief street is the Linden, upon which the most splendid edifices are erected ; it is about 130 feet wide and a mile long, and is adorned with several rows of linden trees, colossal bronze statues, monuments, palaces and gigantic public buildings. Some have compared Berlin with Paris, but it will not bear it. As well might Hercules be compared with Adonis ; both have their superior points. In Berlin everything looks heavy and imperial, even the king assumes to frown like Jove, while in Paris all is light, airy and beautiful, everybody feels gay, and even Napoleon III. looked like a dancing master.

The whole population of Berlin dwell in only 15,000 private houses. In the twelfth century it was a village; it is first mentioned in history in 1244. The house of *Hohenzollern* became masters of the place about 1411. In 1539 the townspeople embraced the reformed faith, and Berlin as well as all Prussia has since been strongly Protestant. At the death of Frederick the Great it had a population of 172,000, and has recently rapidly increased in prosperity, and is now the capital of the great German empire. One of the finest buildings in the city is the old Museum; it is in the Greek style, with eighteen Ionic columns; its front is about 300 feet. It is very elaborately adorned with colossal groups in bronze, and marble statues. The most striking feature of the whole is a very beautiful fresco by Schinkel, which covers the entire front wall under the portico, representing the progress of civilization and the development of the world. The figures are all very large and exquisitely colored. From the square in front, they stand out very boldly and never fail to impress the mind with an emotion of wonder and delight.

The Emperor has expended some of his French treasure in the erection of a monument something after the pattern of the *Colonne Vendome* lately destroyed at Paris. It has just been completed and is undoubtedly a very fine work. It is one hundred and ninety feet high, adorned with reliefs commemorating the Great German victories over the French in 1871. A golden statue of victory, forty-two feet high, crowns the column.

Upon the whole, Berlin is well worthy of a visit, and will richly repay the time expended in exploring its many beauties; the only wonder to me was how so much wealth could be extracted from such a miserable, flat and unsightly country as surrounds it. From the great profusion of gigantic bronze statues with which every vacant place is embellished, one would almost suppose old Vulcan had had his workshop here and had been casting models for the gods. A great feature of Berlin's beauty is the close proximity of all her grand public buildings, of which there are about seven hundred.

Dresden lies due south of Berlin, and is reached in about five hours by rail. The general appearance of the country does not improve until within a few miles of the town when the Jersey-like look of the land begins to put on more of a Pennsylvania appearance.

The city of Dresden in its general appearance is like Berlin; the houses are of the same order of architecture, they are mostly of brick, covered with cement and painted a mellow cream color. It is full of English and American residents, who have taken up their abode here because of its great educational advantages; it is said to have the best schools in the world. Its principal attraction to travellers is its world renowned *Picture Gallery*. It also contains a very rich museum of coins, old gold and silver plate, the crown jewels of the King of Saxony, of which country it was until recently the capital, and some of the finest statuary in ivory executed by Michael Angelo. The gem of the collection of painting is *Raphael's* Sistine Madonna. It cost in 1753, $35,000 in gold, and is now almost priceless; persons come from all parts of the world to look at it. I do not assume to be a connoisseur in paintings, but it seemed to me that there were other pictures in the gallery as meritorious as the *Madonna*. The color is as bright and as delicately shaded to day as when it received its last touch from the hand of Raphael, but the drawing is certainly no better than some modern works. There are paintings in conspicuous positions in this gallery that would be *veiled* in England or America, not that they are without merit or beauty, but because of the *peculiar* subjects they illustrate. As the details of some tragedies will not bear publication, much less should they be presented in all their nakedness on canvas. The rape of Lucretia, and Leda and the Swan, are painted with rather too much perfection for the common eye. The same may be said of some of the statuary, though it must be admitted that even the most fastidious eye can look without emotion upon the most voluptuously chiseled statue where the purity of the marble and coldness of the stone combine to banish from the mind of the beholder all impure thoughts or suggestions. This however is not true of a well executed painting, where every passion is so perfectly delineated and so well colored that the beholder can almost fancy he feels the warm burning breath and sees the heaving and swelling bosom, while his ear may almost hear the throbbing of the enraptured heart, and where every struggling passion is so perfectly portrayed by the painter that it must be understood by every person young or old, pure or impure who chances to gaze upon the picture.

I saw more solid wealth in diamonds and precious stones, gold and silver plate, and finely wrought works in the precious metals than I thought could be collected together in any one place in the world. They are to be seen in the *green vault* of the Royal Palace. There is here exhibited a full communion set in fine gold and ruby-crystal by Benvenuto Cellini.

Before quitting Dresden a young English traveler suggested that we should visit the Zoological Gardens just west of the city; it was late in the afternoon when we entered, and we found the collection so extensive, that before we were aware of it we were in the deep woods among the black swans with darkness fast obscuring all our landmarks for an exit from the place. By the time we reached the gate it was as dark as pitch, a rain storm had commenced and the gate keeper had gone home for the night. We pounded at the gate and hollowed with all our might but no relief came. "Heavens," exclaimed my companion, "Have we to stay with these blasted beasts all night in the rain?" "Not if I can help it," said I, as I commenced scaling the wall, at least twelve feet high. By clinging to the bar of the gate, I got over pretty well, but my poor companion fell from the top of the wall, and came near breaking his neck, beside spoiling a good suit of clothes. He swears he will never forget Dresden, nor will I. To-morrow I start for Prague, and from there to Vienna.

XIX.

Dresden to Vienna—Adventure with a Dutch Girl—Hotel de la Metropole—Beautiful Suburbs—Jews in Vienna—History—The Great World's Fair—Paintings on Exhibition—Playing with the Tiger—Sleeping with One Eye Open—Shipwrecked—Fifteen Miles of Exhibits—Burgomaster's Fete—Cholera in Venice.

Vienna, August, 1873.

I arrived here on the 15th inst. The journey from Dresden requires seventeen hours by rail. I was shut up all night with a bevy of six bouncing German girls and one *baby*, I being the only man in the party. Fortunately for me, one of the girls had been at school at Dresden, and spoke a little English. Her beau was employed at the Exposition in Vienna, and she was about giving him a surprise, by an unexpected visit. About midnight we all got drowsy, and were soon lolling about in all directions, fast asleep. A man is not responsible for his dreams, nor a woman for her talk in her sleep, if the *Bride* of *Ravenna* did lose her life by it, it by no means follows that any other woman who talks in her sleep means all she says. Why should they be responsible then for what they *do* in their sleep? I moralize thus, because about 2 o'clock in the morning, and when the lamp had grown very dim, I was aroused from my slumber and *innocent* dreams by a most loving embrace from my little Dutch girl. She was fast asleep, and no doubt dreaming of her lover. I gently removed her arm and slid my shoulder from under her head, and was soon snoring again. She is none the worse for it, neither am I.

I secured a very excellent chamber at the Hotel de la Metropole, beautifully situated upon the west bank of the canal of the Danube. My chamber window looks down upon the water which presents a very delightful scene in the early evening by moonlight. The waters are quite rapid in their flow and are now very low, and of course not so interesting as when the banks are full. The waters are of a murky lime color, very hard and entirely unfit to drink.

Living here is about as high in a second-class hotel as it is in the first-class ones of New York. The Metropole is the best hotel in the city; I pay 6 florins for my room, and my dinners cost from 3.50 to 5 florins, supper and breakfast about 2½ florins each, so that altogether it absorbs about 15 florins per day, exclusive of cab hire and extras. A florin is about fifty cents in American silver, but as "we are but lookers on here in Vienna," we must of course expect to pay a little more than if we were permanent dwellers in the city. Again we must remember that it is the dwelling place of the Emperor, and the Capital of Austria. The city is very beautifully situated upon both sides of the canal of the Danube. In its details it is just like all other great European cities. It has its splendid avenues, occupying the site of its old bulwarks, its museums, gallery of art, great monuments, palaces, prisons and parks, its old town and new, its narrow streets and its wide ones.

The country around the town is quite mountainous in the distance, and is very much devoted to the culture of the grape. I spent the first day here in surveying the town and its environs, making myself familiar with its streets, and studying the peculiar habits of the people. The manners and customs of the people gradually approach Eastern civilization as we recede from Western nations. Many of the Jews here assume the dress, and keep up the customs of their brethren at Jerusalem. They dwell here in great numbers, and have selected the oldest part of the city for their habitation. They traffic in all manner of cast-off clothing, and gather together everything that other people have thrown away. They trade in the open street ; crowds of them may be seen on Sunday morning, busily engaged in traffic, exchanging hats, coats and even shoes, paying a slight difference in the exchange. They may be found sitting on the bare pavement, trying on shoes, and exhibiting the excellencies of a pair of worn-out pantaloons, a used-up pinch-back watch, or a dilapidated old hat.

After walking around what are here called the rings, occupying the site of the recently removed bulwarks, and which are really fine modern streets, very much like the boulevards of Paris, it is necessary to penetrate the centre of the city, or that part within the rings, to obtain anything like a fair idea of the place. It will be found to be a perfect network of narrow streets, lanes, passages under gloomy arches, and long dismal vaults, with what we would call dirty alleys, running in every conceivable direction. Upon these narrow streets very large houses are erected, often inhabited by fifty families. The entrance is through an arched passage in the centre, generally leading to a court-yard, from which the only light and air is obtained for the chambers not facing the street. In many places the sun never shines upon the street.

It must be remembered that Vienna is a very old city. Marcus Aurelius died here A. D. 180. It was a flourishing town until the Huns invaded the Roman Empire in the fifth century. Charlemagne conquered the inhabitants of the district and made it a part of his empire. During the crusades, we read of Vienna as a city of great importance. In 1276, Rudolph, of Hapsburg, became the ruler of Austria and made

Vienna the seat of his house. It has been twice besieged by the Turks, and near its gates the celebrated battles of Austerlitz and Wagram were fought. The collection of rare paintings of the Belvedere have a world-wide reputation. It requires at least two days to give even a glance at each as you pass ; they are chiefly by the old masters. I confess I am losing my admiration for the old school, and enjoy much better the works of modern masters, many of which are exhibited at the Great Exhibition. There is something wonderfully enchanting in a well executed painting or piece of sculpture.

It is very amusing to observe the passing crowds at the exhibition. Men of all nations, tongues and kindreds of the earth would halt and gaze in rapture on some sleeping venus, nor would they pass without inspection, the venuses awake.

The French department is most admired. A splendid life-size painting representing a naked virgin, rolling upon a bed of roses with a pet tiger, is very suggestive of many living pictures. She sportively caresses his head as he licks her hand ; a lurking fire in his eye indicates that his rough tongue has given him a taste of blood, and when in alarm she endeavors to withdraw her hand, his bristling hair and curved tail imparts to her the startling fact that she is just one minute . too late. He will certainly devour her for no rescuing hand is near. I would advise all my young female friends in America, as well as some of the young gentlemen, to avoid *playing with the tiger.* "*Shipwrecked*" is another beautiful work. A fair young damsel is in a tiny boat wafted by the breath of love far out upon life's smooth sea. Suddenly a terrific tempest wrecks the frail craft, and a great dashing wave casts her lifeless form upon the rugged shore. It needs no explanation. Just opposite is the picture of an angelic form, naked and alone in a deep wood at midnight. She stands erect, holding in her right hand above her head a bright lamp and reflecting mirror. The dim outline of a narrow path is before her. She shows no fear, for she is "*walking in the light.*" This painting is called "La Verita." A little further on I observe a crowd of admirers around a large painting. As usual I find it to be the same old story, a sleeping venus with cupid drawing aside the veil to give Pan a peep. Of course the rustic god is love-struck ; how could any half human beast help it, with all her charms exposed. The poor woman does not know she's naked, for she is *sound* asleep, with one eye *half* open. I have seen women just like her, not only handsome, but they knew it, and they went to sleep just where they knew such half human brutes as *Pan* were wandering about. The *Enchantress* is a charming picture of female beauty, but she walks backward, followed by her admirers till she leads them to an unknown land, the dark confines of which are seen in the background. I wonder if the world ever produced a woman as superlatively beautiful. If it did, we may appreciate Shakespeare's expression : " A fiend like thee could draw my soul to hell !" If Potiphar's wife was half as handsome, Joseph was certainly a saint, or a eunuch.

I shall carry in my mind forever the face of Cæsar. While falling at the base of Pompey's pillar, he seems to say *et tu Brute*, and if he gave to Brutus such a look as the artist has given him here, he would need no other ghost to fright him from the field of Philippi. In the gallery of sculpture are, if possible, some still more attractive works. Here we have Cupid with a golden chain binding together two youthful hearts. It is most exquisitely executed and cannot be looked at without an emotion of pleasure. It recalls a happy hour long years ago, when he chained together a pair of hearts that I could name, and what is better the golden links, though sometimes a little bent, have never yet been broken. Sculpture, when perfect, is always chaste and pure ; the nude figures are supposed to be alone, asleep or surprised ; nothing can so well exhibit the beauty of the human form and at the same time preserve the purity of the imagination. A universally admired work is labeled "I Primi Flori." It represents a sweet maid of sixteen summers, chiseled from marble so pure that it seems transparent. She wears a wreath of the early spring roses, and her face is as bright and hopeful as an angel's smile. Alas ! she little knows how rapidly the winter shall approach and blast her beautiful flowers, or how soon her own loveliness shall fade and pass away forever. And so for days, and even weeks, one could wander among these beautiful images of grace and loveliness and never feel satiated upon the food for thought they so abundantly provide.

The Grand Exposition is simply stupendous ; it is absolutely impossible to give an idea of it. It must be seen to be comprehended or enjoyed. It requires at least fifteen miles of walking to explore it all. Here may be seen the whole world in a nut-shell. Oriental palaces are reproduced, and the markets, bazaars, restaurants and workshops of the East, attended by the veritable merchants, barbers and servants of the lands they represent, in their native costumes The arts, sciences, trades, arms and agricultural implements of all nations are on exhibition. It is but a few yards, often but a step from the habits, customs and manners of a civilized people to the semi-barbarous fashions of Egyptian, Persian or Arabian life. As you march from the East toward the West, the progress of

civilization is distinctly marked by the improved machinery
for manufacturing and the implements of war.

The buildings for the accommodation of the Exhibition,
are of the most beautiful architectural construction.   One can
hardly believe they are to be all removed when the grand display is over.   The park in which they are erected is an ordinary wood, not to be compared with Fairmount Park at Philadelphia, but while we have the advantage in the ground, I
entirely dispair of producing a display approaching the magnitude and grandeur of Vienna.   Those who visited the World's
Fair at London, and the Exposition Universelle at Paris, say
that both combined were not half equal to this.

The Burgomaster of Vienna gave a grand soiree on Saturday evening last.   It was attended by many thousands of
strangers from all parts of the world.   Among other distinguished guests the *Burgomaster of South Chester* (1) was there.
The gardens and halls were splendidly illuminated, while the
guests were welcomed by the most delightful music and a
gorgeous collation.   It lasted nearly all night and was a great
success.

I had intended visiting Venice and Milan, only one day
distant by rail, but the cholera is now so bad in Venice as to
be considered dangerous to strangers.   I met yesterday a
Philadelphia lady direct from there.   She says it was with
difficulty she got into Austria ; not being permitted to land
until the car she occupied was fumigated as well as herself.   I
will therefore postpone my visit to Italy to a more convenient
season, and will leave here to-morrow for Munich, and from
thence to Paris on my way home.

XX.

VIENNA TO MUNICH—LAST LOOK AT THE FAIR—AN AMERI-
CAN IN JAIL—A SUSPICIOUS WINE CELLAR—THE WORLD
IN VIENNA—A BLACK PRINCESS—HIGH ALTITUDE OF MU-
NICH—BAVARIA—MUNICH—ST. BONIFACE—ART GALLERY
—PALACES AND DUNGEONS—THE OLD KING AND LOLA
MONTEZ—THE NEW KING AND MUSIC—BEER DRINKERS—
THE PRIVILEGES OF THE FAIR SEX—A PRIEST-RIDDEN
PEOPLE—REVOLTING SCENE IN A CHARNEL HOUSE.

MUNICH, August, 1873.

Before leaving Vienna I took a long last look at the Grand
Exposition.   It makes the heart sick to think that all this

---

(1) When this letter was written I was the Burgess of South Chester.

gorgeous display of glittering splendor shall so soon, like the "baseless fabric of a dream," vanish and forever pass away. It seems to me that Philadelphia should have had a commissioner here from the beginning, studying the details, for it is folly to suppose that any knowledge worth imparting could be gathered in a week. It would require the whole time to give a hasty glance at each group. Improvements could undoubtedly be made, and just here is where the importance of a competent commissioner is so necessary. Just as an inferior architect might suggest improvements in St. Peter's at Rome, St. Paul's at London, or the Capitol at Washington, so a person of even ordinary ability might be able to give very useful hints, and could profitably observe and note, not the perfection of the display, but its faults and mistakes, so that they could be avoided in our Centennial celebration ; yet I am told by the attendant at the office of the U. S. Commission, that none of the Philadelphia Commission staid over a week. For all they learned in that time they might as well have staid at home.

One of the *sovereigns* of America, at Vienna, is likely to get a taste of Austrian justice instead of her hospitality. He had a dispute at one of the cafes with a waiter, who he says seized his cane as he supposed to strike him, he then drew his revolver and although he replaced it instantly, he was arrested and committed to prison. The laws of Austria are very severe in such cases. It is made a felony to draw a deadly weapon upon a citizen, punishable with fine and imprisonment of *not less* than three years. The most distressing part of the case is, that he has his little son, not over 12 years old, with him. He had better have left his American *institution* at home. There is said to be no necessity for it in this country. I would nevertheless have felt more comfortable last Saturday night if my pocket had contained one The water of Vienna is poison, beer to me is disgusting, and consequently I had to drink wine, which was so frightfully high at the hotel, that none but princes could enjoy it. I was told there were places in the city where good Hungarian wine could be bought by the glass very cheap, and was directed to a place in the old part of the town, which, after some wandering among narrow and winding passages, so contracted that with outstretched arms, I could touch the houses on either side, I came to a low arched vault, which I entered and was conducted through a succession of irregular arches and dark cavernous vaults, to a mouldy cellar lit up with tallow candles, and filled with a crowd of the ugliest, roughest and raggedest set of villains I ever saw. They were seated around dilapidated tables and were smoking common cigars and drinking white Hungarian wine by the

q art. I was the only decently dressed man in the place, and
seemed to be the object of every gaze, as well as the subject of
the common jargon, not a word of which I could understand.
When I thought how easily I could be knocked in the head,
robbed and disposed of, and no one be the wiser of my where-
abouts, I began to feel alarmed and wished myself safely out;
but there was no stopping on a race-course, so I determined to
face it out. I observed the fellow on the other side of the
table, eyeing my diamond breast-pin, which I had forgotten to
conceal and which fairly glittered in the dim candle-light. I
do not suppose there was a particle of danger, but the rogues
did stare at me just like hungry cats at a good fat rat. I
gave the fellow on the other side of the table a defiant look,
and kept my eyes full on his, until with assumed composure, I
gobbled down my pint of wine and quietly felt my way out,
when, I assure you, I breathed much more freely. On inquiry, I learned that it was the Saturday night rendezvous of
the lower classes of Vienna, where they met to smoke bad
cigars and drink cheap wine, and that the probability was,
that they were as much surprised to see me there, as I was to
find myself in their company. I am inclined to think, however, that I was safer at the "Metropole," even if I had to pay
for a whole bottle of wine, in order to get a single drink.

It was a source of great amusement to observe the variety
of races, and the colors and costumes worn by the people of
different nationalities at Vienna. There was at the Metropole
a gentleman of very light complexion, in full European dress,
with a wife, also well dressed, who in America would pass for
a negress. From the attention he paid her, and the politeness
she received from others, I suppose she is a person of some
importance in her own country.

I left Vienna for Munich on the 20th. It requires twelve
hours by express train to make the journey between the cities.
It is much cooler and more pleasant at Munich; although in
about the same latitude it is of much greater altitude, Vienna
being 430, while Munich is 1703 feet above the level of the
sea. The night air here is considered dangerous to sojourners,
because of its sudden coolness and variableness. Bavaria is a
very rich, fertile and beautiful country, much better looking
than either Austria or Prussia. The scenery up the valley of
the Danube and the rapid Iser, is very picturesque. As we
approach Munich the distant Alps can be distinctly seen.
They are but a day's journey distant, and are much visited by
the fashionable citizens as a summer resort. Notwithstanding
the great altitude of the city, it is built upon a vast plain of
about fifty square miles. The ground immediately around the
city is rather sterile, but very highly cultivated. Munich, we

are told, was founded by Henry the Lion, in 1158. It has increased very rapidly in population during the present century;
its present population being about 170,000, nearly all of whom
are very devout Catholics. It is no uncommon sight to see
houses, even of modern construction, ornamented with a niche
containing an image of the blessed virgin and child; while the
churches are very abundant, and most elaborately adorned
with paintings, frescoes and pious statuary. The *Basilica of
St. Boniface*, is one of the most beautiful churches I have ever
seen, and I have visited many hundreds in different countries.
It is an admirable imitation of the ancient Italian Basilica of
the fifth century. It has sixty-six marble columns, each of a
single shaft, supporting round arches richly gilt, forming four
grand aisles. The walls of the entire interior are lined with
polished marble of various colors to the top of the columns,
and above the columns are some of the finest frescoes in
Europe, representing scenes in the life of St. Boniface, and
other old Bavarian saints, with portraits of all the popes from
Julian III. to Gregory XVI. The exterior of the church has
quite an ordinary appearance, being faced with red brick. The
fine marble columns in front of the church are all that would
attract the attention of the passer-by.

Munich has a splendid picture-gallery and a national museum, said to be the finest in Europe. Like most museums the
traveler wearies his mind in endeavoring to comprehend the
immense collections spread before him. He has no time to
deliberately study the historical collections of each epoch or
period so well represented. He might spend months, instead
of hours, in examining and studying the different groups,
chambers and series. One is overwhelmed and confused with
the immensity of the collection, and leaves it with a feeling of
mental fatigue instead of refreshment, the natural result of
cramming the food for a months' reflection into a single meal
of observation. The same may be said of the gallery of paintings in the old *Pinacotheca*; it has works by Rubens, Rem-
brandt, and some of the best efforts of the old masters of Italy
and the Netherlands. It has nine large halls, each set apart
for a separate school. A gentleman of leisure could profitably
spend weeks in this gallery alone, and find ample food for most
delightful thought; for, after all, there is really no end to the
capacity of the mind for reflection. It acts as it is acted upon,
and grows in proportion to what it digests, not to what it de-
vours.

The new part of Munich, with its wide streets and fine
public buildings, monuments in fine bronze, and beautiful
gardens, is more attractive than either Berlin or Dresden.
Some think it superior to Vienna. I visited the King's Palace

and was permitted to look with my plebien eyes into the sacred precincts of royalty. The old palace is now being restored; it covers several acres of ground, has its large court yards, chambers of state, ball and reception rooms, waiting rooms, chapels and bed chambers above ground, and its dark, mouldy vaults and dismal dungeons and cells below ground, where many a poor soul has passed a life of misery and neglect, and where many a royal prisoner, male and female, has died from violence or starvation. If these old walls could speak, they would

> "A tale unfold, whose lightest word
> Would harrow up the soul; * * *
> Make the two eyes, like stars, start from their spheres;
> The knotted and combined locks to part,
> And each particular hair to stand on end,
> Like quills upon the fretful porcupine;
> But this eternal blazon must not be
> To ears of flesh and blood."

I also paid the new palace a visit. It was built by the gay old king of Bavaria a few years ago, for the accommodation of Lola Montez. Though of recent construction, it too could tell some unwelcome tales of the lecherous old reprobate and his merry mistress. Many of us remember how the people, becoming disgusted at the disgraceful scenes enacted in this palace, revolted, and in fury drove Lola from Bavaria, and the foolish old king from his throne. The present king, who I believe is a grand-son of the one previously spoken of, is a model of virtue and propriety, so modest and retiring, that notwithstanding all the efforts of his courtiers, he cannot be induced to wed. Several matches have been made for him, and publicly announced, but he always backs out just at the critical moment—the wedding day. He is what the ladies call a pretty man, soft, effeminate, and of delicate mould; absolutely invulnerable to the charms of beauty, but passionately fond of music.

The citizens of Munich are great beer drinkers, they are absolutely incapable of any form of amusement beyond the enjoyments of a beer garden, where they will sit from morning till night listening to the music, drinking their beer, telling their little stories and smoking their pipes. It is perfectly *comme il faut* for a lady to attend either the gardens, concerts, or even the theatre alone, and she will never be insulted or spoken to except in politeness by any one. While the women have this privilege, it must be added they are also permitted to sweep the streets, make mortar, and carry bricks for the bricklayer saw wood, plough, spread manure, mow and carry burdens large enough for pack-mules. I prefer, with all their faults, our own forms and customs, and I do not think a woman was intended for *all* the uses they make of her in Bavaria.

The lower classes are evidently priest-ridden. A reasonable amount of religion is undoubtedly very good, but while I must admire the Christian devotion of the Bavarians, I cannot without a feeling of pity, see their debased and almost idolatrous saint worship. I was walking through one of the charming gardens, when a fine looking woman, also walking in the garden with a gentleman and two female attendants, suddenly became very sick ; she had all the symptoms of heart disease, and seemed to me in an almost dying state. I saw the attendants run off very rapidly, as I supposed for a physician, instead of which they brought back two priests, who for a full half hour did nothing but oil her hands and put a crucifix to her lips, while they whispered pious ejaculations in her ears. Presently she showed some signs of revival ; then they sent for a doctor. I am told that a rope broke a few days ago and let fall a large stone on the breast of a workman ; his fellow workmen instead of removing the stone and saving his life, ran for a priest. By the time he arrived the man was dead.

I shall never forget a most horrid and revolting sight in the cemetery of the city. Some regulations forbid the burial of the dead until a certain length of time after they are brought to the cemetery for interment. I chanced to observe a funeral halt and deposit a corpse in a large building. As the door opened I looked in ; there lay sixty-three dead bodies in their funeral attire, from babes of yesterday to old men and women of eighty years, young virgins as plump and beautiful as if they were made of wax, lay beside emaciated forms wasted to skeletons by long sickness. Some were absolutely in a state of decay, with black hollow eyes, and lips which had fallen away from the teeth. Most of them were covered with flowers, and all had their faces exposed and were so arranged that a single glance around the hall showed every face. The smell was that of a charnel house. Without depreciating German manners I have come to the conclusion that there is no place like home. I leave here to-morrow for Strasbourg, and am traveling very rapidly westward and homeward.

XXI.

MUNICH TO STRASBOURG--STUTGARDT--THE SUABES--BABIES
AND GRAPES--ULM--DESERTED BADEN-BADEN--CATHE-
DRAL OF STRASBOURG--THE LATE SIEGE--SHELLS FOR
CANDLESTICKS--THE CITY GERMANIZED--THE GREAT
CLOCK--PICKPOCKETS--STRASBOURG TO PARIS--PARIS IN A
STATE OF DECLINE--PROBABLE SHORT-LIVED REPUBLIC--
CONTRAST BETWEEN FRENCH AND PRUSSIAN SOLDIERS--
THE GAY MABILE--ENGLISH AS SPOKEN BY A FRENCH GIRL
BOIS DE VINCENNES--BOIS DE BOLOGNE -ABSYNTH DRINK-
ERS--INFIDELITY--VERSAILLES--USELESS FORTIFICATIONS
OF PARIS.

PARIS, August, 1873.

The time by rail from Munich to Strasbourg is about
twelve hours.   The course is nearly due west, up the valley of
the Danube, which is wide and flat, but seems well cultivated,
although not remarkable for its fertility.   In the vicinity of
Stutgardt the soil as well as the scenery very much improves.
The distant Alps are plainly visible, the rich undulating lands
yield an abundant supply of corn and wine.   Great vineyards
grace all the Southern faces of the mountains, which are terraced with stone walls nearly to their tops, and look very
beautiful.   The city of Stutgardt is of comparatively recent
construction and therefore, although a very pretty town, of no
particular interest to the traveler.   The line of the road from
near Stutgardt follows the valley of the Suabia, from whence
our country has been so liberally supplied with immigrants,
known as *Suabes*.   They are to the Germans what our Pennsylvania Dutch are to the native farmers.   The Prussians or
Bavarians would consider themselves insulted to be called
Suabes.   They are nevertheless a very honest, thrifty and industrious people, and, from the clusters of children everywhere
to be seen, as well in the fields as in their mother's arms, and
other still more comfortable quarters, one would conclude that
the soil was equally as productive of babies as of grapes.

Some of the mountain tops are still graced with old ruined
castles, the remains of feudal times.   I almost wonder that
the shrill scream of the iron horse now so constantly reverber-
ating among the surrounding hills, does not fright from their
rocky graves, the ghosts of some of the old robbers who once
inhabited these ruined piles.

As usual in Germany, the fields are full of women performing the drudgery and common labor of the farm, such as

plowing, spreading manure, mowing and making hay. As a
natural consequence, they are coarse and masculine in appearance. The road passes over some of the most hotly-contested
battlefields of the world. Ulm is a very strong fort; earthworks, thrown up during the recent war, are all around it.
As we passed from Carlsrhue to Oos, my eye recognized the
old castle of Baden. I visited it in 1869, when Baden-Baden
was the battlefield of all the gamblers of the earth. It is said
to have lost its attraction for travelers since its license to gamble has been taken away. The whole country, with the long
range of mountains covered by the Black Forest, seemed as
familiar to my eye as if I had seen it but yesterday. The tall
spire of the Cathedral of Strasbourg can be seen long before
the town is reached. It is one of the highest steeples in the
world, and was a mark for the German gunners in the recent
bombardment of the place. I was surprised to see how thoroughly the town has been deprived of its French appearance.
She looks like an old German woman, and until you hear her
speak, you are not aware that she is a French girl in a German
gown. All the French names of the streets have been taken
off and German jaw-breakers substituted, while the constant
movement of German soldiers and the eternal clatter of the
drum and fife render the illusion still more perfect. At heart
she is devotedly French, and never lets an opportunity slip to
give vent to a secret curse upon her Prussian ravisher. There
is nothing in Strasbourg worth a visit except the cathedral.
It is really a wonderful work. The great piles of stone heaped
up along the aisles, and the new stained glass which has been
substituted for the windows, too plainly indicate how terribly
it suffered from Prussian shot and shell during the siege. It
has, however, been nearly restored to its former appearance.
The organ, which had been blown entirely from its position by
an exploded shell, has been rebuilt and now occupies its old
place. The old priest, whom I bribed to open the church for
me—for I arrived after the hour of public admittance—while
guiding me around the interior of the building gave vent, in
French, to a rather severe curse, for a priest, upon the heads
of the sacreligious heretics who had so nearly destroyed his
idol. The church must indeed have been a rather uncomfortable place during the siege. I counted some thirty marks of
shot and shell, some of which knocked out several tons of
stone. My guide thought that the Prussian king was surely
an infidel; for said he, when we implored him to spare the
cathedral, he sent us back the audacious reply, that "he was
sorry he could not *move* the church out of the range of his
guns," when bang went another shell right into the organ.
But few houses in the city escaped a shot or shell; the hotel

where I stopped received several ; one is still imbedded in one
of the large wooden girders in the coffee room. If it had exploded it would have blown the house to' pieces. Another
came into the landlady's bed chamber, but out of respect for
the lady, did not explode. She has had it unloaded, and it
now ornaments her mantle as a candle-stick. It is ten inches
in diameter and eighteen inches long. The French may abandon all hope of ever recovering Strasbourg. It has been rendered stronger than ever, and so far as human precaution can
make it, it is impregnable. It was one of the gates of France ;
its statue in the *place de la Concorde*, in Paris, is now draped
in mourning.

Before quitting the Cathedral I took a look at the world-
renowned clock. I consider it a great humbug, not worth a
journey of twenty miles to see. So far as its astronomical
construction is concerned, it is undoubtedly a work of some
considerable mechanical ingenuity; but the awkward figures
representing Christ and his Apostles, the crowing cock, and
the figure of death striking the hours on the bell, are anything
but life-like, and could be easily beaten by any ordinary Yankee clock-maker. I have seen in Geneva clock work much
superior to it. The clock at a first glance would hardly attract any particular attention. After gazing upon the graceful
proportions of the architecture of the church, to go into
ecstasies over an old clock with toy men and childish movements, is certainly a step from the sublime to the ridiculous.
It stands upon the ground floor of the church, in one corner of
the building, and looks something like an antiquated organ,
about twelve feet wide by thirty feet high. It may be one of
the world's wonders, but it did not so impress me; perhaps I
expected too much. I really felt ashamed, when I visited it
the second day, to see the great gaping crowd of Americans
anxiously waiting for noon to see the toy figures representing
Christ and his Apostles—the largest figure not exceeding a foot
in stature—make their circular movement, and to hear the
cock crow, which is nothing more than any expert organist
could do much better. The pickpockets reap heavy harvests
just at the moment when the figures begin to move, while the
abstracted fools have all their thoughts on the *He-Biddy*, and
of course none left for their purses. The church itself is, however, all that its enthusiastic admirers claim it to be. It was
founded A. D. 504, and finished in the twelfth century. The
stone work is so mellowed and toned down by age, as to present the appearance of old oak carving. The window called
the "Rose of Marigold," is forty-three feet in diameter. It
radiates like the sun, and from the inside of the edifice, sheds
a flood of gorgeous colors through the rich old stained glass.

The spire is of stone to the highest point, which is 466 feet from the pavement.   It is sixteen feet higher than the great pyramid, and eighteen feet higher than St. Peters at Rome. The view from the tower is very extensive.   The Black Forrest and Vosges mountains can be easily seen.

I left Strasbourg perfectly satisfied with my visit, and continued my journey homeward to Paris, which is about 312 miles west, and requires about twelve hours' travel by express. The French authorities are very particular in their scrutiny of all travelers entering from Germany.   Americans, however, have no trouble in crossing the frontier, which is now between Embermenil and Avricourt.   The cars are stopped, and every passenger is required to pass in single file through a narrow gate, produce his passport, and answer such questions as the official in charge may ask.   Some of the German passengers in our train were under examination several minutes before they were permitted to pass.

I arrived in Paris just a week ago, and have been very busy ever since my arrival in giving a rapid glance at its wonderful and almost exhaustless attractions.   I am satisfied it is in a state of rapid decline.   It is yet the handsomest and most interesting city in the world, but it is not the "*Paris nouvelle de Napoleon III.*"   I saw it in the very acme of its glory, upon the one hundredth anniversary of the birth of Napoleon I—August 15th, 1869.   She then looked like a bride upon her wedding day—she was all smiles and flowers.   There was a beauty and rosy freshness upon her face, only equalled by her rich and glittering attire and brilliant ornaments.   She was surrounded by luxurious splendor, and was overflowing with mirth and happiness.   Now her clothes are soiled, her laces torn, her eyes are red with sorrow, and her face is very, very sad.   The flowers of her fete-day have all withered, and instead of youthful freshness a hectic flush is upon her cheek, a wrinkle upon her brow, and here and there a treacherous gray hair peeps out from her glossy *false* ringlets.

The Parisians are struggling manfully to restore the city to its former beauty, and have made considerable progress in that direction, but it will be a long time before the marks of the lash are removed from her back.   She richly deserved a sound scourging, but I am inclined to think it was laid on a little too heavily.   Some of the public buildings have their ornamental stone fronts completely peppered with musket balls, while others have the deeper indentations of cannon shot.   I counted sixteen marks of cannon balls on the front of the building occupied by the *Corps Legislatif*. On all the public buildings, including the churches, the motto of the Republic has been substituted for the imperial insignia, and the golden

initials L. N , which once graced them all, have been chipped
off and removed. I noticed, however, that "*Liberte, Egalite,
Fraternite,*" was only *painted* on the several buildings with
ordinary lamp-black, which in case of necessity can easily be
removed, and the *arms of royalty* in turn substituted, an event
which will. from present indications, soon transpire. One cannot avoid noticing the marked difference between the French
and Prussian soldiers. The latter are all splendid looking
men, full breasted and sturdy, and march with a firm and confident step; while the former are small, pale, hollow-chested
boys and haggard looking men, apparently unused to arms.
They march with a kind of swagger, and compare with the
Prussians about as a mule with a horse. There can be no
question but that the Frenchmen of Paris have degenerated.
The results of luxury and dissipation have enervated the race.
Their national dissipation is not an over-indulgence in wine,
but a softer and more enfeebling kind of dissoluteness engendered by such places as *le jardin Mabile* and similar places of
debauchery and folly; even they, if possible, have become
more corrupt. I noticed in the *gay Mabile* the same dancers
every night, in disguise as visitors. One of the fair ones seemed
to take a fancy to me. She took me for an Englishman, said
she could not speak English but would soon teach me French.
I excused myself by informing her that I was an American
and could speak French already. "*Ah, vous etes Americain!
Je parle Americain,*" said she. I asked her to favor me with
a little, when up she jumped, and after a hop or two, kicked
the hat from the head of a six-foot looker-on, caught her toe
in her mouth, and whirling like a top, she said in pretty good
English, "*How's tat for high—perty good, eh? Roast-beh!*"
Any government that would tolerate such an establishment as
le Jardin Mabile, must be far advanced in degeneracy.

I visited the Bois de Vincenness, expecting to find it as I
saw it last, but I was sadly disappointed to find what was then
a beautiful garden and ornamented park, now all overgrown
with rubbish and scrub oak, and filled with loungers of the
demi monde, some sleeping on the grass, others making love or
flirting under the shade of some old tree. The Bois de Bologne I found half cut down, and what was once a beautiful
park was now being converted into a race course.

In addition to their other bad habits, the Parisians poison
themselves with absynthe, which they drink almost universally; and they also weaken their naturally acute intellects be
the intemperate use of bad tobacco. A good cigar cannot by
had in Paris under a franc.

The whole city is but a whitened sepulchre, beautiful and
highly ornamented without, but full of corruption and dead

men's bones. I doubt if it is any better than Sodom or Gomorah was; if it contains ten righteous men God only knows where to find them. The great mistake of the Parisian French is their infidelity. They have discarded religion, and have substituted nothing in its place. It is very hard to find a Frenchman who has any idea of a hereafter, and yet he exhibits many excellent traits of character, such as pity, benevolence and generosity, but no veneration for God or respect for religion. There is much more I would like to say of Paris, but the reasonable limits of a letter will not suffice. I would like to speak of my visit to Versailles; of the fine paintings I saw there, among others most excellent portraits of Washington, Henry Clay and Webster; of the miles of galleries devoted to paintings and sculpture; the charming gardens and fountains. I would like also to refer to the battlefields I visited around the city, and the ruined villages and destroyed towns I saw. No city was ever fortified like Paris; all that human skill could suggest was done; yet when the smallest of her forts fell, the entire city was at the enemy's feet. It matters little how many bolts and bars secure the doors of your dwelling; if the burglar can enter a window, all the house is at his mercy. So with Paris; it required more than human vigilance to protect all her gates; the enemy broke open one and all the rest were useless.

XXII.

Homeward—More about Paris—Pere la Chaise—The Catacombs—The Morgue—Museum de Cluny—Siege of Paris—An Old Sailor Sea-sick—Folkstone to London—Thames Embankment—Albert Memorial—Quid pro Quo—The Color Line Abroad—Overcrowded Hotels—Sad Incident on the Ship—A Funeral at Sea—Queer Characters on Board—The Parson—The Professor—The Great Traveler—The Missionary—The Widower—The Blue Stocking—An Old Sailor's Idea of Preachers.

Steamship City of Brooklyn, off Sandy Hook, }
September, 1873. }

"Breathes there a man, with soul so dead,
Who never to himself hath said,
This is my own, my native land!
Whose heart hath ne'er within him burned,
As home his footsteps he hath turned,
From wandering on a foreign strand!"

We are now in a dense fog, lying like a log upon the water, patiently awaiting the rising of the mist, that we may catch a glance of our native land. All is bustle and confusion. The ladies are busy dressing and the gentlemen packing their trunks for a final departure from the ship.

To while away a weary hour, I have concluded to write a final letter. Before leaving Paris I visited some places I had not previously seen. The Cemetery of *Pere la Chaise* and the Catacombs, contains the dust of the millions who once dwelt in, built and beautified this venerable city. The situation of *Pere la Chaise* is most charming. Seated upon a hill in the eastern part of the town, it commands a view of the whole city, and for this alone is well worth a visit. The monuments and sepulchres contrast unfavorably with those of the fashionable cemeteries of America. There is not a cemetery that I have seen comparable with Greenwood or Laurel Hill. There is a sameness about *Pere la Chaise* which makes a detailed examination very tedious. Most of the graves are covered with miniature chapels, filled with small crucifixes and holy candles, artificial flowers and wreaths of immortelles. Most of the walks are straight and narrow; even the trees seem to have been planted without much taste.

The Morgue, which is situated a short distance east of Notre Dame, is a place visited daily by thousands of persons of all classes and from various motives; many visit it like myself, from mere curiosity, many others in search of lost friends and relatives, while still others, to gratify a morbid desire to witness sorrowful scenes and horrible sights. It is said to possess a peculiar fascination impelling a second visit from those who have once entered it. The building is of but one story, with a door for entrance and one for exit. The chamber which contains the dead, is separated from the passage by a glass partition, through which the passing crowd may look upon the dead, who are arranged on marble tables, with as much of the body exposed as decency will permit. It is seldom without a tenant, as all the unknown dead of Paris are deposited there for identification. It is a melancholy study to observe the faces, and read the thoughts and emotions of the myriads who enter it. Fathers look for lost sons; mothers seeking missing daughters, whose anxious faces as they depart, would seem to indicate an increased distress, instead of joy in not finding the lost one there. Perhaps she is lost indeed, worse than dead! She must be sought for in a worse place than the Morgue. When I visited it, one of the tables contained the body of a very handsome young man, with glossy black hair and moustache, and a cleanly shaved face. His chest was full and broad, and his limbs splendidly developed. There was a deep gash above his eye, indicating a death from violence. His clothing was hanging upon a row of pins over his head. He had been found dead in one of the streets, and had been no doubt, like myself, a stranger in Paris.

No one should leave Paris without a visit to the *Hotel de Cluny*. The old curiosities it contains are absolutely unique, and must be seen to be appreciated. It contains among many other very remarkable things, a clumsy contrivance of the old Romans to enforce virtue upon their wives during the husband's absence in the wars. Modesty forbids a description of the singular invention. Suffice it to say that, as a protection from modern *burglary*, it would be but a small impediment ; five minutes would scarcely be required to pick the *lock*.

There is now on exhibition at Paris one of the most perfect panoramas ever painted. It represents the seige of Paris and conveys a better idea of the momentous struggle than could be gathered from volumes of reading. It is no more like the panoramas we are accustomed to see in America, than the light of the sun at noonday is like the glimmer of a tallow candle at midnight. It is with great difficulty that the spectator can convince himself that he is not looking out upon the veritable battlefields around the city ; the burning villages, affrighted and flying citizens, belching cannon, bursting shells, wounded and dying soldiers, and dismounted guns, are all so natural and life-like as to render the illusion perfect. In the foreground the cannon, sand bags and earthworks are real, and none but a connoisseur can discern, without physical inspection, the line where the actual ceases and the artificial begins. It is pronounced by those who are judges to be one of the most perfect pieces of enlarged landscape painting ever produced.

On my way to Boulogne the cars were crowded with returning travelers from the Continent. In the compartment I occupied was a young English Lord, with two ladies, returning from a tour through Switzerland. He was very anxious that none of his fine points should pass unnoticed, to which end he wore a pair of breeches laced tight to the knee, a pair of brogans upon his feet, and heavy woolen stockings up to his knees, the better to exhibit his well developed calves. While dining at Boulogne he warned the ladies to be spare in their diet as the channel was sometimes rough, and *they* might suffer from sea sickness ; as for *him*, he said, *he* was an old sailor and could eat and drink as he liked ; *he* was never sea sick, and would very much like to feel the sensation. We had not been a half hour on the sea before our little ship began to roll and pitch most fearfully. I never saw so many sick persons at once. There were over six hundred on board, and

fully four hundred were sick.   The deck, despite the hundreds
of basins distributed by the stewards, was slippery with the
dinners of the passengers.   Such retching, gagging, and des-
pairing cries of "Oh ! oh, my ! Oh, Lord !" I hope never to
hear again.   I felt a malicious desire to keep my eye on his
lordship, the "old sailor."   He was composedly smoking a
cigar, but I thought he looked a little pale under the gills.
Presently I saw him sit down on a pile of trunks, as I thought,
rather too suddenly for an old sailor.   It was all up ; he made
a rush for the gunwale, and with a tremendous "Oh !" he
gave his entire dinner, including a bottle of Burgundy, to the
fish.   "What is the matter ?" said one of the girls, neither
of whom had shown any symptoms of sickness.   "Oh," said
he, "I ain't *sea* sick, the beastly motion of the boat has
turned my stomach, that's all ; I never was on such a blasted,
stupid ship before."   One of the stewards gave him a basin,
which he kept between "those well-developed calves" the
rest of the voyage, and filled it about three times.   The waves
cross the channel from Boulogne to Folkstone diagonally, and
when the sea is rough the small steamers being about half of
the time in the trough of the sea, roll most terribly.

The country from Folkstone to London is very highly cultivated, the land is rich and rolling, and the dwellings comfortable.   London is constantly improving, new embellishments
being added every year.   The Thames embankment is equal
to anything of the kind in the world.   A splendid new street
has been redeemed from the river and given to the metropolis,
to the great relief of the overcrowded Strand.   The river face
is built of great granite blocks, and when it is remembered
that the tide rises here eighteen feet, the difficulty and extent
of the work can be appreciated.   The Albert Memorial at
Hyde Park has just been finished, and is now one of the
world's most beautiful monuments.   It stands upon an artificial plateau, ascended by granite steps from its four sides.
At the corners are four colossal statues, allegorical of the four
grand divisions of the earth.   The buffalo upon which the
figure of America is seated is open to criticism.   It looks more
like a Durham bull with a lion's mane than a buffalo.   The
base of the monument is embellished with full life-size reliefs
in white marble, representing all the world's greatest geniuses,
above which rises the Gothic spire something similar to the
Scott monument at Edinburgh, the whole of which is heavily
gilt with pure gold, presenting in the bright sunlight a most
gorgeous effect.

The English are great on the *quid pro quo*.   I sat for a
moment in one of the iron chairs distributed over the park, as
I supposed to rest the weary traveler's limbs, and so they

were, but they charged me the equivalent of six cents American money for the privilege ; but when we remember that the
Queen charges sixpence for a sight of her diamonds, and then
only shows a paste copy of the Koh-i-noor, we cannot expect
her to give us a seat in her park for less than half as much.

After a three days' rest in London I left for Liverpool,
which although over two hundred miles distant, is reached in
four and a half hours. It rained all the time I remained there
and had been raining every day for six weeks. At the theatre
in Liverpool, the American doctrine of equality without regard to race, was fully recognized. *Sambo* in full dress, with
a fair British damsel on each side, occupied one of the most
fashionable boxes. We may soon expect to see the House of
Lords graced with a peer from Africa ; yet it is somewhat
remarkable that the Queen rejected the proffered hand of the
King of Abyssinia.

Liverpool was literally crowded with Americans homeward bound ; every ship had its berths all engaged for a
fortnight in advance. Two ships were to sail the day after my
arrival, the *Samaria* of the Cunard, and the *City of Brooklyn*
of the Inman line. I applied first at the Cunard office, but
could not get a berth even by paying a premium ; every corner was secured, even some of the officers' quarters were
purchased. At the Inman office I received no better encour-
agement. As I was on the point of leaving in despair I
learned that berth No. 30 had just been given up, and could
be secured for twenty-one guineas, which I paid at once, and
upon embarking found myself the happy owner of one of the
very best berths in the ship. No one in the city could give
me any information about the "New American Line," nor
could I find any advertisement in the newspapers relating to
it. I met upon the ship a Chicago gentleman with whom I
had traveled in Germany. He had secured his berth two days
before me, and had paid a premium of £10, equal to $50 gold,
over the regular price, and was lucky in getting it at that.

We had 119 cabin and 800 steerage passengers, and as
most of those in the cabin were Americans returning home,
you may imagine we were a jolly party. After trying both, I
much prefer the Inman to the Cunard steamers. The passage
is shorter and the accommodations better. The officers are
more congenial, and the stewards more obliging. The *Samaria*
left Liverpool three hours before the *Brooklyn*, yet we beat her
a day to New York.

Everything went well the first two days out. The sea sickness was passing off—the passengers beginning to become
sociable, and the smoking room to sparkle with wit and humor,
when an event occurred which cast a gloomy cloud over the

whole ship. We had among the passengers an English lady,
with three beautiful little children. She was about joining her
husband in America. He had preceded her several months,
and had provided a home for her reception. He had written
to her of his success, and anticipated happiness in meeting her
and his little ones in New York. She was evidently a woman
of some refinement; her appearance was genteel, and her
children were well clad and clean. She had been very sea-
sick, and became despondent and low spirited. She seemed to
have a deep affection for her husband, but appeared prepossessed with the idea that she would never live to see him again.
We were all enjoying our lunch at noon in the cabin, when
suddenly the machinery stopped, and we were startled by the
tramp of hundreds of feet over head on the deck, rapidly rushing to the stern. My first thought was that the ship was on
fire. I cast a hasty glance out the cabin window and saw the
sailors rapidly cutting away the life boats. In a moment the
tables were deserted, and all hands made a simultaneous rush
for the deck, which was found crowded with passengers greatly excited, looking out upon the sea over the stern of the ship.
Some had clambered into the rigging, and others stood upon
the spanker boom. The woman, with her two youngest children in her arms, had plunged into the sea; she could be seen
about a half mile in the rear, like a little speck floating upon
the waves. In three minutes (which seemed an age) the boat
was cut away, manned and on its way to the rescue. It was
a time of most intense anxiety, as she was expected to
sink every moment. She was soon picked up, when another
speck was observed still further in the rear; it proved to be one
of the children When the boat returned to the ship the child
was dead, and the mother a raving maniac. The little boy
was never seen from the time he was thrown into the ocean.
The next day we buried the little girl according to the rites of
the sea. The body, prepared in the usual way, was coffined
in canvas, with a cannon ball at her feet, borne upon a plank to
the gunwale of the ship, when one end of the plank was
elevated, and while the captain read the service, the corpse
glided under the English flag into the sea, which closed over
it forever. The mother has been confined in the ship's hospital ever since, and although she has shown a few lucid intervals, no hopes are entertained of her recovery. It would have
been better for both her and her husband, if she had followed
her children to their watery grave.

A ship is like a little world ; the saddest scenes are soon
forgotten. In a day or two all was as gay as ever.

There were several passengers on the ship who soon became
known by some characteristic sobriquet. There was the

Parson who never smiled, walked with a measured step, wore a white cravat and enormous spectacles. He preached one night upon *Jonah in the whale's belly*, in which he demonstrated that the *whale* was a kind of *shark*, which had mistaken Jonah for a little shark, and out of paternal regard sheltered him in a kind of pelican-like pouch till the storm was over, when it permitted him to escape and swim ashore. Then there was the *Professor* who was a great calculator, just returning from a course of lectures on figures, in London. He was known in America as Barnum's lightning calculator, and undoubtedly possessed a most wonderful talent. He could stand with his back to the blackboard, filled with several columns of figures by any of the passengers, when he would turn, and in an instant write the correct addition, then turn his back again upon the board, and repeat from memory every figure upon it. One fellow was known as the great *traveler*. Nobody could speak of a spot upon the earth which he had not seen. When asked one day what was the greatest distance he had ever been from home, he replied 40,000 miles He either forgot, or did not know, that the entire circircumference of the earth was not much more than half that much. Tom Pepper was a model of veracity compared with him. Then there was the *missionary ;* he had under his protection a young lady, whom he was escorting to a fellow-missionary in the Sandwich Islands, to whom she was betrothed. From the marked attention he paid her, and their disposition to keep late hours alone upon the deck, the general judgment of the ship was, that they were lovers, and that the other missionary was cheated out of his bride. One of the ladies was known as the *strong-minded* woman, and one of the gentlemen as the *widower*. He was very anxious that every one should know his age— just *forty-five*. He was very fastidious about his dress, shaved every morning, and paid great attention to the young ladies. "You must have been very happy in your matrimonial life," said the *strong-minded* woman? "Oh yes," said he, "we lived together forty years without a single quarrel." ' Were you of age," said she, "when you were married ?" "Yes, 23 years old." She called the *Professor* to solve the problem, how 23 and 40 could make 45.

The last Sunday on the ship was a regular field day for the preachers. We had the regular Episcopal service read by the *Missionary*, a sermon by the *Parson*, who by the way was a Scotch Universalist, and a prayer-meeting in the steerage under the auspices of the *Professor*. Besides which we had a Catholic priest and a Presbyterian minister, who administered private consolation to the members of their respective churches. An old sailor remarked, as soon as he learned that

so many preachers were on board, that he knew we would
have bad luck, for said he, "*what's the use of 'em if we ain't
goin' to die?*"

"Shure," said an old Irish lady as she peeped over my
shoulder, "ye must be writing a very long letter." I informed her that it was a resume of the events of the voyage.
She said she had a son in New York whom she had not seen
since he was a "wee bit of a boy," twenty years ago, that
he was *very rich*, and had sent for her to come and spend her
days with him. "And shure," said she, "I wrote him a
very long letter before I left Ireland, informing him that I
was coming, and for fear it might miscarry I have brought it
with me, and intend to *deliver it myself*." I am in this respect
like the old lady, for I have brought this letter with me and
intend to deliver it myself.

XXIII.

NEW YORK TO ANTWERP—CHANGES IN OCEAN TRAVELING
  SINCE 1873—NEPTUNE IN A RAGE—MUTUAL BLUNDERS IN
  OUR EFFORTS TO SPEAK A FOREIGN TONGUE--THE WARMTH
  OF THE GULF STREAM—THE BEAUTIFUL BLUE AND BRA-
  CING SEA—SMOKING ROOM ENJOYMENTS—EDDYSTONE—
  COAST OF ENGLAND—DOVER—ANTWERP—FAREWELL TO
  THE SHIP AND SHIPMATES.

OFF FLUSHING, April, 1888.

"Now would I give a thousand furlongs of sea for an acre of barren land—
ling, heath, brown furze, anything. The wills above be done! but I would fain
die a dry death."—*The Tempest.*

While waiting for the tide to carry us over the bar and
up to Antwerp, I will economize the time by giving you a
brief note of the interesting events of our voyage. At high
noon, on the fourth of April, with a bright sun, smooth sea
and fair wind—all on board hopeful and happy—we bade farewell to the beautiful New York bay, and facing nearly due
east we fearlessly plunged into the bosom of the tranquil and
lake-like ocean.

Fifteen long years have passed since my last journey
across the sea. The changes in the size, splendor and accommodations of the ocean steamers are very perceptible. The
staterooms and berths are much larger and more comfortable.
We had no bath rooms then, no barber shop or bar room. It

may be doubted whether the last is a real improvement. However great the changes in ships, old ocean remains the same.
The first day out Neptune was all smiles ; the second day his
face was sombre and cloudy ; the third day found him in a
furious rage. About 500 miles out we encountered what I
would call a terrific storm, but what the captain described as
a "right stiff breeze." The ship pitched, lurched and rolled
fearfully. At times her propeller was out of the water, her
leeward bulwarks two feet under water, and her decks at an
angle of forty-five degrees with what should be the level of
the sea. Everything had to be lashed to the ship and the
passengers were gently warned that their safest place was the
cabin. I love the excitement of a storm at sea and secured a
place for myself and daughter leeward of the funnel. While
enjoying the "rage of the tempest's roar," the ship lurched
upon her beam ends and a ten-ton wave struck her in the
windward bilge, sweeping completely over the deck, compan-
ion-house and all, and covering us with water. If our chairs
had not been lashed to the rails we would have been swept
into the sea.

There were but seven passengers at the dinner table that
day. The rest were distressingly sick and remained so for
two days. The tables for the next four days were decorated
with what the English sailors call "fiddles," but what are
now called racks. They are intended to keep the dishes from
sliding off the table. One of the passengers, without thinking of the consequences, took a large dish of salmon from the
steward to help himself to a morsel ; just then the ship gave
another list to the leeward ; in an instant the table was at an
angle of forty-five degrees with its proper level—the salmon
slid across the table and lit upon the sofa on the opposite side ;
dishes flew from the racks, glasses bounced from their sockets
over the table, and a bottle of wine struck one of the gentlemen on his head, nearly fracturing his skull. Another gentleman was thrown from his seat against one of the permanent
cabin chairs, nearly breaking his ribs. He has suffered from
the effects of the accident ever since. The captain informs
me that it is no uncommon thing for passengers in a storm to
have their limbs broken, and sometimes even the most experienced sailors are washed into the sea. After a couple of
days and nights of storm the sky cleared but the winds and
waves continued very high.

Our passengers are of many nations and tongues. The
captain is a German, the officers and crew German, Swiss and
Flemish. The ship's accounts are kept in French francs and
centimes. We have about as much French and German as
English spoken on the vessel. We have a learned professor of

Geology and Philosophy among the passengers. He is a walking encyclopædia of useful knowledge, a very estimable gentleman but a skeptic in orthodoxy. He believes in Heaven but
"takes no stock in *Sheol*." We have also on board a priest of
the Episcopal church, severely orthodox of course. I asked
him why he did not controvert the heresies of the Professor.
His answer was that "none but God could humble a geologist
or take the conceit out of a philosopher. They all think,"
said he, "that they know more than the Almighty." To a
certain extent, I agree with the preacher.

The French and German passengers smile at our efforts
to speak their language, but we laugh at their blunders in
ours. A Swiss gentleman, returning from a tour in South
America, undertook to tell us in English how expert the cow-
boys were in the use of the lasso. He said they could catch
a woman swine by ze foot and take all her little flying porks
before she could get loose. By *woman swine* he meant a *sow ;*
the little flying *porks* meant her *pigs*. Our French cook
thought to surprise us all by writing the *menu* in English.
His blunders were ludicrous. One will suffice as an example.
He described the "hind quarter of lamb" as the "behind
quarter of little sheeps."

Upon entering the Gulf Stream the change in the temperature of the water and air is most remarkable. The water
suddenly becomes fully 20 degrees and the air from 16 to 18
degrees warmer. The thermometer stood at 42 degrees before
entering the stream ; it rose in half an hour to 56 degrees.
The water at the same time was 7 degrees warmer than the
air. There are some things I cannot comprehend about life
on the sea. We have no fire or heat of any kind in our rooms,
most of the time none in the cabin. The temperature is on
an average about 50 degrees ; yet we all sit on the deck and
in the open air, we leave the ports all open when there is no
storm, and we do not feel the cold. It is also most astonish-
ing to see how much we can eat, drink and sleep without any
unpleasant consequences.

Upon a clear night the trail of the ship presents a very
beautiful spectacle. The disturbed water shows a long streak
of phosphorescent light, like myriads of fire-flies upon a summer night. The color of the sea by day is also an interesting
study. It is at times a gray stone color, at other times a dark
blue, then from apple green to the deepest shade of azure.
The various colors are the result of the play of the sun's rays
upon the disturbed waters.

There can be no malaria on the sea, yet I notice that the
ship's doctor gives nothing but quinine to the sick passengers.

He says they bring malaria on board and that the pure sea air develops it.

We have a sweet little ten-months' old boy on the ship, the brightest and among the best babies I have ever seen. He is the favorite of the ship, and laughs and crows from morning till night.

The smoking room was at first a kind of lecture room for the discussion of questions of Theology and Philosophy. Alas! how soon Satan converts even churches to his use. The cozy little tables in the smoking room were soon surrounded with anxious card players, gambling like sinners, while the steward was kept busy answering the bell for wine, brandy and beer. Like all the beginning of sin, the gambling commenced with a penny ante and five cent limit; it ended with a franc ante and Napoleon ($4.00) limit. Some of the foreigners undertook to teach the Yankees some new games. The result was similar to that of the Yankee teaching the heathen Chinee how to play poker. The scholars soon knew the game better than their teachers and the foreigners were cleaned out. Many persons wonder why gambling is permitted on shipboard. The reason is obvious. The sea is the highway of the world, subject to no law but that of nature, which Vatell says is the law of nations. There are no policemen, committing magistrates, courts or even judges on the sea. We all come down to a regular *sea level* and every one does as he pleases, subject to but one condition—he must not interfere with the same rights in others.

At 11 A. M., on the 14th, we passed Lizard Point. The signaling commenced and the news of our safe arrival was at once telegraphed to New York and received there five hours before we sent the despatch. The first land seen was the Scilly Islands, mostly barren rocks. From Lizard the crew began to put the ship in order. The carpets were laid, the covers taken from the red plush upholstery, the brass work scoured, the red curtains put up, the rust on the iron painted, in a word she was rigged out very much like a lady prepared to receive her lover. To look at her dressed up in her Sunday clothes one could not believe she had passed such rough treatment from the sea or had been so buffeted by the angry waves.

On passing Eddystone my mind returned to its namesake at home, and to the kind friend who had given me so much enjoyment on the little ship Comet, in bygone years. The coast of England from Lizard to Dover is plainly seen from the deck. The channel was exceptionally smooth, as tranquil as the Delaware bay, and our ship moved as steadily as the steamer Republic on a Cape May trip. We could see the English coast as distinctly, for two hundred miles, as one could

view the Delaware and Jersey shore from a steamboat. The
English shore is very abrupt, the cliffs in some places rising
very much like the Palisades up the Hudson. The land is cultivated to the edge of the cliff or water as the case may be.
The topography of the country is beautiful, with alternating
hills and vales. The fields divided by stone fences and hedges
are plainly visible. Dover presents a very romantic picture,
nestling in the valley nearly on a level with the sea, with high
hills on both sides and immense cliffs along the sea, below and
above, one hill crowned with Dover Castle and the other with
grand and gigantic fortifications; she conveys to the mind a
sense of beauty, romantic ease and perfect security.

We are now about to bid farewell to the ship. The passengers have become almost one family. We will separate
with regret perhaps never to meet again. We were all strangers two weeks ago, and a fortnight hence will, perhaps, forget
that we have ever met.

XXIV.

ANTWERP TO BALE—THE DYKES AND CANALS OF HOLLAND—
THE CATHEDRAL, BOURSE, ART GALLERY AND ELEVATED
PROMENADE OF ANTWERP—BRUSSELS—MUSEE WIERTZ—
WATERLOO ONCE MORE—EXPENSIVE TRAVELING—GAM-
BLING BY GOVERNMENT LICENSE—A LITTLE DINNER FOR
FOUR—VALLEY OF THE RHINE.

BALE, April, 1888.

My last letter was written upon the ship off the quaint
old town of Flushing. I would like to give you a pen picture
of the place but it is impossible. It is built in the mediæval
style, surrounded with a strong wall, supported by earthworks
and mounted with cannon. The old red tile roofs, of very
irregular heights, appear above the ramparts. The gate to
the city faces up the river Schelde, and, from the sea front,
does not look much larger than the arched front door of an old
mansion. The town stands upon the alluvial deposit from the
mouth of the river, causing a large delta like that of the Mississippi at New Orleans. The deposit from the Meuse, Rhine
and Schelde is very great and changes the channel and bars
of the rivers very frequently. Skillful pilots are required to
take ships up to Antwerp. At times the fogs are so heavy as
to entirely interrupt navigation. We were so unfortunate as
to encounter one about ten miles up the river. The consequence was we lost a whole day and instead of arriving at 7

P. M. on Sunday, did not get there until 5 P. M. on Monday. This was a great disappointment to all on the ship—especially as we arose early and dressed ourselves in our Sunday clothes, and expected to step on shore at sunrise.

I may here say, once for all, that my letters will not attempt to give an accurate description of the places I may see. I will endeavor to convey the impressions made on my own mind. Many letters from abroad are but extracts from guide books. My effort will be to express, as well as I can, the impressions made upon my own mind, and only note that which strikes me as in contrast with the habits and customs of my own country. As a rule, the manners, fashions and habits of the people of Europe are very much like those of America. The means of communication are now so great that men everywhere, and women too, have become cosmopolite.

The first sight of Flushing presented a picture very different from anything seen in America. The depressed soil of Holland, and parts of Belgium is very remarkable. As we sailed up the coast we saw the tops of trees and houses a few feet above the sea banks. The land lies from seventeen to twenty feet below the high water level of the sea. The dykes are immense earthworks against the sea ; an enemy could destroy all Holland if he could but make a breach in the sea walls. The river Schelde is studded with strong forts, and as a still better means of defence—but to be used only as a last resort—sluices have been prepared, by opening of which the whole country for thousands of square miles can be flooded so as to render it impossible for an enemy to move. The people of Holland and Belgium seem to delight in straight lines. There are no fences ; the land is farmed in patches. Around Antwerp it is mostly cultivated with the spade. Long lines of trees can be seen in every direction, all in perfectly straight rows. These long lines of trees generally mark ditches or canals. The canals are constructed on top of what looks like a railroad embankment with the canals where the rails should be. The water is pumped up by windmills from the ditches into the canals and by the canals is carried out to the sea over the dykes.

Antwerp is built upon the left bank of the Schelde about fifty miles from the sea. It is a large and flourishing city, only third in commercial importance to London. It is one of the most interesting cities upon the continent. The Cathedral, very old, and rich with the relics of past ages, is one of the finest specimens of mediæval architecture. It is decorated with statuary and paintings worth millions. It would require volumes to give anything like a full description of the art treasures and relics of this single building. Antwerp has an art gallery equal in gems of art to almost any museum in the world. The old part of the city is very irregular. The wharves, docks and quays are of most substantial masonry. Above the wharf is a very beautiful promenade constructed somewhat on the principle of an elevated road—the part below being the wharf and that above being the promenade. The new part of the city is very much like the new part of Boston ; indeed the whole town reminded me of that city. No traveler should visit the continent without seeing Antwerp.

From Antwerp we went to Brussels, noted as the most complete and beautiful city of its size in Europe. With a good commissioner, a carriage and hard work the town can be pretty well seen in two days. It certainly cannot be properly comprehended in less time. The general site of the city is something like that of Albany, N. Y. Its buildings are equal to the best part of New York but not so heavy, nor are the interior appointments as spacious. The streets are gracefully curved, but few being straight, or at right angles or on parallel lines. It is called, even by the French, " Little Paris." We visited every place of importance in the city, among others the Chamber of Deputies and Senate of the Kingdom. The Deputies were in session. The court language is French. The exterior of the building is not imposing but the inside is very rich with costly carved woodwork, and is decorated with very attractive paintings. Several million francs have been spent in its decoration. The Senate was not in session ; we were, therefore, taken through the whole chamber and had everything fully explained. The new court house is a most imposing and truly grand piece of architecture. It stands on a hill which commands a full view of the city. It has already cost about three million dollars. It will compare favorably with the new municipal building of Philadelphia but is of an entirely different order of architecture.

There is in Brussels a collection of paintings by Wiertz known as " Musee Wiertz." They are all of a most startling and original character. It is not like any other gallery in the world. I would not advise a nervous person to visit it, as he would be apt to have the nightmare for a month after. Some of the pictures made my hair " stand straight on end." A few of his subjects will suffice to give an idea of them all : Such as " A scene in hell " ; " The visions of a decapitated head " ; " The Cholera," etc.

While at Brussels we visited the field of Waterloo, about twelve miles from the city. Upon arriving at the little hotel opposite the Monument I ordered a little dinner for four, to be ready at 1 P. M. I neglected to limit the price. We had a very good dinner but it cost me just $10.50. This is my second visit. I procured the same guide that conducted Victor Hugo over the field in 1860. It is to-day very much as he describes it in "Les Miserables." My guide showed us every important place and position occupied by the contending armies. He was an ardent Frenchman, a great admirer of Boulanger and a firm believer in the future glory of France. He felt quite sure that the time was near when Waterloo will be revenged and Loraine and Alsace be restored to France.

It is the fashion for Americans to attribute the French disaster at Waterloo to unforeseen accidents. No candid observer, however, can fail to see the favorable position secured and held by the Duke of Wellington without admiring his skill and, however much he may worship Napoleon, he can but conclude he was overmatched in strategy at Waterloo.

I find traveling very much more expensive than in 1873. With all the economy I can practice I cannot get along with comfort and reasonable speed under $40 a day for our party of four. It costs about $10 a day for a driver and good carriage without which it is impossible to make any progress in a strange place.

I was surprised to find gambling houses licensed by the government in Brussels. Their signs are hung out in the open street.

From Brussels we journeyed through the Luxemburg passing through Metz, near Sedan and through Strasbourg to Bale, in Switzerland This is a very interesting route, carrying the traveler over and through some of the most historic places and battle-fields of Europe. The road passes through the beautiful valleys of the Moselle and Rhine, whose broad and fertile plains are flanked on either side by mountains upon which the snow has not yet disappeared. The vegetation is far advanced in the valleys but the melting snow upon the mountains keeps the air chilly and the rivers and streams full. Much of the land is cultivated with the spade. Indeed the whole valley of the Rhine looks like a vegetable garden.

XXV.

BALE TO MILAN—AN INTERESTING CITY—BRIDGES AND FER-
RIES OF THE RHINE—THE OLD MINSTER—SPLENDID VIEW
OF THE ALPS — GREAT CHANGES IN EIGHTEEN YEARS —
STREET RAILWAYS WITHOUT RAILS—NO FREE BAGGAGE IN
SWITZERLAND—PASSING THE FRONTIER—CARS WITHOUT
ACCOMMODATIONS—FINE SCENERY—ST. GOTHARD'S TUN-
NEL—AN AVALANCHE AND DESTROYED VILLAGE—A FALSE
IMPRESSION—AN ITALIAN SURPRISED AT THE ABILITY OF
AN AMERICAN TO SPEAK ENGLISH—GREAT DIFFERENCE IN
TEMPERATURE BETWEEN THE NORTH AND SOUTH SIDE OF
THE ALPS.

MILAN, April, 1888.

Bale is called by the Germans Basil, and by the Swiss
Basle. Bale is not much praised by travelers, but to me it is
a very interesting city. Like a modest woman she makes but
little display of her charms, but when you know her better you
love her more. The city is most charmingly situated upon
both banks of the Rhine, which is about twice as wide as the
Schuylkill at Philadelphia, and flows through the town with a
startling rapidity. The river is now very high, caused by the
melting snows upon the surrounding mountains. I timed with
my watch a floating log as it passed the window of the dining
room of our hotel. It floated fifty yards in ten seconds.
The river is walled with substantial masonry on both banks
and is spanned by three bridges. The old bridge is of stone
and is supported by twelve arches. There are also several
rope ferries. By setting the rudder at a certain angle the
rapidity of the current causes the boat to cross the river without oars or steam, the iron rope keeping it in its course. The
houses are built with their foundations under water, and with
balconies overhanging the river. In this respect it is said to
resemble Venice so far as the houses on the river front are concerned. The best hotel in the place is called "Les Trois
Rois,"—in English "The Three Kings." It is a very substantial structure of stone, built upon the site of a hotel which
entertained three kings A. D. 1026. They were Conrad II.,
Henry III., and Rudolph III., the last king of Bourgogne.
It was at a conference here that Rudolph gave up his crown to
Henry III.

The streets of the city are very crooked and narrow in
the old part of the town, but the new city contains many wide,
well-paved and beautiful avenues, gardens and parks. The

old quarters are the most interesting. The topography of the ground is quite hilly. The most interesting building is the "Old Minster." It can be distinguished from the other churches by its peculiar architecture. The roof is of tile, painted and glazed in various colors. At a distance it looks as if it were covered with a bright new piece of oilcloth, or many-colored carpet. Parts of the church are a thousand years old. It has been burnt once, and once partly destroyed by an earthquake. It is now in a very good state of preservation. The latitude of the place is about 500 miles north of Philadelphia, and yet the air is soft and balmy. Vegetation is as far advanced as it would be in the middle of May at Philadelphia. There are no fires in the houses except for cooking, and the ladies are out in their Spring bonnets. Some very fine silks are made here. The industry was introduced about two hundred years ago.

From the rear of the Old Minster the view is very beautiful. The rear yard is about one hundred feet above the river and gives to the eye a range over many miles of meadows and mountains. The Alps, capped with snow, can be distinctly seen without the aid of a glass. The Jura mountains are also plainly visible and the Black Forest as far as the eye can carry the vision, presents its sombre shades. When I visited Bale in 1869 it was a walled town, surrounded with forts and full of troops. It is only by the old landmarks that I would now know it. The walls have disappeared, splendid avenues have taken their place, magnificent residences have sprung up where the old suburbs were and its population has increased from fifty to eighty thousand, among them many millionaires. It is undoubtedly one of the oldest towns in Switzerland. The Emperor Valentinian made it his summer dwelling place as early as A. D. 374. The distance from Brussels is twelve hours by express train. The inhabitants dress and look very much like our own people. A peculiarity I particularly noticed was the street cars, just like our own, with a conductor, bell register and other appliances, but with no rails. They run over the smooth stone streets at will, and move from side to side like our omnibus. I notice, however, that they have the right of way, as all other vehicles turn out in meeting them. The hilly ground and crooked narrow streets exclude the idea of rails for the cars.

We left Bale for Italy on the 21st inst. I had to pay thirteen francs for less than one hundred pounds of baggage to Milan. Travelers must not take Saratoga trunks unless they are prepared to pay very heavily for the luxury. No baggage is now carried free either in Switzerland or Italy, except what you carry in the hand, and that is limited to a carpet bag not over twenty inches long by ten inches square.

Upon entering the frontiers of Italy the trains are stopped and all the baggage, including the little cabas of the ladies, is examined. Although I paid for my baggage and had the registered receipt, it was not brought into the shed for examination. The consequence was I did not get it till I arrived at Genoa.

The cars have no conveniences for sickness or other natural emergencies. There are stated stations where they stop five minutes. The conveniences required by travelers on a long journey must be paid for as used. It makes traveling with ladies very annoying, as well to them as to their male companions. The "toilets" and water closets must be found by the men and the ladies be safely conducted to them and back to the car. It is absolutely necessary to remember the number of your compartment or great difficulty will be experienced in finding it at these hurried stopping places, as all the cars are exactly alike, and they sometimes shift them while the traveler is out.

The entire route from Bale to Milan is grand beyond description. At first we pass over the rich valley of the Rhine, then plunge into the spurs of the Alps; finally we wind through many miles of most rugged and wild mountain scenery. At the entrance of the tunnel of St. Gothard we found two or three feet of snow.

I can only give you an idea of Alpine scenery by comparison. You have passed over our own Allegheny mountains, from the Horseshoe to Altoona and have, no doubt, thought it grand, and so it is; but it is no more to be compared with the Alps than the hills at Lenni, on the Chester Creek Railroad, are to be compared with the Allegheny mountains. This is no exaggeration, but the best truthful comparison I can give to convey a reasonable idea of these stupendous mountains. Another marked difference between the Swiss Alps and our mountain scenery is, that the mountains here, wherever there is earth enough to raise a few blades of grass, are cultivated. In some southern exposures they are terraced by stone walls ten or fifteen feet high, to give one or two feet of ground at the top of the terrace for grape vines. In the heart of the chain, however, they are too wild and craggy for even an attempt at cultivation. Then again, the mountains here are studded with Swiss villages. The villagers live by working in wood and acting as guides, raising goats, etc.

We arrived at Milan about 7 P. M. The name of the town is pronounced differently by English, French and Italians. The English call it Milan, accent on first syllable, and the *i* short. The French pronounce it Milan, with the *i* like our long *e* and the *n* nasal. The Italians call it Milano—the *i* like our *e* long and the accent on the second syllable. Americans should pronounce the name as the English do. The same rule should be observed in pronouncing all proper names. The scenery from St. Gothard tunnel to Milan is very changeable ; from mountains whose tops pierce the clouds and whose crags seem to overhang the road, to vast level plains under the highest state of cultivation. The road is very winding and passes through a great number of tunnels from a few hundred yards to nine miles long. It took our express train twenty minutes to go through the great tunnel of St. Gothard—the longest in the world. On the Italian side we passed the ruined village recently destroyed by an avalanche. Three or four hundred persons were buried under the snow and not a vestige of the village left. The pine trees that stood upon the mountain side above the village were broken and prostrated very much as a drag harrow would break down and tear to pieces a field of green wheat. The timber of which the houses were built lies scattered and broken over many acres of the mountain side. ·

The experience of my life has taught me that first appearances are delusive. I have found my best friends among those who were at first disagreeable to me. Our journey from St. Gothard to Milan was but another illustration of this truth. We bribed the guard at Bale to give us a compartment by ourselves. He did the best he could to preserve us from the intrusion of strangers, but in spite of his efforts a burly, brigandish looking Italian, as we supposed, pulled open the door and *sans ceremonie* thrust himself into the best seat in the compartment. We all looked daggers at the fellow,. at which he only smiled and bowed. He soon began to praise the scenery in Italian. We did not reply. He then asked if any of us could speak German. I told him *no* in a way that would have clearly indicated to an American that no more questions were desirable. I gave him one of my sternest frowns, expecting to freeze the man into silence, but it was all in vain. He began to chat in French. I told him I could not converse much in French but he insisted upon it that I spoke the language elegantly. At this flattery I melted into a smile and he was not slow to perceive that the victory was his. To my surprise, about five minutes afterwards, I found him in an animated conversation, in very good English, with my daughter. From that time till we arrived at Milan he did nothing but chat, laugh and sing. He gave us all the new opera airs and was familiar with several tunes named by my daughter. At Milan he introduced us to his brother, who was an attache of the station, and who spoke perfectly good English. He assisted us in the selection of our hotel and called upon us next day to see that we were comfortable. In a word, the man we took for a brigand and an intruder was the jolliest man I have ever met. I parted with him at Milan with much regret. He declared his intention of calling on us again at Rome.

In my next letter I will try to describe Milan. My impressions of the town are not yet sufficiently formed.

The people of the continent have a very limited idea of America or Americans. In the smoking compartment of the car, just before our arrival at Milan, I overheard a conversation between an Italian and a Frenchman. It was in French. The Italian said there were a great number of American pilgrims visiting Rome, and he was very much surprised to find that they all spoke good English. He asked why it was that they did not study the Italian as well as the English. He seemed very much surprised when the Frenchman informed him that English was our mother tongue. He could not understand why a country discovered by an Italian should choose English for its language.

It is twenty degrees warmer on this side of the Alps than on the Swiss side. Here the temperature is almost at summer heat. Tropical plants and flowers are in bloom in the open air. The gardens and green fields remind one of Paradise, but a passing funeral reminds me that we are still on earth among mortals.

XXVI.

MILAN TO GENOA—THE GREAT CATHEDRAL—ART GALLERY AND PAINTINGS WORTH FORTUNES—STREET RAILWAYS AND ELECTRIC LIGHTS—THE ARCADE VICTOR EMANUEL— THE CAMPO SANTO—HISTORIC GROUND—FIRST SIGHT OF THE MEDITERRANEAN—THE UNIQUE CITY OF GENOA.

GENOA, April, 1888.

The country for miles around Milan is flat and uninteresting. It is drained by ditches and fertilized by a system of flooding. The land, however, is under a high state of cultivation, worked chiefly by the spade and hoe. The farm laborers, as a rule, are three or four women to one man. We saw several bevies of pretty young girls in bare feet and legs, dressed in red petticoats, hoeing the newly dug earth.

My first impression of Milan was favorable. It is built of yellow brick and stone, with a fair proportion of marble.

The brick is invariably covered with cement and painted a soft yellowish color, in imitation of the yellow stone of Paris. The old walls have disappeared. Some of the arched gates remain to mark the places where the ramparts stood. It is rapidly losing its ancient appearance. The most interesting monument of the town is the Cathedral, built about 500 years ago. It is said to be only surpassed by St. Peter's at Rome. The marble was all donated. The ground belonged to the church corporation that preceded the erection of the present edifice, yet the building, when completed, cost the enormous sum of $120,000,000. This will give some idea of the character of the building. The interior is supported by fifty-two colossal stone columns; it contains four thousand pieces of statuary and will hold fifty thousand people. The meridian with the twelve signs of the zodiac is traced upon the marble floor. A hole in the roof a foot in diameter looks like a small star. At noon the rays of the sun fall from the star-like aperture in the roof directly upon the meridian line traced on the floor. The solstices are also marked. On the twenty-first of March the ray of light begins to advance; on the twenty-first of September it stops and begins to recede, thus keeping up a perpetual march, like a sentinel of Time, up and down the same line. The church is a very imposing and conspicuous landmark of the town, of which the inhabitants seem to be very proud.

The art gallery contains paintings by many of the old masters. The chief picture is Raphael's Marriage of the Holy Virgin. It is said it could not be bought for a million dollars. I would not like to offer it if I had the cash to spare.

The city is full of soldiers, drilled every day—a constant reminder to the American traveler of the contrast between the feverish anxiety displayed all over Europe in anticipation of an impending war, and the peaceful quiet and sense of security enjoyed by the people of our own country.

They have a street railway here very much like Philadelphia. The whole city is lighted by Edison's system of electricity. By touching a button above my pillow at midnight my chamber is instantly flooded with a light equal almost to the sunlight of noon. This is the only place in Europe in which I have found this system of light. The ugliest part of the town architecture is the roofs of the buildings—I do not think there is a slate roof in the town. The houses are mostly covered by very rough, half-oval, red tile, presenting the appearance of broken flower pots or red terra cotta drain pipes broken in long pieces and piled up upon the roofs, one row with the belly down and the other with the arched parts up. I notice, however, some new buildings with flat, regular shaped tile, which look very well.

The greatest modern improvement is the Arcade. I can only give you an idea of its appearance by a comparison. Imagine Chestnut Street, Philadelphia, from Seventh to Ninth, uniformly built on both sides with the most attractive buildings on that part of the street. Then spring an arch of glass over the entire street, extending it half a square up and down Eighth Street. At the intersection of Eighth and Chestnut construct a magnificent glass dome. Pave the street from side to side with marble mosaic. Fill the buildings with stores and elegant restaurants, and you will have the Arcade of Milan in Philadelphia. It has a grand triumphal arch at its entrance. The front, facing the Cathedral square, is decorated by a long colonnade. It cost over three million dollars, and was finished in 1865. It is here the citizens do their shopping, gossiping, drinking and other good as well as bad things at night and in bad weather. In the evening it looks like a bee hive.

Milan has a fine Campus Martius and Amphitheatre. Its Campo Santo, or cemetery, is the most remarkable place in the city and is visited by thousands of travelers. It is a large enclosed square of about twenty acres, with a colossal arched gateway, and vaulted colonnade around the inside of the entire wall. This colonnade is filled with most beautiful marble statuary, displaying all imaginable conceptions, some very impressive, others extremely ridiculous. Some of the statuary cannot be looked at without bringing tears to the eyes by reviving recollections of our beloved dead. It is no uncommon thing to see persons on their knees before some monument. Some of the statuary is so full of life as to almost express the hope of a departing soul ; you may almost hear a dying groan, and the flutter of angelic wings in cold marble, all of full life size and some of colossal dimensions. One I shall never forget. It was at least twice as large as life size and represented Time with his scythe and hour-glass just alighting upon a newly made grave, with half-folded wings, peering down as if to read the inscription upon the tomb. His old wings have lost many feathers but he can still fly as fast as ever. The effect is startling in the extreme and caused my hair to feel a peculiar sensation, something like

"Quills upon the fretful porcupine."

No monument under ten feet high is permitted in the place. Those under ten feet must be removed, both monuments and remains, after ten years' repose in the sacred soil. After ten years the bodies of those who cannot afford to buy the ground and erect a monument of the prescribed height are exhumed, and either burned in the crematory, just without the wall, or, if sufficintly decomposed, the bones are laid away in a succession of pigeon holes built in the walls around the ground, with a slab of marble recording the name, etc. It reminded me somewhat of the inside of a safe deposit company's vaults.

The climate of Milan cannot be very healthful; the ground is too low and flat.

Two days with a good guide and carriage is enough to fully explore the city and see all worth the traveler's special notice.

From Milan to Genoa requires a day of twelve hours. After traveling for about thirty miles over a flat and uninteresting country the scenery becomes very beautiful. The mountains again appear with their ever-changing landscapes. Our road passes through several long tunnels, some requiring from five to seven minutes to go through them. The building of the road must have been very expensive. We passed over some historic ground. We were within sight of one of Hannibal's battlefields and some of Napoleon's gigantic struggles. Just before we reached Genoa, by a turn in the road, we had our first view of the Mediterranean sea. It seemed almost like an enchanting dream. We arrived in the old birthplace of Columbus about six P. M., and had a fine view of the town. Our hotel is built upon the old sea wall. It is entered through an ancient arch and looked more like a prison than a place of pleasant rest. But, upon passing through the heavy stone arch, we were delighted to find a very good hotel with an elevator and other modern conveniences. The city is unique and not like any I have seen. It is situated in the extreme bend of a beautiful bay with mountains behind it extending like the horns of a crescent to the right and left. It is nothing like my preconceived ideas of the place. The mountains extend down to the sea; the city is built upon the slopes or mountain sides. The French call it Gene, the Italians call it Genova. The mountains upon which the city is built range from three hundred to two thousand feet in height. Some of the houses are twelve stories high on one street and two stories on the rear street. The courses of the streets which had to conform with the curves of the sea and mountain sides are very crooked and irregular in the old part of the town. The houses are built of stone, plastered and painted mostly in the soft yellow tone of Milan. Many of the buildings are richly frescoed outside and in. False windows, balconies, imitations of carved marble, etc., so well executed as almost to deceive even the citizens, are painted on the smooth walls, giving to the town a much richer appearance than it deserves.

Many of the streets are so narrow that two carriages cannot possibly pass. There are streets in Genoa into which the sun has not shone for a thousand years. Some are not over six feet wide, with seven-story houses on each side. The place is surrounded with immensely strong fortifications. We drove up one of the new streets to a height of 318 feet and had a most charming view of the whole town and harbor for twenty miles around. There were ships lying at anchor before the walls and in the bay from whose masts floated the flags and ensigns of all nations. With a good glass, on a clear day, the island of Corsica can be seen from this point. The town is now in a very thriving condition. It is full of palaces rich in works of art. Among its citizens are some of the world's richest men. I will describe the place more fully in my next letter.

XXVII.

GENOA TO PISA—FIRST IMPRESSIONS OF GENOA—A CITY OF CONTRASTS—BEAUTIFUL WOMEN—ROMANTIC DRIVES—WORLD RENOWNED CAMPO SANTO—A FUNERAL—INNATE DESIRE FOR IMMORTALITY—MR. BLAINE AT PISA—THE LEANING TOWER AND BAPTISTRY—AN UNHEALTHY PLACE —PIGEON HOLES FOR THE BONES OF THE DEAD—MALARIA IN THE VALLEY OF THE ARNO.

ROME, May, 1888.

I have just arrived here direct from Pisa. Genoa is a city of great interest to the American traveler. One of the most beautiful statues in its public squares is of Christopher Columbus. The bay or gulf of Genoa is crescent-shaped. The city is situated in the center. Before the city was built the shore was skirted with mountains rising precipitously from the water's edge from three hundred to two thousand feet high. Upon the sides of these mountains the city has been built.

I must again resort to a comparison to convey a correct idea of the appearance of the place. You must imagine the mountain district of Pennsylvania brought down to the sea shore, shaped like the moon, with high hills running out upon each horn. Then fancy a city of 140,000 inhabitants, built like an enormous amphitheatre, with the houses rising one above the other upon the sides of the mountains, with the streets following the natural conformity of the hills, surrounded by a strong and high wall and with immense fortifications, with very crooked streets, and houses ten stories high on one street and one story on the rear, and you will have a fair idea of this beautiful old city. The new part of the city is regular,

well paved, and contains many palaces. The houses are
mostly built of stone, very abundant here, but all are covered
with cement and painted a soft yellow color. The Italians
are exceedingly fond of painting and sculpture. Nearly all
the houses of the better classes are frescoed very richly within.
There are no paper hangers in Genoa The houses are all
large and high.   In outward appearances it is difficult to distinguish the dwellings of the rich from those of the poor ; but
when you look inside, you are at once undeceived. Some
imposing buildings will be found to have a family in each
room : no carpets on the stone or tile floors ; one chamber
serving as kitchen, bedroom and workshop. In other places
you will find ropes stretched from one side of the street to the
other and the family washing hung cut to dry. I find it,
however, a very attractive and beautiful place.

The temperature here is several degrees warmer in winter
than in Rome. This results from the shelter afforded by the
mountains on the north, and the southern exposure of the city
to the sea. It is a city of contrasts. We see squalor and poverty in one street, in another a few yards off, we find luxuriant
palaces, splendid horses and carriages and beautiful women
and children, and in the same street we meet primitive ox-carts,
barefooted urchins and ragged beggars. While driving to my
hotel, I saw a laborer deliberately strip himself in the street
and change his shirt I have seen other sights in the streets
here that would be shocking to public decency in America.
The citizens are remarkable for their strength and beauty.
The girls are graceful and well formed with large, soft dark
eyes and luxuriant black hair. For their sake I almost wished
myself a boy again, but the frosts of over sixty winters have
frozen the springs of love and have only left a dim but pleasant
recollection of a lost pleasure.

The drives around the city are very fine and afford some
beautiful views of the town and bay. I took several carriage
rides through and outside of the city In a few minutes we
ascended from the sea level to a height of nearly four hundred
feet. Outside the walls you can drive, on a good road, to
points nearly seventeen hundred feet high. All these drives
overlook the city and bay.

The most interesting place without the city wall is the
Campo Santo, or cemetery. It is most romantically situated
in a level valley surrounded by mountains. It is perfectly
square and enclosed by a decorated wall some twenty or thirty
feet high. Around the inside of the wall is a beautiful arched
colonnade, filled with splendid tombs and monuments to the
illustrious dead of Genoa whose remains repose, either under
the monuments, or beneath the marble floor. The statuary is

of the finest marbles and represents every possible poetic conception of Italian genius. A funeral entered while we were
within the walls. Nothing but the heavy black hearse and
some forty or fifty hired mourners entered the grounds. The
bells began to toll and the religious services had just commenced when a discharge of musketry just outside the walls
seemed to startle, at least all the strangers, within the enclosure. The contrast seemed very striking. A whole brigade
of soldiers were going through their drill and target practice
outside of the wall, making the mountains reverberate volley
after volley, while the hired mourners were singing requiems
for the repose of the dead within. To those who are interested
in this subject, a very accurate description of the Campo Santo
of Genoa will be found in the last edition of the Encyclopædia
Britannica. The beautiful monuments and decorations of the
tombs clearly illustrate man's frail efforts to live after he is
dead, if in nothing else, for a few more years in a flattering inscription over his grave. There seems to be a strong desire
implanted in the human heart to rob death of his terrors by
surrounding graves with objects of beauty and attractiveness.
Vain effort! Death in every form is terrible. No wonder
men seek it on the battlefield when the flickering spark can be
extinguished while in full blaze, rather than suffer the gradual
inroads of disease, or the slow approaches of death in the form
of natural decay, and "all the ills that flesh is heir to." In
one corner I noticed an immense sarcophagus, cut from a single block of stone, covered with beautifully carved bas reliefs.
intended to illustrate the supposed immortal actions of the
illustrious dead reposing within. When it was opened a very
small handful of dust was all that remained. The poor but
proud fool who supposed he was immortalized by his imperishable coffin, has been forgotten for, perhaps, two thousand
years, while all that is left for admiration is the work of the
poor sculptor who designed and chiseled his tomb.

Genoa is very strongly fortified, well garrisoned and, I
should say, from my limited knowledge in military affairs,
absolutely impregnable, except by starvation from a regular
siege.

Just as I was leaving Genoa for Pisa, Mr. Blaine and his
family entered the hotel. I had no time to as much as give
him my card. He looks well and, if his outward appearance
is not deceptive, he is certainly able, physically speaking, to
endure the strain of another campaign. On my arrival at
Pisa, I found he had just left there for Genoa. I was very
sorry I had missed the opportunity of a personal interview.
I had hoped to find him at Florence but, like many other disappointments, I had to bear this one too.

From Genoa to Pisa we passed through ninety tunnels. After passing through the mountain region we entered a very flat and uninteresting country. We passed, however, several orange groves and hills planted with olive trees. The olive tree is not pretty but lives to a great age. There are olive groves around Tivoli said to be six hundred years old. I also noticed the enormous size to which the cactus plant grew. Some hedges were formed from these plants. We passed over some historic ground—an old Etruscan town destroyed by the Arabs in the eleven'h century—marble quarries, old ruined castles of the Middle Ages, and many other places of interest to the traveler who has time for details.

Pisa is situated on a flat plain and is built on both sides of the river Arno. As we approach it the Leaning Tower, Cathedral and Baptistry are seen to loom up far above the ancient walls of the city. The climate is damp; rains are very frequent. It is a bad place for rheumatism and *gout*. I gave it two days and left with a slight gouty sensation in my great toe. It is a city of 45,000 inhabitants. It was a flourishing Roman colony 180 years B. C. It is said to be as old as Troy. In the days of Strabo it was built two miles from the sea. Now it is four, the wash of the Arno having formed a delta of two additional miles. At one time it rivaled Venice in commercial importance. It sent out fleets against the infidels, and was one of the first towns of Italy. External prosperity and internal strife which, by the way, are very apt to go together, soon ruined its supremacy, and reduced it to a fourth-rate city. Finally a war with Genoa proved disastrous to Pisa, from which time it has gradually declined and is now of very little importance. Were it not for the leaning tower it would soon be forgotten by travelers.

Like Milan and Genoa, it has its Campo Santo, a very old and interesting cemetery. It is evidently the model of that at Genoa. They have the same practice here as at Genoa and Milan of packing away the decayed bones of the dead in pigeon holes in the walls, called *columbaria*, which signifies pigeon holes or places for pigeons. After the remains are sufficiently decomposed, by lying in the earth, the bones are exhumed and built up in the wall, with a marble slab facing out from the wall and even with its surface, upon which is inscribed the name, etc. The place of original burial is no longer cared for, as hundreds have been buried in the same grave.

The river Arno is beautifully walled up on both sides with marble bridges of three or four arches. Along the river banks are splendidly paved, wide and beautiful streets, affording a fine drive along both sides. The river Euphrates could not have been much better walled in ancient Babylon. I counted my steps over the main bridge and reckoned the width between walls at about three hundred and seventy feet. The river, however, is deep and very rapid. The leaning tower has been described so often as to render further description unnecessary. It is a most remarkable structure and should by no means be passed by the traveler without a careful inspection. In the Baptistry near the tower there is a most beautiful echo. One person singing very slowly and distinctly has the effect of a full choir. The city is now full of pilgrims; indeed I find Europe full of them, on their way to and from Rome. Rome is two hundred and twelve miles south of Pisa. About twenty miles on our journey to Rome I noticed the first post and rail fence I have seen in Europe. The land is not fertile after about twenty miles from Pisa. In some places it is good and undulating, somewhat like Delaware county, in others it is marshy. From Pisa to Rome we pass several of the world's most renowned battlefields. The route from Pisa to Rome follows very nearly the old Via Aurelia. Part of the route is over a district poisoned by malaria. Even the inhabitants fly to the hills in the summer. The present Italian government, however, is spending immense sums in the construction of canals to drain the district and, if possible, make it more healthy. Some of these canals are thirty feet deep, with smaller ditches running into them, full of stagnant water. Thousands of acres of rich alluvial lands have thus been redeemed and I have no doubt the district will soon become a thriving place for farming.

Italy, everywhere, shows signs of energy and recuperation. King Humbert now rules over 35,000,000 souls, and will soon make his kingdom respected by the other powers of Europe. If no reaction takes place and the difficulty with the Pope can be satisfactorily settled, Italy will certainly hold her own with the nations of the earth.

As we approach the sea the Isle of Elba can be seen. Old Etruscan towns of prehistoric origin are passed; places spoken of by Pliny as important cities in his day have descended to villages, now not worth a day's time to see. Tuscany is covered with ruined towns. Old vases and stone coffins are being constantly exhumed. The whole land is now full of interest.

XXVIII.

PISA TO ROME—ETRUSCAN RELICS—CIVITA VECCHIA—THE ETERNAL CITY—NEW EXCAVATIONS AND GREAT DISCOVERIES—THE COLISEUM—RECENT DISCOVERY OF THE SUBTERRANEOUS PASSAGE FROM THE PALACE OF COMODUS TO THE ARENA OF THE COLISEUM—NEW ROME—CRUELTY TO ANIMALS—OLD ROME THIRTY FEET BELOW THE PRESENT SURFACE—THE WORLD'S CONTRIBUTION TO ROME—MILITARY DISPLAY—VILLAS AND PALACES—THE KING AND QUEEN—ROME UNHEALTHY FROM MAY TO SEPTEMBER.

ROME, May, 1888.

One hundred and fifteen miles from Pisa, we enter the former Papal territory, or States of the Church. We cross the river Fiora and soon reach the site of ancient Vulci where thousands of Etruscan vases have been discovered since my own boyhood. The old city was five miles in circuit, but has all disappeared except its tombs. A little further on we passed the town of Corneti, built in the Middle Ages upon the ruins of the ancient Tarquinii. One hundred and fifty-seven miles from Pisa we arrived at Civita Vecchia, the seaport of Rome, with about 13,000 inhabitants. This is a very old city, founded by Trajan. The site and scenery are very picturesque. There are mineral springs and ancient baths found near it. We now approach Rome. Every inch of ground for miles around the city is full of interest. As we draw near the ruined walls and broken arches of the Eternal City, and contemplate its former splendor in contrast with its present humbled aspect, the feeling is one of sorrow tempered, however, with a sense of justice. Time makes all things even. Rome robbed the world of all its treasures of art and beauty. In its turn it has been pillaged for hundreds of years, to enrich the crowns of its former rivals and fill the museums of the world.

I would like to convey a correct idea of this most interesting city. I have read much of Rome but find all my preconceived ideas of the place erroneous. The city is in a state of transition. Those who visited it twenty years ago would hardly know it to-day. Much of the old city has disappeared and is still very rapidly passing away. The streets are being beautified, old buildings torn down, and excavations are being made upon a stupendous scale. New discoveries are being made every day and buried columns, vases, statuary, coins, bronzes and other valuable antiquities are being constantly exhumed. Streets and squares, supposed to be upon the original level of ancient Rome are found to be from five to sixty feet above the old beds.   What was supposed to be the floor of the arena when Byron said

"I've stood within the coliseum's walls
Amid the relics of Almighty Rome,"

was fully fifteen feet above it.   During the Middle Ages it was used as a manufactory ; then as barracks ; then as a magazine for the storage of powder, salt, etc.   The arena was filled with buildidgs to suit it for those purposes.   A part of the arena has been excavated to the original level, showing the dens where the beasts were caged, the places where the gladiators were kept, and the secret passages from the arena to the royal palace, through which the Emperor Comodus entered to play the gladiator, to gratify his insatiable thirst for blood and make Rome howl.

A regular bull fight was displayed in the Coliseum in A. D. 1332.   The bulls won the fight, for of all the hundreds of gallant youths who entered the arena on that occasion only eleven survived.   The city, however, gave a gorgeous funeral to the dead.   The Coliseum was then in ruins very much as it is now.

It has been computed, according to modern prices, that the Coliseum brick work alone would be worth $4,000,000, and this was a very small part of its cost.

While Comodus was returning to his palace one night, he was met by an assassin in the subterranean passageway above mentioned.   As the assailant sprang upon the Emperor he exclaimed : "The Senate sends you this."   He killed his assailant, discovered a conspiracy in his own palace, with his sister at its head, and from that time became one of Rome's most cruel rulers   He called himself the Roman Hercules.   All his statues make him carry a club and no other arm.   He fought in the arena seven hundred and thirty-five times.   He killed from his Imperial seat in the Coliseum one hundred lions with one hundred shots from his bow.   He was at last drugged by a prostitute and strangled by a slave.   The last gladiatorial combat in the Coliseum was in A. D. 404, when a Christian monk sprang into the arena and in the name of Christ separated the combatants.   He was stoned to death.

The debris from Rome, and alluvium, have changed the course of the Tiber.   What was once its bed is now a part of the town, and in appearance is as ancient as the oldest part of the city.   The Tarpeian Rock has had seventy feet of its top quarried off, and has been filled up at its base fully fifty feet ; it is still about seventy feet high.   Many of the most renowned ruins have been converted into churches.   After Rome became Christian, and during the Middle Ages many

old temples were pulled down and pillaged to build and ornament Christian churches.   Constantine robbed it to decorate
his new capital.   The Forum has been partly excavated and
restored to its ancient level.   The old level was found to be
from fifteen to thirty feet below what was formerly supposed
to be the proper floor of the Forum.   The floor level of the
old theatre of Marcellus has been found to be fully thirty feet
under ground.   It is the oldest theatre in Rome and would
seat 28,000 spectators.   Its walls are still well preserved.   The
old Latin quarter has been almost entirely torn down.   An
old fish market has been discovered with beautiful marble
slabs which have been ruthlessly torn from some neighboring
palace to make tables upon which to clean fish.

Rome was formerly subject to disastrous inundations from
the overflow of the Tiber.   This is being corrected by widen-
ing the river.   Two new arches, one on each side of the river,
have been added to one of the oldest bridges of Rome.   The
river has been widened to the extent of the two new arches.
The ugly and irregular old river wall is now being pulled down
and a magnificent new one erected in its place.   In a short
time the Tiber will flow between walls as beautiful as those
of ancient Babylon, the Biblical type of Rome.

Instead of a sleepy old pile of ruins I find Rome a beautiful, well-built, well-paved modern city.   It has a population
of near 400,000 inhabitants.   Its citizens look very much like
the people of Philadelphia.   Its fashions are like ours.   Its
modern improvements, street railways, hotel elevators, cabs
and stores are very much like our own.   The common people
of Rome seem more cruel to their domestic animals than the
same class are in our country.   They overload their horses and
donkeys and use the whip much more freely than would be
permitted in America.   I observe, however, that this is to b
corrected.   The government has recently chartered a " Society
for the prevention of Cruelty to Animals."   In a word, Rome
is a modern city built upon and out of the ruins of an ancient
one.   The material used for building purposes is chiefly stone,
very abundant here.   Brick, however, is much used and was
the material most employed by its ancient builders.   The old
city walls, in many places, were built of brick.   I have not
seen a red brick house in Rome.   Both stone and brick houses
are, as a rule, plastered with cement and painted a mellow
yellow color, like most continental cities.   A striking peculiarity of Rome is the great size of its houses.   Most of the
dwelling houses are six stories high, and in outward appearance there is little difference between the dwellings of the rich
and the poor.   When you take a peep at the inside the difference is but too apparent.   Every room contains a family.

The family washing is seen hanging on the balcony to dry. There are no carpets on the floors, the kitchen, bedroom, parlor, and often the workshop, are in the same room. I doubt whether the Romans have any adequate idea of an English or American home. There are some very fine stores in the city, well managed and doing a prosperous business. The place is full of artists, painters, sculptors and workers in mosaic, musicians and archæologists. The amount of money annually poured into the lap of the world's Old Mistress, is enormous. The city is now full of pilgrims, travelers, pleasure-seekers, students and loungers in high life who have nothing to do but to see or hear something new. All leave their little contributions. I have been ten days in Rome and have left about four hundred dollars here. I met a Philadelphia gentleman yesterday who spent three thousand dollars in two months for works of art here. This will partly account for the wonderful prosperity of the city. A visit to the galleries of the sculptors and painters is always free. Like the spider and the fly, it is very easy to get in but very difficult to get out without leaving an order for your portrait, bust, or some pleasing work of art. Twelve hundred francs ($240) will pay for a highly finished life-size bust of any one ambitious to have his features preserved in marble for the admiration of future generations.

The hotels of Rome are equal to any in the world. We are staying at the "Continental." It is six stories high, has a front of 270 feet and a depth of 150 feet. It occupies the entire square with a fine wide, well-paved street all around it. The cost of hotel life is about the same as in Philadelphia, certainly not less in the first-class hotels.

I was particularly struck with the display of military strength not only here but everywhere on the continent. Soldiers are constantly parading the streets, not in their holiday uniforms, but dressed in fighting trim, with knapsacks and all the accoutrements of actual war. They are required to march twenty miles every day, go through the regular drill and spend the balance of the day upon the fortifications. There is no such thing as playing soldier here. The constant movement of troops and the transportation of cannon and munitions of war reminds me of our own war time. There is a very uneasy feeling at this time all over Europe. Italy has a fine navy and a very efficient though not very large army. On our journey here, I noticed the erection of new earthworks and the strengthening of old ones all along the frontier of Germany, Belgium and Italy. I never saw such fortifications as are being constructed around Metz. I would not be surprised if the smothered fire of former struggles should soon burst into a blaze of war again. Nothing but the general alarm and preparation for the struggle will prevent it. The nation that applies the match to the combustible material will take upon itself a most terrible responsibility.

Rome is not only full of objects of interest within its walls, but is also surrounded with most charming scenery without. The villas of Rome are world-renowned. The word *villa*, without explanation, will convey a very imperfect idea. It means the country seat of some rich Roman Lord. Some of them contain many hundred acres of most beautifully orna- mented and decorated grounds, with splendid drives, gardens and parks, fountains and statuary. Each contains the palace of the owner, and they are generally open to the public. They are enchanting places for an hour's rest and recreation, and most of them without the city walls ; there is no long drive over cobble stones to reach them. The palaces are full of works of ancient and modern art ; many of them have fine collections of Roman antiquities dug up from the grounds of the villa. In these parks and gardens, and in the drives and carriage-ways leading to and through them, the rich and royal citizens of Rome spend their leisure hours. It was my good fortune to meet the King twice and the Queen four times in the villas around Rome.

Rome cannot yet be said to be a healthy city ; it has very much improved in its sanitary condition within a few years. The excavation of so much rubbish must necessarily let loose unhealthy gases confined, perhaps, for hundreds of years. About the first of June the unhealthy season begins. In mid- summer most of the citizens leave the city. The fleas have already begun to invade the hotels ; they are very annoying : they are brought into Rome by the shepherds and goatherds. A mosquito bite is nothing to a flea in your bed.

The King and Queen left Rome yesterday, so the fashion- able season may be considered as over. I will write again before I leave the city for Naples, where I intend to spend a week.

XXIX.

TRAVELING AND ROMANCE — PAST GLORY OF ROME — WEALTHY CITIZENS—POPULATION—PENALTY FOR PROPOS- ING NEW LAWS—HOW TO SEE ROME—A SCHOOL GIRL'S IDEA OF ROME—FOUR HUNDRED CHURCHES — PIOUS FRAUDS—THE BLACK VIRGIN—A WONDERFUL CITY.

ROME, May, 1888.

Nothing takes the romance out of life like traveling. It requires all the sentiment we can command to keep up our preconceived notions of the enchantment supposed to linger around sacred places and among the relics of antiquity. When we travel the same ground over which Paul and Peter walked, and stand where Cicero delivered his orations ; when we look on the very spot where the martyrs died, where great Cæsar fell, or where the gladiators fought and shed their blood to make a Roman holiday, one would suppose a thrill of reverence for the place would inspire our souls ; but the experience of all travelers is the same. Our romantic anticipations all disappear. We find the sacred places of history so much like other parts of the world, so busy with the commonplace affairs of life, so unlike what we expected to see, and so full of false traditions and nonsensical legends as to inspire feelings of disappointment and disgust rather than of reverential awe. But, with all her extravagant inventions and pious frauds, there is a charm still lingering around the undoubted remains of the greatest city of the Old World. The evidence of her lost glory lies all around, but the means of travel and rapid communication are now so great that distance no longer lends enchantment to the view. While, therefore, the antiquities of Rome are greatly instructive as illustrating history and giving us a correct idea of life two or three thousand years ago, they cannot be said to add to our veneration for its lost civilization, or inspire regret for the fall of a power too mighty for the general happiness of mankind.

Rome was certainly a wonderful city. It was but thirteen miles around its walls, but the villas and suburbs extended for many miles outside, and entirely around its walls. After her many disasters, in the time of Justinian, she could put into the field, fully equipped, 30,000 soldiers. Fourteen rivers emptied into the city by aqueducts. Some of the aqueducts were thirty-eight miles long. The city could be flushed at any time.

When Alaric sacked the city in A. D. 410, Gibbon says, it contained 1780 private palaces. Each of these palaces was a little city. They each had their private theatres, hippodromes, temples, baths, porticoes, groves and gardens. The annual income of some of the citizens was nearly $1,000,000. Some of their single feasts cost over $200,000. There were private aqueducts which brought rivers into their villas. It had a population of 2,000,000 within its walls, and at least 3,000,000 without the walls. At some of the games there would be 400,000 spectators.

To govern such a city must have required great power and eternal vigilance. They had one good law which should be adopted in America. They hung the proposer of every new law that failed to pass.

We conclude that the ancient Romans were very much like ourselves, with the same passions, pleasures, likes and dislikes that we have. They had their scholars and their simpletons, wise men and fools, rich men and beggars, lawyers and clients, merchants and farmers. In the early history of Rome a farmer was a gentleman. But as she advanced in wealth and power the farmers became poor, and Cincinatus was supplanted by the Vanderbilts and Goulds of Rome. They soon wrecked the State as they will every other State where they thrive and grow rich on the sweat and toil of the tillers of the soil. I left Rome with regret, but I believe I have seen it more perfectly than most travelers of a fortnight's stay. Many visitors of Rome leave it after a few days, supposing they have seen it. Such visitors are always disappointed and speak of it as a pile of old ruins, broken columns and cracked walls, full of splendid churches and ecclesiastical palaces.

Professor Leslie told us a good story of a school girl's idea of Rome. She was on her return voyage after a tour of Europe to complete her education. The passengers were discussing the interesting cities they had seen and by consensus of opinion agreed that Rome was the most interesting place in the world. Turning to her father, she said : " Pa, were we at Rome ?" The old gentleman rubbed his eye-glasses and examined his diary for a while, and replied : " O, yes ; don't you remember the big church named after Peter, and the burned theatre they called the Colossus of Rome ? (He meant the Coliseum). Nothing worth seeing ; we only stopped there for the eclat of the thing."

It is impossible to fairly comprehend Rome in less than two weeks most industriously spent with the assistance of a carriage and good guide. Even to a person able to speak French or Italian, a guide well versed in the antiquities of the city is essential. More precious time will be wasted in wandering from place to place and in doubling your routes than would pay for two guides.

To persons intending to visit Rome, I would say, before you start re-read " Gibbon's Decline and Fall of the Roman Empire. " Then procure a good map of the city and make yourself familiar with its topography and the nomenclature of its streets. Upon arriving, procure an educated guide—there are several here ; with his aid, a good carriage, and two weeks industriously spent, with six hours a day, you will have a fair conception of what the ancient city was. As to the modern city, you need give it but little attention. It is just like most other European towns. You should first drive around the city, within and without its walls, and take a general glance at the outside of its historic places and buildings. Then commence a systematic internal exploration. You must not forget that the remains of Roman art are only to be found within the three or four hundred churches of the city. Some of these churches are ugly and repulsive in external appearance, but on entering them you will be surprised and amazed at their internal splender, almost invariably made up from old heathen temples which were stripped to decorate the early Christian churches. You must also remember that all you see is what the plunderers of Rome did not consider worth carrying away. You must also not forget that it required three hundred years for Rome to die after she had received her death wound, and that she had been burned, pillaged and torn down by her conquerors, and the nations of Europe had enriched their museums from her works of art before these churches were erected out of what remained. Yet enough has been left to strike us with wonder. I believe I have fairly seen Rome, and I think I can reasonably comprehend what the ancient city must have been. If we find a broken column of jasper, or a fragment of some finely chiseled statuary we can, with reasonable certainty, reconstruct both and form a fair conception of what the original was like. So, looking upon what remains of the ancient city, and making allowances for what has been destroyed and carried away, we can reconstruct its temples, its forum, its palaces, gardens and baths. We can stand by Pompey's statue and see the place where great Cæsar fell. We can occupy the spot where Antony delivered his funeral oration. We can mount the rostrum where Cicero made his speeches. We may stand on the Tarpeian Rock, enter the coliseum, survey the place of the Amphitheatre where so many Christians were given to the flames and to wild beasts while the Roman spectators howled with joy. We may walk through the home of Nero and the halls of the Cæsars, and out to the place where Paul was beheaded and where Peter was crucified, and down in the catacombs and prisons where the early Christians were confined and slain. We can look at buildings, bridges and old city walls, forts and fortifications two thousand three hundred years old, and then we can form some idea of ancient Rome.

I have seen them all, and have visited about thirty of the most interesting churches of the city. I have also been permitted to enter fifteen palaces and villas, rich with statuary and painting. I have seen every work of art of importance in the city as well by ancient as modern masters. I have been able to compare, in my own humble way, the work of Praxitiles and Phidias with that of Conova and Michael Angelo. I have also seen all the magnificent presents sent to the Pope from the crowned heads of the globe, as well as from individuals, all over the world. I have seen the World's Fair at Philadelphia and Vienna, and I affirm without fear of contradiction by those who have seen these splendid displays, as well as the exhibition of the presents to the Pope, that his outshine the other two and throw them both into the shade. This is saying very much, but it is the truth. After spending two days in a hurried walk through the exhibition buildings I felt as I suppose the Queen of Sheba felt when she saw the glory of Solomon, and like her I was constrained to say, '' The half was never told. ''

The above record of what I have seen in Rome is a mere index. Volumes would not fully describe the interesting and beautiful things I have gazed upon while sojourning in that wonderful city. I have also seen some things which have given me pain rather than pleasure. I have no patience with the perpetrators of pious frauds, and I am sorry to say Rome has many of them. They show in one of the churches what the monks affirm is a miraculously preserved corpse of a monk who died 178 years ago. You are not permitted to approach nearer than about one foot of the coffin. It is a most excellent piece of wax work. In another church they show you a spring of oil. In another, the chains with which Peter and Paul were bound, which they allege miraculously linked themselves together when by accident they came in contact with each other. At the place where Paul was beheaded they show three springs of water which they affirm sprung up as soon as the old saint's head struck the ground. In the prison where Paul and Peter were confined before their execution, they show the print of Peter's face in the hard stone, which they allege was caueed by a blow from the keeper of the jail which caused Peter to fall with his face against the wall, when the wall became as soft as wax and left the impression of his face there which has remained ever since. These are all pure inventions of the Middle Ages. The monks give you a quizzical look while repeating the stories. The Italian people, however, are very intense in all their passions and feelings as well religious as secular. They are most devoted Christian believers, and are much to be admired for their religious faith and fervor. Christianity made its first great conquest of the world at Rome and, if it ever dies, its last death struggle will be there.

I was very much surprised to learn that there are many devoted Catholics in Rome who believe the Virgin Mary was black. They exhibit in one of the churches her portrait, said to have been painted by St. Luke. It is only exhibited once a year. I, however, induced the custodian of the picture to show it to me. It is a very ancient looking painting. It represents the Holy Virgin as an Ethiopian of a very dark copper color. I have no faith in the assertion that it was painted by St. Luke. It is perhaps an old Egyptian painting by some artist among the early Christians of that country. I would like to say much more about Rome but I fear I am making my letters too long.

————

XXX

ROME TO NAPLES—LAST LOOK AT ST. PETER'S—A NIGHT
SCENE IN THE COLISEUM — A ROMAN BATH — ANCIENT
ROME CONTRASTED WITH ROME IN THE XVTH CENTURY—
ROMAN JUSTICE IN 1420 — NAPLES — THE DUCHESS OF
EDINBURGH—SIGHTS IN THE STREETS—FLEAS, LICE AND
BEGGARS—A VISIT TO VESUVIUS'S CRATER—GROTESQUE
FORMS OF LAVA—A PAINTER'S IDEA OF HELL—CAPRI
AND THE BLUE GROTTO.

NAPLES, May, 1888.

Although in Naples, my thoughts still linger around Rome. I feel that I have not done justice to the grand old city. Just before my departure we were permitted to visit the palace of the brother of the Pope (Palaza Barberini). It contains many gems of art by Raphael and Guido Reni, besides about 7,000 rare manuscripts. It is a magnificent structure, built by Urban VIII.

Before quitting Rome, perhaps forever, I took a last look at St. Peter's. Every time I see it its beauties multiply and its greatness increases. Yet it is said that of its seven hundred columns, and thousands of pilasters and monuments, statuary and reliefs, no new marble was employed in its construction. All was brought from the ruined temples, baths and palaces of ancient Rome. When we remember that Alaric pillaged the city A. D. 410; and that Attila sacked it A. D. 445; and that it was almost totally destroyed by the Goths A. D. 546; that for hundreds of years it was robbed of all that was considered worth carrying away; that eighty of the most splendid churches of Rome had been built and adorned with their columns of jasper, porphyry and beautiful marbles, statuary and works of art from the ruins of the old city, and that there was yet enough left to build and decorate this most imposing of all the buildings of the world, we can form some imperfect idea of what the ancient city must have been.

Although we received all our ideas of equity jurispru-
dence from the administration of justice in ancient Rome, it
would seem from the records of its courts that its high character for justice must have degenerated.   In 1420, a case is reported in which the question was the ownership of a beautiful statue of Pompey.   It had been found buried many feet
under the earth, with all but the head on the land of the
finder.   The head was over the line, and on a neighbors land.
The court decided that the head should be sawed off and be
given to the owner of the land on which it lay, and the balance should go to the owner of the land on which it was found.
If the Pope had not interfered the sentence would have been
carried out.   He directed the statute to be sold and the pro-
ceeds divided in a fair proportion between the litigants.

The night before leaving Rome there was a grand illumi-
nation of the Coliseum.   I suppose there were at least two
thousand persons in the arena.   We may imagine what it was
when 80,000 spectators were present.   The effect of the different colored lights and Roman candles was very beautiful.
One could almost see the immense audience file in and take
their seats around the tiers, rising almost, in appearance, to
the stars.   We could imagine the Emperor seated under his
purple canopy, and hear the roar of the wild beasts ready to
spring into the arena, or the clash of swords as the gladiators
fought, and the howl of the infuriated spectators for the blood
of the vanquished.   It is affirmed by historians that at the dedication of the Coliseum no less than ten thousand men and five
thousand beasts were killed in the arena to make a Roman
holiday.

"When falls the Coliseum Rome shall fall
And when Rome falls, the world."

I do not remember having described an ancient Roman
bath.   You have often heard of these luxuriant palaces of refreshment and pleasure, but few have any correct idea of their
voluptuous splendor or gigantic proportions.   When you learn
that a river had to be brought into Rome to supply one of
them with water, and that 1000 bathers could swim in one
apartment at the same time ; that one of them covered an area
of 2,628,000 square yards ; that one of the most beautiful
churches (St. Mary of the Angels) has been formed by Michael
Angelo out of one of the apartments of the bath of Diocletian,
and that the Pantheon, with its lofty dome and circular wall
twenty-five feet thick, is but an old Roman bath room, with a
facade and columns added to make it a church, you will have
a faint conception of the meaning of the word " Roman bath."
The Pantheon was built 27 B. C.   The baths of Caracalla
A. D. 212.

Before quitting Rome, I would like to say a word about her fountains. No city in the world, according to its size, has more water emptied into it than Rome. Its fountains are constructed on an immensely grand scale. The water is brought from mountain rivers by aqueducts and is poured out in most lavish extravagance into the open squares of the city. The fountains are decorated with colossal statuary; Neptune, the Tritons, great sea horses, grand cascades of rock work and immense stone basins, over which the water rolls and dashes in the wildest profusion and refreshing beauty. It is said that it requires as much water as the Seine daily discharges into the sea to supply the fountains of Rome. This lavish supply of water is supposed to add very much to the health of the people of the city. I would like to say much more of Rome but I fear I shall weary my readers.

No sterner lesson of the transitory nature of human glory can be taught than in the fall of this great empire. In the sixth century, Rome had dwindled from 5,000,000 to a few thousand miserable wretches, too poor to get away. At that time the bones of St. Peter and St. Paul were supposed to be discovered and it at once became a place of pilgrimage and began to increase; yet in 1709, after over one thousand years, it only contained about 140,000 Christians and 10,000 Jews.

The tomb of Hadrian was once cased with white marble from Paros and was ornamented with statues of gods and great men, the work of Phidias and Praxiteles. Belisarius converted it into a citadel and so it still remains.

Gibbon speaks of the fall of Rome as the most awful scene in the tragedy of the world. The empire that had ruled the world for so many centuries, was reduced in 1425 to a small piece of territory around Constantinople fifty miles long by thirty miles wide.

Farewell to Rome. I feel I shall never look upon its like again, but I shall never forget the pleasure I have enjoyed during the two weeks so profitably spent within its walls.

The distance from Rome to Naples, measured by time on the fastest express trains, is about seven hours. The railroad follows very nearly an old Roman highway. It traverses a rich valley, skirted by beautiful mountain scenery. Here, too, we find women and young girls hard at work cultivating the fields. After a few miles out of Rome the mountains become very barren, with scarcely a green spot to give a smile to their hard rocky faces. The soil of the valley, however, is rich and red, full of vines, olive, fig and orange trees, with here and there a garden of roses. As we approach Naples the mountains become softer and more like high, undulating hills, something like the scenery around York and Gettysburg.

Pa.   We pass towns four hundred years older than our
Christian era, and vineyards of whose excellence Horace sung.
The vines are festooned from tree to tree, presenting a very
pretty appearance.   About forty miles from Naples we catch
the first view of Vesuvius ; a few miles further and we see the
Mediterranean and, before we know it, arrive in the suburbs
of the city.   I was disappointed in the size of Naples.   It is
a much larger town than it appears to be on the first view.   It
is said to contain about 700,000 inhabitants, which would
make it, in population, as large as Philadelphia.   In territorial limits it does not seem more than about one-fourth as
large.   There is nothing very remarkable about Naples except
its world-renowned bay, beautiful isles and grottoes, and its
ever-threatening Vesuvius on the one hand, compared with its
vermin, beggars and bad smells on the other.   The city has
very extensive barracks and is now full of soldiers.   We are
quartered at the Hotel du Vesuve, facing the bay, and the
best hotel in the city.   As evidence of this assertion it will
only be necessary to say that the daughter-in-law of Queen
Victoria, the Duchess of Edinburgh, has a suite of rooms and
is boarding at the same hotel and on the same floor.   We are
trying to keep up the dignity of our country you see.   The
Duchess is a fine looking, well-formed, rather stout woman
and is said to be very exacting in her demands for royal attention.   She is not a beautiful woman but has a very proud,
majestic air, and walks as the daughter of the Czar ought to
carry herself.   I have made it a rule to lodge only at the best
hotels.   My experience is that it is cheapest in the long run
to do so.   We are less liable to imposition and get much better attention.   What one loses in money he gains in comfort.
If I were traveling alone, however, or only with gentlemen, I
would select less expensive hotels.   When traveling with
ladies it is safest to choose the best.

    The best hotel in Naples is not free from fleas.   The
cows and goats are brought into the town to sell the milk and
insure it from adulteration.   The consequence is that while the
citizens get pure milk the town is filled with fleas.   The water
here is not very good.   As a natural consequence the people
are great wine drinkers, yet I have seen no drunken men.   I
have seen sights, however, in the streets of Naples more disgusting, if possible, than drunkenness.   Such as half-naked
men and women ; children of ten, of both sexes, naked ; men
and women amusing themselves on a " flea hunt," or cracking nits and searching each other's heads for vermin.   It is
no uncommon sight to find men taking a quiet nap on the
sidewalk, or to find them in the open street answering all the
calls of nature with perfect nonchalance.   The streets and

public places are cursed with beggars who are permitted to
run after your carriage screaming and yelling for assistance,
while exposing their running sores or the deformity of their
persons.   Some of the sights above described are only seen in
the old parts of the city, but the beggars are everywhere.

The three most interesting excursions from Naples are to
Vesuvius, Pompeii and Capri, each requiring a separate day.
The visit to Vesuvius with ladies is expensive.   Besides twenty-eight francs for your fare and guide, they charge twenty-
five francs for a sedan to carry each lady to the top of the
cone.   The greater part of the ascent is made by a steam elevator or railway on an angle of about forty-five degrees.   The
mountain is over four-thousand feet high.   From the edge of
the cone, which is so hot as to burn your feet, the sight into
the crater is perfect.   It resembles an immense iron foundry
or cauldron one hundred yards in diameter, boiling, bubbling
and seething with molten rock.   Every few seconds it gives
what sounds like a dying groan, the mountain trembles and
then from the whole boiling crater stones and lava are thrown
up two or three hundred feet, falling around the edges of
the cone and thus constantly increasing the height of the
mountain and depth of the crater till the weight of the cone
becomes too heavy for the molten mass below, then the whole
falls in and a great eruption is the consequence.   The smell
of sulphur is almost suffocating.   The top of the cone is yellow with it.   The lava falls around you red hot.   When a piece
falls near you a penny can be pressed into it which soon also
becomes red hot.   I gave my guide a franc to press a penny
from my own pocket into a chunk of lava which fell some
twenty feet from where I stood.   I could light my cigar with it
several seconds afterwards.   I confess that I felt very much as if
I were looking down the chimney of pandemonium and taking
my first, and I hope my last peep into the infernal regions.

To me, the most remarkable thing I saw was the grotesque
forms assumed by the lava of the last great eruption.   It is
seen for miles around the sides of the sterile mountain and, at
a little distance, has the appearance of myriads of naked men,
serpents, animals and reptiles, twisted and contorted into grotesque and unnatural shapes, with the monsters and griffins of
mythology feasting upon the broken and distorted mass.   It
looks as if they had made war upon the mountain, had been
swallowed whole and, after being half digested, had been
vomited out and converted into stone.   I have never seen or
read any description of this most remarkable appearance of the
lava and was, therefore, very much surprised at the spectacle,
as it was altogether unexpected.   I gave a description of it
to some of the English guests of our hotel, and upon their

return next day they all agreed that my description as above given was not an exaggeration. I have no doubt but that Gustave Dore and Weirtz got some of their weird and grotesque illustrations from the forms represented by the lava of Vesuvius. It called to my mind a life-size painting of immense proportions I saw upon the wall of the Campo Santo at Pisa. It was intended to represent the last judgment, and gave us the painter's idea of hell. Satan, in the form of an enormous red hot monster, sat in the center, devouring the damned as they tumbled headlong into his open jaws. He was transparent from heat. The process of digestion could be discovered, and the half-devoured limbs could be seen seeking their disjointed sockets and renewing their former forms, only to be devoured and torn to pieces forever. I have no doubt the painter thought his picture would strike terror to all beholders. They had no Beechers then to rob hell of its terrors.

The drive from Naples to Vesuvius is very dusty and disagreeable at this season of the year. The weather is very dry and the winds from the sea keep up a cloud of white limestone dust very hard on the eyes and generally disagreeable.

The next day we visited the " Blue Grotto," on the isle of Capri, about two hours by boat from Naples. It is a very enchanting little place. The island proper is very high and rocky, with here and there a little cultivated land and flourishing vineyards. The wine of Capri is drunk all over Italy and is accounted very good.

The grotto is entered from the sea by means of small boats, holding about three or four persons. We enter a small hole in the form of an arch about three feet high. It is necessary to bow the head to get in without striking the crown of the arch. The boat almost touches each side as we enter Once in a most delightful spectacle breaks upon the sight. It looks very much like one of the scenes in the Black Crook, or the Naiad Queen. The grotto will hold fifty boats with ample room to row about at pleasure. The color of the water cannot be described. It looked to me like bright sunlight through sapphire. The air within is of a hazy yellow. The water is as clear as crystal. The play of the oars makes the water sparkle like liquid silver. The voices of the visitors are echoed from end to end and from vault to vault. The whole effect is very fairy like. On our return to the ship little naked boys amused us by diving into the sea for pennies thrown overboard, which they almost invariably caught in their teeth before the penny struck the bottom.

XXXI.

NAPLES TO MESSINA—LAST DAYS OF POMPEII—CATANIA AND
MT. ÆTNA—MESSINA TO ATHENS—STROMBOLI—SCYLLA
AND CHARYBDIS—THE CHOLERA AT MESSINA—A JERSEY-
MAN—ITALIAN SHIPS—POLITE CONDUCTORS ACCORDING TO
THE CLASS OF YOUR TICKET—SEASICK PASSENGERS—A
WANDERING SPARROW—THE ISLES OF GREECE—LOVE AND
DEATH—THE PIRÆUS—TIME'S RUINS—THE COUNCIL OF
THIRTY—OLD AND NEW ATHENS—THE NEW ACADEMY—
A COSMOPOLITAN CITY AND DETERIORATED RACE.

ATHENS, MAY, 1888.

Before leaving Naples we spent a day in the exhumed
city of Pompeii. In many respects my anticipations were not
realized. The day was sultry, the dust almost suffocating,
and the beggars disgustingly persistent and annoying. It
takes three hours to reach the place by carriage, and about
two hours to explore the ruins. I am not convinced that the
city was anything like as rich and luxuriant as it is usually
painted by travelers. What remains, however, gives a very
fair idea of Roman life eighteen hundred years ago. Our
ideas of the place have been favorably prepared by Bulwer's
"Last Days of Pompeii." The book, however, I have no
doubt, fairly portrays Roman life at the time of the destruction
of the city. Again, only a small part has been excavated.
The size of its Forum, Bourse, two theatres, municipal buildings and private gardens, would seem to indicate a place of
considerable importance ; nothing, however, when compared
with the cities of our day, or the great ones of that period.
The museum at Naples and the one at Pompeii clearly show
that the people of the city at the time of its destruction were
very much like the people of to-day. They had the same
pleasures and toils, the same trades and professions, merchants
and farmers. The children had the same toys now found at
our firesides. The men played cards, checkers and chess just
as our men do and, from the frescoes on some of the walls, did
many other naughty things practised *sub rosa* to-day. There
were learned men and refined women in Pompeii, and it had
its ignorant, egotistical and vulgar ones. From what remains,
we may fairly judge they managed to extract about as much
good, and suffered about as much evil from life as we do.

From Naples we went to Messina, in Sicily, and from
there to Catania, at the foot of Ætna. The ladies of our party
are showing signs of weariness, at which I am not surprised.

They have never been subjected to such incessant toil, for traveling in Europe means toil in its strictest sense. I only wonder that they have kept up so well. I hope to give them a little rest at Athens, but I intend to carry out my first design and not turn my steps homeward until we have seen Constantinople. Messina is a very old city, but contains nothing that struck me as unusually interesting. Perhaps if I had visited it before seeing Rome, I might have been able to find amusement and instruction here for a week. As it is I shall not stay over a day and a half.

The journey from Naples was delightful. The sea was like a lake and the scenery around the Bay of Naples was exquisitely fine. We came in sight of Stromboli about five o'clock on the morning after embarkation. This island is almost a circle and rises out of the sea like a cone. It was regarded by the ancients as the seat of Æolus. It was considered in the Middle Ages as the entrance to purgatory. It is over three thousand feet high and is one of the volcanoes never entirely inactive. The island of Volcano could also be plainly seen from the ship. It is now in an active state of eruption. Mount Ætna can be seen towering like a giant above the other mountains of Sicily. It is over ten thousand feet high and is always snow-capped, except the cone, which is so hot that the snow melts as soon as it falls. It is the loftiest volcano in Europe. It can only be ascended in summer. One of its eruptions destroyed forty towns and from sixty to one hundred thousand lives. The last violent eruption was in 1886, when it destroyed cultivated fields to the value of one hundred and fifty thousand dollars. The length of the lava stream was four miles. The mountain cannot be seen from Messina. In passing through the Straits of Messina we see what was formerly known as the rock Scylla, represented in Homer's Odyssey as a roaring sea monster On the other side is the fabulous Charybdis of the ancients. The ancient poets and mariners either drew their terrible stories from their imagination, or time and earthquakes have destroyed the rock and filled up the whirlpool, for I could not discern the slightest trace of either.

Messina is quite an extensive seaport, beautifully situated on the sea and backed by mountains. (All Sicily is mountainous). It has a population of 130,000. Its scenery is said to vie with that of Palermo. The cholera last year swept off 40,000 of its citizens. Since then they have introduced purer water into the city and hope to escape a second visitation of the dreadful scourge.

I was surprised at the purity of the English spoken by the chief cook of our hotel. On inquiry I found he was a

genuine Jerseyman from Newark, and knew more about Philadelphia and New York than I did. Most of the attaches or
the hotels of the continent speak a little English. I have
made quite an important discovery. I find, by speaking very
slowly and distinctly, and only using words derived from the
Latin, I can make myself understood when others who speak
much better English than I do cannot be understood at all.
For instance : I never say I *wish* or I *want* anything ; I say
desire. Never say *understand,* but *comprehend.* Never say
begin, but *commence,* etc.

The Italians are a very deliberate people in all their business transactions, and very slow in the performance of all the
duties of life. If you are in haste you cannot hurry an
Italian waiter. If you have but five minutes for the boat or
train, don't trust a cabman or a ferryman. As an illustration
of Italian slowness, our ship from Messina to Athens was
booked to stop at Catania to discharge and take on a part of
her cargo. We were warned by the captain to be on board
punctually at 11 A. M. Instead of starting at eleven, the
ship did not weigh anchor until 5 P. M. A loss of six hours.
A good stevedore of Philadelphia would have done in two
hours what these lazy sailors were six hours working at.

I would not advise my countrymen to travel in an Italian
ship if one of any other nation can be found. I am sorry to
say they are not clean. Fleas, bed bugs and other disagreeable vermin fill every hole and corner. The officers, however,
are very polite and courtly in their attention to the passengers
of the first class. I have noticed, in traveling on the railroads, a most marked difference in the manners of the railroad
officials. When you approach the window and ask for a first-
class ticket, the agent tips his hat and smiles superciliously
while he waits on you and always calls you *Monsieur.* A
second-class ticket is also delivered with common politeness,
no more. The third-class passengers are scarcely noticed.
The guard, who is the same as our conductor, approaches the
window of the third-class car with the abrupt word, ''Tickets!''
The second-class car he approaches with a bow and says,
'' Please show your tickets.'' To the first-class passengers he
always tips his hat and says, '' Will the gentleman be pleased
to exhibit his ticket ?'' and after inspection he says, ''Thank
you : sorry to annoy you.''

Our voyage from Catania was a sad disappointment. Our
ship was not one-eighth laden. In fact she may be said to
have sailed on nothing but ballast. The sea was smooth, the
sky clear ; the sun set behind Mount Ætna most gloriously ;
the passengers were all happy in anticipation of a two days'
rest upon the tranquil bosom of the sea. At the table d'hote

at 7.30 P. M. all were present and enjoyed a hearty meal. To all but the captain and myself it was the last meal for two days. In all my travels by sea, I never encountered anything like it. I was, for the first time in my life, nauseated by the abominable, unaccountable and absolutely indescribable motion of the ship. It was a compound between a roll and a pitch, the most sickening motion I ever felt. After two days and nights, however, we came in sight of land and found a smooth sea again. The passengers began to crawl from their berths like ghosts from their graves, and it was not long before we were as jolly and happy as when we started. The passengers were of different nations—Italians, Greeks, Turks, French, Portuguese and English speaking people. It was surprising how soon we were able to communicate with each other, and it was amusing, after the sea sickness had passed, to see the male passengers playing like children at "hide and seek," "knock in and knock out," and such childlike sports. Men, after all, are but children of a larger growth.

While crossing the Adriatic, two poor little land sparrows, evidently blown by the storm beyond their power to return, took shelter on the ship. They were nearly exhausted, and so hungry and thirsty as to deprive them of all fear of their enemy, man. I could have easily caught them as they hopped about the deck seeking a crumb here and there or a little rain water lying in the hollow places of the ship. I felt that, like myself, they were wanderers and entitled to all the rites of hospitality. They nestled about the ship for a day or so, and as soon as we sighted land made a rapid flight for the shore. Among the steerage passengers was a full-fledged Turk, in the costume of his race. He sat cross-legged and smoked a pipe with a stem four feet long. During the storm it looked very odd to see him with an old English big coat over his gaudy Turkish suit.

As we approached the "Isles of Greece" all my romantic fear of the Nymphs and Sirens, who formerly enticed mariners to destruction by their sweet music, disappeared. If they ever inhabited these barren wastes, I don't wonder that they fed upon the unhappy sailors wrecked upon their inhospitable coasts, for these rocky crags can certainly afford no food for mortals or immortals. The Isles of Greece are apparently mountain peaks, peeping out of the sea. So far as their coast presentation is concerned, they appear to be entirely sterile. Their villages look like mere shelter huts for fishermen. I am only speaking from my own observation. There may be very rich and fertile fields beyond the range of my vision, but I would not like, from present appearances, to be compelled to live on one of them as a condition for the gift of them all.

Many of the scenes of mythology are laid in these Isles.
They abound with wild and wierd shades and enchanted grottoes. There is a beautiful legend of Love and Death getting
their arrows mixed while sleeping in one of these caverns. I
remember, when I was younger than I now am, of writing a
short poem upon this legend. It may not be worth preserving but, as we all love our own children, even if they are
hump-backed and squint-eyed, so I have an affection for my
own early efforts, even if they are halt and lame. Here is
the poem :

THE TWO FRIENDS—LOVE AND DEATH.

Love, weary, threw his arrows down
And went to sleep upon the ground,
While Death, a pleasant hour to spend,
Lay down to rest beside his friend.
While thus they passed the hours away,
Their arrows in confusion lay ;
Death's darts were found in Cupid's quiver,
And there they must remain forever ;
For Love and Death are so allied,
They walk together side by side.
As Hope is followed oft by Fear,
The Altar but precedes the Bier ;
We see together, very often,
An infant's crib and baby's coffin.
A funeral toll and marriage bell
Sound so alike, 'tis hard to tell
Which gives most anguish to the heart,
The shaft of Death, or Cupid's dart.
For Love and Death are so allied
They march forever side by side.

The Piræus, or seaport of Athens, is a very pretty place.
The ancients had two harbors here, the war harbor and the
mercantile harbor. Near here is the supposed tomb of Themistocles, hewn in the rock, but now covered by the water.
It is almost impossible to conceive how completely nearly all
the evidence of the former greatness, beauty and strength of
the Piræus, as described by ancient writers, has passed away.
Scarcely a trace of the immense walls from here to Athens is
to be found. These walls were eighty feet apart and extended
four miles from the city to the Piræus, which was then as now,
the seaport of Athens. The walls were built of dressed granite and were very high and strong. They were intended to
shelter the army as it passed from the city to the port. It was
destroyed by Lysander after the defeat of Alcibiades, 405 B. C.
This same Lysander established the thirty Tyrants, who ruled
the city with such cruelty that in eight months more citizens
were put to death than had been destroyed in thirty years of
war. They ordained the private possession of wealth to be a
capital crime. The Astors, Goulds and Vanderbilts of Athens
were declared public enemies and their property confiscated
for the State.

There is now a railway connecting the place with Athens.
I preferred, however, to take a carriage and guide, and enter

Athens by the old road. In two places we saw a trace of the
ancient wall. This is the dry season; everything is covered
with a white dust; very disagreeable. The Piraeus struck
me as looking very much like the little harbors of New England, and the general appearance of the country is very much
like New Hampshire, Rhode Island and Vermont. The hills
are very rocky, with but very little green grass. Most of the
rivers are now entirely dry. The flow of water from the rains
and snow of winter and early spring is said to be very
abundant, but now scarcely a rivulet is to be seen. Almost
every trace of the ancient city has disappeared. The new city
is just like most other modern European towns. It contains
some very beautiful public and private buildings, among which
I may especially name the New Academy, one of the most
graceful and attractive buildings I have seen in Europe. It
is of pure white marble, partly gilt with gold, and is said to
be an exact copy of some ancient building. In front it is
adorned with two lofty marble columns, surmounted with
finely wrought statues, one of Apollo, the other of Minerva.
No one can look upon these columns without a feeling of
pleasure.

The ruins of the ancient city are much more conspicuous
than those of Rome for the reason that they are mostly exposed to full view, and are not hidden or disfigured by modern
buildings. The site of modern Athens was but a suburb of
the ancient city. Some of the places of interest are in the
modern town, but the finest remains are a short distance further south. As in Rome, learned archæologists are here making new discoveries every day. The treasury of Greece is
nearly empty, but the government is conducting some very
expensive excavations, and is being richly compensated by
startling discoveries. Some splendid pieces of statuary have
been exhumed and set up in the museum and public squares.
Until recently Athens had no museum of Antiquities. She
has supplied the world with ancient statuary and has been
stripped nearly naked to fill the museums of other lands, but
she will soon have as rich relics of the past as any other city.
In my next letter I will be better prepared to describe my impressions of the place. It is a most remarkably cosmopolitan
city. We find people here in strange costumes. The streets
are full of foreigners from Persia, Egypt, Turkey and Syria,
each wearing the costume of his native land. The language
is modern Greek. It looks very odd to recognize upon some
shoemaker's sign, or over the door of a restaurant, such names
as Demosthenes, Pericles, Aristides, etc. The Grecians seem
to take great delight in perpetuating the names of the great
ones of the days of her glory. The disasters of war have,

however, played havoc with the race. The Turk, the Venetians
and the other conquerors of Greece have left their mark upon
the forms and faces of the present race. There is nothing now
in the least remarkable in the beauty of the women or strength
of the men. If anything is to be truthfully said upon this subject, I would say the present type of manhood of the modern
Greeks is something like the mixed Spanish of Mexico and
South America—much deteriorated by the infusion of strange
blood.

XXXII.

ATHENS—A SUNBURNED TRAVELER—THE PARTHENON AND
TEMPLE OF THESEUS—THREE PRINCIPAL HILLS—THE OLD
CITY CARRIED AWAY—EVEN THE SOIL GONE—GROVES OF
DAPHNE—TOMBS OF CIMON AND THEMISTICLES—PRISON
OF SOCRATES—ACROPOLIS AND SITE OF THE SUPREME
COURT—BURIED GRAVEYARDS—PLATO'S ACADEMY—THE
PLACES FROM WHICH DEMOSTHENES AND PAUL SPOKE—
STADIUM AND THEATRE — FALSE TEACHINGS OF OLD
SCHOOLMASTERS — RELICS FROM TROY — BRICKS FOUR
THOUSAND YEARS OLD—ANCIENT EVOLUTIONIST—ELEU-
SIS—SALAMIS—OLD OLIVE TREES—THE KING'S PALACE—
SHINPLASTERS FOR MONEY.

ATHENS, May, 1888.

The sun of Italy has given me the complexion of an Arab.
If I and my friend 'Squire Hazzard were to take a walk together through the streets of Athens we would be taken for
brothers. I am rather proud of my Oriental appearance.
When I arrive at Constantinople I intend to wear a fez. I
find I can stand exposure in the sun better than any of our
party. It is amusing to hear our English fellow-travelers
complain of the *blasted* heat. If the Athenians could only
keep down the disagreeable white dust that floats in clouds and
covers everything, even the green trees of its parks and gardens, their city would be rather a pleasant resort for Americans accustomed to the genial rays of our summer sun. I
have spent a very agreeable week here. The ruins of the
Parthenon and Temple of Theseus are the best I have yet
seen. When we remember that these ruins are the remains
of buildings that were the admiration of the world twenty-five
hundred years ago, and five hundred years before the period
of Roman glory, we can but be astonished at their present preservation. The Temple of Theseus at a little distance looks

like a modern erection, not unlike Girard College, but much smaller. From the hill Lycabettus, no one would take if for a ruin. It was built by Cimon, B. C. 470, to the memory of Theseus whose ghost is said to have appeared at the battle of Marathon and encouraged the Greeks to victory. No cement was used in the masonry of these old ruins. The solid marble blocks are square, dressed smooth on all sides, so as to present a finished inside as well as outside wall. The joints are so nicely fitted that a cambric needle cannot now be inserted between them. In Grecian architecture there is no arch; the ceiling and roof of their temples is formed by immense marble beams, beautifully ornamented, and formerly heavily gilt. The most impressive ruins are those on the Acropolis, a hill of Athens five hundred feet high, around which the ancient city was built. The building of the Parthenon was conducted under the supervision of Phidias, B. C. 488. Until the seventeenth century it stood almost uninjured, when it was left in its present condition by an explosion of gunpowder, caused by a shell during the siege of the place by the Venetians in 1687. The top of the Acropolis was cut off to make a plateau for the Parthenon and other buildings erected thereon.

There are three hills from which a splendid view of Athens can be had. First, the Acropolis; Second, Philopappus, four hundred and fifty-three feet high, and third, Lycabettus, nine hundred and forty-eight feet high. From the latter hill the whole town and country for many miles around, hemmed in by mountains and bordered by the sea, can be distinctly viewed. Athens has been so often painted by pen and pencil that an attempt by me at a further description would be presumptuous. I shall therefore only note such matters as made a special impression on my mind, not mentioned by other travelers. To me, the most striking thing was the complete disappearance of even the material with which the ancient city was built. With the exception of a few noted ruins, not a stone remains of what was once the most beautiful of cities. The question naturally follows, what has become of the imperishable part of the old town? A view of the place suggests the answer. They have been carried away by sea and sold for building purposes all over the earth. The stones that remain of the great four-mile-long walls from the Piræus to Athens, show great labor in their preparation. The rest were carried away to build the quays, wharves and seawalls of Venice and other Italian seaports. The marble blocks, and even the common stone and brick of the houses of the citizens, were well worth removing for building purposes. Some of the broken marble statuary has been found built up in common walls in

Rome. The hills upon which the city was built are of rock. The leveling of the surface of the rock, for foundations, all over the hills, is plainly visible; but even the earth that formed the gardens has been washed away. Small stones, the rocky foundations, and broken pottery, are all that is now left. The trees that once formed the shady groves, where Plato, Socrates and the old Grecian philosophers used to walk and lecture to their disciples, have all been cut down, thus leaving the soil exposed to the hot sun of summer, the dust and winds, and to the wash of winter and spring. In this way hills that were once fertile have lost all their soil, and now show nothing but small stone and a rocky base with scarcely a particle of vegetation.

The Areopagus, where once stood the splendid buildings of the Supreme Court of Athens, is a bare and rugged mass of rock. Steps cut into the stone where the Judges ascended, and a few level places cut into the rock for foundations, are all that remain to mark the spot where Socrates was tried and where Paul preached. Cut into the solid rock, the prison of Socrates still remains, because it could not be carried away without taking the mountain with it. The same may be said of the tomb of Cimon. It has been converted to the basest of uses by the common people, being in an out-of-the-way place.

The Necropolis, a burial place, in its present condition, shows the wonderful changes of the past thousand years. Recent excavations show that the original level of this burial place, was, perhaps, thirty or forty feet below the present surface. The dust, gathered and held by the grass of the neglected graveyard, and the wash caused by the melting snow and heavy rains, have gradually and imperceptibly filled the valley to its present level. The excavations show three distinct periods of Grecian history. In the deeper excavations were found urns, vases, and jars of pottery, which contain the ashes and charred bones of the dead, perhaps three thousand years old; then richly chiseled marble urns and statuary, and beautiful monuments, marking the resting places of the dead of a more luxuriant period; finally, large marble and stone sarcophagi indicating the burial, instead of the burning of the dead.

Every day new discoveries, throwing new light upon the history of the ancient city, are being made. Nothing now remains of the Academy of Plato but a few columns and some broken statuary built into the vegetable garden wall. The old well is still there. The place of the grove, where the old philosophers walked and talked, is now devoted to the raising of cabbages and garden produce for the hungry Athenians of this degenerate age.

Recent excavations clearly prove that Athens, in its glory, must have been a much larger place than we, in our schoolboy days, were taught.

The market place, where Paul heard the Stoics and Epi‑cureans discussing their opposite tenets, would hold perhaps 40,000 persons. The rostrum, still well marked, where De‑mosthenes and Pericles by their eloquence fired the Grecian heart, would hold perhaps 80,000 persons. There was the Stadium, founded by Lycurgus B. C. 350, provided with seats for 50,000 spectators to behold the foot-races. The covering was of an oval shape, six hundred and fifty feet long by one hundred and six feet wide. There was also the Theatre of Dionysus, recently discovered, built 500 B. C., where Æschy‑lus, Sophocles and Euripides played, which would seat 30,‑000 spectators. Besides this was the Theatre of Tragedy, and many other places of amusement and pleasure, and yet I was taught when a schoolboy that Athens, in its greatest glory, did not contain over 20,000 inhabitants. At the same time, I was taught that there never was such a place as Nineveh, and that Troy was a myth of Homer.

By special permission we visited the residence of Dr. Schliemann and inspected his collection of relics exhumed on the plains of Troy. The collection preserved in his own house, and in the Museum here, must strike any reasonably acute mind with wonder and amazement. He undoubtedly discov‑ered the true site of that most ancient city ; a city that was almost prehistoric when Moses was born. We saw arms, tools and ornaments of iron and steel, swords with hilts of solid gold, and gems of the hardest and most precious stones, with engravings upon them only legible through a lens of considerable power. He took from the sarcophagus of Aga‑memnon gold coins as sharply stamped as the products of our best mints of the present day. A gold chain and pair of brace‑lets taken from the same tomb, are most exquisitely wrought and as fresh and beautiful as if they had been the workmanship of yesterday. Every day is throwing new light upon the for‑gotten past and teaching the world the Bible truth that "there is nothing new under the sun," and that man, as we now see him, is just what he was in the olden time. Dr. Schlie‑mann has in his house a brick found by him in Egypt, made of the bitumen of the Nile and sun-baked. The straw, used to hold the substance together and keep it in form while hardening in the sun, is still plainly visible. It is about eleven inches long, five-and-a-half inches wide and five inches thick. It is about three thousand four hundred years old ; just such a brick as the Israelites were compelled to make during their captivity in Egypt.

A most beautiful piece of statuary, by the father of
Praxiteles, was recently found. Nothing is left but the arm
of a female holding a life-sized child of ten or twelve months.
The child is perfect and as well preserved as if it had been
chiseled yesterday.

We visited the famous groves of Daphne, about five miles
from the city. A few straggling laurel trees are all that is
left. A miserable looking monastery occupies the site of the
temple of Apollo (Pythian). Here and there we see a few
columns. The others have been carried off ; some of them
are in the British Museum.

There must have been a change in the topography of the
country—the land at the Piræus has either sunk or the sea
has raised. The tomb of Themistocles, hewn into the solid
rock, is now quite covered with water.

The museum is full of recently exhumed works of the old
masters. They are now erecting a new building in which to
preserve the newly discovered antiquities of the city. The
statuary of the ancients, say 4000 years old, teaches us that
the human form was as beautiful and majestic then as its
best specimens of the present day ; yet I saw in the museum
here, and also at Naples, a male and female statue of a
baboon, man-sized, in a sitting posture, cut from granite, of
unknown antiquity, found side by side with a perfect specimen of a man and woman, seeming to indicate that the sculptor intended to hint that they were of the same race. Perhaps Darwinianism is not as young a philosophy as we have
been taught to regard it. The mere fact, however, that some
old Greek got such a notion in his head is no argument either
for or against the theory. The lessons taught by the museums
of antiquity here and in other places are, that all the relics of
our race indicate man as the same animal in all ages. The
man of 4000 years ago had the same pleasures and passions
as his descendant of to-day. The women were as fair, the
children as lovely, the babes as helpless. They had the same
toys ; they played chess and checkers 4000 years ago ; they
gambled and got drunk; they committed the same crimes and
had the same charities. The probability is that we are much
inferior to them in some of the essential elments of human
greatness, and that they were far below us in many scientific
discoveries.

We visited the ruins of the second great city of ancient At-
tica, Eleusis, about twelve miles from Athens. We followed
very nearly the old sacred road by the groves of Daphne,
before alluded to. On the way we had a view of the bay
Eleusis and Salamis where the great naval battles were fought,
and the Persians were so signally defeated 480 B. C. The

spot in the opposite mountain, called to this day Xerxes' seat,. is pointed out, and is said to be the place where he had his throne erected and where he sat to witness the battle which ended so disastrously to his arms. Marathon and Salamis were two of the world's decisive battles. We enjoy to-day the benefits of these heroic strugles for Western civilization. Had the result been favorable to the Persians the probability is that the manners and customs of the East, including harems and seraglios, would now exist in England and America.

I would like to say more of Athens and of Greece but my letters are becoming too prolix. I must curtail them. The ruins of Eleusis are only surpassed by those of the Acropolis. Excavations made within a few months have exhumed the remains of a great city. I found a coin very well preserved among these ruins. I have no doubt it is over two thousand years old. I quietly put it in my pocket and said nothing about it.

Of the future of Athens I cannot say much. I can see but little hope of any great advance from its present state. The government is very poor and the land sterile. What was spoken of by the ancients as a fertile plain, would not now be considered worth cultivating for farming purposes in America. The celebrated olive groves are still here. They show trees said to be from six hundred to one thousand years old, but they scarcely yield fruit enough to pay for gathering.

The present condition of the currency of Greece is in a deplorable state. Gold is at a premium of thirty-three per cent. They cut up their bank notes to make change. The king has just left his palace for the country. We were per-mitted to visit it and were much pleased with the courtesy shown us by the attendants. It is a fairly good dwelling house, much surpassed by hundreds of private dwellings in Philadelphia and New York.

XXXIII.

CONSTANTINOPLE—EMBARKATION ON THE CONTINENT—
BANDAGED BABES AND EVOLUTION—SITE OF TROY—THE
NARROW DARDANELLES—STAMBOUL—DIRT AND DOGS—
PECULIAR FIRE REGULATIONS—MOHAMMEDAN DISLIKE OF
REPAIRS—CRUELTY TO MEN AND KINDNESS TO BRUTES—
ENGLISH AS SPOKEN BY THE GUIDES—THREE SUNDAYS A
WEEK — SULTAN'S DAY—LADIES AND EUNUCHS BACK-
SHISH — A SELF-RIGHTEOUS MOHAMMEDAN'S PRAYER—
SUPERSTITIONS—THE METEMPSYCHOSIS—STREET SCENES
IN CONSTANTINOPLE.

CONSTANTINOPLE, June, 1888.

After a rough voyage over the Ægean Sea, in a crowded
ship, full of fleas, Turks, Greeks, Armenians and a few English and Americans, most of whom, always excepting the fleas,
were very seasick, I found myself safely moored in the Bosphorus, directly opposite the Golden Horn, and under the
garden walls of the late Sultan's seraglio. Constantinople
from the ship presented a very pretty appearance.   The beautiful green hills, the harems with their luxuriant gardens, the
old walls, towers, mosques and minarets, together with the
soft blue sky and balmy, bracing air, was in pleasing contrast
with the white dust, dry sultry air and barren hills of Athens.
To go by sea from Athens to Constantinople takes about two
days.   We were unfortunate in encountering a strong head
wind, which not only delayed our arrival but caused the ship
to roll very much.   Of the two or three hundred second-class
passengers, not one was in European dress.   Their costumes
were as varied as their nationalities.   I particularly noticed
their heavy clothing.   They all wore woolen fabrics and dressed warmer than we would in midwinter.   Some had suits of
sheep skin with the wool next to their own skins ; others had
great overcoats of goat skin, with the long hair out.   They
wore great turbans and fezes, loose frocks tied in loops around
their ankles, and had long red, yellow and green sashes wound
around their waists, in which they carried ugly knives.   There
was not a new suit in the whole party.   They ate nothing
during the voyage but bread which they always carried about
their persons.   They herded together like sheep and lay cuddled up in their big cloaks, or sat cross-legged on the deck,
smoking long fancy pipes.   The place they selected on entering the ship they kept till the voyage was over.   Some of them
never moved for two days except to cut off a slice of bread for

a meal. On arriving they were very boisterous, and for a full hour kept possession of the gangway of the ship while, with their greasy and stinking luggage, they disembarked.

Continental ports, as a rule, have no docks. The ships do not come up to the wharf, but anchor a short distance from the shore. Small row-boats are in waiting at the wharves, which, for fixed fees, convey the passengers and luggage to and from the ship. In stormy weather it is very inconvenient and often dangerous for ladies and nervous persons. I noticed among the crowd what I had seen in Naples, babies in the warmest weather tightly bandaged in swaddling clothes like the Indian papooses, with arms and legs tightly bound up so that no part of the babe could move except the mouth and eyes. The Darwinians say it was a discovery made by our monkey ancestors, by which they straightened their little monkeys and made them grow up as men. They also point out two very old pieces of statuary in granite, found in Egypt, of prehistoric age, representing a man-sized male and female baboon, in a sitting posture which, they say, were worshiped as the fathers of our race. But we have the stubborn fact that the past five thousand years, so far as the remains of man and his works are concerned, have neither improved nor degenerated his form, feature, or intelligence. The men of Egypt, Nineveh and Troy were just as we find the man of to-day. Perhaps a few thousand years hence, when our civilization shall be broken up, and our religion has either been perfected or destroyed, the relics of buried London or New York will be dug up and be exhibited like those of Egypt and Troy, and our times will be spoken of as either an age of barbarism, or, as we speak of the age of gold. But I must stop moralizing or I will not be able to say anything about Constantinople.

Everything around the city is intensely interesting, even its approaches. Just before entering the Dardanelles we passed the site of Homer's Troy. Our ship went very near the shore. There was Mount Ida and the hills from which Ajax hurled rocks that,

> " Five strong men in this degenerate age
> Could scarcely lift.

Further back were the hills upon which Juno and Venus sat to view the fight. On the opposite side is the Thracean shore where the bodies of the slain were strewn and which

> " Devouring dogs and hungry vultures tore,"

How soon one of our ironclad ships of war would have leveled the " impregnable walls !" and with what ease could we have bombarded the Grecian camp in Europe, and at the same time shelled the city of Troy in Asia.

As we sailed up the Dardanelles I was surprised to see

how narrow the channel is which divides Europe from Asia.
After passing through the Dardanelles, however, it is necessary to cross the Sea of Marmora before reaching the city of
Constantinople. The scenery around the city is undoubtedly
very fine, but the city itself is more beautiful when viewed
from a little distance than when seen within its walls. While
it is the dirtiest and worst paved city in the world (I speak
only of the old part of the town), it is comparatively a healthy
place. The first thing I was struck with was the multitude
of dogs. The city is literally full of them. They lie by
dozens in the streets. The citizens never disturb or hurt
them. If two or three feel inclined to take a nap on the sidewalk, rather than disturb the innocent slumbers of worthless
curs, the people get out of their way and walk in the street.
The dogs have divided the city into districts, and have organized themselves into tribes. Each tribe has its own district. If, by chance, or a desire to rove like old Sampson
among the Philistines, some handsome young pup wanders
beyond the limits of his district all the dogs of the invaded
territory rush upon him and, if not reinforced by his own
tribe, they will kill him in a few minutes. If within reach
of assistance, a general war between the tribes is the result,
till the citizens or police interfere and drive each tribe to its
own particular street. I saw a poor young hound suddenly
pounced upon by at least twenty infuriated whelps. He
yelled and cried most piteously. A workman ran among the
pack and at the risk of being torn to pieces rescued the poor
indiscreet wretch and carried him tenderly in his arms to his
own tribe. I could understand this affection for the dogs if
they were well-bred and beautiful like the dogs of our country ; but I did not, among the thousands of the city, see one
well-bred dog. They are the commonest mongrels, but few
lop-eared, and mostly wolfish looking curs.

The city, in the old district of Stamboul, is largely built
of wood and is subject to great fires, yet they have no municipal fire department. All the city government does is to
maintain a few towers for watchmen to give the alarm when
a fire breaks out. Then the private fire companies, consisting
of ten or fifteen men turn out with a portable engine without
wheels, about half the size of the old one stored away as a
curiosity at the Lazaretto. They are carried by four men
who rush through the streets yelling fire ! fire ! as loud as
they can scream. When they arrive at the scene of conflagra-
tion they coolly look at the flames till the owner makes a bargain with them for their services, or the proprietors of adjoining houses secure their aid to save their homes from destruction.

It is a peculiarity of the Mohammedans never to repair anything. They build beautiful palaces and let them fall into dilapidation for the want of attention. When they get too leaky for habitation they abandon them for new ones They never repair their houses and only, from necessity, put in a new pane of glass. The same may be said of the streets and bridges.

While the Turks are remarkably kind to domestic animals, birds and insects, they have very little regard for their fellow-men. They put saddles on the backs of men and burden them with loads we would hesitate to put upon a horse. I hired a porter for forty cents to take my luggage from the boat to my hotel. It consisted of seven pieces. To my surprise he put on his saddle and had a comrade to pile the whole lot upon his back, which he carried a half mile without a grunt. They carry great loads of marketing and coal and wood about the streets for sale. The only nations of the East not represented in Constantinople are China and Japan. Notwithstanding the Babel of tongues and general mixture of nations, one feels more at home here than in any other continental city. English is spoken in the hotels, and French is used in almost all the shops.

The Sultan goes from the old seraglio to his new palace, through the city, once a year. It happened that the time fixed for the journey was the first Friday after our arrival. Business on that day was suspended along the proposed route. To make the streets smooth for His Majesty's carriage, gravel was hauled and spread over them three or four inches thick. As a consequence the tramway could not be used. I proposed to my guide to take a ride on the tramway. His answer was, "The tramway no walk to-day; this is Sultan's day; burn much powder gun" This is a sample of the English spoken by the guides. He meant that because of the Sultan's journey over the street the tramway would not run and that the day would be celebrated by the firing of cannon.

They have three Sundays here. The Mohammedan Sabbath, (Friday); the Jewish Sabbath, (Saturday), and the Christian Sunday. Sunday is more generally observed here than in other European cities, except in Scotland. The population of the city is fully one million, one-half of whom are Christians. There are about 100,000 Jews; the balance are Mohammedans. The Jews close their shops on Saturday. On Sunday nearly one-half of the stores were shut. This speaks well for the Christians of Constantinople.

For some reason the Sultan saw proper to disappoint his people in making his journey through the city. The streets had been prepared at great expense and soldiers were

stationed at all the cross streets. The scene was very much like
the crowd on Chestnut Street when General Grant returned
from his trip around the world, except that the costumes were
as many as the people. The ladies of the harem passed in
carriages, guarded by strapping big black eunuchs on horseback, in gaudy uniforms. We were permitted to peep at the
fair ones in the carriages, but staring is not permitted under
penalty of the whiplash of the eunuch across your face. Some
of the ladies were as white as milk, others bronze and some
almost black. The Sultan's mother rode in a carriage alone
and amused herself by throwing small coins to the crowd
of beggars that ran after her with outstretched hands crying
"backshish, backshish." When a piece of money was thrown
out there was a general scramble and rough and tumble struggle for the coin. Some great personage, on a white horse,
with a purse in his hand, would take from his wallet a small
coin, hold it up between his fingers, and when the crowd
would surround his horse so that he could not move, he would
bestow the coin on one of the crowd selected by himself, and
then gallop off with a look of great satisfaction, only to repeat
the stupid farce again. All the alms bestowed with so much
display did not exceed ten dollars.

They have no hospitals or almshouses in Constantinople.
The blind, halt and lame must depend upon private charity
or starve. They feed dogs and birds, but let their own helpless ones want.

They have a Mosque dedicated to pigeons. On entering
it, the worshiper purchases a small quantity of grain, kept on
hand for the purpose, which he scatters on the floor. Immediately it will be devoured by thousands of pigeons which live
and breed in the Mosque. They believe that pigeons, doves
and ducks are possessed of the souls of the dead. They say
every time the birds drink and raise their heads to swallow
the water, they are thanking God. They also believe that
the beautiful white water fowl, so plentiful in the Bosphorus,
are possessed of the souls of the unfortunate women of the
harem that have been sewed up in sacks and cast into the
water. On the outside of the Mosques are places for ablutions.
The devout Mohammedan always washes his hands, face and
feet before entering the Mosque. As he washes, he prays.
I saw a very self-righteous looking old Turk at his ablution
in front of St. Sophia. I asked my dragoman to translate his
prayer. As near as I can remember it ran as follows: "O Allah!
I wash my hands, cleanse thou my heart. I wash my feet,
may my walk before thee be clean ; and if I have wronged
any man help me to restore to him that which I have unjustly
taken with five-fold increase, and if I have unjustly scourged

any man, may the stripes of retribution fall on my own back.
Now, O Allah, I wash my face, may it be clean enough for
thee to look upon in the Great Day. ''

The Mohammedans are very superstitious. They believe
in sorcery, witchcraft and the evil eye. In most of the Mosques
they have talismans hung from the ceiling to keep out
bad spirits. The ostrich egg is believed to be a sovereign
amulet against the Evil One. They are hanging from the
roofs of nearly all the Mosques. In the Mohammedan quarters you will see hung over the door of some dilapidated shanty
a piece of brimstone, garlic, and a vial of water, as a charm
against fire. In a word, I can give no better picture of the
Stamboul district of Constantinople than to refer my readers
to the description of Bagdad and Damascus in the Arabian
Nights. Seated on his bench at a street corner you will see
the cobbler pegging away at an old shoe and singing as he
sews ; the barber with his kit, shaving a customer on an old
stool in the street ; old Alla Baba with an air of dignity, and
Cogia Hassin waiting on the three Calenders, sons of kings
and the fine ladies of Bagdad. Here you will see the palace of
rich Sinbad the Sailor, yonder the beggar leaning against his
wall grieving that heaven has not favored him with wealth and
luxury. A little stretch of imagination will reproduce in the
street the old magician offering to give '' new lamps for old
ones. '' You will see men leading horses loaded with water
in leather bags made by stripping the hide from a yearling
calf, with the neck as a spout and the legs tied up to hold the
water. This is peddled about the streets for sale. It was to
bottles of this kind that our Saviour referred when he said new
wine should not be put into old bottles. When the hide is
green it will stretch and make room for fermentation, but when
the leather becomes old the slightest unusual pressure will
cause it to burst. I will say more of Constantinople in my
next letter.

XXXIV.

CONSTANTINOPLE TO BUCHAREST—SCRAPS OF HISTORY PICKED
UP ON THE GROUND—NEW ROME—DUKES AND COUNTS—
THE HIPPODROME—RIOT OF NIKA—THE BLUE AND THE
GREEN—A ROMAN DECREE LIKE OUR XVTH AMENDMENT
—THE DIFFERENCE BETWEEN LIKE AND SIMILAR—STO-
RIES OF IGNORANT GUIDES—VALUABLE MISSIONARY WORK
—THE RUINS OF TIME—AN OLD PROPHECY NEARLY FUL-
FILLED—THE DUNGEON WITHOUT AN ECHO—THE HAND-
WRITING UPON THE WALL—KEEP YOUR MOUTH SHUT—
THE GOLDEN HORN—ARCHERY—WINTER PALACE—SUL-
TAN'S LARGE FAMILY—CRESCENT AND CROSS—A DAY IN
ASIA—CHALCEDON—ST. EUPHEMIA—LOAVES AND FISHES
—BAZAARS—THE BOSPHORUS—HELLESPONT—BLACK SEA
—THE BALKANS—AN OLD MAID.

BUCHAREST, ROUMANIA, June, 1888.

After two weeks' rest at Constantinople, we concluded to
visit two former Turkish provinces, Bulgaria and Roumania.
Within a few years these provinces will, perhaps, be the
theatre of a tremendous struggle on the part of Russia for the
final possession of Constantinople. Before attempting to describe my journey, however, I would like to say a few words
more about Constantinople. It is remarkable what a firm impression little scraps of history, picked up upon the ground,
make upon the mind. Among other things, I learned that
" Constantinople " is not the official name of the city. When
it was founded by Constantine, he, by a most solemn decree,
christened it " The City of New Rome." A beautiful pillar
was erected to commemorate the dedication with the name
just mentioned inscribed upon it in letters of brass. The
common people, however, called it the city of Constantine—
(Constantinople) and for fifteen hundred years it has been
known by no other name.

It was Constantine that created the titles now so common
all over Europe, of Count and Duke. Count means a major-
general ; Duke means a general one degree lower. They are
now hereditary titles and mean nothing.

As I carefully looked at and walked around the oval space
in the center of the city, formerly occupied by the circus, and
now called the amphitheatre, my mind reverted to the terrible
scenes here enacted in the days of Justinian, during the riot of
Nika. The circus was divided into competing companies, one
wore green, the other blue. The excitement ran so high that

the whole city became divided into two bitter factions, the Greens and the Blues. The Blues occupied the same relation to the Court that Tammany now does to the city government of New York. No matter what crimes they committed they could not be convicted. As is always the case, when the law fails to redress wrongs, the Greens determined to be their own avengers and came into the Hippodrome with daggers concealed under their mantles and, in one night, they killed three thousand of the Blues. The Blues appealed to the Emperor who issued a decree which reads very much like the XVth Amendment to the Constitution of the United States. It declares that "all wrongs shall be duly redressed by the courts of law, without regard to condition or *color*." The Blues then commenced the terrible riot of Nika, which means *conquer*, and nearly destroyed the city. It was during this riot that the Church of St. Sophia was burned. It was rebuilt at a cost of $5,000,000. Before the riot could be quelled old Belsarius killed 30,000 of the rioters within the circuit of the Hippodrome.

The religious factions of the city were as bitter in their hatred of each other as the sportsmen. They were divided between the doctrines of Athanasius and Arius. Great volumns were written, expensive counsels were held and bloody battles were fought to settle the difference between the meaning of the words *similar* and *like*, (Homoousian and Homoiousian.)

Some idea of the wealth of the city may be formed by the amount of the spoils which are divided among its captors in its first siege. Gibbon says the spoils amounted to more than seven times the entire revenue of England, yet from this disaster she completely recovered.

Some of the stories told by ignorant guides are amusingly ridiculous. Among other wonderful things about St. Sophia, they tell you that its lofty dome can be seen of a clear day one hundred miles away on the Black Sea, whereas Mount Blanc, 15,000 feet high, can barely be seen from Geneva, only fifty miles away. The church would have to be four thousand feet high to be seen one hundred miles at sea. Mount Olympus is only one hundred and ten miles from Constantinople, and can only be seen by ascending some high place.

Constantinople at one time was a flourishing silk-making city. A *christian* missionary *stole* the art from China. He brought the eggs in a hollow cane. This proved to the Greeks very valuable missionary work.

Nothing is more impressed upon the mind of the traveler than the complete destruction by time of all the monuments of human glory. When we read the glowing accounts of the

city of Constantinople in the days of Justinian ; its splendid
edifices, mighty walls, golden gates and beautiful palaces,
gardens and parks ; its amphitheatre, where the Greens and
Blues contended and quarreled for imperial favor ; its cisterns
of a thousand columns, viaducts, baths and towers, we naturally expect to find some remains of so much vaunted splendor.
We might as well look upon the decayed bones of an exhumed
graveyard for the manly beauty and graceful forms and faces
once possessed by those whose remains are buried there, as to
expect to find many evidences of the former greatness of this
more than dead and buried city. The walls are in ruins.
The Golden Gate has been walled up by the roughest of Turkish masonry. The Happy Gate is a miserable hole in a pile
of old bricks. The seven towers around the Golden Gate are
still standing, but greatly dilapidated. The cistern of a
thousand and one columns is filled up three columns high, and
is used as a place for spinning silk. The Forum, once the
pride of the city, has been arched over and is filled with bazaars. The amphitheatre has been filled up fifteen feet and is
not now more than one-fifth of its former size. St. Sophia's
Church has been converted into a Mohammedan mosque.
That the worshipers may face Mecca, they have built out one
side of the altar further than the other and placed the matting
of the floor diagonally across the building. Every trace of
Christian decoration has been destroyed. Even the mosaic
work representing Christ and the Holy Virgin has been painted
over or covered. When I visited the church it was desecrated
by being converted into a pigeon roost. The Golden Gate
was walled up because of an old prophecy that the enemy
would enter by that gate. The Russians were very near ful-
filling the prophecy seven years ago. From the main tower I
could plainly see with the naked eye their breastworks within
half a mile, apparently, of the Golden Gate. The seven
towers, at the Golden Gate, and the connecting walls enclose
six or eight acres of ground. The enclosure has been used as
a prison for political offenders. Several Sultans and many
Viziers have been murdered here. The walls are covered
with inscriptions cut in the stone by some of the prisoners.
Under the main tower is what is called the "Echoless Dungeon." So called because, no matter how loud the cry of the
tortured prisoner, his voice never reached the surface. The
history will never be written of the thousands of poor wretches
who have suffered and died in this horrid place.

　　　Where the Roman Emperors had their harbor for ships of
war, within the city walls, vegetable gardens are now cultivated, the product of which is carried every morning, on the
backs of the poor farmers, into the city for sale.

In the Stamboul district no repairs, either to the streets or houses, have been made for years.

Notwithstanding the bad government of the city, its natural advantages are so great that it is still one of the most lovely spots of Europe. The new part of the city, on the opposite side of the Golden Horn, is very much like other European cities. The buildings are good and the streets well paved. The Turks seem to realize their fate. The hand-writing is on the wall. They know their lease of power in Europe is nearly ended. Most of the Mohammedans now bury their dead on the other side of the Bosphorus, in Asia.

It is very dangerous for a foreigner to speak disrespect-fully of the Sultan. There are several instances where an in-discreet remark at the table, or in the presence of servants or housekeepers, has resulted in a request to leave the city. It is useless to protest. When such a request comes, even your Minister cannot help you, as the proof is preserved and pro-duced that the hospitality of the city has been violated. In such cases the offender is not permitted to pass out of the city by the " Happy Gate. " He must pass by some other portal, and is escorted to his ship to prevent assassination.

The Golden Horn runs from the Bosphorus about six miles to a point completely dividing the city into two great divis-ions, Stamboul and Pera. As you go up the Horn it gets smaller and finally ends beyond the city limit. Hence the old saying, "Going out at the little end of the horn. "

The Mohammedans, like the Christians, bury their dead and never disturb their final resting place. I saw a funeral in the old graveyard outside the city. It looked very much like one of our own funeral scenes. Evidences, however, of super-stition are found all around their burial places, such as pin-ning or tying small pieces of a sick person's clothing to the tomb or railing around some saintly grave, by which they believe the sickness is cured.

Just outside the city is a large field with several round marble pillars upon which are cut the names of several of the Sultan's courtiers and counsellors. I took it for a burial ground, but on inquiry I found it was the Sultan's field for archery practice. He and his court visit it once a year, and the best shot is rewarded by a pillar planted to his memory with his name and the date the famous shot was made. No matter how far he comes from the bull's eye, all that is required is that he shall be nearer than any of his competitors ; so some one of his courtiers is sure to have a pillar of honor every year.

The Sultan's winter palace is a beautiful white marble building erected at the water's edge of the Bosphorus. It covers several acres of ground. His summer palace is about

a mile further northward on the hill and overlooks the whole
city.   It is said his elder brother and the true heir to the
throne is confined in the winter palace a prisoner of State.   He
was Sultan at the time the Russians were before the city, but
was afterwards deposed in favor of his younger brother, the
present Sultan.   It is also said that of all the courtiers concerned in the overthrow of the former Sultan, not one is now
alive.   They were all *rewarded* by being sent on embassays
and errands of State, but by *some fortuitous accident*, died before
the time for return arrived.   Thus the Sultan has no powerful
friends around him.

The Sultan's household consists of over ten thousand
persons, including wives, children, eunuchs, slaves and servants.   In this respect he is a greater man than Brigham
Young was in the days of his greatest glory.   It is hard to understand how the corrupt teaching of the Crescent has so completely triumphed in the East over the pure doctrines of the
Cross.   The Koran undoubtedly contains some good moral
principles, borrowed from the Bible, but the life of Mahomet
and the doctrines of his religion are wanting in purity and
clouded with superstition.   The great majority, however, of
the Mohammedans, of Turkey, are sincere in their faith.   They
are sober, industrious and honest.   Their belief in predestination and fatalism has dwarfed all their best energies, and must
eventually make them succumb to a race of broader and bolder
views.

Before leaving Constantinople we spent a day in Asia.
We crossed the Bosphorus to the site of ancient Chalcedon.
Nothing of the city remains but a stone fountain said to be
two thousand five hundred years old.   Here we hired a carriage and made an excursion of about twelve miles to the top
of the mountain Bourgourlu (pronounced *Boorgoorloo*).   The
crown of this hill was the former centre of the city.   The
splendid church of St. Euphemia stood on the summit.   It was
one of the most magnificent cathedrals in the world and could
comfortably seat four thousand worshipers.   The fourth general council was held in this church.   Six hundred and thirty
bishops sat in its Nave.   Now not a stone or even a mark remains.   Chalcedon was called the "City of the Blind," because the founders had not seen the site of Constantinople on
the opposite side of the Bosphorus.   Of the Great Walled City,
full of palaces, monuments and magnificent edifices, not a stone
remains.   Great trees are growing where its palaces stood and
sheep graze over the site of St. Euphemia.   It is hard to believe a city ever occupied these cultivated fields and natural
woods.   The road was very rough and stony.   The soil seemed
very much like that of Bethel, in Delaware county.   There

were cherry, peach, plum and apple trees in abundance. If it had not been for the turbans and Turkish costumes, the scenery would have been quite homelike until we got high enough to see the mountains on the South and the city on the West. Here we saw the genuine Asiatic buffalo working like an ox. By the side of the road we saw a peddler, in full Oriental costume, selling cooked loaves and fishes. We could understand the Scriptural scene of Christ feeding the multitude better than before. From my observation of Oriental manners, I am convinced that the habits and dresses of the people of Asia are to-day very much as they were in the days of our Saviour.

From the summit of Bourgourlu the prospect is most charming. Snow-capped Olympus can be plainly seen, though one hundred miles away. One of the high mountains of Asia one hundred and sixty miles to the east, was plainly visible. All the islands of the Sea of Marmora, the Dardanelles, the Golden Horn, the whole city of Constantinople and the beautiful Bosphorus, from Marmora to the Black Sea, could be distinctly seen. I do not remember ever having witnessed a finer view. I thought the view from Lycabettus, over Athens, was the finest I ever saw, but this far surpasses it.

The world-renowned Bazaars of Constantinople occupy the site of the old Forum, which has been arched over in the roughest manner and converted into small shops, where everything of Asiatic or Oriental manufacture may be bought. It is impossible to enter without buying something, no matter how firmly you may have resolved not to do it. The goods are displayed in most fascinating forms. The prices seem low, but are generally about one-third higher than the same goods can be bought at the stores. I priced a silver bracelet and pin with the Sultan's monogram ; to get rid of the merchant I offered him just one-half of his asking price. He refused my offer with a gesture of profound disgust. I smiled and went on, congratulating myself on my success. After I had gone half a square I felt a pull at my arm. The man was there with the articles. He said his children were starving and I would have to take the goods at my own price. I could not go back on my offer. I had firmly resolved on entering not to purchase anything, but I came out several dollars poorer than I went in.

It is somewhat troublesome to enter the city. I had to have the Turkish Consul at Athens give me the necessary papers. Even then the authorities hesitated about admitting my wife and daughter. I also found that it required permission from the American Consul to get out. I presented my passport and got leave to go to Roumania. I then had to call on the Roumanian Consul and get leave to enter that kingdom.

I then presented my papers to the officers at the city gate and had endorsed upon my passport that I had leave to go out by the "Happy Gate." So after many annoyances and much red tape I left Constantinople by the good ship Apollo for Varna, on the Black Sea.

The trip up the Bosphorus was very interesting. It has been the subject of much praise from abler pens. I will not attempt to describe its gardens, palaces and harems. We passed the Hellespont, where Xerxes built his bridge of boats, and where Leander swam to kiss his love. I can only say that I have seen other places just as beautiful, and that I was a little disappointed. Perhaps I expected too much. The Bosphorus is about fifteen miles long and, at places, very narrow. The fact that we gaze upon Asia on the right and Europe on the left for these fifteen miles adds to the interest of the voyage. Upon entering the Black Sea, the temperature fell fifteen or twenty degrees. It is called the Black Sea from the dark shade of its water, caused by the absence of sunshine. The sky is generally overcast and the air damp and chilly. It requires about thirty hours by ship to go from Constantinople to Varna. The sea was rough and most of the passengers very sick. At Varna we took the cars and passed through Bulgaria to Rustchuck, on the Danube. There we crossed the river and again took the cars for Bucharest. We spent a very interesting day at Bucharest. I was surprised to find Bulgaria and Roumania such fertile countries. I never saw better pasture lands or wheat fields. It reminded me very much of the prairie lands ot Illinois. There are, however, no farm houses. The lands are tilled by peasants who live in miserable little huts, or in villages. Our route lay through a spur of the Balkan Mountains and was very picturesque, of course not comparable with the Swiss or Italian Alpine scenery, but very beautiful and entertaining. The tops of the mountains seemed leveled off and crowned with a wall. There were no crags or lofty peaks. The scenery of these mountains is soft and has a soothing rather than a stirring influence upon the beholder.

In my judgment Turkey lost her most fertile territory when she surrendered her sovereignty over Bulgaria and Roumania and, if not torn to pieces in the impending war, these two principalities will soon become rich and prosperous.

Our hotel here is one of the best I have found in Europe ; very few in America are better. I met an English lady, of doubtful age, on the trip from Varna. We had met at Constantinople, where she had set her heart upon capturing a young American traveler. She spoke of the beauties of a moonlight sail on the Bosphorus ; said she would not be afraid to go if *any* young gentleman would take her ; she thought it would be *so* romantic. The young fellow while very polite, would not take the hint, but constantly and adroitly turned the subject. I thought I would inquire about the young gentleman as I found her now alone. I asked her where she had parted with him. "Oh," said she, "I found him so awfully stupid I shook him off and left him at Constantinople. I conversed with him for a whole week and he never could get higher than the weather."

XXXV.

BUCHAREST TO ZURICH—FEMALE MASONS—GREAT WHEAT
FIELDS—UP THE DANUBE—A FEUDAL CASTLE—BELGRADE
—BUDA-PESTH—A SPLENDID CITY OF HALF A MILLION
PEOPLE—ON TO VIENNA—A REJUVENATED CITY—THE
CHANGES OF FIFTEEN YEARS — BEAUTIFUL SUBURBS —
SCHONBRUN—KAHLENBURG—VIENNA TO INNSBRUCK—THE
AUSTRIAN TYROL—OLD CHURCH AT INNSBRUCK—A RIP
VAN WINKLE SLEEP — OVER THE ALPS WESTWARD —
SOURCES OF EUROPE'S THREE GREATEST RIVERS.

ZURICH, SWITZERLAND, June, 1888.

The journey from Constantinople, over the Black Sea, through Bulgaria and Roumania and up the Danube as far as Belgrade, is hard to describe. It differs from any scenery I have yet seen. Bucharest, the capital of Roumania, is a beautiful city of 300,000 inhabitants, well built after the Parisian style, with broad, well-paved streets, and a fine park within easy walking distance from the centre of the city. It is full of delightful gardens, fragrant with roses. French is spoken in nearly all the stores, but the costumes of the common people are Russian. The Russian language seems to be the native tongue of the people. The names upon the signs are peculiar to the place. The family name is given first : as Smith John, Jones Peter, etc. Some of the stores are equal to those of London and New York. I found another of the best hotels in Europe here. I saw women here not only making mortar and digging cellars, but actually using the trowel and doing carpenter work.

From Bucharest we went by rail to Turn-Severin, on the Danube. The route is through some of the richest farm lands on the continent, but they are flat and alluvial, very much like our Western prairies. While the wheat fields are very large, sometimes containing fifty acres, no labor-saving

machinery seems to be used. Labor is so abundant and cheap
as to render improved plows, rakes, mowers and reapers un-
neccessary. I met an agent of the McCormick reaper at Buda-
Pesth. He says it is impossible to introduce their mowers
and reapers here. All the grain is moved by hand in sacks.
It is wonderful how rapidly a cargo of wheat can be put on
board or discharged from a ship.

At Turn-Severin we embarked for a two days' trip up the
Danube. I have gone up the Hudson, the Rhine, and down
the St. Lawrence through the Thousand Isles and over the
rapids ; I have seen Lakes George and Champlain and the
mountain scenery of Pennsylvania, Virginia and Vermont ;
but I have never seen anything finer than the scenery of the
Danube from the Iron Gate up to Belgrade. The river varies
from a few yards, through the mountains, to several miles in
width over the plains. Through some of the mountain gorges
the river seems narrower than it really is because of the precipitous height of the apparently overhanging crags and lofty
mountain peaks. As it winds and twists in its tortuous channel it looks like a succession of little lakes with no outlet.
The boat seems about to butt against some rocky cliff, when
suddenly it wheels about and apparently plunges into another
pond of fifty or a hundred yards in length and, seemingly,
hardly wide enough for the boat to pass. There is an old
Roman road along the water's edge cut into the mountain side
and hewn out of the solid rock, supported here and there by
abutments of masonry, through the entire mountain pass.
Withal the air is balmy and moist, so much so as to cause
green shrubbery to grow in profusion upon the rocky sides of
the mountains wherever there is a fissure or crack in the stone
large enough to permit the fibrous roots to enter and hold the
shrubs and vines. After a few miles the scenery softens, the
crags disappear and gradually we enter a rich, undulating and
highly cultivated country. Then follows a vast marshy district known as the Valley of the Danube, said to be poisoned
with malaria. The river is now very high. At places it
seemed to me to be ten or fifteen miles wide. The ground is
all alluvial below Belgrade and is a great country for grazing.
I saw vast herds of cattle, horses, and immense flocks of sheep
pasturing on the meadows. We passed what seemed to be
groves of willow trees with the water half way up their trunks.
One of the best preserved feudal castles in Europe is seen a
few miles below Belgrade. It covers about thirty acres of
ground. The walls are all perfect. I counted twenty-eight
fine towers. I have no doubt the old baron who built it believed he would live forever in safety within its walls.

Belgrade is a very old town but so much like all the

mediæval cities of Europe as to make a description of it tiresome. It has its old walls, gates, churches, narrow crooked
streets, towers and dungeons, together with its legends and
local stories of tragedies and romances common to all the old
towns of the continent. We stayed there one night.

Next morning we crossed the river and took the cars for
Buda-Pesth, the capital of Hungary. Here we were again surprised. We found Hungary one of the finest farming countries
of the world. A vast rich plain, covered with great wheat
fields and pasture lands, but with no fences or farm houses.
The land is cultivated by peasants. Both sexes work alike
in the fields. The city of Buda-Pesth is one of the finest and
richest in Europe. Like Chicago, it is the great grain centre
of the continent. Everybody seems rich. The streets, parks
and buildings, public and private, are kept in the best of order.
One would say upon a casual glance that it was a new city.
A little inspection, however, will reveal the fact that it has
been built upon the site of a very old one. It has a population of half a million. The river Danube runs through it. Its
streets are from fifty to one hundred and fifty feet wide. It is
surrounded with villas like Rome. The river is walled on
both sides, and has a parapet or bulwark four feet high and a
splendid wide promenade on each side along the water front.
Then a well-paved carriage-way, and palatial residences, hotels
and restaurants looking down upon the beautiful river as it
sweeps rapidly through the city. The river is spanned by a
bridge one-third of a mile long, built on an exact model of the
Brooklyn bridge over the East river at New York. On the
opposite side of the river are the public building, palaces,
gardens, barracks and castles. The hill upon which these
buildings stand is seven hundred and ninety-three feet high
and overlooks the city and country many miles around. At
its foot is a fine natural hot spring with Turkish baths. The
palace gardens are six hundred feet above the level of the
river, looking down upon the town. The people are very
fond of music. The concert hall will hold two thousand persons and is a very beautiful building. We attended a concert
there given in aid of the overflowed peasant villages, by the
world-renowned choir of Vienna. I am not much of a mu-
sician, but I think the singing was the finest I have ever
heard. In a word, Buda-Pesth is a splendid city and cannot
be properly described in the short limit I must give it.

From Buda-Pesth we went by rail to Vienna. I found
my old hotel, the Metropole, so full we could not be accommodated without taking inferior rooms. Our hotels at Bucharest and Buda-Pesth were so good they had spoiled us and
nothing but the best accommodations could now satisfy our

cultivated taste for hotel life. Much to the disgust of the
proprietor we left his house and took up our quarters at the
Hotel Continental, a spacious and well-kept house. I find
Vienna entirely rejuvenated since 1873. I visited it during
the World's Fair of that year. I would hardly know the
place now, so great have been the changes. I am free to say
that it is now what Paris then was : one of the loveliest cities
in the world. The rotunda, or main building of the great
Exposition, is still standing in the Prater and looks as fresh
and well preserved as when the exhibition closed fifteen years
ago. It is still used as an exhibition building and is filled
with the most attractive productions of Austria. It looks
about as well as when the World's Fair was in full course.
While the old city has nearly disappeared the land-marks are
still there ; the old Cathedral, with its tall stone spire ; the
King's Palace and Capuchin vaults where the ashes of Austrian royalty repose ; and the bulwarks of the old city can
still be found, and to one who has seen Vienna twenty years
ago, the picture of the old city may be easily restored ; but
one visiting it for the first time could form no idea of what it
was when its population was only a hundred and twenty or
thirty thousand. It now has a population approaching one
million. The Danube has been straightened, walled and
bridged. It is subjected to great overflows, to prevent which
the channel has been very much improved. The city in 1873,
and for several hundred years before, kept her commercial intercourse with the river by means of a canal which runs through
the town. Now the city has extended to the banks of the
Danube. The principal bridge is nearly a mile long. It has
been built since 1873. It is the full width of the street and
paved from one end to the other. The river is banked and
walled so as to allow a rise of twenty feet without an overflow.
The city is full of new monuments and statuary in marble and
bronze. It contains, however, nothing finer than Canova's
marble group of Theseus and the Minotaur, which is preserved
and exhibited here.

The great charm of Vienna life is its multitude of re-
courses for amusement and pleasure. Like Paris, the people
live in the streets, parks and cafes. The Prater is within a
few minutes' walk from the busiest part of the city, and is
one of the most delightful resorts for refreshment, amusement
or pleasure in the world. In this respect it is much superior
to the Bois de Boulogne of Paris. It is laid out with exquisite
taste ; it has one course in a straight line four miles long. It
is beautifully shaded, full of exquisite drives for carriages or
horseback exercise, enchanting promenades, full of roses and
flowers from every clime. It has its little theatres, concert

halls, and wine and beer gardens ; in a word, it contains everything the human heart can desire or the most fertile imagination conceive of for the promotion of enjoyment and human happiness. If I were compelled to live away from my own country, I would select Vienna as my permanent home, for I believe more genuine happiness could be extracted from life here than in any other place. The people of Vienna are noted for their easy, yet courtly manners.

While wandering through the Rotunda, we met the Emperor, leisurely examining the exhibits. He was dressed in the uniform of an ordinary soldier. There was nothing about him to distinguish him from a high private, and if we had not been told by our commissionaire we would not have known him. He was attended by three or four gentlemen in black suits and dress coats. We saw no armed guards or evidences of precaution for the protection of his person from vulgar obtrusion. In our walks around the building we saw him twice. At one time I was near enough to have touched him. I saw him and the Archduke Charles in the same building in 1873. Although but fifteen years ago, he has sadly changed. He was then in his forty-third year, full of vigor and manly beauty. I did not then notice a gray hair in his head or fine flowing beard. His step was elastic and his whole bearing majestic. He now looks prematurely old. His hair is thin and gray, his eye has lost its fire and his cheek is furrowed with deep lines of care. He is but fifty-eight years old ; I would take him for seventy. He still walks erect and rather briskly, and seems alive with interest for all that affects his empire. As far as I could ascertain by conversation with his subjects, I would say he is a very popular ruler and is much honored and beloved by his people.

The suburbs of the city are very attractive places and are usually gay on every fine afternoon, being crowded by the citizens of the town seeking for country air and rural enjoyment. We visited two or three of the suburban resorts and found them very charming places. Schonbrun is two miles out. It is the seat of the Emperor's summer palace. Kahlenberg, about five miles out, is now reached by rail. It is about one thousand feet high and gives a most perfect view over the city, neighboring mountains and course of the Danube for many miles above and below the city. If time had permitted I would like to have tarried longer in this delightful place. I left it with much regret.

Our next resting place was Innsbruck, via Saltzburg, a very beautiful little town, fifteen hours by express train from Vienna going toward the Alps. I never saw such perfect shades of green as were presented by the hills and mountains

along the route. The road gradually rises until it approaches
the snow line. It follows very near the course of one of the
tributaries of the Danube and passes over some of the wildest
and grandest Alpine scenery. The Tyrol has been so often
described as to become familiar—so far as mere description
can make it familiar—to all who have taken the trouble to
read about it. It is impossible to convey a correct idea of its
grandeur without actually travelling through and over it.

Innsbruck is prettily situated on the River Inn, and is
surrounded with snow clad mountains. The snow, however,
generally disappears about August. It is one of the oldest
towns in Austria and was supposed to have been finished over
a thousand years ago. It is about four hundred miles by rail
west of Vienna. Some of the mountains around Innsbruck
are seven thousand eight hundred feet high. When I looked
out of my chamber window in the morning, it seemed as if one
of the lofty cliffs was about to tumble over and bury me and
my Inn five thousand feet deep. The city itself is about two
thousand feet above the level of the sea. It looks like a pretty
little flower nestling in a mountain cliff, and sheltered by the
surrounding peaks. It contains a very old church full of
bronze life-size statuary, said to be very artistic. The old
town slept for several hundred years, when it was aroused
suddenly one summer morning by the shrill scream of a locomotive on a new railroad which was, after much opposition on
the part of the city authorities, located near its western gate.
From that moment it sprung into importance and now bids
fair to become one of the great commercial frontier cities of
Austria. It is, without exaggeration, one of the prettiest
places in Europe. From Innsbruck we crossed the Alps and
entered Switzerland, our next stop being Zurich two hundred
miles farther west. We passed near the sources of the three
great rivers of Europe—the Danube running east, the Rhine
running northward and the Rhone running southward ; one
emptying into the Black Sea, one into the Mediterranean, and
the other into the North Sea. So it will be seen we have
passed over the highest part of the continent and have now
viewed its finest scenery. We crossed the highest bridge in
Europe, three hundred feet above a chasm cut by a small river
rumbling and tumbling over the rocks below. After passing
through the Arlberg tunnel we began to descend. Great peaks
pierce the clouds in every direction. Mighty cliffs and crags
overhang the rich valleys below, great cataracts tumble down
the mountain sides, while beautiful cascades fall over bluffs
five hundred feet high. But my page is full—and we are at
Zurich.

XXXVI.

ZURICH TO GENEVA—ARLBERG TUNNEL, FOUR THOUSAND
TWO HUNDRED AND NINETY-EIGHT FEET HIGH — SILK
WEAVERS OF ZURICH—BERNE—SUNDAY OBSERVERS SOME-
WHAT INCONSISTENT—OLD CHURCH—BEAUTIFUL NATURE
—GENEVA AGAIN—A SWISS FAMILY—LAKE OF GENEVA—
TOWNS ON ITS BORDERS—THE PRISONER OF CHILLON—
VIEW OF MONT BLANC—AMERICAN WATCHES IN GENEVA
—FUTURE ROUTE.

GENEVA, June, 1888.

My last letter was mailed from Zurich, one of Switzerland's largest towns.   It is most charmingly situated at the
lower end of the lake of the same name.   The lake is about
twenty-five miles long, from two to three miles wide and is at
places nearly 500 feet deep.   It is stocked with several varieties of fine fish and is navigated by both sailing vessels and
steamboats.   On its shores are several villages and manufacturing towns.   The water is clear and of a greenish hue, the
air is cool and bracing, and the people industrous and hospitable.   The altitude of the surface of the lake ia 1345 feet
above the level of the sea.   We passed over mountains 4000
feet high.   The great tunnel of Arlberg, over six miles long,
through which we passed, is 4,298 feet above the level of the
sea.   After leaving the tunnel, we noticed all the rivers and
mountain streams ran northward, into the Rhine ; on the other
side they ran eastward into the Danube.   From this we knew
we had passed over the backbone of the continent.   The effect
of remaining for several days in these high altitudes was to
give a very disagreeable buzzing sensation in the ears.

Zurich has some excellent hotels.   Hotel Baur au Lac, at
which we spent three days, is one of the best in the city.   It
faces up the lake, is surrounded by a beautiful garden fragrant
with roses and full of sweet little bowers, delightfully shaded
and tastefully laid out.   The lake view from our chamber
window is very fine.   We can see up the lake for fifteen miles
and the surrounding mountains, especially upon the right, are
very clearly seen.   The first tier of hills, some of which are
three or four thousand feet high, are green and partly cultivated;
those further off are still higher and barren ; finally the snow-
capped Alpine peaks overtower them all and pierce the clouds.
Just outside of the city is Mount Uetelberg, 3000 feet high
from whose summit a splendid view of the city, lake and surrounding country can be had.   Zurich has a population of

85,000, and is a very busy and enterprising place. Some of
the finest silks are manufactured here, on old-fashioned hand-
looms, by Swiss girls.   I saw them at work on looms of the
simplest construction, but the work produced was of the finest
kind.

After a three days' sojourn at Zurich, we left for Berne.
Here also we found a thriving Swiss city of about 44,000 inhabitants.   It is a very romantic and picturesque old town.
It had the honor of being the birthplace of Delaware county's
present District Attorney.   No wonder he is so proud of his
horses and hounds and takes so much delight in Nature's
charms.   He was born in a land of *bears* and mountains 1800
feet nearer heaven than the highest point in Delaware county.
The waiters at the hotel seemed delighted when I told them
that one of the best offices of the county where I lived was
held by a native born Swiss.

The citizens of Berne are very strict in their observance
of the Sabbath.   The Old Minster, with its high-backed, narrow and most uncomfortable pews, is filled on Sundays with
Protestant worshippers.   It is a naked, cold looking old edifice, but greatly venerated by the people.   It stands upon a
terrace rising perpendicularly one hundred and ten feet, at
the foot of which the river Aare sweeps in a beautiful curve.
The terrace. in the rear of the church, is now a shady grove
with seats and statues, graveled walks and flower beds.   The
view from the terrace is indescribably fine ; the Bernese Alps
present a very grand and thrilling appearance.   We plainly
define the contour of mountains over twelve thousand feet high.

I thought I discovered some inconsistency in their professed respect for the Sabbath.   While the stores were generally closed and the churches well filled on the Sunday I
spent in Berne, I noticed many more people on the drilling
grounds, looking at the evolutions and artillery practice of the
handsome young soldiers, than were in the churches.   Sunday
is a regular drill day in Switzerland.   At sunrise the day is
opened by the booming of cannon, and the constant crack of
the infantry rifle, by battalion as well as in target practice, is
kept up until sunset.   The day is devoted to military reviews,
target practice and warlike parades, of which the people seem
very fond.

The celebrated clock, of Berne, like the one at Strasbourg,
is but a toy, not worth going ten miles to see.

The old part of the town has a very mediæval look, with
high houses, narrow and crooked streets, with sidewalks
under an arched way over which the quaint old houses project.   The new part of the city is like all the other modern
additions to old towns ; that is to say, as beautiful and

convenient as architectural skill can make them. The great attraction of Berne, indeed of all Switzerland, is not its works of Art, but its profuse display of the handiwork of Nature. Its peaceful meadows and placid lakes contrasted with its crags and peaks ; its green forests and barren rocks ; its cataracts, cascades, caverns and grottoes contrasted with its sheepherds and picturesque cottages, sturdy, free and independent people, all crowded within the limits of the little Republic of Switzerland, making it look more like a theatrical spectacle than a living landscape, all unite to make it such a charming retreat for travelers from all parts of the world.

From Berne we went to Geneva in six hours by express train through the best part of Switzerland. We passed Swiss houses with great pitched roofs extending down, porch-like, all around the buildings to within six feet of the ground. Under these patronizing shelters the whole Swiss family rest during winter and repose at night. A Swiss *family* consists of the father, mother, children and often the grand-children, together with the flocks, herds, horses, cows, pigs, goats and other domestic animals, all living in harmony under the same roof.

The Lake of Geneva is the largest in Switzerland. It covers an area of two hundred and twenty-five square miles. It is about fifty miles long and, on an average, eight miles wide. In places it is over one thousand feet deep. Its water is perfectly clear ; objects may be seen sixty feet under water. In color the lake is a deep blue. The deposits of the Rhone at the head of the lake are gradually filling it with a rich alluvial soil and converting what was once a part of the lake into a fertile valley.

There are thirteen towns upon the borders of the lake, in appearance, finished fully a thousand years ago. These towns communicate with the city of Geneva by steamboats which make a daily course of the entire lake. We spent a very agreeable day on one of these boats, only landing once, for two hours, to inspect the famous old castle of Chillon. It stands upon an isolated rock which juts out into the lake. The water at the base of the castle is three hundred feet deep. The castle is in a good state of preservation and is now used as an arsenal. It was built over a thousand years ago and has been the scene of many terrible tragedies. Crimes, in the name of the law and under the guise of justice have been committed here, a recountal of which

"Would freeze the blood."

It contains gloomy dungeons, torture rooms and a gibbet on which thousands of victims have been hung and whose bodies have been thrown down an eighty-feet-deep hole, at the

bottom of which were arranged revolving knives which cut
the poor wretches into twenty or thirty pieces. The fragments
then flowed out into the lake and became food for the fish.
The stone column is shown where Byron's Prisoner of Chillon
was chained for so many years, and until his bare feet wore a
path in the stone floor as he chafed and paced his life away
within the tether of his chain.

"Chillon ! thy prison is a holy place
And thy sad floor an altar—for 'twas trod
Until his very steps have left a trace,
Worn, as if the cold pavement were a sod."

The climate of Geneva is very pleasant. It is never very
warm and seldom cold enough to freeze over the lake. I visited the city nineteen years ago, and can discover but little
change in that part facing the lake. It is the same beautiful
and charming city. Our hotel (De la Paix), fronts upon the
lake and is considered by travelers the best in the city. From
the balcony of our chambers we have a splendid view of Mont
Blanc. It looks like a pyramid of burnished silver rising
above the dim outlines of the lower Alps. The spectacle is
more striking and weird because the sun shines upon the
snowy head of this mountain for several minutes after it has
set at Geneva and the other mountains are partly obscured by
the shades of approaching night. While all around has a
gloomy look, Mont Blanc seems aglow with the reflected rays
of the sun which to us has been under the horizon half an hour.
While gazing upon it we are reminded that we now see the
highest point in Europe.

Geneva is a thriving town of about seventy thousand inhabitants. It used to be the grand centre of watch manufacturers. America has now monopolized this industry. I find
American watches for sale here cheaper than they can be
made by the home manufacturers. French is the native tongue
of Geneva, from which we may infer that we are approaching
the frontier of France. I have concluded to go from here
to Paris, where I shall remain for two weeks and then go to
Meyence and down the Rhine visiting Rotterdam, Amsterdam and perhaps Hamburg, from which I hope to embark for
Scotland.

XXXVII.

GENEVA TO PARIS—FARMING IN FRANCE—LARGE FIELDS
AND WIRE FENCES—SIX OXEN TO A PLOW—THE REPUB-
LIC OF 1873 AND THE EMPIRE OF 1869—HIGH PRICES—
HOTEL CONTINENTAL—PARIS COMPARED WITH VIENNA—
LICENSED BAWDY HOUSES—DUELING—MORALS AND TASTES
—COOK'S TOURISTS IN THE LOUVRE—HOW TO SEE THE
LOUVRE—SHARPERS IN PARIS—PASSPORT ANNOYANCES TO
ENTER GERMANY.

PARIS, June, 1888.

Distance on the continent is measured by time, not by
miles. Paris, by the fastest express train and shortest route.
is twelve hours from Geneva. In our journey here we passed
through the cities of Macon and Dijon. The general face of
the country from Geneva to the French frontier is rather tame
for Switzerland, but, when compared with the flat fields of
France, it is very beautiful. From Macon to Paris one would
almost imagine himself traveling in Pennsylvania and Delaware. The land is good and well tilled. It is, as a rule,
cultivated in small patches, but here and there we find large
farms upon which are used all modern implements, such as
mowers and reapers, horse-rakes and hay-spreaders, sub-soil
plows, steam threshing machines, etc. I saw large flocks of
sheep and hundreds of cows and horses grazing in one-hun-
dred-acre fields surrounded with wire fences. In the mountain
districts the farmers merely scratch the soil as if to tickle it
into a genial smile, but in the alluvial lands they plow very
deep. I saw six large oxen to a plow and it was as much as
they could do to draw it through the stiff sod. The furrow
seemed to me a foot wide and about fourteen inches deep.

I find Paris very much changed since the days of the
empire. It is no longer a city of cheap living and low prices.
The necessaries of life are as dear in Paris as in Philadelphia.
The Bon Marche still keeps up a fair reputation for reasonable
fixed prices. The Palais Royal has degenerated into a set of
street stores, where things can be bought cheap but are always
of inferior quality. I notice around the Palais Royal many
shops " To Let." I do not believe, from present appearances,
that one-tenth as much business is done there now as was done
in 1869. I predict that before many years the Palais Royal
will be among the things that were. The " Grand Magasins
du Louvre " is now one of Paris's popular stores, conducted
somewhat on the principle of Wanamaker's Philadelphia store.

with the difference in favor of the latter. It is worse than
folly to come to Paris to buy cheap goods. There are very
many cheap things here, but just like cheap things everywhere
they are useless and, therefore, dear at any price.

There are several first-class hotels here, but it costs more
to live in one of them than in the same class of hotels in New
York or Philadelphia. We are very comfortably quartered at
the Hotel Continental, an immense establishment in the heart
of Paris, on the Rue Rivoli, directly opposite the Gardens of
the Tuilleries. It covers an entire square. It contains on
Rue Rivoli three hundred and thirty feet ; on Rue Castiglione,
two hundred and fifty-eight feet. It is six stories high and
has five hundred and sixteen sleeping rooms, some of them
with parlors and sitting rooms annexed. The house is well
furnished and has every modern convenience—bar, reading
rooms, restaurant, billiard room, parlors, reception rooms,
elevators, etc. Our rooms front on Rue Rivoli and give us a
fine view over the Gardens of the Tuilleries, directly opposite.
We can see Notre Dame, the tower of St. Jacque, St. Sulpice,
the ruins of Palais D'Orsay, the Hotel des Invalides, with its
gilded dome, Champ-de-Mars, the new iron tower to be the
highest in the world, and Des-Champ-Elysee, as far as the
Arc de-Triomphe ; in a word, we can see nearly the half of
Paris from our chamber window. The hotel is full of English
and American travelers. But few Frenchmen patronize it. If
I were traveling alone I would select an humbler resting place
and could secure better accommodations for less money.

With all its faults, Paris is still a very beautiful city, full
of life and devoted to pleasure. For a month's sojourn, but
few gayer places can be found. For a permanent dwelling
place, I would much prefer Vienna. The vaunted pleasures
of Parisian life are visionary and unreal ; pleasures that cannot be looked back upon with satisfaction. On the other
hand, Vienna is full of solid comfort and real home enjoyments. There the father, mother and all the little ones enjoy a holiday together ; here they take it in pairs. Two is
company, but three a crowd in Paris. The young men and
women of Paris never look beyond the present hour. Their
motto is, "Be merry to-day for to-morrow we may die."
Satan in Paris is the same gentleman of great social culture
and good manners. He is never *publicly* vulgar, but lets no
private opportunity pass to gently insinuate the most disgusting moral sins. He never gets drunk, always wears gloves
and is exceedingly polite. While he would scorn to pick your
pocket, he will not hesitate to recommend all sorts of gambling, from the Grand Prix de Paris to a legalized lottery to
help build the Panama Canal.

A prostitute here holds a license from the government ; her fees are regulated by a tariff of charges fixed by the State authorities. She may recover them in a suit at law.

You are permitted to murder your enemy here with impunity, provided you observe the fixed rules of the so-called code of honor. A trial has just ended before one of the high courts of Paris. I have watched it with great interest. An editor criticised in his paper the work of an artist. The editor was a dead shot, the artist had never discharged a pistol. The criticism was kept up for months, becoming more bitter and sarcastic in each edition. At last the poor artist's wife was attacked and one of his female friends held up to public ridicule. A challenge followed. At the first shot the artist was killed. The only question before the court was, whether the duel had been regularly conducted. After a careful investigation the court found that the code had been followed in all its essential details and the bully, blackguard· and murderer was discharged.

Whatever may be said of the morals of Paris, it must be admitted that the French are very highly cultivated in all that pertains to art and refined taste. The Louvre is still the finest picture gallery of the world. The Luxembourg and the Salon of Paris still display the finest works of modern painters and sculptors. They can make the finest goods and produce the most beautiful fabrics of the world. To do justice to the paintings exhibited in the Louvre, they should be visited once a day for at least a week. I was struck with a visit made to these galleries by a party personally conducted by one of Cook's professional guides. His party consisted of about twenty travelers. He took them through the entire building in one hour and fifty minutes (it requires two hours to walk through the gallery without stopping to examine any pictures). Some of the party were upon a half run·; others, attracted by some work of more than ordinary excellence, were unable to keep up with the crowd ; while all had a confused and bewildered look and were certainly unable to carry away any fixed remembrance of a single painting. When they get home they will think they have seen the world-renowned paintings of the Louvre, but they have not. The proper way to visit the gallery is, first, to take a deliberate stroll through it very much as you would enter and promenade around a ballroom, letting your bewildered eyes rest but for a moment upon the fair faces which most impress you at the first glance ; then take your catalogue and look at every picture. You will often find some perfect gem, unnoticed at your first glance, and many paintings of the greatest merit in some unexpected place.

It takes two weeks, industriously spent, to see Paris.

The place is full of sharpers. I truly pity the greenhorn here. They will relieve him of his money in such a patronizing way as almost to compel him to thank them for robbing him. I will give one instance. While at Versailles, I met an American gentleman with his family. He had gone from the hotel in the coach expressly provided for the guests, that they might not be imposed upon by being overcharged. I asked him how much he paid, and was surprised to learn they had charged him for fare alone, twenty francs per person. I took my family there in the street car for less than one franc each, and we had just as comfortable a ride as he had for twenty francs. I have known instances of American travelers being taken by their guides into restaurants and being compelled to pay twenty francs for what I could get without difficulty for two, or at the outside, four francs.

I leave Paris to-morrow for Meyence and a trip down the Rhine. When purchasing my tickets yesterday the agent declined to sell them until I produced my passport. I was informed that while it would admit me, my wife and daughter could not enter Germany without separate passports. The German authorities are sending back travelers from France every day. I was compelled to call on our Minister for passports for my wife and daughter and, after procuring them, I had to have them vised by the German Consul and pay him forty-eight francs for his permission endorsed upon them to enter Germany. The French government admits travelers from Germany without requiring passports. Some American and English travelers who, without warning, have been turned back at the frontiers of Germany, are very indignant at the conduct of the German authorities. I would not be surprised if another war would soon break out between Germany and France. The result would probably be a further humiliation for France. The French are a brave people, but are not able to measure swords with the powerful German empire. Nothing but one of those unaccountable accidents of war which have so often illustrated the Bible truth that the race is not always to the swift or the victory to the strong, could save France from disaster in a conflict with Germany, in the present condition of her affairs.

XXXVIII

PARIS TO AMSTERDAM—MORE ABOUT PARIS—PETTY MEAN-
NESS OF HOTEL MANAGEMENT -POLITICAL FACTIONS—
RECKLESS DRIVING—METZ—FORTIFICATIONS AND BATTLE-
FIELDS—MARSHAL NEY—BINGEN ON THE RHINE—CHURCH
OF OBERSTEIN—WATCHING THE RHINE—COLOGNE AND
ITS CHANGES SINCE 1869—THE BONES OF ST. URSULA AND
HER ELEVEN THOUSAND VIRGINS.

AMSTERDAM, July, 1888.

We left Paris on the third of this month to visit the battlefields of Metz. I leave Paris with an unfavorable impression.
Travelers in Paris are very much like innocent flies flickering
around the brilliant glare of a gas light. The Parisians look
upon them as legitimate prey. They resort to petty acts of
meanness an Englishman or a German would scorn to practice.
A favorite trick of the hotel keepers is to withhold your bill
until the last moment when you have no time for a critical examination of the long list of trivial items or to correct *mistakes*.
You must be careful not to break a glass, soil the carpet, or
scratch the furniture of your room. If you should happen to
wipe your pen, or let fall a drop of ink upon the gaudy cover
of your table, you may find a charge in your bill for the highest price of a new one. To upset the slop-jar means to pay
for a new carpet no matter how old the soiled one may have
been. Should you indulge in the luxury of blacking your
boots upon one of the elegantly upholstered chairs, you may
expect to pay $10 for a new chair. The only safe way is to
have your bills rendered every few days and closely scrutinize
every item of charge. They have been encouraged in this
system of small swindling, chiefly, by American travelers who
merely glance at their bills and pay them.

I was in the city a little over two weeks and made it a
rule to call for and settle my bill every four days, yet I came
very near being overcharged about four hundred francs. I
called for my bill the evening before my departure, but did
not get it until about five minutes before starting time. I at
once saw that the last payment had not been credited, and so
informed the clerk. He very deliberately asked if I had my
receipt. I informed him that I did not preserve my hotel re-
ceipts, and requested him to look at his cash book. He said
he had no time to examine the book, that was the business of
the book-keeper ; that I could pay the bill and if I could show
a receipt for the money they would take great pleasure in

refunding it. He did not suspect that I was playing with him, for I had the receipt in my pocket ready to produce after I had satisfied myself of his honesty. I then produced my receipt, but did not permit him to take it from my hand. He blushed, begged pardon, said it was a *grand meprise*: examined his books with a provoking slowness ; said it was the first time in the history of the hotel that such a mistake had occurred, and then struck out three hundred and ninety-seven francs from my bill. If I had lost or mislaid my receipt I would have been compelled to pay the bill as rendered.

Before giving me my bill, two men closely examined our rooms, sounded the crockery with a little wooden hammer, and examined everything in the apartments to ascertain whether anything had been damaged. Knowing their habits, we had been very careful not to injure or soil any of the furniture ; indeed we had been very little in our rooms except to sleep there ; the result was no extra charge.

A young American gentleman stopping at the same hotel was not so lucky. He had his hair dressed by the hotel barber, and on leaving paid his bill without examination. He afterwards discovered a charge of forty-seven francs for cutting his hair and furnishing him with a small bottle of worthless hair tonic.

The wife of another American gentleman, in the same hotel, sent for the *coiffeur* to dress her hair. Her husband arrived just as the job had been completed and was coolly presented with a bill of about one hundred francs. The fellow had brought with him new brushes, combs, and half a dozen bottles of perfumes, and had charged for them all, though but a few drops had been used from each bottle. Instead of paying the bill, in true American style, he gave him five francs and kicked him out of the room, bottles, brushes and all. He was lucky in not being served with a "*Proces Verbal*" and severely punished for an assault and battery on the injured barber. A foreigner has no chance for fair play in the inferior courts of Paris. He cannot afford the time and expense of an appeal from the judgment of the petty magistrates and must consequently submit to injustice rather than seek redress in the higher courts.

I particularly noticed the reckless driving by cabmen and others through the crowded streets. Pedestrians seem to have no rights. There are no flagstones for foot passengers. It is no uncommon thing to see a cab in a full gallop, or an omnibus with the horses in a run, in the most frequented streets. To remedy the evil, the city authorities have certain stations, a few squares apart, called "*Secours pour les Blesse*," where they take care of the wounded.

As far as I have been able to form a judgment of the character of the Parisian French, I find them to be a very fickle
and uncertain race, fond of trivial amusements and inclined to
immorality.   A large majority have no religious faith, and
only live for the present day in a state of feverish excitement,
ready at any moment for social or political revolutions.   All
they care for is the gratification of their present desires without any regard to the future.   They are now ready for another
change of government, and are howling for war with Germany.
Paris has many learned, wise and conservative men within its
walls, but they are now the objects of public scorn and ridicule.   There are at least six political factions in the city, each
supporting a newspaper as the organ of the party.   Not a day
passes without some insulting squib or diatribe appearing in
these journals, calculated to embitter the different parties
against each other.   In a word, they are now ready to seize
each other by the throats and inaugurate again the times of
1793 with all the horrors of the Reign of Terror.   No one can
predict the result of war.   It depends upon too many accidents ; but as far as I am able to judge, a war with Germany
at this time would be disastrous to France.   The match is undoubtedly very near the magazine and a very little more friction will cause an explosion that will shake Europe to its very
centre.   The great insecurity of France lies in the settled fact
that Paris is the centre of its political power.   The faction in
possession of Paris rules France.   The people of the Provinces
are thrifty and conservative ; why they suffer the rabble of
Paris to rule and ruin the country is an enigma none can solve.
Germany is ready at a moment's warning for the struggle.   If
it comes it will end either in the complete ruin or in the political regeneration of France.

From Paris to Metz the country is mostly flat, but very
rich.   In many places fine, thrifty young forests are seen.
These have all been planted within the past twenty-five or
thirty years.   Just before reaching Metz the scenery becomes
more broken and attractive.   The weather was bad during my
stay in the city, by reason of which I was much disappointed
in my contemplated tour of its battlefields.   It is at this time
the most interesting spot in Germany.   The decisive battles
around this city have settled for ages the map lines of Europe.
The fate of the German Empire was settled here.   The ambition of France, which had been rapidly growing since she was
so sadly humbled at Waterloo, here received its second and
perhaps its final humiliation.

An American, without seeing them, can form no proper
conception of the immense fortifications around the city of
Metz.   The surrounding country is mountainous, with every

hill strongly entrenched and mounted with guns of a most frightful size. There are new works being constructed every day. The city proper has a population of about 55,000, besides a garrison of 20,000 men. The town is as old as the Roman empire. It was plundered by the Vandals and sacked and almost destroyed by the Huns. In the sixth century it was the capital of the Kingdom of Austria. In 1552 it was captured by the French and strongly fortified by them. They held it against Charles V., but lost it in 1871, when it was again reunited to the German Empire, where it will probably remain as long as the empire lasts. The present lines of successive fortifications extend for fifteen miles around the city. Metz can never succumb to an outward enemy by any force except treachery or starvation. The battlefields lie to the west, on the road to Verdon. It takes a full day and costs about forty francs to visit them. The battle of the 1 th of August, 1870, was very bloody. The French lost about 17,000 and the Germans about the same number of officers and men. The Germans were fortified, while the French fought in the open field.

In the battle of August 18, the Germans had 230,000 men opposed by 180,000 French. The Germans lost over 20,000 officers and men ; the French loss was about 12,000 There were two more battles, one on the 31st of August, the other on the 1st of September. In the last struggle the French were driven back under the guns of Metz.

The city has been much improved by the Germans. The influx of travelers to visit the battlefields has been a source of great profit to the several very good hotels of the place. The new passport system has completely ruined the hotel business. We found a very large and well-appointed hotel with no guests except ourselves. Nearly all travelers now enter Germany from France through Belgium or Switzerland, where no passports are required.

In the Esplanade,—a beautiful park in the centre of the city,—stands the colossal statue of Marshal Ney. I saw his grave in Pere la Chaise, at Paris, with no monument to mark his final resting place. I have often wondered why the Imperialists of France have so neglected one of Napoleon's bravest Marshals, created a Duke by the Emperor in 1805, and Prince of Moscowa 1812. While the other Marshals of France, buried in the same cemetery, have splendid monuments over their remains, Ney has nothing but an iron railing around his grave, and his name cut on the stone step under the gate.

I noticed a peculiarity in the hotel regulations of Metz I have seen in no other place. They reckon from night to night and not from day to day. The traveler's bills commence at

5 P. M. ; the night ends at 8 A. M. the next morning.   If he
holds his room after 5 P. M., he is charged with another night
whether he stays or not.

We left Metz on the 4th of July.   It was uncomfortably cold.
We are all wearing our winter clothing and are none too warm.
We sleep under two or three blankets every night.   Nothing
but violent exercise will cause perspiration here.

Our next resting place was " Sweet Bingen on the Rhine."
The scenery from Metz to Bingen is soft and lovely, here and
there broken by the Vosges mountains which we skirt nearly
the entire route.   We passed the battlefield of Saarbruch,
where a sharp engagement took place between the French and
Prussians August 6th, 1870, in which the French, although
numerically superior, were obliged to retreat.

At Oberstein, there is a church most curiously constructed
in the cliff of a rock four hundred feet high.   The church is
cut out of the face of the rock about two hundred feet up the
precipitous cliff, and presents a very weird and romantic appearance.   The railroad route follows very nearly the course
of the river Nahe, passing through several towns of from five
thousand to twenty thousand inhabitants ; among them Kreuz-
nach, a watering place of great repute, celebrated for its natural
salt springs and baths.   The railroad station is at Bingenbruck,
on the left bank of the Nahe, which we cross by carriage to
Bingen.

Bingen is a town of seven thousand inhabitants, completely
finished several hundred years ago ; a most delightful place to
spend a few days in rest and rural recreation among flower
gardens, vineyards and mountains.   The town is very old.
During the thirty years' war it was almost entirely destroyed
by the French.   From the heights in the rear of the town the
prospect is most charming.   Old ruined castles upon the rocky
hill tops of the Rhine may be seen for many miles down the
river.   On the opposite bank, about five hundred feet up the
hillside, stands the new monument recently erected by the
German Empire, representing "Germania watching the Rhine."
It looks very much like the new monument at New York, of
" Liberty enlightening the World."   A little to the right, on
the opposite side of the river, stands the village of Rudesheim,
surrounded by the celebrated Rudesheimer vineyards, the wine
of which is known all over the world.

We made the trip down the Rhine from Bingen to Cologne
in one day.   Of course I will not be expected to describe
scenery upon which volumes have been written, and upon
which the best painters and landscape artists have exhausted
their skill.   It looks about as it did nineteen years ago when
I saw it last and then thought nothing in the world could be

more beautiful. I had not then seen the Danube, the Dardanelles or the Bosphorus from Constantinople to the Black Sea.
While the Rhine scenery is beautiful, I do not consider it
equal to the scenery of the Danube from the Iron Gate to Belgrade. I can easily imagine how the now barren mountains
of Greece and Judea could have once been terraced as the
mountains of the Rhine now are, and how they could have
been covered with vineyards and verdure as these now are.
If these mountains were neglected for two thousand years as
those of Greece have been, every particle of soil would be
washed off or be blown away and nothing but the barren rock
be left.

We stayed two days at Cologne. It has been very much
improved since my visit in 1869. The cathedral, which has
been five or six hundred years in construction has been finished, and is now one of the grandest Gothic churches in the
world. The spires are five hundred and twelve feet high and
of most perfect proportions. I do not remember ever having
looked upon a construction of human hands more inspiring
with a sensation of awe, than that presented by the first full
view of this cathedral. The latitude of Cologne is nearly
seven hundred miles north of Philadelphia. The Rhine here
is about four hundred and fifty yards wide and flows with
great rapidity. The length of the navigable river from Bale
to the German Ocean is about eleven hundred miles. Its
average width is not over three hundred and fifty yards ; its
average depth about five feet. At Bale the surface of the river
is eight hundred and three feet above the level of the sea ; at
Cologne it is one hundred and twenty-two feet above sea level.
I have been within a few miles of its source, near Toma-See.
where it is seven thousand six hundred and eighty-nine feet
above the level of the sea. It is somewhat remarkable that
the Rhone, running southward, the Rhine, running northward, and the Danube, running eastward, all rise within a
few miles of each other.

The old bridge of boats still crosses the river at Cologne.
Like Bale, Cologne has completely changed since my last
visit. The old houses have nearly all disappeared and splendid modern buildings have taken their places. The old town
walls have been removed and magnificent new boulevards with
houses like the new part of Boston have been built upon the
site of the old bulwarks for miles. The old church of St.
Ursula, with the bones and skulls of the eleven thousand
virgins massacred with her, looks just like it did nineteen
years ago.

XXXIX.

Amsterdam to London—Rotterdam a City on Piles—
Delfthaven and the Mayflower Pilgrims — A Curious
Old City—An Old Friend—The Hague—Diamond Cut-
ting in Amsterdam—Holland, London's Kitchen Gar-
den—Back to London—The Pleasure of Hearing our
Native Tongue Again—Hotel Metropole—Impres-
sions of London After a Long Absence—Off for the
Polar Regions.

London, July, 1888.

From Rotterdam to Harwich by sea, and from thence by
rail to London, requires about one day. We found the North
Sea very rough. Most of the passengers were sick from the
time we entered the Sea until we landed in England. We encountered a wind storm dead ahead and for half an hour went
backward instead of forward It is impossible to describe the
complicated motion of one of the little side-wheel ships of the
line from Rotterdam to London. An ocean steamer never
makes such erratic movements.

We landed safely about 9 A. M. on the day after our embarkation and proceeded at once to this grand old city.

Rotterdam is a very interesting old Dutch town of about
170,000 inhabitants. *Dam*, in Dutch, means to keep out the
water ; Amsterdam, means the dike of the river Amster, which
runs through the town. Rotterdam is built upon a marshy
plain from six to twelve feet below the sea level. The buildings, in the old part of the city, are very irregular, twisted
and out of plumb, leaning in different ways. Some look as if
they were top-heavy and about to tumble into the streets,
while others lean sideways and backward. The cause of this
irregularity is the swampy, alluvial ground upon which the
town is built. No trees can be found to make piles long
enough to reach the firm earth. They now overcome the difficulty by driving the piles up to the head and then driving
others on the ones already sunk until a firm foundation is secured ; even then some of the large modern buildings are out
of plumb and slightly twisted. In Amsterdam they encounter
the same difficulties, but not to the same extent, as the ground
is firmer and nearer on a level with the sea. The whole country around these cities was once a part of the sea and has been
filled up to its present level by the wash of the Meuse, Rhine
and other rivers.

To an American, the most interesting place in Rotterdam

is the old church at Delfthaven and the adjoining wharf from
which the Pilgrim Fathers sailed in the Mayflower, in 1594.
All their names are written in the church records; among
them I read that of Miles Standish. The church has been
preserved in its ancient form, with broad floors covered with
clean white sand. The pews are of unpainted wood, built
very high and uncomfortable, with a board in front upon which
rest great clumsy looking Bibles five inches thick and a foot
square.

The city has its rich, poor, middle class and Jewish quarters. The Jewish quarter is inhabited by about seven thousand
Israelites, who dwell chiefly in the old part. It presents a
very amusing appearance. They seem to live in the streets.
The sidewalks are obstructed by wash tubs and women doing
the family work, cooking, mending and nursing their babies.
I never saw so many little dirty-faced but robust children.
They play all over the street. The men cobble and trade in
the open street, and the parts of the sidewalk not occupied by
the wash tubs and babies is used by them as a place of deposit
for their packs and dog-carts. The pedestrians pay the same
respect to the wash tubs, carts and babies on the sidewalks as
the people of Constantinople pay to their sleeping dogs; that
is to say, they walk in the carriage-way and go around the
obstructions without complaint, as a matter of course.

The most beautiful part of the city is that occupied by
the middle class, which includes merchants and tradespeople
generally, some of whom are very rich. Wealth does not here
raise the class. Each house is of a different order of architecture and is erected in the centre of a garden from one hundred
to one hundred and fifty or more feet square, surrounded by a
canal and approached from the street over a drawbridge and
portcullis. The bridge is down and the portcullis up during
the day; at night the bridge is up and the portcullis down.
The gardens around these beautiful dwellings are laid out
with great taste, with gravel walks, arbors, flower beds and
green, shady trees. The ground is so rich and the climate so
mild that the vegetation is luxuriant and very fresh and green.
There are no dead leaves. I almost doubted whether Death
ever entered this little Paradise, but a piece of black crape
bound by a white ribbon, hanging from one of the door knobs,
dispelled this illusion and convinced me that there were loved
and lost ones here as well as at home. All these pretty dwelling places have fancy names, such as "Felicity," "Paradise,"
"Jerusalem," etc.

The poor quarter is in complete contrast with what I have
endeavored to describe as the quarter of the middle class. The
houses are high, old, ugly and dilapidated; the streets long,

narrow and dark. I visited it on Sunday and will never forget the scene. The street was so crowded with men, women and children as to render it almost impossible to pass in our carriage. The women wore the old Dutch costume of a hundred years ago. They all seemed healthy, and I really believe they were as happy as their more favored brethren of the other quarters.

The whole city is traversed by canals navigated by boats of considerable size, some of them propelled by steam. There are several good hotels in the place. I selected the "Hotel de Pays Bas" because when I visited the city in 1869 it was a new and fashionable house. I was surprised to find the same guide there that showed me the town nearly twenty years ago. In looks he had not grown much older, but his hair showed the frost marks of Time. The hotel is still a comfortable resting place but not equipped with many of the modern hotel improvements.

The city has a fine park running for several miles along the banks of the Meuse. Several old historic houses have been carefully preserved. They show the house where Erasmus was born, and the house where over one thousand citizens were saved during one of the massacres which followed a successful siege of the city. The house was filled with the flying and panic-stricken citizens, while the enemy, flushed with a dearly-bought victory, were sweeping the streets and slaughtering the people. One of the cooler heads killed a sheep and smeared the door with blood. The passing murderers, supposing the house had been already sacked, passed on. Soon after order was restored and the citizens saved from further slaughter. While the city seems to be in a prosperous condition, it is evidently much behind the age as compared with others of the same class.

We went from Rotterdam to Amsterdam and out to the Hague. Amsterdam is a large and prosperous city of nearly half a million inhabitants, well built, but full of canals of green stagnant water. The canals of the city are crossed by about four hundred bridges and are, like those of Rotterdam, navigated by steam and other boats. We visited the King's palace, museum, picture gallery and parks, and took a four hours' drive around the city. We also visited the world-renowned diamond-cutting establishment of Amsterdam. We stopped at Brack's Doelen Hotel, the best in the city and equal to any we have stopped at with a few exceptions.

The Hague is always a place of interest. It has been very much improved during the past few years. It is quite a fashionable watering place, and the residence of the King. He only dwells in his Amsterdam palace about a month in each year.

We have had a fine opportunity to see nearly the whole of Holland and have either visited or passed through all its principal cities and towns. It is a land of ditches, canals, windmills and green luxuriant fields. They raise two crops a year and produce some of the best small fruits in the world. The market for the fruits and general produce of the country is London. Land rents at from ten to thirty dollars an acre. The people are very sober and industrious and apparently as happy as the people of France and Germany, and more contented with their government. There are but few politicians in Holland.

I find London very much improved since my visit in 1873. The Thames embankment was not then finished. It has converted the river front from the ugliest to the most beautiful water front in Europe, if not in the world. While Paris has retrograded London has advanced. To my mind, it is a much handsomer city now than Paris, and a much more pleasant place for an American. After four months of wandering among unknown tongues, it is truly refreshing to hear our native language once more. I have at times, while in the center of some great city, surrounded by hundreds of thousands of people, felt as lonely as if I had been in the center of the sea, or in some great wilderness entirely away from human contact, where every word I heard was as meaningless as the gibberish of a monkey and where I understood the dogs and domestic animals better than my own race. I find the couriers and guides who profess to speak all the European languages very deficient in common conversation. They have learned only what pertains to their business. They understand the language of railroads, steamships, hotels and shops, but nothing more. After all it is not very difficult to acquire a sufficiency of such knowledge. But here, in Old England, we can converse with each other ; we can convey every shade of thought and sentiment ; mind can hold communion with mind without the constant strain and ludicrous mistakes so constantly made when conversing in a foreign tongue.

We are now quartered at the Hotel Metropole, beyond question the finest in the world so far as the building is concerned. I have visited many palaces but have not seen one more completely finished than this hotel. It is one of the largest hotels in the world and is now full to overflowing. The service and attention required by the traveler, to make him comfortable, is not as good as that of the " Continental " of Paris, and not half as good as dozens of hotels we have found of less pretensions. There are now between one and two thousand guests in the house. I have visited again the old landmarks of London and find them about the same as when I saw them last. The appearance of the city, however, as before stated, has been completely changed along the river front. Southwark looks just as it did nineteen years ago ; so do the suburbs of the city. The population of London is now supposed to be over 4,000,000.

I have hired a courier who speaks the languages of Denmark, Sweden and Norway, and have determined to visit those countries. If nothing interferes with my present plans, we will go beyond the Arctic circle as far as the North Cape, and take a look at the midnight sun. This excursion will require at least a month. It is a big undertaking but the ladies of my family think they can endure it and I, therefore, ought not to refuse them such a treat. By the way, they have proved splendid travelers, at which I am agreeably surprised.

XL

LONDON TO THE NORTH CAPE—CHRISTIANIA—RUGGED NOR-
WAY FJORDS, MOUNTAINS AND GLACIERS--LONG TWILIGHTS
AND LOVE MAKING—TEMPERANCE AND LICENSE LAWS OF
NORWAY—DEMOCRATIC MANNERS—THRONDHJEM—BEAU-
TIFUL FLOWERS—ST. OLAF—A GERMAN BRUTE—GRAND
SEND OFF—WHALES—TROMSO—TROGHATTEN—HAMMER-
FEST—LAND WITHOUT VALUE—THE MIDNIGHT SUN—
NORTH CAPE—BIRD-ROOST ROCK—REFLECTIONS.

NORTH CAPE, NORWAY,
On board Steamer Sirius,
Midnight, July, 1888.

We left London on the 12th in a fog, being the tail of a snow storm that passed over the city on the 9th. The weather was disagreeably cold, rousing fires were in all the grates of the hotel, and most of the guests wore their winter clothing. After providing ourselves with rugs, furs and other Arctic attire, we took the train for Tilbury, opposite Grave's End, where we embarked on the British ship Albanos for Christiania. The tide at Tilbury rises nearly twenty-eight feet. The wharf is connected by a long tubular bridge, working on hinges, with a pontoon which rises and falls with the tide.

After a pleasant voyage of three days, we arrived at Christiania, the Capital city of Norway. The whole western coast of Norway, from Christiania to the North Cape, is a network

of rocky islands and fjords (pronounced *feeord*). Some of the
islands are barren rocks, and many of them mountains, from
eight hundred to six thousand feet high, rising either abruptly
or with a gentle slope from the sea. A glance at the map will
convey a better idea of this rough, rugged and barren coast,
with its many thousand island mountains, its fjords, glaciers
and desolate hills of snow, than can possibly be given in the
narrow limits of a letter. We passed one glacier containing
over five hundred square miles of ice. We were on another
nearly fifty miles long and twelve miles wide.

Christiania was, within a recent period, a city of wooden
houses. Commercial prosperity and some extensive confla-
grations have converted it into a very substantial stone and
brick built city, with fine broad, regular and well paved
streets. There is nothing very striking about the town. It
is just such a modern city as the traveler will find all over
Europe. The suburbs, however, are more than ordinarily
beautiful. There are hills fully eighteen hundred feet high,
in close proximity with the town, from which most charming
views can be had over the city and bay. These hills are covered with thrifty green fir trees, which impart to the air an
aromatic perfume of balsam. One of the lady passengers on
the ship thought she smelt the fragrance of the forest pines
as we passed one of the fir clad mountains before landing at
Christiania, but alas! for the uncertainty of our senses, the
delicious perfume was found to come from the newly tarred
shrouds of the ship.

We took a drive around the city and its environs at the
fashionable hour for such amusement, 7 P. M. We returned
at 10 P. M., in full daylight. It seemed very odd to see farmers at work in the harvest field at ten in the *afternoon*. They
don't call it *night* here until about 11.30 or 12 P. M. It is
twilight all night at this season of the year. It takes several
days of sunshine to cure the hay. It must be carefully spread
upon poles, arranged like fences in the fields, so that the air
can circulate through it.

The city has a population of about 124,000. I saw nothing peculiar in the people except their free and easy love-
making. It is no uncommon thing to find lovers, old and
young, sitting on the benches of the park, or strolling among
the trees and reposing upon the grass, in the beautiful suburbs
of the city, nearly all night, always remembering that it is
never very dark. It was as light at eleven P. M. the two
nights we remained there as it is at sundown in summer at
home. I also noticed the horses as being of a different breed
from any I have seen in America. They resemble the ancient
war horses of Greece as they are painted in old pictures, with

great strong necks, very much bowed and with the mane cut short so as to make a crest. They are not very large, but are said to have great strength and endurance.

The Norwegians were formerly heavy drinkers. A strong temperance movement has very much reformed this bad habit. They enacted, in 1877, a very stringent license law. Licenses are sold at public auction to the highest bidder, who is compelled before he receives his license, to give security and pay about one hundred dollars for the privilege. Sometimes a private corporation is licensed upon condition that all profits over a fixed sum shall go to the government. They also have, in some districts, a local option law, by which a majority of the people decide whether any or how many licenses shall be granted. So, you see, the agitation of temperance legislation is not confined to our country alone.

In manners the people are very democratic. Common laborers do not hesitate to set themselves at the same table with the lordly traveller. If you invite your guide to dine with you, he will not hesitate to order a bottle of the best wine and quite innocently invite you to drink with him, but he expects you to pay for the treat. The people, however, are kind, unaffected and polite and less inclined to take advantage of the traveler's necessities than the same class in other parts of Europe. The common people have a peculiar way of expressing their thanks for an act of kindness. They do not speak, but simply bow and shake your hand.

From Christiania, we went by rail to Throndhjem (pronounced *Troneum*). It requires seventeen hours to make the journey. We could see the country as well by night as day. Throndhjem is situated on the west coast, in latitude 63.30 N., on a line with Iceland. It has a population of about 23,000 and is built chiefly of wood. The streets are wide and regular. It has several tastefully kept little gardens of the most beautiful flowers I have ever seen. One of the peculiarities of the latitude and temperature of Norway is to produce larger flowers and broader leaves than the same leaves and flowers are in other places. Butter-cups are nearly all double. Clover heads are twice as large as in England, while the leaves and blades of grass are much longer and broader than in other countries. The perpetual sunlight is supposed to cause this increase in the leaf and blossom of annual plants.

On the spot where St. Olaf was originally buried, a fine church has been erected, which is one of the chief objects of interest in Throndhjem. It is now only a fragment of its former magnificence. In the eleventh and twelfth centuries, the Kings of Norway were all buried here. All the sovereigns of the country are required to repair to Throndhjem to be crowned

Charles XIV., John (Bernadotte), Oscar I , Oscar XV., and the present King, Oscar II., were crowned in this Cathedral. There are several fine views and a beautiful water-fall near the city, well worth a visit.

We were compelled to remain at Throndhjem over a day to meet our ship, which did not arrive at her usual hour because of a fog on her way from Bergan. We went on board about 9 P. M. She was a fine English built iron steamer of about eight hundred tons, one hundred and fifty feet long, with powerful engines and well furnished berths for over one hundred first-class passengers. I was a little surprised to see the American flag at her mizzen masthead and the English colors flying from her foremast   This I suppose was intended as a compliment to the English and American travelers on the ship.   The tourists on board were Americans, English, French, Germans and Italians.   Among the Italians was a veritable prince.   The Germans were also represented by a gentleman from Hamburg, who claimed to be a member of the Imperial Parliament.   The Italian prince was a genial, polite and unassuming gentleman ; the German count was gruff, over-bearing, proud and disagreeable.   He had not been on the ship an hour before he got into a row with a Dutch courier from Rotterdam.   The courier requested him to move his chair, which was in the passage way, to let the lady the courier was escorting pass.   The German flatly refused, whereupon the courier called him a brute.   This offended the gentleman's dignity, and to appease his wounded honor he at once demanded of the captain that the courier should either be sent in irons to Hamburg for punishment, or be put off the ship at the next stopping place.   The captain seemed very much alarmed at the German's rage and actually paid the courier, out of his own pocket, three hundred kronen ($90) to voluntarily leave the ship that night at the next landing.   The enraged fool had not sense enough to know that the only person he was punishing was the poor captain, who, by the way, was a most excellent officer and courtly gentleman.

It takes eight days by steamer to go from Throndhjem to the North Cape and return.   I had no idea that the excursion had created so much excitement.   It seemed to me that the entire population of the city were on the wharf to see us off. A band of most excellent musicians played the national airs of England, France and America, and precisely at 10 P. M. the discharge of four cannon upon the ship announced the hour of departure.   You must always remember that 10 P. M. there means broad daylight.   From Thronhdjem to the North Cape there is no night.   We did not see a star for eight days.   The moon lost its red blush and had a sickly, dying look.   The ship winds its way among thousands of islands and mountain scenery of a most interesting character. Some of the mountains are six thousand feet high, but do not seem near so lofty because of the great distances across the fords or bays which separate them.

We soon arrived at the Arctic Circle 66.50 N., where, from the 21st of June till late in July, the sun never sets. We played for several hours with a school of whales. We nearly ran over a very large one. We were permittsd to land at a place where they convert the captured whales into oil, &c. I counted twenty-three large, dead ones anchored a short distance from the immense vats and steam machinery on the shore. Some had just been brought in, others looked and *smelt* if they had been there for months.

Our first regular coaling place was Tromso, a small wooden built town of about six hundred inhabitants, in N. latitude 69.38. It is sheltered by mountains and is comparatively warm. There was a camp of Laplanders a short distance from the town, which the passengers visited while the ship was being coaled. We are now beyond the line of timber. There is a shrub here and there, and now and then a little green spot, but vegetation is very scarce. The wood with which the town is built has been brought from Russia and exchanged for fish. All the country above the sixty-eighth degree of north latitude was known to the ancients as the land of *Thule*. It was a strange region, supposed to be inhabited by beings different from ordinary mortals. The ancient Greeks never explored it. Indeed, in the reign of Theodoric, the people of Constantinople only knew it by conversations with exiles from those far northern lands. It was in this region that the ceremonies of the Christian celebration of Christmas originated. When the sun disappeared in the South they thought he was buried and their season of mourning began. When some watchman upon a high mountain shouted the glad tidings of the first approaching ray of his return, which was about the twenty-fifth of December, then the joyous festivities of his resurrection began. When these northern nations became Christians, they applied the same ceremonies to their rejoicing for the birth of Christ. Thus, one of our most interesting church festivals had its origin in a heathen custom.

A short distance north of Tromso, we landed to ascend Mount Torghattan, or the *marked hat*. About five hundred feet up the mountain there is a hole, from fifty to a hundred feet square, directly through it. From the sea, it looks as if a large cannon ball had been shot through the mountain. How the tunnel was made no one knows. The inhabitants say it was caused by an arrow from the bow of an old Norwegian giant shot at his rival for the heart of a Norseland maid. They say the arrow struck his high Norwegian hat and went clean and clear through the mountain. The next day the ship stopped at a fishing station to give us an opportunity to visit a seven hundred year old church, about two miles distant. I asked an old fisherman on the wharf, who spoke a little English, why he did not leave these hyperborean regions and come to America. He smiled, shook his head and said there was no better country in the world than Harstahaven. That was the name of the church. On the third day from Throndhjem, we arrived at Hammerfest, the most northern city of Europe. It is also built of Russian timber. It has about two thousand one hundred inhabitants. Its situation is very picturesque, nestling at the feet of mountains of rock in the form of an amphitheatre. It is sheltered from the northern blasts and gets the benefit of the sun's rays upon the bare rock of the mountains. The thermometer stood at 52, while the water showed a temperature of 60. There were twenty-six vessels at anchor in the harbor in front of the town, mostly Russian coasters.

We are now at a point where land has no value. We have left all traces of cultivated fields far behind us. The mind suffers a sense of weariness in contemplating the boundless waste and endless desolation around us. The eye grows tired of perpetual sunshine and longs for the relief of a good old-fashioned night.

Hammerfest is two thousand one hundred miles north of the latitude of Philadelphia. In the same latitude on the American side of the Arctic Ocean we would be in the region of eternal ice. Franklin perished in a latitude south of the North Cape, and the uninhabited regions of East Siberia are south of Hammerfest.

As we sailed out of the harbor of Hammerfest, we got our first glimpse of the midnight sun. The view was very imperfect, and the passengers were very much depressed because of the threatening weather. Many persons come thousands of miles to see it and go home disappointed. There are times when it is not seen for weeks. On the 22d, in latitude 70, we had a superb view of the full orb from 6 P. M. until 2 A. M. At half-past eleven every soul was on deck anxiously looking due north for the last minute of midnight. As the minutes passed slowly away it was an interesting study to observe the excited, care-worn and solicitous faces of the gazing crowd. The sun had gradually skimmed along the northwestern horizon from 6 P. M., at which time it did not seem more than half an hour high. It was about three degrees above the horizon, apparently about four feet high, when we were all

startled by the discharge of one of the ship's cannon, by which
the captain announced the exact minute of midnight. The long
suspense was over and a happy smile lighted up every face.
We had seen the midnight sun. We remained on deck until
2 A. M. and saw the sun begin to gradually rise higher and
higher until he was about five feet above the sea, when most
of the passengers went to bed for a long, happy sleep. At
midnight the sun is due north; at 6 A. M. he is east, not
more than 23 degrees high; at noon he is due south, about
45 degrees high; at 6 P. M. he is west, back to 23 degrees,
and from that hour gradually descends upon an oblique line
northward until he again arrives at a point due north at midnight. If we were at the North Pole the sun would apparently
skim around the horizon at the same altitude. As we are nineteen degrees south of the pole the effect is to give the sun a course
around an imaginary eccentric, with its axis nineteen degrees
south of the centre. The northern part of this ring is just
above the horizon; its southern part is about 45 degrees high.
Around this ring the sun appears to travel daily. Every day the
northern part of this ring descends until it drops below the horizon. The sun then commences to rise and set daily, the southern arc growing gradually less until he at last entirely disappears in the south, where, at his appointed time he appears
again and so on to the end of time.

The next day we started for the North Cape, where we
expected to have a still better view of the midnight sun. The
Cape being farther north and the headland being one thous-
and feet above the sea, the sun at midnight is much higher
than where we saw it. To put in the time, the captain visited
the bird-roost rock, about twenty miles east of the Cape.
When we were opposite the rock, which rises about one thous-
and feet above the sea, a cannon was discharged. Instantly
thousands upon thousands of sea fowl, with a cry of alarm,
took wing and ascended in circles above the rock and over the
ship. I noticed that not more than one-third of the birds roost-
ing upon the ledges of the rock, flew away. The captain said
they had learned that it was all noise and no danger, and only
the young and timid were now frightened at an explosion of
gunpowder. I thought that some men might take a lesson
from the birds.

We soon arrived at the Cape, cast anchor, lowered the
boats and were all on shore. The ascent is very steep, almost
perpendicular. We were about an hour getting to the top. All
were elated at the prospect of a splendid view of the midnight
sun. We were doomed to a most bitter disappointment. We
had scarcely reached the summit when a heavy fog fell upon
the mountain top and completely obscured the sun until long

after midnight. We could barely distinguish where it was, but could not see the orb. While on the mountain, I was very much impressed with our delusive ideas of size and distance. The cape did not seem over two or three hundred feet high, whereas it was fully one thousand. The ship looked about the size of a Delaware river tug. The mountains fifty miles off appeared but a few hundred yards away. If these stupendous mountains and almost boundless seas seem so small to one only a thousand feet above them, how like a microscopic mite must the world appear to the eye that beholds the universe at a single glance.

My letter is too long. I have tried to condense my thoughts, but find it almost impossible. It was written by sunlight at midnight at the North Cape.

XLI.

North Cape to Copenhagen—Last Look at the Midnight Sun—Depressing Silence—Optical Delusions—Once in a Lifetime Enough—Back to Christiania—A Viking Ship One Thousand Years Old—What Will be Said of Our Ships One Thousand Years Hence—Familiar Names—Gin for Breakfast—Ancient Ship Customs—Gotenberg—Prosperity in Europe—Birthplace of Hamlet—Emperor of Germany's Reception—Kings of Denmark and Belgium in Copenhagen—Great Industrial Exposition—Lotteries—Stone Age Relics—All Europe a Camp and Every City an Arsenal—On to Berlin.

Copenhagen, August, 1888.

Just before our arrival at Hammerfest, on our return from the North Cape, we had another view of the midnight sun. As both the sun and the ship were going southward, its disk was not as far above the horizon at midnight as it was at the North Cape. One who has seen the sun just before it goes down on a clear evening at sea, will have a very fair idea of the sun at midnight at Hammerfest at this season of the year. It is apparently about three feet high and casts a long glittering streak of golden rays along the smooth surface of the water. The clouds above are in a blaze of red, while those more distant have a silver lining.

Our return was through different fjords from our course up to the Cape, thus giving us a more extensive view of the rugged mountains and glaciers of Norway. The eternal quiet and absence of the usual signs of civilization in these desolate regions have a very depressing effect upon the mind, hard to express but felt by all travelers who have visited the place. To me it seemed like a journey to the moon, or some dead planet. I was again struck with my inability to measure distances or heights. Before landing upon one of the glaciers I tried to mentally guess its length and breadth. Making full allowance for previous optical delusions, I supposed its breadth to be five hundred yards and its length some two or three miles. It was in fact forty-four miles long and twelve miles broad. I saw a rock upon the side of a mountain which I thought about fifty feet high ; it was in reality higher than the tower of the Public Buildings at Philadelphia which, set beside this mountain, would look like a child's toy. Fjords fully ten miles across do not look over half a mile wide.

North Cape is worth one visit in a lifetime. I would not have missed it for all it has cost, but I would not endure the weariness and fatigue of a second journey there for ten times the cost of the trip. The great drawback to travel in Norway and Sweden is the unexpected distance between the points of interest. For instance, in our journey from London to the North Cape and this far back we have traveled four thousand miles.

On returning to Christiania, we gave the city a more complete examination and found it a very interesting place. It contains one of the world's most wonderful relics, an exhumed Viking ship, in sufficiently perfect condition to convey a very correct idea of the war ships of these people a thousand years ago. This ship is seventy feet long, built very much on the plan of the vessels of the same size of to-day, and gives us a reasonably correct notion of the old mariners of " Norseland " who so successfully invaded England and other lands. As I stood on the deck of our splendid steamer, on our way from Christiania here, and looked down at her powerful compound engines working like great dumb giants, I wondered what the world, a thousand years hence, when our present means of locomotion will most probably be forgotten, will think when one of these wrecked steamers shall be belched up from the bottom of the sea by an earthquake, or the drying up of the sea has exposed it. Perhaps the geologists of that day will pronounce it a fossil sea monster with iron ribs and skin of steel that fed upon coal and drank boiling water. They will, perhaps, be about as near right as our modern philosophers are, in some of their deductions, from fossil remains.

I notice all over Norway, Sweden and Denmark very familiar names, such as Williamson, Clemson, Johnson, Peterson and many other names ending in *son* or *sen*, which has the same meaning here as *Mac* in Scotland and *O'* in Ireland.

Notwithstanding the stringent liquor laws of late years, I
find the Norwegians and Swedes very heavy drinkers. When
you call for a glass of beer, they give you a pint, and they
have free gin on the table for breakfast, dinner and supper.
Withal, I see but few drunken men. There must be something in the chilly atmosphere of this latitude that engenders
a desire for strong drink.

On Norwegian ships they still keep up some of their ancient customs. For instance, the purser still carries the ship's
money in a great bag or purse hung around his neck. It was
from this custom that the ship's treasurer took the name he
still bears, of " purser,"

We came by ship from Christiania to Copenhagen. We
had a very fine view of the coast of Sweden and the southern
part of Norway. We stopped long enough at Gotenberg to
fairly see the city. The coast near the town is very rocky but
interesting. The city is built among the rocks, some of which
project above the loftiest buildings. Most of the rocky eminences are either built upon, or crowned with forts or castles.
The harbor was full of ships of all sizes, from ocean steamers
down to fishing schooners. The streets are wide, well paved
and reasonably regular. I saw nothing very remarkable to
distinguish it from other cities of the same size on the continent, except its rocky site. It has a population of about 82,000,
and appears to be a very busy and thriving place. It may be
that Europe is falling into ruin and decay, but I must confess
I have been unable to see it. All that I have seen points to
great prosperity and a rapid increase of wealth and population.

As we approached Copenhagen the country appeared flat and
uninteresting, somewhat like Holland. Before reaching the
city we passed Elsinore, the scene of Shakespeare's Tragedy
of Hamlet. They show the traveler the brook, in which the
fair Ophelia was drowned, and the grave of the Mad Prince.

Copenhagen is a beautiful, well-built and very strongly
fortified city. Several large forts rise out of the water
along the channel, long before we reach the town. The water
front presents a better appearance than that of most cities. In
approaching the city we passed the old castle of Kronberg
which we afterwards visited ; the guide belonging to the castle not being able to speak English, our visit was not satisfactory. Many historic memories, however, cluster around the
place. It is well preserved and full of objects of interest.
Caroline Matilda, of England, was confined in this castle until
George III., her brother, sent a fleet to escort her to England,
where she soon afterwards died.

The Prince of Wales's wife is the daughter of Christian
IX., King of Denmark. The king seems to be very popular

with the people. I counted four iron-clad ships of war and several torpedo boats lying in the harbor. The city is built upon a flat island, indeed all Denmark is flat. The highest place in the kingdom is only about six hundred feet above the level of the sea. The people of the city seem to be very fond of out-of-door sports and rural pleasures. The city contains sixteen beautiful green squares, devoted entirely to the pleasure of the people. Tivoli Garden, in the centre of the city, is always crowded with old and young pleasure-seekers. On Sundays, and after business hours, one is struck with the bareness of the streets. It is just the opposite in the public squares and gardens, which will be found crowded to overflowing. I know of no town except Hamburg that h s more pleasure grounds and public amusements than Copenhagen. Like all other towns of its size, it has its museums, art gallery, palace, opera house, circus and theatre. We attended the circus once and found it crowded to suffocation. The performance was good ; indeed it could not be better.

The population of the city is about 280,000. The day after our arrival the city, and the Industrial Exhibition now being held there, were visited by Count Bismarck and the young Emperor of Germany. I expected to see a much more enthusiastic reception. I secured places on board one of the reception ships and steamed out some ten or twelve miles to meet the fleet of the Emperor's escort. But few flags were displayed from private houses or ships. Of course the public buildings were decorated with the national colors of Germany and Denmark. The King also sent his splendid yacht to meet and receive the Emperor, and a grand salute was fired from the line of forts as the yacht and royal visitors approached, but any one could see a degree of coldness that must have been anything but pleasant to the pride of the German Emperor. A few days before, the King of Belgium had visited the city, and was received with great enthusiasm. They say there was not a private house in the city that did not display a flag, while the people all along his line of march shouted themselves hoarse in huzzas to his honor. The people of Denmark have not forgotten Schleswig-Holstein.

The exhibition, now being held, is very creditable to the State of Denmark. It looked very much like our Centennial display in 1876, but, of course, was not so extensive or grand. I noticed several lotteries in full operation. The poor peasants were standing in a long line, dropping in their kronen only to see a blank come out. About once or twice a day a prize of from five to ten kronen was drawn, and this seemed to set the people crazy for a chance to gamble.

We had a full look at both the King of Denmark and the

Emperor of Germany as they descended from the ship. There
was no difficulty in seeing them both within the exhibition
grounds. I may be deceived in my estimation of the German
Emperor, but he does not look like a very strong man either
mentally or physically.

There is one of the finest collections of relics of the stone
age here to be found in the world. Hammers, axes, chisels
and other tools in stone are exhibited in the Museum of Antiquities, in the exact form of modern iron and steel tools.

There are also exhibited here two petrified wooden coffins
of a pre-historic age, with skulls and bones well preserved.
The size of each skeleton is about the same as the present human stature, and the shape of their skulls is highly intellectual, showing a volume of brain equal to Daniel Webster or
Victor Hugo. If man is an evolution from a monkey, he must
have attained his present form and intellectual superiority when
these old mummies lived, thousands of years ago.

In my drives around the city and excursions by water along
its front, I was surprised to see the gigantic warlike energy
displayed by such a small kingdom as Denmark. It seems to
me that Europe must soon do one of two things—either enter
upon a general war until the energies of all are exhausted and
the powers be thus again reduced to a level, or agree upon a
general disarming. It is quite certain that one Power cannot
now remain idle while a neighboring State is drilling and arm-
ing to its fullest ability. The result is that all Europe is now
an arsenal and every city a military camp.

The weather has been very unsettled since we left England ; in fact we have been compelled to wear our winter clothing ever since we left Vienna. Cherries and strawberries are
now in season, while the wheat is still green and the grass not
yet harvested. One peculiarity of Sweden and Denmark is
their American mode of farming. They have the same style
of barns, hedges, plows, mowing machines and fences. I have
no doubt but that our idea of farming in Chester and Delaware Counties are largely due to early Swedish emigration.

We leave here to-morrow for Berlin where we will, perhaps, sojourn a week, after which we hope to visit Hamburg
and from there go to Scotland. Our time is now getting short.
We begin to realize that our wanderings are nearly over.

XLII.

Copenhagen to Berlin.—Political Reflections—A Beautiful but Dull City—Bismarck and the Emperor in 1873—The Life of a City Depends Upon the Spirit of its People—First Impression of Berlin the Best—Contrast Between William's and Augusta's Palaces—The Mother of the Young Emperor not Popular—Lessons Taught by the Museum of Arms—An Improved Street Railway Car—On to Hamburg.

BERLIN, August, 1888.

After a few days rest in Copenhagen, I felt an irresistable desire to again visit the capital of the great German Empire. I saw it first in 1873, after the close of the Franco-Prussian war. It had then a population of about eighty thousand. While taking an early morning walk by the Royal Palace, I saw the Emperor and the, then Count, now Prince Bismarck, promenading arm in arm in the Palace Garden. The Emperor looked fresh and vigorous, but the Count seemed to move with pain and had a haggard and careworn countenance. The Crown Prince was then the idol of Germany, young, tall, handsome and strong ; full of health and hope. Since then, both he and his illustrious father have died, and the ponderous crown of the Empire is now upon the head of an untried youth The "man of blood and iron" still lives, but even iron will rust and the warmest blood become chilled with age. Germany is now in the acme of its glory ; great, proud and overbearing. How long she will maintain her exalted position is the problem of the day only to be solved by her conduct in the future. She has wounded the pride of her neighbors. She has mutilated France, dismembered Denmark, humiliated Austria and insulted England. She is now courting the friendship of Russia. If Constantinople is to be the price of that friendship, will England, France, Austria and Italy quietly consent to surrender all the advantages of the Crimean war ?

In our journey from Copenhagen to Berlin. we noticed that the harvest was not yet ripe. We found Denmark, along our route of travel, very fertile but flat. It is covered with farmhouses and barns very much like some parts of our own country. The hedges dividing the fields were very well kept, green and beautiful, giving to the land a very neat and fresh appearance. As we entered Germany and approached Berlin, the land became more sterile and sandy, very much resembling the State of New Jersey from Bordentown to Cape May.

The city of Berlin is situated in the centre of a fifty-mile-wide sandy plateau, at its highest point not over one hundred and twenty feet above the sea. The river Spree, about twice as broad as the creek at Chester, runs through the city. The population of the place has increased with a surprising rapidity since 1873. It now contains, including a garrison of twenty thousand soldiers, a population of 1,300,000, and in size is now the third city in Europe. The built up area of the city is about twenty-five square miles. The streets are splendidly paved, the houses tall and imposing and the general appearance of the city prepossessing. The heart of the city is around the Old Museum, Royal Gallery and Palaces, on both sides of the Spree.

There is a striking resemblance in all European cities. The model of Western Europe was Rome, it is now Paris. As one goes farther East, ancient Babylon and Ninevah are the models. London is a mixture of Roman, Greek and Babylonish architecture. So is Berlin. When one for the first time stands upon the bridge over the Spree and looks towards the Old Museum, Royal Gallery, Palaces, University, Arsenal and other imposing public buildings in close proximity with the splendid street "Unter Den Linden," the city looks like the paintings representing ancient Babylon. While, however, there is a striking similarity in the general features of all European cities, there is in fact, as much diversity of appearance in them as there is in the faces and forms of the people that dwell in them. Some are young, fresh and rosy, others are old, bent and boney ; some are clothed in beautiful apparel, others clad in rags ; some are growing, others dying. Berlin is now rapidly growing in size and beauty. As compared with Vienna, London and Paris, it is, however, a rather dull place. It has a splendid park within a short walk of the centre of the city, but it is not as lively and sprightly as the Bois de Bologne, at Paris or the Prater at Vienna. It is full of theatres and concert halls, but the plays and music are of a grave, heavy and august nature. In a general view, the city looks about as it did in 1873 ; in special details, however, it has greatly improved. The old ramparts have been removed and converted into fine new avenues. The old rough cobble stones have given place to new Belgian blocks, wooden pavements like Chicago, and to asphaltum streets like Paris. Tramways run in every direction and public conveyance is easy and cheap. To my mind Berlin is not as fine a city as either New York or Boston, and a much duller place to live in than either.

To most travelers the first impression of Berlin is the best. As one walks down the broad street, crosses the bridge, looks over at what appears to be a Grecian temple, with tall Corinthian columns, and colossal statuary, flanked wiih hand-

some palaces and spacious hotels, he is apt to form the hasty
conclusion that it is one of the handsomest cities in the world ;
but when he gives the place a closer inspection he finds what
appeared to be grand marble columns and palaces are really
nothing but brick masonry covered with stucco. The feeling
is the same as that experienced when for the first time we discover some idol of female beauty, made up of paint and cotton
pads, or when we suppose we are looking upon a pure diamond
and find it is only a piece of polished glass. Berlin, however,
has some fine modern buildings of cut sandstone, granite and
brick. They are, however, exceptions to the general rule.

We gave the city a thorough examination. We devoted one
day to a drive over the town and through the parks. We visited its best Royal palaces. museums, galleries and monuments.

Every visitor to Berlin should see the Palace of the Old
King and also that of the Empress Augusta. They had separate palaces. The contrast between them is very marked.
That of the Empress is very rich and beautiful, but filled to its
utmost capacity with valuable toys, pretty little articles de vertu,
and useless but very valuable furniture, lace, diamond work,
and a thousand articles that no one but a woman could ever
gather together. It is nevertheless excessively feminine and,
therefore, very pretty. In the palace of the old Emperor, on
the other hand, everything is ample but useful, and in perfect
order. The decorations are of the richest kind. The walls
are covered with splendid paintings by the best masters. The
subjects all touch the pride and glory of Germany. The visitors to a part of this palace are required to wear felt slippers
just as we were made to cover our feet before entering the
mosques of Constantinople. The object, however, is not the
same. In one case the foot of the infidel must not touch the
sacred floor, in the other the slipper is to deaden the noise of
the feet upon the bare polished wood and also to keep the floor
clean. We have entered many royal and princely palaces in
different countries, but have seen none richer or more elegant
than the two seen here. We particularly noticed the portrait of
the widow of the late Emperor Frederick, the daughter of
Queen Victoria. If she was as fair as her picture represents
her, and I have no reason to doubt it, she was a woman of rare
beauty. It is hinted that the German people do not like her.
No one has been able to inform me why. They ought not
only to be proud of her, but also of noble old Queen Victoria,
the grandmother of their Emperor. A very fine view of Berlin can be had from the top of the monument of Victory in the
park.

One of the most interesting places in the city is the Museum of Arms, and the relics of the war with France. A glance

at the monstrous cannon, broken and battered by actual battle, gives some idea of the terrible struggles around Metz and other fields. Some of these guns show the indentations of as many as six cannon balls on a single gun. Some have been struck in the muzzle, others have been broken in two, while many have been bent and dismantled by a single shot. Exact models in plaster and wood of the several battlefields are here exhibited, and afford a most excellent study of the sanguinary scenes of the Franco-Prussian war, so full of glory to Germany and so disastrous to France. This museum is intended to keep up the enthusiasm of Germany for her army, and it seems to have that effect, for it is always crowded and is the scene of many a lecture from some old veteran who is always listened to with pride by the young people of the city. One should never tire of looking at beautiful or interesting objects, yet I confess that I am weary of sight-seeing. I have visited so many museums of art and antiquity, and have seen so many of the world's finest paintings that my desire for picture galleries and museums is almost satisfied. Berlin can boast of a very fine gallery of modern art, and one of the best museums of antiquity in Europe

I noticed in Berlin what seemed to me to be an improvement in street car traveling. The cars have ordinary omnibus wheels, the tires being the width of the iron rails. They have also a fifth wheel, raised and lowered by a lever, which falls into the groove in the iron rail in front of the fore wheels and keeps them perfectly in place upon the rail. By this simple contrivance they can pass each other on a single track by simply raising the fifth wheel, by which they become ordinary omnibuses, and turn out to pass, and then take the track again. We leave here to-morrow for Hamburg.

XLIII

BERLIN TO EDINBURGH—HAMBURG AGAIN—A CITY IN A PARK—DAILY SHOWERS TO REFRESH THE FLOWERS—FOL-LOWING THE TRACK OF SPRING—HAMBURG SOON TO LOSE ITS CHARTER AS A FREE CITY—SUDDEN RISE IN THE PRICE OF GOODS—OLD LUBECK—CURIOUS ARCHITECTURE—THE "DANCE OF DEATH"—ON SHIP FOR SCOTLAND—ALL THE PASSENGERS BUT OURSELVES DEMOCRATS AND FREE TRAD-ERS—EDINBURGH AFTER AN ABSENCE OF NINETEEN YEARS —GLASGOW—THE EXHIBITION AND QUEEN'S JUBILEE PRES-ENTS—OFF FOR YORK.

EDINBURGH, August 1888.

The most direct route from Berlin to Scotland is through Hamburg where we took ship, and in about two and a half days arrived at Leith, the seaport of Edinburgh. The general appearance of the country from Berlin to Hamburg is flat and unprepossessing. Just before reaching Hamburg, however, the prospect improves. We suddenly emerge from a compara-tive desert into a beautiful city of mixed but very striking architecture, green and luxuriant parks, gardens and lawns, lakes and rivers. Except upon the river front, Edinburgh looks like a city built in the centre of a great park. Much of the present splendor of the place is due to the great conflagra-tion of 1842, which destroyed one-third of the city. Enough was left to give a fair idea of the city in the olden time. Before the fire it looked very much like Amsterdam, Rotterdam, Lu-beck and other mediæval towns. The contrast between the old and new town is very striking. The city now has a population of about 475,000, but in commercial importance it is next to Lon-don and Liverpool. The harbor is literally full of ships from all countries, and presents a scene of very busy and active life. Besides the river Elbe, upon which the city fronts, there are two other rivers running through it, with large houses built up from the water on each side giving the city, along the rivers, very much the appearance of Venice. These little rivers empty into the beautiful lakes or basins in the very heart of the city and are crossed by small steamboats and fancy yachts, looking very gay on a fair summer evening.

The suburbs are occupied by rich and elegant villas and country seats, some of them quite baronial in appearance. In many respects the city is unique. Its lakes, canals, rivers, parks, gardens and villas, all within a reasonable proximity of each other, together with the sharp dividing line between the old city and the new, distinguish it from all other cities of the same size. In a word, it is a place of pleasant contrasts. It has a good art gallery, a fine museum, one of the best zoological gardens, and the finest aquarium in the world. Being Protestant in religion, its churches are plain and not very attractive. Like most old cities, the ancient ramparts have been removed and their places converted into splendid drives and avenues, with long lines of trees of the greenest foliage. The luxuriant green fields, lawns, gardens and parks owe their superior verdure to the almost daily rains during the summer. Clear days here are the exception, the rule is a shower or two every day. We wear our heavy winter clothing and never venture into the streets without umbrellas or waterproof overcoats. It is a very bad place for a high silk hat. It looked odd at first, in July, to see the citizens in winter attire and the ladies in furs, but we got used to it. We sleep under blankets every night. It may seem strange but it is nevertheless the fact, that we have been following the track of Spring ever since we left America ; we have not advanced enough to reach Summer yet, and when we get home we will find Autumn with its sere and yellow leaves to greet us, and find one of the Summers of our lives forever lost. We are now enjoying all the early Spring fruits, flowers and vegetables, such as gooseberries, raspberries, strawberries, cherries, green peas (not canned) and asparagus. The farmers are just beginning to mow their grass ; the wheat and oats fields are still green. We have at last reached a land of good butter. I think I have referred to the bad and cheesey butter of Italy and Greece, where the butter was really *grease*.

All imported goods are cheap in Hamburg. 1 find good Havana cigars here cheaper than in America. Hamburg is a free city ; that is to say, no duties are paid on foreign importations. This happy state of affairs is to end with this year. By an Imperial decree, all the free cities of the Old Hanseatic League are to lose their time-honored privilege after 1888. Merchants have already anticipated the supposed rise in goods by marking up their prices about 20 per cent. The prosperity of Germany, like America, depends upon her protective policy. England is nearly ready to abandon her free trade theories. She has already imposed a heavy duty on cigars, spirits, and *silver* plate. Silver, you know, is a great *American* product.

I took a day, while waiting for the sailing time of our ship, to visit the old town of Lubeck, one of the quaintest places I have yet found on the continent. I found the country between Hamburg and Lubeck very highly cultivated and thickly settled with prosperous farmers. In general appearance it looks very much like our own rich farms. The fields are about the same size, the houses and out-buildings have the same air of comfort and the boys and girls seem equally happy and contented. Travelers, as a rule, pronounce rural life and domestic thrift uninteresting. They confine their praise to gay city life or lake, river and mountain scenery ; but to me there is nothing more touching and really beautiful than happy domestic life amid green fields and well-fed herds. It has a charm equal to the gay whirl of city splendor, or mountains, lakes, cascades and grottoes, especially when both can be enjoyed, appreciated and compared.

The city of Lubeck occupies a very commanding position about ten miles from the sea on a small but deep arm of the Baltic. It is chiefly built of red brick, ornamented with terra cotta, very much like the brick work of the present day. Most of the buildings are mediæval and seem to have been erected without the use of the "plumb, level and square." There is scarcely a building in the old part of the town with a straight face or plumb front. Walls, not over fifteen feet high, are crooked and twisted. Two of the old churches have very high steeples which lean almost as much as the Tower of Pisa. One of the side walls is four feet out of plumb at a height of about one hundred feet. To equalize the difficulty the balance of the wall leans about as much the other way. There are no cracks in the walls and the foundations are upon the firm original earth. The conclusion is, therefore, inevitable that they were built so ; why, no one can tell. Even the ten-feet-high stone pillars which support the rich brick vaulting of the ancient cloisters outside the church, are out of plumb. There is not a straight street in the city, but all are of good width and well paved. St. Mary's Church is a most remarkable structure. It is immense in proportion, Gothic in style and constructed entirely of red brick, with grand vaulted arches inside, and whitewashed, to make it look like marble. It has great flying buttresses of brick, in imitation of the stone ones of Notre Dame in Paris. These are necessary to support the heavy brick vaulting over the interior of the building. The walls are visibly out of plumb, while the floor is at least ten feet out of level. It looks within like the enclosure of a graveyard by an immense church. Not an inch of the floor is unoccupied by old flat gravestones recording the merits of those who repose below. The church contains some very interesting relics of the Middle Ages, among which is a very old painting called the "Dance of Death." It is very suggestive of the impartiality of the King of Terrors in the choice of his partners in the dance.

The new buildings are most substantial as well as beautiful in construction and conform with our idea of modern architecture. The town has now a population of about 55,000 ; it once amounted to near 100,000. It was one of the first cities of the Hanseatic League, from the Articles of which many of the ideas in our Federal Constitution were borrowed. I visited the old League Hall, completed in 1443. In the Rathskeller the vaulting is very well preserved. I copied the following inscription from the chimney piece :

"Menich man lude synghet; Wen me em de Brute binget;
Weste he wat men em brochte, dot he wol weuen nochte."

To show my progress in old Saxon I have made the following impromptu translation, in which I claim to have preserved the rhythm as well as the sense of the original :

Many a man loudly sings
When to him a bride one brings;
If he knew what they had brought
He would cry for what he'd caught.

After spending four days in Hamburg, we set sail for Leith, where we arrived in about two days and a half. The sea was smooth and the weather pleasant. Most of the passengers were English and Scotch merchants. They showed great interest in American politics and did not hesitate to express their hope that Mr. Cleveland might be re-elected. The reason they gave for their preference was what they termed "our abominable tariff laws." They said that their correspondents in America had assured them that the Democrats were free traders and that would be of great advantage to the English and Scotch manufacturers. I have now been four days in Edinburg and have made it a point to ascertain the sentiments of the merchants and business men of the city. I have not found a man who is not earnestly anxious for the success of the Democratic party, and all give the same reason—"our unjust tariff laws." It seems to me that if the election of Mr. Cleveland is to be of such immense advantage to the manufacturers of Great Britain, it must necessarily be a corresponding disadvantage to our American manufacturers and workingmen. If they do not hope to profit by it, why are they so deeply interested in Democratic success.

I visited Edinburgh in 1869 and then thought it the most enchanting city I had seen ; now, after nearly 20 years' absence, and after I have seen all the most beautiful cities of Europe, I find no reason for modifying my former opinion of the place. It is without question the most picturesque and charmingly located city I have ever seen. The old castle, five hundred feet above the sea level ; Calton Hill, with its imitation of the Parthenon ; Arthur's seat, nearly eight hundred feet high ; the green and beautiful valley running through the centre of the city, decorated with shrubbery and flowers ; the great waterless bridge crossing the deep ravine connecting the old city with the new ; its parks, monuments, palaces, and substantial cut granite buildings ; all tend to give to the place a grand as well as a romantic appearance, once seen, never to be forgotten. It has been the home of Scotland's greatest poet's and literary men. Scott and Burns have immortalized it, while the sad fate of Mary Queen of Scotts has invested it with a peculiar interest to all the admirers of that unhappy queen. From Arthur's seat the prospect is superb. We can see the North German Ocean ; the Firth and Island of " Macbeth's witches ; " the whole city of Edinburgh down to and including Leith ; the hills of Lammermoor and the scenes of many of Scott's most exciting novels. We visited Roslin Castle and chapel, about nine miles from the city, and were richly paid for the time and trouble. We also paid a flying visit to Glasgow, where we spent a very agreeable day in the Industrial Exhibition now being held there.

Glasgow is one of the world's most busy places. It furnishes ships for all nations ; I have seen them on every sea. The city is full of familiar names such as Simpson, Clyde, McCay, McCall, and other honored Delaware county names. They were making great preparations for an expected visit from the Queen who had promised to attend the exhibition in a few days. The Scotch are among the most loyal subjects of Her Majesty and seem to have a strong personal attachment for her ; in this respect they are in happy contrast with poor Ireland.

The exhibition is very much like the one we saw at Copenhagen, and something like the Centennial Exposition held at Philadelphia in 1876 ; of course not as extensive, but in some respects equally as good. We had the pleasure of seeing all the Queen's Jubilee presents, exhibited in a building erected for the purpose. They are very rich and beautiful, but not equal to those presented to the Pope at his jubilee and on exhibition at Rome when we were there.

We leave here to-morrow for York, where we hope to spend a few days.

XLIV.

London, August, 1888.

Seven weeks ago we left London for a journey to the North
Cape. After wandering over Norway, Sweden, Denmark, Germany and Scotland, here we are back again in this smoky old
town. It is four hundred miles from Edinburgh to London, yet
Ben Johnson walked the entire distance to spend a few days
with a fellow poet. "O Rare Ben Johnson." We have not
been in the habit of traveling by rail more than twelve hours
a day, and never by night; we therefore broke our journey
just half way, at the very remarkable old city of York, where
we remained two days exploring the wonders of that famous
and intensely interesting town. On our journey from Edinburgh we passed Berwick, Durham, Darlington and New Castle, and had a very excellent view of each. They are all noted
places in English history. The cathedral of Durham towers
over the town like the Minster of York.

York is perhaps the oldest city in Great Britain. Some
historians assert that it was a city of considerable importance
when David was King at Jerusalem. It is certain that it is as
old as the Christian religion. It has a well authenticated history since A. D. 79, at which time the Sixth Roman Legion
was quartered there. The Emperor Severus, with his sons
Geta and Caracalla, lived in York A. D. 208. Severus died
there. His son Geta was Supreme Judge of the Tribunal of
Justice, and the great old Roman lawyer Papinianus was his
counsellor. Caracalla murdered his brother Geta and Papinianus was put to death in Rome for refusing, in a public oration, to declare Caracalla innocent. There is a mound a short
distance outside the city walls where Severus's body was burned. His ashes were put into an urn and sent to Rome. There
is another mound about two miles beyond the bulwarks surrounded with hoary old oak trees where, tradition says, one
of the Danish Kings was buried.

The city is situated on the river Ouse, which is navigable
up to its site. It is surrounded by well-preserved Roman walls.
There is not a city in all Great Britain that has preserved its
ancient character so well as York. It has streets with houses

on each side of unknown age. Some of the old houses have recently been reconstructed and their foundations were found to be of Roman masonry. Roman antiquities are constantly being exhumed in the improvement of the city. While in Sicily we made the acquaintance of a gentleman from York whom I at first took for a traveling photographer. He had with him a complete set of instruments and was very industrious in securing good views of all the noted places in that historic country. His manners were so gentle and courtly that we soon concluded I had made another mistake in relying upon first impressions. On parting at Messina we exchanged cards with a kind invitation on his part to call on him if we should visit York. After we were comfortably settled in our hotel, we inquired of the lady in charge of the desk, whether she knew a gentleman in York named Tempest Anderson. "Oh, yes," she replied, "everybody in York knows Dr. Anderson." We had hardly made the inquiry when we were delighted to see our old traveling companion descending the stairway. He had been sent for to visit a sick person in the hotel. The meeting was very pleasant. We found our supposed traveling photographer to be one of the most celebrated physicians of York. He insisted upon our taking tea with him and inspecting his wonderful old house, or rather houses, for he had, at great expense and exquisite taste, repaired and partially restored three of the oldest houses in the city and rendered them a most charming dwelling place for himself, his most agreeable and courtly mother and his two ladylike and highly cultivated sisters. He drove us over the town and surrounding suburbs and gave us historic and other information we could not otherwise possibly have acquired. Through his influence, we were permitted to see places of great interest not open to strangers. On visiting the Museum the next day we were struck by the beauty and systematic arrangement of some rare minerals from Norway. To our agreeable surprise we read upon the label that they had been presented to the Museum by Dr. Anderson. Upon making further inquiry we learned that we had been entertained by one of the best citizens of York and withal a gentleman of culture as well as of great scientific acquirements.

We visited every place of note in and around the city. The most prominent object is the Cathedral or "Minster," as it is called. It is a grand Gothic pile, more imposing than beautiful. Clifford's Tower is a very interesting ruin. It was founded by William the Conqueror, and was the scene of the massacre of the Jews of York, so touchingly referred to in Ivanhoe. Isaac of York and Rebecca, his beautiful and faithful daughter, are two of the best characters in that celebrated novel.

On the 11th of March, 1190, at the beginning of the reign of Richard I., a terrible persecution commenced in England against the Jews. In York, the mob were led by a fanatic monk ; the Jews were massacred without mercy. After the house of the chief Jew of York, named Benet, had been plundered and his wife and children killed, five hundred Jews fled to York Castle, carrying their treasure with them ; all that remained in the town were massacred. Those who took refuge in the castle made their final stand in Clifford's Tower and maintained the seige for several days till hunger overcame them. Finding themselves lost, they resolved to kill each other. Jacen then killed his wife Amia and her sons ; the rest followed his example. The castle was then set on fire by themselves and all perished in the flames. The next day the Register of their bonds and mortgages was taken by the mob and burned in the streets of York. It is only necessary to add that the offenders were never punished except by trifling fines. Nearly one thousand innocent men, women and children were murdered in cold blood by a mob called *Christians*. The tower was repaired by the Earl of Cumberland whose family name was Clifford, from which it has since taken the name of the " Clifford Tower."

The Castle of York, after the fortress was dismantled, was converted into a prison. Among the prisoners confined within its walls were Eugene Aram and the celebrated highwayman, Dick Turpin. We saw the spot where his black mare " Bess " fell dead after his ride from London, two hundred miles, in four hours. Dick had committed a robbery and murder upon Hounslow Heath at 5 o'clock, A. M., and was arrested in the Market Place of York for knocking a butcher down at 9 A. M., on the same day. When the news came to York, several hours later, of the murder and robbery, and Dick was accused of the crime, he successfully pleaded an "alibi" and was acquitted because of the supposed impossibility of traveling, even by the fleetest horse, two hundred miles in two hundred and forty minutes. I remember, when I was a small boy, hearing one of my father's men, who was from York, singing in the peculiar dialect of the peasantry of Yorkshire, a song about " Black Bess," the opening verse of which I can still recollect.

> " Dick Turpin upon the Hounslow Heath,
> His black mare Bess, bestrode ;
> He saw the Bishop's coach and four
> Come galloping down the road ;
> He bade the coachman stop, but he
> Suspecting of the job
> His horses lashed, but he soon rolled off
> With a brace of slugs in his knob.
> Then whispering in his black mare's ear,
> Who luckily was not fagged,
> ' Now travel far and fast, my dear,
> Or I shall be surely scragged,' " etc.

I have no doubt but that many of the traditional feats of
" Black Bess " and Dick Turpin are fabulous, but the jockies
of York believe them all as firmly as they do the Gospel.

The bars and towers of the city wall are full of historic
interest. I can only refer to one of the bars which stands to-
day very much as it appeared after the celebrated battle of
Marston Moor—I refer to Micklegate, at the end of the street
of the same name. The arch is supposed to be Norman. At
the top of this gate were exposed the heads of traitors. During the wars of the Roses the Duke of York, in 1460, had his
head fixed on one of the highest spikes so that " *York might
look over York.*" His son, Edward IV., entered the city after
the battle of Towton and beheld his father's head over the gate
with the inscription above noted pinned above it. He caused
the heads of the Earls of Devon and Wiltshire to replace that
of his father. After the battle of Marston Moor the defeated
Royalists, fleeing from the fatal field, sought admission into
the city by this gate, and tradition says many hundreds died
of exhaustion in sight of the open gate.

We visited the palace of the Archbishop of York where
His Grace lives in regal splendor. The name of Booth is very
common in the city. The ancestors of the Booth family of
Pennsylvania came from York. One of the Archbishops bore
that name, and one of the city gates is called Bootham Bar.
The population of the city is about 80,000. It is rapidly increasing and bids fair soon to regain its old-time importance
as one of the chief cities of Great Britain. It may be interesting to some of your readers to add, that the Quakers of York
founded the first lunatic asylum where kind and gentle treatment to that most unfortunate class of patients was tried as an
experiment, and which is now the accepted treatment all over
the world. My ancestors came from Yorkshire.

I have devoted about ten days to life in London and find
it a little world in itself. One could spend a month here without
knowing much of the city. If we confine ourselves to its avenues of trade and fashionable streets, its grand hotels, places of
amusement and recreation, churches and benevolent institutions, we must concede to it a high state of moral, business and
religious culture ; but, if we explore its dens of vice and districts
of squalor and poverty, we must declare it the Babylon of modern cities and the most wicked place in the world. I have seen
grog shops full of girls and boys, with maids behind the bar
dealing out liquid poison here called " spirits," at three pence
a glass I have seen drunken men and women staggering
through the by-streets and lanes of London on a Sunday afternoon within a stone throw of fashionable churches filled with
pious Christian worshipers. There are places in London to day

where it is dangerous to walk even in daylight. Withal the
city is well governed and has the best and most reliable policemen of any city, perhaps, in the world. When we consider its
enormous population, we can only wonder at the power of the
municipal authority that is able to preserve order as well as it
does, and keep such a restless and discordant mass in anything
like peace and harmony.

This will be my last letter from abroad as I find it tiresome to write of places I have previously visited and formerly
endeavored to describe. We have traveled over Europe from
Brest in the west, to the Black Sea in the east, and from Mount
Ætna in the south, to the North Cape in the Arctic Ocean.
We have been within two days' travel of Africa, and have
stood upon one of the mountains of Asia. We have seen the
site of ancient Troy and looked at snow-clad Olympus.

My letters are only an index of what we have seen, and
have been written without revision or the care I would like to
have given them. I must apologize for their hurried and often
slovenly style. No one knows their imperfections better than
myself. Many of them were written under circumstances of
great difficulty and most of them when I ought to have been
asleep. Travelers will understand this much better than my
readers possibly can.

XLV

From New York to Liverpool Once More—Glimpses at
Life on the Ship—A Good Place to Study Character
—Time Counted not from Wharf to Wharf, but from
Discharging and Taking the Pilot—A Floating City
—Death on Shipboard—Size of the Ship—Moonlight
on the Sea—Latitude and Longitude, How to Find
it by the Stars—Distinguished Passengers—Purse
Proud Travelers—Taken for a Preacher—A Blue-
Stocking.

Liverpool, July, 1889.

After a rather pleasant voyage of seven days, we landed
here early this morning. The weather is cold and disagreeable.
This, however, is nothing new for Liverpool. Many persons
erroneously suppose the time required to cross the sea is reckoned from wharf to wharf. This would not be just to the ship.

The pilot has charge from New York to Sandy Hook, and the journey from Queenstown to Liverpool is often broken by time lost in receiving, discharging and waiting for the mail, and delay caused by the low water at the bar of the Mersey, for these reasons the time is always counted from Sandy Hook to Queenstown. Our ship averaged a run of four hundred and twenty-two miles a day. The ship is well named, "The City of Paris," for she resembles a floating city in more respects than in the number of her passengers. In her present trip, she carried about two thousand persons, including her officers and crew, and among them, it was not difficult to find the follies as well as the pleasures of Paris.

A ship, such as the City of Paris, is a favorable place for the study of human character. Men and women may conceal their true dispositions upon the shore—they may dodge you if they cannot deceive you on the land, but when you catch them on a ship and closely observe their conduct for eight or ten consecutive days, you cannot fail to read their characters and know them, perhaps, much better than they know themselves. The character will crop out if you keep it under your eye long enough to remove restraint and give nature time to work.

This is certainly the iron age. Everything about the ship, even the masts, spars, booms, cross-trees and yards, are of iron. The iron decks are covered with planks and the masts and spars painted to imitate wood, but this is only a sham ; she is an iron ship from stem to stern. When lying at her pier, where she can be compared with other ships she looks rather large, but on the vast ocean she does not at all impress one with her enormous dimensions. One can form some idea of her size by taking a walk around her promenade deck. Fifty yards is cut off for the second cabin promenade, and about the same for the steerage passengers, yet every seven walks around the promenade for the first-class passengers makes one mile. The smoking room is the most interesting place for men, and the deck, in good weather, the favorite spot for the ladies. The smoking room will comfortably seat one hundred and fifty persons and leave ample space for the steward to supply segars and liquors to the guests. The bar is open every day, Sunday not excepted, and yet it is a very rare thing to see an intoxicated person. I have not seen one upon the ship. In this respect there has been a great change within the past twenty years. Gambling is still the great vice of the ship. I may also add that I have seen but little flirting among the young people. During this voyage we have all conducted ourselves with becoming propriety.

Although the weather was not very rough, yet a great

majority of the passengers, from the second to the fourth day out, were very sick. Several of the ship's stewards had to go to their berths. This is a rare occurrence. The third day out, one of the firemen died. They buried the poor fellow the next morning at 4 o'clock. Many of us did not know of his sickness until after he was thrown into the sea.

For two days we passed through a dense fog. The hoarse fog horn blew every two minutes and materially interfered with our conversation by day and our sleep at night. Like many of danger's warnings it was very disagreeable but absolutely necessary. After the fog lifted the sky became beautifully clear, the play of sunlight upon the waves was charming, the spray caused by the dash of the ship through the billows made little rainbows, and the light shining through the white foam gave to the deep blue waves a crest of apple-green. At night the moonlight was superb. There is no place like a ship for the study of the geography of the heavens. As we keep on the 40th degree of north latitude the stars all look familiar and homelike, but as we go northward, for every sixty-nine miles they rise one degree higher. Polaris gets higher up every night. I looked at him the last night I was on the ship and found him about fifty-five degrees, whereas he is only forty degrees high at Philadelphia. With a chronometer, quadrant, and nautical almanac, there is no difficulty in finding our correct latitude and longitude at sea. The degree of altitude of the North star is always the degree of north latitude of the observer. To find our longitude requires only a little calculation. If we see a star rise at nine o'clock which our nautical almanac informs us rises at Greenwich at eight o'clock, we know we are one hour west of the meridian at Greenwich, and as the same star in twenty-four hours makes the entire circumference of the earth, it follows that we are just the one twenty-fourth of the earth's circumference on a given parallel of latitude, west of the meridian of Greenwich.

We have a few distinguished men and women on the ship and a great many who would like to be so considered. It is a great accomplishment in any one to be able to see himself as others see him. Let me illustrate this thought by one or two occurrences during the voyage. As we passed Staten Island, I noticed a large, vulgar-looking man, with a big jaw and heavy eyebrows, standing upon one of the hatches with a large field-glass to his eye and a red handkerchief in his right hand, which he vigorously waved at one of the beautiful mansions upon the shore. I noticed that between each wave of his red flag he would look out of the corners of his eyes to see if anybody was looking at him. After a little while I approached him ; he seemed pleased to be interviewed. I said : " that is a very fine house ; I suppose you know some one that lives there, as I saw you waving your handkerchief. But I saw no one respond. Do you know the happy owner sir ? " "Know the happy owner !" said he, "why, I'm the man myself." I at once congratulated him upon his good fortune, and suggested that he must have had some good luck in money-making. "You're right," said he, "I've made a hundred dollars an hour for the last fifteen years."

A gentleman from Colorado was very talkative about the wonders of Denver. He evidently had a poor memory, for every time I conversed with him he told me the same story as a great secret (which he did not care to have repeated as it might give him too much notoriety on the ship) ; that he had made at least half a million in land speculations around Denver, and now owned five square miles of land. His only trouble was that he only had one daughter and he was very much afraid some English lord would fall in love with her while abroad. I overheard him tell the same story to at least a dozen others on the ship, and always with an air of great confidence.

One evening after dinner, I was standing by the hand-rail, musing over the many curious phases of human character around me, when I was gently touched by a sedate looking old gentleman, with an enormous upper lip, big spectacles on his nose, white cravat and high broad-brimmed hat. He said in a half-subdued tone, " Have I the honor to speak to a minister of the Gospel ? " I said, "My good friend, why do you take me for a preacher ? " "Well," said he, "your sedate manner, the serious cast of your face and your-your-well, your *white* cravat made me think you were one of us." He continued, "there's a kind of free-masonry among us preachers by which we can generally know each other." Now, said he, "of what denomination would you take me to be ? " "Well," said I, "If you will permit me to give an honest answer, I would take you for a Mormon Elder on his way to Europe for recruits." He did not speak to me again during the whole voyage.

I saw a tall, hook-nosed, but very black-eyed woman very busy taking notes. I made the following memorandum in my diary : " That woman is perhaps a blue-stocking from Boston ; I would like to see her diary ; maybe she is an authoress ; perhaps a female lecturer ; wonder what she says in her notes about me." A few days afterwards, when the passengers began to fraternize, I told her if she would show me her notes concerning her first impression of me, I would show her my observations about her. She at once accepted the proposition. Here is an exact reproduction of her note book ; " I do wonder who that tall gentleman with a white cravat and Scotch cap

is? I think he's a preacher—no, he wears diamonds—a gambler, perhaps. He's taking notes—maybe he's criticizing me
—thinks he's good looking—I don't—wouldn't have the best
man on the ship—what horrible conceited things men are any-
how." Every time we met on the deck there was a peculiar
twinkle in her black eye, as much as to say, "Old fellow you
didn't get much the better of me."

But I must bring my letter to a close. I go from here to-
morrow to Stratford-on-Avon, to see the grave of Shakespeare
and from there to old Warwick Castle.

———

XLVI.

LIVERPOOL TO ROUEN—A CRANK—HAPPY CHILDHOOD—A
DAY IN LIVERPOOL — ITS WONDERFUL DOCKS AND SEA
WALLS—ST. GEORGE'S HALL — BIRKENHEAD—BIRMING-
HAM—OLD WARWICK THE KING MAKER'S CASTLE—RURAL
ENGLAND—STRATFORD-ON-AVON—AN ENGLISHMAN'S IDEA
OF PHILADELPHIA--KENNELWORTH--EXPLORING THE SLUMS
OF LONDON—BRIGHTON—NEW HAVEN—SUDDEN CHANGE
FROM ENGLAND TO FRANCE—ROUEN—JEANNE D'ARC—
THE BUTTER TOWER—BIRD'S EYE VIEW FROM MOUNT
GARGON.

ROUEN, July, 1889.

Liverpool is about two hundred and forty miles west of
Queenstown. It took all night and until 11 o'clock next
morning to reach the bar over which, at low tide, vessels drawing more than twenty feet of water cannot pass. The tide falls
about twenty-seven feet. Our ship drew about thirty-two feet
of water and, consequently, six hours were lost waiting for the
rise of the tide. We had to cast anchor ten miles from the
city and entirely out of its sight.

In Liverpool I met one of the cranks of the ship. In my
hurry to get off my last letter I neglected to notice him. He
was six feet two in height, wore his straight black hair six
inches long over his ears and down his back. He had a very
large nose and retreating forehead; he wore a white cravat and
long frock coat; he would be taken for a preacher were it not
for a large cluster diamond pin in his shirt bosom. He was
very exclusive during the whole voyage and was evidently
impressed with his own importance. He was registered on
the ship's catalogue as a Southern Colonel. To my surprise
I found he had registered at the hotel as a D. D. Some wag,
perhaps one of his fellow passengers on the ship, had added
between brackets (D. F.)

I saw, in Liverpool, a procession of romping little children returning from a picnic. They seemed so happy in their holiday dresses that it did my heart good to see and hear them. After all, if they only knew it, children are the happiest of God's creatures. After we arrive at fifty years, life's enjoyments consist chiefly in the recollection of past pleasures. We must not censure an old man if, in a moment of forgetfulness, he acts like a boy, nor blame an old lady for a little girlish coquetry. They are only enjoying the innocent perfume of a few flowers gathered from the thorns and briers along life's pathway.

The city of Liverpool is usually ignored by American travelers, who, in their anxiety to see London and Paris, neglect one of the finest cities in Europe. The commerce of the place is enormous ; its docks are the wonder of the world ; the sea wall and the stupendous floating wharves are more wonderful than the hanging gardens of Babylon. I doubt very much whether any city in the world has such Cyclopean works as the walls, docks and floating wharves of Liverpool. New York will not have such a river front in a thousand years. The city is regular, clean, well paved and well built. It is adorned with some very beautiful and architectural structures, among which is St. George's Hall, a noble building of solid stone supported by fine Grecian columns. The grand arched interior is also supported by finely polished granite columns, some of them monoliths.. The great window of stained glass representing St. George and the Dragon, has a very beautiful effect when seen from the interior. I spent a day riding and walking over the city and suburbs and was richly compensated for my time and labor. At this season the days here are very long; it is daylight at 3 A. M., and one can see to read without artificial light until 9 P. M. Birkenhead, opposite the city, is connected with it by a fine tunnel under the Mersey. It is a suburb of the city and is a charming place, green and refreshing, full of delightful villas where the rich merchants of Liverpool seek repose and the enjoyments of domestic life after their busy hours in the city are over.

From Liverpool, I passed through Birmingham. Its approach looks something like Pittsburg. It is a well-built manufacturing town, of half a million inhabitants. On my way to London, I stopped a day at Warwick and visited the fine old castle so renowned in English history. I found it an intensely interesting place ; by some it is considered even more interesting than Windsor. It was the castle of the Earl of Warwick, so often mentioned in Shakespeare as the " King Maker," during the Wars of the Roses. To be a good traveler it is absolutely necessary to be a good walker. I walked for

miles over and around Warwick. The green fields, limpid
streams, great old oaks and elms, splendid roads, fat flocks of
sheep and thrifty husbandmen, gave to the place an air of great
comfort and rural happiness.

From Warwick, (pronounced *Warrick*) I went by rail to
Stratford-on-Avon, to see the birthplace of Shakespeare.—
After I visited the church, the cottage of, " Sweet Ann Hathaway," and the house where the immortal poet was born, the
custodian requested me to register my name, residence, etc.
He asked me where Thurlow was ? I told him it was near
Philadelphia. He replied that Philadelphia was a very large
place ; that Mr. Childs had told them that it contained over
forty thousand square miles. I saw at once that the poor fellow had confused the words, " Philadelphia " and " Pennsylvania." He evidently thought the State was called, " Philadelphia " and the city. " Pennsylvania." On my return to
Warwick, I was agreeably surprised to find Mr. Richard Young,
of Delaware county, waiting at the station for the train to
Leamington. Thus we are constantly delighted by meeting
our countrymen all over the world.

I can see no signs of poverty in this part of England.
Everybody seems contented and comfortable, healthy and
happy. The trip from Warwick to the old ruined castle of
Kennelworth is made by coach. The place is chiefly inter-
esting as the scene of the Duke of Leicester's flirtations with
Queen Elizabeth, of Sir Richard Varney's villainy, and of poor
Amy Robsart's sorrows, so graphically portrayed in Sir Walter
Scott's novel of the same name.

From Warwick, I went direct to London. It looked as
familiar as the face of an old friend. After wandering for a
day or two among its never-ceasing wonders, I concluded I
would, for a few hours, explore its slums. I dressed myself in
my ship clothing, flannel shirt and Scotch cap ; left all my
valuables behind, and with only a few shillings in my pocket
sallied forth like Don Quixotte in search of new adventures.
I visited The Seven Dials, The District of St. Giles, and the
Alsatia of Sir Walter Scott. I cannot put upon paper what I
saw and heard. Suffice it to say that in my imperfect judgment *hell* must be a pleasant place in comparison with the *slums*
of London. I was so exhausted with my walk that I became
very hungry and got a very good meal in one of the eating
houses, or rather cellars, for nine pence. They would have
taken me for a bloated bondholder if I had spent more. The
weather in London, while I was there, was too cool to stand
or sit in the open air. I could take violent exercise without
perspiration.

From London I visited Brighton on my way to New

Haven. Brighton is to London what Cape May and Atlantic City are to Philadelphia.

New Haven is a place of no consequence. Steamers, small but staunch, with very powerful machinery, run every five hours from New Haven to Dieppe, in France. It requires from two to ten hours to cross the Channel. The passage was very rough. The side wheels were at times completely submerged, and nearly all the passengers distressingly sick. It seems very strange to an American that a little trip on a boat, of four hours, should land him in a foreign country where the laws, manners, and language are, as if by magic, all changed. As no French is spoken at New Haven, so no English is spoken at Dieppe.

I had, for years, felt a strong desire to visit the old city of Rouen, so celebrated in early English history as the scene of so many conflicts between our sturdy English ancestors and the French for the crown of France. The heart of King Richard Cœur de Lion is buried in the old cathedral. The identical spot where Jeanne D'Arc was burned is marked by a tower erected to her memory. I arrived there about 2 P. M., and after securing a resting place at a rickety old French hotel, I commenced my explorations of the city. The city is built on the left side of the Seine, ascending. The new part is very much like all other continental cities, with boulevards, wide, well-paved streets, and handsome modern edifices. The old part is exceedingly quaint and intensely interesting, presenting nearly the same characteristics as Rotterdam, Lubeck, York, and other mediæval towns. The streets are narrow, crooked and rough ; there are no sidewalks ; the houses are built of wood filled in with masonry, each story projecting two or three feet into the street, giving to the houses a top heavy appearance. In some of the narrowest streets, the occupants of the third story can shake hands out of their windows from opposite sides of the street. The city is rapidly losing its ancient appearance. The old houses are being torn down by hundreds annually, the streets are all being widened and re-paved. In a few years it will look like Paris. It has now a population of 150,000 and is rapidly increasing. It contains one of the finest Gothic cathedrals in the world. It will compare very favorably with the one at Strasbourg. The strong and formerly impregnable walls of the city have been removed ; only a few old gates remain. The place where Jeanne D'Arc was burned was near the northern wall. Her ashes were thrown into the Seine, which is about one thousand feet wide and sweeps with a gentle curve through the city. One of the bridges was built by Matilda, the daughter of Henry I., of England. The tower of the cathedral is called, "La tour de

beurre,'' or the Butter Tower, from the fact that it was paid
for by the sale of indulgences to eat butter in Lent ; it is two
hundred and sixty feet high.

The ground upon which the city is built rises from the
river and terminates in a series of hills, several hundred feet
high, from the summits of which the city can be seen with
grand effect.   At the foot of one of these hills is a most beautiful fountain representing a boat, approaching a cataract, saved
from plunging over the waterfall by two rocks.   It is one of
the most striking designs for a fountain I have ever seen.   Before leaving the city I made the ascent of Mount Gargon, an
abrupt hill several hundred feet high, from whose summit the
whole city and twenty miles of surrounding country can be
seen.   It reminded me of Arthur's Seat, near Edinburgh, but
not nearly as high.   The view of the meandering Seine,
from the summit of this hill, is charming.   I counted .
thirteen little islands as I looked up the river ; they reminded
me of a fleet of boats slowly moving down the stream.   The
top of the hill is higher than the highest steeple in the city
and I can look down upon it just as a bird would view it in its
flight over the place.   There are some remains of ancient buildings on this hill.   I sat down on the green turf, sheltered from
a brisk but bracing breeze, and, surrounded by thistles, daisies
and buttercups, wrote these notes upon Rouen—The Roto-
magus of the Romans.

XLVII.

ROUEN TO PARIS—ECONOMY IN TRAVELING—WHAT CAN BE
SEEN IN SIXTY DAYS—AN OLD HOTEL WITH A HISTORY—
PARIS IN SUNDAY CLOTHES—THE GREAT EXPOSITION OF
1889—THE EIFFEL TOWER A MINT—HOW PARIS LOOKS
NINE HUNDRED FEET ABOVE HER—A NIGHT SCENE AT
THE EXPOSITION—ST. GERMAIN—GAS LIGHTS IN PARIS
—BUTTES CHAUMONT.

PARIS, July, 1889.

When I found myself with two months' spare time my
first thought was, how I should spend it so as to get the greatest return with the least expenditure of money.   I had just
finished the story of Phineas Fogg's journey around the world
in eighty days, and I resolved to learn by experience how much
I could see in sixty days.   Even the time necessarily spent on
the ship must not be lost.   A little close observation, a little
exercise of our perceptive faculties, listening with our ears and

looking with our eyes, will secure much to amuse and something to instruct us. I have already given a sketch of my journey as far as Rouen. I had purchased a ticket for the fast train to Paris; the lazy waiter at my hotel forgot to secure a carriage for me in time to make the train; we got to the station just one minute and a half too late, so I had to wait an hour and, instead of getting into Paris at 3 P. M., I did not arrive till nearly 9. The journey was very tedious through an uninteresting country. We passed, however, several very pretty villages and country towns.

To carry out my intention of economizing my money, I selected a thoroughly French hotel with not an American in it. It fronts on a narrow old street about fifteen feet wide, in the oldest part of Paris, but it has a courtyard and a history. During the French revolution, in 1793, they say Robespierre lived in this house, that the narrow street in front has been several times barricaded, and has been more than once red with human blood. My room is in the garret, here called the mansard. I cannot walk about my chamber with my hat on, but, in other respects, it is very comfortable and commodious. I have one of the softest beds I ever rested upon; I get a good breakfast of hot coffee and milk with ham and eggs, or beefsteak and fried potatoes with bread and butter; a good midday meal, and a splendid table d'hôte dinner at 6 o'clock, with service and wine included, for ten francs a day, (about two dollars.) I walk when I wish up to the Continental and Hotel Meurice, not three squares off, and hear the guests complain of the enormous cost of living in Paris. I can ride all over the city for a few cents—not over three cents a mile. I have been here seven days and have visited the whole city, but not once in a cab. I ride in the omnibuses and on the tramways, at three cents per trip, of very often three miles. When my bill was presented this morning for washing and ironing for sixteen days, I was impressed with the practical knowledge of how much labor seventy cents would pay for, for that was the whole bill. At the Grand Hotel or Hotel Continental it would have been about two dollars. There are thousands of Americans now in Paris paying from five to ten dollars a day for their living expenses. I consider my knowledge of the French language worth to me, at least, three dollars a day.

Paris certainly looks very beautiful. No one can stand at the fountain in the gardens of the Tuilleries and look up des Champs Elysees, as far as the Arch of Triumph, and up as far as the Louvre; then walk to the Place de la Concorde, and look over to the Madeline on one side and to the Corps Legislatif on the other, without feeling a peculiar sensation of mingled pleasure and amazement. It is as beautiful as human tact and skill can make it and without doubt the handsomest city in the world. When I visited the place last year it had a weary and somewhat dilapidated appearance, but all now looks clean, fresh and in the best of order. I could hardly believe it was the same old Paris, but when I remember how different a lady looks in a ball room from her appearance when you happen to catch her cleaning house, the riddle was solved. Paris was house-cleaning last year ; this year she is receiving her guests in her best ball-room dress.

The Exposition, of course, is the centre of attraction at present. It is very hard to give a proper description of this grand exhibition of art, industry and science. Suffice it to say, the like was never seen. Those who saw the Centennial Exhibition at Philadelphia, in 1876, can form a pretty fair judgment of this one. In the display of machinery I think the Centennial Exhibition was superior to the present one ; but in all other respects it was far inferior to it. The buildings are of exquisite form and have the appearance of permanent structures, light, airy and substantial. Another advantage over our Centennial display is the easy access to the grounds. The buildings are all erected within the business part of the city on both banks of the Seine, and within a few yards of the Tomb of Napoleon.

The Eiffel (pronounced A-fell) Tower is the eighth wonder of the world. The ground within the four corners of the tower, and covered by the four enormous arches, is about two acres. The entire weight of the tower is only about seven thousand tons. It is about nine hundred feet high, or nearly four hundred feet higher than the highest monument in the world. An elevator conveys eighty persons every fifteen minutes to the top, at a charge of one dollar each. From 9 A. M. till night, there is a line of anxious citizens and strangers awaiting their turn to enter the lift. The tower is at present coining money at the rate of about two hundred dollars an hour. The cost of a ticket to enter the grounds and see the entire exhibition is only nine cents. Before 10 A. M. the price is double. To save the time and the annoyance of wasting two or three hours in the line of persons awaiting their turn to ascend the tower. I got up a little earlier and was at the gate of entrance nearest the tower at 9 A. M. I went directly to the tower and was among the first to enter the elevator. In half an hour from my entrance within the grounds I was on the top of the tower. The morning was cool and windy, but the atmosphere was very clear. With a good field-glass I could see for fifty miles around the city. Distance and size seemed annihilated. Paris looked like a map, and no larger than models of the city I have seen in museums. Indeed, it reminded me very much of a model of the city I saw last year in the Copenhagen Exposition. Horses looked about the size of dogs. In looking directly down on persons walking about, the sight is very comical ; you see nothing but a little head and two enormous legs which appear to be making strides of about five feet at each step.

I made six or seven visits to the Exposition by day, devoting about two hours to each visit. After an hour or two one becomes weary and the senses confused ; it does more harm than good to continue the visit after this feeling of weariness comes upon you. I made one visit at night and never saw a scene so much like my dreams of fairyland. I never saw such a lavish expenditure of gas or such a brilliant display of electric light. The grand arches and the three stories of the tower were brilliantly illuminated, while the summit was crowned with an immense electric lamp that shot its white rays of light with concentrated power, equal to the rays of the sun, upon the fountains in the grounds and the colossal statuary on the domes of the buildings. The rose beds were surrounded with little electric lamps, and the bushes were decorated with them in the form of many colored fruits and flowers. The water from the Trocodero Fountain looked like molten silver, while some of the pools and basins seemed alive with many colored waters. In a word, the spectacle was like an enchanting theatrical representation with a greater sense of reality.

Having a few hours to spare I rested myself by making an excursion to the beautiful suburban town of St. Germain, about thirteen miles from Paris. It is a lovely spot, much frequented by the tired citizens of Paris as a resting place. The Eiffel Tower can be seen in a direct line over Mont Velerian rising far above the summit of the hill.

A stranger entering Paris by night is apt to be dazzled by its appearance and may be disappointed by the reality he sees the next day. To give an idea of the brilliancy of the city by night, it is only necessary to compare its lamp posts with those of Philadelphia. Along the Rue de Rivoli the lamps are only twelve feet apart, while des Champs-Elysees has a thousand lights to a hundred feet.

Yesterday I took my last walk through Paris. I suppose I walked not less than ten miles in different directions, ending my stroll on the Butte Chaumont, in the northwest corner of the city. This was the last great work of Baron Haussman under Napoleon III. It was upon this hill that Admiral Coligny was gibbeted. There is a very instructive museum of Natural History upon the summit and one of the finest views of Paris. It was from their entrenched position on this hill that the Communists, in 1871, threw petroleum shells into the

city, and came very near destroying it.   Take it for all in all.
Paris is a pleasant place, especially for an American who is
always hungry for excitement and like the Athenians in the
days of Paul, constantly desiring to see or hear some new thing.
I leave Paris to-day for Marseilles.

XLVIII.

PARIS TO MARSEILLES—A LONG WALK IN PARIS—IF LONELY,
LOOK UP—OFF FOR LYONS   OLD FASHIONED HARVESTING
—SIX HORSES TO A PLOW—BATTLEFIELDS—STUDY OF
FRENCH IN A RAILROAD CAR—LYONS FROM MT. FOURVIERE
THE SILK OF LYONS—A BLUNDER IN FRENCH—ON TO
MARSEILLES--VALANCE--ANECDOTE OF NAPOLEON--SQUARE
MILES OF COBBLE STONES—FIRST SIGHT OF MARSEILLES—
MARCH—MARCH.

MARSEILLES, August, 1889.
We are now at Marseilles, twenty-one hours by the fastest
express train, south of Paris.   It is a city of dust, sunshine,
straw hats and linen trousers.   Before leaving Paris I took a
long, last walk of about ten miles through the by-streets, and
away from the omnibus routes, to the northwestern part of the
city.   I again ascended "Butte Chaumont."   It is about two
hundred feet high and affords from the plateau on its summit
a charming view of Paris.   On my way I passed the Northern
Railway station and was surprised by its great dimensions.
We think the Broad Street station at Philadelphia a great
affair, and so it is, but Paris has at least five stations fully as
large and some of them twice its size

The Historical Museum on the top of Butte Chaumont is
a very interesting place in which to refresh our recollection of
French history since the Revolution of 1793.   It contains a
regular course of fine paintings illustrating every important
event from that period up to the present time.   Paris can not
be properly seen either by carriage or omnibus ; to see it properly you must do a great deal of good walking.   I did not get
to my hotel till long after sunset.   It was the only perfectly
clear night I have seen since my arrival.   When I came to the
Place de la Concorde the stars were shining most brilliantly.
It reminded me of home, they looked so much like the sparkling eyes of old friends.   They seemed to say, "If you are
lonely look up."

We left for Lyons on the morning of July 30th.   While
very soft, luxuriant and beautiful, the landscape from Paris to

Lyons is not more than ordinarily interesting. The course of the road is over a level but fertile country. As we approach Lyons the face of the country becomes more attractive. It is now the middle of harvest and the country presents some scenes of great rural beauty, such as old fashioned threshing floors, with men and maidens handling the yellow sheaves and horses and oxen treading out the grain. There has been no rain in the south of France for a long time, which gives the fields in some places a parched appearance. After the train strikes the rich valley of the Saone, which it follows through all its sinuosity, the scenery becomes more interesting. It is no uncommon sight to see four and sometimes six strong horses to one great plow, reminding one of some of the beautful paintings of Rosa Bonheur to be seen in all the museums of Europe, engravings of which are quite common in our own country. The country roads are kept in perfect order ; they are as smooth as a floor and as white as chalk, and generally planted with poplar trees on both sides. Before reaching Lyons we pass some small rivers almost dry, but which have the appearance of having been recently full of water. The springtime is said to be the best to see to advantage the vegetation of the south of France. The fruits are now all ripe but the flowers mostly faded. We have delicious grapes, peaches, apricots, plums, melons and small fruits in abundance.

Near the city of Lyons we pass some places of historic interest, such as the battlefield of Montereau, where Napoleon said to his soldiers, when they begged him not to expose himself to the hail of bullets from the enemy's muskets, "My brave boys, the bullet that is to kill me is not yet moulded."

At Blairey, we are near the source of the Seine and enter a more mountainous country. A railway compartment, in a long journey, becomes a very sociable place and affords a fine opportunity to study French. We made the acquaintance of a good natured Frenchman from St. Denis, going to Lyons on business. Much to the amusement of the other passengers we converted him into a school master and for full six hours we made him explain to us the proper pronunciation of every word connected with traveling by rail. He showed great patience and as politely as possible gave us many very valuable lessons in French. My son repaid him for his kindness by beating him most shamefully that night at billiards in Lyons As a consequence of his defeat he had to pay for the use of the table, etc., but as he was the challenger, he did not complain. There is nothing like traveling to give one cheek ; indeed, the necessity of making ourselves understood has completely overcome our natural modesty and proverbial diffidence, for which we are noted among all those who know us. I have made many very amusing blunders, and have very often been the subject of merriment, but I stick at it till I am understood. I always get even with the fellow that laughs at me by telling him that I speak better French than he does English, and then call him a fool or some other bad name, always in English, because I know he don't understand me and thinks I am complimenting him, at which he bows and I smile.

We arrived at Lyons about 11 o'clock at night, having been twelve hours on the fastest express train. We stopped at a French hotel where not a word of English was spoken and, by the help of the lesson we had received on the cars, we had not the slightest trouble in understanding as well as being understood. The only bad mistake we made was in asking the valet why he had not *mended* our chamber. The word we used, in one sense meant to *fix up;* but in the way we used it, it meant to *mend* something broken. The poor fellow looked all over the *chamber* and then informed us that it was not *broken*. After mutual explanation he had a hearty laugh at our expense. Our entire expense of living at this hotel did not exceed three dollars a day. At the hotels most frequented by English and Americans here the cost is double that sum.

The people here complain of the warmth of the weather, but to us it is really charming. At noon it is rather hot, but in the afternoon and morning it is perfectly delightful ; we can take any amount of exercise in our winter clothing without much perspiration, and can sleep at night under a blanket.

Lyons is the second city in France, and only surpassed by Paris in splendor and population. Its natural situation and the surrounding country are much more beautiful than those of Paris. The rivers Saone and Rhone join here and both flow through the city ; the one is about six hundred feet and the other about nine hundred feet wide, both splendidly walled with fine large cut stone, with steps running down to the water's edge and parapets about four feet high, over which the promenading citizen can lean and look at the rapid flow of the beautiful waters from the wide, well-paved and shaded avenues along either side of the rivers. The city is surrounded by hills several hundred feet high. The hill west of the Saone rises from the embankment some three hundred feet and is surmounted by a fine monumental church, from the facade of which the whole city and country lying eastward can be seen for twenty miles. The city lies at the foot of the hill and can be studied from it at great advantage. Every street and all the buildings of any importance can be distinctly seen. The name of the hill is Mt. Fourviere. It is ascended by a railway at an angle of about sixty degrees for two cents. The hill contains ancient Roman ruins. It is beautifully shaded

and laid out in walks and steps, and is ornamented with statuary mostly of a religious character.

One of the principal industries of Lyons is the manufacture of silk goods. It is said the average product of its looms
is 120,000 yards a year. There was a city here five hundred
years before the christian era. The Emperor Augustus Cæsar
was very fond of Lyons and spent much of his time here.
Carracalla and Marcus Aurelius were both born here. The
Saracens captured and held the place for some time, but
were finally driven out by Charles Martel. It was at the siege
of Lyons that the young soldier. Bonaparte, afterwards the
Emperor Napoleon, first showed his great military genius. The
ancient character of the city is, like most other old towns, fast
disappearing before our modern ideas of what a city should be.
They are now erecting some of the grandest stores, magazines
and dwellings to be seen in any city of Europe. We noticed
a store being built of stone dressed on all sides so as to make
the inside finish equal to the outside one, and the joints so
closely fitting as to require very little mortar.

We are highly pleased with our two days' stop at Lyons.
We have ridden and walked all over it and leave it with the
satisfaction of knowing that we have seen it all.

The time by rail, on the fastest trains, between Lyons and
Marseilles is eight hours. The road follows the winding course
of the beautiful Rhone whose picturesque scenery is justly
celebrated all over the world. The scenery varies from the
soft luxuriant verdure of the valley to the rugged and rock-
bound mountains that skirt its edge. We pass several ancient
ruins and some romantic looking old castles. Our general
course is due south and as we advance we can feel the change
in temperature. The country looks very thirsty as if it had
not had a good drink of refreshing rain for a long time. The
leaves of the olive groves are white with dust, but still the
country has a ripe and mellow look. The harvesting near
Marseilles is all done. The peasants are now gathering their
summer fruits. As we pass through Valance we are reminded
that it was here that Bonaparte, when a little boy, was a
scholar at the military school still kept here. It was at Valance that he used to amuse himself by building earthworks in
the sand, and form his contending armies with small gravel
stones, indicating his officers by larger stones, and himself as
General-in-Chief by a stone as big as his fist. One of his schoolmates looked over the wall and made fun of the young soldier,
whereupon he struck him in the head with his "General-in-
Chief" and left a permanent scar upon the mocker's forehead.
Many years afterwards, when Bonaparte the soldier had become Napoleon the Emperor, his old schoolmate sent in his

name and asked for an audience. Napoleon did not remember him till he pointed to the scar on his forehead, which at once brought the long-forgotten occurrence to his mind much to his amusement and to the great profit of his wounded old schoolmate.

We also pass through the old town of Avignon, near which Petrarch lived. As we draw nearer Marseilles the country becomes more barren. Our road passes over a desert plain for many miles, perfectly level and covered with cobble stones; I should say this plain contains cobble stones enough to pave all the streets of the world.

The air soon becomes more cool and bracing. In a short time we quit the broad and beautiful bay of the Rhone to plunge into a succession of tunnels, one of which requires five minutes to get through it; after which we get our first sight of the Mediterranean Sea and Gulf of Lyons, with the city of Marseilles nestling like a coy maiden at the feet of the surrounding hills.

We have spent three days in the city and have seen it all. I must postpone my effort to describe it until my next letter, as I fear this one is becoming tedious. We have taken our berths and embark this morning for Barcellona in Spain, from whence, if possible, we intend to go to Africa. Like the wandering Jew we are not permitted to rest long at any one place no matter how pleasant it may be. We must obey the injunction with which we started—March—March.

XLIX

FRANCE TO SPAIN—MARSEILLES—CAFE'S AND POLITICIANS —ONE OF PLATO'S JOKES—NOTRE DAME DE LE GARDE— THE COURT—FOUNTAINS, BATHS AND FLEAS—TO BARCELONA BY SEA—A BEAUTIFUL SPANISH CITY—MOSQUITOES —BAD PLACE FOR TEE-TOTALERS—FRUITS, FLOWERS AND WINES—HISTORY—PARADISAICAL VILLAS—COSTUMES OF SPAIN DISAPPEARING—DULCENA AND DUENNO—SCANTY BATHING DRESSES.

ZARAGOZA, SPAIN, August, 1889.

The first striking characteristic of Marseilles is its admirable situation. The next thing that strikes one's attention is the great activity and apparent excitement of the people. The city has been built, like Rome, on a succession of hills. There are no level streets in Marseilles; we are either going up or down hill all the time. I sometime think this is true in

life, and that we never walk on the same level, but either advance upward or descend downward, morally as well as intel-
lectually.   The city is fast encroaching on the higher hills
which now surround it in a semi-circle, from the lower to the
upper bay.   It is protected seaward by rocky islands and a
strong stone breakwater.   The old Chateau d'If raises its bold
head just beyond the breakwater   It has become renowned
as the scene of Dumas' novel "The Count of Monte Cristo."
We can plainly see the parapet from which the Count was
thrown, as a corpse, into the sea, and can almost hear him ex-
claim, as he rises to the surface, " Now the world is mine."

Marseilles has a population of 380,000 and is now even
more cosmopolitan than Paris.   The harbor is full of ships
from every country and the streets are thronged by strangers
from every clime.   We see all sorts of costumes and hear the
jargon of every tongue and dialect.

The city, in summer, presents a very dirty and disagreeable appearance.   All the fine old trees ; all the shrubs and
flowers, and even the buildings are covered with a fine, chalky
dust, very annoying and disagreeable.   But little green is to
be seen, either in the city or on the rock bound coast.   Even
the high hills, outside of the city limits, are bleak and of a
whitish gray color.

Marseilles, like all other old towns, is in a state of rapid
transition to a new and well arranged city.   Paris has undoubtedly revolutionized the world in this respect.   Even
Jerusalem and Damascus must soon lose their ancient character and become, like Bucharest, Buda-Pesth and Vienna, beautiful new cities.   The cafes of Marseilles are admitted to be
superior to any in Paris.   They are crowded nightly by excited citizens and strangers, who seem intent on hearing or
telling the news.   But little business is done in the middle of
the day.   From ten to four the banks and public offices are
closed.   The streets and cafes begin to fill about 7 P. M. and
remain crowded until after midnight.   The city seems to be a
paradise for politicians.   As far as I am able to judge, the
great majority of the people are Boulangists, and very radical
in their political views.   They have torch-light processions,
drums, banners and bands of music, bulletins and speech-mak-
ing in the streets.   It reminded me very much of Philadelphia,
opposite the Union League, on the night of a Presidential election.   From my limited knowledge of politics in my own country I have about concluded that the politician is the same animal the world over.   That is to say, a great patriot out of
power, and a great rascal in office.   It would hardly be proper
to leave Marseilles without a glance, at least, at its history.
It was a city of importance twenty-five hundred years ago.

The historians of the place claim that it was founded by the Phœnicians, and that it owes its prosperity to its splendid harbor. It was spoken of by Plato as containing the most patriotic men and virtuous women of any city in the world. He says the manners of the people in his time were irreproachable. He recommends it as a sample of social virtue. From what I have seen of it, it must have retrograded very much since the days of Plato, or the old philosopher was joking.

In the struggle between Cæsar and Pompey, it took sides with the latter. As a consequence, Cæsar laid seige to the city and captured it, broke down its walls and destroyed its navy and all its implements of war.

Before leaving the city we ascended the hill, four hundred feet high, on the south. The view from the summit of this hill is very fine. All Marseilles can be seen below us. There is a fine modern church upon its summit, the interior of which is completely lined with fine many-colored and well-polished marbles. On the opposite side of the city is a very beautiful fountain, said to be one of the largest in the world, composed of columns, facades, grotesque rock work, great stone animals and a beautiful waterfall. I have seen no fountain, except one in Rome, more elaborately designed or better executed. It is situated on a hill, at the union of several streets and has fine, large stone steps leading around the fountain to the Zoological Gardens. The gardens are all that nature and art can make them.

As we passed the splendid Court House we concluded to take a peep at the administration of justice. The Supreme Court for the Province was in session, consisting of three judges, in gowns, but without wigs, and a large number of lawyers. They were arguing some question of encroachment. One of the lawyers reminded me of ex-Judge Broomall, while his opponent was a nervous little fellow, not unlike counsellor Robinson. We thought, from the smiles of the judges and the shrugs of the old lawyer's shoulders and the snapping of his fingers, that the old counsellor was getting the best of the contest, but as I could not understand the technical terms employed, perhaps I was mistaken. The day before we left we jumped into a tramway car and rode out to the public baths on the seashore, just east of the city limits. It reminded me very much of a sea-side bathing place in our own country. The little bath houses are just the same. As there is but little tide in the Mediterranean there is consequently but little beach. The surf, however, is good and we enjoyed very much our first swim in this renowned sea.

The nights at Marseilles are delightfully cool and pleasant, and very promotive of good, refreshing sleep. In this respect it is like Cape May when the sea breeze prevails. The only drawback to our pleasure was a flea hunt the last night we spent in the city. I was awakened about midnight by a yell and an urgent request to get up and strike a light. I supposed that a burglar had entered our room. I sprang upon the floor, stumbled over a chair, nearly knocked over the table, and finally struck a match. Sam had caught a flea ; but, when he raised his hand to show me his captive, as usual he was not there.

The next day, at 10 A. M., we took ship for Barcelona. The voyage was very pleasant. About 4 A. M. the following morning we had our first sight of the hilly coast of Spain. About 8 A. M. we landed. Our hotel was upon the main street of the city, called "The Rambla." It is about one hundred and eighty feet wide, and runs from the harbor straight through the city. We were surprised to find such a well-built, well-paved and beautifully-decorated city. Like Marseilles, the old city has gone, and one modeled after Paris has taken its place. Like Marseillss, also, is is surrounded with hills on the land side. Just at the left, as we enter the port, is a hill over seven hundred feet high, on the summit of which is a strong fort, whose guns cover the harbor and every inch of the city. Hotel bills in Spain are low, but railroad fares are very high. It costs about a dollar an hour to ride first-class on roads where there is no opposition ; second-class in Spain is worse than third-class in an English railway coach. Barcelona is the second city in Spain for size and beauty. It has a population of 430,000, and is rapidly increasing. The old Spanish customs and costumes have been almost entirely driven from the city Paris is now the model for all new cities, and the dress of England is fast driving out of existence all the old fantastic costumes of the world.

The days, at noon, are very warm but the evenings and nights are pleasant. I found my first mosquito at Barcelona. I resolved to leave the place at once, for if there is any one thing in this world I hate more than Satan it is a mosquito. The city has a clean, fresh and very pleasant general appearance. It has a park not ten minutes' walk from the centre of the city, which is one of the most beautiful I have ever seen.

Spain is noted for its fruits and flowers. The flower market of Barcelona is a very attractive place. The fruit market is the finest in the world, the large tables groan under the weight of most delicious fruit. Pomegranates, citron, figs, green-gages, apricots, nectarines, peaches, pears, green almonds, all kinds of small fruits and great clusters of grapes. While feasting upon a fine bunch of white muscats and malagas I thought with pity of my friend Senator Cooper, for he has assured me that a bunch of them will intoxicate him. If he were

here he would be inebriated all the time.   Grapes are not only
abundant but wine flows like water.   It is the common drink
of both rich and poor, yet I have not seen a drunken man on
the continent.   How is this to be harmonized with our American idea of total abstinence and the proposed Constitutional
Amendment.

Barcelona has a fountain almost as beautiful as the one at
Marseilles.   To get an idea of the ancient city, as compared
with the modern one, it is necessary to walk into the little
crooked and filthy streets, which are now mostly the habitation of the poor, but which were once the dwelling places of
the first citizens of the city.

The city is said to have been founded by Hamilcar, the
father of Hannibal, 237 B. C.   The Moors captured it in 713
A. D., but were driven out about ninety years afterwards by
Charlemagne.   They held the city long enough, however, to
give to all succeeding ages their dark and swarthy complexion,
and to fill the language of Spain with their peculiar dialect.

The temperature of Barcelona is never above 87 and seldom below 28° Fahr.   There are not, on an average of one
hundred years, over seventy rainy days in a year.

The villas of the rich are said to be little paradises of rural
beauty, full of orange groves and arbors, vines, fruits and flowers.   Washington Irving has so described them.   They are
undoubtedly most charming retreats.

Here and there we see an original Spanish costume, so
familiar to the readers of Gil Blas and Don Quixote, with
velvet breeches, many-colored ribbons, broad sombreros, white
stockings and sandals, a broad, bright-colored silk sash around
the waist and short jacket covered with lace or embroidery.
Occasionally, only, we meet a Spanish girl with her duenno.
peeping over her fan and pretending to hide her pretty face
with the black lace with which her head is covered.   These
sights are now rare.   The great majority of men and
women look just as they do in Paris, London and New York.
We were told that if we want to see Spanish life and costumes.
we must visit Zaragoza.   So we spent the balance of our time
in taking a ride around the omnibus routes and tramways of
the town, and wound up our visit by a steamboat ride, for two
cents, to the baths on the seashore.   The bathing robes are
very scanty, but enough, as the men and women do not bathe
together as with us.   The bathing place for the ladies is completely covered.   The bathing grounds are only for the pleasure
of a plunge into the sea, and not a place of fashionable display.

We arrived at Zaragoza last night about 9 o'clock, after a
long but interesting, though very warm, ride by rail of twelve
hours.

L.

Zaragoza to Madrid—Size of Spain—Monserrat—Dried
up Rivers—Sunburned Fields—Spain a Great Grave-
yard — Zaragoza-Moorish Manners — Lerida — The
Maid of Zaragoza—The Virgin Mary General-in-
Chief—Steam vs. Romance—A Very Old Town—Ab-
sence of Trees—O'Shea's Guide of Spain—Agreeably
Disappointed in Madrid—A Splendid City in an Arid
Plain—Art Gallery—The Escurial a Humbug.

MADRID, SPAIN, August, 1889.

Spain is quite a large country. It contains 193,000 square
miles ; it is over four times as large as Pennsylvania. It lies
between thirty-six and forty-seven north latitude. Every inch
of its territory that will raise a blade of grass or stalk of corn
is cultivated and, where neither will grow, vines are planted.
In Spring the land is well watered by the melting snow
upon its mountains ; in Summer all the table land is watered
by artificial irrigation. Madrid is located upon the great plateau extending the whole length of the Pyrenees. Its altitude
is two thousand three hundred and eighty-four feet above the
level of the sea. In Winter it is said to be cold and in
Summer very warm. It has a population of over half a million
and is rapidly increasing. We left Barcelona on the 6th and
arrived at Zaragoza in twelve hours. For the first four hours
we ascended, by a very steep grade and winding road, the
mountains on the north of Barcelona. Some of the scenery
was very fine. We completely circled Monserrat, or the Jag-
ged Mountain ; it is eight leagues in circumference. Its rocky
pinnacles rise in perpendicular spires three thousand eight
hundred feet. There is a monastery there, the most celebrated in Spain. It once had an annual pilgrimage of 60,000, but
as true piety is becoming more enlightened, its shrine is more
neglected. It certainly inspires a feeling of indescribable admiration mingled with reverential awe, to gaze upon its imposing peaks of barren rock as they seem, like gigantic cathedral
spires, to pierce the realms of heaven. As we ascend to the
plateau, we see the dried up channels of what, in early
Summer, were rapid mountain streams. For hundreds of miles
along the plateau the ground seems burnt up and all vegetation destroyed by excessive heat and the absence of rain. Here
and there we see empty sheepfolds and little sunburnt villages,

reminding one more of Africa than Europe. The houses are but
one story high, (except in the towns), with flat tile roofs and are
built of baked earth in great square blocks, covered with whitewash.   Why this building material has been chosen in a land
abounding with fine red sandstone formed by Nature into
almost square blocks, I cannot conceive.   I imagine it is a
relic of Moorish dominion, as I am told the houses of the husbandmen in this part of the country are very much like those
in Morocco.   There are but few relics of antiquity to be found
in Spain.   Here and there we see the ruins of an old castle,
generally on the highest hill and without any known history.
In fact, the whole of this part of Spain reminds one of an enormous graveyard devoted to primitive agriculture.   In some of
the fertile spots, where irrigation can be successfully used,
they look like cemeteries converted into gardens.

   Zaragoza is situated upon the river Ebro.   In the Spring
the river is deep and rapid ; now it is nearly dry.   Its valley,
however, is very fertile and cultivated to its fullest extent.
One crop is scarcely gathered before another is planted.   Where
the fields cannot be watered by the little races running in every
direction from the river, donkeys are employed to turn bucket
wheels that raise the water to the desired height to flow into
the little cultivated patches.   Moorish dresses are quite common among the poorer classes in the little villages along the
line of the road.   Men with bright red handkerchiefs tied in
the form of turbans around their heads, and women with their
faces half covered, are an evident relic of the Moorish conquest
and of the harem.   About half way between Barcelona and
Zaragoza we passed through the city of Lerida, a town of
about twenty-five thousand inhabitants.   It is only noticeable
as the place where a celebrated Council was held A. D. 546.
It has been so often sacked by the Goths, Moors and French
that nothing of interest, save the ground on which it stands, is
left.   From what we had been told we expected too much of
Zaragoza ; we fancied a city of ancient Spanish manners, costumes and buildings ; we found it a beautiful modern town of
ninety thousand inhabitants, with great difficulty distinguish-
able from Paris or New York.   It has broad avenues with
fine old trees on each side to shade the promenades.   But
little of the old town remains.   When we found the ancient
part, however, it was very interesting in its narrow winding
streets and great houses almost meeting at the richly carved
and projecting cornices.

   The city is celebrated for the remarkably stubborn resistance
it made to the siege of Napoleon's army in 1808.   Byron has
immortalized the Maid of Zaragoza, who fought by her lover's

side and when he was killed cheered on the soldiers and fought until the city fell.

"Ye who shall marvel when you hear her tale,
Oh ! had you known her in her softer hour,
Mark'd her black eye that mocks her coal-black veil ; ·
Heard her light, lively tones in lady's bower;
Seen her long locks that foil the painter's power ;
Her fairy form with more than female grace;
Scarce would you deem that Zaragoza's tower
Beheld her smile in danger's Gorgon face,
Thin the closed ranks, and lead in glory's fearful chase."

The only way to get a correct idea of what the city was at the time of the seige, is by walking through the streets of the old parts, or at least what remains of them. All the worst part of the city has been torn down and rebuilt ; the remains of the old city now are what formerly was its most aristocratic quarter. Many of the streets are too narrow for two carriages to pass. and have no sidewalks. The balls from cannon, because of the tortuous and zigzag streets, could not fly over one hundred feet without striking the heavy walls of the houses ; the consequence was that after ten thousand French soldiers had gained an entrance over the broken walls they found every house a new fort. The second siege was conducted by four of Napoleon's best generals, well provided with all the necessary implements of war. The walls of the town were but ten feet high and three feet thick ; the people were poorly armed and had but little means of resistance ; yet it required the slaughter of fifteen thousand of the inhabitants and a siege of sixty-two days to reduce the city to capitulation, and not until famine and pestilence had come to the assistance of the besiegers.

The siege of Zaragoza was remarkable in other respects. The citizens were not drilled soldiers ; they refused to have any General in-chief ; in a fit of religious and pathetic frenzy the town authorities elected the Virgin Mary as their General-in-chief. Napoleon smiled when his generals compelled her to surrender, but it is a remarkable historical fact that the siege of Zaragoza was the beginning of the end of the great chieftain. From Zaragoza to Waterloo was one continual succession of disasters and final fall. The heroic resistance of a little unarmed town taught the rest of Spain a lesson of patriotism ; Wellington came to their assistance and the French were driven out of Spain. So the Virgin conquered in the end. The event reminds me of a remark of Victor Hugo. He says : " It was not Wellington ; it was not Blucher ; it was not the allies that won the battle of Waterloo ; it was God. The time had come when God or Napoleon must surrender and Napoleon fell."

There is, as before remarked, but little in Zaragoza to remind the traveler that he is in Spain. Now and then we see a little maiden accompanied by her duenna ; here and there we see scenes like Rebecca and Rachel with their Orienta water jugs, either on their shoulders or being filled at some of the fountains.   Occasionally we meet a country beau with a new sombrero and quaint old Spanish dress ; but these are exceptions, not the rule.   The Spanish Muleteer no longer cheers his poor beast by his songs ; he uses a club or a whip and swears like a *civilized* horse jockey.   I have come to the conclusion that Solomon was right, and that there is nothing new under the sun.   What now is, has been ; and what has been, now is ; humanity is the same all the world over.   In a word, it is only distance that lends enchantment to the view, and as the telegraph and steam engine have annihilated space, the enchantment of former times has been broken.

The monks of Zaragoza insist upon it that the city was founded by Tubal, the nephew of Noah, in the year 242, after the deluge.

The old stone bridge ; the two grand old cathedrals; the ruined convent, where the last struggle was made in the siege, and the old houses in the ancient part of the city, are about all the sights now to be seen.   It is, however, a pleasant place to spend a day, and to break the long journey from Barcelona to Madrid.   We left the city on the 8th at 7 A. M., and did not arrive at Madrid until nearly 10 P. M.   The ride was over the same unbroken plateau, very dusty and dry, with here and there a green valley or mountain range in view.   Scarcely a tree is to be seen and not a soul at work in the parched fields.

Before leaving Paris we went to an English book-seller to buy a guide for travelers in Spain.   He had several for a shilling each, but he assured us they were not reliable.   He advised us to pay four dollars for a book written by Mr. O'Shea, who had traveled all over Spain, and whose book was perfectly reliable.   Seduced by his praises of Mr. O'Shea's " Guide to Spain " I bought the book, but was soon convinced that the author had never seen Spain.   He describes Madrid as a city of gingerbread architecture ; and that it was a furnace hotter than Nebuchadnezzar's, in the summer, and as cold as the North Pole in winter ; that we would be in danger of sunstroke out of the shade and of pneumonia in it ; that from 11 A. M. till 4 P. M. not a soul ventured in the streets, during summer. Instead of a city such as he describes, we found a second Paris. A splendid, well-built, artistically laid out and beautifully decorated city, only surpassed by Vienna, Berlin and Paris.   Its architecture is tasty and substantial.   The streets are very broad—one of them over five hundred feet in width.   The houses are very high, with balconies at each window, where the inmates sit and chat or sup in the shade of a summer evening.   The weather is delightful, we have not seen a cloud since we have been in Spain. At noon it is about as warm as in Philadelphia at this season, but the nights are delightfully cool, with not a mosquito to torment you or a breath of hot air to stifle you. I never enjoyed sweeter sleep than in this much abused city. We wear our heavy spring clothing. I have only seen one linen suit in the city and that was worn by a peasant. The city is shaded by trees and h s several beauti- ful parks and gardens. When we remember that all the trees, as well as flowers and grass in the city and suburbs, must be kept alive in the dry season in summer by irrigation, we can appreciate the beautiful green grass and flowers and form a comparative judgment of the heavy expense necessary to sup- port such a splendid city in such an arid plain. The city pos- sesses one of the finest collections of paintings by the old mas- ters to be found in the world. By some it is considered su- perior to that of Dresden or the Louvre. I was particularly struck with a life-sized painting representing the miraculous conversion of Paul. While gazing upon and trying to study the picture, the thought came into my mind that Paul was either an impostor or Christ was divine. The subsequent life of the old apostle, his enthusiastic ministry and triumphant death ought to convince any fair mind that Paul was honest and terribly in earnest.

We lost an entire day in going and returning, nearly seventy miles, to see the world-renowned Escurial. O'Shea describes it as the eighth wonder of the world and advises us to take our baggage and spend two or three days among its massive wonders. We left our comfortable beds at 5 A. M., took a light breakfast of hot milk, coffee and bread, and em- barked on the first train. In about two hours, over an unin- teresting road, we reached our place of destination. The sta- tion is about a mile from the palace. A short stage ride up an ascending grade brought us to what looked like an immense poor house or state prison. It was O'Shea's eighth wonder of the world, the Escurial. There is nothing in it worth walk- ing a mile to see. It is an enormous pile of roughly cut gran- ite blocks, built into square walls and windows, upon a ground plan formed like a gridiron turned upside down, the several towers representing the upturned feet of the broiling apparatus. The dome and a few of the arches are fair specimens of masonic skill, but I venture to say that there are at least a dozen stone masons in Delaware county who, for the same amount of money, could erect a more beautiful building. The whole thing was the creation of a half crazy old king. Philip II chose St. Law- rence as his patron. He had seen many churches in the form of a cross. He formed the comical idea of building one shaped like a gridiron, commemorative of the martyrdom of his patron saint who, we are told, was broiled alive on that instrument. After having seen the cathedrals at Milan, Cologne, Antwerp, Constantinople and Rome, to call this thing one of the wonders of the world is to descend very rapidly from the sublime to the ridiculous.

We have secured our tickets for two of the best seats in the Amphitheatre and intend to witness the grand royal bull fight, to-morrow afternoon, after which we will bid farewell to Madrid and visit Seville and Cadiz. In my next letter I will endeavor to describe the bull fight.

LI.

MADRID TO SEVILLE—A BULL FIGHT IN THE AMPHITHEATRE —EXCITING SPORT—PECULIAR DESIRE TO SEE ANOTHER FIGHT—ON TO SEVILLE—DROUTH IN SPAIN—A BEAUTIFUL CITY BY NIGHT—A DULL PLACE BY DAY—YUM YUM —THE ALCAZAR—HISTORY—FOUR HUNDRED THOUSAND DEPOPULATION IN ONE YEAR.

SEVILLE, SPAIN, August, 1889.

Before leaving Madrid for this place, we went to see a bull fight in the Amphitheatre, a very large three-story building, copied after the Coliseum at Rome, but not so large. It, however, is large enough to seat seventeen thousand five hundred spectators. The arena is as large as a small race course, being not less than one hundred yards in diameter, perfectly circular and covered with fine clean gravel. Only the two outside tiers are under roof. The main circle is exposed to the weather and consists of twenty-five rows of granite seats, each tier rising fully one foot above the other so that there is no difficulty in seeing over the heads of those in front. The sheltered seats are covered with leather and are comfortable. The Royal box is on the west or shady side ; directly opposite is the stand for the musicians, gaily decorated with flags and streamers. At the right of the music stand is a large gate through which the fighters enter ; on the left is the gate through which the bull comes. There were about ten thousand men, women and children present. The fight began about 5 P. M.

To understand a bull fight it will be necessary to first classify the fighters. The first in rank is the swordsman. (I will avoid the Spanish names). The swordsman is armed with a Toledo blade about the size of an ordinary straight sword. This he holds in his right hand ; in his left he carries a bright red flag. He is gaudily dressed, wears no mail, is generally very handsome and always a great favorite of the ladies. It is his duty, when the others have displayed their several parts, to enter the arena, doff his hat to the occupants of the Royal box and ask permission to kill the foe which he promises to do to the honor of his patron and glory of Madrid. He is required to face the mad bull directly in front and give him his death thrust over or between his horns. The point of the sword must enter the nape of the neck just between the two shoulder blades, and the instrument must be thrust downward into the chest to the hilt. If the bull is killed in any other way he (the bull) can claim a foul and wins the fight, at which the audience hiss the fighter and cheer the *dead* bull. He has not been killed according to the honor of Madrid or the glory of Spain. This paradox reminds one of Shakespeare's Murderers of the Duke of Clarence. "We must not kill him while he sleeps, or, when he wakes, he'll say 'twas foully done."

The next rank among the fighters is the men with barbed sticks gaily wound with different colored ribbons. They fight without flags. Their sticks are about three feet long. They cannot possibly kill the bull but are expected to torment him by planting their barbed sticks in his skin. They too must face the foe and plant their barbs in his shoulders and back directly over his horns. They sometimes succeed in putting six or seven of these barbs into the poor animal and leave them there to dangle and lacerate him every step he takes. These fighters are required, for their own safety, to be very fleet of foot and agile in all their actions.

The third rank is the lancers. They were formerly the first rank and fought the bull fairly in the ring on horseback, armed with nothing but a strong lance. Now they are a low set of wine drinkers, who will take the risk of being killed or hurt for the pay they get. The horses now used are, as a rule, old, crippled or diseased animals intended to be killed. The lancer of modern times wears iron mail under his gaudy dress, protecting his body as high as his chest. If he did not he would certainly be killed, as his horse falls on him, and the bull often attacks him with great fury.

The fourth class is the men with red cloaks or mantles. They are required to madden the bull by flaunting their red mantles in his face and escaping as best they can, while the bull charges and spends his fury on the rag which he tosses about in a great rage.

A great flourish of trumpets announced the opening scene. The gate for the fighters was thrown open, and at the same time two richly dressed horsemen on splendid steeds entered the arena from the gate opposite the Royal box. The object of the two finely dressed horsemen on gallant steeds is to

detract attention from the poor Rosinantes ridden by the
lancers. A grand procession to martial music now marched
around the ring. The poor old hacks had been dosed up with
stimulants and, with their rich caparisons, could scarcely be
distinguished from the most fiery young stallions. As the procession passed the Royal box they took off their hats and
bowed. Whether any of the Royal blood of Spain occupied
the box or not I cannot say, as our seats were on the same tier
but at the right of the box, into which we could not see. The
grand procession had scarcely ended, when the great gate at
the left of the music stand was thrown open and in rushed a
splendid four-year-old bull, with head down and tail up. He
was very much excited and had evidently been tormented by
his torturers before he was let into the ring. He meant business from the start. The men with mantles flaunted their
red rags before his eyes. He made a furious charge upon them :
some jumped aside and left him to toss the cloaks in the air ;
others ran for their lives, dropping their mantles and only escaping by leaping a six-feet-high strong plank barrier. One
of them had scarcely got over before the bull was half over behind him. The horsemen then presented themselves with their
lances. This was really an exciting scene. One of the lancers
kept the bull at bay for several minutes. With one thrust of
his lance he ripped open the skin of the bull, leaving a gash
eighteen inches long. This only made him more furious. In
another desperate charge he took the poor horse clear off his
feet, ripped open his belly and threw him with his rider head
over heels against the barrier. The mantle bearers now rushed
at and surrounded him, taking his attention from the wounded
horse which sprang to his feet ; the lancer mounted him again
and rode him around the ring with his bowels trailing on the
ground and his stomach hanging between his legs. The bull
then made another charge, plunging his long sharp horns into
the poor horse's chest from which the blood ran as from a stuck
pig ; the horse fell dead with his rider on his back. Soon the
bull began to show signs of fatigue. Then the fighters with
their barbed sticks commenced their attack, planting their tor-
menting barbs in his shoulders and back until he again became
maddened with fury and renewed the attack upon the mantle
bearers and lancers. Thus, in less than half an hour, this mad
bull had mortally wounded one and killed outright three horses.
The audience were now in a proper frame of mind to see the
bull killed.

The swordsman entered the arena, bowed to the Royal
box, and asked the usual permission to kill the foe. With
nothing but his sword and red flag, he advanced directly in
front. After many changes by the bull and hairbreadth

escapes of the man, he got the bull in a proper position, with his head down to make a charge when, quick as lightning, he sprang upon him directly between the horns, and planted his sword up to the hilt between his shoulder blades down into his chest. The bull gave a look of surprise, trembled a little, kept up the fight for, perhaps, a minute, with the sword in his chest, then lolled out his tongue and fell upon his knees. In an instant the swordsman sprang upon him again, and with one blow from a short dagger, directly behind the horns, he severed the spinal cord and the brute fell over dead. Three richly caparisoned mules were now driven into the ring and, amid the shouts of the audience, dragged out the dead horse, first and then the murdered bull.

Thus from 5 to 8 P. M. the fight continued, until thirteen horses and four bulls were slaughtered. Some of the horses had their paunches ripped out, others ran around with their bowels trailing on the ground ; some were killed at a single thrust ; others were not finally slaughtered until after several charges. The most cruel part of the sport was the killing of the poor old horses. They were all blindfolded, and, if one showed sufficient strength and spirit to sustain his rider, he would be protected for a while by a dexterous use of the lance ; but as soon as the horse began to show signs of failure, he was invariably placed by his rider in a proper position to receive his death. The bulls showed great courage and enormous strength. One of them threw a horse completely over his head killing him instantly. These bulls are permitted to run wild in parts of Spain and are captured by letting tame bulls run among them. When three or four tame bulls are driven into a coral the wild ones follow them and are captured and then subjected to a system of training by torture and by permitting them to kill old horses.

After the fight was over three wild bulls, with knobs on their horns, were let into the arena for the amusement of the boys. I saw one fellow whose whole ambition, I have no doubt, was to become a bull-fighter, jump with his red flag before one of the bulls, but he was not agile enough to escape ; he was thrown ten feet in the air and as he fell was rolled up into a ball. I was sure the boy was killed, but his companions with their flags took the attention of the bull and the fellow gathered himself up and ran for dear life, leaving his flag behind.

I find it very difficult to describe my feelings during the cruel spectacle. When I saw the first horse killed I felt like leaving the place. I resolved never to witness another, and yet the next day I felt as if I would like to see just one more fight. This abominable feeling still has possession of my heart.

I think when I go back to Madrid I will see one more bull
fight and then swear off forever. Why is it more cruel, after
all, than pigeon shooting or cock-fighting? True, there is not
quite so much danger in the latter, but, if it be true that a
dying insect "feels a pang as great as when a giant dies,"
then it is as cruel to kill a harmless dove as a poor, faithful,
but wornout horse.

We left Madrid for Seville the day after the fight, and
spent fifteen hours in the cars through the most fertile part
of Spain. The large cities of Spain are very far apart. The
most remarkable thing noticed by the traveler along the route,
is the great apparent drouth and absence of all natural trees or
forests. Seville is a very pretty city. Its beauty, however,
has to be sought, it is not seen without searching for it. The
houses are mostly large, old, well-preserved and perfectly white.
The streets are very tortuous and narrow. The houses are
entered from the street through a high wooden gate, well protected with iron spikes. The front windows on the first floor
are barred like prisons. After the outer gate comes the iron
grill. Then the really beautiful and highly decorated court-
yard. This is freshened by a liberal display of exotic trees,
palms, flowers, and great-leaved tropical plants, watered by
beautiful fountains. The time to see Seville is from seven
o'clock in the evening till midnight. All the gates from the
streets to the court yards are then open, the yards in full view
and the well-dressed men, women and maids of rare beauty are
enjoying the evening in various ways in their little apparent
paradises. In the daytime the same houses look repulsive and
prison like. The air of Seville is said to be most salubrious
and its suburbs most charming in the Spring. It is undoubtedly one of the oldest cities in Spain. The Greeks called it
Ispola. Julius Cæsar entered the city 45 B. C. Almost all
the monuments of its early glory have passed away. When
the Moors were driven from Spain there were 12,000 Moorish
families living in Seville, most of whom left the city with all
their wealth. It is said that over 400,000 Moors, Jews and
Arabs abandoned the city in less than one year. Its whole
population, at this time, does not exceed 140,000. The cathedral is a very fine church and covers about as much ground as
the Philadelphia public buildings. The Alcazar, a Moorish
building, by some considered equal to the Alhambra, is well
worth a close inspection. There are in the churches and museum several master-pieces of the old Sevillian painters. Its
bull fights are the most celebrated in Andalusia. The maidens
of Seville are really very beautiful. They have soft black eyes
and profuse black tresses which they wear something like the
Japanese ladies. More than one reminded me of Yum Yum.

They can play most gracefully with their fans, and have most fascinating manners. The young men of the city are also very handsome. Here our praises must end. The middle-aged are homely, the old are repulsive. Some of the girls marry at twelve, are mothers at thirteen and old and ugly at twenty-five. The city is not increasing in population as fast as was expected after the introduction of the railroad. It has a new part but as yet it has no attractions for travelers. In all other respects it looks to me about like other old European cities. The men, women, dogs and cats, especially the dogs, look very much like the same breed at home. Some well bred and some scurvy whelps.

From what I had read of Seville I expected too much. I imagine this is the experience of most travelers. Our anticipations are seldom realized.

Our next resting place will be Cadiz.

LII.

SEVILLE TO CADIZ—CACTI HORSE HIGH AND HOG STRONG——MANKIND THE SAME THE WORLD OVER—THE SAME AS TO DOGS—BEAUTIFUL GIRL BEGGARS—SHERRY WINE—SACRELIGIOUS NAMES—HUNTING WITHOUT DOGS—SALT VATS—CADIZ NIGHT SCENES OF BEAUTY—NO CARPETS—TILE FLOORS, AND WHITEWASHED HOUSES—THE CATHEDRAL—TOO MUCH RELIGION—THE FOSSILS OF SPAIN—DANGERS, DIFFICULTIES AND DISAPPOINTMENTS—NEARLY WRECKED—WAITING FOR SUNDAY.

CADIZ, SPAIN, August, 1889.

By taking a fast train at Seville, we arrived at Cadiz in about five hours. The name is pronounced here *Kadiz;* the *a* being sounded as in the word *fat*, and the *z* like our *s* in kiss. We follow the rich valley of the Guadalquivir to within a few miles of the peninsula upon which the city stands. The fertility of the soil is proved by the rapid succession of its crops. Indian corn is planted in hills not more than one foot apart and yields fine, well-formed ears. The great vineyards and fields of corn, grass and vegetables, are divided by hedges of cacti, some of which are ten feet high, strong enough to keep out a bull and tight enough to defy a hog. Some of them are in bloom, with a centre stock six or eight inches in diameter and thirty feet high. The peasants cut them down like trees, and use them for the same purposes. The whole country is bare of forest trees. The roads are few, mostly

traveled by men on asses, or donkeys loaded with produce in
very large, clumsy-looking pack-saddles. The manners of the
people, from Seville to Cadiz, appear to me more Moorish than
in other parts of Spain. I am still searching, however, for
something I am quite sure I shall never find—men and women
with different hearts, or better or worse souls than those of
our own country. They wear their hair and cut their dresses
a little differently from us, but they all eat, drink and amuse
themselves just the same ; they laugh when they are pleased,
they weep when they are afflicted, just like other people ; some
will lie, steal and swear, others devote their lives to good
works, while a few are standing models of moral and intellectual virtues.

Spain has a great many beggars, but not more than Italy
or Ireland. The beggars here frequent the cafes in the cities,
and sit around the church doors. One class of beggars I
notice reaps a richer harvest than all the rest. I refer to
pretty young girls with sweet little bastard babies in their
arms. Almost every man she asks gives her a penny ; of
course she knows who to solicit from. The poor, old, blind,
halt and crippled beggars do not fare so well, but we see
many a kindly looking man quietly slip a piece of copper in
the outstretched hand of a blind old man or woman sitting
bareheaded in the broiling sun. The policemen seem kind to
almost all the street beggars ; now and then they will interfere with well-known impostors, but the really afflicted beggar
is never ordered out of the most fashionable cafe.

On our journey from Seville to Cadiz we passed through
the world-renowned sherry wine district ; we stopped long
enough to taste the wine ; it is a much lighter wine than the
sherry of our country. It will not keep in our climate as it
comes from the press here. All the wine intended for England
or America is fortified by the addition of sugar which causes
a second fermentation and additional alcoholic strength, and
also changes the flavor of the wine. Dry sherry is made by
adding a sufficient quantity of pure alcohol instead of sugar.
Most of the sherry vineyards have religious names, by which
their wines are known   A name once adopted to distinguish
the wine of any particular proprietor, becomes his trademark
and is not lawfully appropriated by any other wine grower.
The Spaniards are good Catholics and delight in naming their
wines and their children after saints and sacred things. Thus,
it is no uncommon thing to find a plump little boy bearing the
name of Jesus. It sounds very well while he is a little cherub
in his mother's arms, but when some rough, swearing, or
drunken sailor is known by the same name it sounds, to our
ears, a little sacreligious. These thoughts were suggested by

the name adopted by one of the largest vineyard proprietors in the sherry district. To distinguish the peculiar excellence of his wines, he named his vineyard "Jesus, Mary and Joseph." This would be considered a very profane use of a most sacred name in our country, but it is not so looked upon here.

As we traversed some of the pasture lands along the valley, we noticed great flocks of sheep, droves of cattle and horses, and herds of hogs roaming and grazing over immense fenceless prairies. We also saw gentlemen hunting on horseback in the same fields. A peculiarity of the hunt was the absence of dogs. The horses are used to start up the game and the sportsman is expected to shoot it from his seat in the saddle.

Just before entering the little horn upon which Cadiz is built, we passed through several miles of salt vats, dug in the flat marshes near the sea. The evaporation of confined salt water is very rapid here. The sea water is run into thousands of pits dug for that purpose, and then shut off from the sea by flood gates. As the water evaporates the salt precipitates and forms a crust on the water. It is then raked out, dried and heaped up into pyramids, some as large as houses. The whole country for many miles was white with these pyramids of salt, looking very much like large white tents.

The city of Cadiz is most admirably situated on a tongue of land jutting out into the sea. It is almost completely surrounded by water. Its present population is only about seventy thousand, but its commerce is enormous. It and Barcelona are the chief seaports of Spain. The streets are like those of Seville, the houses are high and milk white. The streets are so narrow that, by a municipal regulation, carriages are required to move only in one way as it would be impossible for them to pass. There are no curbstones ; foot passengers must press the walls of the houses when a cart or carriage passes The streets are kept in good order ; indeed, the whole city has the appearance of great cleanliness. The beauty of the city is best seen at night when the gardens and streets are very brilliantly lighted, and the doors and gates of the private houses are open, showing their paradisaical little courtyards and beautiful maidens. The whole city is a fort, surrounded by great walls of stone, seventy feet thick, with parapets armed with cannon. The promenade on the top of the wall is sixty feet wide and gives to the city, when seen from the sea, a very formidable appearance The city could only be captured by being shelled from a distance, or starved into submission. The Spanish government claims to have the most efficient torpedo known to the world. They say, by actual experiment, they can blow the largest man-of-war sixty feet out of water.

There are no steps, staircases or floors of wood in the

houses of Cadiz ; all are made of tile and white marble ; even the bath tubs are marble, giving to the interior of the dwellings an air of delicious coolness.   I have not seen a carpet or piece of matting in Spain ; whether they have them in the winter or not, I cannot say.

The action of the sea air very rapidly decomposes the marble used in the outside walls. Some of the churches, especially the Cathedral, although of comparatively modern construction, have a very old appearance.   To preserve the fine marble dome of the Cathedral they have covered it with vitrified terra-cotta.   Some of the finest modern buildings are now built of brick and painted white.   It is found that brickwork is the most imperishable.   The new theatre, now in course of construction, is composed of this material ; it will be one of the largest theatres in Spain when finished.   The Cathedral is a splendid edifice of greystone, faced inside with various specimens of the finest European marble.   It was finished at a cost of $1,500,000.

Aside from its walls, and the peculiar construction of the city, there are but few wonderful sights to be seen in Cadiz. The days here, in summer, are rather warm, but the nights are deliciously cool.   Spain, like some of the countries of Asia, is cursed with too much religion.   A reasonable religious ardor is healthy and necessary for the happiness and prosperity of every government, but Spain has carried her reverence for holy things too far.   Until within a short time, nearly every other day was a religious holiday and observed more strictly than Sunday.   The people are now struggling to get rid of its excessive number of feast and fast days.   We arrived on the 14th of this month.   We were surprised to find the city in a blaze of gas lights and filled with musicians and citizens in dress suits and holiday attire.   The next day I called on my banker but found his office closed and a notice upon the door that it would be opened the next day between 11 and 4.   It was absolutely necessary that I should have some money, as we had made our arrangements to take ship the next morning at seven for Tangier, in Africa.   After a great deal of annoyance I secured an interview with him.   He informed me that this was the commencement of the festival of the Ascension, and that it was considered, in Spain, a much more sacred day than Sunday ; but as I was in need of money he would procure it for me, as a work of *charity*.   He took my letter of credit and said, if he could succeed in finding any friends with as much spare cash as I wanted, he would call at my hotel with it about 2 P. M.   About 3 P. M. he made his appearance ; he said he could not get access to any of the banks, but had borrowed from different friends the money I wanted.   He informed me.

in a conversation, that the Queen was popular, but there is a
marked dissatisfaction at this time with what the people call
the "Fossils of Spain." The Queen has all her court dressed
in the very best French style, the effect of which has been to
drive the former fantastic costumes of Spanish belles and beaux
almost entirely out of Spain.

Our trouble did not end with the close of Ascension Day.
The ship was to sail at 7 A. M., and no passengers would be
received on board without a ticket, prepaid, to be procured
at the company's office in the city. We went for our tickets
and were informed that, in consequence of this being the eve of
Ascension Day, the office would not be open until after 10 P. M.
We went at the time appointed, paid our one hundred francs
and secured our tickets. We now retired to bed to dream
of Africa, upon whose burning bosom we expected to pass
our next night. At 5 A. M. we arose, got a hasty cup of coffee
and milk and a small roll of bread, and started for the ship,
which was about half a mile from the wharf, lying at anchor.
Our guide put us on a small sailing boat to embark us on our
ship. I noticed that the sea in the bay was very rough, but did
not suppose it was dangerously so. We soon found ourselves
tossed about like a cork in the breakers. For one hour the boatman endeavored to put us on board. His assistant, a boy of
about fifteen, began to pray and cry like a baby. The sails
dashed from side to side over our heads, and the waves every
now and then flew over us. At last the boatman said it was impossible to make the ship and coolly got his anchor ready to
throw over in case of necessity. The ship steamed up and started at full speed, with two forlorn travelers left behind, and a
hundred francs worse than sunk in the sea. All we could understand from the boatman was "Domingo—Reclamacion,"
which we understood to mean that we could take the ship again
on Sunday or get our money back. We returned to our hotel
in high dudgeon, mad as two March hares. We were coolly
informed that it was only a matter of three days. That the same
ticket was good for Sunday, etc. I had encountered too many
disappointments and overcome too many difficulties to let the
mere matter of a furious storm in the Atlantic stop me. I had
started for Africa and there I would go, if it took all summer,
so we went to our rooms to muse on the uncertainties of human
events, and put in the time as best we could for three weary
days. About 5 P. M. one of the waiters came to our chamber
door and knocked with a nervous vigor very different from the
gentle tap of former occasions. He had come to congratulate
us upon our escape. The ship had encountered a terrible storm,
came near being wrecked and had returned to port in distress.
She would start again to-morrow at 6 A. M., if the storm

sufficiently abated to make it safe. We were greatly relieved by this news, as we would now only lose one day. We waited patiently all day, went to bed soon so that we could rise early, but just before putting out our candles the same waiter again knocked at the door to inform us that the ship would start at 3 A. M. and we would have to get up at two, at the same time giving us a gentle hint that it was not certain that she would not abandon the voyage and wait till Sunday. We concluded to wait till Sunday.

We are now patiently waiting, but Sunday seems as far off as Christmas used to in our boyhood days.

LIII.

CADIZ TO TANGIER—LABOR OMNIA VINCIT—AN ORIENTAL CITY—A CONSUL IN BAD REPUTE—SLAVERY, MOHAMMEDANISM AND POLYGAMY—TWENTY-FIVE DOLLARS FOR THE SOUL AND BODY OF A BEAUTIFUL GIRL—NEW WINE IN OLD BOTTLES—A LAWLESS AND DANGEROUS PLACE—GOING UP ON THE HOUSE TOP TO PRAY—SLEEPING, HEELS UP AND HEAD DOWN—THE GRAVEYARD OF THE FAITHFUL— A PILGRIMAGE FOR MECCA—MOORISH MODESTY—MOHAMMEDAN SAINTS—PALACES, JAILS, SCHOOLS AND CONCERTS —A SEA BATH—THE BEGINNING OF THE END.

TANGIER, AFRICA, August, 1889.

By persevering we have prevailed and are now upon the veritable soil of Africa. It is difficult to realize that all around us is not an enchantment, a dream, or a theatrical representation of some Oriental tale. It is impossible to describe this singular, dirty, dreamy old city. Its narrow lanes, called streets, its whitewashed one-story flat-roofed houses, its bare-legged and turbaned inhabitants, its beggars, slaves and bazaars, must be seen to be properly understood. If you want an accurate description of the place read the '' Arabian Night's Entertainment,'' and the pictures it contains will be perfect pen paintings of Tangier. Bagdad and Damascus cannot be more oriental or primitive, in manners as well as architecture, than this equally old city. Its chief sights are the life, manners, and costumes seen everywhere in the streets. Its entire population does not exceed eighteen thousand, and only four hundred wear European costumes. The city is the politico-diplomatic capital of Morocco. The four hundred Europeans residing in the city are chiefly foreign ministers, consuls, with their families and attendants.

The voyage from Cadiz, wind and weather being favorable, is made in about six hours.   The ships are very good sea steamers of English build.   O'Shea had warned us not to attempt to visit Tangier before October, as the heat of August, he said, was unendurable for a white man ; and that we would be also in danger of the African fever.   As we had found him unreliable in his advice about other places, we had concluded to read his book as the old farmer read Dodd's Almanac—when it said rain, the old farmer always looked for fair weather. The sequel proved the correctness of our conclusion.

Our ship "The Mogador" hugged the Spanish coast as far as Cape Trafalgar, from which point, by a sudden tack, we ran across the mouth of the Straits of Gibraltar into the Bay of Tangier.   As we looked towards the Straits, the highlands of both Europe and Africa were plainly visible.   We did not pass over the historic waters off Cape Trafalgar without calling to mind Lord Nelson's famous victory of October 21st, 1805, fought at the very spot over which our ship passed.   We had seen in the British Museum the letter Lord Nelson wrote on the eve of the battle, directed to his mistress, Lady Hamilton. It indicated a premonition of approaching death.   His last wish was for the welfare of his mistress whom he commended to the care of the English people.   They erected countless monuments to the memory of their hero but, very properly,. gave Lady Hamilton the cold shoulder and left her to find another lover or take care of herself.

My former impressions of the African coast were very incorrect.   It is very rough and barren, wind blown and hilly,. not unlike the coast of Spain, but more mountainous.   The Bay of Tangier is very secure against storms ; it is sheltered. by an amphitheatre of mountains.   The city is built in tiers up the sides of the hills at the right, as we enter the bay.   On the top of the hills, overlooking the city, there are several well-built European houses inhabited by the ministers, diplomats and foreign consuls.

Our dragoman seemed to have a very bad opinion of the United States.   He told some very disgraceful stories about our Consul.   I will not repeat them as they are, perhaps, slanders ; but if the one-tenth of what he said is true, our Consul ought not only to be removed, but also severely punished for his conduct here during the past three years.

The inhabitants are not negroes ; they are Arabs and Moors.   The language of the city is Arabic.   The few black people we saw were slaves or servants to their Moorish masters.   I could have bought male or female slaves, fine looking and young, for about five pounds a head (twenty-five dollars). The city is cursed with the three great evils of the earth—

Slavery, Polygamy and Mohammedanism.   It seems to be a
place without law.   The streets are long, narrow and tortuous,
and are never lighted at night,   Men could be murdered here
in the streets, on a dark night, and the crime would not be
discovered before daylight,   A few days ago a Spaniard killed
a Moor in a dispute over a half franc (ten cents),   No arrest
was made and the murderer is now safe in Spain.   A more
filthy place cannot be imagined; it has not been cleaned for
hundreds of years, except by dogs and rains,   All the garbage,
offal of the slaughter pens, sheep's heads, dead animals and
contents of the privies are thrown into the streets.   The streets
are, however, so constructed that a heavy shower will wash
their filth into the sea.   They are very roughly paved and
have not been repaired for, perhaps, a hundred years or more.

The house tops are all flat, often of stone or cement over
the arched chamber below, and are used as places of prayer,
meditation, smoking and amusement, after sunset.   We saw
from the balcony of our hotel several devout Musselmen at
their prayers on their housetops.   I also saw, just after sundown, a loaded camel endeavor to enter the city through one
of the low arched gates.   His burden was too high, whereupon his driver made him kneel and then took from his back
several large sacks.   The camel then got up and entered the
city through the arch.   I could now better understand the
Scriptural expression concerning the rich man, and the camel
going through the needle's eye.   The "Needle's Eye" was
undoubtedly the name of one of the low arched gates of Jerusalem, where the camels had to be unloaded before they could
enter the city.   I could also fully comprehend the story of
Peter's vision, when he was hungry and went up on the house
top to pray.

Water for drinking purposes is drawn from wells and
springs, poured into goat skins and carried about the city on
the backs of peddlers.   We visited one of the famous springs
from which the drinking water is drawn.   The sight was very
disgusting; the spring basin was full of dirty Arabs washing
the filth from their feet and legs, some of them in the water up
to their waists, filling their goat skins, to be sold to the thirsty
citizens at a penny a quart.   These goat skins are called in the
Arabic language, *bottles*, and are the same as those spoken of
in the New Testament as unfit, when old, to be filled with new
wine.   When they are new, that is just stripped from the goat,
they are elastic and yield to the gases of fermentation, but
when old they, like leather, lose this elasticity and the force
of fermentation bursts them.

We found the Arabs and Moors much more bigoted Mohammedans than they were at Constantinople.   They will not

permit an unbeliever to enter their mosques on any pretext ;
we were permitted to look at the exterior, but could not enter
its sacred portals.   There are no chairs, sofas, or even benches
upon which to sit, in the houses, shops, churches or places of
amusement.   They sit cross-legged on mats made from reeds,
or on the bare floor or stone pavement.   They seem to be great
sleepers and can repose in any position.   They have no pillows
and rest as comfortably with their heads hanging down as with
them raised up.   They sleep in the streets, stretched out at
full length on the stone pavement, or cuddled up like dogs in
some nook or corner.   I have no doubt but that Jacob was
accustomed to just such habits, and that he slept as sweetly on
his pillow of stone, when he dreamed of heaven and saw the
angels ascending and descending, as one of us would have reposed upon a pillow of down.

Just outside of the built-up part of the city there is a stony,
barren hill, used as a graveyard, entirely naked and unorna-
mented.   It is now the camping ground of a caravan from the
interior, consisting of many hundred religious devotees on a
pilgrimage to Mecca.   They got here a few days too late for
the ship they were to join to convey them to Syria ; as a consequence they will have to wait here, perhaps, nine months or
a year.   They do not seem to value time.   They are very dirty,
half naked and degraded looking creatures.   Their tents are
made of poles, sticks and old mats, full of vermin and most
forbidding in their general appearance.   About all they do is
to sit around the streets, sleep, read the Koran, say their prayers, and wash their filthy bodies in the wells and springs from
which the drinking water is drawn.

I saw young girls, nearly naked, bending over the walled
well curbs, drawing up water.   Their faces were pretty well
veiled, but all the rest of their bodies were very much exposed.
I also saw them from the balcony of our hotel, bathing in a
little cove of the sea set apart for their special use, as naked as
they were born.   They did not seem to have the slightest idea
of what we would call female modesty.   They, however, consider it very immodest for a beautiful lady to expose her *face*
to public view.

The caravan of pilgrims had in their company several Mohammedan Saints.   They wore white turbans and shirts :
they were evidently religious monomaniacs.   They sit in one
position all day, in the sun, reading aloud portions of the
Koran and making ejaculatory speeches and harangues to
those around them.

We visited the palace of the Emperor, a mean looking
building from the outside view, but very prettily and delicately
finished within, with carved wood and plaster in the form of

fine lace drapery. It must have taken a very long time and great patience to carve out the lace work, as it was all done with a simple knife by the hand of the artist. We also visited the barracks, jail, and place of Justice. The Emperor's horses looked like subjects for a Spanish bull fight at a dollar a head. The Emperor has a great number of excellent saddles, but very few good horses and still fewer soldiers to ride them. We also visited one of the schools where children are taught to read the Koran. It looked like a low stable ; the teacher was sitting on his crossed legs in the centre and the little urchins sitting in the same manner around him. They held little pasteboards in their hands upon which was written the passage they were to learn. The teacher would read it aloud and the scholars repeat after him in concert. This they do from hour to hour and from day to day until they have the entire book committed to memory.

After supper we visited a Moorish cafe and concert room. Our dragoman assured us there was no danger, but we noticed that he provided us with quite a body guard. He walked by our side, a full-fledged Arab went ahead and the landlord, in Moorish costume, brought up the rear. We walked through a very dark, narrow street for some time till we reached the concert room, a miserable one-story building, with bamboo rafters, covered with reed matting and branches of trees. Six Arabs and Moors were the musicians, who sat in the centre of the room on the floor, singing, clapping their hands and sawing upon instruments with one and two strings. There were some ten or fifteen spectators in the room, squatting around on the floor, drinking coffee, which by the way was very good. The whole affair reminded me of the old time plantation songs of our colored people. I confess I did not feel altogether safe until I was in my hotel again. While the concert was progressing, a tall, lank saint entered the room. He did not speak a word. He looked toward Mecca, ejaculated a prayer, bowed his head to the ground several times, then walked around the room and kissed each of the faithful on the top of his head, after which, with great dignity, he left the room.

We retired to our beds about 11 P. M., expecting, after the fatigue of the day, a good night's rest, but we were kept awake nearly all night by the howling, fighting and barking of dogs and braying of asses.

I could not have believed, if I had not seen it, that six hours' travel could carry us from a city of high European culture and comfort to one of such primitive customs and costumes. Before leaving we took a bath in the sea. The water was quite cold, the beach and surf were equal to Cape May. Our dragoman made the necessary arrangements for our bathing *robes*. They were sufficient for Africa, but would hardly do for Cape May. Mine consisted of a napkin and my son's of a bandana handkerchief. A couple of turbaned Moors, evidently of the higher class, as they wore perfectly white clean robes, seemed very much interested in us. They were evidently amused at our white skins.

The weather was very cool and pleasant. The thermometer did not register above eighty-two and the sea breeze was strong and refreshing. We could walk all over the hills of the city without much perspiration. The thermometer is never below sixty in Tangier. Those who wish to see Tangier as we have seen it must visit it soon, for the beginning of the end of this style of life and civilization is very apparent. A new hotel on the plan of those of Paris, and to be conducted by a French company, is now being built. The one we are stopping at is conducted by an Englishman from Gibraltar. While he and all his waiters adopt the Moorish costume, he thinks it will soon be discarded for the European dress. Many of the Moors have European suits, which they wear when they go to Gibraltar or Cadiz. The dresses of the four hundred Europeans who live in the city are no longer objects of curiosity in the eyes of the people. Several fine new houses of European architecture are now being built on the hill overlooking the city and facing the sea. I predict that Tangier, before fifty years, will be like Cadiz and, perhaps, adopt the costumes and manners of Paris and London. I am, to a certain extent, a believer in evolution. The fittest must survive. Electricity and steam, assisted by Peace, must eventually make the world cosmopolite.

Our dragoman promised us a wild boar hunt if we would stay a week, but I remembered the sad fate of Adonis and declined the proffered sport.

I may sum up the whole matter by saying that I would not have missed my visit to Tangier for ten times its cost. It has been one of the most interesting excursions of my life. We leave here this morning at 9 to return again to Cadiz. From there we intend to visit Cordova to see its world renowned Mosque and old Roman bridge over the Guadalquivir. It will require ten hours by rail to make the journey.

LIV

TANGIER TO CORDOVA—CADIZ SEEN FROM THE SEA—DELAP-
IDATED CORDOVA—MOSQUE OF ONE THOUSAND COLUMNS—
ROMAN BRIDGE AND MOORISH MILLS—CORDOVA TO PARIS
—PRIMITIVE FARMING—HIGH TAXES—BACK TO MADRID
—THE COUNTRY OF DON QUIXOTE—AVILA—VALLADOLID
—RELIGIOUS INTOLERANCE—BURGOS—THE LEAD MINES
OF SPAIN—SECOND THOUGHT AS TO THE EXPOSITION—
EMINENT MEN OF THE PAST ONE HUNDRED YEARS.

PARIS, August, 1889.

We left Tangier with some regret, but the fact that we
were now to turn our faces homeward compensated us for our
farewell to Africa. It was our first visit to the dark continent.
The Spaniards call Cadiz the "silver cup in the sea," but to
us, as we approached it and sailed almost entirely around it in
order to enter its beautiful harbor, it seemed like a white pearl
set in azure. It looks like a city of white marble rising from
the sea. The charm was broken when we landed. We found
the same old Cadiz of stone, stucco and whitewash.

As soon as possible we procured our tickets for Cordova,
which we reached in about ten hours. By procuring the services of a good guide we were able to see the whole city in one
day. In the VIIth century Cordova was the rival of Bagdad
and Damascus, with a population of 300,000. It had six
hundred mosques and eight hundred public schools. Its
yearly income was $30,000,000. It was a city of palaces,
mosques, learning and luxury. It now looks like a wrinkled
but royal old widow, mourning beside the dilapidated tomb of
her dead consort and buried children.

In the quarrel between Cæsar and Pompey, Cordova,
unfortunately for it, espoused the cause of the latter. After
his victory of Munda, Cæsar, in cold blood, slaughtered 28,000
of its best citizens.

When St. Ferdinand captured the city from the Moors,
singular as it may seem, it began to decline and has slowly
but steadily continued its downward course till now it can
barely count 50,000 inhabitants. The ground upon which
much of the old city stood is now devoted to agriculture.
When the French were driven from Spain they carried with
them several hundred thousand dollars' worth of silver from
Cordova. The silver chandelier, stolen from the cathedral,
has since been restored.

The mosque of Cordova is now its chief object of attraction. It is certainly a very striking piece of Moorish architecture. It contained over twelve hundred marble columns which, at the first view, one would take to be the works of the Moorish builders, but upon a close inspection all the columns will be found to be the work of Western architects. They were collected by the Moors from all quarters of the earth, from Rome, Greece, and every other country under Moorish dominion or in alliance with them. Many of these columns were presents from Christian kings and emperors. They are all of about the same diameter but of various lengths. Hardly two of the capitals are alike ; on some the capital is too small, on others too large ; some are in true proportion. To give them the appearance of regularity, the columns have no bases, but are buried in the ground at unequal depths, so that the floor, which is of fine marble and mosaic, comes up to the same level and makes the forest of columns look all of the same size. It is said that there is nothing in the world like this mosque. I have never seen any building with which it can be compared. It is but one story high and had originally a flat roof of timber (over the horse-shoe arches, sprung from column to column), which was richly carved in lacework and covered with gold. On entering for the first time, it strikes the mind with a peculiar sensation of vastness and splendor. All the columns are monoliths. Whichever way we turn our faces a vista of columns and arches is presented to the view. During the Moorish occupation, the roof and arches were hung with thousands of gold and silver lamps, giving to the whole an enchanting appearance of oriental beauty. In a word, it looks like "a wilderness of columns and arches." The only credit, to my mind, the Moorish architects are entitled to is the unique design by which they have erected a most charming structure from materials that otherwise would have remained only as objects of curiosity in the museums of the world.

The old bridge of Cordova is chiefly interesting for its great antiquity, grace and beauty. Even now, in its dilapidated condition, its beautiful arches give to the work an appearance of strength and grace. It was built by Octavius Cæsar and is still in reasonably good condition. Just below the bridge are several grain mills erected by the Moors but still in running order. The rapid flow of the Guadalquivir turns the water wheels and keeps the machinery in motion as in the days of yore.

To get out of Spain it is necessary to go back to Madrid. Like the roads of Rome, all the railroads of Spain point toward Madrid.

From Madrid to Paris is 909 miles by the shortest route.

The railroad passes through some of the finest scenery and most celebrated places in Spain. Some of the scenery of the Pyrenees is only surpassed by Switzerland.

We were especially struck with the primitive farming throughout Spain. A good plow, such as is in common use in France and the rest of Europe and America, is seldom seen in Spain ; we have not seen one. They are all home-made, drawn by ropes tied to the horns of oxen, and the best only scratch the ground. The carts are also home made, wheels and all. We are told that some.of the peasant families live on the expenditure of twenty cents a day. The whole family work in the fields. We saw a father, with a six-week-old babe in his arms, driving the oxen while the mother guided the plow and a little seven-year-old urchin ran after them with a club breaking up the clods. Most of the ground in the hilly districts is cultivated with great heavy hoes ; about four persons in a row strike in their hoes at the same time and then turn over the soil which looks very much like plowed ground.

Spain is at least a hundred years behind the rest of Europe. The land, while seemingly the property of the farmers, is really owned by the Crown. The rents are collected in the shape of taxes which, we are told, equal about one-fourth of the gross revenue of the land. All the taxes go directly to . Madrid and never return. The thirsty city drinks dry the river of gold constantly flowing into its ever open mouth.

The whole country is in about the condition of France before the revolution of 1793. Let us hope that the Spanish Government will be wise in time, and by a vigorous State policy get rid of its many drawbacks to prosperity. Otherwise the people will throw off their burdens as they did in France in 1793.

From Cardova to Madrid we passed over the world-renowned " Campus de la Mancha," the birthplace and scene of many of the exploits of the " wisest of fools, and shrewdest of madmen "—Don Quixote de la Mancha. We saw the little village where Cervantes wrote his novel while in jail for debt. The people of the country firmly believe in the actual existence of the doughty old knight.

In our journey from Madrid to Paris we passed some towns of historic interest. Avila has a fine mediæval cathedral and feudal castle of great apparent strength. The town itself has now a very mean appearance. Valladolid, however, is a very handsome town of its kind. It stands 2100 feet above the level of the sea and was the former capital of Spain. It lies about 200 miles north of Madrid. It is chiefly notorious as the birthplace of one of Spain's bigoted and cruel kings, Philip II, who burnt heretics and built the Escurial. The first auto de fe at Valladolid took place May 21, 1559. Seats sold at what would be now equivalent to three or four dollars each. Delicate ladies and little children witnessed the burning alive of fourteen Lutheran christians as they would look at a bull fight. I believe there are bigoted men to-day, of all denominations, who would do the same thing if they had the power. No one church is responsible for that feeling of religious intoleration. St. Lawrence, Philip II's patron saint, was fried on a gridiron as a heretic in his day, and the Puritans of New England hung the Quakers upon the same principle.

The last city of Spain through which we pass *en route* to Paris is old Burgos, up among the Pyrenees, 2867 feet above the level of the sea. It is a cold, cheerless looking place now, but was the gayest city in Spain when it was the capital of Castile. It contains a fine cathedral of mediæval architecture, but we have seen so many old churches and museums that we begin to grow weary of this class of sight-seeing. The old town is chiefly interesting as the birth-place of the Cid. His bones are preserved here in a walnut urn.

> "Corneille has told us the tale of the Cid,
> Of all that he didn't and all that he did."

It will, therefore, not be necessary to repeat here his deeds of prowess It was here that Edward I of England married his fair Eleanor of Castile.

Soon after leaving Burgos we entered France and had a fine view of the sea again. Biarritz is a very fashionable French watering place, beautifully situated near the sea. If travelers wish they can stop off there for a day. The next place of importance is Bayonne and then Bordeaux, a seaport town. The vineyards around Bordeaux are wonderfully productive and are cultivated to their greatest capacity. The balance of the journey was not very attractive. The road passes over the flat lands of France, looking something like the pine groves of New Jersey.

I do not regard Spain as being as fine a country as France. The comparison, however, in its present condition of agricultural cultivation, would hardly be fair. The fruits of Spain are celebrated all over the world ; it is also very rich in undeveloped mineral wealth. Her mines have been known since the days of Solomon, who sent his ships to Tarshish, which was undoubtedly Cadiz.

Very few travelers take the trouble to visit Spain and therefore have a very limited idea of its vastness and the great distances between its chief cities. It has an area over three times that of England. We have traveled nearly three thousand miles in Spain alone and have not been able to see it all. Since leaving Liverpool we have traveled over five thousand miles including our sea trip from Marseiles to Barcelona and from Cadiz to Tangier.

On our arrival back at Paris the weather seemed cold and rather disagreeable, perhaps because we had just left the genial warmth of Spain.

Paris is now crowded to overflowing, even the third class hotels are full. I visited the Exposition again and came to the conclusion, that, if the Eiffel Tower, Edison's phonograph and the magnificent buildings were thrown out of the scale, it would not outweigh the Centennial at Philadelphia very much. Take the tower and the phonograph away and the Exposition presents nothing worthy of calling the world together to see.

In one corner of the Garden of the Tuilleries I found a very interesting panorama presenting, in a very attractive form, life-sized representations of all the eminent Frenchmen of the last one hundred years. They appear before the spectator in the most stirring scenes of their lives. The illusion is so perfect that one is apt to forget that he is only looking upon a painting.

I believe I have seen everything in Paris worth looking at and do not care to waste my time here longer. I would much rather rest at home. I leave here to-morrow for London, by way of Calais and Dover.

———

LV

PARIS TO LIVERPOOL—WHAT CAN BE SEEN IN SIXTY DAYS
—POLITICS AND PROPHECY—THE GREAT MEN OF THE
CENTURY—AN ASTONISHED CABMAN—DOVER—LONDON
FOGS—SUNDAY IN HYDE PARK—FREE SPEECH AND FAIR
PLAY—A CONUNDRUM—COVENT GARDEN AT DAYBREAK—
P. D. Q.—GLIMPSE AT GLADSTONE—HOMEWARD BOUND.

LIVERPOOL, September, 1880.

As my first letter of the present series was written from Liverpool, and as I have now completed my intended circuit. I will close the correspondence from the same place. Since landing here in July, I have traveled over six thousand miles in England, France, Spain and Africa. From this fact alone I should have credit for industry if for nothing else.

I had intended to spend in Paris the few remaining days of my allotted time, but, when I returned, I found the air of Paris damp and chilly, especially so when compared with the balmy atmosphere of Spain. Neuralgia seemed to be epidemic

There were not hip-bath tubs enough in our hotel to accommodate the guests. After a week of suffering I resolved to
leave for London, but, before bidding adieu to the gay capital,
I paid another visit to the panorama in the garden of the
Tuilleries. To persons desiring to know how the men of
French history during the past century looked when in their
glory, this panorama is very suggestive. The illusion is so
lifelike that we are apt to take the first group that catches our
eye to be a party of spectators like ourselves, but we soon discover they are motionless figures, skillfully painted from the
best portraits. We see Napoleon and his brave Marshals just
as they looked when the great Captain made his triumphant
entry into Paris after the termination of his most glorious
camgaign The celebrated characters of the Revolution of '93
—Robespierre, Danton, Murat, Charlotte Corday, Louis XVI.,
Marie Antoinette and the poor little Dauphin—are represented
in some of the most tragic scenes of that terrible period.

Victor Hugo, with folded arms, is leaning against the base
of a column ; Gambetta is just taking le ve of his friends before
making his perilous balloon ascension ; Marshal Ney looks like
an old lion ; Charles X. like a young ass ; Louis Philipe poses
like a demagogue ; Louis XVIII. looks like an overgrown
baby in soldiers' clothes ; Dumas might pass for one of Carncross & Dixey's minstrels about propounding a conundrum ;
Lesseps looks as Mr. Blaine will look ten years hence ; Car-
not looks like William Rhoads, of Newtown, ten years ago ;
Grevy might be taken for lawyer Dick White, of Philadelphia
and George Sand presents a picture not unlike Geoff. Denis in
a lady's dress, but not as good looking. The list is too long
to be repeated in the short confines of a letter. Rochefort is
not only represented in the gallery, but his photograph is exhibited in all the shop windows. If he would cut his hair he
might pass for Judge Broomall.

Although they are on the eve of one of the most important elections ever held in France, politics is in a very lethargic
condition. The fate of the Republic undoubtedly depends
upon the approaching contest. The motto inscribed upon the
banners of the Republicans is " *Vaincre ou Mourir*," yet the
excitement is not half as great as at one of our tamest Presidential campaigns. All parties are united against the Republic, but the admitted fact that it has saved France has given
it a very strong hold upon the French heart. I believe the
French people are growing weary of political excitement and
intend to stand by the Government in the impending struggle.
France has changed her form of government no less than
thirteen times during the past hundred years. She has tried
hereditary Monarchy, citizen kings, the Convention, the

Directory, the Red Republic, Parliamentary government, the Empire and the Republic, and the question now to be submitted to the people is, not shall the Monarchy or the Empire be restored, but shall the Republic be abolished ? The wonderful administrative ability of the French people in the hour of peril has heretofore been sufficient to save the nation from anarchy, and I believe, from what I have seen and heard, the result of the coming contest will be the overwhelming defeat of the enemies of the Republic. *Nous l'errons.*

We will now descend from the fate of the Nation to the cabmen of Paris. The rule of the road requires pedestrians to look out for themselves. A few days ago a young American was leisurely walking up Place Vendome ; the asphaltum pavement was wet and slippery ; a cabman came up on a full run and, without a word of warning, ran his horse against the back of the promenader. Everybody expected to see the young man knocked down, but, to the surprise of all, he wheeled suddenly around and with his fist struck the horse a powerful blow under the left ear knocking him sprawling, head, tail, feet and rump, in a heap in the street. The horse slid upon the smooth pavement fully fifteen feet before he seemed to realize what had happened. It was as much as the cabman could do to keep his seat. The young man neither looked to the right nor left and was soon lost in the crowd. The bystanders helped the fallen horse to his feet and laughed at the cabman whose bewildered look only made the scene more ludicrous.

To vary my route home I took a ticket from Paris to London by the Calais and Dover train. By this line the time between the two cities is only about nine hours. I took a look at Amiens from the cars but was not sufficiently prepossessed with the place to give it a day. Calais is a sleepy old town, not worth an hour of a traveler's precious time. We crossed the Channel on a very smooth sea in less than one hour. The sudden change from France to England seemed magical. We found an almost instantaneous change of language, habits and manners ; an hour before we were in a country where no English was spoken and all accounts were kept in francs and centimes ; we were now in a country where no French was spoken and everything was counted in pounds, shillings and pence, and yet the shores of the two nations were no farther apart than the cities of Philadelphia and Chester. Between Cadiz and Tangier, only six hours apart, we were struck with a more radical change in civilization, religion, dress and manners.

From Dover—whose situation and surroundings are most charming—to London, we pass through the fertile fields of

Kent. The grass is of the richest green ; great flocks of sheep, fat and white, are grazing and reposing in the well-watered meadows. Fine old oak trees line the banks of rivulets and meandering streams. The roadway from Dover to the suburbs of London reminds one of some of Shakespeare's and Milton's descriptions of rural England in the olden time.

I found London enveloped in a dense fog. I tried to take a walk up the Strand but could not see across the street. The dome of St. Paul's looked like a fairy castle floating over the city ; gas was burning in the streets and stores until after 11 A. M., when the fog suddenly lifted and glorious old London appeared as if by magic.

I have never grown weary of London. I like its people, its modes of life, its amusements and its business habits and customs. The English people are said to be unsociable to strangers, but I have never found them so. Amusement in London never forces itself upon you ; you must seek it, and to those who desire a little fun it is not hard to find. I spent almost the entire Sunday in Hyde Park and saw a great many amusing sights illustrative of London life and character. The following little incident will exemplify the fondness of every true Briton for fair play :

There is a little lake in the park where dogs are permitted to swim and play. Upon coming out of the water the dogs had a misunderstanding, commencing with a growl and ending in a free fight. As the battle became general, three dogs jumped upon one that lay by a seat occupied by a well-dressed gentleman reading the *Times*. He at once jumped up and seized two of the three by their collars and held them till the other two had fought it out. When the contest was over, a bystander remarked that the dirty and wet dogs he was holding had ruined his trousers. "You are quite right, sir," said the gentleman, "but the poor brute had to have fair play, you know."

I saw and heard, in Hyde Park, public exhibitions of free speech which would not be permitted in any city in America. There is now a great strike by the stevedores and dock hands of London. The strikers march through the streets with their banners and, by concert, meet in the Park to discuss their grievances.

As the strikers moved through the crowded streets, Her Majesty's policemen cleared the way and marched in two lines, about ten yards apart, on each side of the procession. By a custom so old, as the lawyers say, "that the memory of man runneth not to the contrary," Hyde Park is a spot sacred to free speech. All parties may hold meetings there and say just what they please so long as they refrain from overt acts of treason or breach of the peace. In one place we see a crowd listening to and applauding some half crazy infidel pouring out a tirade of abuse and blasphemy against Christianity. In another place some broken down and seedy old actor will be reciting scenes from Shakespeare, after which he passes around his hat. In another spot, in bad English and most violent gesticulation, we see a half starved socialist cursing the government and counseling all sorts of raids upon the rich for the general benefit of the poor. Even the Queen, Prince Albert, and the little princes do not escape vulgar denunciations. All the banners were blood-red, the inscriptions indicating the sentiments of the societies carrying them, such as "Social Democrats of London;" "By Heavens, our rights are worth fighting for;" "The wages of sin is death—the wages of labor slow but sure starvation," etc.

The speakers were bright, intelligent fellows, who evidently live by their wits. Their ideas were good and well put together but the "H" was thrown about in great confusion. One of the speakers seemed to be a great favorite, as he was repeatedly called for by the crowd and at last appeared amid great applause upon the rostrum. He had white cotton gloves on his great big hands and opened his speech by propounding the following conundrum: "You see, my friends, I wear white cotton gloves; they are of my own make. Do any of you know why old maids wear cotton gloves? Because they don't like *kids*. Now I do like *kids*. That's what I'm here for to-day. I've got four poor little *kids* at home without milk to drink or bread to eat." And so he went on for an hour very eloquently setting forth the struggles of the poor workingman in London to support his wife and *kids*. If he had been an educated man he would, perhaps, have been one of the world's great orators. The sympathy of the masses is clearly in favor of the strikers.

There is no better place to see displays of wealth and beauty than Hyde Park Corner on a Sunday afternoon. It is a free exhibition of the finest horses and handsomest women of the city. Ostensibly they come for air and exercise, but really only to show themselves, their horses, carriages, servants and dogs.

I arose at 6 A. M. on Saturday morning to see the Covent Garden fruit and vegetable market. The streets for many squares were packed with all sorts of carts, wagons and barrows. Little farmers' boys and girls, dressed in their Sunday clothes, sat in the carts almost covered with carrots, beets, cabbages, and cauliflowers. The police are kept busy settling conflicting claims to portions of the street and in keeping the teams in line. One would suppose vegetables enough were vomited into London to glut the market; but I am told that it will all be sold before noon and be devoured by Monday morning.

All the hotels are now full of returning travelers. At Liverpool no rooms can be had without telegraphing a day or two ahead. I suppose that most travelers have noticed the fact that all the hotel waiters in England are German boys. They are the sons of tradesmen in Germany spending a few months in England at very low wages for the purpose of learning the language. Some of them serve for their board and, in the restaurants where it is customary to give the waiters small fees, they pay as much as two shillings a day for the privilege of waiting on the guests. One of these young fellows was the subject of a rather cruel joke by an American gentleman a few days ago. The gentleman ordered his breakfast, P. D. Q. "Vat means dat?" said the waiter. The gentleman informed him that the expression was a *polite* way of requesting immediate attention to the order; in other words, he said it meant as quick as possible. "Oh," said Dutchey, "I vill remember. dat." His next call was from a fidgety old maid, who requested the waiter to bring her coffee "as quick as possible." "Yes, madam," he said, "P D. Q." An explosion of indignation at the supposed familiarity followed, which after due explanation ended in a hearty laugh at his expense, but the poor fellow had to leave the hotel to escape the jeers and twits of his fellow servants who from that time called him by no other name than P. D Q.

Mr. Gladstone, wife and flunky put up at our hotel, the Charing Cross, on his way to Paris. I saw him as he left the hotel for his compartment in the cars. While he carries his age very well, I should say from his appearance it is about time for him to retire from active politics. He is a very plain looking man. He left the hotel alone, his wife and flunky attending to all the details of the journey. The flunky put on some airs.

My route from London to Liverpool was through Derby and Manchester. The country looks very beautiful and fresh. The chief charm of England and Ireland is its deep, refreshing and almost perpetual green.

I went this morning to the office of the steamboat company to see that my baggage was safe and take a glance at the passenger list. I found some of my old shipmates returning home. I also noticed the names of Chauncey M. Depew, Senator John Sherman, Hon. George H. Bates, late Commissioner to Berlin, General Nagle, and other celebrated Americans booked as passengers.

LVI

THE START—THE SHIP—THE PASSENGERS--LOVE, ROMANCE
AND SEASICKNESS—POLITICS—A LOST LEAF FROM A LA-
DY'S DIARY—GULLS, VULTURES AND MEN—A STORM AND
ACCIDENT—UNLUCKY THIRTEEN—REFLECTIONS ON SHIPS,
SAILORS AND SEAS—THE CAPTAIN'S DINNER.

PARIS, February, 1892.

This is my tenth voyage across the Atlantic and the first
one I have made in the winter. During the first five days the
sea was smooth and the weather good. There was but little
seasickness and no dinner at which the table was not reasonably full. We left Chester at noon on the 12th, embarked
about 5 P. M., and sailed at 4.30 A. M. on the 13th. We
arrived here on the 23d about 4 P. M. So it will be apparent that
instead of seven, we have been ten days making the journey.

Upon entering the ship our hearts were gladdened by the
receipt of two telegrams and several letters from kind and
considerate friends, wishing us *bon voyage*. These little
courtesies are exceedingly pleasant. They do not cost much
but they refresh the soul like water the thirsty lip. We feel
that the friends who take the trouble to encourage our parting
will as kindly greet our return. It must be a dry heart that
leaves no loved ones behind, and, to feel that the great ocean
will soon roll between us and the loved ones we are leaving
is apt to chill even the warmest heart. But distance often
lends enchantment to the view, so absence sharpens the appetite
of love.

'Tis sweet to greet the friends we meet :
'Tis sweeter yet to meet again
The friends we've met.

We have chosen for this voyage the ship "La Normandie," of the French line, running directly from New York to
Havre. The distance is about 3175 miles, several hundred
miles greater than that between New York and Liverpool.
La Normandie is not a fast ship, but she is steady and staunch.
I have never sailed upon one that behaved better in bad
weather. As we judge a lady by her conduct under trying
circumstances, so we should approve a ship by her behavior
in a storm. La Normandie is 480 feet long by 50 feet beam.
She sets deep in the water. She has four decks and can carry
over 1000 passengers. Her first-class saloon will comfortably
seat 130 at meals. We have eighty first-class passengers
on this voyage, among them our esteemed fellow-citizen
Samuel A. Crozer, Esq., now talked of as a possible candidate

for Congress from our district. Mr. Crozer's son Edward, accompanied by his charming bride, are also passengers, about to spend their honeymoon in the enjoyment of foreign travel. Luckily for the young and manly husband his wife is a good sailor as well as a sensible woman. I can conceive of nothing more disgusting or trying to a young bride than a sea-sick husband. Sea-sickness not only destroys the romance of love, but it too rudely exposes the frailties of poor human nature. Even the lustre of a crown would lose its brilliancy upon the head of a sea-sick king. Fancy the Emperor William vomiting over the gunwale, or Queen Victoria spewing over her royal robes.

Mr. S. A. Crozer is a first-class sailor. He has crossed the ocean oftener than any other man in Delaware county. He reads French quite freely and speaks it with fluency enough to make himself perfectly understood. He is a man of broad and liberal views and would, undoubtedly, make a first-class Congressman. Although I left home almost as much to escape the entanglements of politics as for the benefit of my health, yet I could not resist the temptation to tamper just a little in Delaware county politics. I had heard, just before leaving home, that the left-handed friends of " Our Jack" were looking for a candidate and had their eyes upon Mr. Crozer. I approached him in the most delicate manner upon the subject. Cæsar, when he pushed away the crown ; Richard III, when he pleaded the scruples of his conscience, or even Mr. Blaine, when he wrote his last letter, were not more non-committal. He candidly admitted that he had been spoken to and only entertained the subject on one consideration. As he seemed to desire my opinion I candidly gave it, but do not propose to publish it just yet.

As the usual time for recovery from sea-sickness approached and the usual means of becoming agreeable had been practiced, the usual results were rapidly developed. The boys began to drink, smoke and gamble, the maids began to spread the nets of love, and the older and more experienced girls began to flirt, while the older boys of the smoking room amused their friends with many a well-told story. Among the stories was the following :

The chief steward while cleaning up the ladies' waiting room, found upon the table a leaf from the journal of a young woman. It read as follows :—First day out · 400 passengers; men stupid ; feel sea-sick ; wish I had stayed home. Second day out—Feel better ; gentlemen more sociable ; made the acquaintance of a real nice fellow ; says he loves me ; glad I came. Third day out—Nice young man proposed ; I refused till Pa had time to find out who he is ; he grew desperate ;

showed me a cigar box full of dynamite ; threatened to blow up the ship if I did not accept him at once ; awful. Fourth day out—I am happy ; I have saved the lives of 400 people.

The little story illustrates the usual course of love-making and flirting upon a ship. It can, to a certain extent, be excused in very young people, but on a ship the disease seizes all the old maids and *unattended* matrons who, in their madness, "play such fantastic tricks as make the angels weep." It is difficult to decide which is the worst flirting place, a ship or a camp meeting.

A flock of sea gulls followed our ship from Sandy Hook to Havre. At least the sailors said so, but I noticed they changed their size and color three times. At first they were snowy white, then smaller and dark brown ; as we approached France they became much larger and more pigeon-colored. There was not however a day, no matter how stormy, that a few gulls were not seen hovering over and following the ship. The seamen say they follow the ship because they love the sailors ; but in this the sailors are undoubtedly *gulled* by the gulls. They follow us at sea very much as some people gull us on shore, to get all they can from us and forsake us when we can give them no more, or when they can steal no more from us. I have no dout but that they think that Providence has provided the several ships that cross the ocean especially to feed the gulls ; just as the fable says the vultures, when they see marching armies on the battlefields of the world, suppose the gods are preparing food for them, and therefore they praise the gods. There is not much difference after all between gulls, vultures and men.

After the fourth day out the sea became angry and boisterous, the winds were contrary and the weather disagreeable. We had to head the ship to the wind and barely held our own for five hours. The ship dipped her nose now and then into the base of a mountainous wave which swept her decks from stem to stern with three or four feet of water. At one time a heavy sea struck the ship under her windward belly and threw her upon her beam end with the saloon deck standing at an angle of about forty-five degrees. The waiters in the saloon, as well as the passengers, were dashed from one side to the other. There is scarcely a winter passage of the Atlantic in which there are not some bruised or broken limbs, sprained joints or cracked skulls. This time it was my turn to be hurt. I was hurled, like a babe in the hands of an enraged giant, fully forty feet from one side of the saloon to the other, striking my shoulder and head with great force against the iron frame of one of the stationary chairs. My scalp was cut to the skull, my left thumb nearly torn from its socket, and my right shoulder was very much bruised. I would not take the risk of another such a fall for the ship with all she contained. The chances would be one hundred to one that neither the ship nor her treasure would be of any value to me. A French gentleman showed me a bad wound on his head which he had received some two months ago on "La Champagne." He was in the hospital five weeks and came near losing his life from just such a fall. My wounds soon healed. In a few hours I recovered from the shock and was on deck again. The next day I learned the cause of all the trouble. I had sat at the table with *thirteen*. Of all the eighty saloon passengers only *thirteen* were at table that day.

> When thirteen 'round a table meet,
> Please make at once a vacant seat
> Or quickly add another friend
> Before grim death the feast shall end ;
> For this thirteen will never meet
> Around a festive board to eat,

· I have, in my short life, sailed upon thirty-two ocean steamers, upon each of which I have spent from two to fifteen days. I have been in English, American, Spanish, Italian, Norwegian, German and French vessels. I have closely observed human life upon them all, and I feel that I could now deliver a very interesting lecture upon my friend Congressman Robinson's favorite subject—"Ships, Sailors and Seas." I have found the toil of the sailor, the care of the captain, and the pains and pleasures of the passengers about the same the world over. With all the luxury of ship life, good weather and good health ; with tranquil seas and jovial companians, but few can endure ten days' confinement upon the finest ship without a sense of weariness and anxious longing for the liberty of dry land. How tedious and heavy must the hours pass to the poor prisoner of a month, a year, or a life in a dungeon. It is only by such comparisons we can fully realize the sad condition of a man buried, as it were, in a prison.

Our second Sunday at sea was passed in true French style by a big dinner and a treat from the captain to champagne all round. On this line all ordinary wines are free, but if you want champagne for dinner you must pay for it. In addition to champagne, the captain presented each passenger at table with a fancy costume in tissue paper, bedizened with silver stars and gilded with gold. Mr. Crozer wore the helmet of Jove ; my cut head was decorated by the crown of Neptune. Juno, Minerva, Diana, Liberty, Terpsichore, Cupid, Venus and all the catalogue of the gods and goddesses of mythology were represented. In a word, we all became children again for a happy hour. A stranger, entering suddenly upon the scene, would suppose himself a spectator to a feast of Deities sipping nectar around the table of the gods.

On the 21st inst., at 4 A. M., we passed the Scilly Islands, soon after we saw Lizard Point and in a short time we got our first sight of France. We had to sleep on the ship and next morning landed and in four hours by rail we were in Paris.

———

LVII.

PARIS TO BORDEAUX—THE BLESSINGS OF NATIONAL EXTRAVAGANCE—PARIS RETROGRADING—HIGH PRICES—SUN OF AUSTERLITZ—ORLEANS—JEANNE D'ARC—ANTIQUITY OF THE TOWN—CATHEDRAL—HOTEL DE VILLE—BORDEAUX —FICKLE FAME IN FRANCE—INCIDENTS IN THE HISTORY OF BORDEAUX—ST. MICHAEL'S MUMMIES.

BORDEAUX, February, 1892.

Just before leaving Paris, I heard a very interesting discussion between two Frenchmen in a cafe, upon what we would call " National extravagance." To my surprise, the one who advocated a lavish expenditure of public money seemed to have the best of the argument. He contended that a nation's wealth did not consist in the treasure it hoarded, but in the results of a proper expenditure of public money. He expressed surprise that the Americans should complain because they were producing more than they could consume. After a certain amount of food, clothing, and materials for the necessaries of life, all the rest is surplus and represents the nation's wealth. The nation receives no benefit from hoarding its surplus. It should be spent in the erection of public works, forts, ships of war, army and navy supplies, docks and works of art. In this way over-production is equalized, laborers, mechanics, artists and manufacturers are taken from the farm, the factory and the workshop, and are transferred to the class of consumers and a market is made for the surplus of goods. In this way the world has produced all its great works from the Pyramids to St. Peters at Rome, none of which would have been constructed if the people who built them had hoarded instead of spent their surplus. So the question is settled, and let us hear no more about Republican extravagance in spending our surplus, to which our Democratic friends are so fond of referring.

I have so often attempted to describe Paris that I will say but little more about it. We found it the same gay and happy place for the young and rich, and the same sad and sorrowful city for the poor and old that it has always been. While I still regard it as the most beautiful city in the world, it is certainly deteriorating every year. It is no more like the Paris of Napoleon III, than a matron of forty, however pretty she may have once been, is like a maid of sixteen. The wrinkles of age cannot be concealed, the marks of dissipation are apparent, and in spite of the skill of her coiffeur, the gray hairs will appear.

I may safely assert that there is now no city in the world where the traveler pays more and gets less for his money. The prices of all the necessaries of life have advanced with great rapidity since the Franco-Prussian war. Gas is three times as high as in America, while coal and coal oil are luxuries only enjoyed by the rich. The chambers of the best hotels are lighted by candles at a franc each, and if we want a lamp we will be charged two francs more. The sleeping rooms are heated by wood fires composed of a few sticks for which we pay three francs for a basketful, and have the room not half warmed. When a tree is cut down in any part of France every twig is carefully bound up in small bundles like sheaves of wheat and sold for kindling wood. Not a chip is wasted. The compartments in the railway coaches are heated by tin feet-warmers. Two are placed in the compartment and contain about five gallons each of boiling water. They will keep the compartment and eight passengers comfortable for four hours.

We left Paris for Orleans on the 26th. On the morning of our departure we saw what the French people call the ''Sun of Austerlitz,'' so called from the great battefield on which Napoleon won one of his most brilliant victories. It is said that at the critical moment in the struggle a peculiar fog hid the French forces until they were in position to strike a fatal blow, when suddenly the sun, bloody red, broke through the fog so that the French forces on the hill could plainly see the enemy in the lower ground without the enemy being able to see the French soldiers. When the fog vanished the victory was won and the French soldiers with one accord shouted aloud, '' *Voila le soleil d' Austerlitz !*'' (Behold the sun of Austerlitz). On the morning of our departure the sun presented the same appearance as it hung in the heavens like a great red ball of fire. We could look at it without inconvenience with the naked eye. The tall buildings, towers and church spires could be dimly seen like spectres keeping watch over a dead city. An ordinary sized building could not be seen fifty feet away. The whole city presented a weird, strange and dreamlike appearance. After a few minutes the spectacle melted away and the unearthly yellow tint was succeeded by bright and natural solar rays.

On our way to Orleans we were struck by the advanced
state of spring vegetables.   While the latitude of Orleans is
far north of that of Philadelphia, yet the spring is much more
advanced.   The fields are green, the spring plowing is done.
Trees are in blossom and peasant women in bare heads and in
some instances, I am sorry to say, in bare feet and legs, are
working in the fields.   The French peasantry are the most industrious and saving people in the world.   They cultivate
little patches of ground with the greatest care and bring from
the earth all it can possibly yield.

We made the acquaintance, on the train, of a French
gentleman from Estampes, just from Australia.   We were
surprised to learn that the people of that country are suffering
from a very severe drought.   He says common drinking water
was selling at six cents a gallon.   Such droughts, he says, are
quite common.   In his opinion Australia has about reached its
greatest prosperity, its great drawback being a scarcity of
water.

We spent a day at Orleans and were both amused and in-
structed in riding over the city and visiting its several places
of interest.   It is not visited much by tourists, but is quite a
charming old city   But little English is spoken by its inhabitants.   Its hotels, with one or two exceptions, are very
primitive in all their appointments.   The floors are made of
tile, the windows are seldom shut and the dining rooms and
bed chambers are without heat.   Frosts are very rare, but
heavy woolen clothing is a necessity, to preserve our natural
heat rather than to depend upon artificial warmth for comfort.

Every shoolboy is familiar with the story of Jeanne
d'Arc and the siege of Orleans in 1429.   The general plan
of the streets in the old part of the city is to-day very much
the same as then.   The city walls have been removed but
the places where the gates stood are still known.   The spot
where Jeanne d'Arc made her successful assault at the
bridge is now marked by a beautiful bronze statue of the
heroine.   The house in which she lodged is still standing and
the armor she wore is said to be still preserved.   This, however, I very much doubt

To say the least, the story of the Maid of Orleans, is a
most interesting and romantic one.   The city is full of statues
set up to her memory, and the walls of nearly all of the public
buildings are decorated with life-size portraits and paintings
representing different scenes in her history from the time she
was a little peasant girl to the day she was burned at Rouen,
by the English, as a witch.   All these statues and paintings
make her a frail, fair and beautiful young girl, just budding
into womanhood.   All history however agrees that she wore

strong iron mail, wielded a heavy sword and rode astride a large and fiery steed. I have no doubt but that one-half of the miraculous power attributed to her was the creation of the superstitious notions of the times in which she lived. She was, perhaps, a strong-minded, raw-boned and intelligent woman, who took advantage of the superstitions of her age to better enforce her influence over the king and his courtiers. Just such a leader as Mrs. George Sand would have made under similar circumstances.

The city of Orleans was known to the Romans and was an important town in the days of Cæsar. By the brave resistance of its citizens Attila, the Hun, was forced to raise the siege he laid around it, although he had sworn to take and destroy it. Its situation is well chosen on a beautiful bend of the river Loire, near its confluence with the Loiret. Its places of interest are in the old crooked and narrow streets. The new part is just like nearly all modern cities of Europe and America. There are very few brick buildings in the new part, but several in the older portions.

The Cathedral is noted as one of the finest in France. Its foundations were laid in 330, A. D. It has been several times destroyed but has always arisen from its ruin more and more beautiful. Henry IV ordered it rebuilt as it now stands. It occupies a whole square and was not finished until 1790. It has two towers like Notre Dame, at Paris, but they are larger and higher. It is certainly a very noble architectural structure and inspires a peculiar feeling of grandeur in the beholder, especially if he stands in the street a hundred yards from the left angle and takes in the whole building at one view.

The Hotel de Ville is built of brick, in the Flemish style, and presents a very pretty appearance. It was formerly a royal palace and was occupied as such by Charles IX, Henry III and Henry IV. Queen Catherine de Medices also lived in it, and also the unfortunate Mary Stuart. It was first converted into a City Hall in 1790.

One full day, with a carriage and good coachman, is sufficient to see everything of interest in the place. Of course the traveler may, if he has the time, spend a week around Orleans and find amusement for every day. He could spend a day in the Museums alone. We gave the principal one an hour.

The next city at which we rested two days, was Bordeaux, one of the most important seaports of France. It is charmingly situated on a grand semi-circle formed by a three-mile bend in the river Garonne. It has 250,000 inhabitants, is clean, regular and well-paved. The old city must have been very small as it has almost entirely disappeared. The present city will compare favorably with any city of its size in France, or perhaps in Europe. The river is, I should say, about five hundred yards wide and is sixty feet deep in front of the city. The docks are nearly equal to those of Liverpool. There are always thousands of ships from all parts of the world in these docks, making them a very busy and interesting place. The principal theatre is a splendid classic edifice with tall and graceful Corinthian columns in front. It was built in 1755.

The French are very fickle in their attachments and tastes. They are constantly removing monuments and erasing inscriptions commemorative of the great deeds of former favorites. During the last empire Louis Napoleon made a great speech in Bordeaux, in which he used the celebrated words, "L' Empire, c' est la paix." (The Empire is Peace). The people of the city erected a grand monument to the Emperor and inscribed upon it, in letters of gold, the above extract from his speech. After the fall of the empire they tore down the monument.

There are other very interesting buildings in the city, but they are of comparatively modern construction and will be objects of interest for the letters of some traveler a thousand years from now.

The old city gates are interesting as landmarks, by which we find the location of the old city walls, and give us a fair idea of its comparatively small size. The old city was the scene of many a bloody struggle between the English and French. Edward the Black Prince held his brilliant court here for many years. His son Richard, of Bordeaux, was born here. It will be remembered by many of my older readers that the Germans captured the place in 1870. They were driven out but again re-took it and held it till peace was made. I would like to say more about Bordeaux but my time is limited. I would like to speak of the old church of St. Michael, with its bell tower three hundred and fifty-four feet high, and of the many dried up mummies fantastically arranged in its vaults. There is something in the soil which preserves the bodies of the dead. The ancient citizens attributed it to the miraculous influence of St. Michael, but they found cats, dogs and even dead serpents were equally petrified when buried there. We leave here to-night for Marseilles, a twelve-hours' ride by the fastest express train.

LVIII.

BORDEAUX TO MARSELLES—BATTLEFIELD OF POITIERS—
TOULOUSE—MARSEILLES ONCE MORE—SUB-TROPICAL CLI-
MATE—ITS WORLD-RENOWNED HARBOR—MARSEILLES TO
ALGIERS—A FRENCH PUNSTER—GAME IN AFRICA DISAP-
PEARING BEFORE THE BREECH-LOADER—ALGEIRS IN 1830
—HOMELY WOMEN—SCORPIONS—ALGIERS TO TUNIS—
FIVE HUNDRED MILES THROUGH THE ATLAS MOUNTAINS
—SETIF—WONDERFUL CONSTANTINE—ROMAN RUINS—
SHEPHERDS WATCHING THEIR FLOCKS BY NIGHT—THE
BIBLE AND THE KORAN.

TUNIS, March, 1892.

We went direct from Bordeaux to Marseilles, a distance
of about five hundred miles. Between Tours and Bordeaux
we passed over the battlefield of Poitiers, where Charles Martel, in the eighth century, at the head of as many Christian
soldiers as he could collect under the banner of Christ and his
country, met and defeated the Moorish hosts and forever
checked the advance of Mohammedanism and the corrupt influences of the harem into the west of Europe. It was the
commencement of a series of bloody battles which finally drove
the Moors from Europe.

It was also at Poitiers that Edward the Black Prince defeated John the Good in 1356, and left eleven thousand of his
soldiers dead upon the field. Between Bordeaux and Marseilles we passed through the very ancient city of Toulouse with a
population, at this time, of 150,000. It is very beautifully
situated upon the river Garonne. If our time had not been
limited we could have spent several days at different places
between Bordeaux and Marseilles.

Marseilles looked even more attractive than when I saw
it last in 1889. It was then too warm to enjoy the walks and
drives in and around the city. She is sheltered from the north
winds by a semi-circle of high, rocky hills, which the rays of
the winter sun strike at right angles and engender a most delicious warmth. The city looks out southward to the sea. In
midwinter it has a climate as warm as that of Bermuda. The
temperature is never below fifty. Sub-tropical fruits and
flowers remain out all winter. Roses are now in full bloom.
There is, as far as I can judge from appearances, but one objection to Marseilles as a permanent dwelling place and that is
its liability to fevers and cholera in the summer. These diseases are supposed to result from the absence of tides in the

Mediterranean. The refuse of the city for two thousand years has been carried into its docks and when an attempt is made to remove this accumulated filth by artificial means, the germs of disease are set free and typhoid is sure to follow.

The new drive along the bluff and rocky shore on the southeast of the city is most charming. It extends for several miles over a splendid road cut into and along the edge of precipitous rocks which are studded with villas, private palaces, fashionable cafes and gay restaurants. The drive ends at the entrance to the Prado, a fine park decorated by sub-tropical trees, plants, flowers, &c. A drive through the Prado brings us back to the city, by another street, to a different part of the town.

The harbor of Marseilles is world-renowned. It has been improved and enlarged by enormous works of masonry running out into the sea, as a breakwater when the southern winds make the waters angry. There are thousands of ships of all nations lying at anchor in the harbor. To satisfactorily visit the docks a carriage and good driver ought to be secured who will take you an hour among these interesting works. I would like to say more of Marseilles, but as I can only give one letter a week, I must leave many interesting subjects untouched. After spending one day at Marseilles we embarked for Algiers, about four hundred and fifty miles southwestwardly, and arrived there in about twenty-eight hours by a very comfortable and fast ship. We made the acquaintance of a French gentleman on the ship who was quite a wit as well as a punster. He asked us where we landed in France. We told him at La Havre. "O !" said he, "You ought to have landed at *Brest*, then you would have come from the bosom of the ocean into the *breast* of France." The soup at dinner was rather thin. Our friend called attention to it by giving my wife a recipe for a very delicate French soup. Here it is : "Take one quart of water, boil it down to one pint to make it strong—dip the wing of a chicken into it three times—season to taste." Some of the passengers were speaking of the great inundations in Spain. "Can you tell me," said he, "why there are no inundations in France ?" We all gave it up. "Because," said he, "water in France is always l' eau." (Pronounced *low*) *l' eau* being the French word for "water." He was a very bright and intelligent fellow but, like most of his kind, he was fully aware of it and laughed a little too much at his own jokes.

Algiers is a very delightful city ; the climate is all that can be desired. For the last thirteen years the temperature has not been below fifty, nor above eighty degrees at any place fifty feet above the sea. Including the suburbs of St. Eugene,

El Bias, and Mustapha, outside of the walls, it has a population of 80,000. Her situation is very charming. A spur of
the Atlas Mountains comes down to the sea which here makes
a regular bend forming the harbor. The city sits with her
back reposing upon the mountains, her head overlooking the
crown of the hills while her feet are bathed by the sea. To
carry out the metaphor, I might say, she is arrayed in white
(*washed*) robes, for every building in the city is white. There
is not a brick building in the place. The hilly streets are
ascended by zigzag terraces beautifully and substantially built.
The new part of the city looks like Paris and other continental
towns. The old Moorish part is very curious ; the streets are
narrow and winding, the shops small, and the whole quarter
is crowded with Arabs and Moors in their peculiar costumes.
The language of the city, especially in the old part, is a babel
of confusion, Turkish, Arabian, Spanish, Moorish and French.
The place is much more sub-tropical than Marseilles. Oranges,
lemons, bananas, palms, and all the catalogue of roses and
flowers are seen growing here.

Game, that was once so plentiful here, has been mostly
destroyed or driven further into the interior by English and
French sportsmen with their breech-loading guns and repeating rifles. Every day or two, however, a wild boar is shot
and brought into the town. Now and then a lion or panther
is killed, but this is now very rare. Small game, such as
partridges, and a small bird rather less than our robin, are still
about as plentiful as quail in Virginia. A sportsman must have
very good luck to bag twenty-five quail in a day. Some
claim to have shot as many as sixty in a day, but from my
own experience, I take such stories *cum grano salis.*

Before 1830, Algiers was a nest of pirates of the worst
kind. France sent a fleet of one hundred and seventeen men-
of-war and four hundred merchantmen, carrying 38,000 soldiers, and took the city by assault. Since then all Algeria has
been under French control. Every ragged Moor we meet in
the street, and most of the Arab porters and laborers of the
place are the descendants of pirates that once infested the
country, yet there are now no rebellions. The French rule
has been firm but beneficial. A walk through the city reminds
one very much of the scenes so well described in the "Arabian
Nights' Entertainment." Some are well dressed in the peculiar Bedouin white robe and head dress, but the great majority
are clothed in dirty and ragged coarse cloth with their feet
and legs entirely bare. They have their heads, necks and
bodies well wrapped up, showing nothing but their faces, while
their feet and legs are exposed to the wind, rain and mud.
When they lie down to sleep, they cover their heads and leave

their bare feet and legs exposed. They prefer to sleep with their heads down and feet up. In other words, they never use a pillow and if they lie down on the side of a hill, you will be sure to find their feet up the hill and their heads down. I saw but few handsome Arab women ; some of the men have a dig-nified and commanding presence, but none were what I would call handsome. The young women are fat, the young men almost skeletons. They have, however, very black and pierc-ing eyes.

There are some very lovely villas, owned by French gen-tlemen and retired merchants, around Algiers. The hotels are all fairly good, but the prices are as high as in Paris. We stopped at St. George's hotel, in the suburb Mustapha. It is about five hundred feet above the sea and presents some very fine views. "Hotel Splendide" is still higher up the mountain and overlooks the harbor and city in a very charm-ing manner I would, however, advise visitors to take a hotel in the heart of the town, where Algerian life can be better seen and studied, but the splendid landscapes can be better seen from the hills.

By a day's drive around the town, the villas, gardens, etc., may be inspected. In walking among the undergrowth and over the hills outside of the city, one should never pick up a stick or stone without first giving it a kick as it may conceal a scorpion or poisonous insect, which are very common around the place. Snakes, however, have been pretty well extirpated. When we landed at Algiers, we thought it such a lovely spot that we would spend at least a week there, but after a busy day we saw it all and began to long for some new sights and scenes. How soon we tire of the most charming scenery and attractive amusements. I sometimes doubt whether we will not grow weary of Paradise. So restless is the spirit of man that heaven will be a prison if he could not go to the other place if he so desired. The government of the Eternal King must necessarily be strong or there would be a rebellion in heaven worse than the one of six thousand years ago. This restless spirit seized our party and, as a natural result, after spending two days in Algiers we started on a five hundred mile trip over the mountains to Tunis. While pursuing this route we were at one time about one hundred and ten miles in the interior of Africa and within nine hours of the great desert of Sahara. We passed through about forty towns and Moorish villages. We stopped one day at Setif, which is three thousand five hundred and twenty-seven feet above the level of the sea. I was kept awake nearly all night by dogs barking and chasing rats about the court yard. We also spent a day at Constan-tine. It is one of the most striking cities I have ever visited.

It is built upon a mass of precipitous rock two thousand one hundred feet above sea level. It is impossible to paint with the pen a picture of Constantine. To paint a perfect pen picture it is necessary to refer to some place like it, with which the reader is familiar. Photographs do not do justice because they only give the outlines of a scene a few yards around the focus. There is no place in the world, that I have seen, bearing any resemblance to Constantine. It is a natural fort. It contains three or four natural bridges, something like the celebrated one in Virginia. It has a canyon running through the town one thousand feet deep. A beautiful bridge spans the chasm six hundred feet above the little stream below which plunges into the earth just at the base of the bridge. The city is built upon the almost perpendicular sides of a mountain of barren rock, with streets and tunnels cut upon its sides so as to utilize all the space and give some most charming landscapes. A gentleman who has seen the renowned scenery of California pronounced this equal to anything he had seen there. He said the Yellowstone Park was grander in its stupendous magnitude but not more striking. Some of the houses in the rear seem to overhang precipices at least six hundred feet deep, while the front of the buildings face upon a handsome street. There is a natural hot sulphur spring at the base of the mountain with artificial baths for skin diseases. It was celebrated for its miraculous cures in the palmy days of Rome. The city is very ancient.

We visited the ruins of a Roman aqueduct with five grand arches at least one hundred feet high still remaining. The masonry is very perfect and without cement. It is about all that remains, as a kind of grave stone, upon which we may read the epitaph of former greatness. I have passed the age of youthful enthusiasm. Twenty-three years of foreign travel have destroyed the romance that naturally clusters around old places of historic interest ; yet I can truly say, I never saw a more interesting place than Constantine. Some of the old streets are too narrow for a carriage, and yet are full to overflowing with what seems to be the over charged surplus of humanity in all its forms, and dressed in every known costume. Turbaned Turks, richly dressed Jews, Bedouin Arabs, Milky-white Moors with hair like a raven's wing and eyes like black diamonds ; veiled Mohammedan women, and half naked and ragged beggars, all in costumes entirely different from the European dress. I saw rings hanging to women's ears four inches in diameter and covered with trinklets. I saw men arrayed in purple and gold, with snowy white turbans ; women in rich lace and flowing satin trousers ; children in gauze robes bedizened with silver and gold tinsel ; and at the same time, fine looking Arab men in bare feet and legs, clothed with coffee bags cut and sewed together so as to make a costume in conformity with Arabian ideas of dress. Some were clean and beautiful, others filthy and extremely ugly. Some of the women looked like the inhabitants of Paradise peeping over the battlements of heaven, while others were as ugly as the hags Macbeth met upon the witches' heath.

We left Constantine well satisfied with our visit. All our preconceived ideas of Africa have been erroneous. Thus far we have met but few black people. The negroes are, as a rule, slaves. All along the route we saw shepherds attending their flocks, just as they did in the days of old. It was often necessary for us to start for our day's journey at four o'clock in the morning. As the light began to dawn, we could see tall Arabs in long white seamless coats, just such raiment as was worn by Christ while he blessed the earth by his presence, standing like dreamy sentinels keeping guard over their flocks. We could see them led from pasture ground to rivulet, and from mountain to mountain in search of food or water. We could better comprehend the Psalm of David : "The Lord is my shepherd, I shall not want ; He maketh me to lie down in green pastures ; He leadeth me beside the still waters." For a hundred miles in the mountain district we saw but few permanent dwellings. Most of the inhabitants dwell in tents or hovels of brush, wood and straw. All their wealth is in their flocks and herds. They are all Mohammedans or Jews, and most of them have four wives. They are not permitted by the Koran to have more, but may own as many concubines as they are able to buy and keep. The Arab husband generally manages to make his wife earn her own living and also be of some pecuniary value to him. He does not hesitate to sell her for a limited season, but always stipulates that she shall be returned in good health, reasonable wear and tear excepted, and be well clothed and nourished. There must be some cause for the great degeneration in the character of the Moor. It can only be attributed to the evil consequences of the harem. It has degenerated the men and demoralized the women. One can hardly believe, when he looks at the Moor of to-day, that he is the son of the energetic race that held Spain for five hundred years and left such monuments of refinement and culture as are still found in that country. The Christian of to-day is what the Moor of the sixth and seventh century was. Can it be possible that we shall ever degenerate into his sad and hopeless condition of to-day, or that he shall advance to the civilization we now enjoy ? Let us never forget that our western civilization is the direct result of Christ's teachings, and that the degeneracy of the Turk, Arab and Moor has been caused by the teachings of the Koran and the religion of the false Prophet.

We arrived at Tunis yesterday. In my next letter I will try to describe the city.

LIX.

TUNIS TO NICE—MOUNTAIN SCENERY OF AFRICA—TUNIS OLDER THAN ROME OR CARTHAGE—THE TRAGIC STORY OF CARTHAGE—DIDO ET DUX—A VERY OLD LOVER—INTERESTING RUINS--AN ARAB GUIDE--THE PALACE AND HAREM OF THE BEY—MORE WIVES MORE WASTE—FORBIDDEN FRUIT — BACK TO MARSEILLES — ALONG THE RIVIERA— CANNES—NICE.

NICE, March, 1892.

It requires nineteen hours by rail from Constantine to Tunis. The country along the route is mountainous and sterile, with here and there a fertile valley devoted to pasture for the flocks and herds of the Arab shepherds. The weather was pleasant but we enjoyed our winter clothing and overcoats. The Atlas chain of mountains is about one thousand five hundred miles long. The mountains we crossed are spurs of the great chain. Some of the scenery was far superior to any of the views of the Alleghenies, not excluding the famous Horse Shoe. A peculiarity of the African mountains is the absence of trees ; they are bare to the summits. As we emerged from some of the tunnels the vistas were supremely fine. A great snow-capped peak at the right ; at the left a stupendous crag ; on the mountain side a cascade ; in the deep chasm a purple mist ; at the bottom a limpid stream ; in the valley below Arab tents and shepherds in their long flowing dresses guarding their flocks.

It was midnight when we arrived at Tunis The city was full of strangers and the hotels crowded. We succeeded, however, in securing very good rooms at the Grand Hotel, a fine new building in the fashionable part of the city. Tunis is very much like a European city. It has its old and new parts. It is not as beautifully situated as Tangier, Algiers or Constantine. The old part of the city has its Arab, Jewish and Moorish quarters. They seem to go in swarms like insects of the same breed. It has its bazars, narrow and crooked streets, covered alleys, *cul de sacs* and lazy as well as industrious citizens. The costumes are as varied as the people.

The chief attractions of Tunis are its great age—being older than Rome or Carthage—and its proximity to the great theatre upon the stage of which the world's greatest tragedies have been performed.   It stands upon the border of a salt lake and is in the centre of a plain of many miles extent.   In this plain many great battles were fought between the Romans and Carthagenians.   Regulus was defeated in the plain between Tunis and Carthage, only nine miles to the northeast.   Every school boy knows his sad end.   A short distance from the city we see the mountains at the base of which Hamilcar murdered, mutilated and annihilated his rebellious mercenary troops.   It took him three years to destroy his hired soldiers, but he was so disgusted at their treachery and cruelty, that he determined to entirely destroy them.   It was around the city that Scipio and Hannibal contended for the empire of the world.   Hannibal had so often invaded the sacred soil of Rome that, for fifteen years, he looked upon it as a conquered nation, but Scipio conceived the brilliant idea of "carrying the war into Africa." His policy eventually changed the result and the conquerors became the conquered.

It was near Tunis that Marius finally defeated Jugurtha and afterwards dragged him in chains behind his chariot through the streets of Rome, where he died from starvation after having lost his mind from his great sufferings.   It was at the city of Tunis, after the end of the second Punic war, that Scipio dictated his cruel terms of peace.   Cruel as they were, Carthage not only complied with them but soon again became the rival of Rome.   Her final fall was due to Cato.   He was sent on an embassy to Carthage and was surprised to find it entirely recovered from the supposed irreparable disasters of the late war. When he returned to Rome he startled the Senate by the concluding words of his great speech—"Carthage must be destroyed."   The decree was made in a secret session of the Senate and Rome only awaited a pretext to renew the war. The third Punic war soon followed.   The only terms of peace for poor Carthage were to give up her best citizens as hostages, to remove the entire population nine miles from the sea, and to permit the Roman army to raze the city to the ground. After a struggle of three years Carthage was destroyed.   When the city fell, all the inhabitants capable of bearing arms, were put to death.   Of the splendid city nothing was left from which it could be rebuilt.   This tremendous and awful disaster, and the struggles that preceeded it, only second to the subsequent fall of Rome, occurred in a little corner of the earth not much larger than Delaware county.

Carthage was founded by Dido, a princess of Troy, B. C. 822.   Virgil, however, in his story of Æneas, and the foundation of Carthage and Rome, is either greatly mistaken in his chronology, or the accepted dates of the fall of Troy and foundation of Rome are erroneous. If the accepted dates are correct, Æneas was over two hundred years old when Dido fell so desperately in love with him as to commit suicide when he deserted her to build his new city of Rome. The spot where she built her funeral pyre is pointed out to the traveler. After the disgrace of Marius, he was found sitting in despair among the ruins of Carthage, the scene of his former glory. In a later period, Cæsar and Pompey contended in the plains between Tunis and Carthage, for the dominion of Rome. Cæsar won and Pompey died. Old Belisarrius fought the Vandals in these same plains near Tunis. Outside of Rome there is no more interesting place, for the student of history, than Tunis.

Most of the land upon which the city of Carthage stood is now cultivated. In every field, however, may be seen, cropping out like the ledge of a natural rock, the veritable ruins of the old city. They extend for miles around. Recent excavations have brought to light many valuable relics. The Museum on the hill is full of very valuable historical marbles, with dates and inscriptions, which completely verify the traditions from which we have extracted our history of the city. Some fine specimens of white m rble statuary have been found which will compare very favorably with the best works of Grecian art. What was supposed to be a hill, about one hundred feet high, is now found to be the debris of an ancient palace. The splendid chapel of St. Louis, who died here in his last crusade, is built upon the vaulted roof of some immense buried building of the destroyed city. We were agreeably disappointed in our visit to Carthage. We were told that but little of the ruins of the old city could be seen. When we remember that it was the rival of Rome for seven hundred years, we can form some idea of what a splendid metropolis it must have been.

Tunis is supposed to have been founded by the Canaanites after they were driven from Palestine by Joshua. It is certainly a very ancient city. Its climate is mild and salubrious from October to May ; after May it is too warm for a comfortable dwelling place. John Howard Payne, the author of "Home, Sweet Home," died here, a homeless wanderer.

Only thirty-seven miles from Tunis is the site of ancient Utica, where Cato the younger committed suicide after his famous soliloquy upon the immortality of the soul. We procured the services of a veritable Arab, named Mustapha, to guide us around the city and show us the sights. He spoke very good French, at least we thought so, for we could perfectly understand him and he us. A native Frenchman speaks too fast for us to keep up with him. Mustapha spoke very slowly and deliberately so that, with a little care on our part, we could communicate our thoughts to each other with great precision. He conducted us through the crowded, narrow streets and lanes of the Moorish and Arab quarters ; through the bazars ; the palace of the Bey, and the harem and its beautiful gardens. The palace covers, I would say from a rough guess, some twenty acres of ground. The exterior is very much dilapidated, but the interior is in very good condition. The Bey is now residing in his new palace about five miles out of town ; we saw it as we went to Carthage. The palace at Tunis, however, could be ready for habitation on a few days' notice. All the furniture, beds, carpets, tapestry, paintings, statuary and ornaments remain. It will comfortably accommodate three or four hundred wives, eunuchs, slaves and children. The present Bey has several hundred wives ; only two, however, enjoy his society. The rest are nurses, minstrels, dancers, etc. The magnificent velvet carpets are very much moth-eaten under the beds and in dark corners. I called Mustapha's attention to the slovenly condition of the Bey's household. He replied, "One wife keep house clean ; two wives hardly keep themselves clean ; more wives, more waste." Then pointing to the marble lions on the grand stairway, he said, "Lion noble beast ; he only have one wife."

In the picture gallery of the palace, we were surprised to find a fine, full life-sized portrait of George Washington, hanging in company with emperors, kings, sultans and other great ones of the earth. The exterior of the palace is now undergoing extensive repairs.

A still more interesting place was the harem. Our Arab guide seemed to be a favorite with the guards. They objected at first to our entrance, but a few words from Mustapha in Arabic had the magic effect of opening the portals even of the sacred seraglio of the Bey We saw the great bed chamber with its two enormous beds, each bed large enough to comfortably accommodate twenty sleepers. The furniture was heavily gilt with gold ; mirrors hung in every position ; the beds were covered with them. The tapestry was of satin, with gold and silver threads interwoven so as to give it the appearance of gold and silver cloth. Every chamber had its peculiar use. Each contained a throne, some were large, others small. The grand concert room had the throne, or Bey's seat, in the centre. His wives amuse him here by singing, dancing and making music. It is impossible to describe the interior of this harem. Suffice it to say, we visited every part of it, from the toilet and bath room to the nursery and bed chambers, and have now a very good idea of the domestic life of the Sultan and great Turkish and Eastern monarchs. Every chamber had its armed guard at the door ; every gate was watched over by an armed eunuch or soldier. The outer walls were also armed with bristling cannon, giving to the whole palace a very strong and formidable appearance. It could, however, be blown to atoms by a few modern shells. Its warlike appearance is more for effect than actual defence.

The lace tracery on the plastered walls is very curious. It was all done with knives and has the appearance of real lace. My wife could hardly be convinced that the vaulted ceiling was not covered with actual lace.

We looked from the windows of the harem out upon a most charming garden of flowers, and orange trees laden with golden fruit. We expressed a desire to visit the garden. Mustapha whispered something to the eunuch at the gate which at once opened and we were admitted. I asked Mustapha what the magic word was at which every gate and door opened. With a sly wink, he said the mystic word was "Backsheesh." It cost me about twelve francs in fees to the different guards and doorkeepers. The seraglio garden was surrounded by a high wall, with no outer gate. It had two little temples to Venus covered with glass where the ladies of the harem sing, play and drink coffee. This is about the sum of a woman's harem life. She eats, bathes, dresses, drinks coffee, sings, plays and dances, and then sleeps or walks about in the garden.

It is a remarkable fact that all mortals, male as well as female, are fond of "forbidden fruit." Eve enjoyed it as well as Adam. As I saw the luscious ripe oranges hanging in tempting clusters, awaiting to refresh the lips of some adventurous thief, I felt a longing desire to steal just one to see if it tasted any better than the ones I could buy in the streets for a penny each. I asked Mustapha what the penalty was for stealing in Tunis. He informed me that a thief in Tunis had his right hand cut off in open court, so I concluded I would buy a few oranges from the eunuch in charge. He gave me four for one franc. I saved my right hand by paying twenty cents, but the oranges did not taste half as sweet as if I had stolen them.

A visit to the beautiful fountains (supplied by a mountain stream, performing the double function of a handsome ornament and water works for the city), about ended our sightseeing.

On the eighth of March we embarked from La Goulette, (the seaport of Tunis, about nine miles from the city and within five hundred yards of the site of Carthage), for Marseilles, which we reached in safety in two days. The sea was rather rough and most of the passengers very seasick. My little party, however, have managed thus far to keep well.

We have not missed a meal on shipboard since we sailed from New York. We were surprised when we arrived at Marseilles to find it snowing; it melted, however, as fast as it fell; it was like the snow we sometimes have at home in May. As we had to spend the day at Marseilles my wife and I visited the chapel of " Notre Dame de la Garde," a most imposing church which crowns one of the highest hills around the city. From the terrace of the church we had a fine view of all Marseilles and of the half-moon ridge of mountains which surround and protect it from the north and northeast winds. We could see for thirty miles out at sea.

The hymn called " The Marsellaise " was not composed, as some suppose, here. It was written by Claude Joseph Rouget de l' Isle, in 1792, at Strasbourg. In our road from Marseilles along the " Riviera " as it is called in Italian, in French " The Littoral," we passed some historic places and saw some very picturesque scenery. At Frejus, the road almost touches the shores of the bay in which the fleet of Mark Antony found shelter after his defeat. Like many another great fool he threw away the world for a woman and received the usual reward for his inordinate love disgrace and death. Some fine Roman ruins may be seen at several places along the line of the road. It was from the same bay at Frejus, that Napoleon sailed for Elbe.

We spent the night and one day at Cannes (pronounced *Can*), a lovely place, with the climate of Jacksonville, Florida, and are now spending a few days at Nice, a most charming place so far as natural beauty is concerned. It is built upon a bay of the Mediterranean. Its principal street extends for two miles along the shore, and is eighty-five feet wide finely paved and walled up from the sea, and is lined with princely villas, that sit back from the street, surrounded with splendid gardens.

Many persons, and among them some preachers of the gospel who, above all others ought to know better, think the great Council of Nice was held here. This is a great mistake. It was held at Nice (Nicia) in Asia Minor, about one hundred and fifty miles from Constantinople.

We leave here to-morrow for Monte Carlo.

LX

FLORENCE, March, 1892.

The much praised winter climate of the French Littoral,
or north coast of the Mediterranean, depends very much upon
the wind and sun.   If the sky is clear and the wind from the
northward, the temperature will be delightful ; but when
cloudy or rainy weather prevails, or the wind comes from the
sea, I know of no more disagreeable place.   We, who were
farmer boys, know what a pleasant place in winter the barn-
yard was, with its southern exposure and sheltered position,
full of clean straw and dreamy cattle, basking in the noontide
sun.   It was a very comfortable place for boys as well as cows.
The same cause produces a like effect along the Littoral.   The
whole coast is sheltered from the cold winds by the high mari-
time Alps.   Their northern slope, when struck by the strong
winds, shoots the cold stratum high up over the little towns
in the sheltered nooks along the coast.   The bluff, southern
face of the mountains receives the direct rays of the sun which
have the same effect upon animated nature as a hot-house has
upon vegetation.   At Nice the stratum of snow-chilled wind
is, perhaps, a mile above the town.   Of all the places we have
yet seen along this coast, Nice is by far the most pleasant.   It
has a population of about 85,000.   The average March temperature is about fifty-two degrees Fahr.   It is a pretty town
and has some very charming drives along the coast and on the
cornices of the mountains.   The old part of the city, around
the ancient port and castle, is very quaint.   Narrow, crooked,
crowded, but clean streets, with houses six and seven stories
high, are a marked feature of the old part of the town.   Castle
Hill is three hundred and fifteen feet high, with houses upon
its steep side next to the port, nearly up to its summit.   The
hill is crowned by the castle or ancient citadel, supposed to
have been built by the Phœnicians, and now a ruin.   The

campo santo, or cemetery, adjoins the castle and is located on
the top of the hill overlooking the city, the country, and the
sea for many miles around. To the right, the view is superb.
Some of the mountains are green and terraced nearly to their
tops, while others are barren rocks, and some are capped with
snow which shines in the rays of the sun like burnished silver.
I have seen but few more delightful views than the one presented from the cemetery on Castle Hill.

Among the tombs of the great ones of Nice, that of Gambetta occupies a consecrated spot on the highest ground in the
cemetery. It is daily decorated with flowers, evergreens,
wreaths of immortelles and votive offerings from the loving
hands of his countrymen. The remains of his mother repose
by his side.

> "How sleep the brave who sink to rest
> By all their country's wishes blest.
> When Spring returns with fingers cold
> To dress again their hallowed mould,
> She then shall tread a nobler sod
> Than Freedom's feet have ever trod."

It was here, on the fifteenth of August, 1542, that a brave
woman, Caterina Segurana, with a devoted band of Christian
followers, attacked and defeated the Turk, Barbarossa (Red
Beard), and with her own hand struck down his standard
bearer. Her mortal remains repose in the cemetery above
mentioned.

Massena, one of Napoleon's bravest marshals, was born
at Nice. He was chosen by the Emperor as the best qualified
of all his marshals to check the victorious march of the Duke
of Wellington in Spain. Massena was ordered to drive the
English with their " Sepoy General " into the sea. Wellington refused to take water and in his turn drove Massena and
the French out of Spain.

Garibaldi was born at Nice. He has a very handsome
marble monument erected to his memory in one of the public
squares.

Nice is now full of travelers spending the Spring months
to escape the disagreeable weather of England and America.
The hotels are overflowing and the landlords happy and saucy.
We found shelter in the " Grand Hotel des Isles Britanique,"
a very imposing and high-priced hotel.

There is a marked difference between the French as spoken in this part of France and in Paris. It is surprising that
Germans and Italians, ' who by the ear,' can detect the slightest
false note in music, for their lives cannot distinguish between
the sounds of the consonants p, b and v. They call " pomme
de terre" *bomme de terre*. " Bon jour " they call *pon jour*,
etc. A Frenchman of Nice became enamored with an English lady. He pressed his suit with such vigor that she

thought it wise to leave the room ; as she passed out the door he cried out in despair, "Madame, Je t'adore." She thought he said, "Madam, *shut that door*." She turned upon him as only an insulted woman can, and said, "Shut it yourself, you impudent puppy." In good French *Je t'adore* sounds very much like "shut that door." *Je t'adore*, literally translated, means "I adore thee."

From Nice we went to Monaco and Monte Carlo. Monaco is built upon a high rock jutting out into the sea and helps to form the cozy nook where Monte Carlo reposes. Monte Carlo is now the greatest gambling resort of the world. The Casino, or gambling palace, is also built on a rock running out into the sea, but not as high as Monaco. Everything that art and gold can do to make the place attractive, has been done. It is filled with groves and gardens, laid out with exquisite taste and is certainly very paradisaical in outward appearance. Splendid streets and roads have been cut in the solid rock. Terraces have been built, the earth of which has been carted from places miles away. As a proper contrast to the beautiful Casino, a magnificent cathedral has been built and paid for from the profits of the gambling bank. Truly extremes meet.

The Casino sits like a sleek tiger, well fed on the blood of the many thousand victims he has eaten up during the past thirty years. This sly beast sleeps during the day but his eyes shine with fascinating power at night. Crouched upon his rocky lair, he bids defiance to the world and never declines a fight. Many thousands contend with him every night and, like the sheep in the fable that went out for wool, they go home shorn. One would suppose the fate of those that have attempted to battle with him would be a warning to others not to play with him, but the crowd of fascinated fortune hunters does not seem to diminish, and the fool-killer seems to have abandoned Monte Carlo.

Aside from metaphor, Monte Carlo seems to be the grand center for the gamblers of the world. I saw as much as $40,000 raked into the bank in less than six minutes. The favorite game is Roulette, in which there are thirty-two little pockets for a revolving ball to fall into. The player that puts his money on any number from 1 to 32, has a chance, if the ball falls into the pocket bearing his number, to get thirty-two times the amount of his stake. The pockets are white and red ; if he puts his money on the red and the ball falls into a red pocket, he wins twice his stake and so on through a variety of complications. He can bet on an even chance, two to one and on up to thirty-two to one. To look at it, it appears perfectly fair, but, somehow, the bank gets enormously rich and the players nearly all quit poor. Some expert gamblers have

come here with immense sums, with the single purpose of
breaking this bank but they have always been the losers. An
English syndicate became convinced that a certain theory, if
it had sufficient capital behind it, could break the concern.
They raised $250,000 and sent an expert player to experiment;
but after a few weeks, Monte Carlo had every cent. The Casino
has eleven tables—around each, at least one hundred players
can be accommodated. These tables are always full. At some
tables they will take a wager of five francs ($1), at others
nothing less than a Louis d'or ($4). Thousands of fortunes
are lost here every year. The average of suicides at Monte
Carlo is about one hundred and twenty-five a year. The bank,
as a matter of policy, buries the suicide and pays his hotel
bill. The "world, the flesh, and the devil," seem to have
possession of the place. I have some doubt whether it contains many more righteous persons than the fated cities of the
plain. I suppose the church at Monaco, paid for from the
earnings of the gaming tables, saves the place from Sodom and
Gomorrah's fate.

It is reported that the net gains of last year reached the
enormous sum of 25,000,000 francs, 2,500,000 more than in
1890. A dividend of two hundred and thirty-five francs was
declared upon each bond of the par value of five hundred francs.
The bonds to-day are quoted at 2300 francs. The directors
also decided to add 100,000 francs to the pension fund for the
1100 officials connected in various ways with the bank.

We made a very pleasant excursion from Monte Carlo to
Mentone by carriage over one of the beautiful mountain roads.
The scenery was really charming. The road, however, is
lined with beggars which detracted very much from the pleasure of the ride. We gave a red-eyed old dwarf ten centimes
for which he thanked us very much and declared as soon as he
got five francs he would try his luck *again* in the bank. So
it seems that even the little charities one dispenses there go
into the coffers of the Casino.

From Monte Carlo we took a twelve-hour ride by rail to
Florence. On our way we passed through San Remo, made
famous as the place chosen by the late Emperor of Germany
as a health resort and place of repose during his last sickness.
We also passed through Genoa which looked about as it did
when I last visited it in 1888. From Genoa we went through
Pisa and took another look at its famous Leaning Tower. The
city does not look as well to me as it did four years ago.

We arrived at Florence about seven P. M. and are now
resting at the Hotel de l' Arno, facing the river from which
the hotel is named. Florence is one of the centers of European
travel. The weather is rather too cold for comfort without

artificial heat and too warm with it. During the day, while the sun shines, it is deliciously pleasant but at night it becomes cold and chilly, caused by the snow upon the mountains, always in sight. The Arno is now rushing through the city and darting with great rapidity under the bridges, muddy and murky from the wash of the mountains. It is about ten feet deep at this season ; in August it will be almost dry. We had heard so much praise of Florence that we expected too much. I was very much disappointed with the general appearance of the city. I have no doubt but that it was, when compared with the other old cities of Europe a very handsome and perhaps a splendid place a few hundred years ago, but it certainly is not, so far as its external appearance is concerned, a very handsome city now.

Like the face and form of some ladies we have met, Florence improves as we become better acquainted with her. As we discover her many concealed virtues and hidden charms we learn to love her more and appreciate her better. With the exception of the world-renowned Cathedral and graceful campanile, or bell tower, the outsides of the churches are all ugly and forbidding in appearance ; but when we enter them we are amazed at the splendor and richness of the work, decorations, statuary and paintings they contain.

Michael Angelo's best sculpture is found in the churches. The gallery Uffizi and its adjunct, the gallery Pitti, contain some of the world's finest paintings. The National Museum contains the sculpture of all the old Italian artists. We see so much of the work of Michael Angelo, Raphæl and Benevenuto Cellini, and so many life-like statues and portaits of Dante, Machiavelli and Galileo, that we almost imagine them alive and walking the streets of Florence.

Some of these old artists must have been fully aware of their skill with the pencil and chisel. They attempted to produce copies of everything from a worm up to the Almighty. It seems to me that Michael Angelo could not have been a very modest man or he would have hesitated before he attempted to paint the face and form of God. If the dignity of the Almighty ever permits him to laugh, and if he ever condescends to look upon the works of man, he must, at least, smile with pity and contempt for the conceited old artist who painted him to look like a Samson, Hercules, or John L. Sullivan.

One of the advantages of Florence is the close proximity of its most interesting places. All its art treasures may be seen within easy walking distance of each other.

The church of S. Croce is the Westminster Abbey or Pantheon of Florence. It contains the tomb of Michael

Angelo, Machiavelli, Galileo and many other illustrious men of
Italy. Among the sacred relics of the church they exhibit a
stone about a foot square that once fell from the vaulted roof,
fully one hundred feet above, and struck a pious monk on the
top of his head while praying to the Virgin. The monk was
not hurt but the stone was *bent* He was certainly a hard-
headed old fellow.

LXI.

FLORENCE TO VENICE—WELL AUTHENTICATED MIRACLES—
JUSTICE EXPENSIVE IN FLORENCE—TREASURES OF ART—
MASONIC EMBLEMS—THE GATE OF PARADISE—CAMPO
SANTO—FLORENCE TO BOLOGNA—LODGED IN A PALACE—
LEANING TOWERS—BOLOGNA TO VENICE—ANOTHER PAL-
ACE—HOTEL—LOW PRICES IN VENICE—NECESSITY FOR
OUR TARIFF LAWS—A UNIQUE CITY—NOT A HORSE IN ALL
VENICE—THE PLAGUE—TITIAN'S FIRST LOVE—OTHELLO
AND DESDAMONA—SHYLOCK VS. ANTONIO—THE INQUISI-
TION NOT A RELIGIOUS INSTITUTION—THE LION'S MOUTH.

VENICE, March, 1892.

I ended my last letter with a history of the miraculous
escape of a pious priest, whose head was harder than a forty-
pound stone that fell one hundred feet from the vaulted roof
of a church where he was praying, and struck him upon the
crown of his cranium without either cracking his skull or
breaking the stone. The stone has been securely chained to
one of the pillars of the church to prevent it from repeating
any more such dangerous freaks. The priest who related the
miracle seemed surprised at an incredulous smile which, despite my will, crept over my countenance. " Do you doubt
the miracle?" said he. I assured him that the evidence was
too conclusive to admit of doubt, for there was the *stone* and I
could not ignore what my eyes so clearly saw. He seemed
pleased at my exhibition of faith and conducted me to the
scene of a still greater miracle, in one of the chapels of St.
Mark's church. The chapel is adorned with a very good life-
size painting, representing several poor monks sitting around
a table praying for food, when suddenly two bright angels
enter with their arms full of bread which they are supposed to
have thrown upon the table. The miracle was performed several hundred years ago in that very chapel which has ever
since been too sacred for any other purpose than a praying
place for the poor and hungry. It reminded me of a miracle

performed some fifty years ago in the State of Delaware. I heard my uncle relate the story when I was a little boy. There was a pious old negro, very poor and too old to work. He had the faith of father Abraham, and when he was out of food, prayed for what he wanted His master was returning from the potato patch, in the dusk of the evening, with a basket of new potatoes. As he passed the open window of the old negro's cabin, he saw him standing in front of his table, full of empty dishes, praying for a few "new taters," whereupon his master threw the basket, potatoes and all, at his old gray head. The potatoes fell in a shower over the table and broke some of his dishes. After the first surprise was over, he raised his eyes toward heaven and said, "Massa Lord, dem's de taters, but please don't throw 'em down quite so hard nex' time." As positive proof of the miracle, the old negro preserved the *basket* and triumphantly showed it to all doubters.

We devoted four days, with a carriage and good guide, to the sights of Florence. We found it full of hidden treasures of art. Including the suburbs, it has a population of about 180,000. The villas without the walls are charming retreats, occupied by the rich natives and English and American sojourners. I am, however, still of the opinion that the beauties of the city, as painted by travelers, are very much overrated.

As we drove over the city to take a glance at its outside appearance our guide, who spoke good French but very bad English, pointed out the several objects of interest—statues, columns, palaces, squares and churches. In one of the principal streets, near the Palace of Justice, is a high column, upon the top of which stands the Goddess of Justice with a pair of scales in her right hand. Our guide tried his hand at a pun in English and, considering his want of experience in the language, he did very well. Pointing to the Goddess on the top of the column he said, "Ze justice is very *high* (dear) in Florence." As we laughed at his pun, he seemed highly pleased.

We visited all the places of interest in the city, including the galleries of painting and sculpture and saw all the famous works of the old masters. We also visited the Palace of the Medicis, which, externally, looks like a prison but internally is very rich with grand old halls, tapestry, statuary and paintings. To those who are fond of sculpture, Florence is rich with the works of the best artists, from Praxiteles and Phidias down to Conova.

With the single exception of Rome, its churches are the richest in internal wealth of any in the world. The Cathedral is a very imposing structure in its architectural design. The campanile is built of different colored marble, like the cathedral, and presents from its summit a splendid view of the city and surrounding country. They show the silver trowel, square, compass and twenty-four-inch guage which, they assure us, were the veritable tools used by the architect in the construction of the church. When I showed the guide the same emblems on my Masonic mark, he took it for granted that I was some great architect and insisted upon showing me the five original plans of the building. I understood the emblems better than he did. They simply meant that the foundations had been laid by some old mason according to the custom of the craft—the same all the world over.

Some travelers affect to go into exstacies over the bronze doors of the Baptistry but, notwithstanding the half hour wasted in a detailed explanation of their allegorical meaning, I could not work myself up to the enthusiasm professed by some of the spectators. The work is undoubtedly very fine. One door took twenty-four years to make. The artist was the celebrated Lorenzo de Berti. When Michael Angelo first saw this door, he declared it fit for the gate of Paradise. It has been called, ever since, the Paradise Door.

One of the commonest old brick churches is called Saint Lorenza. Upon entering the chapel, adjoining the church, the spectator is struck with amazement at the gorgeous profusion of fine colored and highly polished marbles with which the interior is lined. It cannot be described. Some idea can be formed of its beauty and splendor when the cost of its construction is known. Five million dollars was expended upon it at a time when one dollar would produce as much as three dollars will now. When I was a little boy I read the autobiography of Benevenuto Cellini and was, therefore, now very much interested in his work. His masterpiece in bronze stands on the portico opposite the Town Hall. It represents Perseus decapitating Medusa. Critics, however, say it shows too much blood from the neck of the decapitated sorceress. The authorities have put a small metal apron on Perseus which, to a certain extent, spoils the effect of the sculptor's conception of his subject.

We spent the last day in driving around the suburbs. We visited the campo santo, situated, like the one at Nice, on the crown of a hill over three hundred feet high. It commands an excellent view of the city and is a very pretty place to spend an hour. The burial lots, like the compartments of the railroad cars, are divided into first, second and third class. The first class are for the rich, the second class for the ordinary citizen, the third class for the poor. The poor can only rest in holy ground for a few years, not over ten ; the rich are supposed to remain until Gabriel's trump shall awake them. Their tombs are marked—" In perpetuite"—which means "forever."

Just out of the city limits, is a very fashionable drive. We rode over it to see the splendid turnouts of the rich citizens. It is called the Hyde Park of Florence. It is the place to see the beauties of the city airing themselves behind their magnificent carriages and equipments. After our guide assured us he had nothing more to show us we packed our trunks and left for Bologna, four hours distant by express train. We crossed the Appenine mountains ; some of the scenery was very fine. After passing Pistola, an old walled city, we looked down upon a broad valley completely studded with white villas, presenting a most picturesque landscape.

Our hotel at Bologna had the outward appearance of a fine new building, but when we entered the court-yard we discovered we were in a palace over four hundred years old, in which one of the Popes had slept two hundred years ago. The chambers are very large, the ceilings high and frescoed ; but little woodwork is to be seen. The staircase is of pure marble, broad and imposing. It has now had the honor of having an American *Sovereign* to sleep within its walls. It belongs to Count Puscheck, who finds it more profitable to rent it as a hotel than keep it for a residence.

The city seems well built and prosperous, but we are informed its business is now stagnant and its future outlook discouraging. It contains one of the largest unfinished churches in the world, the foundations of which were laid many hundred years ago. It also contains two remarkable leaning towers close together and leaning opposite ways, one finished, the other about half completed. These leaning towers are seen in many of the old towns all over Italy.

We arrived in Venice at six P. M. Although its latitude is as far north as Halifax, the temperature was warm and pleasant. No overcoats were needed in the streets, nor fires in the hotels to keep us comfortable. We were recommended by an Italian gentleman, whose acquaintance we made in the cars, to the Grand Hotel Europa, as the best in the city. It is situated on the Grand Canal, in the heart of the city, and close to St. Mark's. To our surprise, we found ourselves in another four-hundred-year-old palace, belonging to the Giustiniani Family. It is in a remarkably good state of preservation. At a cursory glance one would not take it to be over twenty years old. The room we occupy is very large and looks out upon the Grand Canal and best part of Venice. The ceiling is thirty feet high, vaulted and frescoed. The stairway is of marble and the halls wide and imposing. We at first doubted the landlord's story of his palatial hotel, but, while visiting the Museum, we found a three-hundred-year-old map of the city on which our hotel was marked " Palazzo Giustiniani." So we have occupied rooms in two palaces since our sojourn in Italy.

Everything is cheap in Venice. The very best skilled labor, mechanics and even artists, cannot earn over seventy-five cents a day. Four francs a day is considered very good wages. It does not require much intelligence in the American traveler to see the absolute necessity of our Tariff laws. If it were not for their protection, Italy alone could flood America with most exquisitely wrought glassware, carved woodwork, musical instruments, furniture, tapestry, etc., and sell them at a large profit for prices too low for native competition.

We are highly pleased with Venice. It is one of the most interesting cities we have yet seen. A striking peculiarity of the place is its Sabbath-like quietness ; there is not a horse or carriage in the city and but few dogs, but plenty of rats. The Gondola (pronounced Gundola, with the accent on the first syllable), glides noiselessly through the canals and takes the place of the carrage, wagon and cart in other cities.

The Grand Canal completely bisects the city in a serpentine course from eastward to westward. All the palaces, public buildings and fine residences face upon it or are near by it. Its water is comparatively clear and pure, but the hundreds of small canals all over the city are the most disgustingly filthy places I have ever seen. While going through them, I had to hold my handkerchief to my nose to protect my nostrils from the most execrable of all vile and nasty stinks. They are the open sewers of the city and contain all the offal, garbage and refuse of the town. If it were not for the three-feet tide which rises and falls twice in twenty-four hours, they would certainly be most unhealthy places ; but, while it has been scourged by the plague and cholera, bad fevers are unknown in Venice. During the Plague in the XVIth century the city was nearly depopulated. It is said that 44,000 died in twenty-seven days with the terrible disease. I saw in Florence a representation in wax of the " Plague in Venice." It was the most horrible spectacle I ever looked upon. Titian, the great painter, died of it aged ninety-nine years and eight months. His pictures are found in all the galleries and palaces in the city. When a young man, unknown to fame but celebrated as a portrait painter, a girl of seventeen, of a noble family, sat an hour for her porrtait. She became so violently in love with him that she thought it prudent never to see him again nor call for her picture. A year after he was employed to paint the fresco of the Doge's palace. To the surprise of all Venice he gave to one of the angels in his picture the face of the young lady so perfectly that all who knew her at once recognized her features in the fresco. It is said she died of love, and Titian in all hi

great paintings gave her face to his finest female representations.   There is a very beautiful French novel upon the subject, called " Titian's First Love."   As I had read the novel
I was, of course, very much interested in the picture.

Among the most interesting objects in Venice are St.
Mark's Cathedral ; the Palace of the Doge ; the Bridge of
Sighs ; the Campanile ; the Rialto ; the Church of the Jesuits
and Carmelites ; and the paintings in the gallery containing
the masterpieces of Titian, Tintorello, Paulo Veronese, Bellini,
Lorenzo Venegiano, Ghiberti. Leonardo da Vinci and Dona-
tello.   I do not profess to be sufficiently skilled in the fine
arts to judge of their several merits.   The new school and fine
modern painting in Paris gives me much more pleasure than
all the thousands of religious subjects upon which the old masters exhausted their skill.

While the palaces, prisons, churches, theatres and monuments of the city can be visited by gondola, the walker can
find many cozy nooks and quaint old corners which the traveler
on the canals never sees.

We were shown the reputed bust of Othello the Moor ;
the house of the unfortunate Desdemona ; the place where the
jealous Moor ended his wretched life after the murder of his
wife, and his memorable " Farewell to all the pomp, pride and
circumstance of Glorious War."

We were also shown the place where the celebrated case
of *Shylock the Jew vs. Antonio, the Merchant of Venice*, was
tried, in which it was decided that hard bargains, when committed to writing, are always to be strictly construed.   The
righteous Judge in that case decided that the Jew should have
his bond, a pound of flesh nearest Antonio's heart, but if he
shed a drop of blood he should suffer death, because " 'Twas
not so nominated in the bond."   The Bourse of Venice was
at the foot of the Rialto ; the merchants, brokers and
bankers of Venice, as they went to the Bourse would naturally
meet on the Rialto.   'Twas there that proud and prosperous
Antonio would meet and deliberately insult the poor old Jew
and " rate him about his monies and his usances."   He went
so far as to call him a dog and spit upon him, but when he
became financially involved, the Jew was the only one of all
his *friends* who was willing to lend him money, without security in kind.   The Jew saw his opportunity to get even with
his persecutor but committed the unpardonable sin of undertaking to draw up the bond without the advice of his lawyer.
The case illustrates how dangerous it is for a man to be his
own lawyer, but it also shows how easily a skillful barrister
can get a man out of a very bad difficulty.

St. Mark's, the Clock Tower, the beautiful Square, facing

the Church, with the Palace of the Doges and Bridge of Sighs, leading from the palace to the gloomy prison on the other side of the narrow canal, have been so often painted, by pen and pencil, that any further attempt to describe them would but spoil them by adding paint to a finished picture. Travelers are all disappointed with the Bridge of Sighs. It is a very small enclosed passage-way, leading from one of the upper stories of the palace to the prison on the other side, and would attract no notice were it not for the sad memories connected with the illustrious persons who have, for the last time, looked with a sigh upon the sun through the window of the narrow bridge. We walked half way over it and returned to the palace, which contains, not only the splendid apartments formerly occupied by the Doges, or Grand Dukes of Venice, but also the Senate Chamber, Council Chamber, once occupied by the infamous Council of Ten, and the Chamber of Inquisition, with its instruments of torture and dark, mouldy dungeons, where prisoners of state were confined. In one of the dark narrow passages we were shown the remains of a mechanical contrivance by which the prisoner, while apparently going from his cell to liberty, was suddenly caught by a wooden bar across the throat, when by a powerful spring, another bar would strike his neck from behind and instantly strangle him. In another dark passage we were shown a groove in each side, where a large knife fell and decapitated the prisoner as he leaned forward over an obstacle in the passageway ; his head fell into a hole and was carried to a depository some fifty feet below, full of quick lime ; his body fell into another hole prepared in the same way, so that if the body should be recovered the head could not be recognized. The Inquisition was not, as many suppose, a religious institution. It was founded in Venice as a means of ferreting out plots and conspiracies against the government. The holes in the palace walls where any citizen, without discovering his own name, could deposit letters denouncing others as traitors or conspirators, are yet to be seen. One was concealed by a lion's head. I will describe it more fully in my next letter.

LXII.

VENICE TO PARIS—MORE ABOUT THE INQUISITION—CLASSIC
AND HISTORIC PLACES—ST. MARK'S CHURCH—PALACE OF
THE DOGES—A CITY ON PILES—PADUA—MILAN AGAIN—
ITS WORLD-RENOWNED CATHEDRAL—TRAVELER'S HOB-
BY—A COINCIDENCE—BATTLEFIELD OF MAGENTA—TURIN,
A CITY OF ARCADES—SHIN-PLASTERS IN ITALY—MACON—
AN ENCHANTED CASTLE—LAKE BOURGET—BACK TO PARIS
AND HOMEWARD.

PARIS, April, 1892.

I referred, in my last letter, to the Inquisition of Venice.
It was instituted about A. D. 1310, by the Council of Ten, not
as a religious establishment, but as an adjunct to the criminal
court. Our Grand Jury, or more properly speaking, Grand
Inquest, is but an evolution from the Venitian Inquisition. In
Spain it developed into a religious court to discover and pun-
ish heresies against the established church. When it was instituted in Venice, the noble families were constantly plotting
and conspiring for the overthrow of the Republic. The influence of the rich nobles was so great that it was as much as the
life of an humble citizen was worth to denounce the plotters or
appear as witnesses against them. To give immunity to pro-
secutors for treason, the Inquisition was established. The
mails could not be trusted, so little holes were provided in the
walls of the Palace of the Doge, into which anonymous letters
could be dropped denouncing any citizen, from the Doge down
to a footman. One of these holes was concealed by a carved
lion's head. The letter, dropped into his mouth, fell into a
box with two keys, one held by the Chief Inquisitor and the
other by the President of the Council. The Doge himself
could not have access to the letters deposited in this box.
Unless the denunciation gave the names of witnesses, or referred to circumstances sufficient to make out a *prima facie*
case, no notice was taken of it. If, however, the names of
witnesses were given, the accused was at once put under strict
secret surveillance and the witnesses were brought before the
Council and closely examined. If a case was made out, the
first notice the accused received was an arrest and trial before
the Inquisitor and Council. If condemned, he rarely escaped
death. The institution grew into great favor and, for many
years, preserved the State, but like all good institutions its
virtue depended on the character of the men in possession of
its machinery. Just as a Nero could destroy all the virtues

of the Roman system of government, so a bigoted Chief Inquisitor could convert the Inquisition into an office of unheard
of cruelty and oppression.   Our English ancestors discovered
the necessity of curtailing the existence of the Inquisition to
the shortest period of time, and of changing the Inquisitors
every three months, by which they received all the benefits of
the institution without its evils, and this is what we now call
a *Grand Jury* or *Grand Inquest.*

As in Rome and Florence, so here the richest works of
art are found in the churches.   There are many places
made famous by Shakespeare, Byron, George Sand, Browning
and other poets and novelists.   The Rialto is the scene of the
exciting events in the " Merchant of Venice ;" St. Mark's and
the House of Desdemona, on the Grand Canal   are frequently
referred to in " Othello the Moor ;" Lord Byron has immortalized the Palace of the Doges, and George Sand has thrown
a halo of love around the Hospital where the Maestro (Porpora)
held his free school of music for the poor girls and boys of
Venice, and where poor little Consuelo learned the art of song
which afterwards made her so famous all over Europe and gave
hear a Count for a husband.   Lucretia Borgea also had a
palace in Venice where she practiced her secret art of poison-
ing those she hated or who were in her way.

We were conducted to the spot where the "Jealous
Moor," after realizing that he, "Like the base Judean, had
cast away a jewel richer than all his tribe," ended his miserable existence by plunging into his own heart the same sword
with which he had slain at Aleppo a " malignant and turbaned
Turk " for smiting a Venitian and traducing the State.   Like
many another man, he " Loved, not wisely, but too well."

St. Mark's church is unique in its architecture.   It is a
combination of the Byzantine, Roman, Moorish and Greek
orders.   It never fails, however, to strike the beholder with a
feeling of pleasure and surprise.   All the old churches have
their superstitious legends.   St. Mark's professes to contain
in its crypt the veritable bones of the apostle St. Mark.   It
also possesses a stone, ten or twelve feet square, brought from
Jerusalem, upon which Christ is said to have stood when he
delivered his great Sermon on the Mount.   There was a time,
not many years ago, when, to express a doubt as to the truth
of these legends, would have sent the skeptic to the scaffold or
the stake, but those dark days are past forever.   This church
is undoubtedly rich with holy relics.   It contains pillars from
Solomon's Temple and stones from nearly all the great buildings of antiquity, including Babylon and Nineveh.

There is no more interesting place in Venice than the
Palace of the Doges.   Its grand halls, Council chambers,

Inquisitorial departments, instruments of torture, dungeons and long, dark corridors, leading to the fatal axe or over the " Bridge of Sighs " to perpetual imprisonment, convey a faint but sad picture of the past glory of the Doges of Venice. We visited every part of it.

Venice in her best days had a population of over 200,000. Its greatest prosperity was in the twelfth century. After that it began to decline and its population fell to about 96,000. It is now increasing again in wealth and population. It is built upon alluvial ground with a rock sub-stratum only about twenty-five feet below the surface. The whole city rests upon piles driven down to the rock. There are no leaning buildings in Venice like those of Rotterdam. Some of them lean slightly. We left the city favorably impressed with its many charms. The weather was good while we were there and that added very much to our enjoyment.

We now began to wend our way slowly homeward. We passed through Padua, a town of quite considerable historical importance. It is now very strongly fortified. Its present population is about 80,000. It is said that living in Padua is cheaper than in any other place in Italy. The citizens claim for their town an antiquity equal to Troy. During the reign of Augustus, it was reputed to be one of the richest towns in Italy. We could only look at it for a very short time and form some general idea of its construction. In the route from Padua to Verona (where we stopped a short time), we passed the battle-field of Solferino, and Lake Garda. The lake is thirty-seven miles long by from two to ten miles wide and, in places, one thousand feet deep. Its waters are beautifully blue but often very rough.

Passing over a flat and fertile country we reached Milan and gave it nearly two days. We had seen the city thoroughly in 1888, but now, after having seen most of the renowned cathedrals of Europe, we felt a desire to look once more upon the gem of the world in Gothic architecture—the Cathedral of Milan. St. Paul's, of London, the cathedrals of York, Cologne and Florence are noble, impressive and grand, but they all have a naked internal appearance. Westminster Abbey, Notre Dame, the cathredals at Strasbourg, Orleans, Chester and Brussels are venerable and hoary piles, but are imperfect, not finished, or overcrowded in ornamentation and monuments. They are very interesting places for the student of history, but they never inspire the beholder with that peculiar feeling of awe or wonder which he experiences when, for the first time, he looks up at the dome of St. Peter's in Rome, or St. Paul's in London.

The cathedral at Antwerp is exceedingly beautiful and

striking in its tall, heaven-piercing spire of stone, but it is surrounded with mean shops, built up against its sacred walls which gives it, in other respects, a common appearance. The old cathedral at Vienna is curious to look at because of its mosque-like construction ; in other respects it has no distinctive charms. St. Sophia, St. Mark, and the restored cathedral at Marseilles are curious because of their Byzantine style and great proportions ; but they are naked within. The old Mosque of a thousand columns at Cordova, is only one story high, and from without has a mean look. Of all the cathedrals we have yet seen, St. Peter's at Rome only surpasses the Gem of Milan. Indeed St. Peter's, when first seen, is disappointing but it grows wonderful on acquaintance. The church at Milan strikes the beholder at once as a finished work. It is as perfect as the genius of man can make it. This was consensus of opinion in our little party and has been approved by all the travelers we have met.

Every traveler has his own hobby. They may all, however, be reduced to three heads Nature, Art and Society. Some delight in grand scenery—rocks, crags, mountains, cascades, lakes and plains ; others seek the works of art—old paintings, statuary, temples and ancient ruins ; while many care but little for anything but the social intercourse of men and women. Among the young people we have met the pleasures of society seem to be their chief object in traveling. At Algiers we found our hotel full of society people from London. They spent all their time in balls, drives, billiards and cards and seemed as happy as if they were in Paradise.

When we were shown our room in the hotel at Milan, everything looked familiar. The furniture, the outlook from the balcony, even the chambermaid looked like an old friend. Upon inquiry we found ourselves quartered in the same hotel, on the same story, and the identical room we had occupied four years ago. This was, at least, a singular coincidence and was the result of pure accident.

After a last long look at the cathedral with the somewhat sad impression that we would never look upon its face again, we left Milan for Turin. We passed the great battlefield of Magenta where the French and Sardinians, under Napoleon III. and Victor Emanuel, gained their great victory over the Austrians on the fourth of June, 1859. A few mounds and crosses mark the places where the great ones fell, and a great charnel-house holds the confused and undistinguished bones of the thousands of common soldiers who gave their lives for their country. This victory was the awakening of Italy from its long and deathlike sleep.

Turin is the only city in which we have found bad weather.

It rained nearly all the time we were there. We, however, found time between the showers to drive over the town and thoroughly inspect its outside appearance. Its elevation above the sea is seven hundred and eighty-five feet. It is very romantically situated on the left bank of the Po, with the Alps in full view. The city was the scene of one of Hannibal's victorious marches through Italy and was destroyed by him B. C. 218. It now has a population of 305,000. It is the most regularly laid out city in Europe of its age. Its distinctive mark is its numerous arcades. All the sidewalks on the principal streets are arched over and vaulted, even across the intersections, giving a fine footwalk from ten to twenty feet wide, entirely protected from rain. I walked at least a mile under these beautiful arcades from our hotel to the river, without raising my umbrella, although it rained hard all the time.

We made the acquaintance of the American Consul at Milan. He is a fine looking gentleman, from Cleveland, Ohio, and a staunch Republican. He seemed greatly interested in the debates in Congress on the silver question. He says the people of Italy are naturally very friendly to the United States and have great faith in the financial policy of our government. They think silver and gold ought to be the standards of value, but that silver ought not to be a legal tender over a reasonable sum to be fixed by the government. Silver is now very scarce in Italy and gold is never seen. Italian bank notes are at a discount of four per cent. The smallest note is five francs, about the size of the *shin-plaster* currency we had during the war.

We were somewhat surprised to learn from our friend, the Consul, that there was quite a prosperous Methodist Episcopal church in Milan, of native Italians. While we learn, with age, to love and respect all forms of christian worship, we can but feel a partiality for the church in which our infant lips were first taught to lisp our little prayers to God with a faith that only a child can feel and which, too often, weakens with advancing years.

The city of Turin is strongly fortified and literally full of soldiers. We saw ten thousand well-equipped and well-drilled men, marching out to the Champ de Mars to go through their daily evolutions previous to going to work on the fortifications. They marched through the wide streets in several columns, thirty-two deep, and presented a very fine appearance.

From Turin we went to Macon, twelve hours distant by rail, through the Alps by the Mt. Cenis Tunnel. The scenery over this route is equal to any in Europe. The mountains on the Italian side were partially enveloped in a dreamlike mist. At Ambrogto, an old castle on the mountain top could be distinctly seen with the sun shining upon its ruined towers, while the base of the mountain was entirely hidden by the fog. It looked like an enchanted castle sitting upon a cloud ; more like a fantastic dream than a real mountain scene. Some of the clouds were tinted with the golden rays of the sun ; others were black and threatening while others, like the clouds of life, had beautiful silver lining. And yet I saw travelers asleep in their compartments while this enchanting panorama was passing before them. The great rocky sides of some of the mountains seemed to pierce the clouds and overhang, as if about to fall upon the passing train.

At Aix Les Bains we passed a flowing mountain stream thirty or forty feet wide, of black and smoking water. There are great hot sulphur springs near by, which have, since the days of the Romans, a great reputation for the cure of all forms of skin diseases. We also passed and followed the shore of the beautiful Lake Bourget. At places the tract seemed to touch the water's edge. As we plunge from the lake into a tunnel and then out again, apparently into the lake, the effect is very exhilarating, a new picture being presented as we emerge from each of the forty or fifty tunnels.

We arrived at Macon in the evening. It is not a very interesting town, but served us as a convenient sleeping place for one night. We have made it a rule to travel by day and rest at night as much as possible. Macon is built upon the Soane. It has a population of 280,000 and lies about two hundred and seventy-four miles southeast of Paris. It was the birthplace of La Martine. The route from Macon to Paris is comparatively tame. We arrived back at Paris about seven P. M., having completed our previously arranged itinerary without the slightest deviation.

We have traveled over twelve thousand miles in France, Africa, Italy and on the sea since we left home on the twelfth of February. We intend to now rest nine days in Paris and then set sail for home.

PART II.

———

American Hunts and Travels.

———

The following letters were written at intervals during my European travels. They have been chronologically arranged and may be of some value as faithful pictures of the times and places described. Since they were written, many of the scenes have materially changed. My visit to Gettysburg was only a few years after the battle. Communication by rail was then difficult. Since then it has been greatly improved and the place beautified. Roanoke was then in its infancy ; it is now a flourishing city.

It is only by comparing the past with the present, that the progress of our common country can be intelligently un-. derstood.

T. J. C.

February 21, 1893.

I.

PHILADELPHIA TO NIAGARA FALLS—MANIA A POTU ON THE CARS—INCIDENTS ON THE ROAD—SCENERY—MAUCH CHUNK—WILKESBARRE—A PICNIC DISTURBED—WYOMING —THE BEAUTIFUL GENESEE FALLS—BUFFALO—HOW TO SEE NIAGARA FALLS.

NIAGARA FALLS, August, 1870.

The monotony of the journey from Philadelphia to Bethlehem, was soon broken by the frantic screams of a *lady* passenger with the *mania a potu*. The passengers were kept in a constant state of excitement by her wild and unearthly yells, drowning even the shrill shrieks of the locomotive. She rushed like an affrighted fury from door to door and up and down the narrow aisle of the car, with her babe in her arms, bent upon leaping out to escape some imaginary demon who seemed to pursue her. She was at last secured and held in her seat while her babe was wrested from her arms, and the car in which she remained was switched off at Bethlehem. Scarcely had we exchanged mutual congratulations for our escape from the drunken woman, when the double alarm of the shrill whistle so well known to travelers, and the sudden check caused by the quick application of the brake, admonished us of some new danger. "What's the matter now?" cried a score of voices. Some said a man had been run over ; others said a boy had fallen from a cart which had just crossed the track, and that both his legs were cut off. "Poor fellow !" said a woman in front. (She was just going to Mauch Chunk to see her nephew, who had his leg cut off yesterday by falling from the platform ; he had been a brakeman for sixteen years. So the pitcher which had gone so often to the well had been broken at last). Just then the conductor entered all bows and smiles. "The cruel fellow !" said the woman in front, "to appear so unconcerned after such an accident ;" but we all forgave him when he informed us that they had only run over a cow.

From Bethlehem to the head waters of the Lehigh, the scenery is picturesque and enchanting. The road follows all the courses of the meandering river. I had visited Mauch Chunk about twenty years ago, and am surprised to find it so little changed ; it was then on the stage route to Tamaqua. It is a beautiful place, and were it not for the busy crowd of cars and boats laden with coal and the veritable signs of enterprise and industry everywhere exhibited, it would compare

favorably with a Swiss town. From Mauch Chunk up the
river for many miles the eye is wearied with the constant presence of the debris and wreck caused by the recent great freshet ;
the canal from this place was so completely destroyed that
nothing remains but broken locks and ruptured dams.   It will
never be rebuilt.   The destruction must have been enormous,
and the loss to the company incalculable.   Near the head
waters of the Lehigh, the road diverges to the left, and
courses over the table lands between the Lehigh and the Susquehanna.   The great forests have all fallen before the axe of
the woodman, and the eye of the traveler at one rapid glance
surveys thousands of acres of what was once primeval forest,
but now barren waste.

When within three miles of Wilkesbarre, the line of the
road is twelve hundred feet above the site of the town.   In
order to descend the road winds down the side of the mountain
for sixteen miles before reaching the place.   The town is
beautifully situated on the south bank of the Susquehanna,
which is at this place about five hundred feet wide.   But
few private residences in the most beautiful parts of Philadelphia are more elegant than those along the river front.   It
is the county town of Luzerne and contains about 15,000 inhabitants, and is considered one of the most wealthy towns in
Pennsylvania.   The country at Elmira, and for many miles up
the river, reminds me of the scenery around Baden Baden.
The name of the broad valley above the town, however, is
hardly as romantic as its Rhinish counterpart.   They call the
valley here *Big Flats*.   The whole valley of the Susquehanna
is soft, luxuriant and charming, contrasting finely with the
Lehigh's wild rocky banks, and is well worth a visit from the
American tourist.

On our way from Wilkesbarre to Elmira, we passed a *picnic* party, consisting of a lady, gentleman and horse ; the two
former were enjoying their *lunch* in a beautiful copse-wood
glen by the side of a deep ravine, and as they did not want to
be selfish, they had unharnessed the horse and turned him out
to pasture *on the railroad*.   It was one of the most ludicrous
and serio-comic scenes I ever witnessed.   The affrighted steed
ran several miles ahead of the locomotive, but escaped unhurt.
The last I saw of the *picnic* party, they were endeavoring to
outrun the train with the horse in front of the locomotive.

The reprehensible practice, so common in America, of
constantly changing the names of places, led me astray at the
town of Warsaw.   After expending extravagant praise upon
it, as a charming spot of which I had not so much as heard, I
was informed that it was the old village of Wyoming, in a new
name.   Thousands of acres of fine farm lands, as innumerable

stump fences attest, have recently been redeemed from the forests all along the line of the road from Elmira to Buffalo. In many places large corn and oats fields have no other fences. The stumps seem to have been torn from the ground very much as one would extract a tooth, with the roots all intact ; the stumps are then so arranged as to form very good fences. The spot where the Erie road crosses the Genesee river will be admitted by all as most charming ; the river Esk from Haw- thorden to Roslin Castle in Scotland is not more beautiful. The river seems to have cut its way through the hills from fifty to one hundred feet deep, and has formed a splendid waterfall and cascade ; its beauty is increased by its unexpected dis- covery in such an uninteresting country. From there to Buffalo there is nothing very striking, except perhaps the fact that they have just finished wheat harvest, and are commenc- ing to gather their oats, which in many places is yet too green to cut. We left Philadelphia on Tuesday at one o'clock, P. M., and without traveling by night, arrived at Buffalo on Thursday at four P. M., a distance of four hundred and twenty- six miles by rail. The city of Buffalo claims 180,000 inhabit- ants ; it is situated upon the eastern end of Lake Erie, and from the palatial residences of some of its citizens on Main Street, the tourist at once grants all it claims as being one of the wealthiest cities of the West. We were very agreeably dis- appointed in the place. The buildings are not only substan- tial, but an unusual proportion of them are of a striking and at the same time pleasing architectural design, and surrounded by green, well-shaded lawns, and flowers. There were 20,000 strangers in the town attending the races at the fair grounds, just outside the city. From this place to Niagara Falls is twenty-two miles, making the entire distance from Chester about four hundred and forty-six miles ; the journey is never- theless amply worth the trouble and time required. I was told by others who had preceded me, that I would be disappointed in Niagara, and so I was ; but it was with agreeable surprise, profound wonder, and absolute amazement. I will not attempt to describe the Falls. I have read a description by Dickens, and find it tame. I think I can tell the reason why so many persons are disappointed with Niagara ; they do not take the time, nor have the patience to gaze upon it from the proper places. To see it properly, go first to the Clifton House on the Canada side, walk up the shore to the edge of the Horse Shoe Fall, then descend to the river's edge at the foot of the Falls and gaze up upon the mighty cataract, and if you have a soul and it is not stirred to its very centre, pronounce yourself a stoic, and go home and stay there, for God or Nature have no charms for you. The tourist should also cross the Suspension

Bridge to the American side and from the lower edge of the American Falls look down one hundred and sixty-eight feet, at the glorious, descending, foaming and sparkling sheet of water ; from thence he should cross over to Goat Island and descend the Biddle staircase to the Cavé of the Winds, from which he should re-ascend and walk out to the Tower at the American side of the Horse Shoe, observing the rapids above the Falls and the Three Sisters Islands ; he has then, and not till then, seen Niagara.   I have seen nothing to compare with it in the world.   The cascades and waterfalls of Europe dwindle into insignificance when placed in comparison with Niagara.   The place is full of strangers, every hotel being crowded to its utmost capacity.   We met at the Clifton House, Chief Justice Chase and Mr. Thurlow Weed.   We propose resting here a few days, after which we will pursue our journey over the lakes to Montreal, wending our way homeward *via* Lake Champlain, Lake George, Saratoga Springs, and from Albany down the Hudson to New York.

II.

NIAGARA TO SARATOGA—WHEN SHALL THE LAKES BE EMPTIED ?—MORGAN'S WATERY GRAVE—THE THOUSAND ISLES—THE RAPIDS—FROST IN AUGUST IN MONTREAL—FINE VIEW FROM MONT ROYAL—LAKES GEORGE AND CHAMPLAIN—OLD-FASHIONED STAGES—FORT TICONDEROGA—A SPREAD EAGLE SPEECH—SARATOGA—JOHN MORRISSEY'S GAMBLING ROOMS—VULGAR DISPLAY OF DRESS AND DIAMONDS.

SARATOGA, August, 1870.

We spent two nights on the boat from Niagara to Montreal.   Those who have never seen the lakes have very erroneous ideas of their size.   At Toronto I cast my eye eastward and easily imagined myself at Cape Henlopen, gazing out upon the boundless ocean.   The lake boats are commodious but not as palatial as those of the Hudson ; the state-rooms and table, however, are all the traveler should reasonably require.   In stormy times the lakes are as rough and dangerous to navigate as the ocean, but on a calm summer day they are as smooth as glass.   From Niagara Falls to the town of Niagara, situated at the mouth of the river, where it empties into Lake Ontario, is but a half hour ride by rail over a smooth and apparently stoneless country, with little to interest

the traveler, except the deep cut bed of the river with its perpendicular granite banks, undoubtedly caused by the action
of the water in some remote age, when the great waterfall has
been several miles further down the river than where it now
is.   And so the Falls will continue for hundreds of ages to come
to cut its way slowly, almost imperceptibly, but surely back,
back, inch by inch, until in the remote future it empties the
great lakes into the ocean, and converts what is now their bottoms into rich farms and pasture grounds.   Should the great
city of Buffalo then stand, it will be an inland town.   But we
need not grieve, as we will have slept, peacefully I hope, some
twenty thousand years before the great Falls of Niagara and
the lakes shall disappear.   It is the settled belief of geologists
that the whole country around Worms and the upper valley of
the Rhine was once a lake, which has been emptied into the
German Ocean by the action of the water of the Rhine, as it
has cut its way back from Cologne to Mayence in some pre-
historic age.

Opposite the town of Niagara stands old Fort Niagara, a
place of great interest to the Masonic craft.   It was said they
confined Morgan in the magazine of this fort, a story which no
intelligent Mason at this day believes.   It nevertheless created
a tremendous excitement about forty years ago, when I was a
little boy.   It was undoubtedly a stupendous hoax, invented
by unscrupulous men, for political effect.   I inquired of a very
intelligent old gentleman, (Mr. Thurlow Weed), who at the
time of the alleged murder, was a co-actor in the comedy with
Thaddeus Stevens and other great anti-Masons, as to the truth
of the story.   He assured me most earnestly that the Gospel
was not more true.   He said that *he* entered the fort the morning after the murder, with a *habeas corpus* for the production
of Morgan's body before the Court ; but that the judge who
had granted the writ, being a Mason, gave timely notice to the
brethren having him in charge, and that they, just before daybreak procured two fifty-six-pound weights and a rope, and took
Morgan from the Fort, gagged and tied him, and with one of
the weights tied to his neck and another to his feet, they rowed
him out where the water was at least *six feet deep*, and
with his head and feet *due East and West*, they threw him
into the lake, a *cable's length from the shore*.   Our boat passed
over the very spot where his bones repose, if the story is true.

The boats all cross the lake forty miles to Toronto, from
whence they proceed down the lake one hundred and eighty
miles to Prescot, where it is necessary to change boat in order
to descend the rapids with safety, which no boat drawing over
six feet of water can do.   The most interesting part of the
whole journey, however, is the passage of the Thousand Isles

before arriving at Prescot. The river St. Lawrence is there
several miles wide, and so full of most enchanting little
green islands that in some places it is difficult to navigate the
boat through them. The scenery is very fairy-like; in some
places the green water is so still and glass-like as to mirror the
islands in the streams, where they can be seen as perfectly by
looking down into the water as up on the land. The descent
of the rapids is exciting, but not as much so as I anticipated.
The boat seems to be sinking, bow foremost, as she plunges
over the foaming and angry waters. The steam is all shut off
and six strong men are required at the wheel, to keep the boat
in her true course. At Split Rock, on the Cider Rapids, the
channel between the rocks has not over six feet margin. The
unexperienced passenger naturally holds his breath as he sees
the boat rapidly approach the terrible rock; it would surely
strike it, were it not for the skillful hands at the helm. With
all their skill, however, they sometimes lose their boats; we
passed one, a very fine steamer, completely wrecked upon the
rocks. The rapids of the Rhine, so much talked about in
Europe, are not fit so much as to be named in comparison with
those of the St. Lawrence. We also passed the barge used by
the Fenians, in their worse than foolish raid into Canada.

On the night of the 16th inst., there was frost at Montreal. The town is about eight hundred and sixty miles from
Chester, and four hundred from Niagara Falls. It looks something like Edinburg, Mount Royal, from which the town took
its name, personating Arthur's seat. It is built of cut granite
and seems more like an European town than any I have seen
in America. The French language is spoken altogether in
some parts of the town and surrounding country; this together
with its gold and silver currency,* several times beguiled me
into the belief that I was in Havre, which is built of the same
kind of stone. Montreal contains some of the finest churches
and public buildings on the continent. The Victoria bridge
with its twenty-four piers and tube a mile and a quarter long,
with its single span of three hundred and thirty feet, sixty
feet above summer high water, is alone one of the modern
wonders of the world. A drive around the mountain is full
of interest; it gives a splendid view of the town, bridge and
canal, while in the far distance the Adirondacks and Green
Mountains of Vermont, are plainly visible.

From Montreal we turned our steps homeward, by way of
Lake Champlain, Lake George and Saratoga. The scenery
up Lakes Champlain and George is equal to any lake scenery
in the world. Arriving at Fort Ticonderoga, we took stages

---

*NOTE.—When this letter was written the U. S. had not resumed specie
payment.

for about five miles, over a rough mountain road, where we embarked in the boat upon Lake George. The stage route carried us over the battle ground of Abercrombie's defeat, who in 1758, with 17,000 troops, undertook to storm Fort Ticonderoga. After four days' hard fighting, his shattered and broken army returned to Fort William Henry, leaving 2,000 of the bravest and best of his men dead on the battle field. The capture of Quebec and conquest of Canada rendered the vast military works of Fort Ticonderoga, Fort William Henry and Crown Point useless, and they were dismantled and abandoned. The great hotel at the head of Lake George, occupies part of the site of Fort William Henry, the earthworks being still visible. At Fort Ticonderoga the ruins are in pretty good preservation. As we ascended the hill with a procession of six four-horse coaches, reminding one of the caravan formed by Dan Rice's great Show, the agent of the coaches stopped them all in front of the Fort, and gave us a regular Fourth of July speech, of the most approved spread eagle kind. After recounting in glowing words the glorious deeds of our patriot sires, and a minute recital of the capture of the fort by Ethan Allen, he closed his oration somewhat in this manner : "Thus were the hated tyrants of human liberty and American Independence forever driven from our shore, and our great and glorious Republic founded,

Destined like a rock to stand
Till Gabriel with his *trump* in hand
Shall rouse the living and the dead.
Until the Sun shall cease to burn
And the Moon to ashes turn
Drive on your horses, Ned."

Ned cracked his whip and the caravan advanced.

Lake George is thirty-six miles long by from one to three broad. But little is lacking to make it equal to any of Europe's most favorite pleasure resorts. It sadly needs their romantic castles, mountain roads, and legends which give such an exquisite charm to Heidleburg, and the Black Forrest around Baden Baden. From Lake George we again take the stages, and after a six-mile journey over a very rough and elevated road, from which the Green Mountains of Vermont can be plainly seen, we arrive at Glen Falls, a town of about six thousand inhabitants, where we take the cars, and in two and a half hours arrive at Saratoga, the Baden Baden of America, and the gayest place in the State. It is the resort of the elite of New York, and the sporting men of America. The races are now in full blast, and the *Hon.* John Morrissey is here keeping a first-class gambling house. The ladies here carry the infatuation of dress to a ridiculous extent. They appeared last night at the grand ball of the season in all the gorgeous colors of the rainbow, fairly scintillating with diamonds and glittering with

golden jewels and precious stones. I observed several dowagers
of at least fifty, dressed like damsels of fifteen, with low square-
necked dresses which, instead of exhibiting the charms of
youth, only exposed the ribs and wrinkles of age ; the sear and
yellow leaf instead of the bursting rose bud. One lady was
clothed in what seemed to be a snowflake, with a powdered
wig and frills and a train at least ten feet long. While here
and there I observed some fair faces painted in beauties red and
white " by Nature's own true cunning hand laid on," the
great majority of the gay ones were mere works of art, got up
by nature's journeymen, and botched in the making. A lady
of about forty had on her neck, ears, arms and fingers, about
$25,000 worth of gems and diamonds. The foot of a cluster
cross nestled on her heaving breast, which was liberally exhibited by her square-necked dress. She seated herself with
all a woman's art where two chandeliers cast a flood of light
upon her diamonds. It was amusing to observe her constantly
changing position, obviously made to make her diamonds
sparkle, while her bosom constantly heaved, and with each
heave the diamond cross dazzled the beholder with its brilliant rays. Her last act was to *pick* her *tooth* with her finger
nail to show a magnificent diamond ring. While loath to com-
ment on the frailties of our countrywomen, a sacred regard
for truth requires the exposure. These lavish displays of jewelry, instead of making the wearers, as they suppose, the
centres of attraction, only make them objects of pity with all
well bred people.

III.

BATTLEFIELD OF GETTYSBURG—COMPARED WITH WATERLOO
—THE FIELD AS I SAW IT—THE TERRIBLE STRUGGLE AT
CULP'S HILL—LIBERTY GUARDING HER BATTLEFIELD—
REMAINING EVIDENCES OF THE GREAT BATTLE.

GETTYSBURG, August, 1871.

Two years ago I visited the field of Waterloo, and although the dust and mould of over fifty years had covered many
of its most interesting monuments, yet enough remained to
mark the momentous struggle of the eighteenth of June, 1815.
Hougomont had scarcely been touched since the day of the
battle ; the old red brick wall bore the marks of thousands of
musket balls. The abandoned well from which no water has
since been drawn, and which it is said contains three hundred

skeletons and the charred gates were very much as the battle left them—silent mementos of the memorable day so fatal to the glory of France, but so significant of the liberty and civilization of the world. There also might still be seen " *Le chemin creuz d' Ohain*, so graphically described by Victor Hugo ; the hollow road into which the French cavalry plunged, causing the panic which contributed so largely to the loss of a victory almost won. How little the farmers of Belgium dreamed, as they journeyed over that hollow road, and complained so often of its neglected water courses, which every rain washed still deeper, that God was thereby digging the grave of the great French Empire ; nevertheless, an apparently insignificant lane settled the fate of Napoleon, as well as of the world.

A comparison of the bloody field of Gettysburg with that of Waterloo is by no means far-fetched ; the one was decisive of the liberty of Europe, the other of the freedom of America. The natural position of the ground at Gettysburg, is much stronger for defence than that occupied by the Allies at Waterloo ; but while the Allies had 72,000, and the French 80,000 men, the Federals at Gettysburg had but 60,000, and the Confederates 90,000 men. At Waterloo the Allies lost about 20,000, and the French 40,000 in killed, wounded and prisoners. At Gettysburg the Federals lost about 16,000 killed and wounded and 4,000 prisoners, in all about 20,000. The Rebel loss was 26,500 killed and wounded and 13,000 prisoners and deserters, in all about the same as the French loss at Waterloo. The attack upon *La Poste Hougomont* which was the key to the English position, cost the French about 10,000 men *hors de combat*. The charges upon the works on Culp's Hill were equally disastrous to the Confederates. Both battles were fought for, and won in the cause of humanity. " *Dans la bataille de Waterloo, il y a plus que de nuage, il y a de meteore. Dieu a passe.*" The remark can with equal force be applied to Gettysburg ; it was not Meade, it was not the superior bravery of the Federal forces that won the day, it was God.

The battle cannot be clearly comprehended without viewing the ground. The route from Philadelphia is somewhat tortuous as well as tedious. The first change is at York, which is reached via the Pennsylvania Central, from York via Northern Central to Hanover Junction and thence to Gettysburg. As the train approaches the town, a very good general view of the battlefield can be had from the front platform, or the large side doors of the baggage car. At the right is seen Seminary Ridge, north and west of the town. This ridge was occupied by Reynolds' 1st Corps and Howard's 11th Corps on the afternoon of July 1st. It was in advance of this position

where General Reynolds fell.   Seminary Ridge was occupied by the Rebels on the 2d, 3d and 4th of July, the 11th
Corps having been driven back through the town to the position seen at the left from the cars, and southeast of the Borough,
known as Culp's Hill and Cemetery Hill.   In the distance,
due south from the town, Round Top and Little Round Top
can be easily discerned.   These were the prominent points of
the battlefield.   A carriage, guide and good map of the field,
all of which can be procured for five or six dollars, are absolutely necessary.   The first place visited was the National
Cemetery, a very beautiful and interesting spot,   The monument is a most exquisite work of art, but it seemed to me that
the Goddess of Liberty was either too large, or the column too
small, to be in just proportion to the other parts ; but as I am
not *au fait* in statuary, I will not criticise the work.   From
the Cemetery to Culp's Hill is about a half mile ; the greater
part of the way we traveled by carriage, which we left at the
foot of the hill.   The point where the Louisiana Tigers charged
the works held by the 12th Corps, we attained on foot over
about a third of a mile of very rough and sterile ground.

Gettysburg has this advantage over Waterloo ; the latter
is highly fertile, and under constant cultivation, which to some
extent, has destroyed its characteristics ; but Gettysburg is so
hilly, rough, rocky and sterile, that its features must ever re-
tain the same marks, and like the face of a man, while it may
grow old, the outlines must continue the same.   The grass
will never grow here, but the dew drops on the forest trees
may well grieve

> " Over the unreturning brave—alas !
> Ere evening to be trodden like the grass
>   Which now beneath them, but above shall grow
> In its next verdure, when this fiery mass
>   Of living valor, rolling on the foe
> And burning with high hope, shall moulder cold and low."

Culp's Hill was the key to the Federal position on the
second and third days of the fight ; the remaining evidences of
the tremendous conflict still visible, are truly frightful.   The
enemy had advanced about two miles from his position of
July 1st.   The town had been captured and occupied.   The
capture of the hill was of the first importance, and the flower
of General Lee's army was detailed to the work, but they
never returned ; they captured the works, but had not men
enough left to hold them.   It is said the Rebel dead lay here
four deep, and I verily believe the report.   Acres of forest trees,
as large in diameter as a man's body, were torn into splinters,
not by artillery, but by *musket balls.*   They must have flown
thicker than hail.   How any living being could survive for a
moment under such a fire is a mystery to every one who has

seen the ground. It is said the enemy supposed they were charging the Pennsylvania militia, and first discovered their fatal error when they saw the bronzed faces and faded colors of their old foe behind the works, and in surprise and despair, as they were about leaping over them, cried out : "The army of the Potomac by —" and fell back in disorder and dismay. Others locate this scene at the Peach Orchard. Those who entered the Federal works were beaten back with the butts of the muskets and with stones, the guns being too hot to fire.

In returning from Culp's Hill, looking westward, a charming picture is presented. The wood which skirts the eastern boundary of the cemetery, completely conceals all of the monument, save the Goddess of Liberty upon the top. She appears to be standing on the topmost branch of a tall oak, and looks like a great white angel, with a wreath in her hand, looking down upon her dead and guarding her battlefield. The next point of interest is the Peach Orchard, near the Rose Farm, and Little Round Top. The hill might almost be called a mountain. For its possession a terrific battle was fought at the Peach Orchard on the Emmitsburg road. But few marks of the struggle remain. Save here and there the lead of musket balls on the rocks, and scars or wounds on the intervening trees, nothing more remains to mark the frightful and furious charges upon this part of the field. As we approach from the Emmitsburg road the guide points out a field, now under cultivation, in which are buried over three thousand Confederate dead, who fell in the struggle for Round Top. Not the slightest mark remains to show where the poor fellows sleep. Round Top is two miles due south of the town, and the Peach Orchard is about one mile west of the hill. The hill is a natural fortress, and seems to be an upheaval of rocks and boulders, varying in size from a hogshead to a hay stack, and is somewhat difficult to ascend with no opposing bayonets or batteries. It abounds also with stone, the size of ordinary building stone which, in addition to the rocks, had been formed into a perfect network of breastworks. It cannot be ascended in a straight line, but only by a zigzag course, and by picking our way from rock to rock. It commands the entire field, and its possession secured the victory which otherwise would have been but temporary. When once occupied and armed it was a second Gibraltar, which five hundred men could certainly hold against ten thousand.

Meade's headquarters were at a small frame house on the Taneytown road about half way between Round Top and Culp's Hill. Two shells went through the house, the holes of which are still there. The General was sitting upon a rock in the middle of the road when the dispatch bearer gave him the information that the hill had been occupied and could be held by our forces. A beam of triumph enlightened his somewhat anxious countenance, and he at once caused the news to be signaled to Culp's Hill.

The ravine at the foot of Round Top is also full of boulders. At one place, not inappropriately named "The Devil's Glen," the crevices and fissures of the enormous rocks were found, after the battle, full of rebel dead and wounded. The skill of a General who would attempt the capture of such a position as Round Top may be more than doubted, nevertheless Hood did attempt it ; the 3,000 graves on the Rose farm are the result. While the struggle was being made for Round Top, a flank movement was attempted still further South, which was promptly met and defeated by Kilpatrick's cavalry.

The town of Gettysburg is about the size of West Chester; it shows but few marks of the battle. I noticed, however, one house as we came in from the Taneytown road, completely peppered with musket balls. The relics of the battle, such as shot, shells, swords, guns, bayonets, etc., have been all removed from the field, and can be purchased in the town by those desiring them.

If the visitor desires to examine the rebel lines, he can make it an afternoon's journey. It takes all the forenoon to view the places above indicated. Thousands upon thousands of visitors come annually from all parts of the Union and world to explore this battlefield, and I feel quite sure that none have grudged the time or expense thereby incurred. Philadelphians can return by way of Baltimore, in the same time and for about the same fare, as by Harrisburg or Columbia. The Northern Central road traverses a very beautiful and fertile country from Hanover Junction to Baltimore.

IV.

A Hunt in Arkansas—Pennsylvania Compared With Other States—The Hot Springs—Farm Houses as Hotels—An Amusing Story—A Negro Experience Meeting—Little Rock—Character of the People—Hunting on the Prairies—Rattlesnakes and Whisky—A Case of Buck Fever—River Rail Bird on the Grand Prairie.

LITTLE ROCK, September, 1877.

Every sportsman must be interested in the pleasures of the chase. The intense excitement of the hunt is but a cropping out of a part of our original nature ; a retroactive element of the mind, which carries us back to the period, when our fathers, of ages past, subsisted on the game they killed. It was then that the dog became the friend and companion of man and though not so necessary to our existence now, common gratitude compels us to love him still. When weary of artificial life, and tired of the conventionalties of society, with its hollow amusements and feverish joys, how we long for the freedom of the unplowed fields, and enjoy the peaceful shade of the wild wood. To gratify this innate desire, I left home on the 28th of August, and by traveling day and night, I arrived upon the hunting grounds of Arkansas, on the 2d of September. I traveled about fourteen hundred miles, passing through Pennsylvania, Western Virginia, Ohio, Indiana, Illinois, Missouri, and more than half of Arkansas. To vary the route in returning, I propose to go by the way of Memphis, Louisville and Cincinnati, thus passing through Tennessee and Kentucky. The weary hours of railroad travel can be profitably employed in comparing other countries with our own State. The longer I live and the more I see of the world, the more I am inclined to be cosmopolitan, and yet I never love Pennsylvania so much as when I compare it with other countries. This may seem paradoxical, but it is not, for while we must like our birthplace and naturally be attached to the scenes with which we are familiar, we can also appreciate the excellencies of other lands and enjoy the beauties of other countries.

While Pennsylvania abounds in agricultural and mineral wealth, Arkansas is truly rich in her well-timbered forests, fertile bottom lands, and undeveloped, but rich prairies, every foot of which is capable of cultivation and only awaits the hand of the husbandman, to make them blossom like the rose.

The climate is salubrious, the face of the country varied from broad meadows to rolling prairies, undulating hills and green mountains. The hot springs are among the natural wonders of the world, and can only be appreciated by being visited. The waters are more abundant than any others of the kind ; some of them are so hot as almost to scald the hand when thrust into them. To bathe in them they must be tempered with cold water. They will boil an egg or cook a fish in their natural temperature. They are highly medicinal, and are resorted to by invalids from all parts of the earth. The warm springs and medicinal waters, so celebrated in Europe, dwindle into absolute insignificance when compared with the hot springs of Arkansas.

The people of the State are intelligent, well-informed, kind and universally hospitable. True, the laws are seldom resorted to for the redress of mere personal injuries. No man was ever hung in Arkansas for killing his enemy in a personal rencontre, but murderers for money, thieves and burglars, receive speedy justice, and seldom escape with their lives. No gentleman, however, who knows how to respect himself, need fear his ability to secure the respect of others. The men are a little inclined to profanity and undue indulgence in gaming, but they are generous in disposition and honest in their business intercourse with their fellow-men. They are exceedingly sensitive upon points of personal honor, and quick to resent insult. After close observation, I am satisfied that there is just as much refinement in the city of Little Rock, as can be found in any of our Eastern cities. This is especially true of the ladies. They are unsurpassed in personal beauty ; possess great conversational qualities and really charm one by the ease and elegance of their manners. They possess the peculiar faculty of making one feel at once at home. In the rural districts and on the prairies, the people are very primitive in their habits. No commodious and comfortable farm houses, barns, and out buildings, such as abound in Pennsylvania, are to be seen here. Well-to-do farmers dwell in one-story log houses. without carpets and with only the most indispensable rustic furniture, yet it is truly surprising to see the substantial comfort they manage to extract, from their rude accommodations. There are no country taverns for the entertainment of travelers, but there is no difficulty in finding shelter for the night in the farm houses above described. Some comical stories are told of the embarrassment of Eastern travelers on such occasions.

The following was told of a Jew peddler. We will permit him to tell his own story : " Vell I vas very tired ven I arrive at Jake's house on the grand prairie. Jake said he not have much room ; he said I could schleep on de sofa by the fire, or I could schleep mit der childrens in de bed. Vell, I say Jake, I ish much tired and I gess I schleep on de sofa by myself. I schleep first rate all night. In de morning I vas wakened by the laugh and talk of two bouncing fine girls getten de breakfeast. De most young vas about sixteen. I say, "My deer, whare are de little children ?" She laugh and say *she* vas de baby, and dat she and sister vas de only children in the house. Den I feel awful bad, and I say to myself— "*By Gimminy, ish dat so o-o.*"

A correct idea of life in Arkansas cannot be formed without a glance, in passing, at the negro population. Some of them are quite smart ; all are loquacious and clannish, especially in their religious societies. Carncross & Dixey's exhibitions of negro life, would afford but little amusement here. The veritable scenes witnessed in some of the social gatherings of the race, far surpass in ludicrous extravagance, all the fictitious inventions so ably portrayed by those artists. The Sheriff of Jefferson county vouches for the following :

A bitter feud existed between the Baptists and Methodists on his plantation. The consequence was that any depredation committed by one party was sure to be exposed by the other, and therefore, his hogs, sheep and poultry were more than usually secure. At last a Baptist orother made a feast, and to supply his table, he stole one of his Methodist brother's sheep for which he was sent to jail for three months. Upon his liberation from prison, the Baptist brethren called a great meeting to condole with their afflicted brother, and hear his experience while in jail. With great unction and solemnity, he spoke as follows : " My dear brederin Paul was in jail— Silas was dare, and so was Peter—and, bress de Lord, dis old nigger hab been dare, too. *Nobody knows how near he can git to God, till he gits in jail.*" On another occasion, the Sheriff attended an experience meeting of the Methodist brethren. An old gray-haired saint gave his experience. He told of all his trials and temptations, and how he had withstood them : " And now," said he, " I'se soon gwine home to glory, to dwell forever with de patriarchs and de prophets, de *bims* and de cherubims."

The Sheriff also tells the following war story : He was an officer in the Union army. One night, on the eve of a very severe battle, he was waited upon in his tent by one of his colored soldiers who could neither read or write and who requested assistance in writing a letter to his wife. He took a pen and some paper and told the poor fellow to dictate, and he would write his letter for him. The letter ran thus : "I take my pen in hand to inform you that I am well and that we are going to have a hard fight to-morrow, in which I will most likely be killed and I hope these few lines will find you in the enjoyment of the same blessing. After the battle I will write you again." He then paused, scratched his head and seemed to hesitate ; "well, have you anything else to say," said the Sheriff. "I guess dats about all," said the soldier, "but don't forget to axe her to please excuse *bad writing and spelling.*"

Little Rock is beautifully situated on the high southern bank of the river Arkansas, from which the State takes its name. The name is here pronounced Arkansaw, which I submit, upon the principle that every person must be presumed to know how to pronounce his own name, is the proper pronunciation, Webster to the contrary, notwithstanding.* The city takes its name from a rock which projects into the river at the spot which was the nucleus of the town. It was called *Little* Rock to distinguish it from another very large one also projecting into the river a short distance further up. In 1850 the population of the place was but 2,167. It now contains about 20,000. In 1803 Arkansas was a part of French Louisiana, which accounts for the pronunciation of its name. Its French origin may also be readily discovered from the peculiar pronunciation of all words ending with the French adverbial termination *ment*, such as regiment, government, settlement, &c., the accent here among the descendants of the original settlers, being almost universally placed upon the last instead of the first syllable.

The physical configuration of the State varies from rich alluvial bottoms lands, (annually overflowed by the rivers and intersected with great swamps and small lakes), to hills and mountains, ranging from a few feet to nearly a thousand yards in height, and from vast level prairies to well watered, extensively wooded, and undulating lands. The State is rich in undeveloped mineral wealth, such as coal, iron, zinc, lead and copper. Many of the stories so industriously circulated in the North, of the uncivilized condition of Arkansas, are absolutely false—true it is rather a rough place for a horse thief, and the courts are seldom troubled with personal quarrels—the pistol and bowie knife are the general arbiters of all such conflicts. To live peaceably here, all that is required, is to conduct one's self just as he would in Pennsylvania. Murders are however more frequent, and human life seems to be less secure than in other parts of the Union. Like the rattlesnake, which, by the way, is at home in Arkansas, the offended citizen usually gives his antagonist ample warning before he strikes. When

---

*Note.—Since this letter was written, Webster has corrected his pronunciation of the name.

he straightens himself up with indignant defiance, and says—
" By G—d, sah ! I'm a gentleman, sah ! Ef you dispute it,
sah ! I'll *kearv* (carve) you, sah !" The offender has one of
three things to do ; apologize, retreat, or prepare at once to
kearv or be carved.

But I am occupying too much ground. Instead of descanting upon the life and manners of the people, I desire to
give a brief description of our hunt upon the prairies. Our
party consisted of six hunters, five dogs and one servant.
(Among hunters the dog takes precedence to the servant). The
usual mode is to take a tent and camp out wherever chance
leaves you at the end of the day. We, however, not wishing
to be embarrassed with camp equipments, resolved to rough it,
and sleep under our wagons if we could find no better shelter.
Our provisions consisted of boiled ham, breakfast bacon, bread,
coffee, tea and a *little* whisky. Being all temperance men we
at first resolved to proscribe the whisky, but as rattlesnakes
were abundant on the prairies, we concluded to take a small
quantity as an antidote to their bite, and we unanimously
agreed that *five* gallons would be enough. To our credit be
it known, that we brought *some* of it back to Little Rock, but
unfortunately the keg with its remaining contents was stolen
from us by the ferryman as we crossed the river at midnight,
so we were deprived of the evidence of our own abstemious-
ness.

To reach the grand prairie from Little Rock, we traveled
by rail about forty miles to Carlisle, where teams were in
waiting. From Carlisle, to the commencement of the shooting ground is some ten or fifteen miles further. It was near
night when we set out from Carlisle with two double teams
well loaded with ourselves, our equipments and dogs. The
wagons were comfortable enough but without covers, and as
it threatened rain, which soon descended in torrents, rendering the night pitchy dark, we had the romantic prospect of
spending it under our wagons, wet to the skin. To add to
our trouble, the roads, (which here are only single trails,
never laid out or repaired by any public authority, and often
difficult to follow in daylight and impossible to find at night)
ran through the edge of a wood. We had no lanterns and to
pick our way through it, we had to get out and strike matches.
Emerging at last from the wood, we saw a light, and without
regard to the road, we pulled directly to it. It proved to be
one of the small farm houses before described. The only persons at home were a small boy of nine years and his sister of
about fourteen. Without much ceremony we took possession
of the establishment, tethered our horses and mules, and passed a very comfortable night. We were now on the skirt of

the grand prairie. It is ninety miles long by about thirty broad; looks like a great sea of grass with here and there what seems to be small clumps of wood, called islands, but which proved to be several thousand acres of woodland. These islands are the marks by which the prairie is navigated by day; at night the compass or stars are the guides. The prairie is well stocked with chickens, quail and rabbits. It is no uncommon thing to raise a few deer. They, however are generally found in the wood, or slashes, where from the increased moisture, the grass is very tall and rank, thus affording them better shelter. We commenced shooting soon after quitting our quarters for the first night, and continued the sport throughout the week. We started three fine deer, and could have secured them all if we had been provided with saddles and hounds. They were raised by the dogs about one hundred yards from our wagons. Of course, I got the buck fever, and would hardly have shot at them if they had jumped from under our horses.

The hunting was all done in the wagons. The prairies can be traversed without any regard to the trails or roads. The horses were driven in a trot, and the dogs made to range on each side of the wagons. If a bird rises within range it is shot from the wagon, or if too far off, it is marked and approached in the teams to within about a hundred yards of its alighting place, often a quarter of a mile distant. The hunters then descend from the wagons and follow the dogs till they come to a stand, then advancing slowly till the bird rises, the quickest shot brings him down. But few birds escape when thus raised. When they get up in coveys, the skill of the hunter is shown in his ability to mark the alighting places of the scattered birds, and raise and shoot them, one at a time. We saw several genuine river rail birds in the centre of the prairie. To be sure of it, I shot one and found it plump and fat, just as we find them along the Delaware. In some seasons the chickens are so plentiful that hundreds are shot in a day, but considering the size of the bird no true sportsman would indulge in such useless slaughter. Twenty-five or thirty birds a day are enough to satisfy ordinary ambition. This was our daily average during the week, and furnished ample food for ourselves and dogs and left a large number to be thrown away, the weather being too warm to keep them over a day.

The sport was all that could be expected or desired. The company was agreeable and harmonious, and the enjoyment was a full compensation for its cost. I am very favorably impressed with Arkansas.

V.

A HUNT ON THE BLUE RIDGE—A POLITICIAN AND A FORGET-
FUL PARTY—AN UNPLEASANTNESS AND AN EXPLANATION
—BATTLEFIELDS AND BEAUTIFUL SCENERY—ROANOKE—
A WONDERFUL SPRING—TARIFF DEMOCRATS—WAR REC-
OLLECTIONS—A DIVIDED HOUSE—GOOD SPORT—THE
SLEEP OF INNOCENCE—"THE ELEGANT AND THE BOLD
MCINTYRE"—HUNTING ON HORSEBACK—THE PLEASURES
OF THE HUNT—EPITAPH TO MAHONE.

November 6th, 1883.

On the morning of the General Election, too early to vote,
we took the 1.30 train for Roanoke, Va., for a few days'
quail shooting among the mountains, at the head of the beautiful Shenandoah Valley. We are four true Republicans, and
that our votes might not be lost, we paired with the same
number of honest Democrats at home. A sacred regard for
truth requires me to confess that one of our party was a politician. He boasted of the vile trick he had played upon *three*
confiding Democrats, by pairing with them all instead of one.
It was the same old story, innocence and confidence betrayed
by shrewdness and treachery. "O Liberty, what crimes have
been committed in thy name."

Upon our arrival at Roanoke about midnight, we were
greeted by our genial old friend and former fellow-citizen, Col.
David F. Houston, whose hospitality we enjoyed during our
entire stay.

When a hunter strikes the trail of game, he may forget
the cares at home ; he may, for the time, forget his wife, but
never his dog. Our party were an exception to the general
rule. One of us forgot his dog ; another forgot a ten dollar
box of segars which he left in the car at Baltimore , another
forgot a pack of cards purchased especially to while away the
weary hours of travel, and the other forgot to kiss his wife
before he left home, but he did not forget a good supply of
medicine, pure double distilled extract of rye, a sure remedy
against malaria, snake bites, etc.

The politician of our party was chosen *game* keeper, not
in the English sense of the word, to preserve the game from
poachers, but rather to keep the record of our games at cards.
I have fully made up my mind never to trust a politician—I
caught him, in the most innocent manner, recording the score
in the wrong column. I, in a subdued tone, remarked that
the man who would cheat three confiding Democrats out of

their votes would take advantage of his friends, at card.   He flew into a rage ; sprang to his feet ; thrust his right hand into his hip pocket and in a voice of thunder demanded an explanation.   With a mildness and good temper for which I have always been noted, I told him I could conscientiously swear that he was as honest in cards as Ben Butler was in politics, and could be trusted as far.   This appeased his honor, and, to the great relief of all, instead of pulling out a pistol from his hip pocket, he drew forth a bottle of whisky and we all took a drink.

When his hand went into his hip pocket, all the blooded Virginians in the car jumped to their feet, expecting to be regaled with a scene of blood and carnage for which the South is notorious.   They seemed disgusted at the denouement.

From Hagerstown to Roanoke the scenery is very pretty. We passed very near the battlefield of Antietam.   Gaines' Station was an outpost—every acre around Sharpsburg has been red with war's blood—5,000 Federal soldiers sleep here. Three miles from Sharpsburg the train crosses the Potomac. One mile below is the "Old Pack-Horse Ford."   Just above the ford is a rocky precipice where three thousand Union soldiers fell, among them many of our Corn Exchange Regiment. The scenery around reminds us of the headlines to the war news—

    "All is quiet along the Potomac."

We passed the famous Luray Caves but had not time to enter them.   We also passed within a stone's throw of the renowned Natural Bridge.   While passing over the summit of the Blue Ridge we were within sight of Chambersburg, with the Cumberland Mountains plainly visible in the west.

Roanoke is a thriving town of about six thousand population.   It is in the latitude of Norfolk and longitude of Pittsburgh.   In 1879 it had but six hundred inhabitants.   It is beautifully situated between the Alleghenies and the Blue Ridge and is about eight hundred feet above sea level.   Mountains are all around the town.   Mill Mountain is only two miles away.   From its base gushes a remarkable spring of crystal clear water, flowing 5,000,000 gallons a day.   The water from this spring turns several mills and yields an abundant supply for the water works of the town.   The greatest industrial establishment of the place is the Crozer Steel and Iron Works.   The works closely resemble the plant in South Chester.   The town has a good hotel, a bank, several schools and churches, planing mills, lumber yards and extensive car works.

The Shenandoah Valley is very fertile ; there are also some

good farms on the top of the Blue Ridge. Land is worth about $100 per acre. The country is full of iron and limestone. I prophesy for Roanoke a successful future. The white people are as a rule Democrats, but favorable to a protective tariff.

The Republican party of the South is very different from the same party of the North. The gentleman's party here is the Democratic. It is amusing to listen to the war recollections of the old soldiers. One gentleman told me he was a school boy when the war broke out. He said all the students were anxious to enter the army before the war should end and the Yankees be destroyed. They were taught that no Northern man could ride a horse or shoot a gun, and that the Federal officers tied the cavalry soldiers to their saddles to keep them from falling off or running away.

There is, in the town, a house (now two homes), which had been built by two men. They had been close friends from youth and determined to live and die under the same roof. After the home was built, the friends quarreled over a game of cards. The feud became so furious that they determined to part forever. Each seized a saw and never stopped sawing till they had cut the house in two, from the roof to the ground. They then cut the cards for the choice of the parts, moved the two halves about twenty feet apart, boarded up the ends and have lived neighbors ever since.

We spent two days in hunting. To the uninitiated, a tramp over the mountains, through the valleys, over seven feet high worm fences, under bushes and over ditches, is a little tiresome, especially if one has to carry over two hundred pounds of man and twenty pounds of gun and shells.

We raised the first day six coveys of fine birds and had very good shooting. About 11 A. M., the birds seek cover and are hard to find. Being somewhat fatigued, by common consent we stretched ourselves on the leafy mountain side and were soon sound asleep, dreaming of the election and the defeat of Mahone. In about an hour we were aroused by the stentorian but melodious voice of Geoff. Denis, our companion from Ridley, singing in his best operatic style his favorite song, " The Elegant and the Bold McIntyre." His splendid voice echoed along the mountains like the roar of a locomotive among hollow hills.

We spent most of the next morning upon the plantation of General Smith, on the summit of the Blue Ridge. We hunted on horseback. The horses are well broken and stand fire without a flinch. Our dogs were young, and badly broken ; they flushed the birds and could not "retrieve." We bagged, all told, one hundred and sixty-eight fine, full grown and fat partridges. If our dogs had been well broken, we could have shot twice as many.   There are wild turkeys in the mountains but they, like some voters, can only be caught by a still hunt.

Upon the whole, we had quite an enjoyable time.   The pleasures of a hunt are not all comprised in the amount of game killed.   It is largely made up of congenial companionship, open air exercise, good digestion and, above all, a contented mind.   Our wine, though perhaps not as expensive, is more refreshing, and our food, though not as well cooked, tastes better than at home.   We can look with more complacency upon nature's beautiful. sun-lit face ; we enjoy her wild secluded haunts and can feel " what I cannot express nor cannot all conceal."   In a word we feel *free*, emancipated from the annoyances of civilization ; we feel like Adam felt before he bit that accursed apple.

At 11 A. M., three days after our arrival, we bade farewell to beautiful Roanoke.   On our way home we passed the time in the same merry manner that we spent the fleeting hours on our journey out.

At Charlotteville we saw, written with chalk, on the side of a freight car, the following epitaph upon Mr. Mahone, who had just met his disastrous defeat at the polls :

> "Beneath this sacred slab of stone
> Reposes the body of Billy Mahone.
> He was dwarfed in mind
> And was small in figure ;
> He was cho'ced to death
> By swallowing a nigger."

VI.

A WINTER IN FLORIDA—DOUBLE CELEBRATION OF FEBRU-
ARY 22, 1890—JACKSONVILLE—ST. AUGUSTINE, THE OLD-
EST CITY IN AMERICA—HISTORICAL SKETCH OF FLORIDA
—HOTEL PONCE DE LEON, ITS PROBABLE FATE—AMERI-
CAN DISPOSITION TO EXAGGERATE.

February 22, 1890.

This is a fete day in Florida ; it is not only Washington's birthday, but also the day that Florida was ceded by Spain to the United States of America in 1819.   She did not become a sister State of the Union until March 3, 1845.   The programme for the day is a great base ball contest between the choice players of Jacksonville and St. Augustine in the afternoon, and a grand ball at the Casino in the evening, with a splendid display of fireworks in the park.

The city has about 10,000 inhabitants exclusive of visit-ors, which at this time will swell the population to about 15,000. There are people here from all parts of our common country, but more from the North than from any other part of the United States. The season for visitors opens January 1st and closes May 1st ; after that time it is too warm for comfort. The thermometer now stands at about 80° at noon, but falls to 50° or 60° at night. We sleep under mosquito bars. There are no fires in our rooms ; the windows and doors are all open ; in a word, the temperature is about that of June in the latitude of Philadelphia. Our hotel is named after Juan Ponce de Leon, who sighted the coast off St. Augustine in 1513, and took possession of Florida in the name of the King of Spain. In 1521 he was its Governor. De Soto discovered Tampa in 1539. St. Augustine is the oldest city within the present limits of the United States, and, for this reason, is a very in-teresting place. The Spanish, French, and English had many severe contests for the final possession of Florida. The Eng-lish having possession of Havana exchanged it for Florida. During the Revolutionary struggle, about seven thousand loy-alists from Georgia and the Carolinas moved to Florida. The treaty of peace between the United States and England did not include Florida. England afterwards ceded it to Spain, but just before the war of 1812 our government seized the territory to keep it from again falling into the hands of Great Britain. General Jackson was made Governor. 1 remember very distinctly the breaking out of the Seminole Indian war, which lasted nearly seven years. Osceola was the great Semi-nole chief. The Indians were finally driven to the swamps and by bloodhounds and starvation, were finally compelled to sur-render. In that war Zachary Taylor, Col. Twiggs, Col. Har-ney and Gen. Worth were active participants. They were afterwards noted for their valor in the Mexican war.

In 1845 Florida was admitted as a State of the Union. In 1861 she passed an ordinance of secession and consequently became the scene of many conflicts between the Federal and Confederate forces.

Florida would not be worth much without the Northern blood, money and enterprise injected into it since the close o. the rebellion. Millions of dollars have been emptied into her lap by capitalists of the North and Northwest. Her great attraction is her delightful climate during the winter. We have just received a telegram from Boston, stating that the thermometer there is at zero ; here it is too warm for comfort in the sunshine. Ladies and gentlemen are now promenading in their summer dresses.

Flowers are in full bloom and the ground in the orange

groves is covered with fruit. Insects fly around the electric lights almost as large as birds. Snakes and alligators are abundant and the mosquitoes are as wicked as the same species of New Jersey blood-suckers, in July.

The tourist can take the cars at Philadelphia and need not leave the train until he arrives at Jacksonville. The sleeping cars are comfortable and the meals served in the dining car well cooked and satisfactory. The route is very uninteresting. From Philadelphia to Jacksonville I saw nothing worth opening my eyes to see. The entire scenery is very much like that from Philadelphia to Atlantic City. The time by rail from Philadelphia to St. Augustine is about thirty-six hours.

Jacksonville has a population of about 35,000. Its latitude is 30.24. It was incorporated as a city in 1833. It has several very fair hotels. Most of the streets are unpaved; some are paved with cypress wood, sawed in blocks from the round logs, four inches long by six inches in diameter. These blocks are placed on their ends and make a very good pavement in the sandy soil. There being no frost to break up the streets, when once made, they last several years. The unpaved streets are almost hub deep with sand. The public squares are planted with a very pretty species of wild orange and lemon trees, loaded with tempting fruit. A visitor to the city for the first time naturally wonders how the beautiful yellow oranges are preserved from the depredations of boys and hungry pedestrians; if, however, he tries the fruit, the mystery is solved. They are as bitter as gall and entirely unfit for the palate even of a tramp.

The Hotel Ponce de Leon, of St. Augustine, is said to be one of the largest and best in the world; it is certainly very large and beautiful, especially in design; in execution there is nothing to excite the wonder of the visitor. It is the property of a single individual, one of the kings of the Standard Oil Company; besides the hotel, he is the proprietor of the best part of the city and surrounding country. At first sight, by contrast with the buildings of Jacksonville and other towns in Florida, the hotel strikes the eye with most charming effect. Its Spanish style, grand court yard, gardens and parks of tropical plants, fruits and flowers, when contrasted with the sterile sand banks, swamps and towns of wood and dust through which we have passed in reaching it, give it the effect of an oasis in a desert. The extravagant estimates of its cost, however, must be taken *cum grano salis*. I have no patience with the disposition of our American reporters for the press, to exaggerate everything they attempt to describe. Some of them have gone into ecstasies over this building and have estimated its cost at $5,000,000. A little reflection would at once dispel such an extravagant delusion. The annual interest on five million dollars would be $300,000 ; the cost of repairs and running the hotel added to this would swell the expense of the establishment to, perhaps, $350,000, all of which would have to be earned in four months to pay a decent rent, without any profit to the proprietor. The hotel would therefore lose money unless it earned from $3,000 to $4,000 per day. No one but an idiot would make such an investment. None of the managers of the Standard Oil Company are fools ; ergo, the hotel did not cost over the one-fifth of the sum named.

I was shown a mantel of onyx, in the grand parlor, which I was assured cost $40,000. I do not believe it cost over $2000. As before stated, the design of the building and grounds is strikingly beautiful, but it is very deficient in execution. It is constructed of red brick relieved by artificial blocks of composition resembling grey stone. The interior is finished with carved oak and slabs of very highly polished marble. A fire once under way, would reduce the whole structure to ashes in a very short time. This will probably be its fate.

We have resolved to leave here on Monday morning for Tampa and there take ship for Cuba.

VII.

Florida to Key West—Winter Park—Orange Groves —Hotel Seminole—Lakes, Fish and Game—Kissemee, a Conductor's Mistaken Pronunciation—Sugar and the Tariff—Good Cars but Bad Roads—Port Tampa's Hotel Built on a Pier a Mile Out in the Gulf—Key West and its Wedded Fig Tree—A Portuguese Man-of-War—Havana — Bad Passport Regulations and Worse Money—New Stars—The Ashes of Columbus— Sudden Changes of Temperature—Singular Street Sights—Theatre on Sunday.

HAVANA, March, 1890.

After a few days at St. Augustine the first feeling of surprise at it's soft and summer-like climate passes off. We soon grow weary of warm weather and long for the stimulating breezes of our own active and energetic country.

We found ourselves with a week to spare and resolved to utilize it by a visit to Cuba. After much telegraphy and annoying delays, we secured berths on the ship Olivette, which sailed from Port Tampa on Thursday, February 27th. To economize the interval we stopped at Winter Park, about one

hundred and twenty miles south of St. Augustine. We were
agreeably surprised to find it a most delightful winter retreat,
as warm and pleasant as Atlantic City in July. In the evening
and morning the temperature stood at about 70°. At noon it
reached 82°. There is an excellent hotel and flourishing settlement there. The society now wintering there is of the very
best, having among the guests of the hotel several rich and
ripe widows with fortunes ranging from five hundred thousand
to two millions. I should take it to be a paradise for fortune
hunters. Within a squre of six miles there are some of the
finest orange groves of the State. We took a drive among
them and were permitted to pluck and eat the golden fruit. It
tastes much sweeter when pulled ripe from the trees. We also
saw pine apples growing, but as they are a purely tropical
fruit they were sheltered from the north wind by a board
fence. The hotel "Seminole" has two hundred rooms and can
accommodate five hundred guests. It is situated on the edge
of eleven beautiful little lakes, all of which can be seen from
the promenade on the roof. Some of these lakes are larger
than those of Killarny in Ireland, and are said to be seventy
feet deep. The water is very pure and soft and can be drank
with impunity. This cannot be said of Jacksonville and St.
Augustine.

A little steamboat makes two tours daily of the largest
lakes (each tour takes about an hour). Alligators may be
sometimes seen basking in the sun on the shores, but they are
very shy and are not often visible. The lakes are full of very
fine fish which are caught at all times by the guests of the
house. The fish caught while we were there weighed from
one to three pounds each. Partridges are also plentiful but
the weather is so warm they must be cooked the same day they
are shot. A gentleman sportsman the last day we were there,
with two good setter dogs, brought to the hotel a bag of over
fifty. I am inclined to think he bought some of them for I
noticed they smelt rather strong for a day's shooting. He was,
however, willing to swear that he shot them all in one day.
While taking a ride along the lake road I saw a fine covey of
at least twenty birds, almost as tame as little chickens.

There has been no rain in Southern Florida for about four
months ; as a consequence the roads are very deep, dusty and
sandy. It took our two-horse team two hours to travel, with
four persons and a driver, six miles. The country is very dry
and has a thirsty and barren look. At night forest fires can
be seen in the surrounding pine woods. The place owes all
its prosperity to Northern capital and enterprise. Its latitude
is about 28° ; longitude about 81°. Continuing, upon the
parallel of latitude eastward, would take us about five hundred

miles further south than the Straits of Gibraltar and far into the interior of Africa. If this place possessed the soil of Pennsylvania it would be the paradise of the world. As it now looks, it resembles the lower part of the State of New Jersey stocked with palms, bananas, orange trees, and subtropical fruits and flowers. The soil, however, is not sand but rather a rich sandy loam. The orange trees will not flourish in too much sand. Ugly snakes and poisonous insects are quite numerous in the uncultivated parts of the country.

The lands of Florida can only be profitably cultivated by great labor. The richest lands are reclaimed by canals and ditches. Mr. H. Disston, of Philadelphia, owns about 5,000-000 acres at a place called *Kissemee*, about twenty miles south of Winter Park. A lady on the train asked the conductor what place it was. He innocently replied *Kiss-mee*! She blushed and said he must think she was green to kiss a man in the *day* time on a railroad car.

Mr. Disston is spending a very large amount of money in reclaiming the swamp land. I met him at St. Augustine and received a very cordial invitation to spend a day on his plantation Claus Spreckles, the great anti-Trust sugar king, visited his place a few days ago. From the accounts published in the Florida papers he was very favorably impressed with Mr. Disston's ability to successfully raise sugar cane upon his lands.

The people of Florida are rapidly becoming Protectionists so far as phosphates, oranges and sugar are concerned. Without a protective tariff it will be impossible for Florida to compete with Cuba, the Sandwich, and the Philippine Isles in the cultivation of sugar. Mr. Spreckles says we import $100,000,-000 worth of raw sugar yearly from these islands and get nothing in return. He also says that wages in those countries are only about ten cents a day. Without a tariff to equalize the difference between labor there and here, it will be impossible for us to compete with them.

A great drawback to the pleasure of traveling in Florida is the great distance and uninteresting scenery between the points of interest in the State. The railroads are single tracks; there are constant delays caused by wrecks of freight trains and the want of a perfect system among the different roads ; a delay of from three to seven hours is no uncommon thing. In our journey from Winter Park to Tampa we were delayed two hours, which gave us an opportunity to drive down to the city and get a good dinner while waiting for our train.

Tampa is a town of about 7,000 inhabitants, two hundred and eighty miles south from Jacksonville, and about seven miles from Port Tampa, on the Gulf of Mexico. It is about two hundred and ten miles from Key West and three hundred miles from Havana.

Port Tampa is built on piles and has a very good hotel about a mile out in the bay, where the guests may amuse themselves by fishing from their chamber windows. It is a delightfully cool place and full of fish. It is quite amusing to sit on the pier or look out of your chamber window and see great pelicans, as large as domestic geese, rise some thirty feet out of the water by a lazy flop of their wings, and then suddenly fold them and with head and beak down plunge into the sea like a dart upon some poor little fish that has approached too near the surface and which seldom escapes.

On the evening of the 27th we embarked, and at 3.30 P. M. the next day we landed at Key West, where we spent six hours exploring the little island—only about three miles wide by seven miles long. On our voyage to Key West we saw a kind of Nautilus with its tiny sail set to the wind and gliding over the rough waves like a little boat. They call it " A Portuguese man-of-war " I had never seen one before and was very much interested in the little sailor. Some of them had their sails down and were simply floating on the waves.

Key West is not much of a place. It has a population of about 20,000, most of them employed in the manufacture of Havana cigars. They make the cigars in Key West to save the tariff the Cubans would have to pay on our broad-leaved tobacco, used as a wrapper on the large cigars made here. The Cuban variety has a narrow leaf from which only small sized cigars can be made. By using the Virginia broad leaf for a wrapper, a much larger and more salable cigar can be made. This is the secret of cigar making in Key West. There are a few handsome buildings on the island but the most of the city is built of mean wooden huts None of the houses have chimneys. The finest building on the island is the new Methodist Church. The island is full of fine tropical trees and plants, but has no good water. One of the sights of the place is the wedded fig and palm tree. The fig tree is about twenty-five feet high, and at its root is nearly three feet in diameter ; about twenty feet up the tree a splendid palm tree crops out and has grown fully thirty feet above the highest limbs of the fig tree. The union seems perfect and is certainly very curious.

We sailed for Havana at 11 P. M., and arrived in the harbor at sunrise. No ship is permitted to enter the port until after that hour. We were permitted to enter the city without having our passports *vised*, but were not allowed to depart without having them properly examined by the Spanish authorities at least three days before embarkation. Very much like the privilege the mouse has to enter the trap without objection, but he often finds it difficult to get out again. If the traveler neglects to have his passport *vised* in time he is subjected to the annoyance of securing the service of some hanger-on who as a great favor will get his papers fixed up at an extra cost of two or three dollars. The people of Havana look upon American visitors as legitimate game. The charge for disembarkation to a Cuban is forty cents, and a further charge of forty cents for a cab lands him at his hotel. It cost our party about four dollars each to get from the ship to the hotel. The currency of the country is in a most deplorable condition ; gold is at one hundred and sixty per cent. premium. A $5 U. S. greenback will buy $12.50 in Cuban currency. The hotel prices are charged in gold and are very high for the accommodations offered. I paid fifteen dollars a day, gold, for rooms for three, in the third story.

Havana and Key West are shaded by tropical trees, such as palms, cocoanut trees sixty feet high, date trees, banana plants, etc., presenting a very strange and beautiful scene to the eye of a Pennsylvanian.

The stars look different from the same little twinklers at home. We see stars never looked upon in the latitude of Philadelphia. The brightest stranger to us was Canopus, in the *Argo Navis*. It is a star of the first magnitude, about thirty-six degrees below Sirius. At eight P. M. it is due south about twenty degrees above the horizon. The North star is twenty degrees lower and the stars of the Southern hemisphere about twenty degrees higher than they are in the latitude of Philadelphia. Cuba is about twenty degrees north latitude. Every degree we go south, Polaris descends one degree and the southern stars rise in the same proportion. Under favorable conditions the principal stars in the Southern Cross can be seen from Cuba.

Nobody but laborers leave their beds in Havana before nine A. M. They have but two meals a day and, compared with the bills of fare in Northern hotels, the provisions are poor. The universal motto of the people of Cuba is, " Never do to-day what may be done to-morrow." We were charged ten dollars an hour for a carriage and guide to see the city. The charge, however, was in Cuban money.

The city is fairly built and looks very much like a modern Spanish town ; the houses are covered with stucco of a yellowish tint ; a striking peculiarity of the place is the entire absence of chimneys and smoke ; no fires are in the houses except for cooking. The population of the city is about 250,000. We visited the two principal churches, and drove over the main streets and suburbs. The old Cathedral presents rather a pretty appearance in the interior, but is much better in design than execution. It is covered with stucco and painted in imitation of marble. For a fee of two dollars we were shown the rich vestments of the bishop and the sacerdotal robes of the priests and high church officials ; they were very beautifully and expensively wrought. They also showed us the spot where the ashes of Columbus are said to repose. At Seville, last year, they showed me the tomb of the same old sailor. San Domingo also claims the honor of his grave. The Cubans say that his remains were brought from San Domingo to Havana in 1795. Columbus discovered Cuba October 28, 1492. The island is about seven hundred and ninety miles long by from twenty-two to one hundred and seventeen miles wide. It contains 55,000 square miles and is consequently much larger than the State of Pennsylvania.

I do not believe Cuba is a healthy place. Havana is never free from yellow fever ; the rainy season commences in May and continues till November ; the vegetation is rank and the temperature seldom below 60° ; frosts are unknown and there is nothing to kill the microbes of disease. When we arrived we found the streets, trees, shrubs, flowers and houses covered with a white, disagreeable dust ; there had been no rain since last November ; the temperature stood at about 90° ; the wind was high and great clouds of dust were sweeping through the streets, almost blinding our eyes. About 5 o'clock P. M., on the second day of our visit, a sudden storm swept over the city ; the streets were soon flooded, giving to the houses a fresh and clean appearance, and brightening the trees and flowers ; soon the temperature fell to 65°, which they say is the coldest it has been for a year. We felt very comfortable in our winter clothing. The sea soon lashed itself into a great fury ; the waves dashed against the rock-bound coast, sending their spray entirely over the lighthouse, and Moro Castle, at least one hundred feet high. From the fact that the whole town seemed excited, and crowded the streets to look at the roaring sea and mad waves, I took it for granted that the storm was an unusually severe one for the place.

In some of the streets we saw sights that reminded us of Naples—such as naked men and children. Some were entirely nude, others barely covering the hips and thighs. We also saw great displays of wealth as well as squalor and abject poverty. As we drove out to the cemetery we met and passed eight funerals ; two of the funerals were evidently of grandees. One of the hearses was covered with flowers and was drawn by six horses draped in white ; the driver was dressed in rich livery ; the out-riders wore gold lace and carried great bouquets of flowers, and a long line of splendid coaches followed the remains to the tomb. The other was very much the same but the horses and drapery were black. None but men occupied the carriages ; they were all smoking and seemed to be in rather a jolly mood. Just after this splendid display, came five or six poorly clad men carrying a black pine coffin on their shoulders, in a full run. The lid had not been fastened down and every now and then it flew up several inches exposing the shrouded corpse within. They were running to get the corpse buried before the threatening storm should come to interfere with the funeral. We were told that the coffin had been hired and that the poor corpse was to be thrown into a grave, always ready—a bushel of lime and a little earth were to be its only burial, the coffin was to be returned and perhaps before night some other poor creature was to occupy the same box and the same common grave. We also saw four little boys, of unequal sizes, carrying their little sister to the grave, each boy holding one end of two straps upon which the little coffin was swung. Just behind the funerals came two large droves of horses, five abreast. The first line had riders upon them ; the others had their heads tied to the tails of the horses that preceded them, while another horse was tied to the tail of the horse ahead of it, and so on to the end of the line. As I never saw a drove of horses conducted in this way before it looked quite comical.

There is not much of great interest to be seen in Havana. Its chief attraction is its soft, balmy climate, and its tropical fruits and flowers. The island is very fertile and presents a beautiful picture as it is approached from the sea. We leave for home to-morrow.

Everybody goes to the theatre here on Sunday. We do not intend to be singular in this respect. We are told that the storm has delayed the ship that was to arrive to-day to take us home. We hope, however, to be able to embark to-morrow for a more congenial land and better governed country.

VIII

FLORIDA, JAMAICA AND BERMUDA—JACKSONVILLE—FEBRU-
ARY HERE LIKE OCTOBER IN PHILADELPHIA—THE DE-
GENERATED SUB-TROPICAL EXHIBITION——EMOTIONAL
WORSHIP OF THE COLORED PEOPLE—SUPERSTITIONS OF
THE RICH AS WELL AS THE POOR—RIVER ST. JOHN—
EARLY SPANISH CRUELTY AND ITS REVENGE—FLORIDA,
ORIGIN OF THE NAME—A STATE THROWN UP FROM THE
SEA—REMARKABLE SUBTERRANEAN RIVERS AND SPRINGS
—THE TIME TABLE UNCERTAIN IN FLORIDA—LIVE OAK—
A LANDLORD'S SINISTER SMILE.

FLORIDA, February, 1891.

"Away down upon the Suwanee River,
Far, far away."

On the twenty-third of January we bade farewell for
a while to the chilly air of Thurlow and, by the Florida
Special, we arrived at Jacksonville on the evening of the
twenty-fourth, just in time to escape the blizzard of which we
have heard so much but have seen nothing. It costs more to
ride on the special train but the comforts secured compensate
for the extra expense. We took rooms at the Windsor, a
well-kept, clean and comfortable hotel. The proprietor is a
Northern man, and "knows how to keep a hotel." This
house is homelike, floors carpeted, table good and beds soft
and promotive of sweet sleep. The pompano and shad are
now plentiful and very toothsome.

On our arrival we found the weather rather cold for
Florida. The thermometer stood at night at about 45°, but
during the day it ranged at from 60° to 70° in the shade. The
winter here has been unusually cold, but there has not been
frost enough to materially injure the orange trees, or to kill
the roses. I noticed the bananas and shot plants had been
severely nipped, but young shoots are beginning to sprout.
By comparison, I would say we are enjoying October weather,
as we have it in the latitude of Philadelphia.

Jacksonville (named after Gen. Jackson), is rapidly improving. It now contains about 30,000 souls, besides 10,000
negroes (without souls). Most of the suburban streets are
almost impassable with deep, dirty sand. A few are well but
roughly paved with wood, put down in a most primitive style.
The city, with a few noteworthy exceptions, is built of wood
and of the simplest kind of architecture. Bay Street is the
chief business avenue and contains some really handsome and

rather imposing buildings. It is well paved with wood and looks about as Market Street, in Philadelphia, appeared forty years ago. It runs East and West along the north bank of the St. John's River.

We paid another visit to the Sub-tropical Exposition, expecting to find it as it appeared last winter, but in this we were sorely disappointed. It has degenerated to a third-class show. This is the usual history of all expositions. Some of us remember the miserable fizzle our Philadelphia Centennial Exposition made in trying to keep open after it had formally closed in November, 1876. Instead of setting like the sun in a blaze of glory, it managed to perpetuate a miserable existence for a few years, growing worse and less interesting every year, until its final death from natural decay and absolute neglect. " *Sic transit gloria mundi.*"

The colored people of Jacksonville, like their brethren all over the world, are very emotional and demonstrative in their religious exercises and are very superstitious. In strolling around the city on Sunday, I passed some of their meeting houses and was attracted by the earnestness of their singing and the peculiar energy they exhibited in giving expression to their devotional ejaculations. I passed a dilapidated shanty one story high, the front door hung by hinges made from the soles of old shoes and the shutters swinging on one hinge. Two or three black hogs were rooting in the sand in the yard which was enclosed by old white-washed pickets of different lengths. The house was full to overflowing. Over the front door, painted in lamp-black, was the motto "God is Love." Over the side door an old horse shoe was nailed. I asked an old negro why the horse shoe was nailed over the door. He replied, " Why, massa, don't yo know ? Dat keeps out de witches." " Well," said I, " how about the motto over the front door ?" " O, dat is to keep out de devil." I could but smile at the juxtaposition of the sacred motto with the superstitious use of the horse shoe, and yet it started a train of profitable thought. If the motto had been engraved upon the coat-of-arms of some great man, and emblazoned upon the portals of his palace, how we would admire his piety, even if he did believe that to see, for the first time, the new moon over his left shoulder would bring him bad luck. I knew one of the most intelligent business men of Philadelphia, a man of wealth and culture, who implicitly believed it. I knew a shipping merchant who died leaving immense wealth, who could not be induced for any consideration to permit one of his ships to leave port on a Friday. I knew a very intelligent and successful farmer who always consulted the signs in the almanac before he planted his crops. There is no such thing

as consistency among men.   What we laugh at in the poor
negro, we see every day in the intelligent white man.

There are several daily excursions from Jacksonville, but
of no very great interest except as time-killers.   We grow
ecstatic here over landscapes that would be looked upon with
indifference at home.

The river St. John takes a short turn eastward at Jacksonville and continues in that course for about twenty-three miles
to the sea.   The daily excursion to Mayport, at the mouth of
the river, is of some interest because of the historical events it
recalls.   The remains of two old forts at the mouth of the river
revive some of the tragic history of Florida.   Some French
Huguenots tried to effect a settlement here and built the forts
to defend the river.   They called the river "Rivere de Mai,"
(River May); their settlement they named "Maiporte,"
(Mayport).   A Spanish mariner, named Menendez, captured
the forts and put all his prisoners to death—and this, too, after
they had surrendered and, by all the laws of war, were entitled
to be treated as prisoners.   To excuse his barbarous cruelty
he caused a placard to be set up over the dead prisoners bearing this inscription—"Executed, not as French soldiers, but
as heretics."   Two years later Dominique de Gowzes, a sailor
commanding a French fleet, re-captured the place, and by
authority of the *lex talionis* he hung the entire garrison.   In
imitation of the Spanish conqueror, he also caused a placard
to be nailed upon the trees on which his prisoners were left
hanging, with this inscription painted in black—"Hung, not
as Spaniards, but as murderers."   The retaliation proved
effectual—no more prisoners were hung.   The events above
mentioned transpired about A. D. 1564.

There are several theories as to the origin of the name
"Florida."   The best authenticated theory is that it derived
its name from the Spanish feast day on which it was discovered, "Pascha Floridum," meaning the commencement of
Easter.   Ponce de Leon first discovered the land on that day,
and from "Floridum" the name "Florida" was derived.

Geologically speaking, Florida is a remarkable State.   It
has evidently, at one time, been covered by the sea.   Its sub-
stratum is a shelly rock.   It is full of most remarkable fresh
water springs, some of which are very deep and vomit forth
immense quantities of water.   There is a spring near Tallahasse which has been sounded to the depth of over twelve
hundred feet.   Silver Spring, near Ocala, supplies a river in
itself.   A large three-decked steamboat comes up about five
miles from the confluence of the waters of the spring with the
Ocklawaha river.   The water is twenty feet deep at the spring
and continues of an average depth of ten feet and an average

width of fifty feet for at least five miles, until it empties into
the Ocklawaha. There seems to be a system of subterranean
rivers under the calcareous rock, which break out through its
fissures. After the Charleston earthquake one of the fissures
in the rock at Silver Spring opened about a foot and very per-
ceptibly increased the flow of the spring. This fissure has
been sounded to the depth of eighty feet.

After resting four days at Jacksonville, we settled our
intended itinerary as follows : From Jacksonville to Live Oak,
toward Tallahasse ; Live Oak to New Brandford, at the head
of navigation of the Suwanee ; from there down the river to
the Gulf and over the Gulf to Cedar Key ; from Cedar Key by
rail to Waldo, and from there to Silver Spring ; from Silver
Spring to Ocala (from which I now write), and from there to
Tampa ; thence to Port Tampa, where we will embark for
Jamaica ; a sea voyage of five days ; from Jamaica we will
make a sea voyage to Bermuda and from there by ship to New
York.

We left Jacksonville at seven A. M. and arrived at Live
Oak about eleven A. M. Here we spent a day, which is amply
sufficient. The arrival and departure of the trains is very
uncertain. We concluded, after taking a stroll over the town,
to continue our journey to New Brandford and take the boat
at eight A. M the next day for our trip down the Suwanee.
We were informed by the landlord at Live Oak that the train
would arrive about two P. M. We got our dinner and took
our seats on the porch awaiting the train till after three, when
I thought it best to inquire at the telegraph office when the
train was expected. The operator said it had been delayed
three hours and would arrive at five. We waited till five, when
I ventured to make some further inquiry and was informed
that by reason of some other delay it would not arrive before
seven. We waited until half-past seven, when I got very mad,
engaged a room for the night and went to bed. We were informed the next morning that the train did not get there till
about eleven o'clock at night. We were to take the train the
next morning at 6.40 for New Brandford. The cook seemed
provokingly slow in getting our breakfast ready. We could
not afford to miss the train as the boat was to start at eight
A. M. The landlord smiled. We sat down to breakfast at
seven A. M. ; had hardly taken our seats when along came
the train. We were about siezing what food we could lay our
hands on and running for the train, when the landlord smiled
again. " Don't hurry," said he, " the train always waits till
breakfast is over. I will hold it till you finish your breakfast."
So we deliberately finished our breakfast and took our seats
in the train. I went into the smoker to enjoy a cigar and

discovered the cause of the landlord's sinister smile. There sat the conductor and engineer eating their breakfast, which had been brought over from the hotel.

Live Oak is the county seat. It has a court house and jail, three or four very good stores, a hotel and seven Live Oak trees. The sheriff of the county is a Jew, and is very fond of showing himself to the citizens on horseback. He is a fine looking fellow and rides a good horse with true Southern grace

After the train started I asked the conductor if we would reach New Brandford in time for the boat down the Suwanee. He looked at me rather inquiringly, and I at once saw upon his face the same sinister smile I had noticed on the face of our genial landlord at Live Oak. He simply said, '' The boat won't go till we get there.''

When we arrived at New Brandford we met the obliging purser of the boat at the station. He informed us that the boat had just been supplied with a new boiler, which had not yet been passed by the inspector, and that she could not start without her certificate. He advised us to take rooms at the hotel for the night and that we should have at least an hour's notice before the starting time. We spent just one day at the hotel and, all things considered, we were very well entertained by the kind and obliging landlady who, with her interesting little daughter, did all she could to make our sojourn as agreeable as possible. Of course we did not expect to find Jacksonville or St. Augustine hotels out at the head of the old Suwanee. We had a reasonably good bed and abundance of food, and the kindness and solicitude of the landlady made our pillows soft and gave a relish to our meals.

IX.

NEW BRANDFORD—UNPUNISHED ASSASSINS—LA GRIPPE IN FLORIDA—MORE DELAYS—ONE HUNDRED AND FIVE MILES DOWN THE SUWANEE RIVER—SULPHUR SPRINGS—ALLIGATORS, TURTLES AND WILD TURKEYS—CEDAR KEY—SHUT OUT OF A HOTEL BY THE SHERIFF—A PICNIC—SILVER SPRINGS—THE OCKLAWAHA—HOW THEY SETTLED A DISPUTE OVER THE TITLE TO THE SILVER SPRING HOTEL.—SUGGESTIVE NAMES FOR FLORIDA TOWNS.

FLORIDA, February 11, 1891.

New Brandford is comparatively a new town. I would, at a rough guess, estimate its population as about five hundred.

It has some very good stores. Its people seem industrious and kindly disposed towards strangers. It was here that a United States Marshal was shot by a colored barber. He was shot in the dining-room of the hotel where we stopped. It was here also that a United States Detective was shot about seven months ago. His murderer is now in jail at Live Oak, awaiting trial. His chances for escape are about even, as the people of the place seem to think that he ought to be hung but doubt whether he will be, as he is reported to be well off and has good lawyers to defend him.

The weather at New Brandford is very summerlike, but we were surprised to find almost everybody sick with *la grippe*. It seems to be more fatal here than at home. Unless treated with great care it runs into pneumonia with fatal consequences. The doctors here adopt a most heroic treatment. They bleed, blister, and dose their patients with calomel and quinine. The landlady at the Ivy House, where we rested while at New Brandford, informed us that she used over a bushel of meal in poultices on the chest of one patient. The treatment is said to be very successful in either *curing* or *killing* the patients. Patients from the North seem to recover very rapidly, while those to the manor born are a long time getting well.

About eleven A. M. on the second day of our arrival we received the welcome news that the boat would start in half an hour. We packed up our luggage and were on board in a few minutes. After some delay she started down the river with the inspector on board. After going about two miles she stopped suddenly and began to turn her bow up the river. Something was wrong with the new machinery and she went back to her wharf to be again overhauled. At last, about three P. M., she started again down the beautiful and picturesque stream. It is about one hundred and five miles from New Brandford to the Gulf. The river is remarkable for its dissimilarity to any other river I have ever sailed upon. It is about as wide as the Schuylkill at Philadelphia. At New Brandford there are two beautiful sulphur springs. They are funnel-shaped about one hundred feet in diameter. The water acts almost immediately upon the kidneys and bowels and is as clear as crystal, and sapphire colored. They are from twenty-five to thirty feet deep and are full of large fish. The water is much warmer than that of the river, which causes a slight mist to hang around the springs. They discharge a large volume of water into the river. The smallest object in the bottom can be clearly seen. The water of the river looks almost black, but when dipped up it is perfectly clear and but slightly tinged with amber. It is very good soft water and is drunk freely by the watermen and natives. The river is now about fifteen feet below high water mark. It has bluff banks on each side for many miles ; no marshes and but few flags or splatter docks. Great forest trees of various species grow down to the water's edge. The face of the water is so placid and mirror-like ; so smooth and unrippled that the trees on the shore, the clouds, and even the starry heavens can be seen as distinctly by looking down in the water as by looking up to the sky. The great cypress trees are draped with flowing moss, hanging in pendants from three to ten feet long and waving in the gentle breeze in a very fairy-like manner. The woods on the shores consist of cypress, spruce, maple, bay, pine, live oak and palmetto trees. Some of the palmettos are fifty feet high. The colors of the foliage are as variable as the trees, from the pale gray moss on the leafless cypress to all the shades of green, yellow and red. We saw one alligator, several wild turkeys, any quantity of ducks and turtles, buzzards and eagles without number. The woods on the right bank going down the stream, abound in game, from the shy partridge up to the wild turkey, and from the frisky squirrel to the fleet-footed deer. As we approach the Gulf the river widens and becomes more shallow. Around its mouth are many small islands, some perfectly round, others crescent-shaped ; some oval and others in long strips. The aquatic flags around the islands and along the edge of the river, as we near the mouth, look at a little distance in the sunlight like beautiful embroidery, while the palmetto trees give a charming effect to the background.

Our boat is called the "Belle of Suwanee," and is worthy of her pretty name. She has first-class machinery and is safe and comfortable. She has staterooms for the accommodation of from forty to fifty passengers with a good steward, substantial table and comfortable berths. We spent as pleasant a night on the boat as we have at any of the hotels on our route. We arrived at Cedar Key on the Gulf of Mexico, about six P. M., and through the kindness of the captain we were permitted to keep our stateroom and sleep on the boat the second night. I cannot speak too favorably of the captain and his officers. They were kind, obliging and courteous from the time we embarked till we left the boat. Thus, after all our annoying delays and many disappointments, we were fully compensated for all our trouble. After all, it seems to me that the sweetest enjoyments of life often result from the agreeable surprises of previous disappointments. We would not have missed our trip down the Old Suwanee for ten times its trouble and cost. Hereafter there will be no such delays. The beautiful " Belle of Suwanee " will make regular semi-weekly trips from New Brandford to Cedar Key. Passengers will spend one night on the boat much more agreeably than at any hotel. The navigation of the river is as safe and easy by night as by day. The shadow of the tall trees on the banks at night extends about fifty feet from the shores, leaving a clear, silvery line in the center of the river. All the pilot has to do is to follow this line and he will always be in the middle of the stream. The shores are so bluff that the boat can be moored to a tree anywhere along the river and a landing effected in many places by simply stepping ashore.

At Cedar Key we stepped from the boat to the cars and in three hours we were at Waldo where we changed cars for Silver Spring at which place we expected to take dinner, but as usual in Florida, our engine got out of order and we were delayed about four hours. We had to wait for a freight train to push us to the next station, where we were informed we could lunch. When we arrived, being all hungry, there was a general rush for the hotel, about three hundred yards distant. To our horror and dismay we were informed that the sheriff had just seized the place and that nothing could be had either for love or money. The next break was for the only grocery in the settlement. We bought crackers and sardines and had a very agreeable little picnic under a pine tree. The event made all the passengers friends and we were surprised to find several persons who were acquainted with friends of ours. This agreeable intercourse continued until it was broken up next day, the boat and cars carrying us in different directions perhaps never to meet again.

One day is enough for Silver Spring and yet it ought to be seen by every traveler in Florida. The spring looks like a great mill dam without the *dam*. A full grown river comes suddenly to the surface. The steamboat from Palatka lies moored at the head of the spring ready to start on her daily trip. We made a thirty-mile excursion by boat, down the Spring Run, about ten miles, to its confluence with the Ocklawaha, and up that river as far as we could safely go. The Ocklawaha above its junction with the Silver Spring Run is full of snags ; we struck two while going up the stream. We saw a very large alligator basking in the sun, and caught some very fine large black bass. The large hotel that formerly stood at Silver Spring has been burned. The proprietor had a lawsuit about the title to the land on which it stood. To end the dispute he burned the hotel after which the land was not worth further contention, and so the lawsuit ended.

To read the advertisement of stopping places along the river from Silver Spring to Palatka, one would suppose its banks to be studded with thriving towns. In reality they are but landing places to deliver freight and take on wood. Many

of them have not as much as a single house; some only a small
shed. The names of the different stopping places are very
suggestive—such as "Old Man's Gut," "Hell's Half Acre,"
etc. I believe from what I have seen of some of these landing
places, that to be compelled to live upon one of these "Half
Acres" would be "Hell" enough for the greatest sinner.

We are now very comfortably quartered at Ocala. In a
few days we will leave for the new hotel at Tampa Bay, said
to rival the Ponce de Leon at St. Augustine. On the twelfth
we sail for Jamaica.

X

OCALA TO TAMPA — FARMERS' ALLIANCE EXHIBITION AT
OCALA — SUNSHINE A GREAT SOURCE OF WEALTH — A
TWENTY-TWO-POUND SWEET POTATO—ALL DEMOCRATS—
CARS ON TIME FOR ONCE—THE GREAT TAMPA HOTEL—
SAD FATE OF A YOUNG ENGLISHMAN.

TAMPA, February, 1891.

All the little towns of Florida are called cities. Ocala has
a population of about four thousand. It is the seat of Justice
of the county of Marion. The city is chiefly built of brick.
The principal square with the Court House in the centre looks
very well. It has two National Banks and a Trust Company,
all doing a thriving business. I should say that the city is
situated upon the backbone of the State. The public square
and principal buildings are on the highest ground. The
drainage is from the square both ways to the Ocean and to the
Gulf. The land in Marion county is the best in Florida for
agricultural purposes, so the people of Ocala say, and judging
from its display in the Exposition now being held here, I believe they speak the truth. The only undulating land I have
seen in Florida is in this county. The city has several good
hotels—one of them, "The Ocala House,"—may be classed
among the best in the State. It is quite large and somewhat
imposing, occupying in front the entire length of the square.

The Farmers' Alliance are now holding at Ocala quite a
good exposition of the fruits, flowers and general products of
the State. To me it was much more interesting than the Sub-
tropical Exposition of Jacksonville. One can learn more of
the resources of Florida in a day, by a careful study of the Exposition, than by months of observation while traveling over
the State. It must be remembered that railroads do not pass

through the best part of any country. Florida has many very lucrative sources of wealth. Her timber, turpentine, resin, cotton, oranges and vegetables of all kinds, fruits, flowers and *sunshine* are the best in the world. Her sunshine in winter alone brings millions of dollars to the State. Indeed without it, she would not have secured her present rapid development for many years to come. I saw a sweet potato in the Exposition that weighed twenty-two pounds ; another weighed sixteen pounds. One cluster of cocoas had forty-one full-sized nuts on a single stem. The cluster was as large as a barrel and weighed over one hundred pounds. Beside the ordinary productions of the land, the phosphate deposits throughout the State are immensely valuable. The redeemed swamp territory bids fair to rival Louisiana in the production of sugar cane. It seems to me that Florida has a very bright prospect for further development before her. There is no good reason why her swamps should not be drained and be devoted to the cultivation of sugar and rice.

Among her sister States Florida is but a little girl She has been very much neglected and has not cared to show her many charms. After awhile she will develop into a full grown belle and will, I have no doubt, have many admirers if not lovers, provided, like many other belles, she does not dissipate her charms or put too high a price upon her favors. At present the State is full of Northern enterprise. Politics, for the present at least, seems to have been relegated to the unemployed and is little agitated among business men. Perhaps the quietness in politics may be accounted for on the ground of the absence of necessity. The State is strongly Democratic. Nothing, however, could induce the people to go back to the old lazy days of slavery.

After spending three days very agreeably in Ocala we packed our trunks and came to Tampa, five hours by rail further South. For once the cars were on time. We allowed ourselves fifteen minutes to make the train which, under ordinary circumstances, would have been more than sufficient. Our heavy trunk was sent ahead in an express wagon. On our way to the depot we saw a great crowd of excited people around a wounded and bleeding man. A little further on we found our large trunk lying in the middle of the road. The horse and express wagon were nowhere in sight. We had to find another wagon to carry our trunk to the depot and got there just in time to board the train, which was on time to the second. The horse of the express wagon had run away, broken the wagon and nearly killed the driver.

Tampa is the metropolis of the Gulf as Jacksonville is of the Atlantic. Until recently it was a sleepy old town of dirty

streets and wooden buildings. It has greatly improved within
the past three years. The town is being metamorphosed into
a brick-built city. There are fine foreign steamers now sailing
weekly from Port Tampa. The city is situated at the head of
Tampa Bay at the mouth of Tillsborough river. The great
Tampa Bay Hotel, just opened, stands on an eminence on the
west side of the river and occupies a very conspicuous position.
It is one of the finest hotels in the world. In my judgment it
is superior to the world-renowned Ponce de Leon at St. Augustine. It is very large, about six hundred feet in front, exclusive of the dining room and outbuildings. In approaching
it from the railroad it does not present a very prepossessing
appearance. It is built of rough, reddish brick in the Moor-
esque order of architecture, with six tall minarets, crowned
with the Moorish half moon. All the columns and arches are
Moorish. The grand banqueting hall (dining room) is an immense building in itself, with a very large dome, *a la St. Peter's*.
It is connected with the main building by a semi-circular cor-
ridor, very airy and attractive, and decorated with paintings,
engravings, sofas, antique chairs, columns and statuary. The
building faces the river over a lovely ten-acre lawn, beautifully laid out in walks, flower beds and groves of sub-tropical
trees, such as palmettos, cocoanut, bay, oleander, magnolia,
lemon and orange trees. The river bank has been walled and
the marsh filled with rich river earth. The whole lawn, not
occupied with flower beds, is carpeted by a sward of rich green
grass, kept nicely clipped. This feature is something new in
Florida, as green grass is seldom seen.

The entire building is carpeted, furnished and decorated
in a most luxuriant manner and with exquisite taste. The
walls are hung with fine oil paintings, the alcoves are adorned
with marble, bronze and silvered statuary, while at every turn
richly-gilt mirrors reflect your image and duplicate the gorgeous scenery around. All the decorations are in harmony with
the architecture, and represent Moorish or Spanish scenes and
subjects. It is impossible to give a perfect pen picture of the
building and its surroundings ; it must be seen and closely
studied to be fully appreciated. I have seen most of the
world's great hotels, but have seen few that surpass the "Tampa
Bay." It is remarkable for its originality of design and its
dissimilarity to any other hotel, and will compare favorably
with the best. As before stated at the first view the eye feels
a sense of disappointment but, like all great architectural
structures, it grows in beauty as we become better acquainted
with it.

The whole building is lighted with many thousand electric lights and when fully illuminated presents a fairy-like

spectacle. Some idea will be conveyed of the size of the building and grounds when we consider the fact that it occupies over seventeen acres of land. This includes the lawn and curtilage.

The population of Tampa is now about six thousand. I have no doubt but that in the near future it will be one of the most flourishing cities in Florida. There is but one drawback to the pleasure of a winter sojourn here ; it is too warm and is infested with swarms of hungry and very wicked mosquitoes. We have been sleeping with our windows open all night, with only a sheet for our covering and have been uncomfortably warm. But we cannot expect to enjoy the genial sunshine of summer and at the same time escape the little annoyances incident to all warm latitudes. If we want to get away from the snakes and mosquitoes of Florida we have but to go home.

Speaking of snakes reminds me of a very sad adventure of a young Englishman a few days ago near St. Augustine. His parents are very wealthy and influential citizens of England and sent their son to see America and enjoy the pleasures of traveling and hunting, of which the better class of Englishmen are so fond. With a companion he was out in the woods on a hunting expedition. He had neglected his leather leggins, supposing there were no snakes so near the town. He was bitten by a large rattlesnake and despite every effort to save him, he died in two days after the bite. His companion endeavored to suck the poison from the wound and came near losing his life from a slight fever blister on his lip. This will be sad news to go home to his parents.

We are now killing time as best we can. We do but little more than eat, smoke and sleep. Our amusement after sundown is to look at and study the beautiful heavens, especially those bright stars which are never seen in the latitude of Philadelphia. When we get to Jamaica we expect to see the Southern Cross and the splendid stars of the first magnitude in the Centaur and Ship Argo. We expect to sail on the twelfth and to arrive at Jamaica about the seventeenth. Every berth is taken. If the ship were as large again she would be full of American travelers.

XI.

FROM TAMPA TO JAMAICA—A LEADER IN THE FARMERS'
ALLIANCE—SLIPS OF THE TONGUE—MORE DELAYS—AT
SEA IN AN OLD STEAMBOAT—A SEASICK PARTY—TABLE
SCENE ON THE SHIP—FIRST SIGHT OF THE SOUTHERN
CROSS—LOOKING UPWARD AND DOWNWARD—THE CAP-
TAIN'S IDEA OF DISTANCES—HALF AN HOUR TOO LATE—
SO NEAR AND YET SO FAR.

JAMAICA, February, 1891.

Just before leaving Tampa, our hotel was honored by the
arrival of a distinguished guest. He was anxious that we
should know him as a big man in the Farmers' Alliance. He
wore a slouched hat, talked loud, and had a long grizzly beard.
On entering the dining room he asked the waiter for a seat
where he could "look over the whole plantation." Without
waiting to be shown his seat he took a chair at the head of one
of the center tables. The waiter told him that seat was engaged. "Oh," said he, "I am encroaching on some other
man's reservation, am I?" When the waiter handed him the
menu, he read it all over and leaning back in his chair with an
air of satisfaction, he said, "Well, I rather guess that's pretty
fair provender." The waiter informed him that it was usual
to order a few dishes at a time. "Order is the word, is it?
Well, bring me a dinner." The waiter retired and brought
him soup and fried oysters. "What!" said he, "four dollars
a day for a plate of soup and three little oysters! I don't believe the crop will pay for the seed." Beginning to realize
that he was being laughed at, he put his hand to his forehead
and said in a subdued tone that he believed he was catching
that darned gripe again. The head waiter, with great dignity,
informed the under waiters that they must not treat the guests
with *invicility*. He meant incivility. Of course this was a
lapsus linguæ, but it provoked a titter over the room. All of
us are liable to slips of the tongue. A distinguished friend of
mine of Media, becoming excited over a game of euchre declared most emphatically that a card played by his adversary
was not *gelitimate*. Another friend, of Chester, being elated
over his success in a game of *all fours*, triumphantly announced that he had made "Joe, High, Lack and the Game."
Travelers often find more amusement in the ludicrous scenes
of real life than in those seen on the stage.

Before embarking for Jamaica, and to escape from the
mosquitoes, we spent two very pleasant nights at Port Tampa,

about nine miles from Tampa. The hotel and other buildings are located about a mile out in the bay and rest on piles *a la* Venice. It is a delightfully cool place and the "Inn" is well kept and comfortable. The prices are from four to five dollars per day. In the hall of the Inn they exhibit an enormous fish, hooked by Mrs. Plant, but boated by ex-President Cleveland, about two years ago. It illustrates his usual good luck. It may be doubtful, from present appearances if he will again land the Presidential Fish, hooked by Mrs. Cleveland.

I am inclined to think that we must have seen the new moon over the wrong shoulder before leaving home, for we have suffered more from delays than ever before in our varied travels throughout the world. The ship was advertised to sail at eight P. M. It was midnight before she drew in the plank. She had to wait for the mail train which was three hours late. The vessel in which we expected to sail was a nearly new screw propeller and a very good ship Something was wrong about her machinery and a miserable old side-wheeled steamboat named the "Hewes," from New Orleans, was substituted in her place. She was fully thirty years old, dirty, slow and uncomfortable. Her berths were small, her beds musty and the pillows offensive from the spew of previous seasick passengers. The table was coarse, the drinking water resembled "mud soup," and the steward charged twenty-five cents a glass for rot-gut whisky. I began to realize our helpless condition when I discovered we were being towed by the ship "Olivette," which started at the same time for Havana. We had crossed last year to Havana in the "Olivette," and knew her to be a fine ship. As her bright electric search-light played over the waters of the bay we could distinctly see every buoy and pilot mark a half mile away. After we got out of the bay the Olivette cast off the hawser, leaving us to take care of ourselves and was soon out of sight. We got along very well, making about eight miles an hour till we passed the Isle of Cuba, but as soon as we entered the Caribbean Sea the scene suddenly changed. The winds were directly adverse to the Gulf Stream and very strong, causing waves from twenty to thirty feet high. The course of the ship was diagonal over the waves which caused her to roll most disagreeably. At times one wheel would be out of water while the other would be entirely submerged. The waves repeatedly swept the decks. One incident will suffice to give a fair idea of the whole voyage from Cuba to Jamaica. The captain remained night and day on deck. His place at the head of the table was filled by the purser, a very polite little gentleman, but like most little men he made up in dignity what he lacked in size. The roll of the ship made it very difficult to keep our seats at the table and to keep the dishes and provisions from sliding into our laps or on the floor. The purser tried by his example to show the passengers how gracefully he could keep his seat and eat his soup without spilling it. The ship gave a sudden lurch to the left, causing several chairs, with their occupiers, to tumble over and some of the dishes to slide into the laps of the gentlemen, for there were but few ladies at the table. The purser smiled and remarked that the passengers would have to learn how to accommodate their motions to those of the ship. He had scarcely uttered the words when a tremendous wave struck the side of the ship with almost force enough to lift her out of the water. The ship was on her beam ends, all the dishes and provisions, bottles, glassware and table furniture were swept from the board, covering the passengers with beans, wine, meats and coffee and causing them, in grand confusion, to roll about the slippery and greasy deck. The chair of the purser, with him in it, described a somersault towards the other side of the ship. He was dashed headlong into one of the staterooms and came very near breaking his head as well as his ribs. The purser got decidedly the worst of it. He smelt of benzine which he had used in cleaning his clothes, for two or three days. I have looked upon many ludicrous scenes at the theatre and circus, but I never saw a more laughable one than this table scene on the ship "Hewes."

All we have read of the sickening effect of a two hours' passage across the British Channel read like pleasure trips, when compared with our four days' passage from Cuba to Kingston. The scheduled time from Tampa to Kingston is three days ; we spent six nights upon the ship. We had, however, some compensation for our misery. After we crossed the Tropic of Cancer the Southern Cross could be seen a little after midnight. As we had never seen it, we had a strong desire to enjoy that treat. This beautiful cluster of stars is never seen in the latitude of Philadelphia. It comes to the horizon, almost due South, about one A. M., and is visible for about two hours. My wife is very fond of astronomy and, sick as she was, she crawled out of her berth at two A. M. and stood with me upon the rolling deck for a full half hour gazing in rapture upon the most beautiful of all the Southern constellations. When due south it was at its brightest, and was about eighteen degrees above the horizon. Below the Cross, we saw Alpha Centaur and another bright star of the first magnitude, serving as pointers to the Cross. Sirius was just going down as Alpha Centaur came up. The latter, of all the fixed stars, is said to be the nearest to the earth. It is however so far away that light, which flies at the rate of ninety millions of miles in eight minutes, would require over seventeen years to reach the earth. What a tremendous thought and how hard to comprehend ! The infinity of space and the eternity of matter. I have often thought that man occupies a place in God's creation midway between nothing and his Maker. By the microscope we look downward and the extent of our vision is only limited by the power of the instrument. By the telescope we look up toward God, and our view is only limited by its power.

To descend from the sublime to the ridiculous, I must here relate a conversation between the captain and myself while standing on the deck looking at the Southern Cross. About ten P. M. he had pointed out to some ladies the diamond formed by four third-magnitude stars in *Argo Navis* as the Southern Cross. I knew, from its right ascension, he was mistaken, but I said nothing. When the true Cross appeared in all its splendor and beauty, I called his attention to it and told him he had made a mistake. I pointed out the difference in the magnitude of the stars, these being of the first, while those he had pointed out were of the third magnitude. "Oh," said he, "you must remember we are four hours *nearer* the stars *now* than we were when I showed them to the ladies, and that makes them look so much larger and brighter." Poor fool, thought I, we will not argue the question, but at the rate of speed we were then advancing southward it would take thousands upon thousands of millions of years to make the slightest increase in either the size or brilliancy of the stars we were looking at.

At times it was hard to tell whether we were advancing or going backward. Some days we only averaged four and a half miles an hour. At last we came in sight of the island, and we supposed our troubles would soon end. We were sorely disappointed. It took us a whole day from the time we sighted the coast before we arrived opposite Kingston. To add to our disappointment, we arrived just thirty minutes after sundown, and by the regulations of the authorities, no ship can enter the port between sunset and sunrise. This was the captain's first trip to the Kingston side of the island. He had always before landed his passengers on the north side, from whence they crossed twenty-one miles by land to Kingston. Not being acquainted with the harbor he would not venture to enter, but he assured us he had sent a telegram from Tampa for a pilot, and that he had no doubt upon the signal being given, one would come out and take us into the harbor where our ship could anchor and the passengers have a pleasant night's rest free from further disagreeable motion by the winds and waves. We sent up signal after signal but no pilot came to our relief. The whole night was passed in running up and down between the two lighthouses, blowing the steam whistle and vainly looking at the lights of the city, about two miles off. By good luck, about daylight, a ship from New York came up and, without difficulty, entered the harbor. By following close in her wake we got inside and found our first smooth sea since leaving Tampa. It was like leaving hell for Paradise. The rough sea had broken the cable and our telegram had not been received. The inhospitable citizens of Kingston would have let us perish in the sea rather than come to our relief contrary to the laws of Jamaica. I wonder if the gates of Paradise will be shut forever on the poor wandering soul that, by stress of misfortunes and adversities on life's stormy sea arrives half an hour after the time for shutting them.

XII.

In the Tropics—Kingston—Buzzards as Scavengers—Old Slave Days in Jamaica—Earthquakes—The Story of Lewis Galby—Scraps of History—Three Classes, White, Colored and Black—The World's Fair at Kingston—Canada vs. The United States.

JAMAICA, February, 1891.

All our troubles are now over and we are comfortably quartered at the "Myrtle Bank Hotel." We have a fine large airy room, good soft beds, downy pillows, good fare and excellent service for five dollars per day. Good hotel boarding is higher here than in the *States* (that is what they call our country here). Everything is strange and tropical in comparison with life at home. From our dining room we can look out through the cocoanut and palm trees to the water, only about two hundred yards off. Great iron clad men-of-war are lying at anchor in full view. Every day they fire a salute which is answered from the forts. The weather is delightfully pleasant. The trade winds blow constantly, fresh from the sea, and overcome the heat of the sun. By comparison, I would say the weather here is about as we have it at Cape May in the month of July, with a strong sea breeze prevailing all the time.

The city is hard to describe. It is situated upon low, flat ground, formed by the wash from the mountains behind it. The blue mountains form a kind of amphitheatre, the city being seated in the parquette. There are mountains just outside the city limits, over seven thousand feet high. We have a splendid view of them from our chamber windows. The population of Kingston is about 40,000, from which one would suppose the city a very large place, yet it is not half as large as Chester and, aside from the Myrtle Bank Hotel, it has very few dwellings or stores worth over one or two thousand dollars to build. Most of the houses are but one and two stories high. The streets have but few sidewalks. All the mechanics and working people, shop keepers and merchants, with a few exceptions, are black or colored. I saw a one-story dwelling house in which, I was informed, forty persons slept. This accounts for the large population in so small a city.

Buzzards fly about the streets and walk around the back yards as tame as chickens. They are the scavengers of the city and, like the dogs of Constantinople, they are protected by law. It is impossible to describe the city by comparison with any I have yet seen. From engravings I have seen I would say it resembled modern Bagdad or Damascus more than any European or American town. The houses are mostly enclosed by walls which come out to the street. The walls are irregular and ugly, but after we enter by the street gate, we are surprised to find some palatial residences surrounded by oriental gardens and adorned with fountains and statuary. This, however, is the exception, not the rule. The business part of the town has a very old and dilapidated appearance. Its situation, however, is very charming. Covered in the rear by mountains and constantly fanned by the refreshing breezes from the sea, its climate is the best and most salubrious on the earth. It is shaded by thousands of tropical trees and perfumed by perpetual flowers. We have a large and beautiful bouquet on our private table that could not be bought, at this season, in Philadelphia for less than five dollars. Here it cost a few cents.

The construction of the street walls in front of the houses and gardens gives the city a suspicious appearance, suggestive of danger either to the traveler on the highway or the citizen in his castle. I have no doubt but this mode of building was adopted for the purpose of seclusion as well as defense in the old days of slavery. I remember very well when the English home government took a firm hold of that troublesome question, human slavery, and freed the slaves of Jamaica. The Crown had repeatedly ordered the Governor and Assembly to ameliorate the condition of the slaves. The colonial government looked upon the question as one of local interest only, and at last ordered the certified resolution of the British Government to be burned by the common hangman in the public square. In 1834 the British Government took the question into its own hands, abolished the institution and voted the slave owners $100,000,000 compensation. In 1831 there was a terrible rising of the slaves and many lives were lost. The fire-eaters of

Jamaica threatened to transfer their allegiance to the United States if the British Government should insist in its determination to abolish slavery. England had the moral courage to free her slaves and she has kept and will continue to keep Jamaica.

The chief reason for building the houses only one and two stories high is the repeated earthquakes with which the city has been visited. The island is never entirely free from them. We had a slight shock three days ago. The inside of the houses are not plastered as they are at home. The partitions, ceilings and cornices are all of wood so nicely fitted and painted that, if I had not been told, I would have thought them plastered, stuccoed and corniced with cement. This is to keep the repeated shocks from cracking the plastered ceilings and causing them to fall off. The people tell, with reverence, the story of one Lewis Galby, who, in 1690, was swallowed in a great crevice in the earth caused by the memorable earthquake of that year. He disappeared entirely into the bowels of the earth ; after a short time there was another shock—the earth opened again and vomited him out into the sea still alive. He lived many years after and was always looked upon as miraculously saved.

The population of the island is claimed to be nearly 800,-000. Its area is 4193 square miles. It was discovered by Columbus on his second voyage, May 3d, 1497. It is one hundred and fourteen miles long by from twenty-one to forty-nine miles wide. It is very mountainous, craggy and rocky, full of little fertile valleys with many grottoes, hot and cold mineral springs and beautiful scenery. It has but few carriage roads, fewer railroads, and no rivers of any importance for navigation and trade. Nevertheless the island is well watered, but the greater part of it is entirely unfit for cultivation. The population is divided into three classes, white, colored and black. Most of the people are colored and a few black men here are very rich, but the great majority of the blacks are poor. A colored man considers himself degraded if he marries a black woman and vice versa.

There are a great many Canadians and quite a number of Englishmen here to see and help along the great Industrial Exposition. We visited it yesterday for the first time ; we will give it several visits before we leave. It is quite creditable, indeed a very pretty little display. The main building is constructed very much on the model of the one at Philadelphia in 1876, but, of course, not near so large.

I was surprised to learn from nearly every Canadian to whom I spoke upon the subject, that a settled belief exists in the minds of the people of Canada that it is not only the desire, but the unwritten policy of the United States to absorb their country.

In my next letter I will be able to say more of the manners and customs of the people and the general character of the Island.

XIII.

JAMAICA, AS NEAR THE EQUATOR AS THE NORTH CAPE IS TO THE POLE—MOUNTAINOUS AND FERTILE, BUT NEGLECTED —WOMEN AS LABORERS—WAGES—ONE WHITE PERSON TO FIFTY COLORED—ADVERSE TO WORK BECAUSE UNNECESSARY—LONGITUDE OF PHILADELPHIA—MARKET DAY—A NEW YORK COLORED MAN'S OPINION OF A JAMAICA NIGGER—ENGLISH AS THEY SPEAK IT—THE HARBOR—FATE OF DESERTERS FROM A RUSSIAN IRON-CLAD — UNITED STATES MONEY WORTH MORE THAN STERLING—NO IRISHMEN IN JAMAICA.

JAMAICA, February, 1891.

We have been here ten days. We have seen all that the railway can show and have also had two or three days' coach riding among the mountains. It is too warm to take much exercise between nine A. M. and four P. M. As we have had a constant sea breeze, we have been very comfortable at our hotel. The nights are sufficiently cool to afford refreshing sleep, even in Kingston. We found it uncomfortably cold at night on the mountains at an elevation of two thousand feet.

It will give a better idea of this latitude to extend the line eastward through well-known Southern countries. We are several degrees further south than the most southern part of Europe. The eighteenth degree of south latitude passes through Timbuctoo and Khartoom, extending south of Arabia and through Abyssinia. We are now just about as near the equator as we were to the pole in our visit to the North Cape in 1888.

The island is very mountainous, but even the mountain tops are fertile. It produces, without cultivation, very fine pasturage the year round. The valleys and low lands on the coast are exceedingly rich, but poorly cultivated. I have not seen a scythe, plow, mower, reaper or thresher in Jamaica. The principal agricultural tools are knives to cut the rank guinea-grass and bananas, and shovels, mattocks and hoes. The women do the hardest work. They break stone for the roads, which are kept very good, and have been constructed at great expense. These poor women carry on their heads nearly a wheelbarrow load of stone and earth. The railroad now belongs to a company of Americans. The chief engineer told me that all the grading and tunneling was done by spades and picks. The earth and broken limestone is removed and carried to the dump in baskets carried on the heads of women who are paid thirty-seven cents a day. He said that this is considered very high wages, as the blacks are adverse to work unless stimulated by what they call good pay. When we look at the deep cuts and high embankments through the mountains, and realize that all this mass of earth and stones has been removed in this way, it strikes our mind with incredulous surprise. Most of the merchants, mechanics, railroad clerks and conductors are black and colored men. Of the 800,000 people said to live upon the island not over fifteen thousand are pure white. Many of the officials, and most of the Town Council and Assemblymen are black. All the clerks and carriers in the postoffice and Her Majesty's constabulary are black men. The aristocratic class call themselves *colored people* and hold themselves a degree higher in the scale of respectability than the blacks. The Governor and the Judges of the courts are white men and are paid very good salaries. The Chief Justice receives ten thousand dollars and the Puisne Judges seven thousand dollars a year, which is better pay than the great State of Pennsylvania gives to her Judges. While the wages paid to mechanics and laborers seem very low, when we measure them by the amount of work each person does, they are, perhaps, nearly as high as with us. The rapidity with which work is done here depends more upon the number employed than the amount of work done by each. They move very slowly, go to work very late and stop early. Indeed, the people of Jamaica seem very adverse to, what we would call, hard work. And why should they work? They need but little clothing ; broad-leaved tropical trees give them sufficient shelter ; yams, bananas, mangoes and the other almost innumerable fruits and vegetables of spontaneous growth furnish more food than they can eat ; if they want milk they have but to tap a cocoanut ; and if they are thirsty they need only suck an orange. Necessity is the mother of labor. A desire for luxury alone stimulates the lower classes here to work.

When it is noon at home it is noon here, the longitude of Jamaica and Washington being the same. The island gets its name from a corruption of the Spanish word *Xaymaca*, which means a land of wood and water. It has belonged to the English since Admiral Penn captured it in the days of Cromwell. While it has about seventy streams running every way from the mountains to the sea, it has no rivers worth naming. The

Black River only navigable for very small craft. The cultivation of the island has very much declined since the old slavery days when the laborers were compelled to work. We can see evidences of waste and neglect all around. What were once rich tobacco, coffee and sugar plantations, are now overgrown with logwood and scrub timber, and, where irrigation has been neglected, the land has dried up. There is but very little barren ground, however, in Jamaica. If the Dutch farmers of Pennsylvania had possession of the island for ten years, they would convert it into a little paradise. As it is, there is no doubt but that the people are beginning to improve. They seem to be awaking from a long dreamy sleep. Railroads are being projected, good hotels are being built and American and English enterprise are taking a firm foothold.

If the municipality of New York could only transfer, in a body, the little park in the center of Kingston, to that great city, they would pay millions for it, but without the perpetual summer that nourishes it here it would only delight their eyes for a single season. One winter would kill all the tropical trees, shrubs and flowers it contains. I have no doubt but that the people of Jamaica would find as much pleasure in one of our grand old primeval forests as we enjoy among their cocoas, bananas, bay, cotton wood, lignumvitæs and logwood trees. The eternal fitness of things has properly distributed nature's works. We have in miniature here all the tropics can produce.

Market day is a great event in Kingston. The country people come on foot for thirty miles around the city bringing with them, on their heads and on mules and donkeys, a few shillings' worth of marketing—bouquets of wild roses, yams, vegetables, melons and everything that grows on the island, for which they can get a few cents. Many of the girls and boys have never seen Kingston before, and after the market is over they have a high old time seeing the town and visiting their city cousins and friends. The market houses are very good substantial iron buildings of recent construction, and much superior to anything Chester has of that kind. The sea breeze passes freely through them and keeps them cool and carries off all offensive smell, of which Kingston is full.

The government of the island seems satisfactory to the people. Crime is punished with as much certainty as in other parts of the world. The people are about as honest as other civilized nations but not as industrious because, as before stated, of the absence of necessity for labor. With all its tropical abundance, its luxurious fruits and flowers, its delightful climate its soft, enchanting scenery, its balmy breezes and its perpetual summer sun, I would not be compelled to spend

my life here if my compensation were to be the King of the
Isle.

The colored people look like their brethren of America,
but they are a different race.   Here they are a mixture ot
black, Spanish, English and Creoles.   They are very polite
but never witty.   While getting my money changed from our
own currency to pounds, shillings and pence, to keep from
mixing the silver pieces, I said, "I will put Jamaica in one
pocket and America in the other."   A colored man stepped
up and with a twinkle in his eye, he said, "You may put
Jamaica in one pocket, but you'll have a big job to put the
United States in the other."   I said, "What do you know
about the United States?"   Drawing himself up to his full
standard height, he replied, "I am a *citizen* of that country,
sir ; I belong to New York, and am down here to teach these
niggers how to wait on people at a hotel."

The population are supposed to speak English, but the
lower classes do not speak the language as it is spoken in
England or the United States.   They have a patois of their
own, made up of Spanish, English and some of the old slave
jargon.   I heard two women quarreling in the street and stopped to ascertain, if I could, with the greatest attention, what
they were quarreling about.   I could not understand a single
word.   The speech of the bell boy is very hard to understand
at times when he forgets himself and speaks his common
patois.   One day I forgot to give him his accustomed penny
for answering the bell.   I took the ice water from him and
shut the door.   He knocked gently, and said, "No membra
not de savant, sah."   After some questioning I translated the
sentence, "You have forgotten the servant, sir."

The only articles of general use that may be said to be
cheap are segars.   I like them better than Havanas and they do
not cost half as much.   A very fine and honestly-made segar
can be bought here for thirty dollars a thousand.   They retail
a very fair segar at five for a shilling.   They are about equal
to an ordinary ten cent segar.

We have paid three regular visits to the Exposition, have
driven several times over the town ; been in the markets and
through the business, as well as the fashionable and poor portions of the city, and are prepared to form a correct judgment
of the place.   It is a city of huts and shanties, with here and
there a few good houses.   It is, however, green with trees and
tropical plants.   Land can be bought in the fashionable part
of the town for five hundred dollars a lot, one hundred feet
square ; in the business part of the city it is higher.

The front of the city, on the harbor, is the most valuable
part.   The harbor is really one of the finest in the world.

is never free from foreign ships. Since we have been here we have seen from our dining room and parlor windows, ten or fifteen large ocean ships lying at anchor, among them the United States iron-clad, the Petrel, the Kearsarge, the English ships Ruby, Volage, Calypso and Active. Yesterday the United States ship Enterprise entered the harbor and remained long enough to take on board a quantity of coal, when she immediately departed.

The great Russian iron-clad, Minnie, has been lying at anchor within five hundred yards of the lawn of the hotel which runs down to the water's edge. This ship has created quite an excitement in the city. A few days ago her captain hauled up the English flag and greeted it with a salute of two broadsides. He then came ashore in his launch and in a formal manner asked leave to hang from the yard-arm of his ship three seamen that had attempted to desert, but had been captured. The authorities, of course, peremptorily declined to accede to his request. He then weighed anchor and steamed out of the harbor over three miles from shore. What took place out there no one here knows. After about twelve hours he returned to his old anchorage. It is the general belief that he hung the three deserters and buried them in the sea. In the eyes of international law his ship is a part of the legitimate territory of the Czar, and no one has the power to inquire the fate of the deserters or relieve them from any punishment the laws of Russia may have imposed upon their crime.

The Exposition is fairly good for Jamaica. There are many strangers here from England and Canada, and a fair representation from the United States. All the shop keepers and tradesmen know the value of American money. They will give sixpence more for a five dollar gold piece here than it is worth in England. Currency five dollar bank notes are exchangeable for British pounds.

My attention was called by a gentleman from Toronto to the absence of Irishmen. He offered to wager a five-pound note that there was not an Irishman on the island. I don't know why, but I have been unable to find any; perhaps it may be accounted for from their well-known antipathy to the colored race.

XIV.

Mountain Scenery in Jamaica—Ticks and Lice — No
Game and Few Snakes — Enormous Cisterns—Old
Sugar Plantations—No Farms or Farmers—Spanish
Town—Bog Walk—Grottoes—Constant Spring—One
Visit Enough.

Jamaica, 1891.

Before leaving Jamaica, we made several quite extended
excursions over the island.   We went west as far as the railroad would take us, to a town in the lower mountain district
called Porus ; then we took a two-horse carriage and driver
and went ten miles up to the summit of the mountain, two
thousand feet above the sea level.   It took us three and a half
hours to make the ascent and one hour and a half to come back
the next day.   The town on the mountain is called Mandeville.   It is not much of a place, with a poor country hotel,
hard beds and very poor fare.   We met several very refined
and companionable people at this mountain town, among them
a gentleman from New York, interested in the construction of
the railroad.   Several of the gentlemen stopping at the hotel
are from Canada and are sojourning there for a few days to
enjoy the mountain air and look upon the superb scenery.
The drive from Porus to Mandeville reminds me, so far as the
topography of the country and general contour of the mountains is concerned, of the mountain district of Pennsylvania,
from the Horse Shoe on the Pennsylvania Railroad to Cresson.
The elevation is about the same.   Here, of course, the comparison ends.   The mountains of Jamaica are capable of high
cultivation to their very summits.   The roads abound with
bananas, oranges, cocoanuts, logwood and lignumvitæ trees ;
great cotton wood trees and luxuriant grass grow up to the
mountain top.   Coffee trees can also be seen growing in a wild
state along the road.

After we had lunched, like a gallant man, I invited my
wife to take a walk with me and enjoy some of the fine views
from elevated points hard by.   We enjoyed our stroll very
much, as the air was light and bracing and the temperature
was not above fifty-five degrees.   When we got home we found
ourselves covered with what they call, *grass lice* and *ticks*.
My wife spent three hours in cleaning herself from the annoying little pests.   They burrow into the flesh and, if not removed, are not only troublesome but dangerous.   They kill
the horses and cattle if not taken off.   The herdsmen make it a

rule to "tick" their cattle at least twice a week. The engineer of the extension of the railroad told me that he had been laid up for three weeks from sores and inflammation caused by the ticks. He said they had so burrowed into his flesh that iron nippers had to be used to pull them out. The mosquitoes are very bad in parts of the island, but there are very few snakes. The island is comparatively destitute of game. The largest bird, except the wild water fowl and buzzard, is the crow blackbird. He seems to live and flourish all over the world. Although the island around the coast seems to be pretty well watered, yet water is very scarce in autumn in the mountain districts. Most of the drinking water is secured in cisterns from rains. Some of these cisterns are rather curious. A large hill-top will be plastered over with cement; the base of the hill will be raised by a rim of masonry and cement; all the water that falls on the smooth surface will immediately run into an enormous underground cistern from which it can be pumped by hand as from a great well, for domestic use.

Many of the fences in the mountain district are made of bamboo rails, tied together with creepers from the neighboring trees called nimble jacks. We saw bamboo trees fully fifty feet high and not over three inches in diameter.

On our way from Spanish Town to Porus we passed through a fine old sugar plantation. The water by which it is irrigated is still conveyed by an old Spanish aqueduct built of brick like the aqueducts of Rome, and extending for a long distance to some mountain stream. If it were not for the natural basins up in the mountains which confine the rain water in the spring-time and gradually dispense it by slow percolation to the mountain streams, Jamaica would be dried up.

I do not think the island contains a single farmer, as we Northern people understand the word. They pay no attention to a succession of crops, never plow or replant the fields as before stated. Their only agricultural tools are hoes, mattocks and big knives that look like corn cutters, principally used to cut off bananas and cocoa nuts.

Our second excursion was by rail via Spanish Town to Bog Walk. Spanish Town was the former capital of Jamaica. At present it looks more like an abandoned camp meeting ground covered with miserable dog kennels and tumble-down huts, than a city of eight thousand inhabitants. The scenery, however, from Spanish Town to Bog Walk, is very fine both by rail and coach. There are several tunnels on the road which give beautiful vistas as we enter and emerge from their mouths. We went to Bog Walk by rail and came back by coach over the mountain road. The town of Bog Walk is prettily situated in an amphitheatre formed by the surrounding

mountains.   On the highest parts of the hills may be seen tall
cocoanut trees that look in the early dawn like windmills.
The valley is very rich and is watered by the Rio Cobre, a
small mountain stream not navigable, but very useful for irrigation.   The Bog Walk road follows the stream and in some
places presents scenery equal to celebrated Swiss views.   At
one place the trees up the mountain side were covered from the
water's edge to the mountain's top with a luxuriant growth of
green vines and creepers so thick as to be impenetrable to the
naked eye.

The water from the Rio Cobre in times of floods and
freshets has washed caverns and small grottoes in the soft
limestone mountain sides.   Some of these grottoes are very
beautiful with stalactites and stalagmites.   In the Blue Mountains, about forty miles from Kingston, hot and cold springs
are found in close proximity.   Some of the scenery of Jamaica
presents to the eye, in miniature, truly beautiful landscapes.

Constant Spring, about six miles north of Kingston, has
been highly spoken of, but to me it presented a rather tame
appearance.   It has the best built hotel in Jamaica.   To my
mind, Kingston is a much more pleasant place to live.   It is
called Constant Spring because of its sheltered situation.   I
at first supposed that there was a spring of constantly flowing
water there.   In this I was sadly disappointed ; it is a very
dry place.   Constant Summer would be a more appropriate
name.

The coach route from Annotta Bay to Kingston is very
much admired.   The ships from Tampa have always landed
their passengers there until the last voyage of the "Hewes."
It is about thirty miles by road from Annotta to Kingston,
most of which is through and over the mountains.   It takes a
full day to make a single trip.   The fare to the coachman is
one pound ($5).

We have now seen enough of Jamaica to enable us to
form a fair idea of its topography and the manners and customs
of its people.   It is a tropical world in miniature.   Its lands
are rich and fertile but its people are thriftless, indolent, hand-
to-mouth and easy-going.   I cannot say they are lazy, but
they lack energy and enterprise.   Without a copious infusion
of energetic Anglo-Saxon blood the island will never amount
to much.   If it had better communication with the United
States it would be a most delightful winter resort for our over
worked Northern people.   As it is, the time lost and annoyance suffered in getting here and the uncertainty in getting
away, overbalance the advantages and compel us to say that
one visit to Jamaica is quite enough.

We will sail for Bermuda to-morrow and must spend five days on the sea before reaching that much celebrated winter resort.

———

XV.

JAMAICA TO BERMUDA—MORE ABOUT JAMAICA—THE RAT AND THE MANGOOSE—OLD PORT ROYAL, THE GOMORRAH OF JAMAICA—TURK'S ISLAND—MISCEGENATION—HAYTI'S OPINION OF WHITE PEOPLE—SHIP LIFE, THE SAME OLD STORY—MAY AND NOVEMBER—A LOVE SCENE—LOOKING AT THE STARS—A GAME OF EUCHRE—CANADA VS. THE UNITED STATES.

BERMUDA, March, 1891.

Farewell to Jamaica ! She is black but comely. Travelers have the reprehensible habit of overpainting their pictures. I have endeavored to say nothing of Jamaica that is not true as she presented herself to me. There is something about the place that strikes one who has never visited the Torrid Zone with pleasure and surprise. When we look upon something entirely different from what we have been accustomed to see, it is the contrast and not the new object that startles and at the same time gives us pleasure. The denizens of the desert delight in flowing rivers and rippling streams. The dwellers upon mountains love the rich lowlands and undulating plains. The inhabitants of cities rejoice in the quiet of country life. The boy who for the first time visits the city looks upon it as the centre of all pleasure. So the inhabitants of the Tropics would look with amazement upon a glacier. At first, I took great delight in gazing upon the tall and graceful palmetto, cocoanut, cottonwood, logwood, lignumvitæ and other strange trees, and the countless varieties of fruits, vegetables, sugar plantations, wild groves of oranges and bananas, sapodillas, Mangoes, plantains, yams, grape fruit and pine apples ; but I soon grew weary of the productions of eternal sunshine with their accompanying dust, ticks, lice and pestiferous insects. I soon began to long for the sight of a grand old oak, a tall and graceful pine or even a poplar tree.

A good old-fashioned sleigh ride or even a blizzard would be preferable to the sweltering heat caused by the slightest exercise in the sunshine of Jamaica. A field of corn or wheat would be more beautiful to me than a sugar plantation, an old fashioned apple orchard more attractive than an orange grove. To sum up, I would advise every person who can conveniently

do so, to visit the Tropics once and experience the pleasure of
the contrast with his own country ; but, if he expects to find
anything superior to what he has at home, taken as a whole,
he will be disappointed.

The history of Jamaica demonstrates the danger of human
interference with the harmony of Nature. The early settlers,
that they might enjoy the fruits of the soil without working
themselves, imported great numbers of African slaves. From
natural fecundity the slaves increased so fast that they soon
numbered over fifty blacks to one white man. Insubordination
and insurrections followed until at last the island was surrendered to the former slaves. Plantations were abandoned, fields
uncultivated ; indolence, ignorance and idleness followed and
from a fertile garden, Jamaica declined to little better than an
abandoned and overgrown waste. The ships that came for
produce brought rats ; they, like the slaves, increased so fast
that the land was literally filled with them. As their number
increased their natural food diminished until, from necessity,
they began to devour the young sugar cane, bananas, pine
apples and cocoanuts. The government imported from India
a small carnivorous animal something like a weasel, called the
Mangoose, said to be a deadly enemy of the rat. For a short
time he played sad havoc with the poor rats, just as the English sparrow killed off our caterpillars until he learned to eat
grain. The cunning rat soon learned that the Mangoose only
hunted by day and slept at night, so Mr. Rat kept in his hole
all day and when his enemy slept he sallied forth and committed his usual depredations. The Mangoose and rat soon
became friends and instead of eating each other, they agreed
to live upon the same kind of food, so now they both eat sugar
cane, bananas, cocoanuts, etc. To give some variety to their
bill of fare they climb the tallest trees and crawl into the
smallest holes in search of eggs, and little birds and chicks.
It is next to impossible to raise chickens and even the buzzards
are becoming scarce. As a natural result, nearly all the in-
sectivorous birds have disappeared and pestiferous insects have
increased to such an extent as to threaten the extermination
of all domestic animals. Ticks, grass-lice and fleas have
already shut up all the beautiful promenades and have rendered the pasturing of cattle almost impossible. They will soon
make a complete conquest of the island if something heroic is
not done for their extermination. The Legislature has at last
taken hold of the trouble and has appointed a committee to
examine and report upon the case. They look upon the Mangoose as the disturbing cause in the equilibrium of nature. All
this trouble has come upon Jamaica because the slaves and
the dogs killed off the cats. We will now leave Jamaica to

wrestle with her rats, mangoose and ticks while we seek health and recreation in other places.

On the twenty-eighth of February, on a very hot afternoon, we embarked for Bermuda. Our ship passed over the former site of Port Royal which, like ancient Gomorrah, was swallowed by an earthquake. Not a house, and but one of all the inhabitants escaped. The monument erected to the only survivor can be seen from the deck. I have referred to this earthquake in a former letter. Our ship stopped for a few hours at Turk's Island, about four hundred and twenty-five mile eastward from Jamaica, from thence she sailed nearly due north, seven hundred and fifty miles to Bermuda. We made the voyage in a little less than six days, the sea being rather rough and the winds adverse.

We passed Hayti on the first of March. Our ship ran close to its shores. We could see the houses, horses and green trees very distinctly. It is quite hilly but has a fertile appearance from the ship. While in Jamaica I read an extract from a Haytian newspaper upon the egressions of the white race. It stated that the race problem had been solved in Hayti ; that a white man could only exist there by tolerance ; that he had no rights that a colored man was bound to respect, and if he did not cease plotting and intriguing in the affairs of State he need expect nothing less than absolute banishment from the Island.

We had a very intelligent gentleman on board from Turk's Island. He was a pure Saxon with light hair, blue eyes and fair skin. I endeavored to learn from him all I could about his native island. Among other questions I asked him if the white people intermarried there with the colored folks, as in Jamaica. I noticed that he did not care to converse much on that subject. He simply said that there were some rich and influential colored people on the island that were recognized and received in the best society ; he then turned the conversation upon the manufacture of salt, and the beautiful shell work of the women. When our ship anchored in the harbor, I noticed a beautiful little sailing yacht approaching us. When within hailing distance I saw she was manned by two colored boys. My Saxon friend waved his handkerchief and one of the boys at once cried out : "Hello, Papa, here we are coming to take you home." I guessed the rest.

The Turk's Island group contains nine small island and a rock called Toney's rock. The principal business of the place is the manufacture of salt from the evaporation of sea water. The women and girls make beautiful shell work and seemed to reap quite a harvest from sales to passengers. The people of the island are mostly colored but the proportion of white people is not as small as in Jamaica.

Life on a ship, if well observed, is always very amusing. We see, on a well filled ship, every phase of human character and can find every crack in the human skull and every crank in the human brain. There were two little children on the ship—Sadie, the bright blue-eyed four-year-old daughter of the captain, and Walter, a very manly eight-year-old son of one of the passengers. He evidently felt his importance, as he performed acts of gallantry towards his little shipmate. Both were free from seasickness and great favorites with the passengers as well as crew. Just before reaching Bermuda Walter came to where I was standing and in a confidential way invited me to walk down into the cabin and take a drink with him before we parted, perhaps forever. I accepted his courtesy, anxious to see how he would carry out his intention. Upon entering the cabin he called the steward and coolly called for "one ginger ale and one rum punch." He said I must excuse him for taking something soft, as his father had promised him one thousand dollars, when he was twenty-one, if he would drink no spirits till he arrived at that age, and said he, with a significant wink, " It's the one thousand dollars I'm after you know." I thought it was a pretty good beginning for an eight-year-old boy.

The gossip of the ship was a young woman of perhaps twenty and an old man of not less than sixty-five years. She was fairly good looking, plump and sprightly. He was big, gross, fat and flabby. To use a comparison from nature, she resembled an over-grown lamb and he looked like an over-fed hog. In other words it was December reposing in the lap of May. He was, or pretended to be, very seasick during the entire voyage, and she did nothing but pet and caress him. She fed him with a spoon and then wiped off his ugly mouth with a kiss, at which he would give a grunt of satisfaction. It was their bridal tour, but by close observation one could see behind the mask. He is undoubtedly a rich old fool and she hopes soon to be a gay and dashing widow.

About two o'clock one bright night I arose to take a last look at the stars fast sinking below the southern horizon. My attention was attracted by the rustling of calico and a sudden commotion upon one of the deck settees. I had disturbed the nest of the pretty stewardess and an English midshipman. They were also *looking at the stars*, waiting for *Venus* to rise.

Speaking of the stars calls to my mind a circumstance bearing upon the modern theory that seasickness has its seat in the brain and not the stomach, as is generally supposed. One of the lady passengers would become sick whenever the ship rolled at night, unless she could see the stars. As soon as she saw them she became perfectly well. If the stars should become obscured by clouds, she would at once become sick—but as soon as the clouds passed and the stars appeared again, she recovered. Here is a fact for the medical profession to consider. Her sickness was caused by her mind's inability to comprehend the motions of the ship without something fixed to look upon. I have known seasick passengers to get suddenly well at the first sight of land.

There were several very intelligent Canadian gentlemen on board in a state of great excitement about the election on what they called the crisis in Canada. They had got the absurd notion into their heads that the *States*, as they called our country, intended to annex Canada, peaceably if possible but by force if necessary. I could not convince them that there was no such thought in the public mind in the United States, and that there was no excitement there on the subject. We agreed at last to settle the question by a friendly game of euchre—two Americans on one side and two Canadians on the other. If the Americans should win Canada was to be annexed to the United States, if the Canadians should win the United States was to be annexed to Canada. It is needless to state the result. The United States won seven to one.

When we arrived at Bermuda the first question by our Canadian friends was: "How has the election in Canada gone?" The answer was: "Sir John and the government sustained." "Hip, hip, hurrah! Three cheers for Sir John and Canada!"

We landed at Bermuda on the morning of March sixth. The sun arose in all his splendor; not a cloud could be seen; the deep indigo blue sea had changed to azure. For a full hour we glided among the beautiful little islands, going so near as to almost touch some of them. The green hills and gray rocks, the white houses and cultivated fields and gardens presented a most charming contrast, while the cool bracing air admonished us that we were in a latitude nearly one thousand miles north of Jamaica.

We are pleasantly quartered at the Hamilton House. In my next I will endeavor to give my impression of Bermuda.

XVI.

BERMUDA, March, 1891.

"Thirty days in prison."

It is somewhat difficult to get into Bermuda, but, at this
season of the year, it is absolutely impossible to get out in less
than thirty days. The first impression of the place is so charming that we fancy we would like to die here among the green
hills, cedar groves, coral islands, glorious sunsets, and starry
nights. After a week we suddenly realize that we have seen
it all. At first we buy a bouquet every morning ; after a while
we notice that all the servant girls wear roses, and even the
beautiful Easter lilies remind us of the funeral decorations of a
corpse.

The insatiable desire of the human heart for new scenery
and excitement, after we have seen all one place has to show,
makes us restless and impatient of restraint. So it was with us
in Bermuda ; but when we began to inquire for a stateroom in
a ship to take us away, we learned to our great disappointment
that every berth and even sleeping room on the seats in the
"Social Hall" had been engaged for three weeks in advance.
Then we realized for the first time that we were indeed "prisoners for thirty days." Solicitations, prayers, petitions, in-
terventions of friends and even bribery were of no avail. There
were already a hundred recorded applications for every berth
that might be given up before sailing day. So, having nothing
else to do, we set ourselves to work in a systematic way to
study the history and topography of the islands. Such is the
perversity of my nature, that if I knew I could leave these
islands at will, I would certainly leave them with regret ; but
as I cannot get away, the feeling of restraint overcomes all the
charming allurements of the place and I shall leave it with un-
speakable pleasure.

The history of the islands is interesting. They take their
name from their Spanish discoverer, Juan Bermudez, who,

while sailing for the West Indies with a cargo of hogs, sighted the islands A. D. 1515. He left a few pigs on the island.

Its discovery by the English was due to a frightful shipwreck. Shakespeare's play, entitled "The Tempest," is said to be founded upon a fearful storm and shipwreck upon the coral reefs on the northwest of the islands. The place was the terror of sailors for many years. They supposed it to be infested with devils, sprites, evil spirits and fairies.

> "Full fathoms five thy father lies;
> Of his bones are coral made;
> These are pearls that were his eyes."

They supposed the inhabitants to be half human and half fiend, such as Calaban, "a freckled whelp, hag-born, not honored with a human shape." It soon became a rendezvous for pirates and buccaneers. It was next to impossible for a ship to land because of the absence of harbors on the south, and the coral reefs, extending for many miles out on the north, with but few channels only known to the initiated. When the shipwrecked English crew were driven upon the islands they found them full of hogs, the natural successors of Juan Bermudez's pigs. For many years after the English settled the islands the silver and copper money bore the image of a hog, and was called "Hog money." I have seen some of it in the Museum here. It was adopted to commemorate old Captain Bermudez's swine.

During the American Revolution, the people of Bermuda strongly sympathized with our patriot fathers. By collusions with emissaries sent by General Washington, the magazines on the islands were robbed of an immense quantity of gunpowder which was shipped to Charleston and safely delivered to the Revolutionary authorities, and was the indirect cause of one of our most decisive victories. The English government never succeeded in discovering the persons who aided us in stealing the powder. The people are now intensely loyal to England and rather unfriendly to us. Nevertheless all its prosperity is due to our market for its onions and potatoes and the hundreds of thousands of dollars we annually pour into its lap for two months' enjoyment of its sunshine. Old Æsop was mistaken when he supposed God's sunshine belonged to all his creatures alike. We have to pay very dearly for it here.

Bermuda was a "nest of hornets" for us during the Rebellion. Great shiploads of arms, ammunition and provisions were sent from England, unloaded here, and by swift little blockade runners safely landed on the South Carolina and Florida coast. It was here also that the execrable wretch,

Dr. Blackburn, attempted to export the yellow fever into the cities of the Northern States.

The position of Bermuda is peculiar. By placing one point of a compass in the center of these islands and the other in New York, then by sweeping it to the left through Charleston and around to the West Indies, it will be found almost equi-distant from those points. The nearest land is Cape Hatteras, six hundred and nineteen miles distant. From Turks Island it is about seven hundred miles, and to New York about six hundred and seventy-seven miles. It is undoubtedly the peak of a sea mountain as high from the bottom of the ocean as Mount Blanc is above the level of the sea. It shows no evidence of volcanic origin. It seems to owe its existence above water to the little coral workers assisted by the winds and waves. It is supposed by geologists that the deposits of the coral insect upon the granite peaks of the submarine mountains have built up what we see of the islands.

There are said to be three hundred and sixty-five islands in the group—one for every day in the year. In fact there are only about one hundred worthy of the name of islands. The five largest are situated so as to form, in appearance, but one island. The other islands are scattered over the sounds and are very small, ranging from five to one hundred yards in diameter. From the top of the lighthouse the group looks something like a large fish hook—the bait end being at the dock yard and only a few feet wide, while the line end is nineteen miles northeast, and about two miles wide. The sounds and harbors are in the center and can only be entered from the north or reef side. The reefs extend from the north coast— the bent part of the hook—from ten to twenty miles out in the sea. None of the reefs are above water and there are but three or four channels through which ships can enter. This makes the entrance to the lagoon, or deep water between the reefs and the islands, very dangerous to all but skilled pilots. No ship will attempt to enter the harbor after sunset. If we count the numerous little rocks of coral that peep their noses above the water, we can make three hundred and sixty-five islands with but little trouble and perhaps many more. I counted twenty-seven from one point of view. The whole group only contains about twenty square miles of territory. The land has either subsided or the waters have raised about forty-four feet, which is proved by finding cedar trees, rooted in rich soil and standing vertically, that depth under the present surface of the water. The most elevated ground is only about two hundred and sixty feet above the sea. The whole surface is very hilly. There is but little flat land and only about one acre in twenty worth cultivating. The whole substratum is coral rock, the soil varying from a few inches to, perhaps, two or three feet in the valleys. The soil, however, such as it is, is very fertile and produces three crops a year. In the olden time the islands were covered with cedars, almost equal to the famous trees of Lebanon. The early settlers built great ships wholly of that wood. The ground is cultivated chiefly by the spade and hoe; plows are seldom used. The coral rock is very soft when first quarried. It is sawed out of the quarry by common rip saws, in large blocks, then sawed up into smaller building blocks with common cross-cut and hand saws. It looks strange to see the masons pick up a block of stone and saw it, in a few minutes, into the desired shape. The houses are all built of this rock ; they are roofed with the same material sawed in thin layers about two inches thick and one foot square, joined by the best Portland cement and whitewashed. Most of the houses are but one story high and are always kept white-washed and clean. All the rain water is drained from the roofs into underground reservoirs. This is required by law, as the only drinking water on the islands is what is gathered from rain falls. Some of the barren hill tops are covered with white-washed cement, forming great water-sheds for the public reservoirs. As an exception to the general rule there are some very beautiful mansions and public buildings.

A remarkable peculiarity of the soil and rock is the immediate absorption of water. Fifteen minutes after a heavy rain the roads and walks are dry and entirely free from mud. There is but little dust in the roads or streets ; this gives a fresh appearance to the green cedar trees and abundant flowers. Most of the roads resemble asphaltum streets. They are cut down in some places fifty feet through the soft rock, the sides being perpendicular and the roadbed solid rock ; this, with the cedars and oleander trees, gives a shaded way very pleasant to drive upon. There are but few more cheerful and romantic drives in the world than those over the delightful roads of Bermuda.

The climate is more even than in the same latitude in other countries. While the cold Northern winds cross the warm Gulf Stream, all the icy frost is melted out. It never freezes here ; the temperature is said never to fall below fifty degrees, and during the summer months seldom to rise above eighty degrees. Coming from the hot climate of Jamaica, we at first felt cold and required our winter clothing, including overcoats. The common people have no fires in their houses even in winter ; if they get chilly they go to bed in daytime and stay there till the weather moderates.

For three or four days we did not feel as well as we did in Jamaica ; perhaps this was due to the sudden check of perspiration. I do not believe Bermuda is a healthy place for an invalid, especially for persons suffering from lung diseases. Colds are very common here notwithstanding all the allegations of the inhabitants to the contrary. It is said, however, that malaria is unknown here. It is, undoubtedly, a good place for overworked persons in good health. Most of the visitors from the North complain of insomnia. We have enjoyed but few nights of quiet and refreshing sleep since we arrived.

Much of the sickness among Northern visitors is the result of dissipation and indiscretion. They come from the icy atmosphere of the North and finding the air soft and pleasant here, they throw off their heavy flannels, dress in their summer clothing and expose themselves to the night air when the thermometer is below sixty degrees. This is especially the case with thoughtless girls. We see them at the weekly balls of the Hamilton Hotel in bare arms, bare backs, bare bosoms and *bare faces*, flirting with the red-coated officers of the British army now stationed here. They dance until they are in a state of free perspiration, almost hissing hot, then rush out for fresh air and remain out until completely chilled. The result is : A plump, rosy-cheeked maiden to-night—to-morrow night a sick girl ; a hacking cough and hectic flush in a month, and at the end of the year the *coughing* ends with a *coffin.*

XVII

FOUR BLACK TO ONE WHITE PERSON—A HINT FOR OUR SOUTHERN STATES—AMERICANS NOT PERMITTED TO OWN LAND—AN UGLY REPORT ABOUT GENERAL HASTINGS, OF OHIO — UNUSUALLY HONEST AND PIOUS PEOPLE — SOME INCONSISTENCIES—AMUSEMENTS, INNOCENT AND OTHERWISE—A NEW YORK BELLE WHO LEFT BECAUSE SHE HAD NOTHING TO WEAR—DOCK YARD AND DEFENCES OF THE ISLANDS.

BERMUDA, March, 1891.

The entire resident population of Bermuda does not exceed fifteen thousand. Of these seven-tenths are black or colored. Hamilton, the chief city, has a population of about two thousand. The colored people are polite, well dressed, fairly educated and speak good English. They have no patois like Jamaica. The early settlers attempted to reduce North American Indians to slavery, and to that end sent large numbers of them here. Most of them died under the cruel effort to enslave them. They, however, mixed with the black slaves and have left a distinct trace of Indian blood among the color-ed people. The color line is distinctly drawn, and notwith-standing the disparity in numbers, the white people rule. By the laws of the land the right of suffrage is only enjoyed by male citizens possessed of at least three hundred dollars' worth of property. No person is eligible to office who does not own a freehold estate worth at least twelve hundred dol-lars. The rich colored people vote with the whites and carry every election by large majorities. Here is a hint for our Southern States.

As a rule the people are kind and courteous to strangers. It is their policy to be so ; but the English government early realized the danger of permitting Americans to own land. They knew that in a few years the rich men of America (as they call the United States), would own every inch of land and then what would become of Bermuda's loyalty to the Crown ? To prevent the impending danger they have passed and strictly enforce an alien law making it unlawful for *any* foreigner to hold, inherit. or transmit real estate, and escheat-ing to the Crown all lands held contrary to this statute The *Ohio* General Hastings owns a beautiful villa here called Fairy Land, and there is a very ugly rumor (which I hope is not true) that to keep his villa he has taken the oath of allegiance to the Queen. If this is not true General Hastings ought to deny it, for it is in everybody's mouth here and tends to lower him very much among the American people. If I am not mistaken he now draws a large pension from the United States Govern-ment for the loss of his leg in battle under his country's flag. Allegiance to the Queen must mean disloyalty to the United States, especially if the two countries should become embroiled in war. There are certain suggestions that no honorable man can entertain, no matter what the reward or financial necessity. I do not believe a man can be found in Pennsyl-vania, no matter how poor or humble, who would renounce his allegiance to his country for the whole of Bermuda. Such a suggestion would be as repulsive as an offer to purchase his hope of heaven or his faith in God.

In matters of etiquette the Bermudians are very exacting. They get this from the great number of British officers station-ed here. It is impossible to enter society without a formal introduction. Permission must be formally asked to visit the government docks or gardens and grounds of the private villas, but it is never refused. Indeed, they take great pains to make the visit as pleasant as possible.

The common people are said to be more than usually honest. It is no uncommon thing for a shopkeeper to go to dinner without shutting his store door or leaving any one in charge. I had occasion to make a small purchase in quite a large variety store. The proprietor, without a moment's hesitation, left me in charge of his store while he went out for five or six minutes to hunt change for a half sovereign. I am inclined, however, to attribute this exceptional probity to the certainty of detection and the impossibility of escape. The place is too small and is too much isolated to permit a criminal to get away. He could neither hide himself nor his plunder, nor could he safely sell it. It would not be very difficult to search every suspect on the islands. As an answer, however, to this vaunted allegation of superior honesty, it is difficult to account for the expensive machinery of Justice here, if there is no need of it. I notice quite a large court house and jail ; regular courts, a Chief Justice and two assistant Judges with greater salaries than Pennsylvania pays to her Judges ; an Attorney General with a salary of three thousand dollars, and fees amounting to as much more ; a Solicitor General, Provost Marshal, Prothonotary and all the other necessary officers of a first-class court, and yet the whole population of the islands is not one-fourth that of Delaware county.

They also claim unusual piety in matters of religion. I have no doubt, from the number and splendor of their churches, that they are very devout Christians, but I wish to call attention to a fact in apparent inconsistency with such a claim. The New York steamers arrive every *Sunday* about noon. The event is celebrated by the presence of all the inhabitants of the town. Every hack is on the wharf and all the hotels have their runners there. As I was taught to revere the Sabbath and have made it a rule of my life to attend divine worship every Sunday morning if possible, I arose early on my first Sunday and determined to go to some convenient church. Upon consulting the bulletin board in the hall of our hotel, I was surprised to find that not a church in the city was open on Sunday morning. I could find them in the country by hiring a carriage at a dollar an hour ; but the city churches were only open in the evening. On inquiry I learned the reason. The poor preachers had to talk to empty pews as soon as the signal went up announcing tha. the New York ship had entered the harbor. It reminded me of a camp meeting scene I witnessed a few years ago at Renoboth. The bathing hour arrived while a celebrated preacher was eloquently discoursing upon "The Immortality of the Soul." In less than five minutes a large congregation of devout listeners were in their tents adjusting their bathing robes, and the preacher was compelled to close his sermon without finishing his subject.

The principal amusements here are sailing around the sounds and harbors ; making excursions to the coral reefs some ten or fifteen miles out ; driving over the beautiful roads; exploring the caves, caverns and dens ; visiting the hospitable owners of charming villas ; attending the weekly balls at the Hamilton, and, among the ladies, making love and gossiping ; among the men, getting drunk, smoking and gambling.

The girls, old as well as young, cannot withstand the temptation to display their charms and dresses in the ball room. There are some very gay and rich young widows, and vain mothers with their marriageable daughters boarding at the Hamilton. On every Tuesday night we have a grand ball attended by all Her Majesty's military and naval heroes in their gold lace, tinsel and red, tailless coats. The rich citizens of the islands also attend with their beautiful daughters. It is impossible to describe the glorious display of rich dresses, bare skin and dazzling diamonds. We had a millionaire young lady here for three weeks, from New York—she would have staid longer but "she had nothing to wear." During her three weeks' stay at the Hamilton she came to the table three times a day in a different dress. To cap the climax, she wore *two* dresses on the same evening at the last ball she attended. She first appeared in white satin, waltzing around the room with a fine looking red-coat fop with a one-eye glass, which "ever and anon he shot out, then took it up again." In a half hour after, she appeared on the floor with another red-coat, but this time she was arrayed in black, trimmed with point lace. During her stay she had appeared in sixty four different dresses. I could but moralize upon the pleasure it must afford her father's ghost (for he is dead they say) to realize the results of his lifetime of toil, economy and perhaps his lost soul, in the accumulation of his millions. They were being dispersed by his dashing daughter to advertise some New York silk store, while she is but a walking model for some Parisian *modiste*.

England has spent an enormous sum in improving and strengthening her hold upon these islands While in size they are marked on the map of the world by a pin point, in naval importance they are only equaled by Malta. Every salient point has been fortified ; big guns bristle from forts all over the islands. The great dock-yards are used and are equipped with men and machinery for the repair of the largest ships of war in the British navy. The floating dock, made in England and towed here by four large men-of-war a few years ago, is the largest in the world and will, with ease, bring to the surface the keel of the greatest ship ever built. It would be impossible to capture the place by direct assault, but the improvements and discoveries in modern warfare have rendered most of these costly defenses entirely valueless. Even the splendid harbor, capable of sheltering the entire British navy, would be useless in time of war. The islands are so narrow that an attacking fleet could cover every inch of the harbor with explosive shells at a distance of three or four miles from the shore. If war should ever be declared between England and the United States, the place would be very hard to defend. It could only be saved from destruction by a naval fight. The ships in the harbor would have to come out and fight in the open sea, or be destroyed in their shelter. The people seem to realize that this would be the probable result in case of war.

I had intended to make this my last letter but I am unable to say all of Bermuda that I have observed as worthy of note, in time for the mail which closes to-day at 12.

XVIII

A CHANCE FOR ESCAPE—THE SPANISH ROCK, DEVIL AND HERETICS—VEGETATION INJURED BY THE SALT SPRAY— THE UNFORTUNATE NEW CATHEDRAL—AN OLD FEMALE POKER PLAYER—THE BEAUTIFUL DRIVES—CAVERNS AND GROTTOES—A DAY AT THE DOCK-YARD—AN OLD SAILOR'S PUN—A GENUINE OCTOPUS.

BERMUDA, March, 1891.

By a happy succession of fortunate circumstances I will be able to shorten my term of imprisonment one week. Two young ladies of our hotel are so enamored with the place and have been the objects of such marked attention from certain red-coated young men, that they expressed a desire to remain another week. From pure gallantry, I offered to exchange my splendid stateroom on the new ship Trinidad for a very bad one on the old Orinoco, which is to sail a week earlier. By this simple arrangement we were all made happy. They get another week to flirt with their beaux and I will get home a week sooner than I had hoped to. Thus we see another illustration of the old saying, "One man's misery is another's joy." Now that we feel sure of being able to leave the beautiful islands, we feel less inclined to go. It is certainly a charming place (for a week). The climate is cool and moist without being cold and wet. I, however, love warm weather. I enjoy the long summer days. It is seldom too hot for me, except in politics; then they sometimes make it pretty warm, but I generally manage to live through it and, on the whole, rather enjoy even political—fire.

There is a high coral bluff on the south coast of the main island known as Spanish Rock, before alluded to. It has some cabalistic characters engraved upon its almost perpendicular face, about one hundred feet up from the sea, which is said to be over three miles deep at this place. The engraving on the rock is surmounted by a cross. The tradition among the people is, that the inscription was made by John Bermudez, the discoverer of the islands ; but this is a mistake, as I learned from old records hereinafter mentioned. We visited the rock a few days ago and found the date engraved upon it to be A. D. 1543. By permission of the obliging Librarian of the public library in the Parliament building, I was shown Le Froy's Bermuda, compiled from Colonial Records dating from 1611 to 1652. Among other rare books he showed me one in Old English Black Letter, printed in 1613. From these records it appears that Juan Bermudez merely reported his discovery to the Spanish king ; that afterwards many ships were wrecked upon the treacherous reefs ; that at last the king, being anxious to populate the islands, granted a charter to a Portuguese named Ferdinand Camelo, who, it is said, merely visited the islands and carved his initials and the date of taking possession upon the cliff, since called Spanish Rock, which he surmounted with a cross for the purpose, as he reported, of "frightening off the *Divil* and *Heretics.*" He must have abandoned his grant, for the next authentic record we have is the report of Gonzales Ferdinand d' Oviedo, in 1611. After the frightful shipwreck that cast Sir George Somers on the shore, the English became acquainted with it, and have possessed it ever since. It is very doubtful whether the engraving on the rock was not the work of some shipwrecked sailor, as parts of a wreck have been recently found in the deep water near the rock. The property now belongs to Clarence Peniston, the present Provost Marshal, and a gentleman of great culture and social standing. We became acquainted with him by special introduction and have enjoyed the hospitality of himself and accomplished lady. They are among the oldest families of the islands. I found the name of his ancestors in the old records that I examined in the library.

We have had two or three days of very rainy weather ; I suppose it is the equinoctial storm. It is cool but not frosty. While it never freezes here, the islands are subject to dreadful storms. The trouble with the climate seems to be its sudden changes from sunshine to rain. When the temperature falls below sixty degrees there is great danger of taking cold. They start the fires in the hotel grates when the thermometer falls to fifty-eight degrees. This makes it too warm; then to escape the heat of the house the guests go upon the porches and promenades, and almost before they are aware of it, begin to sneeze and cough. In the great storm of December last the whole surface of the islands was covered with a salt spray for several days. When the sun came out again the inhabitants were surprised to find what looked like a hoar frost on the trees, shrubs, flowers and grass. All the onions, lilies and potatoes appeared to be frost bitten. The leaves of all the sub-tropical plants and trees were killed. The bananas were severely injured and have not yet recovered. The great india rubber tree, with its spreading branches fifty feet long had all its foliage killed. It was found that the spray from the sea for two or three days had left a crust of salt over the islands which had proved very destructive to early and tender vegetables. One of the disastrous effects of this storm was to nearly destroy the splendid new Cathedral, one of the most beautiful and prominent buildings in Bermuda. This church seems to be doomed to more than ordinary misfortunes. It was built in 1850, at a cost of sixty thousand dollars, and was so graceful and beautiful in all its details, that its congregation called it the "Chapel of Ease." In 1884 it was burned to the ground by an incendiary who has never been discovered. The congregation with remarkable energy rebuilt it more beautiful than before. Just as it was nearly completed and was the object of general admiration, the great wind storm of November last nearly ruined it. The new edifice had cost nearly eighty thousand dollars. The congregation, though unfortunate, were not disheartened. They have nearly restored the damage caused by the storm. It stands upon the highest ground in Hamilton and is one of the first objects that strikes the traveler's eye as he enters the harbor.

There is an eccentric old woman now boarding at the Hamilton Hotel, who is an inveterate poker player—not "baby poker" for chips, but the real thing without limit. She is reputed to be very rich. To ease her conscience and bring good luck while she is here she gives all her winnings for the repair of the church, and when at home she devotes her earnings at the game to charity generally. Singular as it may seem she generally wins more than she loses.

There are five or six three-hour drives over excellent roads, and two drives that take all day. In addition to these there are five or six drives of an hour, and two or three sails, with one steamboat excursion to the reefs; these completely show all that is worth seeing in Bermuda. One week is sufficient to see it all. There are no railroads, as the distances are too short to make even a street railway profitable. There are

thousands of persons on these islands who have never seen a
railroad, a snow storm or natural ice.

The drives are mostly through the rich valleys and show
off the place to great advantage.   We see hundreds of acres of
onions, potatoes, tomatoes and Easter lilies, all cultivated, in
small patches, by hand.   The islands have several very pretty
caves.   When you have seen one, however, you have seen them
all.   The guide of the grotto for a fee, shows you what he calls
a Cathedral, with vaulted roof hanging with stalactites and the
floor full of stalagmites, which he calls altars and angels.
They show you dungeons, bridal chambers, sacred fountains,
silver lakes, holy fonts, etc., by candle light and burning
torches of palmetto branches.   It requires about as much imagination to convert these caves—reached by crooked holes,
over boulders and by rough, dirty wooden ladders—into
churches, altars, bridal chambers, etc., as old Polonius requir.d
to convert Hamlet's cloud into a ship, a whale and a camel.
While he could see its likeness to a ship and its resemblance
to a whale, he could only compromise the last questionby admitting that it was "*backed* like a camel."

By making written application, permission will be sent by
mail to visit Her Majesty's dock-yard.   All visitors are required upon presenting their passes to register their names,
country and business or profession.   If the authorities are
then satisfied that no designs are intended against the Majesty
of England, an officer will be detailed to show you through
the machine shops, ship yards and great floating dock, undoubtedly the largest in the world and capable of raising out
of water the heaviest ship in the British navy.   The machine
shops and ship yards are not worth looking at ; they are toys
as compared with Roach's in Chester.   There is an old wooden
war ship lying at the dock, used as a place for sailors to sleep:
it is a very interesting study and clearly represents old-time
naval architecture.   She was built in 1815, and is called "The
Irresistible."   Our grandchildren will have nothing but old
paintings to give them an idea of one of these old wooden
men-of-war, with three gun decks and seventy-four guns,
great masts and full-rigged square sails, and high quarter
deck where the captain and naval officers sat like monarchs of
a wooden world.   They build no new ships at these yards :
they are entirely devoted to repairing disabled vessels.

A fleet of five large war ships entered the harbor a few
days ago.   As soon as the signal was raised all the horses and
carriages were engaged and every person that could get away
drove over to the North shore to view the sight.   It was a very
pretty spectacle to see these great steamers, manned, with their
colors flying, sweeping majestically along the entire North

coast from the entrance through the narrow channel at St.
George's, down to the dock-yards, about nineteen miles. They
have been cruising in Southern seas and are now slowly moving towards Northern waters.

They utilize everything at the dock-yards ; even old condemned boilers are cut up and converted into buoys (the English pronounce the word *boys*). The old officer who showed us
around got off a very bad pun on the word. Looking quiz-
zically at the buoys, he said : " What a good thing it would
be if they could cut us old fellows up after we are worn out
and make *buoys* (boys) of us." Of course we all laughed very
heartily at the wretched pun, which tickled the old fellow
so much that he absolutely refused a proffered *tip* after his
task was done. We learned afterwards, however, that the
commandant had strictly forbidden the ushers to accept tips
from visitors.

I saw at the dock-yard what I had often read about but
never seen before, a genuine Octopus. I had read Homer's
story of the destruction of one of old Ulyses' ships and nine of
his sailors by one of these terrible sea monsters. I also remembered a very vivid description of the one that seized the
villain, Clubin, by the heel and left nothing but his skeleton
in a cavern at the rocks of Dover, so graphically portrayed by
Victor Hugo in his "Toilers of the Sea." I also had a dim
recollection of Congressman Jack Robinson's reference to the
political *Octopus* that gave him so much annoyance in his
Congressional campaign, but I had never seen a living Devil
Fish before. True it was but a baby only four feet long, but
it was large enough and strong enough to kill a man if he
should be so unfortunate as to come within the embrace of its
ugly arms. One of the gentlemen punched it with his cane ;
in an instant it seized the stick with one of its snake-like arms
and it required all the man's strength to withdraw his cane
from the hold its suckers had taken upon it. It had been
caught by a fisherman by making a loop on a rope and quietly
dropping it over its head.

XIX.

A Sail Among the Small Islands—The Coral Reefs—
Rock Studies on the Coast—St. George—A Church
Schism with its Usual Consequences—Prosperous and
Crowded Hotels—Angry Excursionists from Boston
—A Glance at Bermuda Society—Her Majesty's Tail-
less Red Coats—Faded Roses.

BERMUDA, March, 1891.

The trip to the dock-yard is generally made in small
steamers. It gives a very pleasant hour's sail among the
beautiful little islands in the harbor. These small green islands, some of them not fifty yards in diameter, reminded me
somewhat of the Thousand Isles of the St. Lawrence. We
have now explored all the islands, caves, rocks and hills usually visited by strangers here.

Hamilton is situated in about the center of the islands.
It takes a full day by carriage to visit St. George at the extreme Northeast; and about the same time to go to the Lighthouse and Ireland island at the extreme Southeast. The usual
drives require about five days, after which there is nothing more
to see, unless the tourist desires to visit the reefs. To do this
he must hire a tug at a cost of one hundred dollars and small
boats at one dollar each. It will take an entire day to make the
excursion as the reefs are from ten to thirty miles off the North
shore. The water between the reefs and the North shore is
called the Lagoon and, when once within it, it affords a safe
harbor for any sized ship. None but skillful pilots, however,
can enter this harbor. To reduce the expense, travelers generally club together and hire the tug and boats, and provide a
lunch and long sea tongs to secure specimens of coral as souv-
enirs. One of the most pleasant drives is to Tuckertown, on the
South shore. The rocks are very interesting ; in some places
they stand up seventy feet perpendicular. The action of the
waves has made great caverns, natural bridges and other very
interesting rock studies. The old Spanish Rock—described in
my last letter—is on this drive. I found a very pretty piece of
coral and captured a *"Portuguese man-of-war"* (a species of
Nautilus), on this coast. I hope to be able to bring my prize
home if I can do so without bursting his blubber sail. I happened to find the tide unusually low, and by partially undres-
sing and clambering like a ten-year-old boy down the sharp
and rugged edge of the rocks, and then wading out into the
sea, I secured my specimens. We only prize what we secure

by great labor or danger, and as I secured these specimens by
my own labor and not without some danger, I value them far
above their intrinsic worth.   Very fine specimens of coral can
be bought here for a few shillings.

The drive, usually taken first, is along the North shore,
around Harrington Sound and by the "Devil's Hole" and
Joyce's Caves, and back over Prospect Hill, which is crowned
by a fort and gives a fine view of all the islands southwest.
The "Devil's Hole" is a cavern in a hillside having a subterranean communication with the sea.   It is full of all kinds of
enormous fish, crabs, lobsters and turtles.   Some of the fish
are four feet long and very voracious.   They say they will
devour dogs and even children if they happen to fall into the
hole.   This is, however, an *on dit*, and must be taken with due
allowance.   The owner of the hole charges a shilling for a
look into it.   Sometimes he takes as much as twenty-five dollars a day from visitors.

St. George, the oldest part of the islands, can be visited
either by land or water.   The authorities have built a very
substantial causeway at least half a mile long, connecting St.
George with Hamilton.   There are some very interesting rock
studies on the North coast at St. George.   The eternal dash
of the waves against the soft coral rock has washed them into
innumerable fantastic forms, caves, natural bridges, deep
caverns and columns fifty feet high, apparently just ready to
topple over.

On the hill, just back from the harbor, stands the oldest
church in Bermuda.   Near the old church stands what appears
to be a grand ruin.   It is quite large and of fine Gothic architecture.   Nothing stands but the bare walls of cut coral rock.
I supposed I was looking upon some old ruined cathedral   It
only wanted some ivy, and an old gatekeeper with an invented
legend and a charge of sixpence, to make it equal to many of
the interesting ruins of the Old World.   When I learned its
history, the illusion vanished.   Instead of a ruined abbey,
some three hundred years old, it was but twelve years since it
was built.   The church authorities of the old cathedral conceived the idea of erecting a new and more imposing church.
They sent to England for architects and plans and commenced
the work with great energy.   Just as the mason work was
completed, and the structure was ready for its roof, the Devil
entered the church in the form of a schism between the ritual-
ists and low church party.   Singular as it may seem, all the
colored people were extreme high churchmen ; so the colored
question also entered into the quarrel.   Finally the white people withdrew, leaving the Bishop and his colored friends in
peaceable possession of the bare walls and a heavy debt.   For

twelve years no work has been done. Grass, shrubbery and even large trees have grown up in the nave and around the abandoned walls, giving it the ruined appearance before mentioned.

The people say that this has been the most successful year for tourists the islands have ever seen. All the hotels are crowded. The Hamilton has about one hundred more guests than can be accommodated with apartments. They sleep in the neat little houses of the town and take their meals at the hotel at five dollars a day. To add to the plethora of visitors, a ship load of Boston excursionists, for Jamaica, were suddenly emptied into the town a few days ago. They had paid for one day in Bermuda, horses and carriages included. As soon as the agent could land, he hired every free horse and wagon he could for the day. As a natural consequence the other guests could not get a carriage for love or money, and could but give vent to their indignation by cursing the excursionists. About every other man I met used the "big D." The hotel proprietors had to convert the side parlors and bath rooms into sleeping places. There were several very respectable gentlemen with their wives and daughters on the excursion who had been inveigled into purchasing a ticket by reading the highly colored handbills and flaming posters issued by the person who got up the excursion. The voyage from Boston to Jamaica, stopping a day at Bermuda and back to Boston was to be accomplished in twenty days. They were five days reaching Bermuda, and cannot possibly reach Jamaica in less than five days more ; this, with the day spent here, will make eleven days, only allowing them nine days to return ; so they can only look at the shores of Jamaica without landing if they return to Boston within the twenty days for which the ship was chartered.

There is but one opinion among the excursionists, and that is that they have been badly sold. They swear vengeance against the persons who got up the excursion, but can only find about two innocent persons on the ship, hired to show them around, but who had nothing whatever to do with the swindle. When they get home they will probably find no responsible person to answer in damages for the broken contract, to take one hundred and eighty persons from Boston to Jamaica. giving five days on the island, and one on the Bermudas, and return to Boston in *twenty* days. A more demoralized set of half-seasick creatures, as they herded together like swine on the ship, I never saw. Many of them forfeited their tickets and stayed in Bermuda determined to seek redress when they get home, but as before stated, the process will probably be returned— " *Non est inventus.* "

We cannot close our notes on Bermuda without a glance at its social side. The precise meaning of the word Society, is hard to well define. We may call it The general association of refined people. Proper human intercourse, or the enjoyments of human society according to the rules of politeness established by well-bred people. It includes social visits, friendly salutations, agreeable little courtesies, evening parties, teas, dinners, parlor entertainments, rural and manly sports and games, in a word, every enjoyment recognized by the usages of polite and refined people. The crowning glory of Society is a fashionable wedding or a grand ball. In the sense of the word as above defined, I may say that the society of Bermuda is good. The better classes are extremely hospitable, while most of the people, even in the humbler walks, are polite. I am sorry I cannot say as much for some of our countrymen now sojourning in Bermuda. I do not think *Society* in Philadelphia, New York or Boston, is fairly represented here. Our American women are entirely too loud, demonstrative and independent to make a good impression. I only speak, however, of a few. Most of the American ladies here are refined in their manners as well as elegant in their attire. There are, however, a few women here who, daily as well as weekly, make fools of themselves. They wear great flashy diamonds when they ought not ; they wear ball room dresses at the table ; they expose their bare arms even to their arm-pits, and bosoms and backs further than decency permits and they talk too much of their horses, houses and country places. At the weekly balls some of the women who are old enough to be grandmothers dress like girls of eighteen. To see one ball is not to comprehend them all. The last ball was conspicuous more for its wall flowers than its rose buds. One or two old dowagers appeared in very low-necked dresses, exposing their painted ribs, that reminded us more of the shades of death than the fountains of life. What was lacking in youth was made up in pearls, diamonds and gaudy dresses. I saw but one really beautiful woman, over forty, in the ball room. I will not name her for obvious reasons. As long as she is unnamed every old skeleton present on that occasion will think I mean her. There's nothing like a little policy to get along smoothly in this world.

The Queen's guards and naval officers were present in force, decorated with gold lace and in bright red jackets. I think the Queen ought to put *tails* to the *red coats* of her soldiers. It would add very much to their grace in the ball room, and as that is about the only use she puts them to here, she ought to consider their personal appearance in " *Society*, you know."

One fat fellow, with a short neck and big jaw, wore a jacket about two sizes too small. While dancing, bending and bowing, his jacket worked up to his arm-pits, exposing his flannel shirt to the great amusement of his comrades. They don't wear suspenders.

The old girls of from forty-five to sixty reminded me of over-ripe fruit and withered flowers. They had been delicious and fragrant in their day, but they have forgotten that the sweetest roses wither and the finest fruit decays. Where will the lovely white lilies and beautiful flowers that decorate the ball room and repose so temptingly upon the fair bosoms of the gay and happy damsels, be to-morrow night? Some of them will be worn by the servant girls, others will be thrown into the slop jars. But if I continue the comparison further I may be taken for a pessimist, which I am not. I believe in young people enjoying themselves to the full extent of the good things of life, but I do not believe in young people becoming prematurely old, nor in old people trying by paint, powder and perfume, to reverse the order of Nature by counterfeiting youth.

This letter will close my comments on Bermuda. Our ship sails to-day at 1 P. M.

XX.

HUNTING IN VIRGINIA—A MARYLANDER'S OPINION OF YANKEES—VIRGINIA HOSPITALITY—A LOST DOG—WOODCOCK AND WOODPECKERS — OUR FIRST DUCK—COON HUNT— "DEM WEEDS DAT HAB ROOTS AT BOTH ENDS "—THE LOST FOUND—AN ANECDOTE—" MILLIONS OF DUCKS "— A SWEET SLEEP IN THE OPEN FIELD—FIRESIDE STORIES —DILAPIDATION AND WASTE.

EXMORE, VA., December, 1892.

Our party consisted of three boys, under forty, two men, over sixty, five good dogs and two pups. We got a hint that Mr. Cleveland was going to Exmore to shoot ducks, so we organized our little party to see whether we could not kill more partridges than his party did waterfowl.

While on our journey in the cars, we overheard a Maryland "gentleman" express his opinion of Yankees. He said : " One of them came down here four years ago and bought five hundred acres of cripple land for five hundred dollars and *sot* it all out in peach trees. Three years after his 'crap' of peaches paid for his farm. I was fool enough to buy his plantation for five thousand dollars. The next year the trees began to die. I never got a paying 'crap.' If you want to be beat, bargain with a Jew or a Yankee."

We left Chester at eleven A. M., and arrived at Exmore about four P. M. Our point of destination was the farm of W. J. James, Esq., about ten miles from the station. We had written to him three days in advance to meet us at the station with a team to take us to his house. When we arrived no one was there to receive us. On inquiry we learned that the mails went to Jamesville but twice a week, and it was quite probable that our letter had not yet been received. We hired carriages to take us to the nearest hotel, at Dell Haven, about a mile away, but when we were making arrangements with the landlord for accommodations, a team with two fine little Virginia horses came at a very rapid rate down the road. It proved to be the wagon of our host, Mr. James. He was sick in bed when our letter reached him, about two hours before but rather than disappoint us, he had left his bed and came for us. We drove back to the station, loaded his wagon with our trunks, dog-cakes, guns and ammunition, and had a splendid ten miles ride by moonlignt to his mansion. When about eight miles from the station, one of the young dogs gave a yelp and turned back as fast as he could run. We stopped our wagon and ran back after him calling and whistling as we ran, but the fool ran faster than we could, and was soon out of sight. We lost a half hour in our vain efforts to recover the poor brute, then gave it up in despair and slowly wended our way homeward, in the hope that the idiot canine would have natural instinct enough to follow our trail, but we heard nothing more of him, and reluctantly gave him up as lost. We regretted our bad luck very much, as he was a full-bred Irish setter, and was highly prized by his master in Chester, from whom we had borrowed him.

When we arrived at the home of Mr. James, we were cordially received by his excellent and obliging wife, who welcomed us to a warm fireside and a good supper. She had only expected two guests, but showed no embarrassment when she found five hungry men and six dogs emptied into her household. A peculiar trait of Virginia hospitality is the abundance of food upon the family table. She had provided for two and had more than enough for ten. We cannot too highly express our admiration for our kind and obliging hostess. Although her husband was sick, she soon provided comfortable sleeping accommodations for us all. Her beds were soft, he table well supplied and her fireside always cheerful. She ha three bright, well-bred and intelligent boys, ranging from ten to seventeen years of age, who were untiring in their efforts to serve us and make our short sojourn agreeable.

The day after our arrival was Sunday, we took a stroll over the farm, and on our return enjoyed a grand oyster roast upon the shore at the end of the lawn. The mansion is beautifully situated upon a rising knoll, gently sloping to the water's edge. The Chesapeake Bay, at this place is very wide. In looking out upon it, one would suppose he was gazing upon the broad ocean. The shore is very irregular and full of little bays running into the main land from a few hundred yards to many miles. Mr. James' house is built upon the rising shore of one of these little bays. In rough weather we can see the breakers and hear their sea-like roar, while the water in its branches is smooth and lake-like. The branches, or little bays, are planted with the most delicious and finely flavored oysters in the world. A great abundance of them were daily provided for our use and wood was always ready for a roast.

The weather has been very dry for several months ; as a consequence the fresh water springs and little streams are dry and as partridges are great water drinkers, they have migrated to places where they can find fresh springs. We never saw better feeding ground or finer cover for quail than in this part of Virginia, but, for the reason above given, the birds are very scarce and mostly found in the pine thickets and almost boundless woods. It requires long tramps and industrious hunting to find them, and when found, they must be shot upon the "snap."

We were agreeably surprised to learn from Mr. James that there were plenty of woodcock upon his farm. Our surprise increased when he told us that they flew from tree to tree and were mostly shot by boys and negroes. As a woodcock requires soft, spongy ground, and was never known to light upon a tree, we concluded there must be some mistake, and, upon a closer inquiry, we found to our disgust, as well as disappointment, that our host, who was not much of a sportsman, had confounded the name of woodcock with that of woodpecker.

The reader who has never hunted in Virginia, will, perhaps, be surprised to learn that single fields often contain over fifty acres and are generally surrounded by pine wood land. These fields must be carefully hunted. When a covey is raised, one shot at it is all we get. The birds at once fly to the thick pines, where they are found and shot one by one, with great difficulty. We tramped over fully a hundred miles of such ground, hunted faithfully from sunrise till dark, and succeeded in shooting about one hundred birds and several rabbits. When it was too dark to shoot, we had to walk from two to four miles from the "using grounds" to our home, and were often greatly fatigued.

One night, after a busy day, we found ourselves about four miles from home. The young man who was acting as our guide informed us that we could save a half mile by making a short cut over the head of a swampy branch of the Chesapeake by crossing it upon logs and trunks of trees that had been felled for that purpose. When we arrived at the swamp, we found the tide had backed the water, and that the logs upon which we were to cross were, in some places, several inches under the surface. The dampened moss had made the logs very slippery. One of our party ignored gum boots and always wore leather hunting shoes. He could wade very well in four inches of mud or water. To avoid getting his feet wet he took his shoes and stockings off, and, with his trowsers rolled up over his knees, and his gun and shoes in his hand, he was carefully feeling his way over on the logs, when one of the dogs, at a full run from behind, jumped between his legs and threw him into the water up to his hips. He crawled out like a drowned rat, and used some very energetic language to the poor dog. He had at least a mile to walk in his wet clothes, and naturally concluded that "the longest way around was sometimes the shortest way home." He, however, took his mishap like a philosopher, and claimed that he was the only one of our party that had secured a real good duck.

One night we had an old fashioned coon hunt. We were smoking our Havanas, enjoying the genial warmth of a bright and cheerful fire, and the peaceful rest so refreshing to the tired limbs of a weary hunter, when a neighbor entered the room and informed us that his dog was on the trail of a coon and if we desired some sport, we could, he had no doubt, soon secure it. The boys of our party seized their guns and soon forgot their fatigue. The bark of the dog announced the happy news that the coon was treed. After an hour's walk they found him.

> The moon was shining silver bright
> And stars of glory crowned the night,
> High on a limb that same old coon
> Was singing to himself this tune:
> "Get out of the way, you're all unlucky.
> Clear the way for old Kentucky."

Two loads of No. 8 shot hardly tickled him. One of the party had taken the precaution to bring his new choke barrel gun and two cartridges of heavy duck shot. This was too much for the poor coon. The first charge of duck shot killed him stone dead. We intend to have him stuffed and present him to the McClure Gun Club.

Walking across an old field in Virginia at night, requires care and skill. The running briars take root at both ends and

form a sort of loop, which, unless you lift the feet high, is sure
to trip you up. The colored people call them "trip weeds dat
hab roots at both ends."

On our fourth day's hunt we went several miles into new
territory. Being hungry, we hailed a sloop lying at anchor
in one of the little bays and asked the captain if he had oysters
to sell. He had nothing but sweet potatoes, but asked if we
had not lost a dog. We informed him that we had and described our abandoned pup. He said the dog had been wandering about the shore all the morning. In a few minutes we
found him, stinking with the carrion upon which he had fed
since he left us five days before. We were glad to recover
him and be able to restore him to his owner. We kept him a
close prisoner until we landed him safe in the cars for Chester.

In our wandering from farm to farm, we inquired of all
the boys and old colored farm hands we met, if they could tell
us where the quail "used." They all directed us to places
where we could find plenty of *patridges*, but we seldom found
them in the places indicated. It reminded me of a hunt I once
had on the Chowan river in North Carolina. The party were
on Mr. Thomas Simpson's yacht "The Comet." We moored
our little ship to a rickety old wharf and inquired of an old
negro whether there was game around there. "O, yes," said
he, "there's right smart of game out here. Me and another
fellow cotch a fine fat mush rat 'bout a quarter of a mile down
the river about three weeks ago."

The information we got from the old North Carolina negro
was about as reliable as the intelligence communicated by his
brethren of Virginia. I passed a hut full of shiny-faced urchins,
with an old man sitting in the cabin door smoking a corn-cob
pipe. I asked him if there were any ducks around there. "O,
yes," said he, "millions of them ; just sneak down de branch
and you'll get one, sure as falling off a log." This brought
to my mind the duck one of our companions got the night
before by "falling off a log." I crawled down the steep bank,
got scratched by green briars and pricked by the sharp holly
leaves, sneaked for five hundred yards along the ragged shore
and through the thick underbrush to a point where the ducks
ought to be. Just as I passed the point, up jumped one of the
largest black ducks I had ever seen. He was not over twenty
yards from where I stood. I gave him both barrels under the
right wing and tumbled him into the water. Alas, for the
disappointments of a hunter's life ! I had killed an enormous
buzzard, who had been feeding upon a dead rabbit upon the
shore. That afternoon, while crossing a fifty acre field full of
"dem weeds with roots at both ends," I sat down for a few
minutes' rest. Before I knew it, I was sound asleep, with the

bare, sandy soil for my bed and a wood-grass tussock for my pillow. I think I would have slept for hours had I not been awakened by the crack of my companions' guns at a covey of partridges about five hundred yards from my resting place. I did not suffer the slightest injury from my half hour's sleep upon the ground. I would have considered it as a deliberate attempt at suicide to have exposed myself in the same way at home.

We spent the forenoon of our last day upon the farm of Mr. James' brother—a genial, whole-souled man—who left nothing undone that could in any way contribute to our comfort and amusement. In the afternoon his son ferried us over one of the branches, at least half mile wide to entirely new territory. While crossing, he raked up enough oysters to make us a good lunch. We took supper with him that night, and spent an hour around his comfortable fireside. It was no small matter to provide a meal for five hungry men, but Mrs. James was equal to the occasion. Her table groaned beneath provisions enough for twenty guests. After an hour's chat around the fire and the soothing influence of some good cigars, Mr. James harnessed his horses and drove us to his brother's house. This finished our hunt.

The reader must not suppose that killing game is the only pleasure of a sportsman's life. Social intercourse and the companionship of congenial friends, fireside amusements, pleasant stories and exciting games, all contribute to the enjoyment of the occasion.

Of the many fireside tales told by our companions of this hunt, two are worth preserving. One, as a simple illustration of natural affection, the other, a ludicrous example of the fall that always follows human vanity.

A short time after the close of the war one of the gentlemen of our party was taking supper in a fashionable hotel in Washington. He suddenly heard a female cry, whether of joy or sorrow he could not at first tell. Turning his eyes to the place from whence the exclamation came, he saw an old negro woman with her arms around the neck of a tall, handsome, and well dressed white man. His arms were around the poor old woman, and with his hand he patted her upon the back, while she hung upon his neck and kissed him over and over again. The interval between her kisses was filled with sobs and cries. "O, massa, young massa. Now let me die. I never hoped to see young massa again." There was not a scornful sneer upon a single lip, but many moistened eyes among the many guests in the great dining-room of that hotel. The old colored woman had been the gentleman's nurse. To use her expression, "she raised dat boy." His father was a rich planter before the war, and the owner of many slaves. The boy had enlisted in the Southern army. The war had wrecked his father's fortune, freed his slaves and scattered his household. The old nurse had drifted to Washington, and was employed as a sub-cook in the hotel. While attending to her duties she saw through the open door her old master's favorite son, sitting at one of the tables, taking his supper. She had not seen him for many, many years, and thought him dead. When she recognized him she dropped her ladle, rushed unbidden into the dining room, and the scene just described tells all the rest.

It was a simple exhibition of a sudden outburst of a long pent up affection. There is no eloquence more affective than the heart throbs of nature. The other tale told by the same gentleman, is good only because of its ludicrous denouement. A proud old Virginian, tall and straight, with black coarse hair and a dark complexion, claimed to be a descendant of the Indian girl, Pocahontas. When Sitting Bull came to Washington to see the Great Father, the proud old Virginian happened to be in that city. He caused himself to be invited to one of the receptions at which the old Indian Chief was present. He lost no time to inform the Chief that he was of Indian extraction, and the direct descendant of an Indian woman. Some judges of good whisky pour a few drops in the palm of the hand, then after a brisk rub of the hands together, smell the aroma and name the brand. The old Indian with great dignity, took the would-be descendant of Pocahontas by the hand, rubbed their palms briskly for a short time, then smelled the aroma caused by the friction. He then shook his head and only said : "Humph ! no Indian. Nigger."

I would like to describe the dilapidated mansions of the ruined old aristocratic families of Virginia ; their abandoned family grave yards, the wasted lands now overgrown with pines, their many struggles to maintain dignity in their distress and decay, and many other interesting matters I have noted, but my letter is becoming tedious by its length and I must bring it to a close.

When we arrived at Exmore with our game, we met a part of President Cleveland's party with theirs. It was generally conceded that our partridges were worth more than their ducks.

XXI.

A NORTH CAROLINA HUNT IN WINTER — THE HUNTER'S
PARADISE—SUNDRY VICISSITUDES—SNOW, ICE AND SKAT-
ING AT NORFOLK—VALUE OF THE TELEPHONE—A FIVE
MILE RIDE IN AN OPEN WAGON, WITH THE TEMPERATURE
NEAR ZERO—PAIN THE PRICE OF PLEASURE—PARTRIDGES,
RABBITS, TURKEYS AND DEER—A FROZEN THERMOMETER
—COLDEST WINTER IN THIRTY YEARS—A DEER HUNT,
FIVE DEGREES ABOVE ZERO—A TIMELY BLIZZARD—A
MOOT COURT—OLD "WASH" AND HIS TOASTS

BULLOCK, N. C., January, 1893.

Bullock is not a city ; it is a railroad station in Granville
county, North Carolina, and is situated near the confluence of
the rivers Dan and Stanton. The river Roanoke is also within
a short walk of the place. The close proximity of these three
rivers and the immense tracts of waste land, covered with
broom fields, thickets and wood, have made the neighborhood
for miles around a paradise for hunters. Game is abundant,
and the game laws of the State are liberal. These happy hunting grounds are about four hundred miles, by the shortest route,
from Chester. To reach them it is necessary to first go to
Norfolk, thence to Portsmouth, then one hundred and forty
miles, to Clarksville, where another change is made, which
carries the hunter over the Virginia line, some ten or twelve
miles to Bullock. When we left Chester on Saturday night,
January 7th, the weather was cold and disagreeable, and snow
had fallen to the depth of six or seven inches. We thought it
folly to take such a long journey if we were likely to find snow
at the point of our destination, and, therefore, we took the precaution to send a telegram in advance, requesting information
upon that subject. The answer was encouraging.

We were informed that the temperature was rising and
the snow was only two inches deep and rapidly melting and
would probably disappear by the time we would arrive, if we
started at once. After a short consultation, we concluded to
go, "weather or no." Just before taking the cars, one of our
friends suggested that we engage our coffins in advance, so
that they would be ready for our frozen bodies on our return
to Chester. When we arrived at Norfolk we were surprised
to find snow six inches deep and the harbor frozen up. Immense fields of ice stretched from Compostelea Bridge down to
the outer harbor, broken only by the track of the ferry boats.

Several steamers were ice-bound in the docks. Mahone's Lake and Put-in Creek were full of gay and happy skaters, and no such winter weather had been known for thirty years. Our boat was fifteen minutes late, by which our connection with the railroad from Portsmouth would fail unless we could hold the train till we could cross the river. We telephoned from Norfolk that five hunters for Clarkesville would arrive in fifteen minutes after the scheduled starting time and requested the conductor to hold the train for us. The answer came :

"All right."

So by this happy thought we saved a day, as the train only went once in twenty-four hours. This little incident is only important as illustrating the value of a minute in an emergency. By one minute's use of the telephone we saved a whole day for five persons.

We arrived at Bullock about seven P. M. The ground was covered with five inches of snow and the thermometer registered five degrees above zero. There had been another snow fall since the Sunday of our answer to our telegram. To add to our own discomfort and disappointment, we had to ride in an open wagon five miles, over the worst road upon which I have ever traveled. I never suffered more from the biting wind. When we arrived at the house which was to be our headquarters for the next week, we were nearly frozen to death. We were more than an hour on the road, with not as much as a blanket or even straw to protect our shivering knees or ice-cold feet. But pleasure is always bought with pain. Our dearest joys are appreciated because they are dear. If there were no hell I am afraid we would not enjoy Heaven. Our kind and obliging host, had done all he could to make us comfortable. He was not accustomed to such weather and did not anticipate it. His excellent and accomplished wife received us with a gracious smile and welcomed us to two large chambers, each furnished with a rousing pine wood fire and a good, warm, and well-made bed. After a good, hot supper, enjoyed with the best of sauce, a keen appetite, we sought repose and found that peaceful rest only known to children and tired men.

No babe ever slumbered on its mother's bosom with more delight than I reposed upon my downy couch that cold and cheerless night. When I awoke the next morning the fire had burned itself out and I was surprised to find my moustache stiff with my frozen breath. After ten A. M. the mercury had risen to twenty-eight degrees, whereupon we got our dogs and guns and started for our first day's hunt. We saw thousands of rabbit tracks and many foot prints of quail. On the side of the hill covered with oak trees, we saw where turkeys had been scratching for acorns. We also struck the trail of two deer. I do not exaggerate when I say, if the conditions had been favorable, we could have killed a hundred birds and several turkeys. As it was, the birds were very wild and when raised flew fast and far. The snow seemed to destroy their scent, as the dogs could only find single birds with great difficulty. We, however, came home with well-filled bags and with high hopes for the morrow. About ten P. M., Mr. Carrington brought in his thermometer to ascertain the temperature. We all closely examined it and pronounced it worthless, as no mercury could be seen. After a few minutes, however, the warm atmosphere of the room had caused the quicksilver to appear just above the bulb. We found it only registered the temperature from zero upwards. It had fallen to zero, but we could not tell how much below. The streams were frozen over. Ice had formed from four to seven inches thick and the wind blew a howling blizzard. It was the coldest weather North Carolina had seen for many years.

One of Mr. Carrington's neighbors, Mr. Fawcett, whose home was about a half mile away, had visited us the night before and invited us to participate in a deer hunt. Deer were comparatively unknown in this vicinity before the war. The immense quantity of abandoned land, the result of the unhappy struggle, now affords food and shelter for them, and one can be "jumped" almost any reasonably fair day. Mr. Fawcett has a fine pack of hounds and trained horses, who will stand fire from the saddle. It was arranged that we should be at his house by ten sharp the next morning. When we awoke we were told by the colored boy who came to make up our fire that it had snowed again during the night, thus adding three or four inches to what was already on the ground. The thermometer at nine A. M., stood five degrees above zero.

Nothing daunted, we seized our guns, pulled on our high legged gum boots and sallied out for our deer hunt. It came near being a dear hunt to me, for I was never so cold before. When we arrived at Mr. Fawcett's home at the exact minute fixed upon, I detected a smile of surprise. After another cordial *smile* or two, he said, " Gentlemen, I suppose you have come for that deer hunt. We North Carolinians would not dream of a hunt on such a day as this, but if you think you can stand it, I think I can 'jump' a deer for you." He ordered his favorite horse and his sure-footed and trusty mule. With genuine politeness he offered me his horse, which I, of course, declined.

I had never sat on a mule before and I wanted to see how it felt. The rest of the party preferred to walk to keep up animal heat by promoting a more active circulation. While crossing a creek, with banks five or six feet high, my mule's hind feet slipped on the ice ; his fore feet were on the top of the bank. He struggled manfully for a few seconds and then fell back on the ice. Luckily for me, I slipped out of the saddle just in time to escape what might have been a serious fall. While struggling with his fore feet on the bank and his hind feet slipping on the ice, he reminded me of a caricature in one of our illustrated magazines, called "Poor-Lizza."

Lizza was a mule who would not stand hitched. To break her of her bad habit, her owner, an old negro, hitched her in front of a blind on the bank of a mill pond. She, as usual, broke her tether, but went backwards into the mill pond, the banks of which were so high that she could not get out. The skill of the artist was displayed in the woe-begone countenance of the mule as her old owner came to help her out. After that he never broke the tether.

We rode several miles over waste fields, up slashes and through woods, but failed to raise a deer. We then gave up our deer hunt, and sent for the hounds for an old-fashioned rabbit hunt. They were soon running in front of the dogs in every direction. We shot several in a few minutes. If the weather had been favorable, I have no doubt we could have killed two hundred of them in a day.

I never suffered so much from the cold. I thought my feet were frozen. I abandoned my mule and endeavored to warm myself by violent exercise. My only hope was that some of the party would suggest that it was too cold to hunt. I determined that if I died on the field I would not be the first to cry for quarter. Kind Providence came to my relief by sending a blast of wind and snow with terrific force in the face of the youngest of my shivering companions.

"Holy Moses!" he said : "if you fellows want to freeze to death, stay here. I'm going home."

Home he went, with me in his rear. The rest of the party weathered it out, and came home loaded with game, including two fine wild turkeys.

The next day, two of us stayed at home to celebrate the birthday of the junior member of our party. Of course, he stayed with us and expressed himself as satisfied with the celebration. He was foolish enough to lay a wager that the ones who went to the fields would not bring home another turkey. That night they came home with a fine lot of game, including two more turkeys. A dispute arose about the terms of the wager. One side contended that the whole day was included in the time within which the turkey should be shot. The other side insisted that the time was limited to the forenoon.

To settle this momentous question, which bid fair to disrupt the harmony of our little company, the parties agreed that a moot Court should be organized and the testimony should be submitted, and that the verdict should be final. After a good, cheerful supper, we organized the Court. To fill the box, it was necessary to issue a special venire. Mr. Carrington was the sheriff. The first man he summoned was himself, then his wife, daughters and son. The panel was at last filled by his servants. The case will be reported as Gartside *vs.* Flower. The defendant chose as his counsel a fair, bright young lady, Miss Price, the private teacher of Mr Carrington's daughters, and a very interesting and accomplished young lady. The plaintiff pleaded his own cause. The witnesses were called, sworn on a pack of cards, examined and cross-examined. The defendant would have won his case if it had not been for his innocence and carelessness.

After the testimony had closed, his fair counsel moved the Court for leave to abandon the case. The reasons assigned were two. First, that she had received no fee ; second, that, as counsel, she had the right to a private consultation of at least one hour with her client, and that he had not as much as invited her to sit by her side during the trial. The Court held the reasons sufficient and granted the motion. After the testimony was all in and the case duly argued to the jury, the Judge delivered his charge, strongly in favor of the defendant, but the jury, because of the shabby manner in which the defendant had treated his counsel, concluded that no case could be good if a suitor's own counsel abandoned it, and so they found a verdict for the plaintiff, with costs.

The trial consumed the whole evening, and was really well conducted and fairly sparkled with nice points, wit and humor.

There are many more interesting incidents I would like to relate, but my letter is already too long ; suffice it to say that in four short winter days we secured one hundred and sixty-seven quail, twenty rabbits, five wild turkeys, one black duck and one opossum. We saw three deer, but did not get near enough for a shot. If the weather had been favorable we would have brought home at least five hundred quail. Hunters must not expect success without labor. If good luck comes, all right : if bad luck overtakes you, make your own fun and enjoy yourselves all you can. One of the great charms of hunting is its absolute freedom. You are not bound to be home at ten o'clock. You are subject to no boss. You don't even have to go to bed till you get sleepy.

I must not neglect to name General Washington, the old negro servant, who chopped and carried up our firewood. For short, they call him "Wash."   He is a very dignified old negro, with a fine crop of grizzly wool on his head.   He reminded me very much of Mrs. Stowe's Uncle Tom.   Every cold morning, with his master's permission, we gave him a stiff toddy, but we always required him to give us a toast before taking his drink.

Here are some specimens :

> From my lips down to my toes,
> Many a quart and gallon goes ;
> I take dis drink for I don't know,
> If I shall ever get some mo. (More).

> My old Massa promised me,
> When he died he'd set me free ;
> Now old Massa's dead and gone,
> And left me here a hoeing co'n. (Corn).

> Old Massa died de 17th of April,
> They put him in a box made of sugar maple ;
> They dug a big hole down upon the level,
> I really do believe old Massa's gwine to the devil.

The above are only selections from old Wash's many toasts. When he told his old wife what "good drinks de gentlemen up starr gib him" she upbraided him for not giving her some. "My deah," said he, " I tried to hold some in my mouf fo' you, but I had to talk to de Judge, and you know its not perlite to talk to white folks wid yer mouf full."

BIOGRAPHICAL SKETCH

OF THE

CLAYTON FAMILY,

WITH SOME

PERSONAL RECOLLECTIONS OF BETHEL
AND BRANDYWINE HUNDRED.

PART I.

PATERNAL LINE.

Lost Links—Clayton Hall, Yorkshire—Family Arms—
William of Chichester, the Progenitor of the Pennsylvania Branch—Attorney General, John Clayton,
the Founder of the Virginia Family—Joshua, of
England, the First of the Delaware Line—Quakers
and Methodists — How my Grandmother Punished
Her Husband for Becoming a Methodist—Family Con-
nections—Anecdote of John Faulk—Saint Walter
Martin—The Story of Clem Hathaway—Incident in
the Life of John Faulk, Jr—Origin of the Name
Claymont—A Bad Delaware Law—Feasts at Funer-
als—Aunt Lavina—Old Time Carpenters—Why I
Was Named Thomas Jefferson—Origin of the Name,
Whig—Why the Name Tyler was Striken from my
Brother John's Name—Clayton Cider.

The family is the foundation of the State. Great Empires
have sprung from humble lliance between tribes. It is but
reasonable that we should desire to know something of our
ancestors and delight in recounting whatever has contributed
to their fame.

Notwithstanding the important interests connected with
genealogy, it is surprising how soon connecting links are
broken and all traces of former alliances lost. It is, therefore,
the duty, and should be the pleasure, of individual members
of a family to preserve for posterity the information they possess, especially the knowledge that depends upon tradition and
which may die when they die.

The authorities from which I have constructed this sketch
are "Dugdale's Visitations of Yorkshire"—published in 1566 :
"The Historical Magazine of Virginia ;" "Letters of Attorney General John Clayton and his son John, the Botanist ;"
Family letters ; old deeds, wills, court records, inscriptions
upon tombs and conversations with old members of the family.

In the Recorder's office, at West Chester, I have found
deeds from 1684 to 1787, to and from old members of the
family. They are by and to William of Chichester, Thomas,
Samuel, John, Caleb, Abel, David, James and Joshua Clayton.

A deed dated October 13, 1699, from William of Chichester, is for one-half of the street and market place, in the "Town of Chichester," (Marcus Hook). The other half was granted by James Brown, who was the ancestor of the Browns of Chichester, of whom the late Jeremiah Brown was one. Fredrick Brown, the druggist of Philadelphia, is a descendant of James Brown and Hannah Clayton, the daughter of my grand-uncle, Armitt. The late Henry Armitt Brown, Esq., a distinguished orator and member of the Philadelphia bar, was a descendant from this marriage.

The deed last referred to, was dated the same year that William Penn made his second visit to Pennsylvania accompanied by Joshua Clayton, a cousin of William the grantor, named in the above cited deed. Joshua was the ancestor of John M. Clayton, of Delaware. They were all Quakers and friends of William Penn.

I have not been able to trace the family in England further back than 1560, when Thomas Clayton was the owner of "Clayton Hall," in Yorkshire.

The Claytons, according to family tradition, came originally from Sussex, England, where there is a small town of that name. In the olden time, surnames did not indicate relationship but location All the inhabitants of Claytown, (Clayton), took that as their surname. As York was then the political center of the Kingdom, it was quite natural that the bright young man of the sleepy old town should migrate to the fashionable metropolis of England.

The first son of Thomas, of "Clayton Hall," died a minor. His second son was William of Okenshaw. He was a barrister of the Inner Temple. He died in 1627. The estate known as "Clayton Hall," descended to Thomas Clayton (2) who was in possession as heir in 1666. He had a son William, who came to this country in 1671, and is the ancestor of our family, and will be hereafter called William of Chichester, to distinguish him from the many other William Claytons that succeeded him. Thomas (2) had also a son, John, who was a barrister of the Inner Temple. He died April 6, 1666.

William of Okenshaw, the grandfather of William of Chichester, had a son, Jasper, who was knighted by his sovereign for some service which is not stated in the record. He was afterwards called Sir Jasper Clayton.

The family coat of arms, as recorded in the Herald's office, is described as follows : "Arms : Argent, a cross eilgrailed sable, between four torteaux." The legend is : "Probitatem quam divitias." Meaning "Honor rather than wealth." The free translation of this legend would mean "Poor but Proud." The people of this country are not, as a

rule, familiar with the language of Heraldry. I will therefore
presume to translate the record of our family arms. The word
"*Arms*" in heraldry and Norman French means the ensign
of a family consisting of figures and colors, engraved or painted
upon a shield or banner, and which descends from father to
son forever. The word "*Argent*" means that the surface of
the shield shall be silver-white, emblematic of innocence,
purity and gentleness. The "*Cross*" is emblematic of our
christian faith. The word "engrailed" means that the edge
of the cross shall be indented by small conical curves. The
word "*Sable*" means that the cross shall be produced upon
the white surface, by black lines drawn vertically and horizon-
tally, and crossing each other. The word "*Torteaux*" is
the plural of torteau, which means a small circular spot, of a
red color (in our arms there are four red circular spots. The
"*Legend*" is the motto selected by the knight, expressive of
some peculiar trait in himself or his family.

Our coat of arms, as it appears upon the fly-leaf of this
book, is copied from an engraving in the Supplement to the
Virginia Historical Magazine. With the above explanation
it can be understood without difficulty.

Sir Jasper Clayton's son, Sir John of London, was also
knighted July 22, 1664. He was also a barrister, admitted in
1650. His brother George was a haberdasher of London, and
would, perhaps, like many other honest tradesmen of the
family—carpenters, cordwainers and tailors—never have been
again noticed in the family records, if it had not been for his
marriage with Miss Hester Palmer, daughter of Sir Thomas
Palmer.

Sir John had a son John, also a barrister, admitted June
6, 1682. He came to Virginia in 1705. (Nearly all communication with England, at that time, was to and from the port
of Jamestown, Va.).

This John was Attorney General of Virginia until 1737,
when he died. He was also Judge of the Court of Admiralty
and a member of the house of Burgesses. He left a large
volume of letters containing much valuable information concerning the family. He frequently refers to his brother, General Jasper Clayton, who was Governor of Gibraltar and a
Lieutenant General in the English army. He was killed in
the battle of Dettingen, in Bavaria, in 1743. The victory of
the English was celebrated by Handel's famous *Te Deum*.
By his will he left his estate, which was not very large as
measured by the estates of to-day, to be about equally divided
among all his children except his daughter, Juliana. The
clause referring to her reads as follows : " I give and bequeath
to my very undutiful and lost daughter, Juliana, the reputed

wife of Peter Hoo)er, who was my servant, one shilling and
no more." This would seem to sustain my translation of the
legend on the family arms—" Poor but proud."

I do not assume to make an absolutely correct record of
the family connections, nor do I profess that all my deductions
are beyond the possibility of mistake. I, however, believe
the facts stated to be substantially correct. My chief difficulty
has been to harmonize the great confusion in family names.
There can be but little doubt that the Claytons of Virginia,
Georgia, Delaware and Pennsylvania are descendants of the
Claytons of " Clayton Hall " in Yorkshire, England. There
is a strong family resemblance in the individual members of
the several branches. This is corroborated by an occurrence
related by one of my brothers in Arkansas. He was on a
Mississippi steamboat after the war and was spoken to in a
familiar way by a stranger who addressed him as " Mr. Clayton." The mistake was soon discovered. The stranger was
from Georgia and had mistaken my brother for one of his
neighbors, bearing the same name, and with whom he was well
acquainted. He affirmed that the two looked so much alike
that their wives would not be able to tell one from the other.
The Claytons of Georgia, I am informed, are the descendants
of Rev. John Clayton, an Episcopal clergyman, a contempo
rary and friend of John Wesley, the founder of Methodism.
Joshua Clayton who, as before stated, came to this country in
1699, with Penn on his second visit, was the ancestor of the
late John M. Clayton, and was a cousin of William Clayton
of Chichester, from whom our family are descended. Joshua
had a son, James, who had two sons, Joshua, Jr., and James,
Jr. Joshua, Jr. was a surgeon in the Revolutionary army and
a graduate of the University of Pennsylvania. He was afterwards Governor of Delaware and U. S. Senator from that
State. He died in 1798. His son, Thomas Clayton, was
Chief Justice of Delaware and also U. S. Senator from that
State.

John M. Clayton's father was James, a brother of Joshua,
Jr. He and the Chief Justice, Thomas Clayton, were cousins.

William Clayton of Chichester, the ancestor of our family
before coming to America in 1671, procured a patent from the
British government for five hundred acres of land in Upper
Chichester. This was before Penn became proprietor of the
Province, and before the Duke of York's charter. He also
owned a tract of land at Maylandville, near Philadelphia.
A part of the city, known as " Forty-ninth " Street, is built
on land formerly of William Clayton. It is said that his wife
was named Prudence. I, however, have not been able to
verify this tradition. All his deeds are signed simply,

"William Clayton." His wife must have died shortly after his arrival or, perhaps, before. He had a daughter named Prudence, who married Henry Reynolds. The wedding was celebrated at Burlington, N. J., Nov. 10, 1678. Mr. Reynolds afterwards purchased land and came to Chichester, where he died August 7, 1724. His widow, Prudence, died in 1728. She had ten children. Their eldest son, Francis, married Miss Aston, of Salem. Francis had a son named Henry, who married the daughter of John Davis, of Radnor. Their daughter, Elizabeth, married George Martin, of Chichester, whose daughter, Sarah, was the mother of Hon. John M. Broomall. Washington Townsend, John M. Sharpless, John Sharpless and Dr. George Martin, of West Chester, are descendants of Henry Reynolds and Prudence Clayton. William Clayton, the father of the said Prudence, was one of the nine justices who sat at Upland (Chester) in 1681. Henry Reynolds, his son-in-law, was one of the jurors of said court. William was also a member of Penn's Council.

William of Chichester had a son, William (2) Clayton, born about 1675. His wife was named Elizabeth. He died about February, 1727. He left five sons, named William (3) Edward Richard, Abel and Ambrose.

William (3) married Mary, the daughter of Walter Martin. He died about January 9, 1758. The land upon which St. Martin's Church, at Marcus Hook stands, was donated by Walter Martin, by deed dated 1699. Book A, p. 236. In consideration of the gift, the church canonized him and named the church *Saint* Martin. As an evidence of his saintly character he made one of the conditions of his grant, that the mortal remains of no Quaker should ever be permitted to repose in the burial ground which was a part of his grant, and that there might be no mistake he endorsed his deed with an explanation of what he meant by the word "Quaker." He said he did not mean to exclude Kethites or Christian Quakers, but only Quakers who did not acknowledge the divinity of Christ, be baptized by water, take the Lord's Supper and believe in the resurrection of the dead. Also such Quakers as refused to take an oath upon the Bible should be excluded.

Richard Clayton, son of William (2) had a son, Curtis, and a son Richard—my great-grandfather Richard married Abigail, daughter of Robert and Mary Powell, of Concord. Abigail's mother was Mary, daughter of Joseph Rhoads, of Marple. Richard had three sons, Powell my grandfather, Curtis and Armitt. Powell has since been a favorite name in the family. Curtis was the ancestor of the Claytons of Philadelphia and Colorado. During the Revolutionary war, my great-grandfather Richard, was the keeper and proprietor of the hotel at the head of the pier at Port Penn, Delaware. He had a hostler named Clem. Hathaway. When the British Fleet sailed up the river, a few enthusiastic patriots secured an old cannon which they planted upon the pier and opened fire upon the passing fleet, which immediately poured a broadside into the town.

Clem. was half asleep, with his head resting between his hands, and his elbows on his knees, sitting in front of the old-time fireplace, when he was suddenly aroused by a cannon ball which pierced the wall about six inches above his head, imbedding itself in the brick chimney and covering him with red dust. Without a word he arose and walking deliberately out to the end of the pier, he turned his back to the enemy, bending himself forward so as to present a mark for the British sharp-shooters on the ships. He remained in this defiant position for about ten minutes. The musket balls fell like hail around him but did not as much as scratch his skin. He then straightened himself up, adjusted his clothing and deliberately returned to the hotel. It is needless to add that from that time till his death, a few months after, he was the hero of the town. His daring defiance of the British Fleet gave him a free "admittance to the bar," and too much indulgence in his new privilege soon ended his days.

I had the above anecdote directly from my father's lips, who assured me that his father gave it to him just as I have related it, but in rather plainer language.

After my great-grandfather left Port Penn, he lived for several years at Marcus Hook, where my grandfather was born. His dwelling was situated on the southerly side of the main street, nearly opposite the Old Market House. In 1786, Richard purchased his Bethel farm from John Ford. He spent the balance of his life upon this farm. At his death he gave it to his son Powell, my grandfather.

He gave his Port Penn property to his son Curtis, who afterwards moved to Philadelphia. He was the direct ancestor of the Philadelphia and Colorado Claytons. His son Curtis has but recently died in Philadelphia, aged ninty-two. Much of the information contained in this sketch I obtained from him a few years ago.

My great-grandfather Richard had two daughters. Hannah and Elizabeth. Hannah married Stephen Faulk by whom she had two sons—William and Clayton—and a daughter named Mary. Stephen Faulk, a merchant of Philadelphia, is a descendant from this marriage. Mary married Philip Jones, of Wilmington, Delaware. His son, Philip, was a dentist in Wilmington, in 1848. Stephen Faulk, the husband of Hannah (Clayton) Faulk, died before his wife. She afterwards married a man named McKnight, whom she also survived. She died when I was about eleven years old, Nov. 12, 1837. My grandfather died about six months before. These were the first funerals of which I have any recollection. They were my first object lessons upon the certainty of death. I shall never forget the terrible impression made upon my mind as I looked down upon the cold dead face of "Aunt Hannah."

Elizabeth, his sister, married John Tweed, of Delaware. She had a son named Curtis, whom I remember very well. He was killed in an accident upon the Philadelphia, Wilmington and Baltimore Railroad, about 1840.

Elizabeth had also a son named John, a wheelwright, of Wilmington, Delaware. He was lame from a wound, by the broad axe, in his knee. She had three other sons whom I did not know, named James, Clayton and Columbus. Columbus died in Philadelphia June 27, 1892.

Elizabeth had three daughters, named Abigail, Mary and Elizabeth. Abigail married Mr. Moore, a gentleman of Illinois, where she died highly respected. Elizabeth was a fine looking woman and a frequent visitor at my father's house before her marriage, in 1845. She married Mr. Harrison Justison, of Hancock county, Illinois, where she died November 16, 1891.

Powell Clayton had three wives. His first wife, my grandmother, was Sarah, a daughter of John Faulk, of Delaware. They were married May 27, 1790. I have heard my father say that his mother was reputed to be a woman of rare beauty. We must pardon him for that expression as most men think their mothers the most beautiful of women. She died when he was very young. It was said that, when she stood erect, her loosened hair swept the floor at her feet. She also had the reputation of being somewhat proud of her personal charms and social standing. She despised the Methodists but tolerated the Quakers. When my grandfather became a Methodist, she thought the family disgraced. She shut herself up in her room over a week and wept from shame. All the efforts of her disconsolate husband to soothe her sorrow were vain. She held the fort for about eight days. Her only terms of surrender was his immediate withdrawal from the church. At the end of eight days she partially relented and received her husband with her wonted grace. Before her death, however, which soon followed on November 1, 1795, she requested that she might be buried in the Quaker Burying Ground, in Upper Chichester, where her body now reposes without a stone to mark her resting place—(In those days the Quakers were opposed to tomb-stones).

Methodism, in those days, was much more primitive than it now is. The early Methodists did not condemn shouting aloud their praises to the Lord. They sung and prayed with great spiritual fervor and did not believe in church music or educated preachers. They regarded religion as a *Faith* rather than as a *Philosophy*.

They adopted the plain dress, and many of them used the "*Thee* and the *Thou* of the Quakers." They however substituted the word *Brother* for the appellation of *Friend* used by the Quakers. There was no substantial difference between the faith of the Quakers and Methodists until after the schism in the Society of Friends caused by the preaching of Elias Hicks. The Quakers of the olden time were more aristocratic than the Methodists and more clannish and secluded. This may account for my grandmother's prejudice against the Methodists. Her father, John Faulk, was fine looking and rather proud in his bearing. He wore buckskin breeches, silk stockings and silver knee and shoe buckles. The following anecdote of my great-grandfather, Faulk, I received from the lips of my father :—He was a skillful stonemason. When the jail at New Castle was erected he did the stone work which was considered, at that time, as a very fine specimen of masonic skill. After the jail had been finished a short time, a prisoner sawed off the iron bars of his cell window and escaped. The two ends of the cell bars had been set in sockets drilled in the sill and head stone. The question was, how to restore the bars without tearing out the sill and head stone and rebuilding the window and disfiguring the wall ? The commissioners finally concluded that, at least, the head stone would have to be taken out in order to get the ends of the new iron bars into the sockets. Proposals were invited for the work. The bids ranged from seventy-five to one hundred dollars. On the day the contract was to be awarded, John Faulk appeared before the commissioners and proposed to do the work for nothing, without tearing down any of the wall, provided the commissioners would pay the blacksmith's bill, which should not exceed ten dollars, and, that the work should be finished to the satisfaction of the commissioners in half a day. They at first thought the old man had lost his wits, but as they could detect no signs of insanity, and as he was a man of responsibility, they told him to go ahead.

He went to a blacksmith and in a few minutes had new bars cut. He then brought the blacksmith with his portable forge to the jail, and after heating the bars red hot he bent them in the form of a bow until the two ends could enter the sockets in the stone, then with a few strokes of the hammer the bars were straightened and chilled by dashing some water

upon them. The whole job was completed to the perfect satisfaction of the commissioners, but to the surprise and disgust
of the contractors, in less than five hours.

The Faulks, of Delaware, are descendants of my great-
grandfather Faulk. I knew his grandson, John, of Brandywine Hundred, Delaware, very well. In his younger days he
was one of the handsomest men I ever saw. He was an athlete,
worthy of comparison with the best specimens of manhood in
ancient Greece or Rome, as represented by their statues in
marble. He could fell an ox with a blow from his fist. I
have seen him lift seven hundred pounds dead weight. When
he was at his best, I doubt if there was a man living could
stand before him. About 1840, the Methodists held a camp
meeting, at Penney's Wood, near a hotel called the Practical
Farmer. A crowd of rowdies from Philadelphia created some
disturbance, whereupon, John Faulk, who was a member of
the church, ejected them from the ground. Nine of them,
some of whom were known prize fighters, made an attack
upon him the same afternoon in the bar-room of the hotel. In
less than forty minutes, five of them were lying senseless upon
the floor ; of the other four, one had his arm broken, one had
two ribs fractured and the other two had their noses smeared
over their faces. It was necessary to call in a doctor before
the wounded bullies could be conveyed to the railroad station.
It is needless to say there were no more disturbances during
the continuance of the meeting. Some of the fervent old
Methodists actually believed that God had interfered and gave
to John Faulk the strength of Sampson. I have seen John
Faulk, with one hand, swing a twenty-five-pound sledge hammer three times around his head and then hurl it from ten to
fifteen yards further than any other person could throw it.
Withal he was exceedingly kind and good natured. At the
age of thirty, before he had reached his prime, he was attacked
with rheumatism from which he suffered all the balance of
his life. It completely ruined the symmetry of his form.
Some of his joints were destroyed, his right hip was displaced,
his back was bowed and for twenty years he could scarcely
stand erect. Why nature made him so strong and then destroyed her work, is hard to understand. If he had been a
dissipated man, moralists would have attributed his afflictions
to that cause, but he was sober, industrious, abstemious and
a christian man all his life.

We will now return to my grandfather, Powell Clayton.
He had two sons by his first wife Sarah (Faulk). Richard
the elder was born March 6, 1791. John, my father, was
born December 6, 1792. Richard married Miss Grubb, of
Delaware. Upon his marriage, my grandfather purchased for

him a beautifully situated farm near the present railroad station at Claymont. The mansion stood upon the hill nearly opposite the late residence of Rev. Mr. Clemson. He named his residence "Claymont"—an abbreviation of Clayton's Mount. This name has remained as the name of the railroad station but all dominion of the old proprietor of the mansion has long since departed. I doubt whether the oldest residents now know the origin of the name. The mansion was burned many years ago and the property was purchased by Thomas Clyde, the founder of the Clyde line of steamers.

My uncle Richard died of yellow fever when it was epidemic in Philadelphia, September 14, 1820. He left an infant son only a few days old. It died eight days after its father. His widow afterwards married a man named Buck. She died childless and intestate.

By the laws of Delaware, Richard's infant son inherited his father's estate, subject to the dower of its mother. When it died, within a week of its father's death, its mother, as its next of kin inherited the estate. When she died her brothers and sisters took it as her heirs at law. Thus a fine estate bought by my grandfather, by the accident of the babe's death a week after its father's decease, vested in entire strangers to his blood. By the laws of England this could not be. There the heir, to inherit the land must be of the blood of the first purchaser. Such ought to be the law of America, and is the law of Pennsylvania.

Powell Clayton died, as before stated, in 1837, in the house now occupied by Mr. Hinkson, on the road running from Naaman's creek to Booth's Corner, in the township of Bethel. From all that I can learn of him, he was a good, rather than a great man. He was a consistent christian and a man of some influence in his church. I have heard my old and esteemed friend Samuel Hance, of Bethel, recently deceased at the advanced age of ninety-four years, say that my grandfather was the direct means of bringing him into the church, and was his class-leader. He told me once that he always loved me because my grandfather showed so much love for him.

My grandfather was content to move upon the level plane upon which his contemporaries walked without jostling any of them. He never aspired to be a leader either in the church or State. He, therefore, led a comparatively happy life and died a peaceful death, loved and respected by all who knew him.

The greater part of his life was spent upon his farm, the mansion house of which is now occupied by J. Wesley Hance, in Bethel. When his son Nelson married Miss Jemima Booth, a daughter of James Booth, late of Bethel, he moved to the house a little further up the road and now occupied, as before stated, by Mr. Hinkson. He died very suddenly of heart disease while taking his wonted morning walk around his farm.

In those days, funerals were great events. The whole community turned out *en masse* to help bury a friend who could afford a funeral feast. It was the fashion then to announce at the grave, "That the relatives and *friends* of the deceased are earnestly invited to return to his late home for dinner." All the old women in the neighborhood were improvised as cooks and all the laboring men were employed as assistants. The little pigs, chickens and turkeys seemed to know that their time had come and, by instinct, calmly surrendered to the inevitable with remarkable resignation.

It was truly wonderful to see how many devoted friends a dead man had as measured by the guests at his funeral feast. The funeral procession reached from his house to the church, over a mile. The feast began about noon and did not end until after dark. I was then about eleven years old and thought a funeral a real jolly thing. My old aunt Hannah, grandfather's sister, died about six months after. Her funeral was very plain and slimly attended. She could not afford a funeral feast. As I have already remarked, her death made a deep and lasting impression upon my mind. I looked upon the Grim Monster as the only Mortal enemy of man. Since then the visits of Death have been so frequent as to entitle him to be saluted as a "friend of the family." I have followed eleven funerals from my father's home to the graveyard at Bethel, ending with my mother's.

My grandfather's second wife was Mary Mattson. They were wedded June 16, 1796. By her he had a son named Mattson, born May 7, 1797. He was a rover and was lost at sea about 1819.

My grandfather's second son by his wife Mary, was Nelson, born December 12, 1800. He lived all his life in Bethel where he died May 6, 1866. She left two surviving daughters, Levina and Mary. Mary married a man named Lamplieugh. Levina never married. She was a highly intelligent and very strong minded woman. A short time after her father's death, she made her home at my father's house where she died.

I cannot pay too high a tribute of respect to the memory of Aunt Levina. She was a remarkable woman—a great reader and profound reasoner—she wrote some very good poetry and was well posted upon all the scientific questions of the day. I never knew a person with a better memory. She was very fond of my twin brothers, John and William. Before they were five years old she taught them to read. When I commenced reading law, she followed me by reading every book that I had read. She used to examine me in Blackstone, Kent, Cruise on Real Estate and Stephen's Pleading. When I was admitted in 1850, my old aunt knew about as much law as I did. Withal, she was exceedingly modest. Outside of our own family, but few knew much of her many virtues.

Powell Clayton's third wife was Sarah Elliot, a widow, whose maiden name was Sharpless. They were married March 10, 1814. She survived her husband many years. By her he had but one son, named Curtis, born April 1, 1816, who died in Bethel, leaving one son William Torbert Clayton, born September 21, 1838, and one daughter, Sarah Jane, born June 20, 1840, both living. William T., I believe, now resides in Texas.

John Clayton, my father—as before stated—was born December 6, 1792, in Bethel, in the house now occupied by Wesley Hance.

He served a regular apprenticeship as a carpenter, under a somewhat celebrated builder of Wilmington, named John Newlin. My father followed his business for several years with some success. He worked at his trade in the cities of Wilmington, Baltimore, Philadelphia and New York. About 1846, he took me to New York to show me a house, I think on Bond street, that he had planned and built and of which he was very proud. His greatest pride was in the very elaborate wooden mantel, which was certainly a work of merit. It looked very much like the hard-wood mantels, now so fashionable and which are only a renascence of the style of the early part of this century. In those days the carpenter was also the architect. He not only drew all the plans, but he laid out and made all the ornamental work of the building.

My father and mother were married on the first day of January, 1822. They had ten children of whom only three are now living. Six of my brothers and sisters died in early life. I, the oldest son, was born July 26, 1826. At that time my father was a staunch Jeffersonian Democrat. As an evidence of his politics, he named me Thomas Jefferson. In 1828, two years after my birth, when the Presidential contest was between Adams and Jackson, Henry Clay, who had been a Democrat, commenced the organization of the Whig party. My father followed his fortunes and in 1831, became a Whig.

There are two theories of the derivation of the word *Whig*. We were taught that it was a word formed from the initials of a motto upon the banner of the opposition party in England, during the early days of the Commonwealth: "We Hope In God." Instead of the words in full, they painted in letters of gold upon their ensigns and banners the initials only—

W. H. I. G., (Whig).   Whether this is the true derivation of
the grand old party name or not, it serves to illustrate the
purity of its hopes, but the sequel proved that its hopes were
vain.   Others hold that the name was derived from the Scotch
word "Whiggam"—meaning *Whey*, a great drink of the
covenanters.

My father remained an earnest and energetic Whig until
the party died ; he then became an enthusiastic Republican.
He was a delegate to the Baltimore convention, in 1840, which
nominated General Harrison for President.   In that year my
twin brothers, John and William, were born, (Oct. 13, 1840).
They were named John Tyler and William Henry Harrison
Clayton.

After the death of President Harrison and Tyler's treacherous abandonment of his party, my father, with his own
hand erased the name "Tyler" from the family record, and
had the boy baptized "John Middleton Clayton," after John
M. Clayton, of Delaware, which name he bore to the time of
his tragic death in Arkansas, where he was cowardly assassi-
nated for presuming to contest the election of Hon. R. C.
Breckenridge, to a seat in Congress.   He was shot, at night,
through a window in Plummersville, while conversing with a
friend, on the twenty-ninth of January, 1889.   A biographic
sketch of his life will be found in the "Secretary's Report of
the Annual Reunion of the Survivors' Association, 124th
Regiment, P. V."   Published in 1889.

My father never presumed to take much part in public
affairs.   After his marriage he devoted his life to farming, and
by industry and ecomony, succeeded in maintaining and edu-
cating his large family of children.   He devoted his energies
chiefly to the cultivation of fruit—apples, cherries and peaches.
He had the reputation of making the best cider in the market.
I have known him to make over one hundred hogsheads in a
year.   It very much resembled champagne wine and would
keep for years without becoming sour.   His secret for the
preparation of his cider died with him.   I can only remember
a part of the process.   In the first place, none but sound Gray
House apples were used and the cider was always made in
cold weather.   It was invariably run into *hogsheads*, never in
barrels.   It was stored in the cellar and when at its highest
alcoholic state, it was rectified with the best Russian isinglass
and racked off into new hogsheads.   This, I believe to be the
whole secret.   It reads as if it were a very easy thing to do,
but the skill consisted in knowing just when the cider was in
its highest alcoholic state.   By years of practice my father
could tell by placing his ear at the bunghole just when to
treat it with the isinglass.   He would sometimes fail but not

often. He had an apple orchard of not over three acres from which I have heard him say he reaped a clear profit of over one thousand dollars a year. My father died October 16, 1871, in the 79th year of his age. He was always fond of young society and bore his years well. I have no doubt but that he would have lived to be a very old man but for an accidental fall a few years before his death from the effects of which he died in the possession of all his faculties and in other respects hale and strong.

χ

MATERNAL LINE.

GRANDFATHER CLARK—AN OLD TORY—HIS SWORD TURNED INTO A CORKSCREW—A MORTAL INSULT—CAPTAIN WILLIAM GLOVER—COMMODORE DECATUR—SIXTY-FOUR YEARS A METHODIST—RELIGION AND GOOD SENSE—FAMILY CONNECTIONS—MY BROTHERS.

My mother's father, Captain George Clark, was born in New Jersey, in 1755. He was twenty-one years old when the Colonies declared their independence. His father was an Englishman and a Tory. His son George, my grandfather, espoused the English side of the controversy and became an officer in the British colonial army. He received his pay from the Crown up to the day of his death, February 26, 1812. He lived the greater part of his life in Brandywine Hundred, New Castle county, Delaware.

I have the following anecdote from the late Stephen Cloud, Sr., of Bethel, who was my father's first cousin, his mother being a daughter of John Faulk, the elder :

After the close of the Revolutionary war, the Tories and Patriots did not fraternize as freely as fellow countrymen should. In order to be prepared to measure swords with England again, if it should become necessary, the State government by law required the militia to be regularly enrolled and on stated times, called "Training Days," to be drilled and inspected. It so happened upon one of those training days, several years after the close of the war, that no one present was sufficiently educated in the manual of arms to act as "Training Master." Making a virtue of necessity, my grandfather was requested to lend a hand and help put the boys through the drill. He accepted the honor and appeared upon the ground in his full military dress, including, most unfortunately, a *Red* coat.   He also carried his sword and a silver mounted musket, which had been presented to him by his old companions in arms when the army was disbanded and which he highly prized.   Scarcely had he formed the men in line, before there was a vigorous protest from the old patriots against being drilled by a *Red Coat*.   The better class of the patriots endeavored to quell the impending storm but with no success.   The *soldiers* made a break and, before the danger was realized, they knocked down the red-coated tory, tore off his sword, took his gun and rent his coat into shreds.   To add insult to injury they thrust his sword in the hard ground up to the hilt, then broke his gun over a stump, and, with the barrel for a lever with one end in the guard of the sword, they turned it round and round till it came out of the ground in the form of a long corkscrew.

I have heard my mother say that her father never got over the indignity thus put upon him, and always said that America would come to no good until the Crown of England should wipe out the disgrace put upon a British soldier by these riotous and low-bred *Republicans*.

The grave of my grandfather Clark may be found near the south line of the Bethel graveyard and is marked by an old-fashioned marble tombstone.   He married Miss Ann Glover, a daughter of William Glover, a sea captain whose ship sailed from Philadelphia to London.   Among family relics in my possession is his fine marine spy-glass ; it is three feet long and is an excellent instrument.   I have also a fine mahogany work table made in England, and six heavy table spoons in solid silver, hand-made, bearing the initials of my grandmother's maiden name, ''A. G.''   They were wedding presents from her father.   She was born in 1773, and died March 3, 1830.   Captain Glover was born in 1741.   He died at his residence in Philadelphia, August 6, 1806.   Our relationship to Commodore Decatur came through this branch of the family, but although I have often heard my mother give the connecting link, I have not been able to now find it.   The Glovers were strong patriots during the Revolutionary war The Toryism of grandfather Clark was a cause of constant irritation and some bitterness in the families, until after my grandfather's death and until after the death of Decatur in 1820, about two years before my mother's marriage when all further dissensions ceased.

My mother was born October 3, 1803.   At the early age of sixteen years she became an active Methodist and for sixty-four years she mantained her standing in the church as a consistent and energetic christian woman.   While devoted to her own church, she respected all other forms of christian worship.

She never permitted her attachment to her own form of worship to lessen her respect for other creeds. During the Native American excitement, when St. Augustine's church was burned in Philadelphia, my mother was earnest in her outspoken condemnation of that sacreligious outrage. She gathered her little family around her and tried to explain to us that the forms of worship were but paper walls dividing christian denominations, that we all worshipped the same God and trusted in the same Savior, and that we should be careful to say nothing that would offend others in their religious faith. Our laboring man, Patrick, was a devoted Catholic. He and my mother were the only two in the family that eat no meat on Friday or during Lent, a rule which she strictly observed to the day of her death. She used to tell us that in religion as well as in politics we were all largely creatures of circumstances; that if our parents had been Catholics we most likely would be of the same faith. She said to me during the heated campaign of 1840, when every man, woman and child in the county were tremendously excited over politics : "Son, have you ever thought that if your father had been a *Loco Foco* (Democrat) you would, perhaps, be one ?" I was so thoroughly imbued with the principles of the Whig party, that I could not then believe it possible under any consideration, that I should be anything but a Whig.

During her long, patient and useful life, she had her full share of sorrow but no one heard her complain. She followed to the grave seven of her children ; two in infancy, and five when they were just entering manhood and womanhood. She was a woman of strong character and of an unbending will. She did not fear to drive the most headstrong horse, and, what was often remarked, the horse most always seemed to know that it was in the hands of its mistress.

She met her approaching end of life with true christian fortitude—willing to live but not afraid to die. Death had no terrors for her. She met him as a friend and not an enemy. She died May 12th, 1883, in the eightieth year of her age

Grandfather Clark had two sisters, named Margaret and Laurana. Margaret married a Mr. Wallace ; they had a son named Wesley, who was a Methodist preacher. Laurana married John Tettimary, of Philadelphia. Laurana had a daughter named Sarah, who married Peter Williamson, of Philadelphia. Beside my grandmother (Ann Glover), Captain William Glover had a daughter named Brandling, she was my great aunt, and was married to Isaac Grubb, of Delaware. In this way I am related to the Grubbs of that State. My mother's brother, Wesley Clark, of Bethel, is still living; her sisters Letitia, Priscilla, Brandling, Charlotte and Laurana are dead. Letitia mar-

ried Rev. John Talley, of Delaware. Priscilla married Lewis
Talley, of Delaware ; her daughter, Letitia, married Humphrey
Pyle, recently deceased, of Chester Heights, Delaware county.
Her daughter Priscilla, married William McCracken, of Delaware county. Laurana married Rev. William Cooper, a very
eloquent Methodist preacher. Brandling married John Johnson, the son of Robert Johnson, late of Bethel, who was the
second husband of my grandmother Clark, *nee* Glover. Charlotte married Thomas Hance, a brother of Samuel Hance of
Bethel, who recently died at the age of ninety-four. My uncle
Wesley married Charlotte Pool, a sister of Wesley Pool, of
Bethel. Of myself and living members of our family I ought
not to be expected to say much. My brother, Powell, is well
known both as a soldier and a citizen. By profession he was
a civil engineer in Kansas. When the war of the rebellion
broke out he entered the Union army as a Captain of the First
Kansas Volunteer Infantry. He fought his way from Wilson's
creek to Arkansas, and when hostilities ceased, he had advanced from Captain to Brigadier General, commanding a division. He stopped where the war left him, and made Arkansas
his home. He now resides at Eureka Springs, in that State.
His name is intimately connected with the political history of
Arkansas since its reconstruction. He was at one time Governor and afterwards U. S. Senator of that State. He married
an estimable lady of his adopted State, and has now a large
and interesting family. His eldest son, Powell, Jr., although
barely in his majority, is now Second Lieutenant in the Fifth
Cavalry of the regular U. S. Army.

My brother William, also served as Second Lieutenant of
Company H, 124th Regiment of Pennsylvania. He partici-
pated in the battles of South Mountain, Antietam and Chan-
cellorville. When the war ended he settled in Pine Bluff, Arkansas. By profession he was a lawyer. He was appointed
Judge of the First Circuit of Arkansas, a court of the highest
original jurisdiction in the State. After two years' service as
Judge, he resigned for the more lucrative office of U. S. District Attorney for the Western District of Arkansas. He was
appointed to the office by President Grant, in 1874, which
office he still holds. He also married a lady of Arkansas and
has a large and interesting family.

PART II.

THE CIRCUMSTANCE THAT DECIDED MY CHOICE OF A PROFESSION : OR WHY I BECAME A LAWYER.

MY MOTHER'S AMBITION—MY FATHER'S ADVICE—EARLY
EFFORTS AT ANATOMY—A FIST FIGHT IN CHURCH—CHOIR
AND ANTI-CHOIR—THE TRAGIC AND COMIC SIDE OF THE
CHURCH QUARREL—AN OLD MAN'S IDEA OF SCIENTIFIC
MUSIC—A CHURCH TRIAL—FIRST EFFORTS AS AN ADVO-
CATE—A PREACHER OUTWITTED—HISTORY OF A BUSINESS
CARD—HISTORY OF AN OLD LETTER—PERSONAL INSPEC-
TION OF ANOTHER MAN'S WORK WORTH TEN THOUSAND
DOLLARS—AN ANGRY OLD LAWYER.

My mother intended me for a preacher ; my father recommended me to study medicine but, by a mere accident, I chose
the profession of law. In my youth I showed some taste for
anatomy. I purchased a quantity of human bones from Dr.
S. A. Barton and from a colored doctor of Philadelphia and
spent my nights in my bedroom in arranging and wireing them
together. I succeeded in preparing a fair skeleton of the
human frame. I could then name the fifty bones of the head,
trunk, legs and arms ; the twelve bones of the hand and wrist,
and the fourteen bones of the foot. I have derived some advantage from this knowledge in the practice of my profession.
After months of labor I finished my work. I named it Pompey and, from pure bravado, I laid it in my bed and slept with
it the night I completed it. I afterwards sold it to a secret
society of Delaware. I am told they still possess it and use
it in their initiatory ceremonies as "a sad memorial of man's
mortality."

I also attempted the preparation of the anatomy of a babe
but the sutures of the skull bones had not sufficiently ossified
to hold the little cranium together, so I gave this undertaking
up in disgust.

I had the name of being a bad boy, but this was unjust.
After fifty years, I can look back and conscientiously deny
the charge. I was wild, untamed, overflowing with animal
spirits and keenly alive to everything of a ridiculous nature,
but I was not bad at heart. My bad reputation was largely

the result of an unfortunate disturbance in Bethel Church during a protracted meeting. I was then about seventeen years old. My father always dressed well and took pride in seeing his children fashionably clad. In those days the young men dressed with more taste and elegance than they do now. In the winter, the Spanish circular mantles were very fashionable. They were made of black broadcloth, lined with red satin and ornamented with long silk cords and tassels. When thrown over the shoulder, with the red satin delicately exposed, held in a loop by the cord and tassel, they were very dressy. While sitting in the church one night I threw my mantle over the back of the seat and was, like a good christian, intently listening to the fine singing and earnest praying of the good old fathers of the church. I heard a tittering laugh behind me when, turning my head, I saw a low-bred fellow (whom I will not now name because he was of a respectable family) with his pocket knife cutting a long slit in the back of my mantle. Without thinking of the consequences, I dealt him a stunning blow in the face, felling him to the floor between the benches. He began to scream murder, but before assistance came his face was covered with blood. The scene that followed cannot be described. The church was crowded. The congregation jumped upon the benches and made a rush for the place, where they supposed a man was being murdered. The women and children began to scream; the aisles were jammed up with struggling men and women; some of the seats were broken and each person seemed intent to outdo all others in rendering confusion more confounded. My father was the first to seize my upraised arm. When I realized what I had done I at once surrendered. After quiet was restored and the congregation dismissed, I was informed that I must go to New Castle jail. I felt that a crisis had come in my life but, in all the trying events of my subsequent career, I never felt more perfect command of my faculties. I asked my captors, in a subdued but calm and earnest voice, if they would hear me before condemning me. Father King was the preacher in charge. Father Samuel Hance was then a local preacher of great eloquence and power and one of the most popular men in the church. By his upright christian life he had deservedly earned the respect and confidence of the entire people. "Brethren," said Father King, "do not be too hasty; let us hear what the young man has to say." "Certainly, certainly," said Father Hance, "we will hear the boy before condemning him." I then felt that the victory was mine. I stated my case in a most respectful manner. I expressed my profound regret that I had permitted my indignation to get the better of my judgment. I told them of the tittering laugh

I had heard, and that I saw the man I had chastised with his
knife cutting my mantle. That it had cost my father seventy-
five dollars only a month or two before, and that it was now
ruined. Then, spreading out the folds before them, I pointed
out the cut very much as Antony is supposed to have pointed
out the "rent the envious Casca made" in dead Cæsar's
mantle ; after which I turned to my father and saw great big
tears rolling down his honest cheeks. "Father," said I,
" will you go my security for future good behavior and, if the
church wish to prosecute me, that I will appear before any
magistrate when required ?" With some emphasis he said :
" I certainly will, and will defend you, too, if it takes all I am
worth." I was let off on my good behavior, upon my father
agreeing to produce me when wanted. This little incident in
my history has had a beneficial effect upon my whole after
life. I never now condemn a man or boy without hearing
him, and the experience of my life has taught me that there
is generally some extenuating cause for every assault and battery. In two cases out of three the man that gets beaten is
in fault. Of course there are exceptions to this rule. This
church disturbance, however, was the direct cause of the name
I afterwards had of being a "bad boy." The man who was
really in fault and who so maliciously commenced the assault
by cutting my mantle left the State soon after and I never saw
him again. It was reported in the neighborhood that he died
in jail in Ohio, where he was convicted of some infamous
crime and sentenced to a long term of imprisonment.

In 1847, Bethel Church was one of the most flourishing
in the State of Delaware. There were but few Sundays that
it was not crowded. During religious revivals which were
repeated every winter it was filled to overflowing. Services
were sometimes continued nightly for over a month without
abatement in the religious excitement. The congregation
possessed several good singers, but there was no regular church
choir. They had a sort of organization in the form of a singing society, which met at stated times at each other's houses
to practice and prepare for the ensuing church service. About
this time, the singers petitioned the trustees, of whom my
father was one, to set apart two benches prepared by a four-
inch-wide board nailed upon the back of each bench, for their
especial use. The board on the back of the bench was to
hold their open note books while they sung. The request was
granted but, like most sudden innovations upon settled customs, instead of proving an improvement it turned out to be
the ruin of the church. The primitive Methodists looked
upon it as a step toward Ritualism and High Church practices. The friends and enemies of the *choir*, as the singing

party called themselves, soon became divided into separate parties and, as the controversy advanced, the schism widened until, at last, it split the church and almost destroyed the congregation. Friends of a lifetime became enemies ; families were divided ; law suits were engendered ; church trials were instituted ; in a word, the Devil, under the guise of a *note book*, entered and ruined the church. At last the *choirists* triumphed in the tribunals of the church, but the victory was barren and, perhaps, so far as the cause of religion was concerned, worse than a defeat. It resulted in the withdrawal in a body of a large and influential part of the congregation and membership, and the building of the church called Siloam, only a short half mile from the old church.

It may be doubted whether all the bad feeling engendered by this most unfortunate church feud of nearly a half century ago, has yet been entirely eradicated from the hearts of all of the old participants in the quarrel. I shall never cease to regret the part our family took in the unfortunate controversy. After forty-five years of reflection we can see our errors. There was no wrong in advocating improved church music ; the fault was in the *way* it was attempted to be done. Most of the fathers of Methodism had left the Church of England because of its extreme ritualism. The old Methodists of Bethel thought they saw signs of a return to High Church practices and conscientiously resented it. The time was not ripe for the innovation and its advocates pressed it with too much force. It is always dangerous to force even our conviction of right upon those who honestly differ with us. This spirit in the church was deeply regretted by my mother and was a source of great anxiety to her during the balance of her life. Every tragedy has a comic side. I had an old friend named Samuel Grubb, a blacksmith, at Grubb's cross-roads, in Delaware. Coming up from Wilmington one day on horseback I stopped to have my horse shod. He was very much excited over the church trouble and expressed his determination to take his hammer with him the next time he went to church and knock those strips the choir used as rests for their note books, off the backs of the benches. I undertook to reason the matter with him. I cited David and his harp, the music of the spheres, and even quoted Shakespeare's opinion of " The man that had no music in his soul," winding up my remarks by referring to the Scriptural admonition to sing not only with the spirit but with the *understanding* also. He listened until I had finished, when he entirely demolished the structure of my argument by a reply something like this : " Singing with the understanding does not mean that one must understand the cabalistic signs of a note book, it means you must understand the sense of the hymn ; it means you must understand the difference between the black art of the devil, witches and evil spirits, and good spirits. Anybody with common sense ought to know that it will not help the voice to look, when you sing, upon those things you call *keys*, and *bars*, with black and white *tadpoles*, some with their tails up, some with their tails down, decorated with black flags, and trying to crawl through the fence. It's all the work of the devil.''

To shorten my story, we will return to the church trials growing out of the excitement created by the introduction of the *Cabalistic* Note Books. Among others the preacher was tried for maladministration, and my uncle Curtis and my father were brought before the church for violating that clause in the Discipline which forbids the drinking of spirituous liquors as a beverage. At first my father became very angry and determined to leave the church, but better counsels prevailed and he resolved to stand his trial. He had taken an active part in the impeachment of the preacher and, to make things even the preacher, as the prosecutor, presented the charges against him and my uncle. Remembering the successful manner in which I had defended myself on my trial, my father requested me to act as his counsel. Upon reflection, and after due deliberation in a family council, it was arranged that I should defend my uncle, and that Mr. John B. McCay should act as my father's counsel, but that I should prepare the points upon which he should base his defense. I commenced by a careful study of the Discipline and a commentary upon it, written by one of the Bishops who had been a lawyer. The book laid down three general principles : 1st, That the trial must be in accordance with, and under the forms of, the canon law ; 2nd, That the rules of evidence must conform to the laws of the State in which the trial is held ; and 3rd, That the offense charged must be one made punishable by the civil law. Offenses merely against the Discipline of the church do not, in the first instance, subject the offender to expulsion, but only to admonition and reproof. That is to say, offenses not *malum in se*, that is, not criminal in themselves, but which are made offenses by the church Discipline only, subject the offenders, 1st, to a private admonition. If he does not heed the private reproof, then he may be admonished by the preacher in the presence of witnesses. If he continues recusant, he may be brought to trial. In the book referred to, Greenleaf on Evidence, and several books on English ecclesiastical law were cited as authority. I procured a copy of Greenleaf and studied it very closely. I found in the canon law that some substantial person must be named as prosecutor,

and that the charges must be clearly expressed and must be
followed up by specifications of time, place and circumstances,
consecutively numbered, and if the minister should be the
prosecutor, he could not *preside as a judge* on the trial.   I
prepared these points in form, with full instruction how to use
them, citing the authority for each point.   On the day appointed for the trial, the church was crowded.   It was rumored
that there were, at least, fifty witnesses, and that the trial
would continue several days.   We had taken the precaution
to have the Presiding Elder present, as the immediate superior
of the preacher in charge, to whom we could appeal upon our
points of law.   As we had anticipated, the charge was read
naming the offence as " The drinking of intoxicating liquors
as a beverage," and was signed, as we had hoped, by the
preacher in charge as the prosecutor.   After the court was
opened, the preacher assuming to preside, at once proceeded
to name the committee of trial.   We at once raised the question of competency in the judge and produced the authority.
" He was the prosecutor and could not be the judge."   The
Presiding Elder held the point well taken and, being the next
in authority by the rules of the church, he took his seat as
President of the court.   This was the first point gained and
presaged final victory.   A committee friendly to the accused
was appointed.   The Presiding Elder naming one, the accused
named one, and the two so chosen, the third.

The preacher then proceeded to call his witnesses.   We
asked the ruling of the court upon the following point :   " No
witness will be permitted to testify to any fact except from his
own personal knowledge ; and shall not state anything derived
from information received from other sources than his own
personal knowledge."   The point was sustained.   The result
was that of the forty or fifty witnesses present only three could
testify from their own personal knowledge.   One was a woman
who said she saw the accused drink a glass of ale with his
dinner at a market tavern in Philadelphia.   One man said he
had seen him take a glass of brandy with a friend in a hotel
in Chester, and the third testified that the accused had treated
him at the bar of the Black Bear hotel on Christmas Day, in
Philadelphia.   After the testimony had closed we presented
our first point :   " That drinking intoxicating liquor as a
beverage is not a crime or misdemeanor under the laws of the
State, and that the defendant, according to the Discipline of
the church and the canons of ecclesiastical law, could not be
brought to trial until after admonition from the preacher."
The result was an acquittal both of my father and uncle without
" the jury leaving the box."   The Presiding Elder came to
my father's house after the trial was over, and complimented me

very highly upon the "masterly manner in which I had conducted the defense." He then suggested that I should study law and volunteered to speak to Mr. Bates, then in full practice in Wilmington, Delaware, with whom I was registered as a student and read law in his office for two years. Mr Bates was then Secretary of the Commonwealth and was afterwards Chancellor of the State. He was a man of most remarkable ability, possessing a finely cultured mind but a frail body. He died a few years ago respected and honored by all who knew him. By his advice, I chose the city of Philadelphia as the field of my future efforts. I read law for six months under Hon. Edward Darlington, of Media. and on his motion was admitted November 24, 1851. I was admitted to the Philadelphia bar soon after, and practised my profession in that city for about twenty five years and up to the time I took my seat upon the Bench in Delaware County.

The above incidents in my life are only useful as illustrations of the general truth, that "man is a creature of circumstances." The difficulty I had with the man that cut my mantle, and for which, if it had not been for the forbearance of the good old Christian men then at the head of the church, I would have been tried for a crime, was the indirect cause of the choice of my future profession. The trial of my father, which we all keenly felt as tending to disgrace the family, was the direct cause.

Of all the interesting circumstances in my life, as a lawyer, only three will be of any interest to the general reader, and they are only valuable as illustrating the great results of small things in the life of a professional man.

In 1852, while I was courting the lady I afterwards married, she was spending a few days with one of her former schoolmates who lived near the old Navy Yard in Philadelphia. It was about four miles from my cousin's home at Seventeenth and Market, where I was then boarding. I, of course, spent a few hours in her society every evening while she was there. One night about eleven o'clock, when I started for home, I found myself in a furious snow storm. The snow was at least a foot deep in the streets, the omnibuses had all stopped, and I had four miles to walk. I managed to wade through the snow about three squares to the old frame " Ferry Hotel," and spent the balance of the night by the fire in the bar-room. The next morning I took a look at myself in an old fly-stained looking-glass that hung upon the smoky wall of the bar-room. I noticed the edge of the frame full of business cards, stuck between the glass and the wood so as to attract the attention of persons vain enough to look at themselves in the glass. Without expecting any resulting I, in a mechanical

ical way, took a card from my pocket and stuck it in the frame. A few days after, a carriage stopped in front of my office and a gentleman on crutches came in with my card in his hand. He was a merchant from Newborn, North Carolina, and stated that he had been badly injured by a collision on the Camden and Amboy road, in which a great number had been killed and wounded. He wanted to commence proceedings against the corporation for negligence and recover damages for his injuries. I asked him who had recommended him to me. He said, being a stranger, he had taken the wrong ferry-boat from Camden, and had landed at the Navy Yard instead of Market Street; that he had gone into the old Ferry Tavern to warm himself while waiting for the omnibus to bring him up town, and had, while casually taking a look at himself in the glass to see what kind of an appearance he would present after the accident, seen my card, and, as he would want a lawyer, he concluded to call on me. A minute history of the details of the results that followed this little incident will be too long to here recount. Suffice it to say, I recovered heavy damages against the company, the case was finally settled and, for twenty-three years, I attended to all the business of the firm of which my client was a member in Newborn, and through his recommendation I secured many other clients from that city. At a rough estimate, that little card was worth to me at least five or six thousand dollars.

The next incident which will serve to encourage vigilance in young lawyers happened four or five years afterwards. I had for a client an old shoemaker whose shop and dwelling were up in Kensington. After his death, his wife, in order to collect a few outstanding bills, was compelled to incur the expense of an administration upon his estate. I was employed as her attorney. I inquired about his estate but found it very small. His widow asked me what she should do with a quantity of papers she had found in his desk which, as far as she could learn, were of no value. I told her to pack them in a shoe box and send them to me and I would examine them. I spent several nights examining and reading every paper. I was tempted several times to throw the entire batch into the waste box, but as the decedent had thought the papers of sufficient importance to be preserved, I resolved to patiently finish my task so that I could, with certainty, inform my client that they were worthless. After having nearly finished my examination, I found a letter from Calcutta, India. It was seventeen years old, and was from a firm of lawyers in that city, addressed to the decedent, informing him of the death of a merchant of that city without known heirs and, as he was of the same name, requesting information as to whether he was in any way related to the Calcutta merchant. I sent for my client, the administratrix, read the letter to her and asked if she knew anything about it. She said she remembered hearing her husband say, on several occasions many years ago, that he was heir to some money in Calcutta, but for the last ten years he had never mentioned it. I concluded it would not cost much to write. I accordingly wrote a letter, informing the attorneys that I represented the dead man and that he had said in his lifetime that he was heir to some money in Calcutta, naming the estate, and that I was informed they could give me some information. About six months afterwards, and when I had almost forgotten the whole affair, I received a letter from the Judge of the court in Calcutta, stating that he was the survivor of the firm to whom I had written. That his partner was dead and that there was a large sum of money there invested in English funds at two per cent. interest, under the control of the Bank of England, China and India, in Calcutta, awaiting the identification of the heirs of the decedent in America—the English heirs having long since received their share. The balance of this story is too long for recounting the details. After unheard-of labor, and spending a good round sum of money, I found the American heirs, scattered over the different States of the Union. One was a servant girl in Philadelphia ; one was a bar-tender in New York, and one was a herdsman in Texas. In all there were only eight entitled to participate in the fund. The proofs were all regularly made before the British Consul and duly certified to at Calcutta. About five years after the discovery of the letter, I received a draft on London worth, at that time, forty per cent. premium, and after deducting the fee agreed upon, amounting to several thousand dollars, the smallest sum paid to any one heir was to the servant girl and her brother, the bar-tender. They received four thousand dollars each. I had heard much of great fortunes awaiting claimants in the old country, but this is the only case I have ever known to prove successful in its results.

The last circumstance connected with my early practice, to which I wish to refer, will illustrate the importance of depending on ourselves and never taking anything for granted simply because some one, who ought to know more than we do, says so.

A firm of distillers on Market Street was dissolved by the death of its senior member. The surviving partner was appointed by the court receiver of the firm's assets. He was represented by one of the first lawyers of the city who had the reputation of being very skillful in adjusting complicated accounts. I was taken into the case to do the drudgery necessary to be done in all contested cases, but I had no discretionary powers and was expected to implicitly obey the orders of the senior counsel. At the end of the year allowed by law, the Receiver was required to file an account. I was ordered to examine the books, arrange the vouchers and lay all the papers, books and accounts before a celebrated accountant whose name I will not mention because the story I am about to tell might be offensive to his surviving family. The accounts were prepared with a great display of statements, sheets and balance sheets, supposed to conclusively prove the result to which the accountant had arrived. When the court appointed a Master to pass upon the account and report distribution, the senior counsel appeared before him, presented the voluminous papers, *as his own personal work*, and assured the Master that *he* had carefully examined every item and voucher and could certify that the account as stated was absolutely correct. I noticed that the counsel representing the dead partner, seemed highly pleased with the result of the account. He stated to the Master that he had no objections to interpose. That he was glad the estate had fallen into the hands of such able gentlemen as our senior counsel; that it was unnecessary to prolong the proceedings, and he therefore agreed that the Master might certify the account as correct and proceed to make distribution of the estate without further delay—all of which tickled the pride of our senior very much. Now it so happened that our client had requested me, after the accounts were filed, to give him an opinion as to what his balance would probably be. To do this I took the books which had been returned by the accountant, and, in my own way, struck the balance and found the share of our client to be about $104,000. To our surprise the expert accountant had only awarded us $94,000, a difference of $10,000. Our client was very much annoyed that I should have made such a mistake. I looked over the great number of statements, debtor and creditor sheets and balance sheets of the expert, but could not find where the error was. At last I threw all his work aside and commenced a statement of the account in my own simple and common sense way, by first charging the Receiver with all the estate that had come to his hands, then crediting him with all the debts he had paid and all the proper expenses of settling the estate. The balance was certainly the clear estate of the firm. I then divided the balance which made the sum of $104,000 for each partner. I then found by the books that he had paid to the widow of the deceased partner at sundry times during the year many large sums of money, but instead of charging them to the *personal* account of the deceased partner, he had simply credited his Receiver's account with these several payments. It was quite clear that all payments to the estate of the deceased partner should be charged against his share of the balance of the estate and not against the general fund, and here was the whole error, making the difference against our client of $10,000. Elated with my discovery, I went at once to the senior counsel with my re-statement of the account, but to my surprise and disgust I found that I could not beat into his head the demonstration of the mistake. I found that his great reputation for unraveling complicated accounts was entirely due to the skill of his old expert bookkeeper and, with all his brilliancy as a lawyer, he absolutely knew nothing about mathematics and could hardly add up four columns of figures without great labor and many mistakes. At last he got angry and in a sarcastic manner informed me that I knew almost too much for one man and not quite enough for two, and that my interference would make delay and trouble in the final settlement of the estate ; that his expert accountant knew more in a day than I would be able to learn in a lifetime, and that he preferred to take the account of a man who had served him for twenty years without making a mistake in as much as a farthing, to the figures of a boy who was interested in sustaining a mistake by which he had raised false hopes in his client. I had always before this treated him with great deference and respect ; but now, being convinced of his shallow pretensions, I calmly told him that I had not yet informed our client of my discovery, but that I would now do so, and take the responsibility of filing, in my own name, exceptions to the account. I called upon our client, who, being a common sense business man, saw the error at once, and suggested that instead of filing exceptions we should call on the Master and state our discovery to him. The Master saw it in a moment and at once applied to the court to have the account recommitted and the error corrected. The result was that I had saved my client $10,000 by trusting to myself rather than taking the conclusions of one that ought to know much more than I did. My client immediately discharged the senior counsel, gave me a handsome fee, and made me his sole attorney from that day until I retired from the bar in 1875. He also sent me a great many valuable clients and never ceased, when the opportunity presented itself, to speak well of me and to tell his business friends the service I had done him.

My experience at the bar has had its sad as well as its happy side—its tragedies as well as its comedies. I could unfold many interesting tales of sorrow; open the wounds of many bleeding hearts and expose skeletons in many closets.

"But this eternal blazon must not be!"

It would not only violate my oath of office but would open wounds long since healed.   Why exhume the putrid carcasses of dead and buried contentions ?

PART III.

RECOLLECTIONS OF BETHEL AND BRANDYWINE HUNDRED SIXTY YEARS AGO.

Ante-Railroad Times—First Temperance Society—The Old Post Road—Hotel Keepers of the Olden Time— The Fireside and Bake Oven—Anglo-Phobia—The Schoolmaster—Five Miles Around Bethel Church— Beauties—Woodmen—Whimsical Men, Witches and Fortune-Tellers—Fireside Tales—Aunty Burnett's Snake Story—Granny Eastick—Emmor Lloyd—Polly Pudding—The Bewitched Rabbit—The Hunter's Revenge—Mousley's Adventure at the Devil's Rock— An Old Man Turned Into an old Mare—Planting According to the Signs—The Lucky Bone—Bewitched Churn—The Water Wizard and the Weather Wise— Ante-Mowing Machine Days—The Country Store—A Chronic Liar—Old Fanny Cherry—Molly Shade's Speak-easy—Postscript.

When I was born, there was not a steamboat, steamship, railroad or electric telegraph in the world. There had been experiments in steam locomotion and navigation, but no practical results had been attained. The year 1830 may be adopted as the birth-year of steam locomotion. The first patent in the United States was granted in 1828. All the ships of that day were built of wood ; the iron age had not yet commenced. The manners and customs of the people were very different from the habits of to-day. The drinking of intoxicating liquors was almost universal. Every family, making the slightest pretensions to gentility, had its side-board well stocked with liquors. A decanter of spirits was upon every dinner table. To make a social call and not be invited to the side-board, would be a polite intimation that your company was not agreeable. The first regular temperance society was formed in 1826, the year of my birth. It made but little headway until after 1833. In that year the first National Temperance Convention was held. It adopted the following resolution : " The traffic in ardent spirits as a drink and the use of the same as such are morally wrong and ought to be abandoned throughout the world." This resolution made a ripple of excitement among the people and was generally regarded as an undue interference

with the social rights of a free people ; very much like the
ridicule and condemnation that followel the first resolution of
the society for the abolition of human slavery.   It cannot be
doubted but that we were, at that time, rapidly becoming a
nation of drunkards.   The only difference between the aristocratic clergyman and the poor layman in this respect was, that
one drank French brandy while the other drank whisky.

The radius of daily news did not extend beyond thirty or
forty miles from the county town.   It required a month or six
weeks to get the news, by the fastest sailing ships from Europe.   The old Post Road from Wilmington to Philadelphia,
was the central artery for the circulation of general news. Important messages were carried by post riders on fast horses
which were changed every ten miles.   Taverns were located
all along the road about ten miles apart.   In those days the
"keeper of a public house," as tavern keepers invariably called
themselves, were looked upon as important persons, several
degrees above the common herd in social and political standing.
I have seen the U. S. mail coach, with an armed guard and
trumpeter come up the Post road in a full gallop, and when
the horn was blown, all the farmers on the road to the Philadelphia market, immediately pulled out to give free passage to
the " United States Mail."

Wood was the only fuel ; coal had not yet come into general use, even in the cities.   Hickory wood was hauled by
horses all the way to Philadelphia, Chester and Wilmington.
There was a city officer called the " Corder."   It was his duty
to measure every cord of wood brought for sale to the city.
Every farmer carefully preserved his woodland, as he supposed
the supply would soon become exhausted and his timber lands
would bring fabulous prices.   The city of Philadelphia was
illuminated by whale oil lamps.   Gas had not been yet introduced.   Great whaling fleets sailed at stated periods from
various ports, including Wilmington, to procure whale oil for
lubricating and illuminating purposes.   Coal oil was only
known as a quack medicine, and was sold in small bottles by
the druggists to cure rheumatism. The houses, at night, were
ligh ed by oil lamps, candles, and, in winter, by a rousing fire
in the great old-time fireplace.

The social meaning of the word " fireside" is derived from
the old baronial fireplaces of merry England, around which
the family gathered for social enjoyments and the entertainment of sojourners, neighbors and friends.   Some of these
fireplaces were so large that an ordinary sized man could walk
into them under the mantel, without stooping, while in breadth
they were from eight to ten feet; and at least four or five feet
deep.   The backlog was the trunk of a tree, from eighteen

inches to two feet in diameter and six feet long. Andirons, two and three feet long, supported the cord wood while it burned, sending out a bright but cheerful light and generous warmth throughout the large family room, while the blue smoke could be seen by the children on the stone seats in the chimney corner, curling and ascending to the chimney top. These great fireplaces were only in the principal family room, which was usually very large and served as kitchen, dining room, family sitting room, spinning and working room and a place for family intercourse and enjoyment.

Every farm house had an enormous bake-oven from six to eight feet long by three to four feet wide of an oval shape, in which a dozen large loaves of bread, forty or fifty pies, a little pig, a great roast, or two turkeys and several chickens could be baked all at the same time. The preparation of oven wood was a serious matter to the farm hands, so much so, that in the rustic parties and sham weddings with which the young people amused themselves, they required the supposed groom to promise that

> "He would be true, and would be good
> And keep his wife in *oven wood*."

As a rule the people loved the French and hated the English. This was because of the friendship of France during the Revolution; the recent visit of Lafayette and the bitterness engendered by what was then called the "Late War." (1812)

There was no common school system in those days. The school houses were erected like the churches, by individual generosity; by the union of a few families or by general contribution. The "Master" formed and ruled his own school by a regular scale of prices per quarter, none being admitted without paying a fixed sum for tuition. In mathematics and English Grammar the schools were as good if not better than the schools of to-day. The trouble of the system was that the children of the poor and many of the middle classes were neglected and grew up without as much as acquiring the rudiments of an education. I have known many worthy, bright and highly intelligent men who could neither read or write. Some of the respectable families of to-day are descended from such grandfathers.

The schoolmaster had to be a man of courage as well as learning, and able to whip the biggest boy in the school, which he generally had to do before he was properly respected. Discipline was enforced by a small switch for the girls but a great ox-gad for the boys. While the boys were good-hearted and robust fellows, it must be confessed they were inclined to be a little belligerent. All questions of importance were settled by a personal combat. The one that could whip the other was always considered in the right.

By the foregoing general outline of the situation sixty years ago, the reader will be better able to account for the peculiarity and eccentricity of some of the people of Bethel and Brandywine Hundred at that time. I ought, however, to say that my personal recollections do not cover the whole of either Bethel or Brandywine Hundred. "The Hundred," as we used to call it, extends from Wilmington to the Pennsylvania line, and from the river Delaware westward the entire breadth of the State. Its general population were as highly cultivated and were as polite as the best citizens of Pennsylvania. The parts of Bethel and "The Hundred" to which I wish to confine myself lie within a radius of five miles around Bethel M. E. church and about equi-distance from Wilmington, Chester and West Chester. The elevation is very high; Malaria was unknown; the people lived to be very old; the men were robust and sturdy ; the women were handsome, strong and motherly; the girls were noted for their beauty in form and feature. They had sweet engaging manners and exceedingly kind hearts. I may say without fear of successful contradiction, that in all my travels I have never seen young women with better complexions, fairer faces or better forms than many of the young women of Bethel and Brandywine Hundred fifty years ago. The little piece of territory above described has also turned out several good and useful men. The country was heavily wooded from the river up to Brandywine Summit. If we desired we could hunt all day without leaving the continuous wood from Hickman's mill up through the lands of Preston Eyre and William Larkin and as far as Concord ; or we could take the south branch of Naaman's creek at the Post road and keep in the woods as far up as Brandywine Summit. Game was quite plentiful. With our old-fashioned flint lock guns six feet long we could shoot pheasants, partridges, wild pigeons, woodcock, wild ducks, English snipe and squirrels. Foxes were so common as to make the preservation of our chickens somewhat difficult. During the hunter's moon the young fellows, with good trained dogs, amused themselves by successful 'possum and coon hunts. Rabbit hunting with hounds was great sport. There were a class of workmen in those days called "woodsmen." They were one degree higher in the social scale than "farm hands," who, in their turn, were one degree above "laborers." These woodsmen spent their whole time in the woods chopping fire wood, getting out fencing materials and ship timber. I have seen them with a rip saw, one man on an elevated log and one standing under it, the man above lifting the saw and the one below drawing it down, sawing out great three-inch plank for shipping. The "ship stuff," as it was called, would be transported on great timber wheels, drawn by five or six horses in a single file, to the shipyards in Wilmington. There was another distinct class of workmen, called "team drivers." They did nothing but attend to and drive their teams by which they transported all articles of heavy merchandise. All the business now done by railroads was then done by these "teams."

My readers will now understand why many of the good people of the neighborhood above described were cranky, eccentric and superstitious. While this little spot of earth contained its full share of bright, intelligent and well-bred people, it must be confessed it had more than its share of singular and quaint characters. The belief in witchcraft had, unfortunately, taken a firm hold upon the minds of many very respectable citizens. It was nearly universal among the farm hands, woodsmen, teamsters and working people. I am told that traces of its slimy trail can yet be discovered in some of the descendants of the old believers in the black art. It was useless to argue the question with them. They were well posted in all the passages of Scripture upon that subject. They pointed to the case of Saul and the Witch of Endor, and cited the commandment, "Thou shalt not suffer a witch to live." As the Bible, in those days, was supreme authority upon all disputed questions, they had the best of the argument ; just as the priests are said to have silenced the argument of Galileo, that the earth was round, by pointing to the passage of Scripture which declared, that at the second advent of Christ he should descend from heaven and all the world should see him ; which could not be if the earth was round, unless the inhabitants in the antipodes could look through the earth ; so, the believers in witchcraft said, "If the Bible is true, there were witches in the olden time and, if there ever was a witch, there can be witches now."

The belief in witches, wizards, ghosts, dreams and fortune-tellers was the direct result of fireside stories told by old women, nurses and weak-minded men to while away the long winter nights. When a little boy, I have listened to them by the hour until I was so excited with fear that I would not go to bed in the dark or sleep alone.

Many wonderful snake stories were told. It was said they would milk the cows and charm birds and children. That if a child should be charmed by a snake and the reptile should be killed, the child would die. Snakes were then quite plentiful and some were very venomous, especially the yellow viper and copperhead. I remember killing one when I was quite small. It had coiled itself in my path as I was going

to school through the woods about a mile from my father's
house. When I told my father that the snake flattened its
head and hissed at me like a goose, he turned deadly pale and
made me take him to the place where I had killed it. When
he looked at it he said, " My son, that is a viper ; if it had
as much as scratched your skin it would have killed you." I
have seen black snakes six and seven feet long and large
enough to swallow a half-grown rabbit. I have often found
them in a half-dreaming state with toads and frogs in their
bellies.

There was an old midwife in the neighborhood named
Aunty Burnett. She had no settled home ; her skill in her
profession made her welcome in every house. It was hardly
necessary to have a doctor if Aunty Burnett could be secured.
She had an exhaustless supply of most startling and marvellous stories. When I was about seven years old I heard her
relate the following incident : She was employed to nurse a
dying old man whom she named, and who was well known in
Delaware. He had the reputation, while in a fit of anger of
having whipped to death one of his old slaves, named Pompey.
Just before his death they raised him up in bed when, with a
stare of horror, he stretched out his emaciated arm and with
his bony finger he pointed to a corner of the room and cried
out aloud, " Pompey ! Pompey !" They looked at the place
at which he had pointed and there was an enormous black
snake slowly crawling towards the bed. The old man gave a
frantic scream and fell over dead. When they looked for the
snake it was gone.

There was another old woman in "The Hundred"
named Granny Eastick, who, as far as I have been able to
learn, had no enemies and whose only fault was her age. She
was a widow, dressed oddly, walked half bent with a home-
made cane, lived alone in a log house in the woods and gathered chestnuts, shellbarks, walnuts and hazelnuts, which she
sold for a living. In the winter, when pinched with hunger,
she would sometimes solicit alms in the form of cold victuals
and cast-off clothing. Yet she had the reputation of being a
witch. She got her reputation in this way : One of her
neighbors who, by the way, was a distant relation of mine on
my mother's side, had a very sick cow. From its strange
actions, the cow doctor said it was bewitched. It would sit
like a dog, roll its eyes, and try to stand on its head. The
doctor consulted his *witch book* and found that the remedy to
break the charm, when a dumb animal should be bewitched,
was to cut off its right ear, stick it full of new needles and
then boil it in spring water. The effect would be that the
witch, whoever she might be, would make her appearance,

tormented by the pain of the needles in her ear. Then, without speaking, some of the boiling water should be thrown upon her and the charm would be broken. While this ceremony was being performed, poor old Granny Eastick happened to come up the lane with her basket on her arm to request some cold victuals. Without a word, some of the boiling water was thrown on her. She screamed and ran away and, as the cow got well, she was ever after reputed a witch. The following story of old Granny Eastick, I heard from an old man named Emmor Lloyd. He was a wood-chopper. His terms were fifty cents a day and a quart of whisky. He regularly drank his quart of whisky every day for forty years and, of course, died in the Poor House a very old man. He was chopping our winter firewood when he told the story one winter night, in front of a rousing fire, with a pitcher of hard cider by his side. The story ran thus: There was a very interesting girl of about fourteen years, the daughter of a respectable farmer in "The Hundred," who was afflicted with a most singular disease. She would run on all-fours like a dog; she would mew like a cat; sometimes she would (on all-fours) run backwards, and if not watched would go into very dangerous places. (No doubt she had St. Vitus' dance). It was thought the child was bewitched. Emmor was then chopping wood for the girl's father and he determined to break the spell and save the child. A witch doctor was consulted who said, if the witch could be compelled, in the presence of the person under her spell, to say "God bless the child," the spell would be broken; provided, the blood of the witch could be drawn with a rusty iron instrument before she had time to repeat her curse. Emmor provided a rusty table fork and then sent for Granny to come and see the child. As soon as she entered the room he seized her by the throat, charged her with the crime, and commanded her to look at the girl and say "God bless the child." She at once raised her hands and said, "My God bless the child." He gave her a terrible shake and tightened his grip upon her throat saying: "You must not say *my* God, *your* God is the devil; say 'God bless the child.'" Nearly dead from his grip, she repeated the words as directed. He instantly drew blood from her forehead by scratching her with the prongs of the rusty fork and the child got well.

Many good old women in the neighborhood were believed to be witches. I will only relate one more case—that of Polly Pudding. That was not her proper name. When Hickman's mill was being built Polly's husband, whose name was Benjamin, was one of the millwrights. It was the custom when a new mill was ready to be started to give a big dinner to the workmen. On this occasion a very large pudding had been provided. At dinner Ben made a hog of himself and ate nearly the entire pudding. When the mill was started one of the men turned to Ben and said: "Can you tell me what the clapper says?" "Yes," says Ben, "It says *pitta patta, patta pitta.*" "No," said the other, "It says *Benny Pudding— Pudding Benny.*" The rest of the workmen at once took up the refrain and began to sing, *Pudding Benny, Benny Pudding*, which, very much to Benny's annoyance, they kept up all the afternoon, and from that day to the day of his death he was known by no other name than Benny Pudding. After his death his widow was called Polly Pudding, even the children were called Puddings. After her husband's death Polly lived in a small house in the woods near Faulk's Cross Roads. She was a sober, industrious and economical old woman. She did not meddle with the affairs of her neighbors, but bent all her energies to the support of herself and children and yet they called here a witch, simply because some hunters stopped at her home one day to get a drink of milk and while partaking of her hospitality laid their guns in a heap on the floor, which she stepped over and jokingly said: "A penny for all the rabbits these guns will shoot to-day." The hunters had scarcely left the door before a fine rabbit jumped out of her garden. The dogs at once started on the trail and chased it all the balance of the day. It ran through thickets, greenbriers, swamps, hedges and among the rocks. At one time the dogs were within a few feet of it when it suddenly stopped and ran back between the legs of one of the hunters. They all shot at it over and over again until night stopped the hunt and their ammunition was exhausted. They then remembered the magic words: "A penny for all the rabbits these guns will shoot to-day," and came to the unanimous conclusion that Polly Pudding had bewitched their guns and had turned herself into a rabbit and in that form had been playing with them all the afternoon. During all the balance of her life she was reputed to be a witch. One of the hunters lived in Bethel near Booth's Corner. When he arrived at home that night he found one of his cows dead. He cut her open and found a *witch ball* in her stomach. (A witch ball is a small roll of hair about as large as a walnut often found in the stomach of cows, supposed to be taken into the stomach by the cow licking itself when shedding its coat). He at once consulted an old woman named Joanna Thompson, a fortune-teller, as to how he could break the spell. She informed him that the spell could be broken by drawing a profile picture of the supposed witch upon a sheet of white paper with a new goose quill, using his own blood for ink. Then with a silver bullet, twelve steps away, naming one of the twelve Apostles at each step, he should shoot at the picture. If he should hit it, and the person he suspected was the true witch, she would be wounded in the same part of her body as might be struck on the picture by the silver bullet. He strictly followed the directions, took deliberate aim, pulled the trigger, but the gun did not go off. Upon examination he found the mainspring of the lock had broken. He kept his place and sent his hired man to the house for a live coal, which he applied to the touch-hole and the gun went off. The silver bullet struck the picture in the leg. He then made his man mount one of his fastest horses and ride over to Polly Pudding's to ascertain the effect. The man met one of her sons going after the doctor. Just at the time the gun went off she had fallen down stairs and broken her leg. I heard this story told by the man who shot the picture. He related it in all its particulars, much more at large than I have repeated it, to eight or ten men at the old log blacksmith shop at Booth's Corner, then occupied by a man named Mousley. A learned discussion followed the story, some holding that the coincidents tending to establish the fact that old Polly was a witch were but accidents, others taking the ground that the law ought to protect the people from such evil influences. Some of the young fellows present boldly announced their skepticism as to the existence of witches or even the devil himself. This seemed to shock Mr. Mousley very much, and to convince the young skeptics of their error he related an adventure of his own still more startling and supernatural than the tale of Polly Pudding.

To understand the story the reader must be made acquainted with the surroundings. A short mile from my father's house, nearly due south and just over the Delaware line, there was a very remarkable rock known as "The Devil's Seat." It sloped to the eastward and had upon it a well-defined print of a large cloven foot and a hollow place as if made by a large man sitting upon it while it was in a soft state. I have no doubt but that it was a landmark made during the stone age. Stone arrow heads, spear heads and what were called Indian axes made of stone have been found around the place. Perhaps it was intended to mark the boundary of the territory of Sitting Bull, the Indian chief whose tribe once occupied Delaware and a part of Pennsylvania. There are many persons now living who have seen this singular rock. There is another very remarkable rock on the farm formerly occupied by John B. McCay, deceased, covered with hieroglyphics which was, perhaps, another landmark of a long lost tribe.

"The Devil's Seat" was in about the centre of a twenty acre field, very poor, and which had not then been cultivated

within the memory of the oldest inhabitants.   It was called
the Indian Field and was believed, by the class of persons I
am trying to describe, to be haunted.   I have seen as many as
four or five holes, three or four feet deep and in diameter as
large as an ordinary well, dug in different places in the field
by unknown persons, supposed to be searching for hidden
treasure.   Because of its bad reputation hunters at night generally avoided this field, for many strange stories had been told
of valuable dogs who had chased game at night into the field
and had never been seen again.   The rock was destroyed a
few years ago by being blasted with gunpowder; the person
who destroyed it was the owner of the farm and, it was said,
he expected to find a pot of gold under it.   Whether he did
or not I have never heard.   It is certain, however, that he
succeeded in destroying one of the most interesting remains of
a pre-historic age.

The scene of Mousley's terrible adventure was in this
field at midnight and upon the above described rock.   He had
been hunting with three excellent dogs and had caught two
coons and an opossum.   While wending his way slowly homeward, the moonlit sky was suddenly overcast with black,
ominous clouds ; the dogs seemed terrified and ran trembling
to where he stood under an old chestnut tree, about twenty
yards from the " Devil's Seat."   He heard a rumbling sound
under his feet like smothered thunder, then he saw a sudden
flash of light.   Turning his face toward the place from whence
the flash came, he saw a most terrible sight.   There sat the
Devil in his seat upon the rock.   He was blowing a blue flame
out of his mouth and nostrils, as if trying to warm his hands.
His eyes looked like two balls of fire.   He had no clothes
upon him, and was as red as blood.   Mousley, half dead with
fright, dropped his game at his feet.   Satan then threw up
both arms above his head and yawned.   His mouth, when
opened by his yawn, looked like the open door of a blast furnace.   Just then Mousley's best old dog picked up one of the
coons and started in a full run toward the rock and, without
stopping, plunged head foremost into the devil's open mouth,
coon and all, and disappeared.   The other two dogs immediately
followed suit, each with his game in his mouth.   Just then a
great old owl flew out of the tree above his head with a loud
hoot, and hovered over the rock.   The devil looked up at the
owl and with an unearthly Ha ! ha ! ha ! he sunk into the earth
dogs, game and all.   The dogs were never seen again.   This
story was told, not as a joke, but as a solemn truth, by a
Christian man of a good reputation for truth and veracity.
He was, perhaps, temporarily insane from excessive fright and,
in his demented state, believed the fancies of his heated

imagination to be realities.   I leave the question for psychologists to solve.   It is too deep for my comprehension.

It was a common custom in my boyhood days, after their own harvesting was done, for farmers to assist each other at "harvest wages" (which was about four times the wages of common labor) in securing their crops.   There were no reapers, mowers, or even horse rakes in those days, say sixty years ago.   The wheat was reaped by hand with a common sickle and the grass was mowed by the scythe.   One of our neighbors, who lived over the line, (whose name I will suppress because some of his descendants are now very respectable people and would perhaps blush to know their ancestor's weakness) was assisting my father during harvest.   One morning he came to the farm very late.   He looked very much out of sorts, complained of soreness in his joints, stiff limbs and backache.   Being a conscientious man and member of Bethel church he hesitated to undertake to do a full day's work at "harvest wages."   Taking my father aside, he said he had been so *abused* the night just passed that he did not feel able to do the work of a full hand.   My father asked him who had abused him.   He replied that he had been turned into an old horse and had been ridden by witches all night under whip and spur and that he was so tired he could scarcely walk, much less work   My father laughed at him and told him that instead of being an old *horse* he had a night-*mare*.   The poor fellow did not see the point and hobbled off home.   He had evidently caught cold and had bad dreams.

Many of the old farmers planted their crops in strict conformity with the zodiacal signs in the almanac.   They would not plant beets, carrots or parsnips when the sign was in the head, nor corn, cabbage or turnips when it was in the feet. Many persons believed in faith cure for all diseases.   There were persons who believed they had the power to pow-wow away warts, skin excrescences, tumors and the like, while others believed in some occult influence possessed by certain persons born with a cowl, who, by repeating a secret passage of Scripture, could stop hemorrhages and relieve pain.   Many of my readers will remember an old gentleman named Jehu Forwood, of Brandywine Hundred, who was said to possess this wonderful power.   When accidents happened from runaway horses, falls from trees, or bad wounds from the unskillful handling of edged tools, two horses were at once saddled, one was sent at full speed to Jehu Forwood, to have him stop the blood and relieve the pain, the other was sent for the doctor.   I am unable to explain the miracle, but almost invariably the blood and pain stopped about the time the rider reached Mr. Forwood's house.   It was said that persons injured at a great distance from his house were relieved more certainly than his near neighbors. He attributed this to more earnest faith. The probability is that the blood had more time to coagulate and the pain was perhaps soothed by the mucilaginous exudations from the blood protecting the fresh wound from the action of the air.

A very common custom with the young girls was to secure the forked bone of a fowl's breast, called the "Lucky-bone," and place it over the front door of the house. The first young man that entered under the bone was to be the future husband of the maid that placed it there. This was a sign that seldom failed. The reason is quite obvious. As both parties believed their union was decreed by heaven, they naturally submitted to the divine predestination. The witch-hazel tree was supposed to possess invincible powers over the charms of magicians. It entered into almost all domestic medicines and was a specific against all the arts of sorcery.

I remember when I was a little boy one of our neighbors had great difficulty in churning his butter. He had churned continuously for seventeen hours and the butter would not come. He concluded that the churn was bewitched and at once went to the woods for a withe of witch-hazel which he bound around the churn and in a few minutes the butter came. It was, however, very white and cheesey. The fact was that he had half starved his cows ; the weather was cold and wintry and the milk had but little butter-producing substance in it.

As late as 1842 respectable people professed to have the power to tell where to dig wells in order to strike water nearest to the surface, and many intelligent persons believed it. There was an old and highly respected jeweler of Wilmington, well known by almost everybody in the State, who boldly professed to possess this power. The corporation of Wilmington lost the record of one of its old water mains and had spent much time in vain endeavoring, by a system of digging, to find the lost water pipe. At last after digging up many streets where it was supposed the main might be but without success, one of the city fathers suggested that they try the skill of the old jeweler. The suggestion was adopted. He went to a neighboring wood and procured two wands of witch-hazel which he placed before him in the form of St. Andrew's cross and commenced walking over the streets where it was thought the pipe might be. In about half an hour, with hundreds of men and boys following him, he suddenly stopped and directed the workmen to dig. They did so and to the joy of the city authorities the lost main was found.

One of our neighbors was a great weather-wise. He had digested a system of rules and signs by which he foretold the

state of the weather for several days in advance. Some of his
rules were based upon meteorological influences and can be
explained upon scientific principles of which he had not the
slightest knowledge. Many of his signs were exceedingly
absurd. He believed in the prophecy of St. Swithin (ground-
hog day) as firmly as he did in the book of Revelation. His
faith in the influence of the moon was equally as strong. A
hazy ring around the moon meant approaching rain. The
number of stars within the ring indicated the days within
which the storm would come. When he saw the leaves of the
willow tree turn upwards and the smoke from the chimney refuse to ascend, or when the chickens perched upon the fence
and with their bills began to arrange their feathers, rain was
sure to come within a day. A pig in the late fall with straw
in his mouth meant a hard winter. A great harvest meant a
long winter ; a scant crop of hay meant a short and mild winter. His rule was : "If your crop is short, save it all and
you'll have enough ; if you have a great crop don't waste any
for you'll need it all."

His theory of the moon's control of the weather was ri-
diculously absurd. When the new moon appeared with her
belly down and horns up (convexo-concave) he predicted a dry
month. His reasons were that the water in the moon could
not run out. When the new moon appeared concavo convex
—belly up and horns down—of course all the water in the
moon ran out upon the earth and a wet month was the consequence.

My father used to laugh at his theories and, by many
well-made arguments, try to convince him of the absurdity of
his signs. One beautiful moonlight night, our old neighbor
came to our house with a beam of triumphant satisfaction upon
his honest face, and a great roll of foolscap paper in his hand.
"Well, John," said he, "I've come over to convince you that
the moon does control the weather." He then unfolded his
manuscript which contained the results of a year's observations. He had kept a record of every rain during the year
and his record clearly showed that every storm had occurred
within three days of a change of the moon. My father was
at first inclined to dispute the record, but as our neighbor was
a man of spirit as well as physical strength, such an intimation
might have led to unpleasant results. After a few moments'
thought, my father burst into a derisive laugh. "Why,"
said he, "you old fool, don't you know that by no possibility
could a storm come beyond three and a half days of a quarterly
change of the moon ? A lunar month is twenty-eight days ;
there are four changes in the month, or one every seven days ;
if the rain is four days from the last quarter it must be only

three days from the ensuing one, because four and three make seven   I shall never forget the look of bewildered amazement in the face of our old neighbor as he began to realize the truth.   "Dod Zounds," said he, "I'll hardly believe the Bible any more."

Even the forms of religious worship in those days were very different from the practices of to-day.   Whether the modern doctrine of evolution applies to the spiritual as well as the physical world, is a question too deep for me.   I do not wish to be misunderstood.   In my religious views I am orthodox, but it is quite certain that great advances have been made, not only in the forms but in the creeds of many Christian denominations during the past sixty years.   I have witnessed most boisterous and extravagant ebullitions of religious excitement at protracted meetings and revivals in Old Bethel Church.   I have seen religious fervor approach so near insanity as to be hard to draw the dividing line, and which would not be approved by the sentiment of the most fervent worshiper of to-day.   And yet the persons who were guilty of the absurd antics caused by what they called the "Blessing," were undoubtedly good, honest Christians.   Under intense religious excitement they lost control of themselves and ignored the restraints and conventionalities of society.   Among the many earnest old Methodist preachers of my boyhood days I can recall two whose preaching made a lasting impression upon my mind. They were eloquent to a remarkable degree.   Their ideas were original and often startling.   They were great revivalists and always drew together crowded congregations.   I shall never forget the conclusion of a prayer made upon the occasion of a great revival meeting by one of these old preachers.   After informing the Lord that his Christian soldiers had overcome the devil and driven him from the field of battle, he concluded thus :   " Now, O Lord, lash the devil—lash him till he lolls out his dry and blistered tongue upon the blasted and burning shoals of eternal damnation and howls for mercy, but show him none for Christ's sake, Amen !' "

The other old preacher to whom I have referred was appointed to Chester circuit, which extended from Brandywine creek to Philadelphia and from the river back to Downingtown.   With his horse and saddle bags he rode over this great circuit and preached three times each Sunday at his different appointments.   He was a man of most remarkable genius, with a mind well stored with historical illustrations and ludicrous anecdotes.   A new church was to be dedicated and an effort was to be made to raise funds to pay off the church debt.   His text was :   " The Lord loveth a cheerful giver "   While descanting upon the love of the Lord for a liberal man, he took occasion to express what contempt he must have for a stingy soul. He said that there were great souls that God could not look upon the earth without seeing them, and there were other souls so small that the Almighty had to use a microscope to find them. "So small that ten thousand of them could dance a jig upon the point of a cambric needle and have more room to jump about than a tadpole would have to wriggle in the Atlantic ocean."

It was quite fashionable to preach eulogistic funeral sermons over the coffins of all the old sinners in the neighborhood. The custom became such an intolerable nuisance that the preachers were compelled to set their faces against it. To illustrate the ridiculous extent of this foolish custom, I may be pardoned for relating an anecdote told in my father's house by the Rev. J. B. Ayars, then the traveling preacher of Chester circuit. He was aroused late one night by the son of one of his congregation, a boy of about ten or twelve years, who had come to request him in the name of his father to preach a funeral sermon over the remains of his brother, who had just died. The preacher took out his memoranda book to make some notes about the deceased so that he could intelligently speak of him in his sermon.

The following dialogue ensued :
" What was your brother's name ?"
" He hain't got no name."
" How old was he ?"
" He was no old at all, he died a *bornen.*"

The country store, at the cross-roads, was a great place for loungers, loafers and idlers. They met by mutual affinity and drank cider, smoked common segars and talked politics. Theological questions and the affairs of State were often discussed, jokes were cracked and amusing stories were told. It was a real pleasant place to spend the long autumnal nights. Among the frequenters of the place was a man named Batten. He had the name of telling very improbable stories and was never known to hear a marvelous tale without being able to tell a still more extravagant one. One of the old men of the neighborhood was very fond of starting Batten by telling himself some improbable story. One night, when my uncle Wesley Clark, now a very old man, was playing a game of checkers at the store, Batten entered. The old gentleman, to whom I have just referred, turned to my uncle and said, " Wesley, have you ever heard of a larger eel than the one you and I caught down at Grubb's Landing when we were boys ? It weighed just twenty pounds." Batten pricked his ears and remarked that he, upon one occasion, when he was working at Charley Pusey's mill, saw a very large eel. He said the mill suddenly stopped without any apparent cause. The headgate was open but no water flowed upon the great over-shot wheel. At last they found an enormous eel had got fast in the wooden trunk which carried the water from the headgate to the wheel. With great difficulty they got it out. "Well," said uncle Wesley, "how large was it?" "Weel," said he, "we weighed it very carefully on the scales and, singular as it may seem, it just weighed twenty pounds and *one ounce*."

On another occasion he told of a remarkable shot that he once made while at Pusey's mill. He said a party of gentlemen from Philadelphia came to see Mr. Pusey and brought with them very expensive double-barreled guns with which to astonish the country people on a squirrel hunt. They got an early breakfast and started out to a shellbark tree in the woods, near the mill. It was not long before they commenced to shoot. They shot so rapidly and so long that Mr. Pusey sent him out to see what was the cause of such incessant firing. When he arrived he found the hunters had been shooting all the morning at the same squirrel on the top branch of the tree. He had taken Mr. Pusey's gun with him and asked leave to make one shot at it. The hunters laughed at his old flint-lock gun, and told him he might try what he could do. He went to the butt of the tree, stepped off one hundred yards so as to have a fair sight on the squirrel, and banged away. At the first shot down came the squirrel, stone dead. He picked it up and was surprised at its extraordinary weight but, giving it a shake, the cause of its extra weight was explained—fully two pounds of shot had *lodged in its hair*, and about another pound had *just penetrated its hide*, but none had gone into its body far enough to kill it except the heavy shot from Pusey's gun.

Pusey's mill was in Upper Chichester and is now a ruin, having been burned a few years ago and never rebuilt.

When my father was building the home in which I was born, Batten's father was one of the carpenters. A large chicken hawk had been carrying off the poultry and my father determined to watch for him in the early morning and, if possible, shoot him. He, however, did not get up early enough. When he went out with his gun, he saw the hawk on the opposite side of the field at least a hundred yards away, making his breakfast on a fine young hen. He did not expect to hit it but shot at it to frighten it away when, to his surprise, the hawk fell dead. A single slug had, by chance, struck it in the head. "Well," said he, "Batten, that was a very remarkable shot." "Yes," said Batten, "that was a very fair shot, but if I were to tell you how far off *I* shot a hawk once with my old gun, you would say, 'O, pshaw! that's one of Batten's lies.' "

There were several other quaint old characters I would like to introduce to my readers if time and space would permit. Some of my older readers will remember Old Fanny Cherry. Her proper name was Frances Chervine ; she was an old maid of gigantic size ; I should say she was at least six feet in height and large in proportion. She could lay an ordinary man over her knee and spank him as a mother would an unruly boy. She used to boast that no man ever insulted her. She had no special calling, but migrated from house to house. Wherever she could hang her shawl she considered her home. She usually carried her entire wardrobe with her ; I have seen her come up the back lane to my father's home, with six petticoats and three frocks on, an umbrella under her arm, a parasol over her head and a band-box in her hand. Whenever she appeared thus equipped it indicated a two weeks' visit. She was a devout Methodist, and a great shouter. She never went to church without indulging in her favorite form of worship, which was, as soon as the preacher said anything that pleased her, to jump up, clap her hands and whirl round and round, like a top until she became dizzy, which she mistook for a manifestation or divine approval and then sat down content.

There was another old female known as Molly Shades. Her home was about a mile south of my Uncle Nelson's house. It was completely isolated, being a half mile from any other dwelling. Its seclusion adapted it to the purpose for which it was used. It was an old-time *speak-easy* where all who wished could drink whisky and smoke tobacco on the sly. While gunning one day with my father, when I was a boy, he pointed out the old house and said : "If these old trees could speak they would tell many unsavory tales of drunken carousals, ribald songs and scenes of revelry." Many of the old, good fellows of the neighborhood would meet there to spend their leisure hours. Sometimes their festivities would not end until '' the wee small hours of the morn." Amid the fumes of common segars, four for a cent, hard cider at a cent a glass, whisky at twenty cents a gallon, and pig-tail tobacco at a cent a yard, we may imagine how the old revelers spent their long winter nights.

My father said the first time he visited the place was just after his return from the city of New York, where he had lived for several years. He went into the house to buy a plug of her best Cavendish tobacco. She said she had nothing but '' Pig Tail.'' He informed her that he did not chew pig tail. '' Now John," said she, '' Don't put on any of your New York airs here. Why don't you talk like other people ? Why don't you say you don't *chaw* pig-tail ? I'll declare how some people do put on !''

My book must now be brought to a close. Whatever my readers may think of it or of me, I feel they will at least admit that my life has not been a lazy one.

POSTSCRIPT.

I have submitted the manuscript of my personal recollections of Bethel and Brandywine Hundred to an old friend from Massachusetts. He assures me that there were in the neighborhood in which he was born, sixty or seventy years ago, just such quaint old customs, whimsical characters and superstitious people as I have described.

I am inclined to the belief that there was a class of people in all the rural districts of our common country very much like those I have mentioned, and that their peculiarities and eccentricities resulted from their social isolation and the absence of free schools, newspapers, railroads and telegraphs, which have now made mankind cosmopolite.

T. J. C.

January 1, 1893.

www.ingramcontent.com/pod-product-compliance
Lightning Source LLC
Chambersburg PA
CBHW022007110726
47901CB00006B/1436